Algorithms and Computation in Mathematics • Volume 5

Editors

E. Becker   M. Bronstein   H. Cohen
D. Eisenbud   R. Gilman

Springer
Berlin
Heidelberg
New York
Barcelona
Budapest
Hong Kong
London
Milan
Paris
Singapore
Tokyo

Dieter Jungnickel, 1952 –

Graphs, Networks and Algorithms

With 200 Figures
Translated from the German by Tilla Schade

 Springer

Dieter Jungnickel
Universität Augsburg
Lehrstuhl für Diskrete Mathematik
Optimierung und Operations Research
Universitätsstr. 14
D-86135 Augsburg
e-mail: jungnickel@math.uni-augsburg.de

Mathematics Subject Classification (1991): 05-01, 68R10, 68Q25

The English edition is based on the third German edition published
by Bibliographisches Institut Wissenschaftsverlag in 1994.

Library of Congress Cataloging - in - Publication Data applied for

Die Deutsche Bibliothek – CIP-Einheitsaufnahme

Jungnickel, Dieter:
Graphs, networks and algorithms / Dieter Jungnickel. - Berlin;
Heidelberg; New York; Barcelona; Budapest; Hong Kong;
London; Milan; Paris; Singapore; Tokyo:
Springer, 1999
(Algorithms and computation in mathematics; Vol.5)
ISBN 3-540-63760-5

ISSN 1431-1550

ISBN 3-540-63760-5 Springer-Verlag Berlin Heidelberg New York

© Springer-Verlag Berlin Heidelberg 1999
Printed in Germany

Typesetting: Camera-ready copy from the author
Cover design: design & production GmbH, Heidelberg

SPIN: 10559386   46/3143 - 5 4 3 2 1 0 – Printed on acid-free paper

Preface

During the last few decades, Combinatorial Optimization and Graph Theory have – as the whole field of Combinatorics in general – experienced a particularly fast development. There are various reasons for this fact; one is, for example, that applying combinatorial ways of deduction has become more and more common. However, two developments on the 'outside' of mathematics may have been more important: First, a lot of problems in Combinatorial Optimization arose immediately from everyday practice in engineering and management, for example determining shortest or most reliable paths in traffic or communication networks, maximal or compatible flows or shortest tours, planning connections in traffic networks, coordinating projects or supply and demand problems. Second, practical instances of these tasks, which belong to Operations Research, have become accessible by the development of more and more efficient computer systems. Furthermore, Combinatorial Optimization problems are also important for Complexity Theory, an area in the common intersection of Mathematics and Theoretical Computer Science which deals with the analysis of algorithms. Combinatorial Optimization is a fascinating part of mathematics, and a lot of its fascination – at least for me – comes from its interdisciplinarity and its practical relevance.

The present book concerns mainly that part of Combinatorial Optimization which can be formulated and treated by graph theoretical methods; neither the theory of Linear Programming nor Polyhedral Combinatorics are considered. Simultaneously, the book gives an introduction into Graph Theory, where we restrict ourselves to finite graphs. We motivate the problems by practical interpretations wherever possible.[1] Also, we use an algorithmic point of view, that is, we are not content with knowing that an optimal solution exists (this is trivial to see in most cases anyway), but we are mainly interested in the problem of how to find an optimal (or at least almost optimal) solution as efficiently as possible. Most of the problems we treat have a 'good' algorithmic solution, but we also show how even difficult problems can be treated (for example by approximation algorithms or complete enumeration) using a particular 'hard' problem (namely the famous 'travelling

---

[1] Most of the subjects we treat here are of great importance for practical applications, for example for VLSI-Layout or for designing traffic or communication networks. We recommend the books by Bermond (1992), Korte, Lovász, Prömel and Schriver (1990) and Lengauer (1990).

salesman problem') as an example. Such techniques are interesting even for problems where it is possible to find an exact solution because they may decrease the amount of calculation work considerably. To be able to judge the quality of algorithms and the degree of difficulty of problems, we introduce the basic ideas of Complexity Theory (in an informal way) and explain one of the main open problems of modern mathematics (namely the question 'P=NP?'). In the first chapters of the book, we will present algorithms in a rather detailed manner but turn to a more concise presentation in later parts. We decided not to include any explicit programs in this book; it should not be too difficult for a reader who is used to writing programs to transfer the given algorithms. Giving programs in any fixed programming language would have meant that the book is likely to be obsolete within a short time; moreover, explicit programs would have obscured the mathematical background of the algorithms. However, we use a structured way of presentation for our algorithms, including special commands based on PASCAL (a rather usual approach). The book contains a lot of exercises and, in the appendix, the corresponding solutions or hints for finding the solution. As in any other discipline, Combinatorial Optimization can be learned best by really working with the material; this is true in particular for understanding the algorithms. Therefore, we urge the reader to work on the exercises seriously (and do the mere calculations as well).

The present book is a translation of a revised version of the third edition of my German text book 'Graphen, Netzwerke und Algorithmen'. The translation and the typesetting was done by Dr. Tilla Schade in collaboration with myself.

The text is based on two courses I gave in the winter term 1984/85 and in the summer term 1985 at the Justus-Liebig-University in Gießen. As the first edition of the book which appeared in 1987 was received quite well, a second edition became necessary in 1990. This second edition was only slightly changed (there were only a few corrections and some additions made, including a further appendix and a number of new references), because it appeared a relatively short time after the first edition. The third edition, however, was completely revised and newly typeset. Besides several corrections and rearrangements, some larger supplements were added and the references brought up to date. The lectures and seminars concerning Combinatorial Optimization and Graph Theory I continued to give regularly (first at the University of Gießen, since the summer term 1993 at the University of Augsburg) were very helpful here. I used the text presented here repeatedly; I also took it as the basis for a workshop for high school students organized by the 'Verein Bildung und Begabung'. This workshop showed that the subjects treated in this book are accessible even to high school students; if they are motivated sufficiently, they approach the problems presented with great interest. Moreover, the German edition has been used regularly at various other universities.

I thank my students and assistants and the students who attended the workshop mentioned above for their constant attention and steady interest. Thanks are due, in particular, to Priv.-Doz. Dr. Dirk Hachenberger and Prof. Dr. Alexander Pott who read the whole manuscript of the (German) third edition with critical accuracy; the remaining errors are my responsibility.

Augsburg, May 1998   Dieter Jungnickel

Table of Contents

1. Basic Graph Theory

The history of Graph Theory begins with a paper by Euler (1736)[1] where he solved the well-known 'Königsberger Brückenproblem'. This problem consists in finding a circular tour through Königsberg using each of the seven bridges over the river Pregel exactly once.

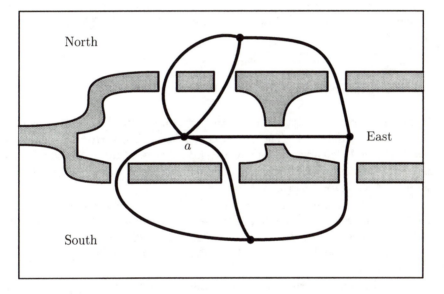

Fig. 1.1 Map of Königsberg and the corresponding graph

When trying to solve this problem one soon gets the feeling that there is no solution. But how can this be proved? Euler realized that the shapes of the islands and of the banks of the river are not important; the solvability depends only on the 'connection properties'. We represent the two islands and the two banks of the river by points (called vertices), and the bridges by lines

---

[1] see Wilson (1986) and Biggs, Lloyd and Wilson (1976).

between the respective points. Thus we get the 'graph' of the above picture. Trying to find a circular tour, we now begin a tour, say, at the vertex called a. When our tour returns to a for the first time, we have used two of the five bridges connected with a. At our next return to a we have used four bridges. Now we can leave a again using the fifth bridge, but there is no possibility to return to a without using one of the five bridges again. This shows that the problem is indeed unsolvable. Using a similar technique, it can be shown that it is impossible even to find any tour, not necessarily circular, using each bridge exactly once (that is, the tour might end at a different vertex than it begins). Euler proved even more in his paper and gave a necessary and sufficient condition for an arbitrary graph to have a circular tour of the above kind. We will treat his theorem in Section 1.3. But first, we have to introduce some basic notations.

The present chapter contains a lot of definitions. We recommend the reader to work on the exercises to get a better idea of what the terms really mean. Even though the present chapter has a more introductory nature, we will also prove a couple of nontrivial theorems and give two interesting applications. We warn the reader that the terminology in Graph Theory is rather unhomogeneous (although this improved a little after the book by Harary (1969) appeared).

1.1 Graphs, Subgraphs and Factors

A *graph* G is a pair $G = (V, E)$ consisting of a finite[2] set $V \neq \emptyset$ and a set E of two-element subsets of V. The elements of V are called *vertices*. An element $e = \{a, b\}$ of E is called an *edge* with *end vertices* a and b. We say that a and b are *incident* with e and that a and b are *adjacent* or *neighbours* of each other, and write $e = ab$ or $a \overset{e}{\longrightarrow} b$.

There are two important series of examples: The *complete graph* K_n has n vertices (that is, $|V| = n$) and all two-element subsets of V as edges. The *complete bipartite graph* $K_{m,n}$ has as vertex set the disjoint union of a set V_1 with m elements and a set V_2 with n elements; edges are all the sets $\{a, b\}$ with $a \in V_1$ and $b \in V_2$.

We will often illustrate graphs by pictures in the plane. The vertices of a graph $G = (V, E)$ are represented by (bold type) points and the edges by lines (preferably straight lines) connecting the end points. We give some examples:

---

[2] In Graph Theory, infinite graphs are studied as well. However, we restrict ourselves in this book – like Harary (1969) – to the finite case.

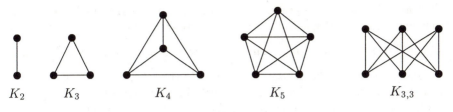

K_2 K_3 K_4 K_5 $K_{3,3}$

Fig. 1.2 Some graphs

We emphasize that in these pictures the lines merely show with which vertices the edges are incident. In particular, the 'inner points' of these lines as well as possible points of intersection of two edges (as in Figure 1.2 for the graphs K_5 and $K_{3,3}$) are not significant. In Section 1.5 we will study the question which graphs can be drawn without such additional points of intersection.

Let $G = (V, E)$ be a graph and V' be a subset of V. By $E|V'$ we denote the set of all edges e which have both their vertices in V'. The graph $(V', E|V')$ is called the *induced subgraph* on V' and is denoted by $G|V'$. Any graph $G' = (V', E')$ where $V' \subset V$ and $E' \subset E|V'$ is called a *subgraph* of G. A subgraph with $V' = V$ is called a *spanning subgraph*. Some examples are given in Figure 1.3.

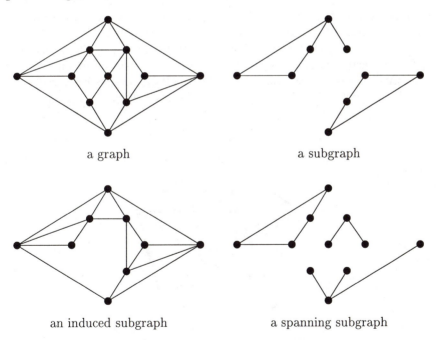

a graph   a subgraph

an induced subgraph   a spanning subgraph

Fig. 1.3 Subgraphs

For any vertex v of a graph, the *degree* deg v of v is the number of edges incident with v. We have the first (almost trivial) result:

Lemma 1.1.1. *In any graph, the number of vertices of odd degree is even.*

Proof. Summing the degree deg v over all vertices v, each edge is counted exactly twice (once for each of its vertices). Thus we have $\sum_v \deg v = 2|E|$. As the right hand side is even, the number of odd terms deg v in the sum on the left hand side must be even. $\square$

If all vertices of a graph G have the same degree r, G is called a *regular* graph, more precisely an *r-regular* graph. The graph K_n is $(n-1)$-regular, the graph $K_{m,n}$ is regular only if $m = n$ (in which case it is n-regular). A *k-factor* is a k-regular spanning subgraph. If the edge set of a graph can be divided into k-factors, such a decomposition is called a *k-factorization* of the graph. A 1-factorization is also called a *factorization* or a *resolution*. Obviously, a 1-factor can exist only if G has an even number of vertices. Factorizations of K_{2n} can be interpreted as schedules for a tournament of $2n$ teams (in soccer, basketball etc.). The following exercise shows that such a factorization exists for any n. The problem of setting up schedules for tournaments will be studied in Section 1.7 as an application.

Exercise 1.1.2. We use $\{a, b_1, \ldots, b_{2n-1}\}$ as the vertex set of the complete graph K_{2n} and divide the edge set into subsets E_i for $i = 1, \ldots, 2n - 1$, where $E_i = \{ab_i\} \cup \{b_j b_k : j + k \equiv 2i \pmod{2n - 1}\}$. Show that the E_i form a factorization of K_{2n}. (The case $n = 3$ is shown in Figure 1.4.) 1-factorizations were introduced by Kirkman (1847); interesting surveys are given by Mendelsohn and Rosa (1985) and Wallis (1992).

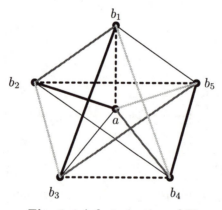

Fig. 1.4 A factorization of K_6

At the end of this section, we introduce one more series of graphs. The *triangular graph* T_n has as vertices the two-element subsets of a set with n elements. Two of these vertices are adjacent if and only if their intersection is not empty. Obviously, T_n is a $(2n - 4)$-regular graph. But T_n has even stronger regularity properties: the number of vertices adjacent to two given vertices x, y depends only on the fact whether x and y themselves are adjacent or not. Such a graph is called a *strongly regular graph*, abbreviated by *SRG*. These graphs are of great interest in Finite Geometry; see the books by Cameron and van Lint (1991) and Beth, Jungnickel and Lenz (1998). We will not look at SRG's any further in this book and only give some exercises concerning this concept:

Exercise 1.1.3. Draw the graphs T_n for $n = 3, 4, 5$ and show that T_n has parameters $a = 2n - 4$, $c = n - 2$ and $d = 4$, where a is the degree of any vertex, c is the number of vertices adjacent to both x and y if x and y are adjacent, and d is the number of vertices adjacent to x and y if x and y are not adjacent.

For the next exercise, we need another definition. For a graph $G = (V, E)$, the graph $\overline{G} = (V, \binom{V}{2} \backslash E)$ is called the *complementary graph*. Two vertices of V are adjacent in $\overline{G}$ if and only if they are not adjacent in G.

Exercise 1.1.4. Let G be an SRG with parameters a, c and d having n vertices. Show that $\overline{G}$ is also an SRG and give its parameters. Moreover, prove the formula
$$a(a - c - 1) = (n - a - 1)d.$$

(Hint: Count the number of edges yz for which y is adjacent to a given vertex x, and z is not adjacent to x.)

1.2 Paths, Cycles, Connectedness, Trees

Before we can go on to the Theorem of Euler mentioned in Section 1.1, we have to give a formal definition of what a 'circular tour' really means. Let $(e_1, \ldots, e_n)$ be a sequence of edges in a graph G. If there are vertices $v_0, \ldots, v_n$ such that $e_i = v_{i-1} v_i$ for $i = 1, \ldots, n$, the sequence is called a *walk*, for $v_0 = v_n$ a *closed walk*. A walk for which the e_i are pairwise distinct is called a *trail*, a closed walk with that property is a *closed trail*. If, in addition, the v_j are pairwise distinct, the trail is a *path*. A closed trail with $n \geq 3$, for which the v_j are pairwise distinct (except, of course, $v_0 = v_n$), is called a *cycle*. In any of these cases we use the notation

$$W : \quad v_0 \overset{e_1}{\rule{1.5cm}{0.4pt}} v_1 \overset{e_2}{\rule{1.5cm}{0.4pt}} v_2 \rule{1.5cm}{0.4pt} \quad \cdots \quad \rule{1.5cm}{0.4pt} v_{n-1} \overset{e_n}{\rule{1.5cm}{0.4pt}} v_n$$

and call n the *length* of W. The vertices v_0 and v_n are called the *start vertex* and the *end vertex* of W, respectively. We will sometimes specify a walk by the sequence of vertices $(v_0, \ldots, v_n)$, provided that $v_{i-1}v_i$ is an edge for $i = 1, \ldots, n$. In the graph of the following picture, (a, b, c, v, b, c) is a walk, but not a trail; and (a, b, c, v, b, u) is a trail, but not a path. Also, (a, b, c, v, b, u, a) is a closed trail, but not a cycle, whereas (a, b, c, w, v, u, a) is a cycle. We suggest the reader to consider some more examples.

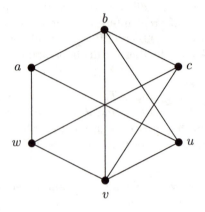

Fig. 1.5 An example for walks

Exercise 1.2.1. Show that a closed walk of odd length contains a cycle. What do closed walks not containing a cycle look like?

Two vertices a and b of a graph G are called *connected* if there exists a walk with start vertex a and end vertex b. If any two vertices of G are connected, G is called *connected*. For any vertex a, we consider (a) as a trivial walk (of length 0), so that any vertex is connected with itself. Then connectedness is an equivalence relation on the vertex set of G. The equivalence classes of this relation are called the *connected components* of G. Thus G is connected if and only if its vertex set V is a connected component. Components which contain only one vertex are also called *isolated vertices*. We give some exercises concerning the above definitions:

Exercise 1.2.2. Let G be a graph having n vertices and let any vertex of G have degree at least $\frac{n-1}{2}$. Show that G must be connected.

Exercise 1.2.3. A graph G is connected if and only if, for any decomposition $V = V_1 \,\dot\cup\, V_2$ (that is, $V_1 \cap V_2 = \emptyset$) of the vertex set of G, there exists an edge $e = vw$ such that $v \in V_1$ and $w \in V_2$.

Exercise 1.2.4. If G is not connected, the complementary graph $\overline{G}$ is connected.

If a and b are two vertices in the same connected component of a graph G, obviously there is a path of shortest length d between a and b. (Why?) Then a and b are said to have *distance* $d = d(a, b)$. The notion of distances in a graph is a very fundamental one in Graph Theory; we will investigate it (and a generalization) thoroughly in Chapter 3.

The rest of this section is devoted to characterizing and examining the minimal connected graphs. First, some more definitions and an exercise. A graph is called *acyclic* if it does not contain a cycle. For a subset T of the vertex set V of a graph G we denote by $G \backslash T$ the induced subgraph on $V \backslash T$. This graph arises from G by omitting all vertices in T and all edges incident with these vertices. For a one-element set $T = \{v\}$ we write $G \backslash v$ instead of $G \backslash \{v\}$.

Exercise 1.2.5. Let G be a graph without isolated vertices having n vertices and $n - 1$ edges (where $n \geq 2$). Show that G contains at least two vertices of degree 1.

Lemma 1.2.6. *Any connected graph on n vertices contains at least $n - 1$ edges.*

Proof. We use induction on n; the case $n = 1$ is trivial. So let G be a connected graph on $n \geq 2$ vertices. Choose an arbitrary vertex v of G and consider the graph $H = G \backslash v$. H is not necessarily connected, so suppose H has connected components Z_i having n_i vertices $(i = 1, \ldots, k)$, that is, $n_1 + \ldots + n_k = n - 1$. By induction hypothesis, the subgraph of H induced on Z_i has at least $n_i - 1$ edges. Moreover, v must be connected in G with each of the components Z_i by at least one edge. Thus G contains at least

$$(n_1 - 1) + \ldots + (n_k - 1) + k = n - 1$$

edges. □

Lemma 1.2.7. *Any acyclic graph on n vertices has at most $n - 1$ edges.*

Proof. If $n = 1$ or $E = \emptyset$, the statement is obvious. For the general case, choose any edge $e = ab$ in G. Then the graph $H = G \backslash e$ has exactly one more connected component than G. (Note that there cannot be a path in H from a to b, because such a path together with the edge e would give rise to a cycle in G.) Thus, H can be decomposed into connected, acyclic graphs $H_1, \ldots, H_k$ (where $k \geq 2$). By induction, we can assume that each graph H_i contains at most $n_i - 1$ edges, where n_i is the number of vertices of H_i. But then G has at most $(n_1 - 1) + \ldots + (n_k - 1) + 1 = (n_1 + \ldots + n_k) - (k - 1) \leq n - 1$ edges. □

Theorem 1.2.8. *Let G be a graph with n vertices. Then any two of the following conditions imply the third:*

(a) G is connected.
(b) G is acyclic.
(c) G has $n - 1$ edges.

Proof.

(i) Let G be acyclic and connected. Then Lemmas 1.2.6 and 1.2.7 imply that G has exactly $n - 1$ edges.

(ii) Now let G be a connected graph having $n - 1$ edges. Suppose G contains a cycle C, then the graph $H = G\backslash e$ (where e is any edge of C) is a connected graph with n vertices and $n - 2$ edges. This contradicts Lemma 1.2.6.

(iii) Suppose G is an acyclic graph having $n - 1$ edges. Then Lemma 1.2.7 implies that G cannot contain an isolated vertex (note that omitting such a vertex would give an acyclic graph with $n - 1$ vertices and $n - 1$ edges). By Exercise 1.2.5, G then has a vertex of degree 1, so that $G\backslash v$ is an acyclic graph with $n - 1$ vertices and $n - 2$ edges. By induction it follows that $G\backslash v$ and hence G are connected.

$\square$

Exercise 1.2.9. Give a different proof for Lemma 1.2.6 using the technique of omitting an edge e from G.

A graph T for which the conditions of Theorem 1.2.8 hold is called a *tree*. Any vertex of T having degree 1 is called a *leaf*. A *forest* is a graph whose connected components are trees. We will have a closer look at trees in Chapter 4.

In Section 4.2 we will prove the formula for the number of trees on n vertices due to Borchardt (1860) using rather sophisticated techniques from Linear Algebra. Now we give a much more elementary proof which furthermore has the advantage of proving a stronger result[3]. By $f(n, s)$ we denote the number of forests G having n vertices and exactly s connected components, for which s fixed vertices are in pairwise distinct components. Then the number of trees on n vertices is $f(n, 1)$. The following theorem due to Cayley (1889) gives a formula for the numbers $f(n, s)$; we give a simple proof due to Takács (1990a).

Theorem 1.2.10. *We have $f(n, s) = sn^{n-s-1}$.*

Proof. We begin by proving the following recursion formula:

$$f(n, s) = \sum_{j=0}^{n-s} \binom{n - s}{j} f(n - 1, s + j - 1), \qquad (1.1)$$

---

[3] The reader might skip the rest of this section during the first reading, but should come back after having read Section 4.2 for comparison.

where we set $f(1,1) = 1$ and $f(n,0) = 0$ for $n \geq 1$. How can an arbitrary forest G with vertex set $V = \{1,\ldots,n\}$ having precisely s connected components be constructed? Let us assume that the vertices $1,\ldots,s$ are the specified vertices which belong to distinct components. The degree of vertex 1 can have values $j = 0,\ldots,n-s$ (so that the neighbours of 1 form some arbitrary subset $\Gamma(1)$ of $\{s+1,\ldots,n\}$). Obviously we have – after choosing the degree j of 1 – exactly $\binom{n-s}{j}$ possibilities to choose $\Gamma(1)$. Note that the graph $G\backslash 1$ is a forest with vertex set $V\backslash\{1\} = \{2,\ldots,n\}$ and exactly $s+j-1$ connected components, where the vertices $2,\ldots s$ and the j elements of $\Gamma(1)$ are in different connected components. After having chosen j and $\Gamma(1)$, we still have $f(n-1, s+j-1)$ possibilities to construct the forest $G\backslash 1$. This proves the recursion formula (1.1).

We now prove the formula of the theorem by using induction on n. The case $n = 1$ is trivial. Thus, we assume $n \geq 2$ and that

$$f(n-1, i) = i(n-1)^{n-i-2} \qquad \text{holds for} \quad i = 1,\ldots n-1. \qquad (1.2)$$

Using this in equation (1.1) gives

$$
\begin{aligned}
f(n,s) &= \sum_{j=0}^{n-s} \binom{n-s}{j}(s+j-1)(n-1)^{n-s-j-1} \\
&= \sum_{j=1}^{n-s} j\binom{n-s}{j}(n-1)^{n-s-j-1} + (s-1)\sum_{j=0}^{n-s}\binom{n-s}{j}(n-1)^{n-s-j-1} \\
&= (n-s)\sum_{j=1}^{n-s}\binom{n-s-1}{j-1}(n-1)^{n-s-j-1} + \\
&\qquad\qquad + (s-1)\sum_{j=0}^{n-s}\binom{n-s}{j}(n-1)^{n-s-j-1} \\
&= \frac{n-s}{n-1}\sum_{k=0}^{n-s-1}\binom{n-s-1}{k}(n-1)^{(n-s-1)-k}\cdot 1^k + \\
&\qquad\qquad + \frac{s-1}{n-1}\sum_{j=0}^{n-s}\binom{n-s}{j}(n-1)^{n-s-j}\cdot 1^j \\
&= \frac{(n-s)n^{n-s-1} + (s-1)n^{n-s}}{n-1} = sn^{n-s-1}.
\end{aligned}
$$

This proves the theorem.   □

Note that the rather tedious calculations in the induction step could be replaced by the following (not shorter, but more elegant) combinatorial argument. We have to split up the sum we got from using equation (1.2) in (1.1) in a different way:

$$f(n,s) = \sum_{j=0}^{n-s} \binom{n-s}{j}(s+j-1)(n-1)^{n-s-j-1}$$

$$= \sum_{j=0}^{n-s} \binom{n-s}{j}(n-1)^{n-s-j} -$$

$$- \sum_{j=0}^{n-s-1} \binom{n-s}{j}(n-s-j)(n-1)^{n-s-j-1}.$$

Now the first sum counts the number of words of length $n-s$ over the alphabet $V = \{1,\ldots,n\}$: The binomial coefficient counts the number of possibilities to distribute j entries 1 (where j has to be between 0 and $n-s$), and the factor $(n-1)^{n-s-j}$ gives the number of possibilities how to fill the remaining $n-s-j$ positions with entries $\neq 1$. Analogously, the second sum counts the number of words of length $n-s$ over the alphabet $V = \{0,1,\ldots,n\}$ which contain exactly one entry 0. As there are obvious formulas for these numbers, we directly get

$$f(n,s) = n^{n-s} - (n-s)n^{n-s-1} = sn^{n-s-1}.$$

The theorem of Borchardt (1860) is now an immediate consequence of Theorem 1.2.10.

Corollary 1.2.11. *The number of trees on n vertices is n^{n-2}.*   □

It is remarkable that n^{n-2} is also the cardinality of the set $\mathbf{W}$ of words of length $n-2$ over an alphabet V with n elements. The question arises whether we could prove Corollary 1.2.11 by constructing a bijection between $\mathbf{W}$ and the set $\mathbf{T}$ of trees with vertex set V. This is indeed possible according to Prüfer (1918). We will now, following Lüneburg (1989), construct the 'Prüfer code' $\pi_V : \mathbf{T} \to \mathbf{W}$ recursively. As we will need an ordering of the elements of V, we assume in what follows w.l.o.g. that V is a subset of $\mathbb{N}$.

So let $G = (V, E)$ be a tree. For $n = 2$ the only tree on V is mapped to the empty word, that is, we set $\pi_V(G) = ()$. For $n \geq 3$ we use the 'smallest' leaf of G to construct a tree on $n-1$ vertices. We set

$$v = v(G) = min\{u \in V : deg_G(u) = 1\} \tag{1.3}$$

and denote by $e = e(G)$ the unique edge incident with v, and by $w = w(G)$ the other end vertex of e. Now let $G' := G\backslash v$. Then G' has $n-1$ vertices, and we can assume by induction that we know the word corresponding to G' under the Prüfer code on $V_G := V\backslash\{v\}$. We define recursively

$$\pi_V(G) := (w, \pi_{V_G}(G')). \tag{1.4}$$

It remains to show that we have indeed constructed the desired bijection. We need the following lemma which shows us how to determine the minimal leaf of a tree G on V from its Prüfer code.

Lemma 1.2.12. *For any tree G on V, the leaves are precisely those elements of V which do not occur in $\pi_V(G)$. In particular,*

$$v(G) = min\{u \in V : u \text{ does not occur in } \pi_V(G)\}. \tag{1.5}$$

Proof. First suppose that an element u of V occurs in $\pi_V(G)$. Then u was added to $\pi_V(G)$ at some stage of our construction, that is, some subtree H of G was considered and u was adjacent to the minimal leaf $v(H)$ of H. Now if u were also a leaf of G (and thus of H), then H would have to consist only of u and $v(G)$, so that H would have the empty word as Prüfer code, and u would not occur in $\pi_V(G)$, contradicting our assumption.

Now suppose that u is not a leaf. Then there is at least one edge incident with u which is discarded during the construction of the Prüfer code of G (because the construction only ends when a tree on two vertices remains of G). Let e be the edge incident with u which is omitted first. At that point of the construction, u is not a leaf, so that the other end vertex of e has to be the minimal leaf of the respective subtree. But then, by our construction, u is used as the next coordinate in $\pi_V(G)$. $\qquad\qquad\square$

Theorem 1.2.13. *The Prüfer code $\pi_V : \mathbf{T} \to \mathbf{W}$ defined by equations (1.3) and (1.4) is a bijection.*

Proof. For $n = 2$, the statement is clear, so let $n \geq 3$. First we show that π_V is surjective. Let $\mathbf{w} = (w_1, \ldots, w_{n-2})$ be an arbitrary word over V, and denote by v the smallest element of V which does not occur as a coordinate in $\mathbf{w}$. By induction, we may assume that there is a tree G' on the vertex set $V \backslash \{v\}$ with $\pi_V(G') = (w_2, \ldots, w_{n-2})$. Now we add the edge $e = vw_1$ to G' (as Lemma 1.2.12 suggests) and get a tree G on V. It is easy to verify that $v = v(G)$ and thus $\pi_V(G) = \mathbf{w}$. To prove injectivity, let G and H be two trees on $\{1, \ldots, n\}$ and suppose $\pi_V(G) = \pi_V(H)$. Now let v be the smallest element of V which does not occur in $\pi_V(G)$. Then Lemma 1.2.12 implies that $v = v(G) = v(H)$. Thus G and H both contain the edge $e = vw$, where w is the first entry of $\pi_V(G)$. Then G' and H' are both trees on $V \backslash \{w\}$, and we have $\pi_V(G') = \pi_V(H')$. Using induction, we conclude $G' = H'$ and hence $G = H$. $\qquad\qquad\square$

Note that the proof of Theorem 1.2.13 (together with Lemma 1.2.12) gives a constructive method for decoding the Prüfer code.

Example 1.2.14. Figure 1.6 shows some trees and their Prüfer codes for $n = 6$ (one for each isomorphism class, see Exercise 4.1.5).

Exercise 1.2.15. Determine the trees with vertex set $\{1, \ldots, n\}$ corresponding to the following Prüfer codes: $(1, 1, \ldots, 1)$; $(2, 3, \ldots, n-2, n-1)$; $(2, 3, \ldots, n-3, n-2, n-2)$; $(3, 3, 4, \ldots, n-3, n-2, n-2)$.

Exercise 1.2.16. How can we determine the degree of an arbitrary vertex u of a tree G from its Prüfer code $\pi_V(G)$? Give a condition for $\pi_V(G)$ to correspond to a path or a star (where a *star* is a tree having one exceptional vertex z which is adjacent to all other vertices).

Exercise 1.2.17. Let $(d_1, \ldots, d_n)$ be a sequence of positive integers. Show that there is a tree having n vertices whose degrees are $d_1, \ldots, d_n$ if $d_1 + \ldots + d_n = 2(n-1)$. (Hint: use the Prüfer code). Construct the tree with degree sequence $(1, 1, 1, 1, 2, 3, 3)$. We remark that the determination of the possible degree sequences of a graph on n vertices is a considerably more difficult problem; see, for instance, Sierksma and Hoogeveen (1991) and Barnes and Savage (1995).

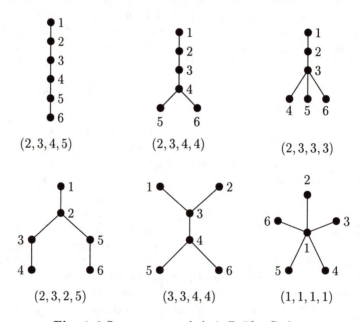

Fig. 1.6 Some trees and their Prüfer Codes

We have now seen two proofs for Corollary 1.2.11, which are examples for two important techniques in solving enumeration problems, namely using recursion formulas on the one hand and using bijections on the other. In Section 4.2 we will see yet another proof which will show the application of algebraic tools (like determinants or permanents). In this text, we cannot treat the most important tool of Enumeration Theory, namely generating functions. The interested reader can find the basics of Enumeration Theory in any good book on Combinatorics; for a more thorough study we recommend the extensive monograph of Goulden and Jackson (1983), which is a standard reference.

Concluding this section, we note that the number $f(n)$ of forests on n vertices has also been studied several times, see Takács (1990b) and the references given there. Takács proves the following simple formula (which is not easy to derive):

$$f(n) = \frac{n!}{n+1} \sum_{j=0}^{\lfloor n/2 \rfloor} (-1)^j \frac{(2j+1)(n+1)^{n-2j}}{2^j j!(n-2j)!}.$$

We mention an interesting asymptotic result due to Rényi (1959) comparing the number of all forests with the number of all trees:

$$\lim_{n \to \infty} \frac{f(n)}{n^{n-2}} = \sqrt{e} \approx 1.6487.$$

1.3 Euler Tours

In this section we will solve the Königsberger Brückenproblem for arbitrary graphs. The reader should note that the 'graph' of Figure 1.1 is not really a graph according to the definitions given in Section 1.1, because it contains pairs of vertices which are connected by more than one edge. Thus, we generalize our definition: For a *multigraph* $G = (V, E)$, E is allowed to be a family (instead of a set) of two-element subsets of V. To be able to distinguish the different edges connecting the same pair of vertices, we have to define a multigraph as a triple (V, E, J), where V and E are disjoint sets, and J is a mapping from E to the set of two-element subsets of V, the *incidence map*. The image $J(e)$ of an edge e is the set $\{a, b\}$ of end vertices of e. Edges e and e' with $J(e) = J(e')$ are called *parallel*. Then all the notions introduced so far carry over to multigraphs. However, in this book we will – with just a few exceptions – restrict ourselves to graphs.[4]

The 'circular tours' occuring in the Königsberger Brückenproblem can be described abstractly as follows. An *Eulerian trail* or an *Euler tour*[5], respectively, is a trail or a closed trail, respectively, which contains each edge of the multigraph G exactly once. A multigraph is called *Eulerian* if it contains an Euler tour. The following theorem of Euler (1736) characterizes the Eulerian multigraphs.

---

[4] Some authors denote the structure we call a 'multigraph' by 'graph'; graphs according to our definition are then called 'simple graphs'. Moreover, sometimes even edges e for which $J(e)$ is a set $\{a\}$ having only one element are admitted; such edges are then called *loops*. The corresponding generalization of multigraphs is often called a *pseudograph*.

[5] Sometimes one also uses the term 'Eulerian cycle', even though an Euler tour usually contains vertices more than once.

Theorem 1.3.1 (Theorem of Euler). *Let G be a connected multigraph. Then the following statements are equivalent:*

(a) G is Eulerian.
(b) Each vertex of G has even degree.
(c) The edge set of G can be partitioned into cycles.

    Proof:

(a) $\Rightarrow$ (b): Let C be an Euler tour of G. Each time a vertex v occurs in C adds 2 to its degree. As each edge of G occurs exactly once in C, any vertex v must have even degree.

(b) $\Rightarrow$ (c): Suppose G has n vertices. As G is connected, it has at least $n-1$ edges by Lemma 1.2.6. G does not contain vertices of degree 1, so that, by Exercise 1.2.5, G must have at least n edges. Then, by Lemma 1.2.7, there is a cycle K in G. Removing K from G we get a graph H in which any vertex still has even degree. Considering the connected components of H separately, we can, using induction, partition the edge set of H into cycles. Hence, the edge set of G can be partitioned into cycles.

(c) $\Rightarrow$ (a): Let C be one of the cycles in the partition of the edge set E into cycles. If C is an Euler tour, we are finished. Otherwise there exists another cycle C' having a vertex v in common with C. We can w.l.o.g. use v as start and end vertex of both cycles, so that CC' (that is, C followed by C') is also a tour. Going on with this procedure we finally get an Euler tour. $\qquad\square$

Corollary 1.3.2. *Let G be a connected multigraph having exactly $2k$ vertices of odd degree. Then G contains an Eulerian trail if and only if $k = 0$ or $k = 1$.*

Proof: The case $k = 0$ is clear by Theorem 1.3.1. So suppose $k \neq 0$. Similar to the proof of Theorem 1.3.1 it can be shown that an Eulerian trail can exist only if $k = 1$; in this case the Eulerian trail has the two vertices of odd degree as start and end vertices. Let $k = 1$ and name the two vertices of odd degree a and b. By adding an (additional) edge ab to G, we get a connected multigraph H whose vertices all have even degree. Hence H contains an Euler tour C by Theorem 1.3.1. Omitting the edge ab from C then gives the desired Eulerian trail in G. $\qquad\square$

Exercise 1.3.3. Let G be a connected multigraph having exactly $2k$ vertices of odd degree ($k \neq 0$). Then the edge set of G can be partitioned into k trails.

    The *line graph* $L(G)$ of a graph G has as vertices the edges of G; two edges of G are adjacent in $L(G)$ if and only if they have a common vertex in G. For example, the line graph of the complete graph K_n is the triangular graph T_n.

Exercise 1.3.4. Give a formula for the degree of a vertex of $L(G)$ (using the degrees in G). In which cases is $L(K_{m,n})$ an SRG?

Exercise 1.3.5. If G is Eulerian, then $L(G)$ is also Eulerian; the converse is false in general. Find a necessary and sufficient condition for $L(G)$ to be Eulerian.

Finally we recommend the very nice survey of Fleischner (1983), which treats Eulerian graphs and a lot of related questions extensively; another survey was written by Lesniak and Oellermann (1986). A much more extensive treatment of these subjects can be found in the monographs by Fleischner (1990) and Fleischner (1991). For a survey of line graphs, see Prisner (1996).

1.4 Hamiltonian Cycles

In 1859 Sir William Hamilton (known to every mathematician for the quaternions and the Theorem of Cayley-Hamilton) proposed the following game called 'around the world'. The corners of a regular dodecahedron were labelled with the names of cities; the task was to find a circular tour along the edges of the dodecahedron visiting each city exactly once (where sometimes the first steps of the tour were also prescribed). Thus, in the corresponding graph, we look for a cycle which contains each vertex exactly once. Such a cycle is therefore called a *Hamiltonian cycle*. In Figure 1.7 we give a solution for Hamilton's original problem.

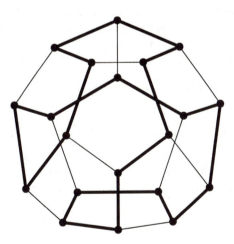

Fig. 1.7 Around the world

More about the game can be found in Ball and Coxeter (1947). Although Euler tours and Hamiltonian cycles have similar definitions, they are quite different. For example, there is no nice characterization of *Hamiltonian graphs*, that is, of those graphs containing a Hamiltonian cycle. As we will see in the next chapter, there are good reasons to believe that such a 'good' characterization cannot exist. However, we know many sufficient conditions for the existence of a Hamiltonian cycle; most of these conditions are statements about the degrees of the vertices. Obviously, the complete graph K_n is Hamiltonian.

We first prove a theorem from which we can derive several sufficient conditions on the sequence of degrees in a graph. Let G be a graph on n vertices. If G contains non-adjacent vertices u and v such that $\deg u + \deg v \geq n$, we add the edge uv to G. We continue this procedure until we get a graph $[G]$, in which, for any two non-adjacent vertices x and y, we always have $\deg x + \deg y < n$. $[G]$ is called the *closure* of G.(We leave it to the reader to show that $[G]$ is uniquely determined.) Then we have the following theorem due to Bondy and Chvátal (1976).

Theorem 1.4.1. *A graph G is Hamiltonian if and only if its closure $[G]$ is Hamiltonian.*

Proof. If G is Hamiltonian, $[G]$ is obviously Hamiltonian. As $[G]$ is derived from G by adding one edge after the other, it is sufficient to show that adding an edge – as described above – does not change the fact whether a graph is Hamiltonian or not. So let u and v be two non-adjacent vertices with $\deg u + \deg v \geq n$, and let H be the graph which results from adding the edge uv to G. Suppose that H is Hamiltonian, but G is not. Then there exists a Hamiltonian cycle in H containing the edge uv, so that there is a path $(x_1, x_2, \ldots, x_n)$ in G with $x_1 = u$ and $x_n = v$ containing each vertex of G exactly once. Consider the sets

$$X = \{x_i : vx_{i-1} \in E \text{ and } 3 \leq i \leq n - 1\}$$

and

$$Y = \{x_i : ux_i \in E \text{ and } 3 \leq i \leq n - 1\}.$$

As u and v are not adjacent in G, we have $|X| + |Y| = \deg u + \deg v - 2 \geq n - 2$. Thus, there exists i with $3 \leq i \leq n - 1$ such that vx_{i-1} as well as ux_i are edges in G. But then $(x_1, x_2, \ldots, x_{i-1}, x_n, x_{n-1}, \ldots, x_i, x_1)$ is a Hamiltonian cycle in G (see Figure 1.8), a contradiction.   □

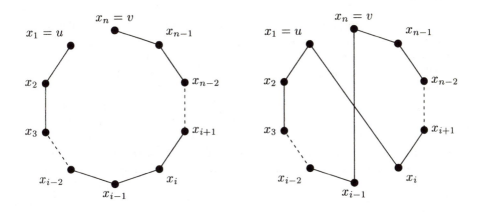

Fig. 1.8

In general, it will not be much easier to decide whether $[G]$ is Hamiltonian. But if, for example, $[G]$ is a complete graph, G has to be Hamiltonian by Theorem 1.4.1. Thus, we obtain the following two sufficient conditions for the existence of a Hamiltonian cycle, which were proved by Ore (1960) and Dirac (1952), respectively.

Corollary 1.4.2. *Let G be a graph having $n \geq 3$ vertices. If, for any two non-adjacent vertices u and v, we have $\deg u + \deg v \geq n$, then G is Hamiltonian.*   □

Corollary 1.4.3. *Let G be a graph having $n \geq 3$ vertices. If any vertex of G has degree at least $\frac{n}{2}$, then G is Hamiltonian.*   □

More sufficient conditions for the existence of a Hamiltonian cycle were derived by Bondy and Chvátal (1976) using Theorem 1.4.1, in particular they derived the result of Las Vergnas (1972). We refer the reader to Gondran and Minoux (1984). More results about Hamiltonian graphs can also be found in Harary (1969), Berge (1973), Bermond (1978) and Chvátal (1985).

Exercise 1.4.4. Determine the minimal number of edges a graph G with 6 vertices must have if $[G]$ is the K_6.

Exercise 1.4.5 (Ore(1961)). Let G be a graph having n vertices and m edges, and assume $m \geq \frac{1}{2}(n-1)(n-2) + 2$. Show that G is Hamiltonian (Hint: Use Corollary 1.4.2).

Exercise 1.4.6. If G is Eulerian, then $L(G)$ is Hamiltonian. Does the converse hold?

We digress a little and look at one of the oldest problems in popular mathematics, the *Knight's Problem*. This problem consists of moving a knight on a chessboard – beginning, say, in the upper left corner – such that it reaches each square of the board exactly once and returns with its last move to the square where it started. As mathematicians tend to generalize everything, they want to solve the problem for chess boards of any size, not even necessarily square. Thus we look at boards having $m \times n$ squares.[6] If we represent the squares of the chessboard by vertices of a graph G and connect two squares if the knight can move directly from one of them to the other, a solution of the Knight's Problem corresponds to a Hamiltonian cycle in G. We define G formally as follows: The vertices of G are the pairs (i, j) with $1 \le i \le m$ and $1 \le j \le n$; as edges we have all sets $\{(i, j), (i', j')\}$ with $|i - i'| = 1$ and $|j - j'| = 2$ or $|i - i'| = 2$ and $|j - j'| = 1$. Most of the vertices of G have degree 8, except the ones which are too near the edge of the chessboard. For example, the vertices at the corners have degree 2. In our context of Hamiltonian graphs, this interpretation of the Knight's Problem is of obvious interest. However, solving the problem is just as well possible without looking at it as a Graph Theory problem. Figure 1.9 gives a solution for the ordinary chess-board of $8 \times 8 = 64$ squares; the knight moves from square to square according to the numbers with which the squares are labelled. Moreover, Figure 1.9 shows the Hamiltonian cycle in the corresponding graph.

1	52	25	38	3	54	15	40
24	37	2	53	26	39	4	55
51	64	27	12	29	14	41	16
36	23	62	45	60	43	56	5
63	50	11	28	13	30	17	42
22	35	46	61	44	59	6	57
49	10	33	20	47	8	31	18
34	21	48	9	32	19	58	7

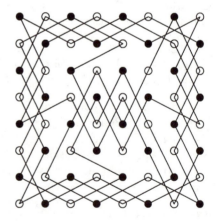

Fig. 1.9 A Knight's Cycle

---

[6] This problem was considered by Euler and Vandermonde and others; see the paper by Wilson (1989) about the history of Hamiltonian graphs, which is worth reading anyway.

The following theorem solves the Knight's Problem for arbitrary rectangular chessboards, see Schwenk (1991):

Result 1.4.7. *There is a 'knight's cycle' for any chessboard of size $m \times n$ (where $m \le n$), with the following three exceptions:*

(a) m and n are both odd.
(b) $m = 1, 2$ or 4.
(c) $m = 3$ and $n = 4, 6$ or 8.

$\square$

The proof (which is elementary) is a nice example of how such problems can be solved recursively, combining the solutions for some small sized chess-boards. (Solutions for boards of sizes 3×10, 3×12, 5×6, 5×8, 6×6, 6×8, 7×6, 7×8 and 8×8 are needed, and these can easily be found by computer.) The version of the knight's problem where no last move closing the circuit is required has also been studied. We refer to Conrad, Hindrichs, Morsy and Wegener (1994) and the entertaining presentation by Conrad, Hindrichs, Morsy and Wegener (1992).

Exercise 1.4.8. Show that knight's cycles are impossible for the cases (a) and (b) in Theorem 1.4.7. (Case (c) is more difficult.)
Hint: For case (a) use the ordinary colouring of a chessboard in black and white squares; for (b) use this same colouring as well as another appropriate colouring (say, in red and green squares) and look at a hypothetical knight's cycle.

At the end of this section we look at one of the most popular problems in Combinatorial Optimization, the *Travelling Salesman Problem*, or, for short, the *TSP*. This problem will later serve as our standard example of a 'hard' problem, whereas most of the other problems we will consider are 'easy'.[7]
We look at a travelling salesman who has to take a circular journey visiting n cities and wants to be back in his home city at the end of the journey. Which route is – knowing the distances between the cities – the best one? To translate this problem into the language of Graph Theory, we consider the cities as the vertices of the complete graph K_n; any circular tour then corresponds to a Hamiltonian cycle in K_n. To have a measure for the expense of a route, we give each edge e a 'weight' $w(e)$. (This weight might be the distance between the cities, but also the time the journey takes, or the cost, depending on the criterion subject to which we want to optimize the route.) The expense of a route then is the sum of all weights of edges in the corresponding Hamiltonian circuit. Thus the formal version of our problem is as follows:

---

[7] The distinction between 'easy' and 'hard' problems can be made quite precise; we will explain this in Chapter 2.

Problem 1.4.9 (Travelling salesman problem, TSP). On the complete graph K_n, we have a given weight function $w : E \to \mathbb{R}^+$. Find a cyclic permuation $(1, \pi(1), \ldots, \pi^{n-1}(1))$ of the vertex set $\{1, \ldots, n\}$ such that

$$w(\pi) := \sum_{i=1}^{n} w(\{i, \pi(i)\})$$

is minimal. We call any cyclic permutation π of $\{1, \ldots, n\}$ and the corresponding Hamiltonian cycle

$$1 \;\underline{\quad\quad}\; \pi(1) \;\underline{\quad\quad}\; \ldots \;\underline{\quad\quad}\; \pi^{n-1}(1) \;\underline{\quad\quad}\; 1$$

in K_n a *tour*. If $w(\pi)$ is minimal among all tours, we call π an *optimal tour*.

It is convenient to look at Problem 1.4.9 as a problem on matrices, where we write the weights as a matrix $W = (w_{ij})$. Of course, we have $w_{ij} = w_{ji}$ and $w_{ii} = 0$ for $i = 1, \ldots, n$. The cases of a TSP on n vertices thus correspond to the symmetric matrices in $(\mathbb{R}^+)^{(n,n)}$ having entries 0 on the main diagonal.

In the following example we have rounded the distances for the (with the exception of Basel, German) cities Aachen, Basel, Berlin, Dusseldorf, Frankfurt, Hamburg, Munich, Nuremberg and Stuttgart to units of 10 kilometers, and set $10w_{ij}$ to be the rounded distance.

Example 1.4.10. Determine an optimal tour for

	Aa	Ba	Be	Du	Fr	Ha	Mu	Nu	St
Aa	0	57	64	8	26	49	64	47	46
Ba	57	0	88	54	34	83	37	43	27
Be	64	88	0	57	56	29	60	44	63
Du	8	54	57	0	23	43	63	44	41
Fr	26	34	56	23	0	50	40	22	20
Ha	49	83	29	43	50	0	80	63	70
Mu	64	37	60	63	40	80	0	17	22
Nu	47	43	44	44	22	63	17	0	19
St	46	27	63	41	20	70	22	19	0

An optimal tour and a tour which is slightly worse (which we get by replacing the edges *MuSt* and *BaFr* by the edges *MuBa* and *StFr*) are shown in Figure 1.10. Note that looking at all the possibilities for tours is a lot of work: even for only nine cities we have $\frac{8!}{2} = 20160$ possibilities. (We can always take the tour to begin at vertex 1, and fix the direction of the tour.) Of course it would be feasible to look at all these tours – at least by computer. However, for 20 cities we get about 10^{17} possible tours, making this approach more or less impossible. We will have a closer look at the TSP in Chapter 14 and will explain the various techniques studied there using Example 1.4.10.

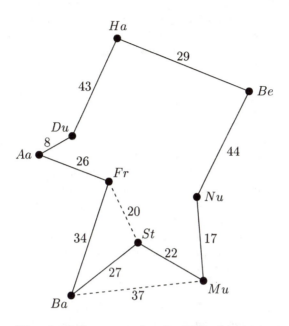

Fig. 1.10 Two tours for the TSP of 9 cities

Even though the number of possible tours grows exponentially with n, there still might be an easy method to solve the TSP. For example, the number of closed trails in a graph may also grow very fast as the number of edges increases; but, as we will see in Chapter 2, it is still easy to find an Euler tour or to decide that no such tour exists. On the other hand, it is difficult, as we have already mentioned, to find Hamiltonian cycles. We will use these three examples in the next chapter to think about the complexity (that is, the degree of difficulty) of a problem.

1.5 Planar Graphs

This section is devoted to the problem how to draw graphs in the plane. First, we need the notion of isomorphism. Two graphs $G = (V, E)$ and $G' = (V', E')$ are called *isomorphic* if there is a bijection $\alpha : V \to V'$ such that we have $\{a, b\} \in E$ if and only if $\{\alpha a, \alpha b\} \in E'$ (for any a, b in V). Let E be a set of lines in (three-dimensional) Euclidean space and V the set of end points of the lines in E. Identifying each line with the two-element set of its end points, we can consider (V, E) as a graph. Such a graph is called *geometric* if any two lines in E are disjoint or have one of their end points in common.

Lemma 1.5.1. *Any graph is isomorphic to a geometric graph.*

Proof. Let $G = (V, E)$ be a graph on n vertices. Choose a set V' of n points in $\mathbb{R}^3$ such that no four points lie in a common plane (Why is that possible?), and map V bijectively to V'. Let E' contain, for each edge e in E, the line connecting the images of the vertices on e. Then, obviously, (V', E') is a geometric graph isomorphic to G. □

As we have only a plane piece of paper to draw graphs, Lemma 1.5.1 does not help us a lot. We call a geometric graph *plane* if its lines all lie in one plane. Any graph isomorphic to a plane graph is called *planar*.[8] Thus, the planar graphs are exactly those graphs which can be drawn in the plane without additional points of intersection between the edges, see the comments after Figure 1.2. We will see that most graphs are not planar; more precisely, we will show that planar graphs can only contain comparatively few edges (compared to the number of vertices).

Let $G = (V, E)$ be a planar graph. If we omit the lines of G from the plane in which G is drawn, the remainder splits into a number of connected (open) regions; the closure of a region is called a *face*. We have the following theorem.

Theorem 1.5.2 (Euler's Formula). *Let G be a connected planar graph with n vertices, m edges and f faces. Then $n - m + f = 2$.*

Proof. We use induction on m. For $m = 0$ we have $n = 1$ and $f = 1$, so that the statement holds. Now let $m \neq 0$. If G contains a cycle, we discard one of the edges contained in this cycle and get a graph G' with $n' = n$, $m' = m - 1$ and $f' = f - 1$. By induction hypothesis, we have $n' - m' + f' = 2$, and hence $n - m + f = 2$. If G is acyclic, then G is a tree, and by Theorem 1.2.8 we have $m = n - 1$, and, as $f = 1$, again $n - m + f = 2$. □

Originally, Euler's formula connects the numbers of vertices, edges and faces of a convex polyhedron and is used, for example, to determine the five regular polyhedra (or *Platonic solids*, namely the tetrahedron, octahedron, cube, icosahedron and dodecahedron), see, for instance, Coxeter (1973). We now use Theorem 1.5.2 to derive bounds on the number of edges of planar graphs.

We need two more definitions. An edge e of a connected graph G is called a *bridge* if $G \backslash e$ is not connected. The *girth* of a graph containing cycles is the length of a shortest cycle.

Theorem 1.5.3. *Let G be a connected planar graph on n vertices. If G is acyclic, then G has precisely $n - 1$ edges. If G has girth at least g, then G can have at most $\frac{g(n-2)}{g-2}$ edges.*

---

[8] In the definition of planar graphs, one often allows not only straight lines, but curves as well. However, this does not change the definition of planarity as given above, see Wagner (1936). For multigraphs, it is necessary to allow curves.

Proof. The first statement follows from Theorem 1.2.8. Thus let G be a connected planar graph having n vertices, m edges and girth at least g. Then $n \geq 3$. We use induction on n; the case $n = 3$ is trivial. Suppose first that G contains a bridge e. Discarding e, G is divided into two connected induced subgraphs G_1 and G_2 which have disjoint vertex sets. Let n_i and m_i be the numbers of vertices and edges of G_i, respectively, for $i = 1, 2$. Then we have $n = n_1 + n_2$ and $m = m_1 + m_2 + 1$. As e is a bridge, at least one of G_1 and G_2 contains a cycle. If both G_1 and G_2 contain cycles, they both have girth at least g, so that by induction

$$m = m_1 + m_2 + 1 \leq \frac{g((n_1 - 2) + (n_2 - 2))}{g - 2} + 1 < \frac{g(n - 2)}{g - 2}.$$

If, say, G_2 is acyclic, we have $m_2 = n_2 - 1$ and, similar to the above argument,

$$m = m_1 + m_2 + 1 \leq \frac{g(n_1 - 2)}{g - 2} + n_2 < \frac{g(n - 2)}{g - 2}.$$

Now suppose that G does not contain a bridge. Then each edge of G is contained in exactly two faces. If we denote the number of faces whose border is a cycle consisting of i edges by f_i, we get

$$2m = \sum_i i f_i \geq \sum_i g f_i = g f,$$

as each cycle contains at least g edges. By Theorem 1.5.2, this implies

$$m + 2 = n + f \leq n + \frac{2m}{g}, \quad \text{and hence} \quad .m \leq \frac{g(n - 2)}{g - 2}.$$

$\square$

Corollary 1.5.4. *Let G be a connected planar graph with n vertices, where $n \geq 3$. Then G contains at most $3n - 6$ edges.*

Proof. This follows directly from Theorem 1.5.3, as G is either acyclic, or has girth at least 3. $\square$

Examples 1.5.5. (i) By Corollary 1.5.4, K_5 is not planar, as a planar graph on five vertices can have at most nine edges.

(ii) $K_{3,3}$ has girth 4 and, as it has more than eight edges, this graph is not planar by Theorem 1.5.3.

We want to state one of the most popular theorems of Graph Theory, namely the characterization of planar graphs due to Kuratowski, see Kuratowski (1930). We refer the reader to Harary (1969), Aigner (1984) or Thomassen (1981) for the elementary but rather lengthy proof. Again we need some definitions: A *subdivision* of a graph G is a graph H which can be derived from G by applying the following operation once or several times:

Replace an edge $e = ab$ by a path $(a, x_1, \ldots, x_n, b)$, where all the x_i are 'new' vertices, that is, vertices which have not been contained in G so far. Two graphs H and H' are called *homeomorphic* if they are subdivisions of the same graph G.

Exercise 1.5.6. If (V, E) and (V', E') are homeomorphic graphs, we have $|E| - |V| = |E'| - |V'|$.

Result 1.5.7 (Theorem of Kuratowski). *A graph G is planar if and only if it does not contain a subgraph which is homeomorphic to K_5 or $K_{3,3}$.*   □

It is clear, using Examples 1.5.5, that a graph having a subgraph homeomorphic to K_5 or $K_{3,3}$ cannot be planar. For the converse we refer to the sources given above. There is yet another interesting characterization of planarity. If we identify two adjacent vertices u and v in a graph G, we get an *elementary contraction* of G; more precisely, we omit u and v and replace them by a new vertex w which is adjacent to all vertices which were adjacent to u or v before. Figure 1.11 shows a subdivision and a contraction of $K_{3,3}$. A graph G is called *contractible* to a graph H if H arises from G by a sequence of elementary contractions. For the proof of the following theorem see Wagner (1937), Aigner (1984) or Harary and Tutte (1965).

Result 1.5.8. *A graph G is planar if and only if it does not contain a subgraph which is contractible to K_5 or $K_{3,3}$.*

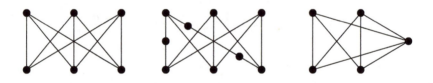

Fig. 1.11 $K_{3,3}$, a sudivision and a contraction

Exercise 1.5.9. Show that the *Petersen graph* (see Figure 1.12, cf. Petersen (1898)) is not planar. Give three different proofs using 1.5.3, 1.5.7 or 1.5.8, respectively.

Exercise 1.5.10. Show that the Petersen graph is isomorphic to the complement of the triangular graph T_5.

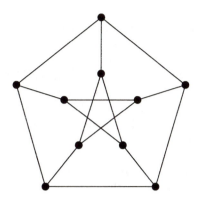

Fig. 1.12 The Petersen graph

The isomorphisms of a graph G onto itself are called *automorphisms*; they form a group called the *automorphism group* of G. In this book we will not have a closer look at the automorphisms of graphs (except for some comments on Cayley graphs in Chapter 8); we refer the reader to Yap (1986), Harary (1969) and Cameron and van Lint (1991). However, we give an exercise concerning this topic.

Exercise 1.5.11. Show that the automorphism group of the Petersen graph contains a subgroup isomorphic to the symmetric group S_5. (Hint: Look at Exercise 1.5.10.)

Exercise 1.5.12. What is the minimal number of edges which have to be removed from K_n to get a planar graph? For each n, construct a planar graph having the maximal number of edges.

The last exercise in this section shows that planar graphs have to contain many vertices of small degree.

Exercise 1.5.13. Let G be a planar graph on n vertices. By n_d we denote the number of vertices of degree at most d. Show that

$$n_d \geq \frac{n(d-5) + 12}{d+1}$$

and apply this formula to the cases $d = 5$ and $d = 6$. (Hint: Use Corollary 1.5.4.) Can the given formula be strengthened?

More on planarity (including algorithms) can be found in the monograph by Nishizeki and Chiba (1988).

1.6 Digraphs

For a lot of applications (especially for problems concerning traffic and transportation), it is useful to give a direction to the edges of a graph, for example to signify a one-way street in a city map. A *directed graph* or *digraph* is a pair $G = (V, E)$ consisting of a finite set V and a set E of ordered pairs (a, b), where $a \neq b$ are elements of V. The elements of V are called *vertices* again, those of E *edges*; the term *arc* is also used instead of 'edge' to have a distinction between the directed and the undirected case. Instead of $e = (a, b)$, we again write $e = ab$; a is called the *start vertex* or *tail* and b the *end vertex* or *head* of e. We say that a and b are *incident* with e, and call two edges of the form ab and ba *antiparallel*. To draw a directed graph, we proceed as in the undirected case, but indicate the direction of an edge by an arrow (see Figure 1.13). *Directed multigraphs* can be defined analogously to multigraphs; we leave the precise formulation of the definition to the reader.

There are some operations connecting graphs and digraphs. Let $G = (V, E)$ be a directed multigraph. Replacing each edge of the form (a, b) by an (undirected) edge $\{a, b\}$, we get the *underlying multigraph* $|G|$. Replacing parallel edges in $|G|$ by a single edge, we get the *underlying graph* (G). Conversely, let $G = (V, E)$ be a multigraph. Any directed multigraph H with $|H| = G$ is called an *orientation* of G. Replacing each edge ab in E by two arcs (a, b) and (b, a), we get the *associated directed multigraph* $\overrightarrow{G}$; we also call $\overrightarrow{G}$ the *complete orientation* of G. The complete orientation of K_n is called the *complete digraph* on n vertices. Figure 1.13 illustrates these definitions.

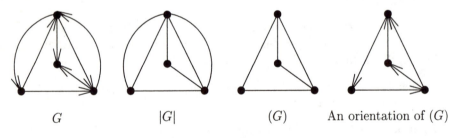

| G | $\lvert G \rvert$ | (G) | An orientation of (G) |

Fig. 1.13 (Directed) Multigraphs

We can now transfer the notions introduced for graphs to digraphs. There are some cases where two possibilities arise; we only look at these cases explicitly and leave the rest to the reader.

Let us consider trails first. Let $G = (V, E)$ be a digraph. A sequence of edges $(e_1, \ldots, e_n)$ is called a *trail* if the corresponding sequence of edges in $|G|$ is a trail. We define walks, paths, closed trails and cycles accordingly. Thus, if $(v_0, \ldots, v_n)$ is the corresponding sequence of vertices, $v_{i-1}v_i$ or v_iv_{i-1} must be an edge of G. In the first case, we have a *forward edge*, in the second a *backward edge*. If a trail consists of forward edges only, it is called a *directed trail* ; analogous definitions can be given for walks, closed trails, etc. In contrast to the undirected case, there exist directed cycles of length 2 (namely cycles of the form (ab, ba)).

A *directed Euler tour* in a directed multigraph is a directed closed trail containing each edge exactly once. We want to transfer the Theorem of Euler to the directed case. Some more definitions: By $d_{in}(v)$ we denote the number of edges having head v (the *indegree* of v), and by $d_{out}(v)$ the number of edges having tail v (the *outdegree* of v). A directed multigraph is called *pseudo-symmectric* if $d_{in}(v) = d_{out}(v)$ holds for each vertex v. Finally, a directed multigraph G is called *connected* if $|G|$ is connected.

Theorem 1.6.1. *Let G be a connected directed multigraph. Then the following statements are equivalent:*

(a) G has a directed Euler tour.
(b) G is pseudo-symmetric.
(c) The edge set of G can be partitioned into directed cycles.

Proof. As the proof is similar to the proof of Theorem 1.3.1, we leave the details to the reader. (Hint: The part '(b) implies (c)' needs a somewhat different argument). $\square$

For digraphs, there is another obvious way of defining 'being connected' besides the ordinary definition of connectedness given above. We say that a vertex b of a digraph G is *accessible* from a vertex a if there is a directed walk with start vertex a and end vertex b. As before, we allow walks to have length 0, so each vertex is accessible from itself. A digraph G is called *strongly connected* if any vertex is accessible from any other vertex. A vertex a from which any other vertex is accessible is called a *root* of G. Thus, a digraph is strongly connected if and only if each vertex is a root.

Note that a connected digraph is not necessarily strongly connected. For example, a tree can never be strongly connected (where a digraph G is called a *tree* if $|G|$ is a tree). If G has a root r, we call G a *directed tree*, an *arborescence* or a *branching* with root r. Obviously, an undirected tree has, for any vertex r, exactly one orientation as a directed tree with root r.

At the end of this section, we look at the question which connected multigraphs can be oriented in such a way that the resulting graph is strongly connected. Such multigraphs are called *orientable*. Thus, we ask which connected systems of streets can be made into a system of one-way streets such that people can still move from each point to any other point. The answer is given by the following Theorem of Robbins (1939).

Theorem 1.6.2. *A connected multigraph is orientable if and only if it does not contain any bridge.* $\square$

We want to prove a stronger result which allows to orient the edges one by one (in any arbitrary order). We need some more terminology. A *mixed multigraph* has edges which are either directed or undirected. (We leave the formal definition to the reader.) A *directed trail* in a mixed multigraph is a trail in which each oriented edge is a forward edge, but the trail might also contain undirected edges. If each vertex is accessible from any other vertex by a directed trail, a mixed multigraph is called *strongly connected*. The Theorem of Robbins can then be derived from the following result of Boesch and Tindell (1980) using induction.

Theorem 1.6.3. *Let G be a mixed multigraph and e an undirected edge of G. Suppose that G is strongly connected. Then e can be oriented in such a way that the resulting mixed multigraph is still strongly connected if and only if e is not a bridge.*

Proof. Obviously, the condition that e is not a bridge is necessary. So suppose that e is an undirected edge of G such that none of the two possible orientations of e gives a strongly connected mixed multigraph. We have to show that e is a bridge of $|G|$. Let u and w be the vertices incident with e, and denote the mixed multigraph we get by omitting e from G by H. Then there is no directed trail in H from u to w; because otherwise we could orient e from w to u and get a strongly connected mixed multigraph. Analogously, there is no directed trail in H from w to u.

Let S be the set of vertices which are accessible from u in H (by a directed trail). Then u is, for any vertex $v \in S$, accessible from v in H for the following reason: u is accessible in G from v by a directed trail W; suppose W contains the edge e, then w would be accessible in H from u, which contradicts our observations above. Now put $T = V \backslash S$; as w is in T, this set is not empty. Then any vertex $t \in T$ is accessible from w in H, because t is accessible from w in G, and again: if the trail from w to t in G needed the edge e, then t would be accessible from u in H, and thus t would not be in T.

We show next that e is the only edge of $|G|$ having a vertex in S and a vertex in T, which shows that e is a bridge. By definition of S, there cannot be an edge (s,t) or an edge $\{s,t\}$ with $s \in S$ and $t \in T$ in G. Finally, if G contained an edge (t,s), then u would be accessible in H from w, as t is accessible from w and u is accessible from s.   □

Exercise 1.6.4. Let G be a multigraph. Prove that G does not contain a bridge if and only if each edge of G is contained in at least one cycle. (We will see another characterization of these multigraphs in Chapter 7: Any two vertices are connected by two edge-disjoint trails.)

Mixed multigraphs are an obvious model for systems of streets. However, we will restrict ourselves to multigraphs or directed multigraphs, respectively, for the rest of this book. One-way streets can be modelled in directed multigraphs as well, and 'ordinary' two-way streets can then be represented by pairs of antiparallel edges.

Exercise 1.6.5. Let G be a connected graph all of whose vertices have even degree. Show that G has a strongly connected, pseudo-symmetric orientation.

Some relevant papers concerning (strongly connected) orientations of graphs are Chvátal and Thomasson (1978), Chung, Garey and Tarjan (1985) and Roberts and Xu (1988).

1.7 An Application: Tournaments and Leagues

In this section we look at the application of factorizations mentioned before, namely setting up schedules for tournaments[9]. If we want to design a schedule for a tournament, say, in soccer or basketball, where each of the $2n$ participating teams should play against each of the other teams exactly once, we can use a factorization $\mathbf{F} = \{F_1, \ldots, F_{2n-1}\}$ of K_{2n}. Then each edge $\{i, j\}$ represents the match between the teams i and j; if $\{i, j\}$ is contained in the factor F_k, this match will be played on the k-th day. (That means we have to choose an ordering of the factors!) If there are no additional conditions on the schedule, we can use any factorization. At the end of this section we will make a few comments on how to set up 'balanced' schedules.

Of course, the above method can also be used to set up a schedule for a league (like, for example, the German soccer league), if we consider the two rounds as two separate tournaments. But then there is the additional problem of planning the home and away games. Look at the first round first. Replace each 1-factor $F_k \in \mathbf{F}$ by an arbitrary orientation D_k of F_k, so that we get a factorization $\mathbf{D}$ of an orientation of K_{2n} (that is, a 'tournament' as defined in Exercise 7.5.5). Then the home and away games of the first round will be fixed as follows: If D_k contains the edge ij, the match between the teams i and j will be played on the k-th day of the season as a home match for team i. Of course, when choosing the orientation of the round of return matches, we have to take into account how the first round was oriented; we look at that problem later.

Now, as we want home and away games to alternate for each team (as far as possible) during the first round, we cannot use any arbitrary orientation $\mathbf{D}$ of any arbitrary factorization $\mathbf{F}$. This problem was solved by de Werra (1981) who obtained the following results. Define a $(2n \times (2n-1))$-matrix $P = (p_{ik})$ having entries A and H as follows: We have $p_{ik} = H$ if and only if team i has a home match on the k-th day of the season (that is, D_k contains an edge of the form ij). De Werra calls this matrix the 'home-away-pattern' of $\mathbf{D}$. A pair of consecutive entries p_{ik} and $p_{i,k+1}$ is called a *break* if the entries are the same (that is, there are two consecutive home or away games, a situation we want to avoid as far as possible). Before determining the minimal number of breaks, an example might be useful.

---

[9] This section will not be used in the remainder of the book, and thus can be skipped during the first reading.

Example 1.7.1. Look at the case $n = 3$ and use the factorization of K_6 shown in Figure 1.4, cf. Exercise 1.1.2, where we write i instead of b_i (for $i = 1, \ldots, 5$) and use the symbol ∞ for the vertex a. We choose the orientation of the five factors as follows: $D_1 = \{1\infty, 25, 43\}$, $D_2 = \{\infty 2, 31, 54\}$, $D_3 = \{3\infty, 42, 15\}$, $D_4 = \{\infty 4, 53, 21\}$ and $D_5 = \{5\infty, 14, 32\}$. Then we have the following matrix P:

$$
P = \begin{pmatrix}
A & H & A & H & A \\
H & A & H & A & H \\
H & A & A & H & A \\
A & H & H & A & H \\
H & A & H & A & A \\
A & H & A & H & H
\end{pmatrix},
$$

where the lines and columns are ordered $\infty, 1, \ldots, 5$ and $1, \ldots, 5$, respectively. Note that the matrix contains four breaks; the next lemma shows that this is best possible (for $n = 3$).

Lemma 1.7.2. *Any oriented factorization of K_{2n} has at least $2n - 2$ breaks.*

Proof. Suppose $\mathbf{D}$ has at most $2n - 3$ breaks, then there are at least three vertices for which the corresponding lines of the matrix P do not contain any breaks. At least two of these lines (the lines i and j, say) have to have the same entry (H, say) in the first column. As both lines do not contain any breaks, they have the same entries, and thus both have the form

$$H \quad A \quad H \quad A \quad H \ldots$$

Then, none of the factors D_k contains one of the edges ij or ji, a contradiction. (In other words: If the teams i and j always have either both a home match or both an away match, they cannot play against each other.)   □

The main result of de Werra (1981) shows that the bound of Lemma 1.7.2 can always be achieved.

Theorem 1.7.3. *The 1-factorization of K_{2n} given in Exercise 1.1.2 can always be oriented in such a way that the corresponding matrix P contains exactly $2n - 2$ breaks.*

Sketch of proof. Again we write i instead of b_i (for $i = 1, \ldots, 2n - 1$) and ∞ instead of a. We give an edge $\{\infty, k\}$ of the 1-factor E_k of Exercise 1.1.2 the orientation $k\infty$ if k is odd, and the orientation ∞k if k is even. Moreover, the edge $\{k + i, k - i\}$ of the 1-factor E_k is oriented as $(k + i, k - i)$ if i is odd, and as $(k - i, k + i)$ if i is even. (Note that the orientation in Example 1.1.3 has been chosen using this method.) Then it can be shown that the orientated factorization $\mathbf{D}$ of K_{2n} defined in this way has indeed exactly $2n - 2$ breaks. The lines corresponding to the vertices ∞ and 1 do not contain any breaks, whereas exactly one break occurs in all the other lines. The comparatively long, but not really difficult proof of this statement is left to the reader. Alternatively, the reader may consult the papers of de Werra (1981) or de Werra (1988).   □

Sometimes there are other properties an optimal schedule should have. For instance, if there are two teams from the same city or region, we want one of them to have a home game and the other to have an away game on each day of the season. Using the optimal schedule from Theorem 1.7.3, this can always be achieved.

Corollary 1.7.4. *Let* **D** *be the oriented factorization of* K_{2n} *with exactly* $2n - 2$ *breaks which was described in Theorem 1.7.3. Then, for any vertex* i, *there exists a vertex* j *such that* $p_{ik} \neq p_{jk}$ *for all* $k = 1, \ldots, 2n - 1$.

Proof. The vertex 'complementary' to vertex ∞ is vertex 1: Team ∞ has a home game on the k-th day of the season (that is, ∞k is contained in D_k) if k is even. Then 1 has the form $1 = k - i$ for some odd i, so that 1 has an away game on that day. Similarly it can be shown that the vertex 'complementary' to $2i$ (for $i = 1, \ldots, n - 1$) is the vertex $2i + 1$.   □

Now we still have the problem of finding a schedule for the return round of the league. Choose oriented factorizations $\mathbf{D}_H$ and $\mathbf{D}_R$ for the first and second round. Of course, we want $\mathbf{D} = \mathbf{D}_H \cup \mathbf{D}_R$ to be a complete orientation of K_{2n}; hence ji should occur as an edge in $\mathbf{D}_R$ if ij occurs in $\mathbf{D}_H$. If this is the case, $\mathbf{D}$ is called a *league schedule* for $2n$ teams. For $\mathbf{D}_H$ and $\mathbf{D}_R$, there are home-away-patterns P_H and P_R, respectively; we call $P = (P_H P_R)$ the home-away pattern of $\mathbf{D}$. As before, we want a league schedule to have as few breaks as possible. We have the following result:

Theorem 1.7.5. *Any league schedule* **D** *for* $2n$ *teams has at least* $4n - 4$ *breaks; this bound can be achieved for any* n.

Proof. As P_H and P_R both have at least $2n - 2$ breaks by Lemma 1.7.2, P obviously contains at least $4n - 4$ breaks. A league schedule having exactly $4n - 4$ breaks can be obtained as follows: By Theorem 1.7.3, there exists an oriented factorization $\mathbf{D}_H = \{D_1, \ldots, D_{2n-1}\}$ of K_{2n} with exactly $2n - 2$ breaks. Put $\mathbf{D}_R = \{E_1, \ldots, E_{2n-1}\}$, where E_i is the 1-factor having the opposite orientation as D_{2n-i} (that is, $ji \in E_i$ if and only if $ij \in D_{2n-i}$). Then P_H and P_R each contain exactly $2n - 2$ breaks; moreover, the first column of P_R corresponds to the factor E_1, and the last column of P_H corresponds to the factor D_{2n-1} which is the factor oriented opposite to E_1. Thus, there are no breaks between these two columns of P, and the total numer of breaks is $4n - 4$.   □

In reality, the league schedules described above are unwelcome, because the return round begins with the same matches with which the first round ended (though with home and away games exchanged). Instead, $\mathbf{D}_R$ is usually defined as follows: $\mathbf{D}_R = \{E_1, \ldots, E_{2n-1}\}$, where E_i is the 1-factor oriented opposite to D_i. Such a league schedule is called *canonical*. The following result can be proved analogously to Theorem 1.7.5.

Theorem 1.7.6. *Any canonical league schedule* $\mathbf{D}$ *for $2n$ teams has at least $6n - 6$ breaks; this bound can be achieved for any n.* □

For more results about league schedules and connected problems we refer to de Werra (1980), de Werra (1982), de Werra (1988) and Schreuder (1980). In practice, one often has a lot of secondary conditions (sometimes even conditions contradicting each other), so that the above theorems are not sufficient for finding a solution. In these cases, computers are used to look for an adequate solution satisfying the most important conditions. The problem of finding a schedule for the soccer league in the Netherlands for the season 1988/89 was discussed by Schreuder (1992). Another such real problem having secondary conditions was treated by de Werra, Jacot-Descombes and Masson (1990), and a survey of some European soccer leagues was given by Griggs and Rosa (1996).

Back to tournaments again! Basically, any factorization of K_{2n} can be used. But in reality, in most cases there are additional conditions the schedule should satisfy. For example, the teams should play an equal number of times on each of the n playing fields (because they might vary in quality, for example). The best one can ask for in a tournament with $2n-1$ games for each team is, of course, that each team plays twice on each of $n-1$ of the n playing fields and once on the remaining field. Such a schedule is called a 'balanced tournament design'. Any schedule can be written as a $(n \times (2n-1))$- matrix $M = (m_{ij})$, where the entry m_{ij} is given by the pair xy of teams playing in round j on field i. Sometimes it is required that, for the first as well as for the last n columns of M, the entries in each row of M form a 1-factor of K_{2n}; this is then called a 'partitioned balanced tournament design' (PBTD) on $2n$ vertices. Obviously, such a tournament schedule represents the best possible solution concerning a uniform distribution of the playing fields. We give an example for $n = 5$, and cite an existence result for PBDT's (without proof) proved by Lamken and Vanstone (1987) and Lamken (1987).

Example 1.7.7. The following matrix describes a PBTD on 10 vertices:

$$\begin{pmatrix} 94 & 82 & 13 & 57 & 06 & 23 & 45 & 87 & 91 \\ 83 & 95 & 46 & 02 & 17 & 84 & 92 & 05 & 63 \\ 56 & 03 & 97 & 81 & 42 & 67 & 01 & 93 & 85 \\ 12 & 47 & 80 & 96 & 53 & 90 & 86 & 14 & 72 \\ 07 & 16 & 25 & 43 & 98 & 15 & 37 & 26 & 04 \end{pmatrix}$$

Result 1.7.8. *Let $n \geq 5$ and $n \notin \{9, 11, 15, 26, 28, 33, 34\}$. Then there exists a PBTD on $2n$ vertices.* □

Finally, we recommend the interesting survey by Lamken and Vanstone (1989) about tournament designs, which are also studied in the book of Anderson(1990).

2. Algorithms and Complexity

In Theorem 1.3.1 we gave a characterization for Eulerian graphs: A graph G is Eulerian if and only if each vertex of G has even degree. This condition is easy to verify for any given graph. But how can we find an Euler tour in an Eulerian graph ? The proof of Theorem 1.3.1 only shows that such a tour exists, but does not tell us how to find it (though it contains a hint of how to achieve this). We are looking for a method for constructing an Euler tour, an 'algorithm'. In this book we generally look at problems from the algorithmic point of view: we want more than just theorems about existence or structure. As Lüneburg (1982) said: It is important that we can finally compute the objects we are working with. However, we will not go as far as giving concrete programs (in PASCAL, say); our algorithms will be described in a less formal way. Our main goal is to give an overview over the basic methods used in a very large area of mathematics; we can only achieve this (without exceeding the limits of this book) by omitting the details of programming techniques. Readers interested in concrete programs are referred to Syslo, Deo and Kowalik (1983) and Nijenhuis and Wilf (1978), where programs in PASCAL and FORTRAN, respectively, can be found.

Although a lot of algorithms will occur in the rest of this book, we will not try to give a formal definition of what an 'algorithm' really is. Such a definition belongs to both Mathematical Logic and Theoretic Computer Science and is given, for instance, in Automata Theory or in Complexity Theory; we refer the reader to Hopcroft and Ullman (1979) and Garey and Johnson (1979). As a general introduction, we also recommend the books by Aho, Hopcroft and Ullman (1974) and Aho, Hopcroft and Ullman (1983).

In this chapter, we will try to show, in an intuitive way, what an algorithm is, and develop a way to measure the 'quality' of an algorithm. In particular, we look at some basic aspects of graph theoretic algorithms, for example the problem of how to represent a graph. Moreover, we need a way to formulate the algorithms we deal with. We shall illustrate and study these considerations more thoroughly using two examples (Euler tours and acyclic digraphs). At the end of the chapter we introduce a class of problems (called NP-complete problems) which plays a central role in Complexity Theory; we will meet this type of problems over and over again in this book.

2.1 Algorithms

First we want to give the reader an intuitive notion of what an algorithm is. Algorithms are techniques for solving problems. Here the word 'problem' is used in a very general sense: A *problem class* consists of infinitely many *instances* having a common structure. The problem class *ET* ('Euler tour'), for example, means the task to decide, for a given graph G, whether it is Eulerian or not, and, if possible, to construct an Euler tour for G. Each graph is an instance of *ET*. An algorithm is a technique which can be used to solve each instance of a given problem class.

According to Bauer and Wössner (1982), an algorithm should have the following properties:

(1) *Finiteness of description*: The technique can be described by a finite text.
(2) *Effectiveness*: Each step of the technique has to be feasible (mechanically) in practice.[1]
(3) *Termination*: The technique has to stop for each instance after a finite number of steps.
(4) *Determinism*: The sequence of steps has to be uniquely determined for each instance.[2]

Of course, an algorithm should also be *correct*, that is, it should indeed solve the problem correctly for each instance. Moreover, an algorithm should be *efficient*, which means it should work as 'fast' and 'economically' as possible. We will look at this property more closely in Sections 2.5 and 2.7.

Note that – like Bauer and Wössner (1982) – we make a difference between an 'algorithm' and a 'program': an algorithm is a general technique for solving a problem (that is, it is problem-oriented), whereas a program is the concrete formulation of an algorithm as it is needed for being executed by a computer (and is therefore machine-oriented). Thus, the algorithm is the essence of the program. A very detailed study of algorithmic language and program development can be found in Bauer and Wössner (1982), see also Wirth (1976).

Now let us look at the problem class *ET*! The following example gives a trivial technique for solving this problem.

---

[1] It is probably because of this aspect of mechanical practicability that some mathematicians think that algorithms are not a part of mathematics. I think this is a misunderstanding: Performing an algorithm in practice does not belong to mathematics, but development and analysis of algorithms (including the translation into a program) do. Like Lüneburg (1982), I am of the opinion that treating a problem algorithmically means understanding it more thoroughly.

[2] In most cases, this property will not be required in this book.

Example 2.1.1. Let G be a graph, and thus an instance of ET. Then carry out the following steps:

(1) If G is not connected[3] or if G contains a vertex of odd degree, STOP: The problem has no solution.
(2) (All vertices have even degree). Choose an edge e_1, look at each permutation $(e_2, \ldots, e_m)$ of the remaining edges and check whether $(e_1, \ldots, e_m)$ is an Euler tour, until such a tour is found.

This 'algorithm' is correct by the Theorem of Euler, but there is still a lot to be said against it. First, it is not really an algorithm in our sense, because it does not determine how the permutations of the edges can be found and in which order they are examined. (The problem of generating permutations of a given set can be formulated in a graph theoretic way, see Exercise 2.1.3. Algorithms for this can be found in Nijenhuis and Wilf (1978) and Even (1973).) Moreover, it seems that examining up to $(m-1)!$ permutations is not really a very intelligent way of solving the problem. Analyzing the proof of Theorem 1.3.1 (compare also the directed case in 1.6.1) leads to another technique first given by Hierholzer (1873):

Example 2.1.2. Let G be an instance of ET, that is, G is a graph. Then carry out the following steps:

(1) If G is not connected or if G contains a vertex of odd degree, STOP: The problem has no solution.
(2) Choose a vertex v_0 and construct a closed trail $C_0 = (e_1, \ldots, e_k)$ as follows: for the end vertex v_i of the edge e_i choose an arbitrary edge e_{i+1} incident with v_i and different from $e_1, \ldots, e_i$, as long as this is possible.
(3) If the closed trail C_i constructed is an Euler tour: STOP.
(4) Choose a vertex w_i on C_i incident with some edge in $E \backslash C_i$. Construct a closed trail Z_i as shown in (2) (having start and end vertex w_i) in the connected component of w_i in $G \backslash C_i$.
(5) Form a closed trail C_{i+1}: Take the closed trail C_i with start and end vertex w_i, and append the closed trail Z_i. Continue with (3).

This technique yields a correct solution: As each vertex of G has even degree, for any vertex v_i reached in (2), there is an edge not yet used leaving v_i, except if $v_i = v_0$. Thus, step (2) really constructs a closed trail. In (4), the existence of the vertex w_i follows from the connectedness of G. However, the technique is not yet deterministic, but that can be helped by numbering the vertices and edges and, whenever something is to be chosen, choosing the vertex or edge, respectively, having the smallest number. In the future, we will not explicitly state how to make such choices deterministically. The steps in 2.1.2 are still rather big; at least in the first chapters we will give

---

[3] We can check whether a graph is connected with the BFS technique presented in Section 3.3.

more detailed versions of the algorithms. Toward the end of the book – when the reader is more used to our way of stating algorithms – we will often give rather concise versions of algorithms. A more detailed version of 2.1.2 will be presented in Section 2.3.

Exercise 2.1.3. A frequent problem is to order all permutations of a given set in such a way that two subsequent permutations differ by only a transposition. Show that this problem leads to the question whether a certain graph is Hamiltonian. Draw the graph for the case $n = 3$.

Exercise 2.1.4. We want to find out in which cases the closed trail C_0 constructed in Example 2.1.2 (2) is already necessarily Eulerian. An Eulerian graph is called *arbitrarily traceable* from v_0, if any maximal trail beginning in v_0 is an Euler tour. (Here 'maximal' means that all edges incident with the end vertex of the trail occur in the trail.) Show that:

(a) G is arbitrarily traceable from v_0 if and only if $G \backslash v_0$ is acyclic.
(b) If G is arbitrarily traceable from v_0, then v_0 is a vertex of maximal degree.
(c) If G is arbitrarily traceable from at least three different vertices, then G is a cycle.
(d) Give examples of graphs which are arbitrarily traceable from exactly two vertices.

The results in Exercise 2.1.4 are due to Ore (1951), who introduced the concept of arbitrarily traceable graphs, and to Bäbler (1953) and Chartrand and White (1970).

2.2 Representing Graphs

If we want to execute some algorithm for graphs in practice (which usually means on a computer), we have to think first about how to represent a graph. We do this now for digraphs; an undirected graph can then be treated by looking at its complete orientation.[4] So let G be a digraph, for example the one shown in Figure 2.1. We have labelled the vertices $1, \ldots, 6$; it is common practice to use $\{1, \ldots, n\}$ as the vertex set of a graph with n vertices. The easiest method to represent G is to list its edges.

---

[4] This statement refers only to the representation of graphs in algorithms in general. For each concrete algorithm, we still have to check whether this substitution makes sense. For example, we always get directed cycles by this approach.

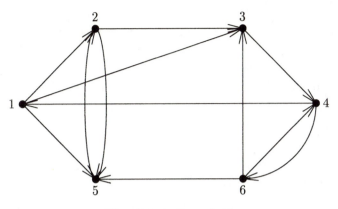

Fig. 2.1 A digraph G

2.2.1 List of Edges

A directed multigraph G on vertex set $\{1, \ldots, n\}$ is specified by:

(i) its number of vertices n;
(ii) the list of its edges, given as a sequence of ordered pairs (a_i, b_i), that is,
$e_i = (a_i, b_i)$.

The digraph G of Figure 2.1 is then given by:

(i) $n = 6$;
(ii) $12, 23, 34, 15, 52, 65, 46, 64, 41, 63, 25, 13.$[5]

The ordering of the edges was chosen arbitrarily.

A list of m edges can, for example, be implemented by two **arrays** $[1 \ldots m]$ (named 'head' and 'tail') of type **integer**; in PASCAL we could also define a type **edge** as a **record** of two components of type **integer**, and then use an **array**$[1 \ldots m]$ of **edge** to store the list of edges.

Lists of edges need few space in memory ($2m$ places for m edges), but they are not easy to work with: If we need, for example, all the vertices adjacent to a given vertex, we have to search through the whole list, which takes a lot of time. We can avoid this disadvantage by ordering the edges in a reasonable way or by using adjacency lists.

---

[5] We write simply ij instead of (i, j).

2.2.2 Incidence Lists

A directed multigraph G on vertex set $\{1, \ldots, n\}$ is specified by:

(i) the number of vertices n;

(ii) n lists $A_1, \ldots, A_n$, where A_i contains the edges beginning in vertex i. Here an edge $e = ij$ is recorded by listing its name and its head j, that is, as the pair (e, j).

The digraph of Figure 2.1 is then repesented as follows:

(i) $n = 6$;

(ii) $A_1 : (1, 2), (4, 5), (12, 3); A_2 : (2, 3), (11, 5); A_3 : (3, 4); A_4 : (7, 6), (9, 1);$
    $A_5 : (5, 2); A_6 : (6, 5), (8, 4), (10, 3).$

We have numbered the edges in the order given in 2.2.1. Note that incidence lists are basically the same as edge lists, given in a different ordering and split up into n separate lists. However, in the undirected case, each edge occurs now in two of the incidence lists, whereas it would have been sufficient to put it in the edge list just once. But working with incidence lists is much easier, especially for finding all edges incident with a given vertex. If G is a digraph or a graph (so that there are no parallel edges), it is not necessary to label the edges, and we can use adjacency lists instead of incidence lists:

2.2.3 Adjacency Lists

A digraph having vertex set $\{1, \ldots, n\}$ is specified by:

(i) the number of vertices n;

(ii) n lists $A_1, \ldots, A_n$, where A_i contains all vertices j for which G contains an edge (i, j).

The digraph of Figure 2.1 is represented by adjacency lists as follows:

(i) $n = 6$;

(ii) $A_1 : 2, 3, 5; A_2 : 3, 5; A_3 : 4; A_4 : 1, 6; A_5 : 2; A_6; 3, 4, 5.$

If, in the directed case, we often need all edges with a given end vertex as well as all edges with a given start vertex, it might be helpful to store 'backward adjacency lists' (where the end vertices are given) as well. For implementation, it is common to use ordinary or doubly linked lists. Then it is easy to work on all edges in a list consecutively, and to insert or remove edges. We give one more method for representing digraphs.

2.2.4 Adjacency Matrix

A digraph G with vertex set $\{1,\ldots,n\}$ can be specified by an $(n \times n)$-matrix $A = (a_{ij})$, where $a_{ij} = 1$ if and only if (i,j) is an edge in G, and $a_{ij} = 0$ otherwise. A is called the *adjacency matrix* of G. For the digraph of Figure 2.1 we have

$$A = \begin{pmatrix} 0 & 1 & 1 & 0 & 1 & 0 \\ 0 & 0 & 1 & 0 & 1 & 0 \\ 0 & 0 & 0 & 1 & 0 & 0 \\ 1 & 0 & 0 & 0 & 0 & 1 \\ 0 & 1 & 0 & 0 & 0 & 0 \\ 0 & 0 & 1 & 1 & 1 & 0 \end{pmatrix}.$$

Adjacency matrices can be implemented simply as an **array** $[1\ldots n, 1\ldots n]$. As they need a lot of space in memory (n^2 places), they will only be used to represent digraphs having many edges. Though adjacency matrices are of little practical interest, they are an important theoretical tool for studying digraphs.

If not stated otherwise, we always represent (directed) multigraphs by incidence or adjacency lists. We will not consider procedures for input or output or algorithms for treating lists (for instance, for operations such as inserting or removing elements, reordering or searching through a list) here. These techniques are not only used in Graph Theory but belong to the basic algorithms (searching and sorting algorithms, fundamental data structures) used in many areas. We refer the reader to the literature, for instance, Aho, Hopcroft and Ullman (1983), Mehlhorn (1984) and Corman, Leiserson and Rivest (1990). We close this section with two exercises about adjacency matrices.

Exercise 2.2.5. Let G be a (directed) graph having adjacency matrix A. Show that the (i,k)-entry of the matrix A^h is the number of (directed) walks of length h beginning at vertex i and ending at k.

Exercise 2.2.6. Let G be a strongly regular graph with adjacency matrix A. Give a quadratic equation for A. (Hint: Use Exercise 2.2.5 with $h = 2$.)

Looking at the adjacency matrix A (in particular, at the eigenvalues of A) is one of the main tools for studying strongly regular graphs, see Cameron and van Lint (1991). In general, the eigenvalues of the adjacency matrix of a graph are important in Algebraic Graph Theory, see Biggs (1993) and Schwenk and Wilson (1978) for an introduction and Cvetkovich, Doob and Sachs (1980) and Cvetkovic, Doob, Gutman and Torgasev (1987) for a more extensive treatment. Eigenvalues have a lot of interesting applications in Combinatorial Optimization as well; the reader might want to consult the interesting survey by Mohar and Poljak (1993).

2.3 The Algorithm of Hierholzer

In this section, we study the algorithm sketched in Example 2.1.2 in more detail. More precisely, we formulate the Algorithm of Hierholzer (1873) which is able to find a (directed) Euler tour in a (directed) Eulerian multigraph. We skip the trivial checking of the condition on the degrees.

Throughout this book, we will use the symbol $\leftarrow$ for assigning values: $x \leftarrow y$ means that value y is assigned to variable x. Boolean variables can have values 'true' and 'false'.

Algorithm 2.3.1. Let G be a (directed) Eulerian multigraph having vertex set $\{1, \ldots, n\}$. Moreover, let s be a vertex of G. We construct an Euler tour K with start vertex s.

1. Data structures needed

a) incidence lists $A_1, \ldots, A_n$; for any edge e, we denote the end vertex by end(e);

b) lists K and C for storing sequences of edges forming a closed trail. We use 'doubly linked' lists; that is, each element in the list is linked to its predecessor and its successor, so that these can be found easily;

c) a Boolean mapping 'used' on the vertex set (used(v) has value true if v occurs in K, and value false otherwise), and a list L containing all vertices v for which used(v) = true holds;

d) a pointer $e(v)$, which points, for each vertex v, to an edge in K beginning in v ($e(v)$ is undefined at the beginning of the algorithm);

e) a Boolean mapping 'new' on the edge set (new(e) has value true if e is not yet contained in the closed trail);

f) variables u, v (for vertices) and e (for edges).

2. Procedure TRACE(v, new; C)

The following procedure constructs a closed trail C consisting of edges not yet used, beginning at a given vertex v.

(1) If $A_v = \emptyset$, then **return**.

(2) (Now we are sure that $A_v \neq \emptyset$.) Find the first edge e in A_v and delete e from A_v.

(3) If new(e) = false, go to (1).

(4) (We know that new(e) = true.) Append e to C.

(5) If $e(v)$ is undefined, assign to $e(v)$ the position where e occurs in C.

(6) Assign new(e) $\leftarrow$ false and $v \leftarrow$ end(e).

(7) If used(v) = false, append v to the list L and set used(v) $\leftarrow$ true.

(8) Go to (1).

Here **return** means that the procedure is ended: thus a 'go to the end of the procedure' is performed, and the execution of the program continues with the procedure which called TRACE. We have already seen in Section 2.2 (more precisely, in the proof of 1.6.1) that the above procedure indeed constructs a closed trail C beginning in v.

3. Procedure EULER$(G, s; K)$.

(1) $K \leftarrow \emptyset$, used$(v) \leftarrow$ false for all vertices v, new$(e) \leftarrow$ true for all edges e.
(2) used$(s) \leftarrow$ true, append s to L.
(3) TRACE(s, new; K);
(4) If L is empty, **return**.
(5) Let u be the last element of L. Delete u from L.
(6) $C \leftarrow \emptyset$.
(7) TRACE(u, new; C).
(8) Insert C in front of $e(u)$ in K.
(9) Go to (4).

In step (3), a maximal closed trail K beginning in s is constructed, and all vertices occuring in K are stored in L. In steps (5) to (8) we then try, beginning at the last vertex u of L, to construct a detour C consisting of edges that were not yet used (that is, which have new$(e) =$ true), and to insert this detour into K. Of course, this detour C might be empty. As G is connected, the algorithm ends only if, for each vertex v of G, we have used$(v) =$ true, and no more detours are possible. If G is a directed multigraph, the algorithm works without the function new; we can then just delete each edge from the incidence list after it has been used.

We close this section with a somewhat lengthy exercise. We need some definitions: Let S be a given set of s elements, a so-called *alphabet*. Then any finite sequence of elements from S is called a *word* over S. A word of length $N = s^n$ is called a *de Bruijn sequence*, if, for any word w of length n, there exists an index i such that $w = a_i a_{i+1} \ldots a_{i+n-1}$, where indices are taken modulo N. For example, 00011101 is a de Bruijn sequence for $s = 2$ and $n = 3$. These sequences take their name from de Bruijn (1946). They are closely related to shift register sequences of order n, and are, particularly for $s = 2$, important in Coding Theory and Cryptography, see, for instance, Golomb (1967), MacWilliams and Sloane (1977) and Rueppel (1986); an extensive chapter on shift register sequences can also be found in Jungnickel (1993). We now show how the Theorem of Euler for directed multigraphs can be used to show the existence of de Bruijn sequences for all s and n. However, we have to admit loops (a, a) as 'edges' here; the reader should convince himself that Theorem 1.6.1 still holds.

Exercise 2.3.2. Define a digraph $G_{s,n}$ having the s^{n-1} words of length $n-1$ over an s-element alphabet S as vertices, and the s^n words of length n (over the same alphabet) as edges. The edge $a_1 \ldots a_n$ has the word $a_1 \ldots a_{n-1}$ as tail and the word $a_2 \ldots a_n$ as head. Show that the de Bruijn sequences of length s^n over S correspond to the Euler tours of $G_{s,n}$, and hence prove the existence of de Bruijn sequences for all s and n.

Exercise 2.3.3. Draw the digraph $G_{3,3}$ with $S = \{0, 1, 2\}$ and use Algorithm 2.3.1 to find an Euler tour beginning at vertex 00; where there is a choice, always choose the smallest edge (smallest when interpreted as a number). Give the corresponding de Bruijn sequence.

The digraphs $G_{s,n}$ can also be used to determine the number of de Bruijn sequences for given s and n; see Section 4.8. Algorithms for constructing de Bruijn sequences can be found in Ralston (1981) and Etzion (1986).

2.4 How to Write Down Algorithms

In this section, we introduce some rules for how algorithms are to be described. Looking again at Algorithm 2.3.1, we see that the structure of the algorithm is not easy to recognize. This is mainly due to the jump commands which hide the loops and conditional ramifications of the algorithm. Here, what Jensen and Wirth (1985) say about PASCAL is true: 'A good rule is to avoid the use of jumps to express regular iterations and conditional execution of statements, for such jumps destroy the reflection of the structure of computation in the textual (static) structures of the program.' Thus, we borrow some notations from PASCAL which will help us to display how an algorithm is structured. In particular, these notations, which are used often in the literature, emphasize the loops and ramifications of an algorithm.

In the remainder of this book, we will use the following notations:

2.4.1 Ramifications

if B **then** $P_1; P_2; \ldots; P_k$ **else** $Q_1; Q_2; \ldots; Q_l$ **fi**

means: If condition B is true, the operations $P_1, \ldots, P_k$ are executed; if B is false, operations $Q_1, \ldots, Q_l$ are executed. The alternative is optional; so that we might also have

if B **then** $P_1; P_2; \ldots; P_k$ **fi**.

In this case, if condition B is not satisfied, no operation is executed.

2.4.2 Loops

for $i = 1$ **to** n **do** $P_1; \ldots, P_k$ **od**

means: The operations $P_1, \ldots, P_k$ are executed for each of the (integer) values the 'control variable' i takes: for $i = 1$, $i = 2$, $\ldots, i = n$. It is also possible to decrement the values of i:

for $i = n$ **downto**   1   **do** $P_1; \ldots; P_k$ **od**.

2.4.3 Iterations

while B **do** $P_1; \ldots; P_k$ **od**

means: If condition B holds (that is, if B has Boolean value 'true'), operations $P_1, \ldots, P_k$ are executed; this is repeated as long as B holds.

repeat $P_1; \ldots; P_k$ **until** B;

means: The operations $P_1, \ldots, P_k$ are executed; if condition B is not satisfied afterwards, the operations are repeated, until finally condition B holds.

The main difference between these two ways of describing iterations is that a **repeat** is executed at least once, whereas the operations in a **while** loop are possibly not executed at all (namely if B is not satisfied).

for $s \in S$ **do** $P_1; \ldots; P_k$ **od**

means that the operations $P_1, \ldots, P_k$ are executed $|S|$ times, once for each element s in S. The order of the elements, and hence of the iterations, is not specified.

Moreover, we write **and** for the Boolean operation 'and' and **or** for the Boolean operation 'or' (not the exclusive or). As before, we shall use $\leftarrow$ for assigning values. The 'blocks' of an algorithm arising from ramifications, loops and iterations will be shown by indentations. As an example, we translate the algorithm of Hierholzer into the new notation.

Example 2.4.4. Let G be a (directed) Eulerian multigraph and s a vertex of G. The algorithm constructs a (directed) Euler tour K of G. The data structures we use are as in 2.3.1. Again, we have two procedures.

Procedure TRACE$(v, new; C)$

(1) **while** $A_v \neq \emptyset$ **do**
(2)   delete the first edge e from A_v;
(3)   **if** new$(e) = $ true
(4)   **then** append e at the end of C;
(5)   **if** $e(v)$ is undefined
(6)   **then** assign the position where e occurs in C to $e(v)$
(7)   **fi**
(8)   new$(e) \leftarrow$ false, $v \leftarrow$ end(e);
(9)   **if** used$(v) = $ false
(10)   **then** append v to L;
(11)   used$(v) \leftarrow$ true
(12)   **fi**
(13)   **fi**
(14) **od**

Procedure EULER$(G, s; K)$

(1) $K \leftarrow \emptyset, L \leftarrow \emptyset$;
(2) **for** $v \in V$ **do** used$(v) \leftarrow$ false **od**;
(3) **for** $e \in E$ **do** new$(e) \leftarrow$ true **od**;
(4) used$(s) \leftarrow$ true, append s to L;
(5) TRACE$(s,$new$;K)$;
(6) **while** $L \neq \emptyset$ **do**
(7)   let u be the last element of L;
(8)   delete u from L;
(9) $C \leftarrow \emptyset$;
(10)   TRACE$(u,$ new$; C)$;
(11)   insert C in front of $e(u)$ in K
(12) **od**.

We needed some more lines than in 2.3.1 to write down the algorithm, but it is obvious that the new notation reflects much more of its structure. Of course, this is mainly useful if we use a structured language (like PASCAL) for programming, but even for programming in a language which depends on jump commands it is helpful first to understand the structure of the algorithm. We will look at another example in detail in Section 2.6. Before, we consider the question of how to measure the quality of algorithms.

2.5 The Complexity of Algorithms

Complexity Theory studies the time and memory space an algorithm needs depending on the 'size' of the input data; this approach is used to compare different algorithms for solving the same problem. To do this in a formally correct way, we would have to be more precise about what an algorithm is; we would also have to make clear how input data and the time and space needed by the algorithm are measured. This could be done using Turing machines (introduced by Turing (1936)), but that would lead us too far away from our original subject.

Thus, we will use the number of vertices or edges, respectively, of the (directed) multigraph we are dealing with, for measuring the size of the input data. The *time complexity* of an algorithm A is the function f, where $f(n)$ is the maximal number of steps A needs to solve an instance of a problem having input data of length n. The *space complexity* is defined analogously for the memory space needed. We do not specify what a 'step' really is, but count the usual arithmetic operations, access to arrays, comparisons, etc. as one step. This does only make sense if the numbers in the problem do not become really big, which is the case for graph theoretic problems in practice (but usually not for arithmetic algorithms).

Note that the complexity is always measured for the worst possible case (for a given length of input data). This is not always realistic; for example, the Simplex Algorithm in Linear Programming has exponential complexity although it does work very fast in practice. Thus, it might often be better to use an 'average complexity'. But then, we would have to set up a probability distribution for the input data, and the whole treatment becomes much more difficult.[6] Therefore, it is common practice to look at the complexity for the worst case.

In most cases it is impossible to calculate the complexity $f(n)$ of an algorithm exactly. We are then content with an estimate of how fast $f(n)$ grows. We use the following notations: Let f and g be two mappings from $\mathbb{N}$ to $\mathbb{R}^+$. We write

- $f(n) = O(g(n))$, if there is a constant $c > 0$ such that $f(n) \leq cg(n)$ for all sufficiently large n;
- $f(n) = \Omega(g(n))$, if there is a constant $c > 0$ such that $f(n) \geq cg(n)$ for all sufficiently large n;
- $f(n) = \Theta(g(n))$, if $f(n) = O(g(n))$ and $f(n) = \Omega(g(n))$.

If $f(n) = \Theta(g(n))$, we say that f has *rate of growth* $g(n)$. If $f(n) = O(g(n))$ or $f(n) = \Omega(g(n))$, respectively, then f has at most or at least rate of growth $g(n)$, respectively. If the time or space complexity of an algorithm is $O(g(n))$, we say that the algorithm has complexity $O(g(n))$.

We will mostly consider the time complexity only, and just talk of the *complexity*. The space complexity is at most as large as the time complexity, because the data taking up memory space in the algorithm have to be read first.

---

[6] How difficult it really is to set up such a distribution can be seen in the probabilistic analysis of the Simplex Algorithm, see Borgwardt (1987).

Example 2.5.1. For a graph G, we obviously have $|E| = O(|V|^2)$; if G is connected, Theorem 1.2.6 implies that $|E| = \Omega(|V|)$. Graphs with $|E| = \Theta(|V|^2)$ are often called *dense*, graphs with $|E| = \Theta(|V|)$ are *sparse*. Corollary 1.5.4 tells us that the connected planar graphs are sparse. Note that $O(\log|E|)$ and $O(\log|V|)$ are the same for connected graphs, because the logarithms differ only by a constant factor.

Example 2.5.2. Algorithm 2.3.1 has complexity $\Theta(|E|)$, because each edge is treated at least once and at most twice (during the procedure TRACE); each such examination of an edge is done in a number of steps bounded by a constant, and constants can be disregarded in the notation we use. Note that $|V|$ does not appear because of $|E| = \Omega(|V|)$, as G is connected.

If, for a problem P, there exists an algorithm having complexity $O(f(n))$, we say that P has complexity at most $O(f(n))$. If each algorithm for P has complexity $\Omega(g(n))$, we say that P has complexity at least $\Omega(g(n))$. If, in addition, there is an algorithm for P having complexity $O(g(n))$, then P has complexity $\Theta(g(n))$.

Example 2.5.3. The problem of finding a (directed) Euler tour in a (directed) Eulerian multigraph has complexity $\Theta(|E|)$, because we have given an algorithm having this complexity, and obviously any algorithm for this problem has to consider all the edges to be able to put them into a sequence forming an Euler tour.

Unfortunately, in most cases, it is much more difficult to find lower bounds for the complexity of a problem than to find upper bounds, because it is hard to say something non-trivial about all possible algorithms for a problem. The reader might have realized another problem working with the above notations for the complexity of algorithms: Disregarding constants when looking at rates of growth means that the rates of growth are only asymptotically significant (that is, for very large n). For example, if we know that the rate of growth is linear, that is $O(n)$, but the constant is $c = 1000000$, this would not tell us anything for the cases of relatively small n. In fact, the asymptotically fastest algorithms for integer multiplication are only interesting in practice if the numbers treated are large, see, for instance, Aho, Hopcroft and Ullman (1974). However, for the algorithms we are going to look at, the constants will always be small (mostly ≤ 10).

In practice, the *polynomial* algorithms, that is, the algorithms of complexity $O(n^k)$ for some k, have proved to be the most useful. Such algorithms are also called *efficient* or – following Edmonds (1965b) – *good*. Problems for which a polynomial algorithm exists are also called *easy*, whereas problems for which no polynomial algorithm can exist are called *intractable* or *hard*. This terminology becomes clear if we consider the difference between polynomial and exponential rates of growth. The following table illustrates this difference which is most evident for large values of n:

$\frac{f(n)}{n}$	10	20	30	50	100
n	10	20	30	50	100
n^2	100	400	900	2,500	10,000
n^3	1,000	8,000	27,000	125,000	1,000,000
n^4	10,000	160,000	810,000	6,250,000	100,000,000
2^n	1,024	1,048,576	$\approx 10^9$	$\approx 10^{15}$	$\approx 10^{30}$
5^n	9,765,625	$\approx 10^{14}$	$\approx 10^{21}$	$\approx 10^{35}$	$\approx 10^{70}$

Table 2.1 Rates of Growth

The difference between polynomial and exponential rates of growth becomes even more obvious when thinking about the consequences of improved technology. Suppose we can at present – in some fixed amount of time, say an hour – solve an instance of size N on a computer (at rate of growth $f(n)$). What effect does an increase in computer speed of, say, a factor 1000 then have on the size of instances we are able to solve? If $f(n)$ is polynomial, say n^k, we will be able to solve an instance of size cN, where $c = 10^{3/k}$; for example, if $k = 3$, this still means a factor of $c = 10$. If the rate of growth is exponential, say a^c, there is only an improvement of constant size: we will be able to solve instances of size $N + c$, where $a^c = 1000$. For example, if $a = 2$, we have $c \approx 9.97$; for $a = 5$, $c \approx 4.29$.

We see that, from a practical point of view, it makes sense to consider a problem well solved only if we have found a polynomial algorithm for it. Moreover, if there is a polynomial algorithm, in most cases there is even an algorithm of rate of growth n^k with $k \leq 3$. Unfortunately, there is a very large class of problems, the so-called *NP-complete* problems, for which not only no polynomial algorithm is known, but there is good reason to believe that such an algorithm cannot exist. These questions are investigated more thoroughly in Complexity Theory, see Garey and Johnson (1979). Most algorithms we look at in this book are polynomial. Neverthelesss, we will explain in Section 2.7 what NP-completeness is, and show in Section 2.8 that determining a Hamiltonian cycle and the TSP are such problems. In Chapter 12, we will develop strategies for solving such problems (for example, approximation or complete enumeration) using the TSP as an example (the TSP is often used as the standard example for NP-complete problems). A lot of NP-complete problems will appear in various parts of this book.

It has to be admitted that most problems arising from practice tend to be NP-complete. It is indeed rare to be able to solve a real-world problem just by applying one of the polynomial algorithms we shall treat in this book. Nevertheless, these algorithms are of practical importance, since they are regularly used as sub-routines for solving more involved problems.

2.6 Directed Acyclic Graphs

In this section, we look at one further algorithm to illustrate once more the definitions and notations introduced in the last sections. The algorithm deals with directed *acyclic* graphs (or short 'dag'), that is, directed graphs which do not contain directed closed trails. This sort of graphs occurs in many applications, for example in the planning of projects (see 3.6) or for representing the structure of arithmetic expressions having common parts, see Aho, Hopcroft and Ullman (1983). First we give a mathematical application:

Example 2.6.1. Let $(M, \leq)$ be a *partially ordered set*, for short, a *poset*. This is a set M with a reflexive, antisymmetric and transitive relation $\leq$. Note that M corresponds to a directed graph G having vertex set M and the pairs (x, y) with $x < y$ as edges. G is obviously acyclic.

A frequent problem is to find out whether a given directed graph is acyclic, and if it is, to find a *topological sorting* of its vertices. That is, we are looking for an enumeration of the vertices of G (labelling them with the numbers $1, \ldots, n$, say) such that, for each edge ij, we have $i < j$. We show that such a sorting exists for any directed acyclic graph using the following lemma.

Lemma 2.6.2. *Let G be a directed acyclic graph. Then G contains at least one vertex with $d_{in}(v) = 0$.*

Proof. Choose a vertex v_0. If $d_{in}(v_0) = 0$, there is nothing to show. Otherwise, there is an edge $v_1 v_0$. If $d_{in}(v_1) = 0$, we are done. Otherwise, there exists an edge $v_2 v_1$. As G is acyclic, $v_2 \neq v_0$. Continuing this procedure, we get a sequence of pairwise distinct vertices $v_0, v_1, \ldots, v_k, \ldots$. As G has only finitely many vertices, this sequence has to terminate, so that we reach a vertex v with $d_{in}(v) = 0$.   □

Theorem 2.6.3. *For any directed acyclic graph, there is a topological sorting.*

Proof. According to Lemma 2.6.2, we can choose a vertex v with $d_{in}(v) = 0$. Look at the directed graph $H = G \backslash v$. Obviously, H is acyclic as well and can (using induction on the number of vertices) be sorted topologically. Suppose the enumeration of the vertices is $v_2, \ldots, v_n$. Then $(v, v_2, \ldots, v_n)$ is a topological sorting of G.   □

Corollary 2.6.4. *Any partially ordered set can be embedded into a linearly ordered set.*

Proof. Let $(v_1, \ldots, v_n)$ be a topological sorting of the corresponding directed acyclic graph. Then, if $v_i < v_j$, we always have $i < j$, so that $v_1 < \ldots < v_n$ is a complete linear ordering.   □

Next we present an algorithm which finds out whether a given directed graph is acyclic and, if this is the case, gives a topological sorting. The technique is taken from the proof of Theorem 2.6.3: We look for vertices with $d_{in}(v) = 0$ and delete them successively. To make the algorithm more efficient, we use a list of the $d_{in}(v)$ and bring it up to date whenever a vertex is deleted (so that we do not have to search through the whole graph for vertices with $d_{in}(v) = 0$). Moreover, we keep a list of the vertices having $d_{in}(v) = 0$. The following algorithm was originally given by Kahn (1962).

Algorithm 2.6.5. Let G be a given directed graph. The algorithm checks whether G is acyclic, and determines a topological sorting if possible.

Data structures needed

a) adjacency lists $A_1, \ldots, A_n$ (where G has vertex set $\{1, \ldots, n\}$);
b) a function 'ind', where $\text{ind}(v) = d_{in}(v)$;
c) a function 'topnr', where $\text{topnr}(v)$ gives the index of vertex v in the topological sorting ;
d) a list L of the vertices v having $\text{ind}(v) = 0$;
e) a Boolean variable 'acyclic' and an integer variable N (for counting).

Procedure TOPSORT $(G; \text{topnr}, \text{acyclic})$

(1) $N \leftarrow 1, L \leftarrow \emptyset$;
(2) **for** $i = 1$ **to** n **do** $\text{ind}(i) \leftarrow 0$ **od**;
(3) **for** $i = 1$ **to** n **do**
(4)   **for** $j \in A_i$ **do** $\text{ind}(j) \leftarrow \text{ind}(j) + 1$ **od**
(5) **od**;
(6) **for** $i = 1$ **to** n **do if** $\text{ind}(i) = 0$ **then** append i to L **fi od**;
(7) **while** $L \neq \emptyset$ **do**
(8)   delete the first vertex v from L;
(9) $\text{topnr}(v) \leftarrow N; N \leftarrow N + 1$;
(10)   **for** $w \in A_v$ **do**
(11) $\text{ind}(w) \leftarrow \text{ind}(w) - 1$;
(12)   **if** $\text{ind}(w) = 0$ **then** append w to L **fi**
(13)   **od**
(14) **od**;
(15) **if** $N = n + 1$ **then** acyclic $\leftarrow$ true **else** acyclic $\leftarrow$ false **fi**.

Theorem 2.6.6. *Algorithm 2.6.5 finds out whether G is acyclic, and if it is, constructs a topological sorting; the complexity is $O(|E|)$, if G is connected.*

Proof. The discussion above shows that the algorithm is correct. As G is connected, we have $|E| = \Omega(|V|)$, so that initializing the function ind and the list L in step (2) and (6), respectively, does not take more than $O(|E|)$ steps. Each edge is treated exactly once in step (4) and at most once in step (10), which means that the complexity is $O(|E|)$. $\square$

When checking whether a directed graph is acyclic, each edge has to be treated at least once. This observation gives:

Corollary 2.6.7. *The problem of checking whether a given connected digraph is acyclic or not has complexity* $\Theta(|E|)$. □

Exercise 2.6.8. Show that any algorithm which checks whether a digraph given by its adjacency matrix is acyclic or not has complexity at least $\Omega(|V|^2)$.

The above exercise shows that the complexity of an algorithm might depend considerably upon the way of representation chosen for the directed multigraph.

Exercise 2.6.9. Apply algorithm 2.6.5 to the directed graph shown in Figure 2.2.

In the remainder of this book, we will present algorithms in less detail than we did up to now. In particular, we will not explicitly explain the data structures used; they should be clear from the context. If not stated otherwise, all (directed) multigraphs are represented by incidence or adjacency lists.

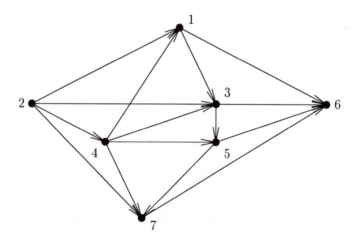

Fig. 2.2 A digraph

2.7 NP-Complete Problems

Up to now, we have only looked at algorithms whose complexity is polynomial, that is, $O(f)$ for a polynomial f in the size of the input data. Problems which can be solved by such an algorithm are called *polynomial* or – as in Section 2.5 – *easy*. Now we look at another class of problems. First, we restrict ourselves to *decision problems*, that is, to problems whose solution is either 'yes' or 'no'. The following problem HC is an example for such a decision problem; other such problems which we have solved already are the question whether an Euler tour exists in a (directed) multigraph, or the question whether a directed graph is acyclic.

Problem 2.7.1 (Hamiltonian cycle, HC). Let G be a given connected graph. Does G have a Hamiltonian cycle?

We will see that Problem 2.7.1 is just as difficult as the TSP given in 1.4.9. To do so, we make an excursion into Complexity Theory. The following problem is another, very important decision problem.

Problem 2.7.2 (Satisfiability, SAT). Let $x_1, \ldots, x_n$ be Boolean variables (that is, they can have values 'true' or 'false'). We consider formulae in $x_1, \ldots, x_n$ in *conjunctive normal form*, that is, terms of the type $C_1 C_2 \ldots C_m$, where each of the C_i has the form $x_i' + x_j' + \ldots$ (with $x_i' = x_i$ or $x_i' = \overline{x_i}$), that is, each C_i is a disjunction of some (possibly negated) variables.[7]. The problem SAT consists in deciding whether any of the possible combinations of values for the x_i gives the whole term $C_1 \ldots C_m$ the value 'true'. In the special case where each of the C_i consists of exactly three literals, the problem is called '3-satisfiability' (3-SAT).

Most of the problems in this book are not decision problems but *optimization problems*: Between all possible structures of a given kind (for example, for the TSP considered in Section 1.4, between all possible tours), we look for the optimal one with respect to a certain criterion (for example, the shortest tour). Examples for such problems (which we will solve in this book) are finding shortest paths, minimal spanning trees, maximal flows, maximal matchings, etc. However, each optimization problem corresponds to a decision problem; we illustrate this using the TSP. For a given matrix $W = (w_{ij})$ and a positive integer M, the corresponding decision problem is the question whether there exists a tour π such that $w(\pi) \leq M$. Between decision problems and optimization problems one might consider *evaluation problems*, where the value of an optimal solution is asked for, without requiring the explicit solution itself (for example, we ask for the length of an optimal tour without wanting to know the optimal tour itself). Obviously, any algorithm

---

[7] We write $\overline{p}$ for the negation of the logical variable p, $p + q$ for the disjunction 'p or q', and pq for the conjunction 'p and q'. The x_i' are called *literals*, the C_i are *clauses*.

for an optimization problem solves the corresponding evaluation problem as well; analogously, solving an evaluation problems also gives a solution for the associated decision problem. It is not clear whether the reverse of these statements is true. In general, using binary search, we can solve an evaluation problem using the solutions of the corresponding decision problem. But in general, we do not know how to construct an optimal solution if we only know its value.[8] Anyway, an optimization problem is at least as hard as the corresponding decision problem, which is all we will need to know.

We denote the class of all polynomial decision problems by P (for 'polynomial').[9] The class of decision problems for which a positive answer can be verified in polynomial time is denoted by NP (for 'non-deterministic polynomial'). That is, we do not only require the answer 'yes' or 'no', but the explicit specification of a *certificate* which allows to verify the correctness of a positive answer. We explain this concept by example, first using the TSP. If a possible solution (for the TSP, a tour) is presented, it has to be possible to check in polynomial time whether (i) the object has the required structure (whether it is really a tour, and not, say, just a permutation with several cycles) and whether (ii) the object satisfies the condition imposed (whether the tour has length $w(\pi) \leq M$, for example, where M is the given bound). Our second example is the question whether a given connected graph is not Eulerian. A positive answer can be verified by giving a vertex of odd degree. (We do not know an analogous certificate for the question whether a graph is not Hamiltonian!) However, the definition of NP does not demand that a negative answer can be verified in polynomial time. The class of decision problems for which a negative answer can be verified in polynomial time is denoted by Co-NP.[10]

Obviously, we have P ⊂ NP ∩ Co-NP: Any polynomial algorithm for a decision problem gives the correct answer in polynomial time, and thus can be used to verify a given answer. On the other hand, it is not clear whether every problem from NP is also in P or in Co-NP, respectively. For example, we do not know any polynomial algorithm for the TSP. Nevertheless, we can verify a positive answer in polynomial time (by checking whether the certificate π is a cyclic permutation of the vertices, calculating $w(\pi)$ and comparing it with

---

[8] In problems from Graph Theory, it is often sufficient to know that the value of an optimal solution can be determined polynomially. For example, for the TSP, we would check in polynomial time whether there is an optimal solution not containing a given edge. In this way, we can find an optimal tour by sequentially using the algorithm for the evaluation problem a linear number of times.

[9] To be formally correct, we would have to state how an instance of a problem is 'coded', so that the length of the input data could be measured, and what an 'algorithm' is. This can be done by using the concept of a Turing machine introduced by Turing (1936). For a detailed treatment of Complexity Theory, we refer to Garey and Johnson (1979) and Lewis and Papadimitriou (1981).

[10] For NP as well as for Co-NP we look at a kind of 'oracle' which presents some (positive or negative) answer to us; and this answer has to be verifiable in polynomial time.

M). However, we do not know any polynomial algorithm which could check a negative answer for the TSP (namely the answer: 'There is no tour of length $\leq M$' for some arbitrary given M). In fact, the questions whether P = NP or NP = Co-NP are the outstanding questions of Complexity Theory. As we will see, there are good reasons to believe that the conjecture P $\neq$ NP (and NP $\neq$ Co-NP) is true. To this end, we consider a special class of problems within NP.

A problem is called *NP-complete* if it is in NP and if the polynomial solvability of this problem would imply that all problems in NP are solvable in polynomial time as well. In other words: Each problem in NP can be 'transformed' (in polynomial time) to the given NP-complete problem such that a solution of the NP-complete problem also gives a solution of that other problem in NP. We will soon see some examples for such transformations. Note that NP-completeness is a strong condition on a problem: If we found a polynomial algorithm for such a problem, this would imply that P = NP. Of course, we do not even know yet whether NP-complete problems exist. The following theorem of Cook (1971) answers this question. For the rather technical and lengthy proof we refer to Garey and Johnson (1979) or Papadimitriou and Steiglitz (1982).

Result 2.7.3 (Cook's theorem). *SAT and 3-SAT are NP-complete.*   □

Having found a first NP-complete problem (such as 3-SAT), other problems can be shown to be NP-complete by transforming the known NP-complete problem in polynomial time to these problems. Thus, it has to be shown that a polynomial algorithm for the 'new' problem implies that the given NP-complete problem is polynomially solvable as well. For example, 3-SAT can be polynomially transformed to HC; so that we get the following result of Karp (1972), which we will prove in Section 2.8.

Theorem 2.7.4. *HC is NP-complete.*   □

Next we use Theorem 2.7.4 to show that the TSP (as a decision problem) is NP-complete; this proof will give a first relatively simple example for the method of transforming one problem into another. (The proof of Theorem 2.7.4 will be considerably more involved.)

Theorem 2.7.5. *TSP is NP-complete.*

Proof. TSP is obviously a problem in NP (see above). Suppose there exists a polynomial algorithm for TSP; we construct a polynomial algorithm for HC. Let $G = (V, E)$ be a given connected graph, and $V = \{1, \ldots, n\}$. Let K_n be the complete graph on V with weights

$$w_{ij} := \begin{cases} 1 & \text{for } ij \in E, \\ 2 & \text{otherwise.} \end{cases}$$

Obviously, G has a Hamiltonian cycle if and only if there exists a tour π of weight $w(\pi) \leq n$ (and then, of course, $w(\pi) = n$) in K_n. Thus, if there is a polynomial algorithm for TSP, then we can also decide HC in polynomial time. By Theorem 2.7.4, this implies that TSP is NP-complete.   □

Meanwhile hundreds of problems, some of which had been studied for decades, have been recognized as NP-complete; a lot of these problems are important in practice. A detailed list of such problems can be found either in Garey and Johnson (1979) or in the contributions 'The NP-completeness column: An ongoing guide' by David S. Johnson appearing periodically in the 'Journal of Algorithms'. For none of these problems, a polynomial algorithm could be found in spite of enormous efforts, which gives at least empirical evidence to the conjecture P $\neq$ NP.[11] Meanwhile, there has also been some theoretical progress, so that a proof of the conjecture P $\neq$ NP seems conceivable, see Johnson (1986). The study of this problem has led to the development of 'structural complexity theory'; see, for instance, Book (1994) for a survey. Anyway: Proving that NP-complete problems are in fact hard (that is, not solvable in polynomial time), would not help us when we have to deal with these problems in practice. Some possibilities how to treat these problems practically will be discussed in Chapter 14. At the end of this section, we give two (not really hard) exercises:

Exercise 2.7.6. Show that the problem DHC ('directed Hamiltonian cycle') is NP-complete, where DHC is the question whether a directed graph G contains a directed Hamiltonian cycle.

Exercise 2.7.7 (Hamiltonian path, HP). Show that the problem HP is NP-complete, where HP is the problem of deciding whether a given graph G contains a *Hamiltonian path* (that is, a path containing each vertex of G).

One more notation: A problem which is not a decision problem, but whose polynomial solvability would imply P = NP is called *NP-hard*. In particular, any optimization problem corresponding to an NP-complete decision problem is an NP-hard problem.

2.8 HC is NP-Complete

In this section (which can be skipped during the first reading) we prove Theorem 2.7.4 and show that HC is NP-complete. Following Garey and Johnson (1979), our proof makes a detour over another very important, NP-complete graph theoretical problem. First a definition: A *vertex cover* of a

---

[11] Thus, we can presumably read 'NP-complete' also as 'non-polynomial'. However, one sometimes finds the reverse conjecture P = NP, or the suggestion that the problem might not be decidable.

graph $G = (V, E)$ is a subset V' of V such that each edge of G is incident with (at least) one vertex in V'.

Problem 2.8.1 (Vertex Cover, VC). Let $G = (V, E)$ be a graph and k a positive integer. Does G have a vertex cover V' with $|V'| \leq k$?

Obviously, the problem VC is in NP. We prove a further result of Karp (1972) and show that VC is NP-complete by transforming 3-SAT polynomially to VC and applying Result 2.7.3. Our technique for the proof is used often for this kind of proof: we construct, for each instance of 3-SAT, a graph consisting of some 'special purpose components' combined in an elaborate way. We hope the strategy will become clear in the proofs of Theorem 2.8.2 and Theorem 2.7.4.

Theorem 2.8.2. *VC is NP-complete.*

Proof. We want to transform 3-SAT polynomially to VC. So let $C_1 \ldots C_m$ be an instance of 3-SAT, $x_1, \ldots, x_n$ are the variables occuring in $C_1, \ldots, C_m$. For each variable x_i we consider a copy of the complete graph K_2, namely

$$T_i = (V_i, E_i) \quad \text{where} \quad V_i = \{x_i, \overline{x_i}\} \quad \text{and} \quad E_i = \{x_i\overline{x_i}\};$$

the purpose of these subgraphs (called 'truth setting components' by Garey and Johnson (1979)) is to determine the Boolean value of x_i. Note that each vertex cover of the graph G we want to construct has to contain, for each i, at least one of the vertices x_i or $\overline{x_i}$. Analogously, for each clause C_j $(j = 1, \ldots, m)$, we define a copy $S_j = (V'_j, E'_j)$ of K_3, where

$$V'_j = \{c_{1j}, c_{2j}, c_{3j}\} \quad \text{and} \quad E'_j = \{c_{1j}c_{2j}, c_{1j}c_{3j}, c_{2j}c_{3j}\};$$

the purpose of these 'satisfaction-testing components' is to check the Boolean value of the clauses. Note that each vertex cover of G has to contain, for each j, at least two of the three vertices in V'_j.

The graphs T_i $(i = 1, \ldots, n)$ and S_j $(j = 1, \ldots, m)$ are the 'special components' of our graph G; they do not depend on the explicit structure of the term $C_1 \ldots C_m$, but only on n and m. The only part of the construction of G where the literals occuring in the clauses are used is the part we turn to now: Fixing the edges connecting the S_j and the T_i ('communication edges'). For each clause C_j, let u_j, v_j and w_j be the three literals occuring in C_j, and define a set of edges

$$E''_j = \{c_{1j}u_j, c_{2j}v_j, c_{3j}w_j\}.$$

Finally, we define $G = (V, E)$ by

$$V := \bigcup_{i=1}^{n} V_i \cup \bigcup_{j=1}^{m} V'_j \quad \text{and} \quad E := \bigcup_{i=1}^{n} E_i \cup \bigcup_{j=1}^{m} E'_j \cup \bigcup_{j=1}^{m} E''_j,$$

and put $k := n + 2m$. Obviously, the construction of G can be performed in polynomial time (in n and m). Figure 2.3 shows, as an example, the graph corresponding to the instance

$$(x_1 + \overline{x_3} + \overline{x_4})(\overline{x_1} + x_2 + \overline{x_4})$$

of 3-SAT. We claim that G has a vertex cover W with $|W| \leq k$ if and only if there is a combination of values for $x_1, \ldots, x_n$ such that $C_1 \ldots C_m$ has value true. Any vertex cover has to contain at least $n + 2m = k$ vertices (see our observations above), so that we get even $|W| = k$. Moreover, we know that, if W exists, it has to contain, for each i, exactly one of the vertices x_i and $\overline{x_i}$, and for each j, exactly two of the three vertices of S_j.

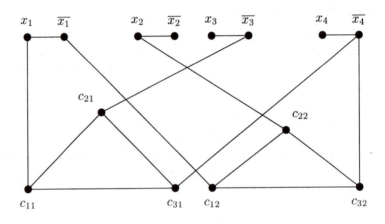

Fig. 2.3 An instance of VC

Now suppose W is such a vertex cover. Then we can use W as follows to obtain a combination w of Boolean values for the variables $x_1, \ldots, x_n$: If W contains x_i, we set $w(x_i) = $ true; otherwise W has to contain the vertex $\overline{x_i}$, and we set $w(x_i) = $ false. Now consider some arbitrary clause C_j. As W contains exactly two of the three vertices in V_j', these two vertices are incident with exactly two of the three edges in E_j''. As W is a vertex cover, it has to contain a vertex incident with the third edge ($c_{3j}w_j$, for example), and hence W contains the corresponding vertex in one of the V_i (in our example, the vertex corresponding to the literal w_j, that is, either x_i or $\overline{x_i}$). According to our definition of the assignment w of Boolean values, this literal has the value true, so that the clause C_j also is true. As this holds for all j, the combination w of Boolean values gives the term $C_1 \ldots C_m$ also the Boolean value true.

Conversely, let w be an assignment of Boolean values for the variables $x_1, \ldots, x_n$ such that $C_1 \ldots C_m$ takes the value true. We define a subset $W \subset V$

as follows: If $w(x_i) = $ true, W contains vertex x_i, otherwise W contains $\overline{x_i}$ (for $i = 1, \ldots, n$). Then, all edges in E_i are covered. Moreover, for each clause C_j (which has value true using w), at least one edge e_j of E_j'' is covered. Adding the end vertices in S_j of the other two edges of E_j'' to W, obviously all edges of E_j'' and of E_j' are covered and W is a vertex cover of cardinality k.   □

Exercise 2.8.3. An *independent set* or a *stable set* in a graph $G = (V, E)$ is a subset U of the vertex set V such that no two vertices in U are adjacent. A *clique* in G is a subset C of V such that any two vertices in C are adjacent. Show that:

(a) The following problem 'Independent Set' (IS) is NP-complete: Does a given graph G contain an independent set of cardinality $\geq k$?
(b) The following problem 'Clique' is NP-complete: Does a given graph G contain a clique of cardinality $\geq k$?

Hint: Think about how these problems are connected with VC.

Now we prove the NP-completeness of HC by transforming VC polynomially to HC; then, the assertion follows from Theorem 2.8.2. Again, we follow Garey and Johnson (1979). Let $G = (V, E)$ be a given instance of VC, and k a positive integer. We have to construct a graph $G' = (V', E')$ in polynomial time such that G' is Hamiltonian if and only if G has a vertex cover of cardinality $\leq k$. Again, we begin by defining some special purpose components. First, there are k special vertices $a_1, \ldots, a_k$ (called 'selector vertices') used to select k vertices from V. For each edge $e = uv \in E$, we define a subgraph $T_e = (V_e', E_e')$ having 12 vertices and 14 edges as follows (see Figure 2.4):

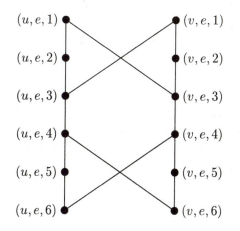

Fig. 2.4 Cover-testing component

$$V'_e := \{(u, e, i) : i = 1, \ldots, 6\} \cup \{(v, e, i) : i = 1, \ldots, 6\};$$
$$E'_e := \{\{(u, e, i), (u, e, i+1)\} : i = 1, \ldots, 5\} \cup$$
$$\cup \{\{(v, e, i), (v, e, i+1)\} : i = 1, \ldots, 5\} \cup$$
$$\cup \{\{(u, e, 1), (v, e, 3)\}, \{(u, e, 3), (v, e, 1)\}\} \cup$$
$$\cup \{\{(u, e, 4), (v, e, 6)\}, \{(u, e, 6), (v, e, 4)\}\}.$$

The subgraph T_e (called a 'cover-testing component') will make sure that the vertex set $W \subset V$ determined by the selectors $a_1, \ldots, a_k$ contains at least one of the vertices incident with e. In G', the only vertices of T_e incident with further edges will be the 'outer' vertices $(u, e, 1), (u, e, 6), (v, e, 1)$ and $(v, e, 6)$. The reader can easily convince himself that each Hamiltonian cycle of G' then has to 'run through' each of the subgraphs T_e using one of the paths shown in Figure 2.5:

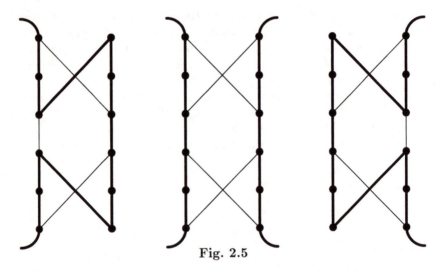

Fig. 2.5

To describe the other edges of G', we order, for each vertex $v \in V$, the edges incident with v in some arbitrary order and label them $ev_1, \ldots, ev_{\deg(v)}$. The $\deg(v)$ corresponding graphs T_{ev_i} are connected by the following edges:

$$E'_v := \{\{(v, ev_i, 6), (v, ev_{i+1}, 1)\} : i = 1, \ldots, \deg(v) - 1\}.$$

These edges create a path in G' which contains precisely the vertices (x, y, z) with $x = v$, see Figure 2.6.

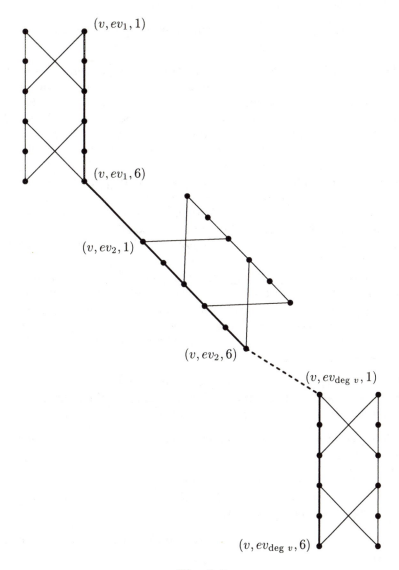

Fig. 2.6

Finally, we connect the start and end vertices of all these paths to each of the selectors a_j. Thus, we define a further edge set as follows:

$$E'' := \{\{a_j, (v, ev_1, 1)\} : j = 1, \ldots, k\} \cup \{\{a_j, (v, ev_{deg(v)}, 6)\} : j = 1, \ldots k\}.$$

Then we have

$$V' := \{a_1, \ldots, a_k\} \cup \bigcup_{e \in E} V'_e \quad \text{and} \quad E' := \bigcup_{e \in E} E'_e \cup \bigcup_{v \in V} E'_v \cup E''.$$

Obviously, G' can be constructed from G in polynomial time. Now suppose that G' contains a Hamiltonian cycle K. Let P be a trail contained in K beginning at a selector a_j and not containing any further selector. It is easy to see that P runs through exactly those T_e corresponding to all the edges incident with a certain vertex $v \in V$ (in the order given in Figure 2.6). Each of the T_e appears in one of the ways shown in Figure 2.5; no vertices from other cover-testing components T_b (not corresponding to edges f incident with v) can occur. Thus, the k selectors divide the Hamiltonian cycle K into k trails $P_1, \ldots, P_k$, each corresponding to a vertex $v \in V$. As K contains all the vertices of G', and the vertices of an arbitrary cover-testing component T_f can only occur in K by occuring in a trail corresponding to one of the vertices incident with f, the k vertices of V determined by the trails $P_1, \ldots, P_k$ form a vertex cover W of G.

Conversely, let W be a vertex cover of G, and $|W| \leq k$. We may assume $|W| = k$ (if $|W| < k$, we can add some arbitrary vertices to W). Write $W = \{v_1, \ldots, v_k\}$. The edge set of the Hamiltonian cycle K we look for is determined as follows. For each edge $e = uv$ of G we choose the edges in T_e drawn bold in one of the three graphs of Figure 2.5; our choice depends on the intersection of W with e as follows:

– if $W \cap e = \{u\}$, we choose the edges of the graph on the left,
– if $W \cap e = \{v\}$, we choose the edges of the graph on the right,
– if $W \cap e = \{u, v\}$, we choose the edges of the graph in the middle.

Moreover, K has to contain all edges in E'_{v_i} (for $i = 1, \ldots, k$) and the edges

$$\begin{array}{ll}
\{a_i, (v_i, (ev_i)_1, 1)\} & \text{for} \quad i = 1, \ldots, k, \\
\{a_{i+1}, (v_i, (ev_i)_{deg(v_i)}, 6)\} & \text{for} \quad i = 1, \ldots, k-1 \quad \text{and} \\
\{a_1, (v_k, (ev_k)_{deg(v_k)}, 6)\}.
\end{array}$$

The reader is invited to check that this defines indeed a Hamiltonian cycle K for G'. $\qquad\qquad\qquad\qquad\qquad\qquad\qquad\qquad\qquad\qquad\qquad\qquad\quad \square$

A proof of Theorem 2.7.4 which transforms 3-SAT directly (without the detour using VC) to HC can be found in Papadimitriou and Steiglitz (1982).

3. Shortest Paths

One of the most common applications of graphs in everyday life is the representation of networks for traffic or data communication. The survey map of german motorways in the official guide 'Autobahn Service', the railroad or bus lines in some system of public transportation, or the network of routes an airline offers are represented as graphs without anybody being aware of it. Thus, it is obviously of great practical interest to study paths in such graphs. In particular, we often look for paths which are 'good' or even 'best' in some respect: Sometimes the shortest or the fastest route is required, sometimes we want the cheapest path or the one which is 'safest' (for example, we want the route where it is most unlikely that we encounter a speed control installation). We will mainly consider shortest paths in (directed) graphs in this chapter, and we will see that this question is not only of interest in traffic networks.

3.1 Shortest Paths

Let $G = (V, E)$ be a graph or a directed graph on which a mapping $w : E \to \mathbb{R}$ is defined. We call the pair (G, w) a *network*; the number $w(e)$ is called the *length* of the edge e. Of course, this terminology is not intended to exclude other interpretations (such as cost, duration, capacity, weight, probability, ...); we will see some examples later. For instance, in the context of studying spanning trees, we usually interpret $w(e)$ as the weight of the edge e. However, in the present chapter, the reader should keep the image of lengths in a network of streets in mind for better illustration. Then the next definition follows naturally: For any (directed) walk $W = (e_1, \ldots, e_n)$, the *length* of W is the number $w(W) := w(e_1) + \ldots + w(e_n)$. For digraphs, of course, W has to be a directed walk. The *distance* $d(a, b)$ between two vertices a and b in G is the minimum of all lengths of walks starting at a and ending at b. There are two difficulties with this definition: First, b might not be accessible from a, and second, there might be walks of arbitrarily short length. The first problem can be solved by defining $d(a, b) = \infty$ if there is no (directed) path from a to b. The second problem comes from the possible existence of cycles of negative length. For example, in the network shown in Figure 3.1, we can find a walk of arbitrarily short length from a to b by using the cycle

(x, y, z, x) as often as needed. This problem can be avoided by restricting the definition to trails. Most of the networks we will deal with, however, will not contain any (directed) cycles of negative length. Then the distance between two vertices is well-defined even if we allow walks in the definition.

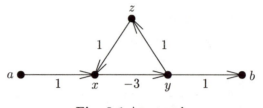

Fig. 3.1 A network

The reader might ask why negative lengths are allowed at all and whether they occur in practice. The answer is yes, they do occur, as the following example (which is also an example for another interpretation of the 'length' of an edge) from Lawler (1976) shows: A trading ship travels from port a to port b, where the route (and intermediary ports) are free to be chosen. The routes are represented by trails in a digraph G, and the length $w(e)$ of an edge $e = xy$ signifies the profit gained by going from x to y. For some edges, the ship will have to travel empty (because there is no load to carry), so that, for these edges, $w(e)$ is negative: the 'profit' is really a loss. Replacing w by $-w$ in this network, the shortest path represents the route which yields most profit. Clearly, the practical importance of this example is small. We will encounter really important applications later when treating flows and circulations. Then the existence of cycles of negative length (and finding these cycles) will be an essential tool for solving the problem of determining an optimal circulation.

Thus, we allow negative values for w in general and define distances as explained above. A *shortest path* from a to b then is a (directed) trail of length $d(a, b)$ from a to b. If G does not contain any (directed) cycles of negative length, we can also talk of shortest walks. We remark that always $d(a, a) = 0$, because an empty sum is defined to have value 0.

If we talk of shortest paths and distances in a graph (or a directed graph, respectively) without any given length function, we always use the length function which assigns length $w(e) = 1$ to each edge e.

Finally, we give an example for an interpretation of shortest paths which allows us to formulate a problem (which at first glance seems to be completely out of place here) as a problem of finding shortest paths in a suitable graph.

Example 3.1.1. In a lot of applications, the length of an edge signifies the probability of its failing (for instance, in networks of telephone lines, TV broadcasting systems, computer networks or roads used for transportation). In these cases, one is looking for the route having the highest probability for not failing. Let $p(i,j)$ be the probability that edge (i,j) does not fail. Assuming that failings of edges occur independently of each other (which is not always realistic), we have $p(e_1)\ldots p(e_n)$ as the probability that the walk $(e_1,\ldots,e_n)$ can be used without interruption. We want to maximize this probability over all possible walks with start vertex a and end vertex b. Note first that the maximum of the product of the $p(e)$ is reached if and only if the logarithm of the product, namely $\log p(e_1) + \ldots + \log p(e_n)$, is maximal. Moreover, we always have $\log p(e) \leq 0$ (because of $p(e) \leq 1$). Now put $w(e) := -\log p(e)$; then $w(e) \geq 0$ for all e, and we have to look for a walk from a to b for which $w(e_1) + \ldots + w(e_n)$ becomes minimal. Thus, our problem has been reduced to a problem of finding shortest paths. By the way, this technique can also be used to solve the problem mentioned above, namely, when going by car, finding the route where it is most unlikely that our speed will be controlled by the police (if we know the probability for each 'edge' that there is a control).

In principle, a technique for finding shortest paths can also be used to find longest paths: Substituting w by $-w$, a longest path with respect to w is just a shortest path with respect to $-w$. However, good algorithms for finding shortest paths are known only for the case where G does not contain any (directed) cycles of negative length. In the general case we basically have to look at all possible paths. Note that substituting w by $-w$ often creates cycles of negative length.

Exercise 3.1.2 (Knapsack Problem). There are n given objects , to each of which there is associated a 'weight' a_j and a 'value' c_j. We look for a subset of these objects such that the sum of their weights does not exceed a certain bound b and such that the sum of their values is maximal. (For the practical basis of the problem, look at the name!) The a_j and the c_j have to be positive integers. Reduce this problem to finding a longest path in some appropriate network. (Hint: The network has a start vertex s, an end vertex t and, for each object, $b + 1$ vertices; moreover, it is acyclic.)

3.2 Finite Metric Spaces

Before looking at algorithms for finding shortest paths, we want to show that there is a connection between the notion of distance and metric spaces. We recall that a *metric space* is a pair (X, d) consisting of a set X and a mapping $d : X^2 \to \mathbb{R}_0^+$ satisfying the following conditions (for all x, y, z from X):

(MR 1) $d(x, y) \geq 0$, and $d(x, y) = 0$ if and only if $x = y$;
(MR 2) $d(x, y) = d(y, x)$;
(MR 3) $d(x, z) \leq d(x, y) + d(y, z)$.

The value $d(x, y)$ is called the *distance* between x and y; the inequality in (MR 3) is referred to as the *triangle inequality*. The matrix $D = (d(x, y))_{x, y \in X}$ is called the *distance matrix* of (X, d).

Now consider a network (G, w), where G is a graph and w is a positive valued mapping $w : E \to \mathbb{R}^+$. Then a walk beginning at vertex a and ending at vertex b can have length $d(a, b)$ (where the distance between a and b is defined as in Section 3.1) only if it is a path. The following result shows that the notation 'distance' is justified; the proof is easy and therefore left to the reader.

Lemma 3.2.1. *Let $G = (V, E)$ be a connected graph with a positive length function w. Then (V, d) is a (finite) metric space, where the distance between two vertices is defined as in Section 3.1.* $\square$

Lemma 3.2.1 suggests the question whether any finite metric space can be 'realized' by a network. More precisely: Let D be the distance matrix of a finite metric space (V, d). Does a graph $G = (V, E)$ with length function w exist such that its distance matrix with respect to w agrees with D? Hakimi and Yau (1964) answered this question as follows.

Proposition 3.2.2. *Any finite metric space can be realized by a network with a positive length function.*

Proof. Let (V, d) be a finite metric space. Choose G to be the complete graph with vertex set V, and let the length function w be the given distance function d. By d' we denote the distance in the network (G, w) as defined in Section 3.1; we have to show that $d = w = d'$. Let $W = (e_1, \ldots, e_n)$ be a trail having start vertex a and end vertex b. For $n \geq 2$, an iterative application of the triangle inequality yields:

$$w(W) = w(e_1) + \ldots + w(e_n) = d(e_1) + \ldots + d(e_n) \geq d(a, b).$$

As the path ab (consisting only of the edge ab) has length $d(a, b)$, we are finished. $\square$

Exercise 3.2.3 (Kay and Chartrand (1965)). Find a condition under which a finite metric space can be realized by a graph (that is, by a network all of whose edges have length 1).

We have only considered the case that a metric space (V, d) is to be realized by a network having vertex set V. More generally, we could examine a realization by a network on a graph $G = (V', E)$ with $V \subset V'$; in this case the distance $d_G(a, b)$ in G for two vertices a, b of V has to be the same as their distance $d(a, b)$ in the metric space. Such a realization is called *optimal* if the sum of all lengths of edges is minimal of all possible realizations. It is not obvious that such optimal realizations do exist, but they do, as was proved by Dress (1984) and Imrich, Simões-Pereira and Zamfirescu (1984).

The following simple example shows that the realization given in the proof of Proposition 3.2.2 is not necessarily optimal: Let $d(a,b) = d(b,c) = 4$ and $d(a,c) = 6$. The realization on K_3 has total length 14, whereas there is a realization on four vertices having total length seven (see Figure 3.2).

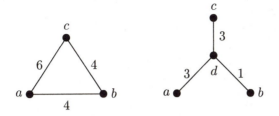

Fig. 3.2 Two realizations of a distance matrix

Realizations of metric spaces by networks have been intensively studied; in particular, the question whether a given metric space can be realized on a tree has found great interest. As Hakimi and Yau (1964) showed, a realization on a tree is always optimal. Bunemann (1974) proved that such a realization is possible if and only if, for any four vertices x, y, z, t of the given metric space, the following condition holds:

$$d(x,y) + d(z,t) \leq \max\,(d(x,z) + d(y,t), d(x,t) + d(y,z)).$$

A different characterization (using ultra-metrics) is due to Bandelt (1990). We also refer the reader to Simões-Pereira (1988) and Althöfer (1988). The problem of finding an optimal realization is difficult in general: Winkler (1988) showed that this problem is NP-hard.

3.3 Breadth First Search and Bipartite Graphs

We turn to examining algorithms for finding shortest paths. All techniques presented here could be transferred to multigraphs; but this generalization would be useless, because, when looking for shortest paths, out of a set of parallel edges we only use the one having smallest length. In this section, we look at the special case of distances in graphs (that is, each edge has length 1), which is particularly easy. The following algorithm was suggested by Moore (1959) and is known as *breadth first search*, or, for short, BFS.

Algorithm 3.3.1 (BFS). Let G be a (directed) graph given by adjacency lists A_v. Moreover, let s be an arbitrary vertex of G and Q a queue.[1] The

---

[1] Recall that a *queue* is a data structure for which elements are always appended at the end, but removed at the beginning ('first in – first out'). For a discussion of the implementation of queues we refer to Aho, Hopcroft and Ullman (1983) or Corman, Leiserson and Rivest (1990).

vertices of G are labelled with integers $d(v)$ as follows:

Procedure BFS$(G, s; d)$

(1) $Q \leftarrow \emptyset$; $d(s) \leftarrow 0$;
(2) Append s to Q;
(3) **while** $Q \neq \emptyset$ **do**
(4)   remove the first vertex v from Q;
(5)   **for** $w \in A_v$ **do**
(6)   **if** $d(w)$ is undefined
(7)   **then** $d(w) \leftarrow d(v) + 1$;
(8)   append w to Q
(9)   **fi**
(10)   **od**
(11) **od**.

Theorem 3.3.2. *Algorithm 3.3.1 has complexity $O(|E|)$. At the end of the algorithm, for any vertex t of G, we have:*

$$d(s, t) = \begin{cases} d(t) & \text{if } d(t) \text{ is defined}, \\ \infty & \text{otherwise.} \end{cases}$$

Proof. Obviously, any edge is examined by BFS at most twice (in the directed case, only once), which yields the assertion about the complexity. Moreover, $d(s, t) = \infty$ if and only if t is not accessible from s, and thus $d(t)$ stays undefined throughout the algorithm. Now let t be a vertex such that $d(s, t) \neq \infty$. Then, obviously, $d(s, t) \leq d(t)$, because t was reached by a path of length $d(t)$ from s. We show that equality holds by using induction on $d(s, t)$. For $d(s, t) = 0$, this is trivial, because $s = t$ in that case. Now let $d(s, t) = n + 1$ and suppose $(s, v_1, \ldots, v_n, t)$ is a shortest path from s to t. Then $(s, v_1, \ldots, v_n)$ is a shortest path from s to v_n, and by induction hypothesis, we have that $d(s, v_n) = n = d(v_n)$. Thus, $d(v_n) < d(t)$, so that BFS treats v_n before t during the **while**-loop. On the other hand, as G contains the edge $v_n t$, BFS treats t when examining the adjacency list of v_n (if not earlier). It follows that $d(t) \leq n + 1$ and hence $d(t) = n + 1$. $\qquad \square$

Corollary 3.3.3. *Let s be a vertex of a graph G. Then G is connected if and only if, at the end of BFS($G, s; d$), $d(t)$ is defined for each vertex t .* $\qquad \square$

We can also use BFS to determine the connected components of some graph G:

Exercise 3.3.4. Design an algorithm COMP(G) which determines the connected components of a graph G.

Note that the statement analogous to Corollary 3.3.3 for directed graphs is not true. If we want to check whether a given directed graph is connected, we can apply BFS to the corresponding graph $|G|$. Applying BFS$(G, s; d)$

for each vertex of a directed graph, we can find out whether G is strongly connected: G is strongly connected if and only if, for each s, BFS$(G, s; d)$ always reaches all vertices t and assigns values to $d(t)$. This method, however, is not really efficient: it has complexity $O(|V||E|)$. In Chapter 9, we will see a technique with complexity $O(|V|)$.

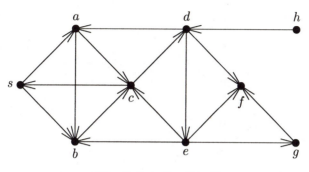

Fig. 3.3 A digraph G

Let us consider an example for how BFS is executed (see Figures 3.3 to 3.5). The figures show a directed graph G and the output of BFS for G and for $|G|$. If there are choices to be made during the algorithm (in step (5) of the BFS), we always used the alphabetical order of the vertices. The vertices are drawn in *levels* of same distance to s for better illustration. Moreover, we have omitted all edges leading to vertices already labelled.

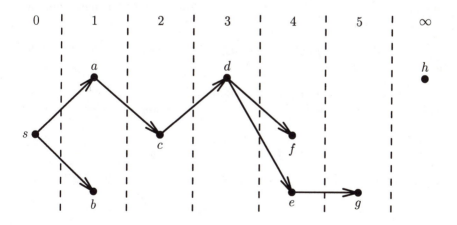

Fig. 3.4 BFS-tree for G

Thus, all we see of $|G|$ is a *spanning tree* , that is, a spanning subgraph of G which is a tree. This kind of tree will be studied more closely in Chapter 4. Note that distances in G and in $|G|$ do not always coincide (which was to be expected). However, we always have $d_G(s,t) \geq d_{|G|}(s,t)$.

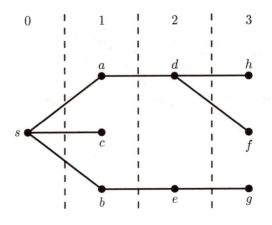

Fig. 3.5 BFS-tree for $|G|$

At the end of this section, we look at an important class of graphs, namely the bipartite graphs. We will see that BFS can be used to find out whether a graph is bipartite or not. A graph $G = (V, E)$ is called *bipartite* if there is a partition $V = S \,\dot\cup\, T$ of its vertex set such that the sets of edges $E|S$ and $E|T$ are empty, that is, all edges in G are incident with one vertex in S and one vertex in T. The following theorem gives an interesting characterization of bipartite graphs.

Theorem 3.3.5. *A graph G is bipartite if and only if G does not contain any cycles of odd length.*

Proof. First suppose that G is bipartite and let $V = S \,\dot\cup\, T$ be a partition of its vertex set satisfying the condition of the definition. Consider an arbitrary closed trail in G, say

$$C = v_1 \text{——} v_2 \text{——} \ldots \text{——} v_n \text{——} v_1,$$

and suppose $v_1 \in S$. As there are no edges within S (or T), it follows that

$$v_2 \in T, \quad v_3 \in S, \quad v_4 \in T, \quad \ldots \quad, \quad v_n \in T, \quad v_1 \in S,$$

so that n must be even.

Conversely, suppose that G does not contain any cycles of odd length. We may assume that G is connected. Choose some vertex x_0. Let S be the set of all vertices x having even distance $d(x, x_0)$ from x_0, and let T be the complement of S. Now suppose there is an edge xy in G such that $x, y \in S$. Let W_x and W_y be shortest paths from x_0 to x and y, respectively. By our definition of S, W_x and W_y have even length. Moreover, let z be the last common vertex of the two paths (beginning in x_0). Call the parts of W_x and W_y going from z to x and y, respectively, W_x' and W_y'. Then

$$x \xrightarrow{W_x'} z \xrightarrow{W_y'} y \xrightarrow{xy} x$$

is a cycle of odd length in G; the details are left to the reader. Analogously, it can be shown that G cannot contain an edge xy with $x, y \in T$. Thus, $S \cup T$ is a partition of V such that there are no edges within S or T, and G is bipartite.   □

The proof of Theorem 3.3.5 shows how the distances $d(s, t)$ in G (from a given start vertex s) can be used to find the corresponding partition of the vertex set of a given bipartite graph G. These distances can be determined using BFS; we only have to modify Algorithm 3.3.1 in such a way that it detects cycles of odd length (in case G is not bipartite). It is easy to see that, at the time when BFS examines an edge e for the first time, a cycle of odd length containing e exists if and only if e has both its vertices in the same level. That gives us the desired criterion for checking whether G is bipartite or not. If G is bipartite, the vertices in the part of G determined by s are exactly the vertices having even distance from s, so that we have found one part of the partition of the vertex set. We obtain the following algorithm.

Algorithm 3.3.6. Let G be a connected graph and s a vertex of G.

Procedure BIPART $(G, s; S, T, \text{bip})$

(1) $Q \leftarrow \emptyset$, $d(s) \leftarrow 0$, bip $\leftarrow$ true, $S \leftarrow \emptyset$;
(2) Append s to Q;
(3) **while** $Q \neq \emptyset$ and bip $=$ true **do**
(4)   remove the first vertex v of Q;
(5)   **for** $w \in A_v$ **do**
(6)   **if** $d(w)$ is undefined
(7)   **then** $d(w) \leftarrow d(v) + 1$; append w to Q
(8)   **else if** $d(v) = d(w)$ **then** bip $\leftarrow$ false **fi**
(9)   **fi**
(10)   **od**
(11) **od**;
(12) **if** bip $=$ true **then for** $v \in V$ **do**
(13)   **if** $d(v) \equiv 0 \pmod 2$ **then** $S \leftarrow S \cup \{v\}$ **fi**
(14)   **od**;
(15) $T \leftarrow V \backslash S$
(16) **fi**.

The above discussion yields the following result; we leave the details to the reader.

Theorem 3.3.7. *Algorithm 3.3.6 has complexity $O(|E|)$. It checks whether a given connected graph G is bipartite or not, and if it is, finds a bipartition of its vertex set.*   □

Exercise 3.3.8. Describe a BFS-based algorithm with complexity $O(|V||E|)$ which finds a shortest cycle in (and thus the girth of) a given graph G.

The problem of finding a shortest cycle was extensively studied by Itai and Rodeh (1978) who also treated the analogous problem for directed graphs. The best known algorithm is due to Yuster and Zwick (1997) who achieved a complexity of $O(|V|^2)$.

BFS can also be used to find a shortest cycle of even or odd length, respectively, see Monien (1983).

3.4 Bellman's Equations and Acyclic Digraphs

We turn to the problem of determining shortest paths in a general network; the known algorithms for this problem always find a shortest path from a start vertex s to every possible end vertex t (which is accessible from s). Choosing t in a special way does not decrease the complexity of the algorithms. As remarked in Section 3.1, we always assume that G does not contain any cycles of negative length. Moreover, we assume from now on that G is a directed graph; the undirected case can (for non-negative length functions) be treated by considering the complete orientation $\overrightarrow{G}$ instead of G.[2] Without loss of generality, we may assume that G has vertex set $V = \{1, \ldots, n\}$. We write $w_{ij} := w(ij)$ if G contains the edge ij, and $w_{ij} = \infty$ otherwise. Furthermore, u_i is the distance $d(s, i)$, where s is the start vertex (in most cases, we take $s = 1$). Any shortest path from s to i has to contain a (last) edge[3] ki; deleting ki yields a shortest path from s to k. Thus, the distances u_i (for $s = 1$) have to satisfy the following *Bellman's equations* (due to Bellman (1958)):

(B) $u_1 = 0$ and $u_i = \min\{u_k + w_{ki} : i \neq k\}$ $(i = 2, \ldots, n)$.

We want to show that the system of equations (B) has exactly one solution if G does contain cycles of positive length only; this solution then consists of the distances u_i in G. First, let u_i $(i = 1, \ldots, n)$ be any solution of (B). Choose some vertex j; we look for a path of length u_j from 1 to j. We can choose some edge kj with $u_j = u_k + w_{kj}$, then choose an edge ik with

---

[2] If we want to allow negative lengths of edges, we need a construction which is considerably more involved, see Section 13.6.

[3] Recall again that all paths are directed.

$u_k = u_i + w_{ik}$, etc. We have to show first that this construction cannot yield a cycle. So suppose we would get a cycle

$$C = v_1 \quad\rule[0.5ex]{1.5em}{0.4pt}\quad v_2 \quad\rule[0.5ex]{1.5em}{0.4pt}\quad \ldots \quad\rule[0.5ex]{1.5em}{0.4pt}\quad v_m \quad\rule[0.5ex]{1.5em}{0.4pt}\quad v_1.$$

Then the following equations hold:

$$
\begin{aligned}
u_{v_1} &= u_{v_m} + w_{v_m v_1} \\
&= u_{v_{m-1}} + w_{v_{m-1} v_m} + w_{v_m v_1} \\
&= \ldots \\
&= u_{v_1} + w_{v_1 v_2} + \ldots + w_{v_m v_1}.
\end{aligned}
$$

This implies $w(C) = 0$, contradicting our assumption that G contains cycles of positive length only. Thus, our construction has to stop at vertex 1 and yield a path from 1 to j. For any i, the part of this path leading to vertex i always has length u_i. By doing the same for all other vertices not yet occuring in the path(s) constructed so far (where we construct the path backward only until we reach some vertex on one of the paths constructed earlier), we get a directed spanning tree with root 1 (we can assume w.l.o.g. that each vertex is accessible from 1). In particular, we can apply this technique to the distances in G (because they satisfy the Bellman equations).

Theorem 3.4.1. *If* 1 *is a root of* G *and if* G *contains cycles of positive length only, then* G *contains a spanning arborescence with root* 1 *for which the path from* 1 *to any other vertex in* G *always is a shortest path.*   □

Such an arborescence is often called a 'shortest path tree' ; we will use the abbreviation *SP-tree*. Now let $u_1, \ldots, u_n$ be the distances in G, and let $u'_1, \ldots, u'_n$ be another solution of (B). Suppose we have $u_j \neq u'_j$ for some j. The above construction shows that u'_j is the length of some (not necessarily shortest) path from 1 to j. As $u_j = d(1, j)$, this means $u'_j > u_j$. Let kj be the last edge in a path of length u'_j from 1 to j. By induction, we can assume $u_k = u'_k$. But then, $u'_j > u'_k + w_{kj}$ contradicting (B). Thus, it follows that $u_j = u'_j$ for all $j = 1, \ldots, n$.

Theorem 3.4.2. *If a given network contains cycles of positive length only, and if* 1 *is a root of* G, *then Bellman's equations have exactly one solution, namely the distances* $u_j = d(1, j)$.   □

Thus, to determine the distances and the shortest paths, we have to solve the system of equations (B). We begin by looking at the easiest possible case, namely the case of an acyclic directed graph. As we saw in Section 2.6, it is possible to find a topological sorting of G in $O(|E|)$ steps. After having executed TOPSORT, we replace each vertex v by its number topnr(v). Now, if there is an edge ij in G, we always know that $i < j$, and it is easy to solve Bellman's equations recursively:

$$u_1 = 0 \quad \text{and} \quad u_i = \min\{u_k + w_{ki} : k = 1, \ldots, i-1\} \quad (i = 2, \ldots, n).$$

Obviously, this system of equations can be solved in $O(|E|)$ steps using backward adjacency lists, where each list contains the edges with a common head.

Theorem 3.4.3. *Let N be a network on an acyclic directed graph G having root s. Then shortest paths from s to all the other vertices can be determined with complexity $O(|E|)$.* $\square$

Exercise 3.4.4. Show that, under the same conditions as in Theorem 3.4.3, we can also determine a system of longest paths from s to all other vertices with complexity $O(|E|)$. Does this yield an efficient algorithm for the knapsack problem of Exercise 3.1.2? What happens if we drop the condition that the graph should be acyclic?

A larger class of graphs (containing the acyclic directed graphs) for which it is possible to determine the distances with respect to a given vertex with complexity $O(|E|)$ was found and characterized by Mehlhorn and Schmidt (1986). At the end of this section, we return to SP-trees.

Exercise 3.4.5. Let T be a spanning arborescence with root s in a network (G, w) not containing directed cycles of negative length. Show that T is an SP-tree if and only if the following condition holds for each edge $e = uv$:

$$d_T(s, v) \le d_T(s, u) + w(uv),$$

where $d_T(s, u)$ is the distance from s to u in the network $(T, w|T)$.

The following important theorem strengthens the result of Theorem 3.4.1.

Theorem 3.4.6. *Let G be a directed graph with root s and $w : E \to \mathbb{R}$ a length function on G. If the network (G, w) does not contain any directed cycles of negative length, then there exists an SP-tree with root s for (G, w).*

Proof. Let v be an arbitrary vertex of G. By hypothesis, v is accessible from s; let W be a path of shortest length (that is, of length $d(s, v)$) from s to v. As (G, w) does not contain any directed cycles of negative length, W is even a shortest walk from s to v. Let u be the last vertex on W before v, so that the last edge of W is $e = uv$. Then $W \backslash e$ is a shortest path from s to u: if W' were a path from s to u shorter than $W \backslash e$, then $W' \longrightarrow e$ would be a shorter walk from s to v than W. Thus,

$$d(s, v) = d(s, u) + w(uv). \tag{3.1}$$

As we chose v arbitrarily, we may, for any vertex $v \ne s$, choose an edge $e = e_v = uv$ satisfying condition (3.1). Thus, we get $|V| - 1$ edges which together form a spanning arborescence T of G with root s. (The reader should check this for himself as an exercise; a formal proof can be found in Lemma 4.8.1). It is now clear that T is an SP-tree for (G, w), since all edges of T satisfy condition (3.1). $\square$

Exercise 3.4.7. Show that the condition that no cycles of negative length exist is necessary for proving Theorem 3.4.6: If (G, w) contains a directed cycle of negative length, there cannot be an SP-tree for (G, w).

3.5 An Application: Scheduling Projects

We saw in Exercise 3.4.4 that it is easy to find longest paths in an acyclic digraph. We want to use this fact to solve a (very simple) problem instance of making up a schedule for a project. For executing a complex project (such as, for example, building a dam, a shopping center or an airplane), the various tasks have to be well co-ordinated to avoid loss of time and money. This is the goal of network planning, which is, according to Müller-Merbach (1973) 'the tool from Operations Research used most'. Taha (1992) states that these techniques 'enjoy tremendous popularity among practitioners in the field'. We restrict ourselves to the simple case where we have restrictions on the chronological sequence of the tasks only: there are some tasks which we cannot begin before certain others are finished. We look for the shortest possible time the project takes, and for the points of time when each of the tasks should be begun. Two very similar methods to solve this problem, namely the *critical path method (CPM)* and the *project evaluation and review technique (PERT)* were developed between 1956 and 1958 by two different groups, cf. Taha (1992) and Müller-Merbach (1973). CPM was introduced by E. I. du Pont de Nemours & Company to help scheduling construction projects, and PERT was developed by Remington Rand for the U.S. Navy for scheduling the research and development activities for the Polaris missile program. CPM-PERT is based on determining longest paths in an acyclic directed graph. We shall use a formulation where the activities in the project are represented by vertices; alternatively, one could also represent them by arcs, cf. Taha (1992).

First, we assign a vertex $i \in \{1, \ldots, N\}$ of a directed graph G to each of the N tasks of our project. We let ij be an edge of G if and only if task i has to be finished before beginning task j. The edge ij then has length $w_{ij} = d_i$ equal to the time task i takes. Note that G has to be acyclic, because otherwise the tasks in a cycle in G could never be started. As we have seen in Lemma 2.6.2, G contains at least one vertex v with $d_{in}(v) = 0$ (and, analogously, at least one vertex w with $d_{out}(w) = 0$). We introduce a new vertex s (the start of the project) and add edges sv for all vertices v with $d_{in}(v) = 0$; similarly, we introduce a new vertex z (the end of the project) and add edges wz for all vertices w with $d_{out}(w) = 0$. All the new edges sv have length 0, whereas the edges wz are given length d_w. In this way, we get a larger directed graph H with root s; by Theorem 2.6.3, we may assume H to be topologically sorted.

Now we denote the earliest possible point of time we could start task i by t_i. As all the tasks immediately preceding i have to be finished before, we get the following system of equations:

(CPM) $t_s = 0$ and $t_i = \max \{t_k + w_{ki} : ki$ an edge in $H\}$.

This system of equations looks like Bellman's equations and describes the longest paths in H (compare Exercise 3.4.4). As in Theorem 3.4.2, (CPM) has a unique solution, which again is easy to calculate recursively (because H is topologically sorted and thus contains edges ij with $i < j$ only). The minimal amount of time the project takes is the length $T = t_z$ of a longest path from s to z. If the project is to be finished at the point of time T, the latest point of time T_i where we can still start task i is given recursively by

$$T_z = T \quad \text{and} \quad T_i = \min \{T_j - w_{ij} : ij \text{ an edge in } H\}.$$

Thus, $T_z - T_i$ is the length of a longest path from i to z. Of course, we should get $T_s = 0$, which is useful for checking our calculations. The difference $m_i = T_i - t_i$ between the earliest point of time and the latest point of time for beginning task i is called *float* or *slack*. All tasks i having float $m_i = 0$ are called *critical*, because they have to be started exactly at the point of time $T_i = t_i$, as otherwise the whole project would be delayed. Note that each longest path from s to z contains critical tasks only; for that reason each such path is called a *critical path* for H. In general, there is more than one critical path.

In practice, H will not contain all edges ij for which i has to be finished before j, but will only contain those edges for which i is an immediate predecessor of j (that is, there are no intermediate tasks between i and j). As an example, we have a simplified look at building a house. First, we need a list of the tasks, the amount of time they take, and which tasks have to be finished before which other tasks; this information can be found in Table 3.1. The corresponding directed graph is shown in Figure 3.6. We have drawn the edges as undirected edges to make the figure somewhat simpler; all edges are meant to be directed from left to right.

As the directed graph is drawn in Figure 3.6, it is not necessary to state a topological sorting of the vertices explicitly (see Exercise 3.5.2). Using (CPM), we calculate consecutively

$$t_s = 0, \quad t_1 = 0, \quad t_2 = 0, \quad t_3 = 3, \quad t_4 = 5, \quad t_5 = 7, \quad t_8 = 7,$$
$$t_6 = 14, \quad t_{11} = 14, \quad t_{13} = 17, \quad t_7 = 17, \quad t_9 = 18, \quad t_{10} = 18,$$
$$t_{12} = 20, \quad t_{14} = 22, \quad t_{15} = 25, \quad t_{16} = 28, \quad T = t_z = 33.$$

Table 3.1 Project of Building a House

Vertex	Task	Amount of Time	Prec. Tasks
1	prepare the building site	3	–
2	deliver the building material	2	–
3	dig the foundation-trench	2	1,2
4	build the foundation	2	3
5	build the walls	7	4
6	build the roof supports	3	5
7	cover the roof	1	6
8	plumbing outside the house	3	4
9	plasterwork outside	2	7,8
10	put the windows in	1	7,8
11	put in the ceilings	3	5
12	lay out the garden	4	9,10
13	plumbing inside the house	5	11
14	put insulation on the walls	3	10,13
15	paint the walls	3	14
16	move	5	15

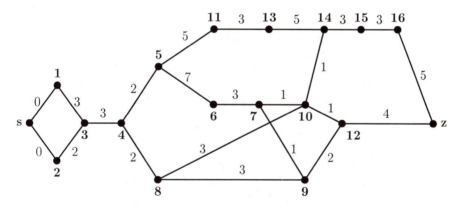

Fig. 3.6 Digraph for the project of building a house

Analogously, we get the T_i and the floats m_i as

$$T_z = 33, \quad m_z = 0; \quad T_{16} = 28, \quad m_{16} = 0; \quad T_{15} = 25, \quad m_{15} = 0;$$
$$T_{12} = 29, \quad m_{12} = 9; \quad T_{14} = 22, \quad m_{14} = 0; \quad T_9 = 27, \quad m_9 = 9;$$
$$T_{10} = 21, \quad m_{10} = 3; \quad T_7 = 20, \quad m_7 = 3; \quad T_{13} = 17, \quad m_{13} = 0;$$

$$T_6 = 17, \quad m_6 = 3; \quad T_{11} = 14, \quad m_{11} = 0; \quad T_5 = 7, \quad m_5 = 0;$$
$$T_8 = 18, \quad m_8 = 11; \quad T_4 = 5, \quad m_4 = 0; \quad T_3 = 3, \quad m_3 = 0;$$
$$T_1 = 0, \quad m_1 = 0; \quad T_2 = 1, \quad m_2 = 1; \quad T_s = 0, \quad m_s = 0.$$

Thus, the critical tasks are $s, 1, 3, 4, 5, 11, 13, 14, 15, 16, z$, and they form (in this order) the critical path (which is, in this case, unique).

Further information on project scheduling can be found in the books by Taha (1992), Chapter 12, and Müller-Merbach (1973), §7.5.1, and in the references given there. Of course, there is more to scheduling than the simple method we considered. In practice there are often further constraints that have to be satisfied, for instance, scarce resources like limited amounts of machinery or restricted numbers of workers at any given point of time. For a good general overview of scheduling, the reader is referred to Lawler, Lenstra, Rinnooy Kan and Shmoys (1993). We close this section with a couple of exercises.

Exercise 3.5.1 (Müller-Merbach (1973)). A factory wants to substitute an old production facility by a new one; the necessary tasks are given in Table 3.2. Draw the corresponding network and determine the values t_i, T_i, and m_i.

Table 3.2 Project: Substitute Production Facility

Vertex	Task	Amount of Time	Preceding Tasks
1	ask for offers, compare and order	25	–
2	take apart the old facility	8	–
3	remove the old foundation	5	2
4	plan the new foundation	9	1
5	time of delivery for the new facility	21	1
6	build the new foundation	9	3,4
7	install the new facility	6	5,6
8	train the staff	15	1
9	install electrical connections	2	7
10	test run	1	8,9
11	acceptance test and celebration	2	10

Exercise 3.5.2. Let G be an acyclic directed graph with root s. The *rank* $r(v)$ of a vertex v is the maximal length of a directed path from s to v. Use the methods introduced in this chapter to find an algorithm which determines the rank function and checks whether G is acyclic.

Exercise 3.5.3. Let G be an acyclic directed graph with root s (given by adjacency lists A_v). Show that the following algorithm also determines the rank function on G and determine its complexity:

Procedure RANK$(G, s; r)$

(1) create a list S_0, whose only element is s;
(2) $r(s) \leftarrow 0; k \leftarrow 0;$
(3) **for** $v \in V$ **do** $d(v) \leftarrow d_{in}(v)$ **od**;
(4) **while** $S_k \neq \emptyset$ **do**
(5)   create a new list S_{k+1};
(6)   **for** $v \in S_k$ **do**
(7)   **for** $w \in A_v$ **do**
(8)   **if** $d(w) = 1$
(9)   **then** append w to S_{k+1};
(10) $r(w) \leftarrow k + 1; p(w) \leftarrow v;$
(11)   **fi**;
(12) $d(w) \leftarrow d(w) - 1$
(13)   **od**
(14)   **od**;
(15) $k \leftarrow k + 1$
(16) **od**.

How can we determine $d(w)$? How can a longest path from s to v be found? Can RANK be used to find a topological sorting of G?

3.6 The Algorithm of Dijkstra

In this section, we consider networks having all lengths non-negative. In this case, Bellman's equations can be solved by the Algorithm of Dijkstra (1959), which is probably the most popular algorithm for finding shortest paths.

Algorithm 3.6.1. Let (G, w) be a network, where G is a graph or a directed graph and all lengths $w(e)$ are non-negative. The adjacency list of a vertex v is denoted by A_v. We want to calculate the distances with respect to a vertex s.

Procedure DIJKSTRA$(G, w, s; d)$

(1) $d(s) \leftarrow 0, T \leftarrow V;$
(2) **for** $v \in V \backslash \{s\}$ **do** $d(v) \leftarrow \infty$ **od**;
(3) **while** $T \neq \emptyset$ **do**
(4)   find some $u \in T$ such that $d(u)$ is minimal;
(5) $T \leftarrow T \backslash \{u\};$
(6)   **for** $v \in T \cap A_u$ **do** $d(v) \leftarrow \min(d(v), d(u) + w_{uv})$ **od**
(7) **od**.

Theorem 3.6.2. *The Algorithm of Dijkstra determines the distances with respect to some vertex s in (G, w) with complexity $O(|V|^2)$. More precisely, at the end of the algorithm, we have*

$$d(s, t) = d(t) \quad \text{for each vertex } t.$$

Proof. Obviously, we have $d(t) = \infty$ if and only if t is not accessible from s. If $d(t) \neq \infty$, it is clear that $d(s,t) \leq d(t)$, because then there exists a directed path of length $d(t)$ from s to t. We want to show that also $d(t) \leq d(s,t)$ by using induction on the order in which vertices are removed from T. The first vertex being removed is s; trivially $d(s) = 0 = d(s,s)$. Now suppose that the inequality is true for all vertices t that were removed from T before u. We may assume that $d(u)$ is finite. Moreover, let

$$s = v_0 \xrightarrow{\ e_1\ } v_1 \xrightarrow{\ e_2\ } \ \ldots\ \xrightarrow{\ e_n\ } v_n = u$$

be a shortest path from s to u. Then, for $h = 0, \ldots, n$,

$$d(s, v_h) = \sum_{j=1}^{h} w(e_j).$$

Choose i to be the maximal index such that v_i was removed from T before u. Then, by induction hypothesis, we know that

$$d(s, v_i) = d(v_i) = \sum_{j=1}^{i} w(e_j).$$

Now suppose that $v_{i+1} \neq u$, that is, $i \neq n - 1$. Then, after v_i was removed from T in the **while** loop, $d(v_{i+1}) \leq d(v_i) + w(e_{i+1})$ holds. As $d(v_{i+1})$ can only be decreased in the following iterations, this inequality is still true when u is removed. Thus,

$$d(v_{i+1}) \leq d(v_i) + w(e_{i+1}) = d(s, v_i) + w(e_{i+1}) = d(s, v_{i+1}) \leq d(s, u). \quad (3.2)$$

Now if $d(s, u) < d(u)$, then also $d(v_{i+1}) < d(u)$, and that means that v_{i+1} has been removed from T before u, contradicting the fact that we chose i to be maximal. Thus, we must have $d(u) \leq d(s, u)$ as asserted. For $u = v_{i+1}$, this inequality follows directly from Equation (3.2). We have now shown that Dijkstra's algorithm is correct. For the complexity, note that in step (4) the minimum of the $d(v)$ has to be calculated (for $v \in T$), which can be done by $|T| - 1$ comparisons. In the beginning of the algorithm, $|T| = |V|$, and then $|T|$ is decreased by 1 with each iteration. Thus, we need $O(|V|^2)$ steps altogether for the execution of (4). It is easy to see that the other steps can also be done in $O(|V|^2)$ steps. $\quad\square$

We remark that the Algorithm of Dijkstra might not work if there are negative weights in the network, even if no cycles of negative length exist. Note that the estimate in Equation (3.2) does not hold any more if $w(e_{i+1}) < 0$. An algorithm which works also for negative weigths can be found in Exercise 3.6.9.

Exercise 3.6.3. Modify Algorithm 3.6.1 such that it finds a shortest path from s to t as well (not only the distance). If s is a root of G, construct an SP-tree for (G, w).

Example 3.6.4. Consider the network given in Figure 3.7 with vertex set $V = \{1, \ldots, 8\}$:

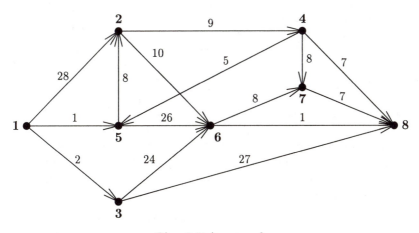

Fig. 3.7 A network

With $s = 1$, Algorithm 3.6.1 is executed as follows (where the final values for d are printed in bold face):

start values: $\mathbf{d(1) = 0}$, $d(i) = \infty$ for $i = 2, \ldots, 8$, $T = V$.

Iteration I: $u = 1$, $T = \{2, \ldots, 8\}$, $d(2) = 28$, $\mathbf{d(3) = 2}$, $\mathbf{d(5) = 1}$;

Iteration II: $u = 5$, $T = \{2, 3, 4, 6, 7, 8\}$, $d(2) = 9$, $\mathbf{d(3) = 2}$, $d(6) = 27$;

Iteration III: $u = 3$, $T = \{2, 4, 6, 7, 8\}$, $\mathbf{d(2) = 9}$, $d(6) = 26$, $d(8) = 29$;

Iteration IV: $u = 2$, $T = \{4, 6, 7, 8\}$, $\mathbf{d(4) = 18}$, $d(6) = 19$;

Iteration V: $u = 4$, $T = \{6, 7, 8\}$, $\mathbf{d(6) = 19}$, $d(7) = 26$, $d(8) = 25$;

Iteration VI: $u = 6$, $T = \{7, 8\}$, $\mathbf{d(8) = 20}$;

Iteration VII: $u = 8$, $T = \{7\}$, $\mathbf{d(7) = 26}$;

Iteration VIII: $u = 7$, $T = \emptyset$.

Exercise 3.6.5. Calculate the distances with respect to $s = 1$ for the underlying undirected network (see Figure 3.5).

We have a closer look at the complexity of Dijkstra's Algorithm. Initializing the variables in (1) and (2) takes $O(|V|)$ steps. During the **while** loop, in

(6), each edge is treated exactly once, because, for given u, only those edges uv are considered for which v is in T. In particular, vertices v which are not adjacent to u are not treated in (6). Thus, this part of the iteration has complexity $O(|E|)$, which is, at least for sparse graphs, much better than $O(|V|^2)$. Thus, for graphs having few edges, it makes sense to try to reduce the number of compare operations in (4) by using an appropriate data structure. A *priority queue* (sometimes also called *heap*) is a data structure consisting of a number of elements each of which has a given real value (its 'priority') associated with it; we can then apply operations such as inserting elements or determining and removing the element having the least priority ('DELETEMIN'). Computer scientists showed that a priority queue with n elements can be implemented such that these two operations can be executed with complexity $O(\log n)$. We refer the reader to Aho, Hopcroft and Ullman (1983) or Corman, Leiserson and Rivest (1990). We need a modification of this implementation which enables us also to remove a given element or reduce its priority with complexity $O(\log n)$, see Aho, Hopcroft and Ullman (1974) or Corman, Leiserson and Rivest (1990). Using these results (we do not go into the details), we can then put the vertex set of the graph into a priority queue T in Dijkstra's Algorithm (using d as priority function) and get the following modified algorithm:

Algorithm 3.6.6. Let (G, w) be a given network, where G is a graph or a directed graph and all lengths $w(e)$ are non-negative. We denote the adjacency list of v by A_v. Moreover, let T be a Priority Queue with priority function d. The algorithm calculates the distances with respect to a vertex s.

Procedure DIJKSTRAPQ$(G, w, s; d)$

(1) $T \leftarrow \{s\}, d(s) \leftarrow 0$;
(2) **for** $s \in V \backslash \{s\}$ **do** $d(v) \leftarrow \infty$ **od**;
(3) **while** $T \neq \emptyset$ **do**
(4) $u := \min T$;
(5)   DELETEMIN (T);
(6)   **for** $v \in A_u$ **do**
(7)   **if** $d(v) = \infty$
(8)   **then** $d(v) \leftarrow d(u) + w_{uv}$;
(9)   insert v with priority $d(v)$ into T
(10)   **else if** $d(u) + w_{uv} < d(v)$
(11)   **then** change the priority of v to $d(v) \leftarrow d(u) + w_{uv}$
(12)   **fi**
(13)   **fi**
(14)   **od**
(15) **od**.

Each of the operations during the **while** loop has complexity $O(\log |V|)$; altogether we need at most $O(|E|) + O(|V|)$ such operations. If G is connected, we get the following result.

Theorem 3.6.7. *Let (G, w) be a connected network, where w is non-negative. Then Algorithm 3.6.6 (the modified Algorithm of Dijkstra has complexity $O(|E| \log |V|)$.* $\square$

The discussion above is a first example for the fact that sometimes we can say more about the complexity of a Graph Theory algorithm if we look more thoroughly at the data structures used. It is interesting to note that, conversely, Graph Theory is one of the most important tools when studying the implementation of data structures; for example, for implementing a priority queue, a certain kind of tree is used (for instance, 2-3-trees). Many examples for the close relationship between Graph Theory algorithms and data structures can be found in Tarjan (1983).

Exercise 3.6.8. Let s be a vertex of a planar network having a non-negative length function. Which complexity does the calculation of the distances with respect to s have?

Using even more involved data structures, the results of Theorem 3.6.7 and Exercise 3.6.8 can still be improved. Implementing a priority queue appropriately (for instance, as a 'Fibonacci Heap'), inserting an element or reducing the priority of a given element can be done in $O(1)$ steps; DELETEMIN still needs $O(\log n)$ steps. Thus, Fredman and Tarjan (1987) were able to reduce the complexity of Algorithm 3.6.6 to $O(|E| + |V| \log |V|)$. The best theoretical bound known at present is $O(|E| + \frac{|V| \log |V|}{\log \log |V|})$, see Fredman and Willard (1994); however, their algorithm is of no practical interest, as the constants hidden in the big-O notation are too large. If all lengths are relatively small (say, bounded by a constant C), Ahuja, Mehlhorn, Orlin and Tarjan (1990) have shown that a complexity of $O(|E| + |V| (\log C)^{\frac{1}{2}})$ can be achieved. For the planar case, Frederickson (1987) has given an algorithm with complexity $O(|V| (\log |V|)^{\frac{1}{2}})$. For a short but nice discussion of various algorithmic approaches of practical interest, see Bertsekas (1993). More information about practical aspects may be found in the papers of Gallo and Pallottino (1988) and Hung and Divoky (1988).

At the end of this section, we present an algorithm which can also treat instances where negative lengths occur, as long as no cycles of negative length exist. It is due to Ford (1956) and Bellman (1958).

Exercise 3.6.9. Let (G, w) be a network without cycles of negative length. Show that the following algorithm calculates the distances with respect to a given vertex s and determine its complexity:

Procedure BELLFORD$(G, w, s; d)$

(1) $d(s) \leftarrow 0$;
(2) **for** $v \in V \backslash \{s\}$ **do** $d(v) \leftarrow \infty$ **od**;
(3) **repeat**
(4)   **for** $v \in V$ **do** $d'(v) \leftarrow d(v)$ **od**;
(5)   **for** $v \in V$ **do** $d(v) \leftarrow \min(d'(v), \min\{d'(u) + w_{uv} : uv \in E\})$ **od**
(6) **until** $d(v) = d'(v)$ for all $v \in V$.

Apply this algorithm to Example 3.6.4, treating the vertices in the order $1, \ldots, 8$.

3.7 An Application: Train Schedules

In this section, we treat a real world problem which can be solved using the Algorithm of Dijkstra: finding optimal connections in a public transportation system.[4] Such a system consists of several lines (of trains or buses) which are served in regular intervals. Typical examples are the German Intercity network or the American Greyhound bus lines. If someone wants to use such a system to get from a certain starting point to some destination (both of them being stations of the network), it is necessary in general to change lines a couple of times, each time having to wait until the next train or bus of the respective line leaves. Often, there might be a choice between several routes; we are interested, of course, in finding the fastest one. This task is already done in practice by interactive information systems, giving travellers the optimal routes to their destinations. For example, the state railway company of the Netherlands uses such a schedule information system based on the Algorithm of Dijkstra, as described by Siklóssy and Tulp (1989). We now illustrate (using a somewhat simplified example) how such a problem can be modelled in such a way that the Algorithm of Dijkstra applies. For the sake of simplicity, we always talk of trains, train stations and lines, although there are various other interpretations of the basic problem; any set of events occuring at regular intervals can be treated similarly.

We begin by constructing a directed graph $G = (V, E)$ which has the train stations as vertices and the railway tracks between two stations as edges. With each edge e, we associate a time $f(e)$ for travelling. (Parallel edges might be used to model trains going at different speeds.) Edges always connect two consecutive points of a line where the train stops, that is, stations a train just passes through do not occur on this line. Thus, lines are just paths in G; cycles are allowed. With each line L we associate a time interval T_L (the amount of time between two trains of this line). For each station v on a line L, we define the *time cycle* $t_L(v)$, which specifies at which times the trains of line L leave station v. This time has to be stated modulo T_L. Let

---

[4] I owe the material of this section to my former student, Dr. M. Guckert.

$$L = v_0 \xrightarrow{\ e_1\ } v_1 \underline{\qquad} \ \cdots \ \underline{\qquad} v_{n-1} \xrightarrow{\ e_n\ } v_n$$

be a line. Then the values $t_L(v_i)$ are determined as follows[5]:

$$t_L(v_0) := s_L (\text{mod } T_L)$$
$$t_L(v_i) := t_L(v_{i-1}) + f(e_i) \ (\text{mod } T_L) \quad \text{for } i = 1, \ldots, n. \tag{3.3}$$

That is, the time of departure at station v_i is the sum of the time of departure at station v_{i-1} and the travelling time $f(e_i)$ from v_{i-1} to v_i (modulo T_L)[6]. The schedule of line L is completely determined by (3.3); the trains leave station v_i (modulo T_L) at the time of departure $t_L(v_i)$ at intervals of length T_L.

Next, we have to calculate the waiting-times when changing lines. Let $e = uv$ and $e' = vw$ be edges of lines L and L', respectively. A train of line L' leaves the station v at the times

$$t_{L'}(v), t_{L'}(v) + T_{L'}, t_{L'}(v) + 2T_{L'}, \ldots$$

and a train of line L reaches station v at the times[7]

$$t_L(v), t_L(v) + T_L, t_L(v) + 2T_L, \ldots.$$

It is quite obvious that, if L and L' have different time cycles, the waiting-time does not only depend on the time cycles, but also on the precise point of time modulo the least common multiple T of T_L and $T_{L'}$. We illustrate this by an example: Suppose the time cycle of line L is 12 minutes, that of L' 10 minutes, and we have $t_L(v) = 0$, $t_{L'}(v) = 5$. Then $T = 60$, and we get the following schedules at v:

Line L:	0	12	24	36	48	
Line L':	5	15	25	35	45	55

We see that the waiting-time for the next train of line L' varies between 1 minute and 9 minutes. To make things simpler, we now assume that all time cycles are the same. Then the waiting-time at station v is

$$w(v_{LL'}) := t_{L'}(v) - t_L(v) \quad (\text{mod } T).$$

(For $L = L'$, we get $w(v_{LL'}) = 0$ of course, because, in this case, we do not have to change trains.)

---

[5] Note that, as different lines may leave their start stations at different times, we cannot just define $t_L(v_0) = 0$!

[6] We have neglected the amount of time a train stops at station v_i; this could be taken into account by either adding it to the travelling time $f(e_i)$, or by introducing an additional function $w_L(v_i)$, which then has to be added to $t_L(v_{i-1}) + f(e_i)$.

[7] More precisely, the trains of line L leave station v at these times, that is, they reach v a little bit earlier. We assume that this short time interval suffices for the process of changing trains, so that we can leave this out of our considerations as well.

Exercise 3.7.1. Reduce the case of different time cycles to the special case where all time cycles are equal.

Our next step is to construct a new directed graph $G' = (V', E')$ which allows us to find an optimal connection between two stations (including the waiting-times when changing trains) directly by finding a shortest path. Here, a *connection* between two vertices v_0 and v_n in G is a path

$$W = v_0 \; \xrightarrow{\quad e_1 \quad} \; v_1 \; \xrightarrow{\rule{1cm}{0pt}} \; \ldots \; \xrightarrow{\quad e_n \quad} \; v_n$$

in G together with the specification of the line L_i corresponding to edge e_i (for $i = 1, \ldots, n$). The travelling time of this connection then is

$$f(e_1) + w(v_{L_1 L_2}) + f(e_2) + w(v_{L_2 L_3}) + \ldots + w(v_{L_{n-1} L_n}) + f(e_n). \quad (3.4)$$

That leads to the following definition of G': For each vertex $v \in V$ and each line L serving station v, we have two vertices $(v, L)_{in}$ and $(v, L)_{out}$ in V'; for each edge $e = vw$ contained in some line L, there is an edge $(v, L)_{out}(w, L)_{in}$ in E'. Moreover, for each vertex v contained in both lines L and L', E' contains an edge $(v, L)_{in}(v, L')_{out}$. Then a directed path from v_0 to v_n in G' corresponds in fact to a connection between v_0 and v_n (including the information which lines to use and where to change trains). We want to obtain the travelling time (3.4) as the length of the corresponding path in G'. Thus we define the weight function w' on G' as follows

$$w'((v, L)_{out}(w, L)_{in}) := f(vw)$$
$$w'((v, L)_{in}(v, L')_{out}) := w(v_{LL'}).$$

Then our original problem can be solved by applying the Algorithm of Dijkstra several times to the network (G', w'): To find all optimal connections from station v, we apply Dijkstra's Algorithm (modified as in Exercise 3.6.3) to all vertices of the form $(v, L)_{out}$ in (G', w').

In this context, we mention some other problems concerning the *design* of a schedule for several lines having certain time cycles, that is, the problem of how to choose the times of departure s_L for the lines L (for given time cycles T_L). In general, the desired schedule should be optimal with respect to one of the following criteria:

- the longest waiting time should be minimal (or the sum of all waiting-times)
- the shortest time interval between the departure of two trains from a station should be maximal (that is, we want a safety interval between two trains)
- the sum of all travelling times between any two stations should be minimal (we might even give each of the routes a weight in this sum corresponding to its importance, maybe according to the number of travellers).

These problems are considerably more difficult; in fact, they are NP-hard in general, although polynomial solutions are known for a small number of lines. We refer to the literature, in particular for the first two problems, to Guldan (1980), Burkard (1986), Brucker, Burkard and Hurink (1990). The last problem was studied in detail by Guckert (1996), and the related problem of minimizing the sum of waiting-times of all travellers was treated by Domschke (1989). Both these authors described and tested various heuristics.

3.8 The Algorithm of Floyd-Warshall

Sometimes it is not enough to calculate the distances with respect to a certain vertex s in a given network, but we need to know the distances between any two vertices. Of course, we could apply one of the algorithms treated above several times, varying the starting vertex s over all vertices in V. That technique would solve the problem with the following complexities:

Using the   Algorithm of Moore: $O(|V||E|)$;
            Algorithm of Dijkstra: $O(|V|^3)$ or $O(|V||E| \log |V|)$;
            Algorithm of Bellman-Ford: $O(|V|^2|E|)$.

These complexities could be improved a bit according to the remarks at the end of Section 3.6. Takaoka (1992) presented an algorithm with complexity $O(|V|^3 (\log \log |V| / \log |V|)^{1/2})$. In the planar case, we can, according to Frederickson (1987), achieve a complexity of $O(|V|^2)$.

In this section, we study an algorithm for this problem which has a complexity of $O(|V|^3)$ as well, but which has the advantage of having a clear structure. Thus, we do not get a better complexity than we have for the simple modification of the Dijkstra Algorithm; but we can also treat instances with negative lengths (though, of course, we cannot allow cycles of negative length). The following algorithm for determining the distance matrix is due to Floyd (1962), see also Warshall (1962).

Algorithm 3.8.1 (Floyd-Warshall). Let (G, w) be a network not containing any cycles of negative length, where we assume $V = \{1, \ldots, n\}$. Define $w_{ij} = \infty$ if ij is not an edge in G.

Procedure FLOYD$(G, w; d)$

(1) **for** $i = 1$ **to** n **do**
(2)   **for** $j = 1$ **to** n **do**
(3)   **if** $i \neq j$ **then** $d(i, j) \leftarrow w_{ij}$ **else** $d(i, j) \leftarrow 0$ **fi**
(4)   **od**
(5) **od**;
(6) **for** $k = 1$ **to** n **do**
(7)   **for** $i = 1$ **to** n **do**

(8)   **for** $j = 1$ **to** n **do**
(9) $d(i,j) \leftarrow \min(d(i,j), d(i,k) + d(k,j))$
(10)   **od**
(11)   **od**
(12) **od.**

Theorem 3.8.2. *Algorithm 3.8.1 has complexity* $O(|V|^3)$. *After execution, d is the distance function for* (G, w).

Proof. The complexity of the algorithm is obvious. Let $D_0 = (d_{ij}^0)$ denote the matrix defined in step (3) and $D_k = (d_{ij}^k)$ the matrix generated during the k-th iteration in step (9). Then D_0 contains all lengths of paths consisting of one edge only. It can now be seen (using induction) that (d_{ij}^k) is the shortest length of a (directed) path from i to j containing vertices from $\{1, \ldots, k\}$ only (and i and j, of course). As we assumed that (G, w) does not contain any cycles of negative length, the statement follows for $k = n$. $\qquad\square$

Exercise 3.8.3. How can Algorithm 3.8.1 be modified to not only calculate the distance matrix, but to find shortest paths between any two vertices as well?

Example 3.8.4. For the network shown in Figure 3.8, the Algorithm of Floyd-Warshall computes the following matrices:

$$
D_0 = \begin{pmatrix} 0 & 2 & 4 & \infty & 3 \\ 2 & 0 & 8 & \infty & 1 \\ 6 & 2 & 0 & 4 & 3 \\ 1 & \infty & \infty & 0 & 5 \\ \infty & \infty & \infty & 1 & 0 \end{pmatrix}
\qquad
D_1 = \begin{pmatrix} 0 & 2 & 4 & \infty & 3 \\ 2 & 0 & 6 & \infty & 1 \\ 6 & 2 & 0 & 4 & 3 \\ 1 & 3 & 5 & 0 & 4 \\ \infty & \infty & \infty & 1 & 0 \end{pmatrix}
$$

$$
D_2 = \begin{pmatrix} 0 & 2 & 4 & \infty & 3 \\ 2 & 0 & 6 & \infty & 1 \\ 4 & 2 & 0 & 4 & 3 \\ 1 & 3 & 5 & 0 & 4 \\ \infty & \infty & \infty & 1 & 0 \end{pmatrix}
\qquad
D_3 = \begin{pmatrix} 0 & 2 & 4 & 8 & 3 \\ 2 & 0 & 6 & 10 & 1 \\ 4 & 2 & 0 & 4 & 3 \\ 1 & 3 & 5 & 0 & 4 \\ \infty & \infty & \infty & 1 & 0 \end{pmatrix}
$$

$$
D_4 = \begin{pmatrix} 0 & 2 & 4 & 8 & 3 \\ 2 & 0 & 6 & 10 & 1 \\ 4 & 2 & 0 & 4 & 3 \\ 1 & 3 & 5 & 0 & 4 \\ 2 & 4 & 6 & 1 & 0 \end{pmatrix}
\qquad
D_5 = \begin{pmatrix} 0 & 2 & 4 & 4 & 3 \\ 2 & 0 & 6 & 2 & 1 \\ 4 & 2 & 0 & 4 & 3 \\ 1 & 3 & 5 & 0 & 4 \\ 2 & 4 & 6 & 1 & 0 \end{pmatrix}
$$

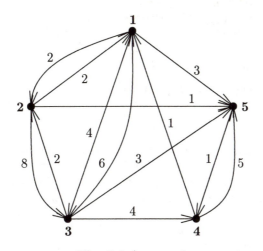

Fig. 3.8 A network

Exercise 3.8.5 (Lawler (1976)). Apply Algorithm 3.8.1 to the network in Figure 3.9.

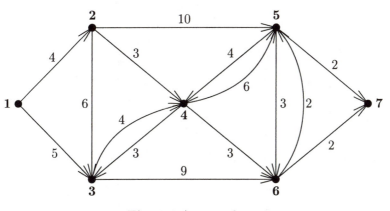

Fig. 3.9 A network

In Section 2.6, we looked at acyclic directed graphs associated with partially ordered sets. Any such directed graph is *transitive*: if there is a directed path from u to v, it follows that there is also an edge uv. Now let G be an arbitrary (acyclic) directed graph. For each pair of vertices (u, v), for which uv is not an edge, but v is accessible from u, we add the edge uv to G. This operation yields the *transitive closure* of G. It is obvious that the transitive closure of an acyclic directed graph is again acyclic and thus corresponds to a partially ordered set. The Algorithm of Floyd-Warshall can be used to compute the transitive closure of an (acyclic) directed graph with complexity $O(|V|^3)$: Two vertices u and v have distance $d(u, v) \neq \infty$ if and only if uv is an edge of the transitive closure of G.

Exercise 3.8.6 (Warshall (1962)). Simplify Algorithm 3.8.1 for computing the transitive closure by interpreting the adjacency matrix of an (acyclic) directed graph as a Boolean matrix.

We mention another possibility to associate an acyclic directed graph to a partially ordered set. More generally, let G be any acyclic directed graph. If uv is an edge in G, and there exists a directed path of length ≥ 2 from u to v in G, we remove this edge uv from G. That operation yields a directed graph called the *transitive reduction* G_{red} of G. If G is the directed graph associated with a partially ordered set as in Section 2.6, G_{red} is also called the *Hasse diagram* of G. Drawing such a Hasse diagram, we usually put the vertices of equal rank on the same horizontal level. Figure 3.10 shows the Hasse diagram of the partially ordered set of the divisors of 36. The orientation of the edges is not shown explicitly; it is understood that all edges are oriented from bottom to top. As an exercise, the reader might draw some more Hasse diagrams.

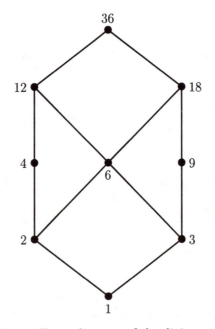

Fig. 3.10 Hasse diagram of the divisors of 36

Exercise 3.8.7. Design an algorithm for constructing the reduction of an acyclic directed graph with complexity $O(|V|^3)$. (Hint: The Floyd-Warshall Algorithm can be used here to determine longest paths.) Show that G and G_{red} have the same transitive closure.

More about the transitive closure and the transitive reduction of an acyclic directed graph can be found in §IV.3 of Mehlhorn (1984). Schnorr (1978) gave an algorithm for constructing the transitive closure with an average complexity of $O(|E|)$.

We look at a further application of the Algorithm of Floyd-Warshall: Sometimes we are interested in finding the 'center' of some network. (It is obvious how this could be applied in the context of traffic or communication networks.) Let (G, w) be a network not containing any cycles of negative length. Then the *excentricity* of a vertex v is defined as

$$\varepsilon(v) \quad := \quad \max \{d(v, u) : u \in V\}.$$

A *center* of the network is a vertex having minimal excentricity. The centers of a given network can be determined easily using the Algorithm of Floyd-Warshall: After having executed the algorithm, $\varepsilon(i)$ simply is the maximum of the i-th row of the matrix $D = (d(i, j))$, and the centers are those vertices for which this maximum is minimal. For example, the vertices of the network of Example 3.8.4 have excentricities $\varepsilon(1) = 4$, $\varepsilon(2) = 6$, $\varepsilon(3) = 4$, $\varepsilon(4) = 5$ and $\varepsilon(5) = 6$, so that 1 and 3 are centers of the network. It is obvious that the complexity of the additional operations (finding maxima and minima) is dominated by the $O(|V|^3)$ operations needed by the Algorithm of Floyd-Warshall. Thus we have:

Theorem 3.8.8. *Let N be a network without cycles of negative length. Then the centers of N can be determined with complexity $O(|V|^3)$.* $\square$

If we take all edges in a given (directed) graph to have length 1, the above definition yields the excentricities of the vertices and the centers of the graph in the Graph Theory sense. Sometimes we are interested in the maximal excentricity of all vertices of a graph. This value is called the *diameter* of the graph; it is, for example, of interest in communications networks (see Chung (1986)). For more on communication networks, see also Bien (1989) and Bermond (1992). It is a difficult (in fact, NP-hard) problem to choose and assign centers for networks under the restrictions occuring in real world applications; we refer the reader to Bar-Ilan, Kortsarz and Peleg (1993).

To close this section, we look at the 'dynamic' variant of the problem of determining shortest paths between any two vertices in a network. Suppose we have, using an appropriate algorithm, found a solution for some optimization problem. Then we want to change the input data a little bit and find an optimal solution for the changed instance using the optimal solution we know already, without having to execute the whole algorithm again. For our problem of finding shortest paths, this means keeping the distance matrix D and some information needed for constructing shortest paths (as, for example, the matrix $P = (p(i,j))$ used in the solution of Exercise 3.8.3) up to date while inserting some edges or reducing lengths of edges, instead of calculating all the entries of the matrices D and P again. If all lengths $w(e)$ are integers in the interval $[1, C]$, it is obvious that at most $O(Cn^2)$ such operations can be performed because any edge can be inserted at most once, and the length of each edge can be reduced at most C times. While the repeated application of the Algorithm of Floyd-Warshall for a sequence of such operations would need $O(Cn^5)$ steps, it is also possible to solve the problem, using an adequate data structure, with complexity only $O(Cn^3 \log nC)$. If we are treating an instance with graph theoretic distances, that is, for $C = 1$, a sequence of $O(n^2)$ insertions of edges needs $O(n^3 \log n)$ steps only. We refer the reader to Ausiello, Italiano, Marchetti Spaccamela and Nanni (1991).

3.9 Cycles of Negative Length

Later in this book (when treating flows and circulations in Chapter 9), we will need a method to find out whether a given network contains a directed cycle of negative length; the algorithm should also be able to find such a cycle in case one exists. We can modify the Algorithm of Floyd-Warshall to perform this task. It is easy to see that a network (G, w) contains a directed cycle of negative length containing vertex i if and only if Algorithm 3.8.1 yields a negative value for $d(i, i)$.

Algorithm 3.9.1. Let (G, w) be a network with vertex set $V = \{1, \ldots, n\}$.

Procedure NEGACYCLE $(G, w; d, p, \text{neg}, K)$

(1) neg $\leftarrow$ false, $k \leftarrow 0$;
(2) **for** $i = 1$ **to** n **do**
(3)   **for** $j = 1$ **to** n **do**
(4)   **if** $i \neq j$ **then** $d(i,j) \leftarrow w_{ij}$ **else** $d(i,j) \leftarrow 0$ **fi**;
(5)   **if** $i = j$ **or** $d(i,j) = \infty$ **then** $p(i,j) \leftarrow 0$ **else** $p(i,j) \leftarrow i$ **fi**
(6)   **od**
(7) **od**;
(8) **while** neg $=$ false **and** $k < n$ **do**
(9) $k \leftarrow k + 1$;
(10)   **for** $i = 1$ **to** n **do**
(11)   **if** $d(i,k) + d(k,i) < 0$
(12)   **then** neg $\leftarrow$ true; CYCLE$(G, p, k, i; K)$
(13)   **else for** $j = 1$ **to** n **do**
(14)   **if** $d(i,k) + d(k,j) < d(i,j)$
(15)   **then** $d(i,j) \leftarrow d(i,k) + d(k,j)$; $p(i,j) \leftarrow p(k,j)$

(16)   **fi**
(17)   **od**
(18)   **fi**
(19)   **od**
(20) **od.**

Here CYCLE is a procedure which uses p for constructing a cycle of negative length containing i and k. Note that $p(i, j)$ is, at any given point of the algorithm, the predecessor of j on a (at that point of time) shortest path from i to j. CYCLE can be described informally as follows: First, set $v_0 = i$, then $v_1 = p(k, i)$, $v_2 = p(k, v_1)$, etc., until, for some index a, $v_a = k = p(k, v_{a-1})$. Then continue with $v_{a+1} = p(i, k)$, $v_{a+2} = p(i, v_{a+1})$, etc., until an index b is reached for which $v_{a+b} = v_0 = i = p(i, v_{a+b-1})$. Now the cycle we have found uses each edge in the direction opposite to its orientation, so that $(v_{a+b} = v_0, v_{a+b-1}, \ldots, v_1, v_0)$ is the directed cycle of negative length containing i and k we looked for. It can then be stored in a list K. We leave it to the reader to state the procedure in a formally correct way.

If (G, w) does not contain any directed cycles of negative length, the variable neg has value false at the end of Algorithm 3.9.1; then d contains the distances in (G, w) as in the Algorithm of Floyd-Warshall. The matrix $(p(i, j))$ can be used – as shown above for the procedure CYCLE – to find a shortest path between any two given vertices. Altogether, we get the following result.

Theorem 3.9.2. *Algorithm 3.9.1 decides with complexity $O(|V|^3)$ whether a given network (G, w) contains cycles of negative length or not; in case it does, such a cycle is constructed. If the network does not contain cycles of negative length, the algorithm yields the distance matrix $(d(i, j))$ for (G, w).* □

Exercise 3.9.3. Let G be a directed graph having n vertices and root s, and let w be a length function on G. Modify the Algorithm of Bellman-Ford (see Exercise 3.6.9) such that it determines whether (G, w) contains a cycle of negative length. If there is no such cycle, the algorithm should determine an SP-tree with root s using a procedure SPTREE. Write down such a procedure explicitly.

Exercise 3.9.4. Modify the Algorithm of Floyd-Warshall such that it determines the shortest length of a directed cycle in a network not containing any cycles of negative length.

3.10 Path Algebras

In Section 3.4, we learned about Bellman's equations: the distances u_i with respect to a vertex i in a network (G, w) satisfy the conditions

(B) $u_1 = 0$ and $u_i = \min\{u_k + w_{ki} : i \neq k\}$ $(i = 2, \ldots, n)$.

We now look at the question whether such a system of equations could be solved using methods from Linear Algebra. In fact, this is possible by introducing the appropriate algebraic structures (called path algebras). We only sketch the basic ideas here, for details we refer to the literature, in particular Carré (1971), Carré (1979), Gondran and Minoux (1984) and Zimmermann (1981).[8]

First, we have to transform the equations (B) a little. Recall that we defined $w_{ij} = \infty$ if ij is not an edge of our network. Thus, we extend $\mathbb{R}$ to $\overline{\mathbb{R}} = \mathbb{R} \cup \{\infty\}$. Moreover, we introduce two operations $\oplus$ and $*$ on $\overline{\mathbb{R}}$:

$$a \oplus b := \min(a, b) \qquad \text{and} \qquad a * b := a + b,$$

where, as usual, we define $a + \infty$ to be ∞. Obviously, (B) can be written as

$$u_1 = \min(0, \min\{u_k + w_{k1} : k \neq 1\}) \qquad \text{and}$$
$$u_i = \min(\infty, \min\{u_k + w_{ki} : k \neq i\});$$

note that (G, w) does not contain any cycles of negative length. Using the operations introduced above, we now get the system of equations

$$(B') \qquad u_1 = \bigoplus_{k=1}^{n}(u_k * w_{k1}) \oplus 0, \quad u_i = \bigoplus_{k=1}^{n}(u_k * w_{ki}) \oplus \infty,$$

setting $w_{ii} = \infty$ for $i = 1, \ldots, n$. We can now define matrices over $\overline{\mathbb{R}}$ and apply the operations $\oplus$ and $*$ to them in analogy to the usual definitions from Linear Algebra. Then (B') (and hence (B)) can be written as a linear system of equations:

$$(B'') \qquad u = u * W \oplus b,$$

where $u = (u_1, \ldots, u_n)$, $b = (0, \infty, \ldots, \infty)$ and $W = (w_{ij})_{i,j=1,\ldots,n}$.

Thus, Bellman's equations are a linear system of equations over the algebraic structure $(\overline{\mathbb{R}}, \oplus, *)$. Then the Algorithm of Bellman-Ford (Exercise 3.6.9) can be interpreted as follows. First set

$$u^{(0)} = b \qquad \text{and then recursively} \qquad u^{(k)} = u^{(k-1)} * W \oplus b,$$

until the sequence eventually converges to $u^{(k)} = u^{(k-1)}$, which in our case occurs for $k = n$ or earlier. Thus, the Algorithm of Bellman-Ford is analogous to the technique of Jacobi from classical Linear Algebra over $\mathbb{R}$, see, for instance, Stoer and Bulirsch (1993).

These observations lead to studying algebraic structures which satisfy the same conditions as $(\overline{\mathbb{R}}, \oplus, *)$. A *path algebra* or *dioid* is a triple $(R, \oplus, *)$ such that $(R, \oplus)$ is a commutative monoid, $(R, *)$ is a monoid, and both

---

[8] This section is not used in the rest of the book, and can for that reason be passed over.

distributive laws hold; moreover, the neutral element o of $(R, \oplus)$ satisfies the absorption law. This means that the following laws hold, where e denotes the neutral element for $(R, *)$:

(1) $a \oplus b = b \oplus a$;
(2) $a \oplus (b \oplus c) = (a \oplus b) \oplus c$;
(3) $a \oplus o = a$;
(4) $a * o = o * a = o$;
(5) $a * e = e * a = a$;
(6) $a * (b * c) = (a * b) * c$;
(7) $a * (b \oplus c) = (a * b) \oplus (a * c)$;
(8) $(b \oplus c) * a = (b * a) \oplus (c * a)$.

Exercise 3.10.1. Show that $(\overline{\mathbb{R}}, \oplus, *)$ is a path algebra with $e = 0$ and $o = \infty$.

Exercise 3.10.2. Let $(R, \oplus, *)$ be a path algebra. We define a relation $\geq$ on R by

$$a \geq b \quad \Longleftrightarrow \quad a = b \oplus c \quad \text{for some } c \in R.$$

Show that $\geq$ is a preordering (that is, it is reflexive and transitive). If $\oplus$ is idempotent (that is, $a \oplus a = a$ for all $a \in R$), then $\geq$ is even a partial ordering (that is, it is also antisymmetric).

Exercise 3.10.3. Let (G, w) be a network not containing any cycles of negative length. Give a matrix equation for the distance matrix $D = (d(i, j))$.

We now transfer the notions developed in the special case of $(\overline{\mathbb{R}}, \oplus, *)$ to arbitrary path algebras. For the remainder of this section, a *network* means a pair (G, w) such that G is a directed graph, $w : E \to R$ is a length function, and $(R, \oplus, *)$ is a path algebra. The *length* of a path $P = (v_0, v_1, \ldots, v_n)$ is defined as

$$w(P) := w(v_0 v_1) * w(v_1 v_2) * \ldots * w(v_{n-1} v_n).$$

The *AP-problem* (short for 'algebraic path problem') then consists in calculating the sums

$$w_{ij}^* = \oplus \ w(P) \qquad \text{(where P is a directed path from i to j)}$$

and finding a path P from i to j such that $w(P) = w_{ij}^*$ (if the above sum and such a path exist). For the case $(\overline{\mathbb{R}}, \oplus, *)$, the AP-problem reduces to the *SP-problem* ('shortest path problem') of determining the distances and shortest paths.

As before, we introduce a matrix $W = (w_{ij})$, whose (i, j)-entry is the length $w(ij)$ if ij is an edge of G. We set $w_{ii} = o$ for $i = 1, \ldots, n$ and $w_{ij} = o$ if $i \neq j$ and ij is not an edge in G. Note that, for the special case $(\overline{\mathbb{R}}, \oplus, *)$ above, we looked at the matrix $W' = W \oplus E$ (see Exercise 3.10.5 below). Here E denotes the *unit matrix*, that is, $e_{ii} = e$ for $i = 1, \ldots, n$ and $e_{ij} = o$ for $i \neq j$. As usual, we write A^k for the k-th power of A; moreover, we define $A^{(k)} := E \oplus A \oplus A^2 \oplus \ldots \oplus A^k$.

Lemma 3.10.4. *The (i,j)-entry of the matrix W^k (or the matrix $W^{(k)}$, respectively) is the sum $\oplus w(P)$ over all directed walks from i to j consisting of exactly (or at most, respectively) k edges.*

Proof. Use induction on k. □

We look again at the special case of the SP-problem. In a network (G, w) not containing cycles of negative length, distances can always be realized by paths, so that we need at most $n - 1$ edges. Thus, we have $D = W^{(n-1)}$; moreover, $W^{(n-1)} = W^{(n)} = \ldots$. It is easy to see that $W^{(n-1)}$ indeed satisfies the matrix equation of the solution of Exercise 3.10.3:

$$\begin{aligned}
W^{(n-1)} * W \oplus E &= (E \oplus W \oplus \ldots \oplus W^{n-1}) * W \oplus E \\
&= E \oplus W \oplus \ldots \oplus W^{n-1} \oplus W^n = W^{(n)} = W^{(n-1)}.
\end{aligned}$$

This kind of element, called a *stable* element (that is, an element a with $a^{(p)} = a^{(p+1)}$ for some p), is also important for general path algebras. In fact, the matrix $W^* = (w_{ij}^*)$ of the AP-problem is an 'infinite sum' $\oplus W^k = E \oplus W \oplus W^2 \oplus \ldots$, that is, it is the 'limit' of the matrices $W^{(k)}$ for $k \to \infty$. If W is stable, these formulas make sense: if $W^{(p)} = W^{(p+1)}$, then $W^* = W^{(p)}$. That is the reason why criteria for stability play an important part in the theory of path algebras; see Zimmermann (1981). For the theory of convergence, see also Kuich and Salomaa (1986).

Exercise 3.10.5. Let $(R, \oplus, *)$ be a path algebra such that $\oplus$ is idempotent. For any matrix A, we define $A' := E \oplus A$. Show that $(A')^k = A^{(k)}$ and, using this fact, find a technique for calculating $A^{(n)}$ and discuss its complexity.

Now suppose that W is stable; we call $W^* = W^{(p)} = W^{(p+1)}$ the *quasi-inverse* of W. Then we have in general – as in the special case $R = \overline{\mathbb{R}}$ above –

$$W^* = W^* * W \oplus E = W * W^* \oplus E;$$

thus the matrices $Y := W^* * B$ and $Z := B * W^*$ (where B is any arbitrary matrix), respectively, are solutions of the equations

$$Y = W * Y \oplus B \quad \text{and} \quad Z = Z * W \oplus B. \tag{3.5}$$

In particular, we can choose a column or row vector b for B and get a linear system of equations analogous to the system (B'').

Exercise 3.10.6. Let $(R, \oplus, *)$ be a path algebra. Show that the $(n \times n)$-matrices over R also form a path algebra, and that we can, as in Exercise 3.10.2, define a preordering (or, in the idempotent case, a partial ordering) on this path algebra. Show that $W^* * B$ and $B * W^*$ are minimal solutions of Equation (3.5), and that, in the idempotent case, the system (3.5) has a unique minimal solution.

Equations having the same form as (3.5) can be solved using techniques analogous to the well-known methods of Linear Algebra over $\mathbb{R}$. We have already seen that the Algorithm of Bellman-Ford corresponds to the technique of Jacobi; this technique can also be used for the general case of a stable matrix W over any path algebra R. It can also be shown that the Algorithm of Floyd-Warshall corresponds to the technique of Gauss-Jordan elimination. For more on this result and other general algorithms for solving (3.5), we refer to Gondran and Minoux (1984) and Zimmermann (1981).

At the end of this section, we want to use some examples to show that the abstract concept of path algebras makes it possible to treat various interesting network problems with just one general method. However, the SP-problem is still the most important example; here the case of positive lengths – that is, the path algebra $(\mathbb{R}_+, \min, +)$ – was already studied by Shimbel (1955). Longest paths can be treated analogously: We look at the path algebra $(\mathbb{R} \cup \{-\infty\}, \max, +)$.

Example 3.10.7. Consider the path algebra $(\{0, 1\}, \max, \min)$, that is, the Boolean algebra having two elements, and set $w_{ij} = 1$ for each edge of G. Then Lemma 3.10.4 has the following meaning: There exists a directed walk from i to j consisting of exactly (or at most, respectively) k edges if and only if the (i, j)-entry of W^k (or $W^{(k)}$, respectively) is 1. The matrix $W^* = W^{(n-1)}$ is the adjacency matrix of the transitive closure of G; see Exercise 3.8.6.

Example 3.10.8. Consider the path algebra $(\mathbb{R}_+, \max, \min)$, and think of the length $w(ij)$ of an edge ij as its 'capacity'. Then $w(P)$ is the *capacity* of the path P, that is, $w(P)$ is the minimum of the capacities of the edges contained in P. Here, the (i, j)-entry of W^k (or $W^{(k)}$, respectively) is the largest capacity a walk from i to j consisting of exactly (or at most, respectively) k edges has. It follows that $W^* = W^{(n-1)}$, and that w^*_{ij} is the largest capacity of any walk from i to j, see Hu (1961).

Example 3.10.9. Consider the path algebra $(\mathbb{N}_0, +, \cdot)$, where each edge of G has length $w(ij) = 1$. Then W is simply the adjacency matrix of G. The (i, j)-entry of W^k or of $W^{(k)}$, respectively, is the number of walks from i to j consisting of precisely, or at most, respectively, k edges, see Exercise 2.2.5. Note that W^* does not exist in general, as there might be infinitely many walks from i to j. If G is an acyclic directed graph, W^* is well-defined; then we have $W^* = W^{(n-1)}$, and w^*_{ij} is the number of all directed walks from i to j.

Exercise 3.10.10. Find a path algebra which is suitable for treating the problem of Example 3.1.1, where $w(i, j)$ is the probability $p(i, j)$ as given in 3.1.1, see Kalaba (1960).

Exercise 3.10.11. Any commutative field $(K, +, \cdot)$ is obviously also a path algebra. Show that A is stable over K if G is acyclic, and give a formula for A^* under this condition. Does the converse hold?

The reader can find a lot of further examples for path algebras in the literature given above, in particular in Gondran and Minoux (1984) and Zimmermann (1981); see also Kuich and Salomaa (1986) for applications in Automata Theory. Finally we mention an example from practical Operations Research.

Example 3.10.12. We construct a directed graph G, whose vertices are the single parts, modules, and finished products occuring in an assembly line. We want the edges to signify how many single parts or intermediary modules are needed for assembling bigger modules or finished products. That is, we assign weight $w(i, j)$ to edge ij if we need $w(i, j)$ units of part i for assembling product j. G is called the *Gozinto graph*. In most cases, the modules and products are divided into levels of the same rank, where the finished products have highest rank, and single parts (which have not been assembled from any smaller parts) lowest rank; that is, the products and modules are divided into 'disposition levels'. The notion of ranks used here is the same as in Exercise 3.5.2; it can be calculated as in Exercise 3.5.3. Often the Gozinto graph is taken as reduced, that is, it contains an edge ij only if part i is used directly for module j, without any intermediary step of assembly, see Section 3.8. Here the reduced graph G_{red} can be determined as in Exercise 3.8.7; we always assume G to be acyclic. (This is not always true in reality; in chemical production, Gozinto graphs containing cycles occur quite often, see Müller-Merbach (1966)).

Now suppose that we have a Gozinto graph which is reduced already. Sometimes one wants to know how much of each part used directly or indirectly is needed. We consider the path algebra $(\mathbb{N}_0, +, \cdot)$ and the given weights $w(ij)$. As G is acyclic, there are only finitely many directed paths from vertex i to vertex j. Thus, the matrix W^* ($= W^{(n-1)}$) exists; and entry w_{ij}^* gives the total number of units of i needed for the assembly of j (as the reader can check easily). The matrix W^* could, for example, be determined using the Algorithm of Bellman-Ford (that is, the generalized Jacobi technique), or using the technique analogous to the Algorithm of Floyd-Warshall (see Müller-Merbach (1969)).

More about Gozinto graphs can be found in the book by Müeller-Merbach (1973) as well as in the two papers of the same author cited above. Note that the entries of a column of W^* give the numbers of parts and modules needed for the corresponding product; whereas the entries in the lines show where (and how much of) the corresponding part or module is needed.

4. Spanning Trees

In this chapter, we have a closer look at trees which were introduced in Section 1.2. We begin by giving some further characterizations of trees and determining the number of trees on n vertices and, more generally, the number of spanning trees in a connected graph. The main part of this chapter is devoted to problems of the following kind: In some given network, we look for a spanning tree for which the sum of all lengths of edges is minimal. This problem has a lot of applications: For example, the vertices might represent cities we want to connect to a system supplying electricity; then the edges represent the possible connections and the length of an edge states how much it would cost to build the respective connection. Other possible interpretations are tasks like establishing traffic connections (for cars, trains or planes: 'Connector Problem'), or building a network for TV broadcasts. Finally, we consider Steiner trees (these are trees where it is allowed to add some new vertices) and arborescences (the directed analogue of trees).

4.1 Trees and Forests

We defined a tree to be a connected acyclic graph, and in Theorem 1.2.8, we gave some equivalent conditions. The following lemma gives some further characterizations for trees:

Lemma 4.1.1. *Let G be a graph. Then the following conditions are equivalent:*

(1) G is a tree.
(2) G does not contain any cycles, but adding any further edge yields a cycle.
(3) Any two vertices of G are connected by a unique path.
(4) G is connected, and any edge of G is a bridge.

   Proof.

$(1) \Rightarrow (2)$: Let G be a tree and $e = uv$ any new edge. As G is connected, there is a path W from v to u. Then $v \overset{W}{\underline{\hspace{1cm}}} u \overset{e}{\underline{\hspace{1cm}}} v$ is a cycle. G itself is acyclic by definition.

(2) $\Rightarrow$ (3):   Let u and v be two vertices of G. If there were no path between u and v, adding an edge uv to G could not yield a cycle. Thus, G must be connected. Suppose G contained two different paths W and W' from u to v. Then $u \ \overset{W}{\rule{2cm}{0.4pt}} \ v \ \overset{W'}{\rule{2cm}{0.4pt}} \ u$ would be a closed walk in G, so that G would have to contain a cycle, a contradiction.

(3) $\Rightarrow$ (4): G is connected by hypothesis. Let $e = uv$ be an edge in G. Suppose e is not a bridge, then $G\backslash e$ is still connected. ($G\backslash e$ denotes the graph arising from omitting e from G.) But that means there have to be two disjoint paths from u to v in G.

(4) $\Rightarrow$ (1): G is connected by hypothesis. Suppose G contains a cycle K. Then any edge of K could be omitted from G, and the resulting graph would still be connected. In other words, no edge of K would be a bridge, a contradiction.

$\square$

Here are some exercises concerning trees and forests:

Exercise 4.1.2. A connected graph is called *unicyclic* if it contains exactly one cycle. Show that the following statements are equivalent (see Anderson and Harary (1967)):

(1) G is unicyclic.
(2) $G\backslash e$ is a tree for some appropriate edge e.
(3) G is connected, and the number of vertices is the same as the number of edges.
(4) G is connected, and the set of all edges of G which are not bridges forms a cycle.

Exercise 4.1.3. Any tree has either exactly one center or exactly two centers (see Section 3.8). What is the relationship between the excentricity and the diameter of a tree?

Exercise 4.1.4. Let G be a forest having exactly $2k$ vertices of odd degree. Then the edge set of G is the disjoint union of k paths.

Exercise 4.1.5. Determine all isomorphism classes of trees on six vertices and calculate the number of trees in each isomorphism class, as well as the number of all trees on six vertices. Moreover, find the corresponding automorphism groups.

Note that the number t_n of isomorphism classes of trees on n vertices grows very fast with n; the following table is taken from Harary (1969) (for $n = 1, 2, 3$, $t_n = 1$).

Table 4.1 Number t_n of isomorphism classes for trees on n vertices						
n	4	5	6	7	8	9	10
t_n	2	3	6	11	23	47	106
n	11	12	13	14	15	16	17
t_n	235	551	1301	3159	7741	19320	48629
n	18	19	20	21	22	23	24
t_n	123867	317955	832065	2144505	5623756	14828074	39299897

An interesting exposition of the question how to check whether two given trees (where a root is marked) are isomorphic can be found in Campbell and Radford (1991).

Exercise 4.1.6. Let T be a tree. Suppose the complementary graph $\overline{T}$ is not connected. Describe the structure of T and show that these graphs $\overline{T}$ are precisely the disconnected graphs having maximal number of edges.

4.2 Incidence Matrices

In this section we define a further matrix associated with a directed graph. We will use this matrix to give another characterization of trees and to find a formula for the number of spanning trees of an arbitrary connected graph.

Definition 4.2.1. Let G be a directed graph with vertex set $V = \{1, \ldots, n\}$ and edge set $E = \{e_1, \ldots, e_m\}$. Then the matrix $M = (m_{ij})$ $(i = 1, \ldots, n;$ $j = 1, \ldots, m)$, where

$$m_{ij} = \begin{cases} -1 & \text{if } i \text{ is the tail of } e_j, \\ +1 & \text{if } i \text{ is the head of } e_j, \\ 0 & \text{otherwise}, \end{cases}$$

is called the *incidence matrix* of G.

For example, the directed graph of Figure 2.1 has (numbering vertices and edges as in 2.2.1) the following incidence matrix:

$$\begin{pmatrix} -1 & 0 & 0 & -1 & 0 & 0 & 0 & 0 & +1 & 0 & 0 & -1 \\ +1 & -1 & 0 & 0 & +1 & 0 & 0 & 0 & 0 & 0 & -1 & 0 \\ 0 & +1 & -1 & 0 & 0 & 0 & 0 & 0 & 0 & +1 & 0 & +1 \\ 0 & 0 & +1 & 0 & 0 & 0 & -1 & +1 & -1 & 0 & 0 & 0 \\ 0 & 0 & 0 & +1 & -1 & +1 & 0 & 0 & 0 & 0 & +1 & 0 \\ 0 & 0 & 0 & 0 & 0 & -1 & +1 & -1 & 0 & -1 & 0 & 0 \end{pmatrix}$$

Thus, each column of an incidence matrix contains exactly two non-zero entries, namely one entry $+1$ and one entry -1; summing the entries -1 (or $+1$, respectively) in row i gives $d_{out}(i)$ (or $d_{in}(i)$, respectively). Note that we assume that the vertices and edges are numbered in some given order, so that the matrix M is determined by G only up to permutations of rows and columns. The entries $0, 1$ and -1 are often considered as integers, and the matrix M is considered as a matrix over $\mathbb{Z}$, $\mathbb{Q}$ or $\mathbb{R}$; we could also use any other ring of characteristic $\neq 2$ (so that $1 \neq -1$).

Adding all the rows of the incidence matrix of a directed graph gives a row having all entries 0. This yields the following lemma.

Lemma 4.2.2. *Let G be a directed graph having n vertices. Then the incidence matrix of G can have rank at most $n - 1$.*   □

Later, we will determine the precise rank of the incidence matrix. But first, we give a characterization of those directed graphs which are forests, where a directed graph G is called a *forest* if $|G|$ is a forest (analogous to our terminology for trees).

Theorem 4.2.3. *A directed graph with incidence matrix M is a forest if and only if the columns of M are linearly independent.*

Proof. We have to show that $|G|$ contains a cycle if and only if the columns of M are linearly dependent. Suppose that

$$K \quad = \quad v_0 \ \frac{e_1}{\rule{2cm}{0pt}} \ v_1 \ \frac{e_2}{\rule{2cm}{0pt}} \ \ldots \ \frac{e_k}{\rule{2cm}{0pt}} \ v_k$$

is a (undirected) cycle in G. Let $s_1, \ldots, s_k$ be the columns of M corresponding to the edges $e_1, \ldots, e_k$. Moreover, let $x_i = 1$ if e_i is a forward edge, and $x_i = -1$ if e_i is a backward edge in K (for $i = 1, \ldots, k$). Then we have $x_1 s_1 + \ldots + x_k s_k = 0$.

Conversely, suppose the columns of M are linearly dependent. Then there are columns $s_1, \ldots, s_k$ and integers $x_1, \ldots, x_k \neq 0$ such that $x_1 s_1 + \ldots + x_k s_k = 0$. Let E' be the set of edges corresponding to the columns $s_1, \ldots, s_k$ and V' the set of vertices of G incident with the edges contained in E'. Then the directed subgraph $G' = (V', E')$ does not contain any vertices of degree 1, so that $|G'|$ (and hence $|G|$) cannot be a forest by Exercise 1.2.5.   □

Theorem 4.2.4. *Let G be a directed graph with n vertices and p connected components. Then the incidence matrix M of G has rank $n - p$.*

Proof. According to Theorem 4.2.3, the rank of M is the number of edges of a maximal forest T contained in $|G|$. If $p = 1$, T is a tree and has exactly $n - 1$ edges; M has rank $n - 1 = n - p$ in this case.

Now suppose $p \neq 1$. Then G can be partitioned into its p connected components, so that T is the disjoint union of p trees. Suppose these trees have $n_1, \ldots, n_p$ vertices. Then the incidence matrix of G has rank $(n_1 - 1) + \ldots + (n_p - 1) = n - p$. $\square$

Next, we show that the incidence matrix of a directed graph has a very special structure. We need the following definition: A matrix over $\mathbb{Z}$ is called *totally unimodular* if any square submatrix has determinant 0, 1 or -1. These matrices are particularly important in Combinatorial Optimization. For example, the theorem about integral flows in networks, which we will treat in Chapter 6, is based on the following result (see also Lawler (1976), §4.12), even though we will give a different proof.

Theorem 4.2.5. *Let M be the incidence matrix of a directed graph G. Then M is totally unimodular.*

Proof. Let M' be any square submatrix of M, say with k rows and columns. If $k = 1$, it is trivial that M' has determinant 0, 1 or -1. So let $k \neq 1$. We assume first that each column of M' contains two non-zero entries. Then the rows and columns of M' define a directed graph G' having k vertices and k edges. By Theorem 1.2.7, $|G'|$ cannot be acyclic, so that G' is not a forest. Therefore, the columns of M' are linearly dependent by Theorem 4.2.3, and we have det $M' = 0$. Now, if our assumption that each column contains two non-zero entries does not hold, we can choose some column of M' having at most one entry $\neq 0$. Calculating the determinant of M' by expanding it with respect to this column, we get a factor 0, 1 or -1 multiplied with the determinant of a square $((k - 1) \times (k - 1))$ submatrix M''. Now the statement follows using induction on k. $\square$

Corollary 4.2.6. *Let G be a directed graph with n vertices and $n - 1$ edges. Let B be the matrix we get from the incidence matrix M of G by deleting an arbitrary row. If G is a tree, then det $B = 1$ or det $B = -1$, otherwise det $B = 0$.*

Proof. Note that the row deleted from M is a linear combination of the other rows. Thus, by Theorem 4.2.4, B has rank $n - 1$ if and only if G is a tree. Now the statement follows immediately from Theorem 4.2.5. $\square$

Now we use the incidence matrix to determine the number of spanning trees of a directed graph. Here, a *spanning tree* is a directed subgraph T of G such that $|T|$ is a spanning tree for $|G|$.

Theorem 4.2.7 (Matrix Tree Theorem). *Let B be the matrix arising from the incidence matrix of a directed graph G by deleting an arbitrary row. Then the number of spanning trees of G is det BB^T.*

Proof. Let n be the number of vertices of G. For any set S of $n - 1$ column indices, we denote the matrix consisting of the $n - 1$ columns of B

corresponding to S by $B|S$. Now the Theorem of Cauchy and Binet (see, for instance, Hadley (1961)) implies

$$\det BB^T = \sum_S \det (B|S)(B|S)^T = \sum_S \det (B|S)^2.$$

By Corollary 4.2.6, $\det B|S \neq 0$ if and only if the edges of G corresponding to S form a tree; moreover, in this case, $(\det B|S)^2 = 1$. This proves the theorem.   □

Theorem 4.2.7 is contained implicitly in Kirchhoff (1847). Of course, the theorem can also be used to determine the number of spanning trees of a graph G by considering the incidence matrix of any orientation of G. We will do this below for the complete graphs. First, let us state a lemma and the general result.

Lemma 4.2.8. *Let A be the adjacency matrix of a graph G, and M the incidence matrix of an arbitrary orientation H of G (where both matrices use the same order of the vertices for numbering the rows and columns). Then $MM^T = diag(deg\ 1, \ldots, deg\ n) - A$.*

Proof. The (i, j)-entry of MM^T is the scalar product of the i-th and the j-th row of M. For $i \neq j$, this entry is -1 if ij or ji is an edge of H and 0 otherwise. For $i = j$, we get the degree $\deg i$.   □

Theorem 4.2.9. *Let A be the adjacency matrix of a graph G and A' the matrix $-A + diag\ (deg\ 1, \ldots, deg\ n)$. Then the number of spanning trees of G is the common value of all minors of A' arising from deleting one row and the corresponding column from A'.*

Proof. The statement follows directly from 4.2.7 and 4.2.8   □

In Section 4.8, we will give a different proof for Theorem 4.2.9 which avoids using the Theorem of Cauchy and Binet. The matrix A' is called the *degree matrix* or the *Laplacian matrix* of G. Now look at the case $G = K_n$. Theorem 4.2.9 gives a formula for the number of all trees on n vertices; note that this formula counts the different trees, not the isomorphism classes of trees. Obviously, the degree matrix of K_n is $A' = nI - J$, where J is the matrix having all entries $= 1$. By Theorem 4.2.9, the number of trees on n vertices is the determinant of a minor of A', that is

$$\begin{vmatrix} n-1 & -1 & \cdots & -1 \\ -1 & n-1 & \cdots & -1 \\ \multicolumn{4}{c}{\cdots\cdots\cdots\cdots\cdots\cdots\cdots} \\ -1 & -1 & \cdots & n-1 \end{vmatrix} = \begin{vmatrix} n-1 & -n & -n & \cdots & -n \\ -1 & n & 0 & \cdots & 0 \\ -1 & 0 & n & \cdots & 0 \\ \multicolumn{5}{c}{\cdots\cdots\cdots\cdots\cdots\cdots\cdots} \\ -1 & 0 & 0 & \cdots & n \end{vmatrix}$$

$$= \begin{vmatrix} 1 & 0 & 0 & \dots & 0 \\ -1 & n & 0 & \dots & 0 \\ -1 & 0 & n & \dots & 0 \\ \hdotsfor{5} \\ -1 & 0 & 0 & \dots & n \end{vmatrix} = n^{n-2}.$$

This gives a third (non-constructive) proof for Corollary 1.2.11.

Exercise 4.2.10. Use Theorem 4.2.9 to show that the number of spanning trees of the complete bipartite graph $K_{m,n}$ is $m^{n-1}n^{m-1}$.

The result in Exercise 4.2.10 is due to Fiedler and Sedlacek (1958); a simple direct proof can be found in Abu-Sbeih (1990), who also applied this result to give a further proof for Corollary 1.2.11.

Note that we can also define incidence matrices for graphs: the matrix M has entry $m_{ij} = 1$ if vertex i is incident with edge e_j, and $m_{ij} = 0$ otherwise. But the statements analogous to Lemma 4.2.2 and Theorem 4.2.3 do not hold; for example, the three columns of a cycle of length 3 are linearly independent over $\mathbb{Z}$. However, the situation changes if we consider the incidence matrix M as a matrix over $\mathbb{Z}_2$.

Exercise 4.2.11. Prove the analogues of 4.2.2 through 4.2.4 for graphs, where M is considered as a binary matrix.

The incidence matrix M of a graph (considered as a matrix over the integers) is not unimodular in general, as the following exercise shows. Moreover, it gives a further important characterization of bipartite graphs.

Exercise 4.2.12. Let G be a graph with incidence matrix M. Show that G is bipartite if and only if M is totally unimodular (as a matrix over $\mathbb{Z}$). Hint: The proof that unimodularity of M is necessary is similar to the proof of Theorem 4.2.5. The converse can be proved indirectly.

Exercise 4.2.13. Let e be an edge of K_n. Determine the number of spanning trees of $K_n \backslash e$.

Exercise 4.2.14. Let G be a forest with n vertices and m edges. How many connected components does G have?

Sometimes, a list of all spanning trees of a given graph is needed, or an arbitrary choice of some spanning tree of G (a 'random' spanning tree). These tasks are treated by Colbourn, Day and Nel (1989). In particular, it is shown that the latter problem can be solved with complexity $O(|V|^3)$.

4.3 Minimal Spanning Trees

In this section, we look at spanning forests in networks. So let (G, w) be a network. For any subset T of the edge set of G,

$$w(T) = \sum_{e \in T} w(e)$$

is called the *weight* of T. A spanning forest or a spanning tree of G, respectively, is called a *minimal spanning forest* or a *minimal spanning tree* if its weight $w(T)$ is minimal of all the weights of spanning forests (or trees, respectively). We restrict ourselves to spanning trees; the general case can be treated by considering a minimal spanning tree for each connected component of G. Thus, we assume G to be connected from now on.

Minimal spanning trees were first considered by Boruvka (1926a) and Boruvka (1926b). Shortly after 1920, the rural area of Southern Moravia was to be connected to electrical supply; the problem of finding as economical a solution as possible for the network to be constructed was presented to Boruvka. He found an algorithm for constructing a minimal spanning tree and published it in the two papers cited above. We will look at his algorithm in the next section. The papers of Boruvka remained unnoticed for a long time; often the solution of the problem of finding minimal spanning trees is attributed to Kruskal (1956) and Prim (1957), although both of them quote Boruvka (1926a). An interesting article concerning the history of the problem was written by Graham and Hell (1985). It also contains references to various applications reaching from the obvious examples of constructing a network for traffic or communication to more remote examples in classification problems, automatic speech recognition, picture processing etc.

If the weight function w is constant, any spanning tree is minimal of course. In this case, determining a minimal spanning tree could be done – as described in Section 3.3 – using a BFS (with complexity $O(|E|)$). For the general case, we give three efficient algorithms in the next section. Corollary 1.2.11 and Exercise 4.2.10 show that the examination of all spanning trees would be a method having non-polynomial complexity. First we characterize the minimal spanning trees. We introduce the following notation: Let T be a tree and e an edge not contained in T. According to Lemma 4.1.1, the graph arising from T by adding e contains a unique cycle. We denote this cycle by $C_T(e)$. (As the orientation of edges is insignificant when looking at spanning trees, we may assume that G is a graph.) The following theorem is of fundamental importance.

Theorem 4.3.1. *Let (G, w) be a network, where G is a connected graph. A spanning tree T of G is minimal if and only if, for each edge e in $G \backslash T$, we have*

$$w(e) \geq w(f) \qquad \text{for all edges } f \text{ in } C_T(e). \tag{4.1}$$

Proof. First suppose that T is minimal. If (4.1) is not satisfied, there is an edge e in $G \backslash T$ and an edge f in $C_T(e)$ with $w(e) < w(f)$. Removing f from T divides T into two connected components, since f is a bridge. Adding e to $T \backslash f$ gives a new spanning tree T', and as $w(e) < w(f)$, T' has smaller weight than T. This contradicts the minimality of T.

Conversely, suppose that (4.1) is satisfied. We choose some minimal spanning tree T' and show that $w(T) = w(T')$, which proves that T is minimal as well. We use induction on the number k of edges in $T' \backslash T$. The case $k = 0$ (that is, $T = T'$) is trivial. So let e' be an edge in $T' \backslash T$. Again, we remove e' from T', so that T' is divided into two connected components V_1 and V_2. If we add the path $C_T(e') \backslash \{e'\}$ to $T' \backslash \{e'\}$, V_1 and V_2 are connected again. Thus, $C_T(e')$ has to contain an edge e connecting a vertex in V_1 to a vertex in V_2. Note that e cannot be an edge of T', because otherwise $T' \backslash \{e'\}$ would still be connected. The minimality of T' implies that $w(e) \geq w(e')$: replacing edge e' by e in T', we get another spanning tree T'', and if $w(e) < w(e')$, this tree would have smaller weight than T' contradicting the minimality of T'. On the other hand, (4.1) states that $w(e') \geq w(e)$, so that $w(e') = w(e)$ and $w(T'') = w(T')$. Thus, T'' is a minimal spanning tree as well. T'' has one more edge in common with T than T', and, using induction, we have $w(T) = w(T'') = w(T')$. □

There is another characterization of minimal spanning trees. We need two definitions: Let G be a graph having vertex set V. A *cut* is a partition $S = X \overset{.}{\cup} X'$ of V into two non-empty subsets. By $E(S)$ or $E(X, X')$ we denote the set of all edges incident with one vertex in X and one vertex in X'. Any such edge set is called a *cocycle*. Here, we need cocycles constructed from trees.

Lemma 4.3.2. *Let G be a connected graph and T a spanning tree of G. For each edge e of T, there is exactly one cut $S_T(e)$ of G such that e is the only edge T has in common with the corresponding cocycle $E(S_T(e))$.*

Proof. If we remove e from T, the tree is divided into two connected components and we get a cut $S_T(e)$. Obviously, the corresponding cocycle contains e, but no other edge of T. It is easy to see that this cut is the only one having this property. □

Theorem 4.3.3. *Let (G, w) be a network, where G is a connected graph. A spanning tree T of G is minimal if and only if, for each edge e of T, we have*

$$w(e) \leq w(f) \quad \text{for each edge } f \text{ in } E(S_T(e)). \tag{4.2}$$

Proof. First let T be minimal. Suppose that there is an edge e in T and an edge f in $E(S_T(e))$ with $w(e) > w(f)$. Then, by removing e from T and adding f instead, we could construct a spanning tree of smaller weight than T, a contradiction.

Conversely, suppose that (4.2) is satisfied. We want to reduce the statement to Theorem 4.3.1, so that we have to show that (4.1) holds. Let e be an edge in $G \backslash T$ and $f \neq e$ an edge in $C_T(e)$. Consider the cocycle $E(S_T(f))$ defined by f. Obviously, e is contained in $E(S_T(f))$, so that by (4.2), $w(f) \leq w(e)$. □

Exercise 4.3.4 (Boruvka (1926a)). Let (G, w) be a network, where any two edges have different weights. Show that (G, w) has a unique minimal spanning tree.

4.4 The Algorithms of Prim, Kruskal and Boruvka

In this section, we treat three algorithms for determining minimal spanning trees, all of which are based on the characterizations given in the previous section. We begin with a generic algorithm for determining minimal spanning trees, which also allows a rather simple and easily understandable proof. The three subsequent algorithms are special cases of this general method which was discovered by Prim (1957).

Algorithm 4.4.1. Let $G = (V, E)$ be a connected graph with vertex set $V = \{1, \ldots, n\}$ and $w : E \to \mathbb{R}$ a weight function for G. The algorithm constructs a spanning tree T having minimal weight.

Procedure MINTREE$(G, w; T)$

(1) **for** $i = 1$ **to** n **do** $V_i \leftarrow \{i\}$; $T_i \leftarrow \emptyset$ **od**;
(2) **for** $k = 1$ **to** $n - 1$ **do**
(3)   choose V_i with $V_i \neq \emptyset$;
(4)   choose an edge $e = uv$ with $u \in V_i$, $v \notin V_i$ and $w(e) \leq w(e')$
           for all edges $e' = u'v'$ with $u' \in V_i$, $v' \notin V_i$;
(5)   determine the index j for which $v \in V_j$;
(6) $V_i \leftarrow V_i \cup V_j$; $V_j \leftarrow \emptyset$;
(7) $T_i \leftarrow T_i \cup T_j \cup \{e\}$; $T_j \leftarrow \emptyset$;
(8)   **if** $k = n - 1$ **then** $T \leftarrow T_i$ **fi**;
(9) **od**.

Theorem 4.4.2. *Algorithm 4.4.1 determines a minimal spanning tree for* (G, w).

Proof. We use induction on $t := |T_1| + \ldots + |T_n|$ to prove the following statement:

> For $t = 0, \ldots, n - 1$, there exists a minimal spanning tree T (4.3)
> of G containing $T_1, \ldots, T_n$.

For $t = n - 1$, this statement implies that the algorithm is correct. It is obvious that (4.3) holds at the beginning of the algorithm, before the loop (2) to (9) is executed for the first time, because $t = 0$ at that point of time. Now suppose that (4.3) holds for $t = k - 1$, that is, before the loop is executed for the k-th time. Look at the edge $e = uv$ with $u \in V_i$ constructed in the k-th iteration. If e is contained in the tree T satisfying (4.3) for $t = k - 1$, there is nothing to show. Thus, we assume $e \notin T$, so that $T \cup \{e\}$ contains the unique cycle $C = C_T(e)$. Obviously, C has to contain another edge $f = rs$ with $r \in V_i$ and $s \notin V_i$. By Theorem 4.3.1, $w(e) \geq w(f)$. On the other hand, we choose e in step (4) such that $w(e) \leq w(f)$. This means that $w(e) = w(f)$ and $T' = (T \cup \{e\}) \backslash \{f\}$ is also a minimal spanning tree of G, so that T' satisfies (4.3) for $t = k$. $\square$

Of course, we cannot give the precise complexity of Algorithm 4.4.1, because it depends as well on the choice of the index i in step (3) as on the details of the implementation. We now turn to the three special cases of Algorithm 4.4.1 mentioned above. All of them are derived by introducing precise statements for steps (3) and (4) in MINTREE. The first algorithm was favoured by Prim (1957) and is therefore known as the *Algorithm of Prim*, although it was already given by Jarník (1930).

Algorithm 4.4.3. Let G be a connected graph with vertex set $V = \{1, \ldots, n\}$ and $w : E \to \mathbb{R}$ a weight function for G, where G is given by adjacency lists A_v.

Procedure PRIM$(G, w; T)$

(1) $g(1) \leftarrow 0, S \leftarrow \emptyset, T \leftarrow \emptyset$;
(2) **for** $i = 2$ **to** n **do** $g(i) \leftarrow \infty$ **od**;
(3) **while** $S \neq V$ **do**
(4)   choose $i \in V \backslash S$ such that $g(i)$ is minimal, and set $S \leftarrow S \cup \{i\}$;
(5)   **if** $i \neq 1$ **then** $T \leftarrow T \cup \{e(i)\}$ **fi**;
(6)   **for** $e \in A_i \cap E(S, V \backslash S)$ **do**
(7)   let v be the vertex incident with e in $V \backslash S$;
(8)   **if** $g(v) > w(e)$ **then** $g(v) \leftarrow w(e)$ and $e(v) \leftarrow e$ **fi**
(9)   **od**
(10) **od**.

Theorem 4.4.4. *Algorithm 4.4.3 determines a minimal spanning tree T of G with complexity $O(|V|^2)$.*

Proof. It is easy to see that Algorithm 4.4.3 is a special case of Algorithm 4.4.1 (written a bit differently): if we always choose V_1 in step (3) of MINTREE, we get the Algorithm of Prim. (The function $g(i)$ introduced in 4.4.3 is used to make it easier to find the shortest edge leaving $V_1 = S$.) Thus, it follows from Theorem 4.4.2 that the algorithm is correct. Now look at the complexity. The **while**-loop is executed $|V|$ times. During each of these iterations, the comparisons in step (4) can be done in at most $|V| - |S|$ steps, so that we get a complexity of $O(|V|^2)$. As G is simple, this is also the complexity of the whole algorithm, because in step (6), each edge of G is examined exactly twice. $\square$

Example 4.4.5. We look at the undirected version of the network of Figure 3.5.

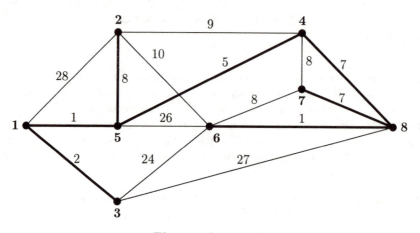

Fig. 4.1 A network

Let us label the edges as follows: $e_1 = \{1,5\}$, $e_2 = \{6,8\}$, $e_3 = \{1,3\}$, $e_4 = \{4,5\}$, $e_5 = \{4,8\}$, $e_6 = \{7,8\}$, $e_7 = \{6,7\}$, $e_8 = \{4,7\}$, $e_9 = \{2,5\}$, $e_{10} = \{2,4\}$, $e_{11} = \{2,6\}$, $e_{12} = \{3,6\}$, $e_{13} = \{5,6\}$, $e_{14} = \{3,8\}$, $e_{15} = \{1,2\}$. Thus, the edges are ordered according to their weight. We do not need this ordering for the Algorithm of Prim, but will use it later for the Algorithm of Kruskal. The Algorithm of Prim is then executed as follows:

Iteration 1: $i = 1$, $S = \{1\}$, $T = \emptyset$, $w(2) = 28$, $e(2) = e_{15}$, $w(5) = 1$,
$\qquad\qquad$ $e(5) = e_1$, $w(3) = 2$, $e(3) = e_3$

Iteration 2: $i = 5$, $S = \{1,5\}$, $T = \{e_1\}$, $w(2) = 8$, $e(2) = e_9$, $w(4) = 5$,
$\qquad\qquad$ $e(4) = e_4$, $w(6) = 26$, $e(6) = e_{13}$

Iteration 3: $i = 3$, $S = \{1,5,3\}$, $T = \{e_1,e_3\}$, $w(6) = 24$, $e(6) = e_{12}$,
$\qquad\qquad$ $w(8) = 27$, $e(8) = e_{14}$

Iteration 4: $i = 4$, $S = \{1,5,3,4\}$, $T = \{e_1,e_3,e_4\}$, $w(7) = 8$, $e(7) = e_8$,
$\qquad\qquad$ $w(8) = 7$, $e(8) = e_5$

Iteration 5: $i = 8$, $S = \{1,5,3,4,8\}$, $T = \{e_1,e_3,e_4,e_5\}$, $w(6) = 1$,
$\qquad\qquad$ $e(6) = e_2$, $w(7) = 7$, $e(7) = e_6$

Iteration 6: $i = 6$, $S = \{1, 5, 3, 4, 8, 6\}$, $T = \{e_1, e_3, e_4, e_5, e_2\}$
Iteration 7: $i = 7$, $S = \{1, 5, 3, 4, 8, 6, 7\}$, $T = \{e_1, e_3, e_4, e_5, e_2, e_6\}$
Iteration 8: $i = 2$, $S = \{1, 5, 3, 4, 8, 6, 7, 2\}$, $T = \{e_1, e_3, e_4, e_5, e_2, e_6, e_9\}$

The corresponding spanning tree is indicated by the bold edges in Figure 4.1.

Next we look at another special case of Algorithm 4.4.1 due to Kruskal (1956).

Algorithm 4.4.6. Let G be a connected graph with vertex set $V = \{1, \ldots, n\}$ and $w : E \to \mathbb{R}$ a weight function. The edges of G are ordered according to their weight, that is, $E = \{e_1, \ldots, e_m\}$ and $w(e_1) \leq \ldots \leq w(e_m)$.

Procedure KRUSKAL$(G, w; T)$

(1) $T \leftarrow \emptyset$;
(2) **for** $k = 1$ **to** m **do**
(3)   **if** e_k does not form a cycle together with the edges of T
            then append e_k to T **fi**
(4) **od**.

We see that the Algorithm of Kruskal is the special case of MINTREE where V_i and e are chosen in such a way that $w(e)$ is minimal among all edges which could still be chosen (that is, among all those edges which do not have both end vertices in one of the sets V_j and would therefore create a cycle). Theorem 4.4.2 implies that the algorithm is correct. Alternatively, we could also use Theorem 4.3.1: In step (3), we choose the edge which does not create a cycle with the edges already in the forest and which has minimal weight of all edges with this property. Thus, the set T of edges constructed satisfies (4.1), and therefore T is a minimal spanning tree.

Let us consider the complexity of Algorithm 4.4.6. For ordering the edges according to their weight and for removing the edge of smallest weight, we use the data structure priority queue already described in Section 3.6; then these operations can be done in $O(|E| \log |E|)$ steps. However, it is difficult to estimate the complexity of step (3) of the algorithm: How do we check whether an edge creates a cycle, and how many steps does this take? It helps to look at the algorithm as a special case of Algorithm 4.4.1. In step (1), we begin with a (totally) disconnected forest T on $n = |V|$ vertices which consists of n trees without any edges. During the iteration, an edge is added to the forest T if and only if its two end vertices are contained in different connected components of the forest constructed so far; these two connected components are then joined by adding the edge to the forest T. Thus, the checking for cycles can be substituted by keeping a list of the connected components. To do this, we need a data structure appropriate for treating partitions. In particular, operations like disjoint unions (MERGE) and finding the component containing a given element should be easy to perform. Using this, we give the following more precise version of Algorithm 4.4.6.

Algorithm 4.4.7. Let G be a connected graph with vertex set $V = \{1, \ldots, n\}$ and $w : E \to \mathbb{R}$ a weight function on G. We assume that E is given as a list of edges.

Procedure KRUSKAL $(G, w; T)$

(1) $T \leftarrow \emptyset$;
(2) **for** $i = 1$ **to** n **do** $V_i \leftarrow \{i\}$ **od**;
(3) put E into a priority queue Q with priority function w;[1]
(4) **while** $Q \neq \emptyset$ **do**
(5) $e := \text{DELETEMIN}(Q)$;
(6)   find the end vertices u and v of e;
(7)   find the components V_u and V_v containing u and v, respectively;
(8)   **if** $V_u \neq V_v$ **then** MERGE(V_u, V_v); $T \leftarrow T \cup \{e\}$ **fi**
(9) **od**.

Now it is easy to determine the complexity of the iteration: Finding and removing the minimal edge e in the priority queue takes $O(\log |E|)$ steps. Merging the connected components (there are n of them at first) successively, and finding the components in step (7), can be done with a total effort of $O(n \log n)$ steps (see Aho, Hopcroft and Ullman (1983) §5.5 or Corman, Leiserson and Rivest (1990) §24.2). As G is connected, G has at least $n - 1$ edges, so that the overall complexity is $O(|E| \log |E|)$. We get the following result.

Theorem 4.4.8. *The Algorithm of Kruskal (as given in 4.4.7) determines a minimal spanning tree with complexity $O(|E| \log |E|)$.* $\square$

Note that, for sparse graphs, this complexity is much better than the complexity of the Algorithm of Prim. In practice, the Algorithm of Kruskal often contains one more step: after each merging of components, it is checked whether there is only one component left; in that case, T is already a tree and the algorithm can stop.

Example 4.4.9. We apply the Algorithm of Kruskal to the network of Figure 4.1. The edges $e_1, e_2, e_3, e_4, e_5, e_6$ and e_9 are chosen successively, so that we get the same spanning tree as with the Algorithm of Prim (although there the edges were chosen in a different order). The reason for this is that our example has only one minimal spanning tree. In general, however, the Algorithms of Prim and Kruskal yield different minimal spanning trees.

Now we turn to the third special case of Algorithm 4.4.1 which is due to Boruvka (1926a). His algorithm treats the case where all edge weights are different. In that case, we can combine several iterations of MINTREE: during

---

[1] It is not absolutely necessary to use a priority queue here. It is also possible to use any other sorting technique to arrange the edges according to increasing weight.

each iteration, we add, for each nonempty V_i, the shortest edge 'leaving' V_i. We give a comparatively short description of the resulting algorithm.

Algorithm 4.4.10. Let G be a connected graph with vertex set $V = \{1, \dots, n\}$ and $w : E \to \mathbb{R}$ a weight function, where two distinct edges always have different weight.

Procedure BORUVKA$(G, w; T)$

(1) **for** $i = 1$ **to** n **do** $V_i \leftarrow \{i\}$ **od**;
(2) $T \leftarrow \emptyset$; $M \leftarrow \{V_1, \dots, V_n\}$;
(3) **while** $|T| < n - 1$ **do**
(4)   **for** $U \in M$ **do**
(5)   find an edge $e = uv$ with $u \in U$, $v \notin U$ and $w(e) < w(e')$
           for all edges $e' = u'v'$ with $u' \in U$, $v' \notin U$;
(6)   find the component U' containing v;
(7) $T \leftarrow T \cup \{e\}$;
(8)   **od**
(9)   **for** $U \in M$ **do** MERGE(U, U') **od**
(10) **od.**

Theorem 4.4.11. *The Algorithm of Boruvka determines a minimal spanning tree with complexity $O(|E|\ log\ |V|)$.*

Proof. It follows from Theorem 4.4.2 that the algorithm is correct. The condition that all edge weights are different makes sure that no cycles are created during an execution of the **while**-loop. As the number of connected components is at least halved in each iteration, the **while**-loop is executed at most $\log |V|$ times. We leave it to the reader to give a precise formulation of steps (5) and (6) leading to the complexity of $O(|E| \log |V|)$. (Hint: For each vertex v, we should originally have a list E_v of the edges incident with v.) □

Example 4.4.12. We apply the Algorithm of Boruvka to the network shown in Figure 4.2. When the **while**-loop is executed for the first time, the edges $\{1, 2\}$, $\{3, 6\}$, $\{4, 5\}$, $\{4, 7\}$ and $\{7, 8\}$ (drawn bold in Figure 4.2) are chosen and inserted into T. That leaves only three connected components, which are merged during the second execution of the **while**-loop by adding the edges $\{2, 5\}$ and $\{1, 3\}$ (drawn bold broken in Figure 4.2).

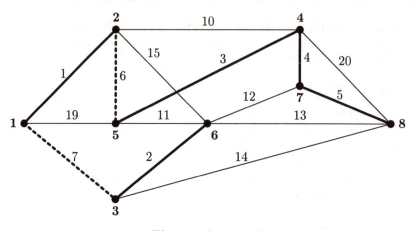

Fig. 4.2 A network

Exercise 4.4.13. Show that the condition that all edges have different weights is necessary for the correctness of the Algorithm of Boruvka.

The complexity of the algorithms given above can sometimes be improved by using appropriate data structures. It is possible to implement both the Algorithms of Prim and Kruskal such that they have complexity $O(|E| \log |V|)$, see Johnson (1975) and Cheriton and Tarjan (1976). A version of the Algorithm of Prim using Fibonacci heaps which has complexity $O(|E|+|V| \log |V|)$ can be found in Ahuja, Magnanti and Orlin (1993). The Algorithm of Boruvka (or appropriate variations, respectively) can likewise be implemented with complexity $O(|E| \log |V|)$, see Yao (1975) and Cheriton and Tarjan (1976). Fredman and Tarjan (1987) and Gabow, Galil, Spencer and Tarjan (1986) gave almost linear bounds; finally an algorithm with linear complexity was discovered by Fredman and Willard (1994). Of course, this supposes that the edges are already sorted according to their weights. Unfortunately, the best theoretical algorithms tend to be of no practical interest because of the large size of the implicit constants. Matsui (1995) gave a simple algorithm with complexity $O(|V|)$ for planar graphs.

The problem of finding a new minimal spanning tree if we change the weight of an edge and know a minimal spanning tree for the original graph already was discussed by Frederickson (1985) and Eppstein (1994). On the average, an update may be done in $O(\log |V|)$ steps (under suitable assumptions). Finally, it can be verified in linear time (that is, with complexity $O(|E|)$) whether a given spanning tree is minimal. A similar result holds for the 'sensitivity analysis' of minimal spanning trees. By *sensitivity analysis* we mean the question how much the weight of a given edge e can be increased without changing the minimal spanning tree already known. For the latter two problems, see Dixon, Rauch and Tarjan (1992).

We close this section with some exercises.

Exercise 4.4.14 (Bondy and Murty (1976)). The following table gives the distances (in units of 100 miles) between the airports of the cities London, Mexico City, New York, Paris, Peking and Tokyo:

	L	MC	NY	Pa	Pe	To
L	-	56	35	2	51	60
MC	56	-	21	57	78	70
NY	35	21	-	36	68	68
Pa	2	57	36	-	51	61
Pe	51	78	68	51	-	13
To	60	70	68	61	13	-

Find a minimal spanning tree for the corresponding graph.

Exercise 4.4.15. The *tree graph* $T(G)$ of a connected graph G has the spanning trees for G as vertices; two of these trees are adjacent if they have $n - 2$ edges in common (where $n = |V|$). Show that $T(G)$ is connected. What can be said about the subgraph of minimal spanning trees (for a given weight function w)?

4.5 Maximal Spanning Trees

For some practical problems, it is necessary to consider *maximal spanning trees*, that is, we want to determine a spanning tree whose weight is maximal among all spanning trees of a given network. We give an example taken from Christofides (1975).

Example 4.5.1 (Optimization of a communication network). We consider the problem of sending confidential information to n persons. We define a graph G having n vertices (corresponding to the n persons); two vertices i and j are adjacent if it is possible to send information directly from i to j. For each edge ij, we denote by p_{ij} the probability that the information sent is overheard. Suppose that these probabilities (for being overheard) on the different edges are independent of each other. Now substitute p_{ij} by $q_{ij} = 1 - p_{ij}$, that is, by the probability that the information is sent without being overheard. Now, to send the information to all the n persons, we are looking for a spanning subgraph of G for which the product of the q_{ij} (over the edges occuring in the subgraph) is maximal. Replacing q_{ij} by $w(ij) = \log q_{ij}$, we have reduced the problem to finding a spanning tree of maximal weight.

Example 4.5.1 can be considered as a special case of the 'network reliability problem', if we take the vertices to be the nodes of a communication network and interpret p_{ij} as the probability that the connection between i and j fails. A maximal spanning tree then is a tree which maximizes the probability for undisturbed communication between all nodes of the network. This interpretation (and its algorithmic solution) is already contained in Prim (1957).

So suppose (G, w) is a given network; we are looking for a maximal spanning tree. Obviously, a spanning tree T for (G, w) is maximal if and only if T is minimal for $(G, -w)$. Thus, we can find a maximal spanning tree by replacing w by $-w$ and using one of the algorithms of Section 4.4. Alternatively, we could also stay with w and just replace 'minimum' by 'maximum' in the Algorithms of Prim, Kruskal and Boruvka and, in Kruskal's Algorithm, order the edges according to decreasing weight. Here is another problem where we are interested in finding a maximal spanning tree:

Problem 4.5.2 (Bottleneck Problem). Let (G, w) be a network, where G is a connected graph. For any path

$$W \ = \ v_0 \ \xrightarrow{\ e_1\ } \ v_1 \ \xrightarrow{\ e_2\ } \ v_2 \ \ldots \ \xrightarrow{\ e_n\ } \ v_n,$$

$c(W) = \min \{w(e_i) : i = 1, \ldots, n\}$ is called the *inf-section* or the *capacity* of W. (Think of the cross-section of a tube in a supply network or the capacity of a road.) For each pair (u, v) of vertices of G, we want to determine a path from u to v with maximal capacity. The following theorem due to Hu (1961) reduces this problem to finding a maximal spanning tree.

Theorem 4.5.3. *Let (G, w) be a network on a connected graph G. Moreover, let T be a maximal spanning tree for G. Then, for each pair (u, v) of vertices, the unique path from u to v in T is a path of maximal capacity in G.*

Proof. Let W be the path from u to v in T, and e some edge of W with $c(W) = c(e)$. Suppose there exists a path W' in G having start vertex u and end vertex v such that $c(W') > c(W)$. Let $S_T(e)$ be the cut of G defined in Lemma 4.3.2 and $E(S_T(e))$ the corresponding cocycle. As u and v are in different connected components of $T \backslash e$, the path W' has to contain some edge f of $E(S_T(e))$. As $c(W') > c(W)$, we must have $w(f) > w(e)$. But then $(T \cup \{f\}) \backslash \{e\}$ would be a tree of larger weight than T. $\square$

The Algorithms of Prim, Kruskal and Boruvka can be used (modified for determining maximal spanning trees) to solve Problem 4.5.2 as well.

Exercise 4.5.4. Determine a maximal spanning tree and the maximal capacities for the network of Figure 4.1.

Exercise 4.5.5. Prove the converse of Theorem 4.5.3: If T is a spanning tree such that, for any two vertices u and v, the unique path from u to v in T is a path of maximal capacity in (G, w), then T is a maximal spanning tree for (G, w).

The following problem is related to the 'bottleneck problem' discussed in 4.5.2:

Problem 4.5.6 (Most Uniform Spanning Tree). Let G be a connected graph and $w : E \to \mathbb{R}$ a weight function for G. We look for a spanning tree T such that the difference between the weights of the edge (in T) having largest weight and the edge having smallest weight is minimal. This problem can be solved using a modification of the Algorithm of Kruskal with complexity $O(|V||E|)$; using a more involved data structure we can get a complexity of $O(|E| \log |V|)$. We refer the reader to Camerini, Maffioli, Martelli and Toth (1986) and Galil and Schieber (1988).

Note that analogous problems can be treated for directed graphs as well. For example, for a directed graph having a root, we might want to determine a directed tree of minimal (or maximal) weight. We will return to this problem briefly in Section 4.8.

Exercise 4.5.7. Show that a directed tree of maximal weight in a network (G, w) on a directed graph G does not necessarily contain paths of maximal capacity (starting at the root).

4.6 Steiner Trees

If we have the problem of connecting n points in the Euclidean plane by a network of minimal total length, we can of course determine a minimal spanning tree (minimal with respect to Euclidean distances). For example, think of the problem to connect n cities by a telephone network. But, as we saw in Section 3.2 already, it is possible (at least for some arbitrary metric) that there is a better solution if we are allowed to add some more vertices (in our example, some switch stations not located in one of the n cities). Any tree in the plane which is allowed to contain, on top of the n given vertices, any number of additional vertices (the so-called *Steiner points*), is called a *Steiner tree*. The *Euclidean Steiner Problem* (called 'Geometric Steiner Tree' by Garey and Johnson (1976)) is the problem of finding a minimal Steiner tree for the given n vertices.[2] This problem (for $n = 3$) goes back even to Fermat and was considered in the last century, between others, by Jacob Steiner (that accounts for the name). A fundamental study of the problem was given by Gilbert and Pollak (1968); these authors have, among other

---

[2] Note: Some authors use the term 'Steiner tree' for what we would call a minimal Steiner tree!

things, suggested the problem of finding a lower bound ρ for the ratio between the total length of a minimal Steiner tree and the total length of a minimal spanning tree for a given set of vertices. They were able to show $\rho \geq \frac{1}{2}$ (we will prove this result in 14.4.9) and gave the *Steiner ratio conjecture* that even $\rho \geq \sqrt{3}/2$ holds. This bound which is optimal (as can be seen rather easily), was shown to be correct by Du and Hwang (1990a) and Du and Hwang (1990b). In other words: A minimal Steiner tree for a given set of n vertices is at most 14 % (roughly) better than a minimal spanning tree. We note that minimal Steiner trees are very hard to determine (the problem is NP-complete, see Garey, Graham and Johnson (1977)), whereas it is easy to find minimal spanning trees. Hence, for practical applications, one will be satisfied either with minimal spanning trees or with better, but not necessarily minimal, Steiner trees. A relatively good algorithm for determining minimal Steiner trees can be found in Trietsch and Hwang (1990); in Du and Zhang (1992), the reader can find heuristics for finding good Steiner trees.

The Steiner problem has also been studied extensively for metric spaces other than the Euclidean plane. In this section, we study the graph theoretic version of the Steiner problem, called the *Steiner Network Problem*. We have a given network (G, w) with a positive weight function, where the vertex set V of G is the disjoint union of two sets R and S. Now we want to find a *minimal Steiner tree*, that is, a minimal spanning tree T for an induced subgraph whose vertex set has the form $R \cup S'$ with $S' \subset S$. The vertices in S' are again called *Steiner points*. Note that the Steiner network problem is a common generalization of two problems for which we have already found an efficient solution: the case $S = \emptyset$ is the problem of determining a minimal spanning tree, and for $|R| = 2$, the problem consists of finding a shortest path between the two given vertices. However, the general Steiner network problem is NP-hard, see Karp (1972). Lawler (1976) gave an algorithm whose complexity is polynomial in the cardinality s of S and exponential only in the cardinality r of R. Before stating this algorithm, we show that, in the metric case (that is, if G is complete and w satisfies the triangle inequality), we need only relatively few Steiner points. This result is due to Gilbert and Pollak (1968).

Lemma 4.6.1. *Let* $G = (V, E)$ *be a complete graph whose vertex set is the disjoint union* $V = R \dot\cup S$ *of two subsets. Moreover, let w be a positive weight function on E satisfying the triangle inequality. Then there is a minimal Steiner tree for the network* (G, w) *which contains at most* $r - 2$ *Steiner points (where $r = |R|$).*

Proof. Let T be a minimal Steiner tree for (G, w) containing exactly p Steiner points. By x (and y, respectively) we denote the average degree of a vertex of R (or S', respectively) in T. Then the number of all edges in T satisfies

$$r + p - 1 = \frac{rx + py}{2}.$$

It is trivial that $x \geq 1$. As w satisfies the triangle inequality, we may assume that any Steiner point in T is incident with at least three edges, hence $y \geq 3$. Thus, we get

$$r+p-1 \geq \frac{r + 3p}{2}, \quad \text{so that} \quad p \leq r-2. \qquad \square$$

The next lemma shows that the general case can easily be reduced to the metric case.

Lemma 4.6.2. *Let $G = (V, E)$ be a graph whose vertex set is the disjoint union $V = R \, \dot\cup \, S$ of two subsets. Moreover, let w be a positive weight function on E and d the distance function in the network (G, w). Then the weight of a minimal Steiner tree for the network (K_V, d) is the same as the weight of a minimal Steiner tree for the original network (G, w).*

Proof. First let T be any Steiner tree for (G, w). Then each edge $e = uv$ of T has weight $w(uv) \geq d(u, v)$, so that the minimal weight of a Steiner tree for (K_V, d) is at most $w(T)$. Conversely, if we replace each edge uv in a minimal Steiner tree T' for (K_V, d) by the edges of a shortest path from u to v in G, we obviously get a Steiner tree T'' of the same weight for (G, w). (No edge can occur twice and there cannot be a cycle after this operation of replacing the edges, because otherwise we could discard at least one vertex of T'', and – as we saw above – this would give an upper bound $< w(T')$ for the weight of a minimal Steiner tree for (K_V, d), a contradiction.) $\qquad \square$

Algorithm 4.6.3. Let $G = (V, E)$ be a given connected graph with a positive weight function $w : E \to \mathbb{R}$. Let the vertex set $V = \{1, \ldots, n\}$ be the disjoint union $V = R \, \dot\cup \, S$ of two subsets and $|R| = r$. The algorithm constructs a minimal Steiner tree T for R in (G, w).

Procedure STEINER$(G, R, w; T)$

(1) $W \leftarrow \infty$; $T \leftarrow 0$; $H \leftarrow K_n$;
(2) FLOYD$(G, w; d, p)$;
(3) **for** $i = 1$ **to** $r - 2$ **do**
(4)   **for** $S' \subset S$ with $|S'| = i$ **do**
(5)   PRIM$(H|(R \cup S'), d; T', z)$;
(6)   **if** $z < W$ **then** $W \leftarrow z$; $T \leftarrow T'$ **fi**;
(7)   **od**
(8) **od**;
(9) **for** $e = uv \in T$ **do**
(10)   **if** $e \notin E$ **or** $w(e) > d(u, v)$
(11)   **then** replace e in T by the edges of a shortest path from
                u to v in G
(12)   **fi**
(13) **od**.

Here, FLOYD is a modified version of the procedure given in Section 3.8 which uses a function p (giving the predecessor as in Algorithm 3.9.1) to determine not only the distance between two vertices, but a shortest path as well. We need this shortest path in step (11). Analogously, PRIM is a procedure modified (in an obvious way) to compute not only a minimal spanning tree, but also its weight.

Theorem 4.6.4. *Algorithm 4.6.3 computes a minimal Steiner tree for* $(G, R; w)$ *with complexity* $O(|V|^3 + 2^{|S|}|R|^2)$.

Proof. It follows immediately from Lemma 4.6.1 and (the proof of) Lemma 4.6.2 (and from the correctness of the procedures FLOYD and PRIM) that the algorithm is correct. Procedure FLOYD called in step (2) has complexity $O(|V|^3)$ according to Theorem 3.8.2, and each call of procedure PRIM in step (5) has complexity $O(|R|^2)$ (see Theorem 4.4.4). (Note that PRIM is applied to $O(|R|)$ vertices only, see Lemma 4.6.1.) The number of times PRIM is called is obviously

$$\sum_{i=0}^{r-2} \binom{|S|}{i} \leq 2^{|S|}.$$

That proves the statement about the complexity.   □

In particular, Theorem 4.6.4 shows that Algorithm 4.6.3 is polynomial in $|V|$ for fixed s. However, the estimate for the complexity given in the proof of Theorem 4.6.4 is rather bad if we assume r to be fixed; in that case the number of calls of PRIM could be estimated better as about $|S|^{r-2}$. Thus, Algorithm 4.6.3 is polynomial for fixed r as well, and we have proved the following corollary (generalizing the fact that the Steiner network problem can be solved efficiently for the cases $r = 2$ and $s = 0$ as stated above).

Corollary 4.6.5. *For fixed r or for fixed s, respectively, the Steiner network problem can be solved with polynomial complexity.*   □

Finally, we refer to the survey of Maculan (1987), who considers a version of the Steiner network problem for directed graphs. An extensive exposition of the various Steiner problems can also be found in the book by Hwang, Richards and Winter (1992). Steiner trees have important applications in VLSI-layout, see Korte, Prömel and Steger (1990) and Martin (1992). In this context, one is particularly interested in good heuristics, see Voß (1992), Du and Zhang (1992) and Berman and Ramaiyer (1994).

4.7 Spanning Trees with Restrictions

In reality, most of the problems we meet cannot be solved by determining just any (minimal) spanning tree; the solution will have to satisfy some further restrictions. Unfortunately, this often leads to much harder, quite often NP-hard, problems. In this section, we state some of these problems without looking for possibilities to solve them (like heuristics); that will be done in Chapter 14 using the TSP as the standard example. Even if there is no weight function given, restrictions can make the task of finding an appropriate spanning tree NP-hard. The following four problems are NP-complete, see Garey and Johnson (1979).

Problem 4.7.1 (degree constrained spanning tree). Given are a connected graph G and a positive integer k. We want to find a spanning tree T for G having maximal degree $\Delta \leq k$.

Problem 4.7.2 (maximum leaf spanning tree). Let G be a connected graph and k a positive integer. Is there a spanning tree for G having at least k leaves?

Problem 4.7.3 (shortest total path length spanning tree). Given a positive integer k and a connected graph G, we are looking for a spanning tree T such that the sum of all distances $d(u,v)$ over all pairs of vertices $\{u,v\}$ is at most k.

Problem 4.7.4 (isomorphic spanning tree). Let G be a connected graph and T a tree. Does G have a spanning tree isomorphic to T? (Note that the case where T is a path is the problem of finding out whether G has a Hamiltonian path.)

We cannot expect to solve these problems efficiently by some algorithm. Thus, we can even less expect to find, for example, a nice formula for the maximal number of leaves a spanning tree of G might have. Nevertheless, it is still possible to find some interesting results, such as, for example, lower or upper bounds for the respective value. We illustrate this for Problem 4.7.2 and give a result of Kleitman and West (1991), stating that a connected graph having large minimal degree has to contain a spanning tree with a lot of leaves.

Result 4.7.5. *Let $l(n,k)$ be the largest positive integer m such that each connected graph having n vertices and minimal degree k contains a spanning tree with at least m leaves. Then*

(i) $l(n,k) \leq n - 3\frac{n}{\lfloor k-1 \rfloor} + 2$;

(ii) $l(n,3) \geq \frac{n}{4} + 2$;

(iii) $l(n,4) \geq \frac{2n+8}{5}$;

(iv) $l(n,k) \geq \left(1 - \frac{b \ln k}{k}\right) n$ *for sufficiently large k, where b is a constant with $b \geq \frac{5}{2}$.*

$\square$

We do not give the relatively long (though not really difficult) proof and recommend the reader to look at the original paper cited above. The proof is constructive and contains a method for finding a spanning tree with the given number of leaves.

Finally, we give some problems with restrictions where a weight function is involved.

Problem 4.7.6 (bounded diameter spanning tree). We have a given connected graph G with a weight function $w : E \to \mathbb{N}$ and two positive integers d and k. Does G have a spanning tree T whose weight satisfies $w(T) \leq k$, and whose diameter is at most d?

According to Garey and Johnson (1979), this problem is NP-complete. Thus, it is NP-hard to find, out of all minimal spanning trees, a tree having smallest possible diameter. This is true even if the weight function takes the values 1 and 2 only. However, it is easy to solve the case where all weights are equal.

Exercise 4.7.7. Give a polynomial algorithm for determining a spanning tree whose diameter is at most 1 larger than the smallest possible diameter. Hint: look at Theorem 3.8.8 and Exercise 4.1.3.

A variation of Problem 4.7.6 was studied by Ho, Lee, Chang and Wong (1991): we look for a tree satisfying $w(T) \leq k$ and $d(u,v) \leq d$ for all $u,v \in V$ where $d(u,v)$ is the distance in the network (G,w). This variation is NP-complete as well. However, in a Euclidean graph (that is, the vertices are points in a space $\mathbb{R}^m$ and the weights $w(u,v)$ are given by the Euclidean distance), it is possible (with complexity $O(|V|^3)$) to find a spanning tree such that the maximum of the $d(u,v)$ is minimal.

Problem 4.7.8 (minimal cost reliability ratio spanning tree). Let G be a connected graph with weight function $w : E \to \mathbb{N}$ and a reliability function $r : E \to (0,1]$. The value $r(e)$ is meant to be the probability that edge e works, and $w(e)$ is the cost of using e. For a spanning tree T, $w(T)$ is (as usual) the sum of all $w(e)$ with $e \in T$; $r(T)$ is defined to be the product of the $r(e)$ for $e \in T$. Thus, $w(T)$ is the total cost of T, and $r(T)$ is the probability that no edge in the tree fails (see Section 4.5). We look for a spanning tree T such that the ratio $w(T)/r(T)$ is minimal.

For this problem, a polynomial algorithm is known. Counting arithmetic operations as one step each, Problem 4.7.8 can be solved with complexity $O(|E|^{5/2} \log\log|V|)$, see Chandrasekaran, Aneja and Nair (1981) and Chandrasekaran and Tamir (1984). As some of the arithmetic operations occurring are exponentiations, this estimate of the complexity might be considered somewhat optimistic.

Our final example involves two functions on E as well. This time, the two functions are coupled non-linearly, and the goal is to minimize the resulting function.

Problem 4.7.9 (optimum communication spanning tree). Let G be a connected graph with a weight function $w : E \to \mathbb{N}_0$ and a request function $r : \binom{V}{2} \to \mathbb{N}_0$, and let k be a positive integer. Does G have a spanning tree T such that

$$\sum_{\{u,v\} \in \binom{V}{2}} d(u,v) \cdot r(u,v) \leq k,$$

where $d(u,v)$ denotes the distance in the network (T, w) (that is, $d(u,v)$ is the sum of all weights $w(e)$ of edges occuring in the path from u to v in T)? In practice, $d(u,v)$ signifies the cost of the path from u to v and $r(u,v)$ is the capacity we need for communication between u and v (for example, the number of telephone lines needed between cities u and v). Then the product $d(u,v)r(u,v)$ is the cost of communication between u and v, and we want to minimize the total cost.

Problem 4.7.9 is NP-complete even if the request is the same for all edges ('optimum distance spanning tree'), as was shown by Johnson, Lenstra and Rinnooy Kan (1978). However, the special case where all weights are equal can be solved in polynomial time; Hu (1974) gave an algorithm of complexity $O(|V|^4)$. But even this special case of Problem 4.7.9 (called 'optimum requirement spanning tree') is much more difficult to solve than determining a minimal spanning tree is, and the solution is found by a completely different method. We return to this problem in Section 10.4.

The general problem of finding spanning trees which are optimal with respect to several functions is treated by Hamacher and Ruhe (1994).

4.8 Arborescences and Directed Euler Tours

In this section, we look at the statement analogous to Theorem 4.2.9 for the directed case and at an application to directed Euler tours. First we give a simple characterization of arborescences which we used in Section 3.4 already.

Lemma 4.8.1. Let G be an orientation of a connected graph. Then G is a spanning arborescence with root r if and only if

$$d_{in}(v) = 1 \quad \text{for all } v \neq r \quad \text{and} \quad d_{in}(r) = 0. \tag{4.4}$$

Proof. Let v be an arbitrary vertex of G. As $|G|$ is connected by hypothesis, there is a path W in G from r to v. This path even has to be a directed path: Suppose W contained a backward edge. Then $d_{in}(r) \geq 1$ or $d_{in}(u) \geq 2$ for some vertex $u \neq r$ on W. Thus r is a root for G. A similar argument shows that G cannot contain a cycle. $\qquad \square$

Analogous to the degree matrix of a graph, we now introduce the *indegree matrix* $D = (d_{ij})_{i,j=1,...,n}$ for a directed graph $G = (V, E)$ with vertex set $V = \{1, \ldots, n\}$, where

$$
d_{ij} = \begin{cases} d_{in}(i) & \text{for } i = j \\ -1 & \text{for } ij \in E \\ 0 & \text{otherwise.} \end{cases}
$$

We denote the submatrix of D obtained by deleting the i-th row and the i-th column by D_i. The following analogue of Theorem 4.2.9 is due to Tutte (1948).

Theorem 4.8.2. *Let $G = (V, E)$ be a directed graph having indegree matrix D. Then the r-th minor $\det D_r$ is equal to the number of spanning arborescences of G with root r.*

Proof. We may assume $r = 1$. First note that it is not necessary to look at edges having head 1 if we want to construct spanning arborescences with root 1 and that the entries in the first column of D do not occur in the minor $\det D_1$. Thus, we may assume w.l.o.g. that G does not contain any edges having head 1 and that the first column of D is the vector having all entries 0. (This assumption makes the remainder of the proof easier.) Now suppose there exists a vertex $i \neq 1$ with $d_{in}(i) = 0$. In this case, obviously, G does not have any spanning arborescence. On the other hand, the i-th column of D then has all entries equal to 0, so that $\det D_1 = 0$. Thus, the statement is true for this case.

We now turn to the case where the condition

$$
d_{in}(i) \geq 1 \quad \text{for each vertex } i \neq 1 \tag{4.5}
$$

holds. We use induction on $m := d_{in}(2) + \ldots + d_{in}(n)$. (As we assumed that $d_{in}(1) = 0$, we have $m = |E|$.) The more difficult part of the induction here is the induction basis, that is, the case $m = n - 1$. We have to show that G is an arborescence (with root 1) if and only if $\det D_1 = 1$. So let G be an arborescence, then condition (4.4) holds for $r = 1$. As G is acyclic, G has a topological sorting by Theorem 2.6.3. Thus, we may assume $i < j$ for all edges ij in E. Then the matrix D is an upper triangular matrix with diagonal $(0, 1, \ldots, 1)$ and $\det D_1 = 1$.

Conversely, suppose $\det D_1 \neq 0$; we have to show that G has to be an arborescence (and, in that case, actually, it follows that even $\det D_1 = 1$). It follows from condition (4.5) and $m = n - 1$ that $d_{in}(i) = 1$ for $i = 2, \ldots, n$. Thus, G satisfies condition (4.4), and, using Lemma 4.8.1, all we have to show is that G is connected. According to Theorem 1.2.8, we can show instead that G is acyclic. Suppose G contains a cycle C:

$$
C = i_1 \longrightarrow i_1 \longrightarrow \ldots \longrightarrow i_k \longrightarrow i_1.
$$

We consider the submatrix U of D_1 consisting of the columns corresponding to $i_1, \ldots, i_k$. As each of the vertices $i_1, \ldots, i_k$ has indegree 1, U can have entries $\neq 0$ only in the rows corresponding to $i_1, \ldots, i_k$. Moreover, the sum of all rows of U is the zero vector, so that U has rank $\leq k - 1$. Thus, the columns of U, and hence also the columns of D_1, are linearly dependent; it follows that $\det D_1 = 0$ which contradicts our hypothesis. Therefore, the statement of the theorem holds for $m = n - 1$.

Now let $m \geq n$. In that case, there has to be a vertex having indegree ≥ 2, say

$$d_{in}(n) = c \geq 2. \tag{4.6}$$

For each edge e of the form $e = jn$, let $D(e)$ denote the matrix obtained by replacing column n of D by the vector $v_e = -\mathbf{e}_j + \mathbf{e}_n$ (where $\mathbf{e}_k$ is the k-th unit vector, so that v_e has entry -1 in row j, entry 1 in row n and all other entries 0). Then $D(e)$ is the indegree matrix for the graph $G(e)$ arising from G by deleting all edges with head n except e. Now (4.6) implies that $G(e)$ has at least one edge less than G, so that, by induction hypothesis, we know that the minor $\det D(e)_1$ is equal to the number of spanning arborescences of $G(e)$ with root 1. Obviously, this is the number of spanning arborescences of G which have root 1 and contain the edge e. Thus, the number of all spanning arborescences of G with root 1 is the sum

$$\det D(e_1)_1 + \ldots + \det D(e_c)_1,$$

where $e_1, \ldots, e_c$ are the c edges of G having head n. It is clear immediately that the last column of D is the sum $v_{e_1} + \ldots + v_{e_c}$ of the last columns of $D(e_1), \ldots, D(e_c)$. Then the multilinearity of the determinant implies

$$\det D_1 = \det D(e_1)_1 + \ldots + \det D(e_c)_1,$$

and the statement follows. $\qquad\qquad\qquad\qquad\qquad\qquad\qquad\qquad\qquad\qquad\square$

Theorem 4.8.2 can be used to obtain another proof for Theorem 4.2.9. Even though this proof is not shorter than the proof given in Section 4.2, it is more elementary, as it avoids using the Theorem of Cauchy-Binet (which is not all that well-known).

Corollary 4.8.3. *Let* $H = (V, E)$ *be a graph with adjacency matrix* A *and degree matrix* $D = diag(deg\ 1, \ldots, deg\ n) - A$. *Then the number of spanning trees of* H *is the common value of all minors* $\det D_r$ *of* D.

Proof. Let G be the complete orientation of H. Then there is a one-to-one correspondence between the spanning trees of H and the spanning arborescences of G having root r. Moreover, the degree matrix D of H is the indegree matrix of G as well. The statement now follows from Theorem 4.8.2. $\qquad\square$

Now let G be a directed Eulerian graph; then G is a connected pseudo-symmetric directed graph by Theorem 1.6.1. The following theorem of de Bruijn and van Aardenne-Ehrenfest (1951) describes a connection between spanning arborescences and Euler tours of G.

Theorem 4.8.4. *Let $G = (V, E)$ be a directed Eulerian graph. For $i = 1, \ldots, n$, let a_i denote the number of spanning arborescences of G having root i. Then the number e_G of directed Euler tours of G is given by (for arbitrary i)*

$$e_G = a_i \cdot \prod_{j=1}^{n} (d_{in}(j) - 1)! \tag{4.7}$$

Sketch of Proof. Let A be a spanning arborescence of G having root i. For each vertex $j \neq i$, let e_j denote the unique edge in A having head j, and choose e_i as a fixed edge having head i. Now we construct a cycle in G (using the method shown in the Algorithm of Hierholzer) using all edges backward (so that, reversing the order of the edges in the cycle, we get a directed cycle). That is, we leave vertex i using edge e_i and, for each vertex j we reach (using an edge having tail j!), we use (as long as this is possible) some edge with head j not yet used to leave j again. In contrast to the method shown for the Algorithm of Hierholzer, we choose e_j for leaving j only if all other edges with head j have been used already. It can be seen as usual that the construction can only terminate at the start vertex i (because G is pseudo-symmetric). Moreover, for each vertex j, all edges having head j (and hence all the edges of G) are used exactly once because of the restriction that e_j is chosen last. Thus, we indeed get an Euler tour. Obviously, each choice of the edges (where we are free to choose) in our construction gives a different Euler tour. We can choose the edges with head j in $(d_{in}(j) - 1)!$ ways, so that the product in (4.7) gives the number of distinct Euler tours of G which can be constructed using A. It is obvious that distinct arborescences having root i also lead to distinct Euler tours. Conversely, it is easy to construct a spanning arborescence with root i from any directed Euler tour in a similar way.   □

Corollary 4.8.5. *Let G be a directed Eulerian graph. Then the number a_i of spanning arborescences of G with root i does not depend on the choice of i.*   □

From Exercise 2.3.2 we know that the deBruijn sequences of length $N = s^n$ over an alphabet S of cardinality s correspond bijectively to the directed Euler tours of the digraph $G_{s,n}$ defined there. Combining Theorems 4.8.2 and 4.8.4, we can now calculate the number of such sequences originally found by de Bruijn (1946). See also van Lint (1974); a similar method can be found in Knuth (1967).

Theorem 4.8.6. *The number of deBruijn sequences of length* $N = s^n$ *over an alphabet* S *of cardinality* s *is*

$$b_{s,n} = s^{-n}(s!)^{s^{n-1}}. \tag{4.8}$$

Sketch of Proof. As each vertex of $G_{s,n}$ has indegree s, Theorem 4.8.4 yields

$$b_{s,n} = a((s-1)!)^{s^{n-1}}, \tag{4.9}$$

where a is the common value of all minors of the indegree matrix D of $G_{s,n}$. Thus, it remains to show that

$$a = s^{s^{n-1}-n}. \tag{4.10}$$

To do this, Theorem 4.8.2 is used. (We have to be a bit careful here, because $G_{s,n}$ contains loops. Of course, these loops should not appear in the matrix D.) As the technical details of calculating the determinant are rather tedious, we will not give them here and refer to the literature cited above. $\square$

At the end of the present chapter, we mention some references where the interested reader can find more information about determining an arborescence of minimal weight in a network (G, w), where G is a directed graph. This problem is considerably more difficult than the analogous problem of determining minimal spanning trees in the undirected case; for this reason, we have not treated it in this book. A minimal arborescence can be determined with complexity $O(|V|^2)$ or $O(|E| \log |V|)$; the respective algorithm was found independently by Chu and Liu (1965) and Edmonds (1967b). An implementation having the above complexity was given by Tarjan (1977), see also Camerini, Fratta and Maffioli (1979), where some details of Tarjan's paper are corrected. This method can also be found in Gondran and Minoux (1984). The best result up to now is due to Gabow, Galil, Spencer and Tarjan (1986), who used Fibonacci heaps and reached a complexity of $O(|V| \log |V| + |E|)$.

5. The Greedy Algorithm

In this chapter, we look at a generalization of the Algorithm of Kruskal, the so-called Greedy Algorithm. This algorithm can be used for maximization on 'independence systems' (as, for example, in the case of the Algorithm of Kruskal, the system of spanning forests of a graph). However, the strategy used is rather short-sighted: we always choose the element which seems best at the moment (that is, of all the admissible elements, we choose the element whose weight is maximal) and add it to the solution we are constructing (this explains the name!). In general, this strategy does not work, but for a certain class of structures, the so-called matroids (which play an important part in Combinatorial Optimization), it indeed leads to an optimal solution. In fact, this class of structures is characterized by the fact that the Greedy Algorithm works for them, but there are other possible definitions for matroids. We will see some other characterizations of matroids and look at the notion of duality of matroids.

Next, we consider the Greedy Algorithm as an approximation method for maximization on independence systems which are not matroids and examine its efficiency, that is, we want to derive bounds for the ratio between the solution given by the Greedy Algorithm and the optimal solution. We also look at the problem of minimization on independence systems. Finally, in the last section, we discuss some further generalizations of matroids and their relationship to the Greedy Algorithm.

5.1 The Greedy Algorithm and Matroids

First, recall the Algorithm of Kruskal for determining a maximal spanning tree or forest, respectively. Let G be a simple graph and $w : E \to \mathbb{R}$ a weight function on G. We order the edges according to decreasing weight and treat them consecutively; we insert an edge into the set T if it does not form a cycle with the edges which are already in T. At the end of the algorithm, T is a maximal spanning forest (if G is connected, a maximal spanning tree). We can describe the technique used by the Algorithm of Kruskal as follows: Let $\mathbf{S}$ be the set of all subsets of E which are forests. Then the edge e examined at the moment is added to T if and only if $T \cup \{e\}$ is also in $\mathbf{S}$. This strategy – namely choosing the edge which is maximal of all edges satisfying certain conditions – can of course be applied to other systems $(E, \mathbf{S})$, too. We give some definitions.

An *independence system* is a pair $(E, \mathbf{S})$, where E is a set and $\mathbf{S}$ is a subset of the power set of E closed under inclusion: from $A \in \mathbf{S}$ and $B \subset A$ it follows that $B \in \mathbf{S}$. The elements of $\mathbf{S}$ are called *independent sets*. The optimization problem associated with $(E, \mathbf{S})$ is the following: for a given weight function $w : E \to \mathbb{R}_0^+$, we want to find an independent set A whose *weight*

$$w(A) := \sum_{e \in A} w(e)$$

is maximal. (The restriction to non-negative weight functions makes sure that there is a maximal independent set among the independent sets of maximal weight. We can drop this restriction if we assume A to be a maximal independent set, see Theorem 5.5.1.)

Thus, determining a maximal spanning forest is the optimization problem associated with $(E, \mathbf{S})$, where E is the edge set of the graph G, and $\mathbf{S}$ is the set of all edge sets which are forests. We generalize the Algorithm of Kruskal to work for an arbitrary independence system.

Algorithm 5.1.1. Let $(E, \mathbf{S})$ be an independence system and $w : E \to \mathbb{R}_0^+$ a weight function.

Procedure GREEDY $(E, \mathbf{S}, w; T)$

(1)   order the elements of E according to their weight, e.g. $E = \{e_1, \dots, e_m\}$ with $w(e_1) \geq w(e_2) \geq \dots \geq w(e_m)$;
(2) $T \leftarrow \emptyset$;
(3)   **for** $k = 1$ **to** m **do**
(4)   **if** $T \cup \{e_k\} \in \mathbf{S}$ **then** append e_k to T **fi**
(5)   **od**.

Theorem 4.4.8 states that the Greedy Algorithm solves the optimization problem associated with the system of forests of a graph. For arbitrary independence systems, however, the simple strategy ('always take the biggest piece!') of this algorithm does not work. We call an independence system $(E, \mathbf{S})$ a *matroid* if the Greedy algorithm solves the associated optimization problem.[1] Hence, the next theorem gives just a different way of stating Theorem 4.4.8.

---

[1] Originally, Whitney (1935) and van der Waerden (1937) introduced matroids as an abstract generalization of the notions of linear and algebraic independence, respectively. In the next section, we give some other possible definitions. The generalization of the Algorithm of Kruskal to matroids was found independently by Gale (1968), Welsh (1968) and - a bit earlier - by Edmonds (see Edmonds (1971)). However, beginnings of these ideas can already be found in Boruvka (1926a) and Rado (1957).

Theorem 5.1.2. *Let $G = (V, E)$ be a graph and* **S** *the set of those subsets of E which are forests. Then $(E, \mathbf{S})$ is a matroid.*   □

The matroid described above is called the *graphic matroid* of the graph G. Next we treat a class of matroids coming from directed graphs.

Theorem 5.1.3. *Let $G = (V, E)$ be a directed graph and* **S** *the set of all subsets A of E for which no two edges of A have the same head. Then $(E, \mathbf{S})$ is a matroid, the so-called head-partition matroid of G.*[2]

Proof. Obviously, an independent set of maximal weight can be found by choosing, for any vertex v of G with $d_{in}(v) \neq 0$, the edge having head v of maximal weight. Thus, the Greedy Algorithm solves the corresponding optimization problem.   □

Here is an example where it is trivial that the Greedy Algorithm works:

Example 5.1.4. Let E be a set of n elements and **S** the set of all subsets X of E with $|X| \leq k$ (for $1 \leq k \leq n$). Then $(E, \mathbf{S})$ is called a *uniform matroid* (of degree k). For $k = n$, it is also called the *free matroid* on E.

Exercise 5.1.5. Let G be a graph. A *matching* in G is a set of edges which do not have any vertices in common. We will look more closely at these objects later. Show that the matchings in a graph G do not form a matroid in general, even if G is bipartite. The independence system of matchings in G will be examined in Section 5.4.

5.2 Characterizations of Matroids

We begin by giving two characterizations of matroids which show that these structures - as mentioned already - can indeed be considered as generalizations of the notion of linear independence.

Theorem 5.2.1. *Let $M = (E, \mathbf{S})$ be an independence system. Then the following conditions are equivalent:*

(1) M is a matroid.
(2) For $J, K \in \mathbf{S}$ with $|J| = |K| + 1$, there always exists some $a \in J \backslash K$ such that $K \cup \{a\}$ is also in $\mathbf{S}$.
(3) For any subset A of E, all maximal independent subsets of A have the same cardinality.

---

[2] The tail-partition matroid is defined analogously.

Proof.

(1) $\Rightarrow$ (2): Suppose M is a matroid for which (2) is not satisfied. Then there are $J, K \in \mathbf{S}$ with $|J| = |K| + 1$ such that, for any $a \in J\backslash K$, $K \cup \{a\}$ is not in $\mathbf{S}$. Let $k = |K|$. We define a weight function w by

$$w(e) := \begin{cases} k + 2 & \text{for } e \in K, \\ k + 1 & \text{for } e \in J\backslash K, \\ 0 & \text{otherwise.} \end{cases}$$

Note first that K is not the solution of the associated optimization problem, because $w(K) = k(k + 2) < (k + 1)^2 \leq w(J)$. On the other hand, the Greedy Algorithm first chooses all elements of K, because they have maximal weight. After having chosen all elements of K for the solution, however, the weight of the solution cannot be increased any more: all remaining elements e either have $w(e) = 0$ or are in $J\backslash K$, so that $K \cup \{e\}$ is not in $\mathbf{S}$, according to our assumption above. Thus, M is not a matroid, a contradiction.

(2) $\Rightarrow$ (3): Let A be an arbitrary subset of E and J and K two maximal independent subsets contained in A (that is, there is no independent subset of A which contains J or K, except J or K, respectively, itself). Suppose we have $|K| < |J|$. As $\mathbf{S}$ is closed under inclusion, there is a subset J' of J with $|J'| = |K| + 1$. By (2), there exists an element $a \in J'\backslash K$ such that $K \cup \{a\}$ is independent. This contradicts the maximality of K.

(3) $\Rightarrow$ (1): Suppose that M is not a matroid, but satisfies condition (3). Then the Greedy Algorithm does not work for the corresponding optimization problem. Thus, there is a weight function w such that Algorithm 5.1.1 constructs an independent set $K = \{e_1, \ldots, e_k\}$ although there exists an independent set $J = \{e'_1, \ldots, e'_h\}$ of larger weight. We may assume that the elements of J and K are ordered according to decreasing weight and that J is a maximal independent subset of E. By construction, K is maximal too. Then (3) implies (with $A = E$) that $h = k$. We use induction on m to show that the inequality $w(e_i) \geq w(e'_i)$ holds for $i = 1, \ldots, m$. Then, for $m = k$, we get a contradiction to our assumption $w(K) < w(J)$. The Greedy Algorithm chooses e_1 to be an element of maximal weight, so that the inequality holds for $m = 1$. Now suppose we have shown that the inequality holds for m and assume $w(e_{m+1}) < w(e'_{m+1})$. Look at the set $A = \{e \in E : w(e) \geq w(e'_{m+1})\}$. Then $\{e_1, \ldots, e_m\}$ is a maximal independent subset of A, because, if e were an element such that $\{e_1, \ldots, e_m, e\}$ would be independent, then $w(e) \leq w(e_{m+1}) < w(e'_{m+1})$ (because the Greedy Algorithm chose the element e_{m+1} after having chosen e_m), and hence

$e \notin A$. But as $\{e'_1, \ldots, e'_{m+1}\}$ is also an independent subset of A, we have derived a contradiction to condition (3).

$\square$

Note that condition (2) of Theorem 5.2.1 is analogous to the exchange theorem of Steinitz from Linear Algebra; this condition is therefore also called the *exchange axiom*. Similarly, condition (3) is analogous to the fact that any two bases of a linear subspace have equal cardinality. In fact, condition (2) implies immediately:

Theorem 5.2.2. *Let E be a finite subset of a vector space V and $\mathbf{S}$ the set of all linearly independent subsets of E. Then $(E, \mathbf{S})$ is a matroid.* $\square$

Any matroid which can be described as in Theorem 5.2.2 is called a *vectorial matroid* or *matric matroid*. The second name comes from the fact that the subset E of a vector space V can be given as the set of columns of a matrix. The independent sets are then the linearly independent subsets of that set of columns. An abstract matroid is called *representable over K* (where K is a given field) if it is isomorphic to a vectorial matroid in a vector space V over K. (We leave it to the reader to give a formal definition for 'isomorphic'.)

Exercise 5.2.3. Any graphic matroid is representable over K for any field K. (Hint: Use the incidence matrix A.)

We mention some terminology which is analogous to the terms of Linear Algebra. The maximal independent sets of a matroid $M = (E, \mathbf{S})$ are called *bases*. The *rank $\rho(A)$* of a subset A of E is the cardinality of a maximal independent subset of A. Any subset of E not contained in $\mathbf{S}$ is called *dependent*.

Exercise 5.2.4. Let ρ be the rank function of a matroid $M = (E, \mathbf{S})$. Show that ρ has the following properties:

(1) $\rho(A) \leq |A|$ for all $A \subset E$;
(2) ρ is *isotonic*, that is, for all $A, B \subset E$, we have $A \subset B \Rightarrow \rho(A) \leq \rho(B)$;
(3) ρ is *submodular*, that is, for all $A, B \subset E$,
$\rho(A \cup B) + \rho(A \cap B) \leq \rho(A) + \rho(B)$ holds.

Conversely, matroids can be defined using their rank function: Let E be a set and ρ a function from the power set of E to $\mathbb{N}_0$ satisfying conditions (1), (2) and (3) above. Then the subsets X of E satisfying $\rho(X) = |X|$ are the independent sets of a matroid on E, see Welsh (1976) for example. Submodular functions are important in Combinatorial Optimization and Matroid Theory, see, for instance, Pym and Perfect (1970), Edmonds (1970), Frank and Tardos (1988), Qi (1988), and the monograph by Fujishige (1991). To solve Exercise 5.2.4, we need a result worth noting explicitly, although it is a direct consequence of condition (2) of Theorem 5.2.1.

Theorem 5.2.5 (Basis Completion Theorem). *Let J be an independent set of the matroid $M = (E, \mathbf{S})$. Then J is contained in a basis of M.*   □

We introduce another useful term using the rank function. The next lemma is clear.

Lemma 5.2.6. *Let J be an independent set of the matroid $(E, \mathbf{S})$. If J is a maximal independent set of X as well as of Y, then J is also a maximal independent set of $X \cup Y$.*   □

Theorem 5.2.7. *Let $M = (E, \mathbf{S})$ be a matroid and A a subset of E. Then there is a unique maximal set B containing A such that $\rho(A) = \rho(B)$, namely*

$$B = \{e \in E : \rho(A \cup \{e\}) = \rho(A)\}.$$

Proof. First let C be any set containing A with $\rho(A) = \rho(C)$. Then $\rho(A \cup \{e\}) = \rho(A)$ holds for any $e \in C$, because otherwise we would have $\rho(C) \geq \rho(A \cup \{e\}) > \rho(A)$. Thus, all we have to show is that the set B of the statement of the theorem above satisfies the condition $\rho(A) = \rho(B)$. Let J be a maximal independent subset of A, then J is also a maximal independent subset of $A \cup \{e\}$ for each $e \in B$. Hence, by Lemma 5.2.6, J is also a maximal independent subset of B .   □

The set B described in Theorem 5.2.7 is called the *span* of A and is denoted by $\sigma(A)$. Analogous to the terms used in Linear Algebra, a set A with $E = \sigma(A)$ is called a *generating set* of M. If a set A satisfies $\sigma(A) = A$, it is called *closed*. A *hyperplane* is a maximal closed subset of E which is not E itself. Now matroids could be characterized by systems of axioms using the notion of span or hyperplane; we refer again to Welsh (1976). We give some exercises concerning the terms introduced above.

Exercise 5.2.8. Let $M = (E, \mathbf{S})$ be a matroid. Then the *span operator σ* has the following properties:

(1) $X \subset \sigma(X)$ for all $X \subset E$;
(2) $Y \subset X \Rightarrow \sigma(Y) \subset \sigma(X)$ for all $X, Y \subset E$;
(3) $\sigma(\sigma(X)) = \sigma(X)$ for all $X \subset E$;
(4) If $y \notin \sigma(X)$ and $y \in \sigma(X \cup \{x\})$, then $x \in \sigma(X \cup \{y\})$.

Property (3) shows why the sets $\sigma(A)$ are called 'closed'; property (4) is again called *exchange axiom* because it is basically the same as condition (2) of Theorem 5.2.1. Conversely, the conditions given above can be used for an axiomatic characterization of matroids by the span operator.

Exercise 5.2.9. Show that the bases of a matroid (that is, the maximal independent subsets) are precisely the minimal generating sets.

We introduce one more term; this time it is taken from the terminology of Graph Theory. A *circuit* in a matroid is a minimal dependent set (analogous to a 'cycle' in a graph). We have the following theorem; the special case of a graphic matroid should be clear from the above discussion.

Theorem 5.2.10. *Let $M = (E, \mathbf{S})$ be a matroid, J an independent set of M and e any element of $E \backslash J$. Then either $J \cup \{e\}$ is independent or $J \cup \{e\}$ contains a unique circuit.*

Proof. Suppose that $J \cup \{e\}$ is dependent. Set

$$C = \{c \in E : (J \cup \{e\}) \backslash \{c\} \in \mathbf{S}\}.$$

Then C is dependent, because otherwise C could be completed to a maximal independent subset K of $J \cup \{e\}$. As J is independent itself, we would have $|K| = |J|$, so that $K = (J \cup \{e\}) \backslash \{d\}$ for some element d. But then d would have to be an element of C, a contradiction. Thus, C is dependent; C even is a circuit: If we remove any element c, we get a subset of $(J \cup \{e\}) \backslash \{c\}$, which is, by definition of C, an independent set. It remains to show that C is the only circuit contained in $J \cup \{e\}$. So let D be another circuit contained in $J \cup \{e\}$. Suppose there exists an element $c \in C \backslash D$, then D is a subset of $(J \cup \{e\}) \backslash \{c\}$, which is an independent set. It follows that $C \subset D$, and hence $C = D$. □

At the end of this section, we show how matroids can be characterized by the circuits they contain. The first lemma is trivial.

Lemma 5.2.11. *Let $(E, \mathbf{S})$ be a matroid. A subset A of E is dependent if and only if $\rho(A) < |A|$. If A is a circuit, we have $\rho(A) = |A| - 1$.* □

Theorem 5.2.12. *Let $M = (E, \mathbf{S})$ be a matroid and let $\mathbf{C}$ be the set of all circuits of M. Then $\mathbf{C}$ has the following properties:*

(1) If $C \subset D$, then $C = D$ for all $C, D \in \mathbf{C}$;
(2) For any $C, D \in \mathbf{C}$ with $C \neq D$ and for $x \in C \cap D$, there always exists some $F \in \mathbf{C}$ with $F \subset (C \cup D) \backslash \{x\}$.

Conversely, if a pair $(E, \mathbf{C})$ satisfies conditions (1) and (2), then there is a unique matroid $(E, \mathbf{S})$ having $\mathbf{C}$ as its set of circuits.

Proof. First, let $\mathbf{C}$ be the set of circuits of M. As circuits are minimal dependent sets, condition (1) is trivial. The submodularity of ρ yields, together with Lemma 5.2.11

$$\rho(C \cup D) + \rho(C \cap D) \leq \rho(C) + \rho(D) = |C| + |D| - 2 = |C \cap D| + |C \cup D| - 2.$$

As C and D are minimal dependent sets, $C \cap D$ is independent, so that

$$\rho(C \cap D) = |C \cap D|,$$

and thus

$$\rho((C \cup D)\backslash\{x\}) \leq \rho(C \cup D) \leq |C \cup D| - 2 < |(C \cup D)\backslash\{x\}|.$$

By Lemma 5.2.11, $(C \cup D)\backslash\{x\}$ is dependent and therefore contains a circuit.

Conversely, suppose $\mathbf{C}$ satisfies the conditions ('circuit axioms') (1) and (2). If there exists a matroid $(E, \mathbf{S})$ with set of circuits $\mathbf{C}$, the independent sets are obviously

$$\mathbf{S} = \{J \subset E : J \text{ does not contain any element of } \mathbf{C}\}.$$

Now $\mathbf{S}$ is obviously closed under inclusion. It remains to show that $(E, \mathbf{S})$ satisfies condition (2) of Theorem 5.2.1. Suppose that condition is not satisfied, so that we can choose a counterexample (J, K) such that $|J \cup K|$ is minimal. Let $J\backslash K = \{x_1, \ldots, x_k\}$. Note $k \neq 1$, because otherwise, as $|J| = |K| + 1$, K would be a subset of J and $J = K \cup \{x_1\}$ would be independent. Our assumption is that $K \cup \{x_i\} \notin \mathbf{S}$ for $i = 1, \ldots, k$. In particular, there exists $C \in \mathbf{C}$ with $C \subset K \cup \{x_1\}$; as K is independent, x_1 must be in C. As J is independent, there is an element $y \in K\backslash J$ which is contained in C. Consider the set $Z = (K\backslash\{y\}) \cup \{x_1\}$. If Z is not in $\mathbf{S}$, then there exists $D \in \mathbf{C}$ with $D \subset Z$ and $x_1 \in D$. Condition (2) above yields that there exists a set $F \in \mathbf{C}$ with $F \subset (C \cup D)\backslash\{x_1\} \subset K$, contradicting $K \in \mathbf{S}$. Thus, Z must be independent. Note that $|Z \cup J| < |K \cup J|$. As we chose our counterexample (J, K) to be minimal, (J, Z) has to satisfy condition (2) of Theorem 5.2.1. That means that there exists some x_i, say x_2, such that $Z \cup \{x_2\} \in \mathbf{S}$. But $K \cup \{x_2\} \notin \mathbf{S}$, so that there is a circuit $C' \in \mathbf{C}$ with $C' \subset K \cup \{x_2\}$. We must have $x_2 \in C'$, because K is independent; and $(K\backslash\{y\}) \cup \{x_1, x_2\} \in \mathbf{S}$ yields $y \in C'$. Thus, $C' \neq C$, and $y \in C \cap C'$. Using condition (2) above again, there exists a set $F' \in \mathbf{C}$ with $F' \subset (C \cup C')\backslash\{y\} \subset (K\backslash\{y\}) \cup \{x_1, x_2\} \in \mathbf{S}$. This contradicts the definition of $\mathbf{S}$. Using condition (1) above, $\mathbf{C}$ is indeed the set of circuits of the matroid $(E, \mathbf{S})$. $\square$

Exercise 5.2.13. Show that the set $\mathbf{C}$ of circuits of a matroid $(E, \mathbf{S})$ satisfies the following stronger version of condition (2) of Theorem 5.2.12 (Lehman (1964)):

(2')   For all $C, D \in \mathbf{C}$, for any $x \in C \cap D$, and for each $y \in C\backslash D$, there exists a set $F \in \mathbf{C}$ with $y \in F \subset (C \cup D)\backslash\{x\}$.

Exercise 5.2.14. Let $(E, \mathbf{S})$ be a matroid. Show that:

(a) The intersection of closed sets is closed.
(b) $\sigma(X)$ is the intersection of all closed sets containing X.
(c) X is closed if and only if, for any $x \in E\backslash X$, the condition $\rho(X \cup \{x\}) = \rho(X) + 1$ holds.

Exercise 5.2.15. Let $(E, \mathbf{S})$ be a matroid of rank r (that is, $\rho(E) = r$). Show that $(E, \mathbf{S})$ contains at least 2^r closed subsets.

5.3 Duality of Matroids

In this section we construct, for any matroid M, the so-called 'dual' matroid M^*. The notion of duality of matroids is different from the duality we know from Linear Algebra: The dual matroid of a finite vector space is not the matroid formed by the dual space. Duality of matroids has an interesting meaning in Graph Theory, see Theorem 5.3.4 below. The following theorem, which shows the construction of the dual matroid, is due to Whitney (1935).

Theorem 5.3.1. *Let $M = (E, \mathbf{S})$ be a matroid. Then $M^* = (E, \mathbf{S}^*)$, where*

$$\mathbf{S}^* = \{J \subset E : \text{there is a basis } B \text{ of } M \text{ with } J \subset E \backslash B\},$$

is a matroid as well. The rank function ρ^* of M^* is given by

$$\rho^*(A) = |A| + \rho(E \backslash A) - \rho(E).$$

Proof. Obviously $\mathbf{S}^*$ is closed under inclusion. Thus, we only have to verify condition (3) of Theorem 5.2.1 for $\mathbf{S}^*$. More precisely, we have to show that, for any subset A of E, all maximal subsets of A which are independent with respect to $\mathbf{S}^*$ have the same cardinality $\rho^*(A)$ as given in the assertion. So let J be such a subset of A, that is, there exists a basis B of M such that $J = (E \backslash B) \cap A$; moreover, J is maximal with this property. As J is maximal, B is chosen such that $A \backslash J = A \backslash ((E \backslash B) \cap A) = A \cap B$ is minimal (with respect to inclusion). It follows that $K := (E \backslash A) \cap B$ is maximal with respect to inclusion. Thus, K is a basis of $E \backslash A$ (with respect to $\mathbf{S}$), and has cardinality $\rho(E \backslash A)$. Therefore, the minimal subsets $A \cap B$ all have cardinality

$$|B| - \rho(E \backslash A) = \rho(E) - \rho(E \backslash A);$$

and all maximal subsets $J \in \mathbf{S}^*$ of A have cardinality

$$|J| = |A| - |A \backslash J| = |A| - |A \cap B| = |A| + \rho(E \backslash A) - \rho(E). \qquad \square$$

The matroid M^* constructed in Theorem 5.3.1 is called the *dual matroid* of M. According to Exercise 5.2.9, the sets in $\mathbf{S}^*$ are precisely the complements of generating sets of M:

Corollary 5.3.2. *Let $M = (E, \mathbf{S})$ be a matroid. Then the independent sets of M^* are precisely the complements of the generating sets of M. In particular, the bases of M^* are the complements of bases of M. Hence, $(M^*)^* = M$.* $\square$

The bases of M^* are called *cobases* of M; the circuits of M^* are called the *cocircuits* of M.

Example 5.3.3. Let $M = M(G)$ be the matroid corresponding to a graph G. If G is connected, the bases of M are the trees in G; the bases of M^* are the *cotrees*, that is, the complements of trees. The circuits of M are the cycles in G and the circuits of M^* are the simple cocycles of G (that is, all those cocycles which are minimal with respect to inclusion). More general, if G has p connected components, n vertices and m edges, then, by Theorem 4.2.4, $M(G)$ has rank $n - p$ and $M(G)^*$ has rank $m - (n - p)$.

We state a result of Whitney (1933) which shows the meaning of duality of matroids in Graph Theory. A proof can be found in Chapter 6 of Welsh (1976).

Result 5.3.4. *A graph G is planar if and only if the dual matroid $M(G)^*$ is graphic.* □

To illustrate Result 5.3.4, we show how, for a planar graph G, the dual matroid can be recognized as being graphic. Suppose G is drawn in the plane. We construct a new graph $G^* = (V^*, E^*)$ whose vertices are the faces of G (see Section 1.5). Two such faces are connected by an edge in G^* if and only if they have a common edge in G. Then $M(G)^* = M(G^*)$.

Exercise 5.3.5. Let $M = (E, \mathbf{S})$ be a matroid and A and A^* two disjoint subsets of E. If A is independent in M and A^* is independent in M^*, then there are bases B and B^* of M and M^*, respectively, such that $A \subset B$, $A^* \subset B^*$ and $B \cap B^* = \emptyset$. (Hint: note $\rho(E) = \rho(E \backslash A^*)$.)

Exercise 5.3.6. Let $M = (E, \mathbf{S})$ be a matroid. A subset X of E is a basis of M if and only if X has non-empty intersection with each cocircuit of M and is minimal with respect to this property.

Exercise 5.3.7. Let C be a circuit and C^* a cocircuit of the matroid M. Show that $|C \cap C^*| \neq 1$. (Hint: Use Exercise 5.3.5 for an indirect proof.)

Exercise 5.3.8. Let x and y be two distinct elements of a circuit C in a matroid M. Then there exists a cocircuit C^* in M such that $C \cap C^* = \{x, y\}$. (Hint: Complete $C \backslash \{x\}$ to a basis B of M and consider $B^* \cup \{y\}$, where $B^* = E \backslash B$ is a cobasis.)

We mention that Minty (1966) has given a system of axioms which characterizes a pair (M, M^*) of dual matroids by the properties of their circuits and cocircuits; an important condition here is that $|C \cap C^*| \neq 1$, see Exercise 5.3.7.

We will return to matroids several times in the remainder of this book. For a thorough study of Matroid Theory we recommend the book by Welsh (1976), which is still the standard reference for this area. The monographs by Recski (1989) and Oxley (1992) are interesting as well, the first one in particular because of its presentation of the applications of matroids. A series of recent monographs concerning Matroid Theory was edited by White (1986), White (1987) and White (1992).

5.4 The Greedy Algorithm as a Technique for Approximation

In this section we look at independence systems $M = (E, \mathbf{S})$ which are not matroids. For these systems, by definition, the Greedy Algorithm does not yield an optimal solution for the optimization problem

$$(\text{P}) \qquad \text{Maximize} \quad w(A) \quad \text{such that} \quad A \in \mathbf{S},$$

where $w : E \to \mathbb{R}_0^+$ is a given weight function. Of course, we can apply the Greedy Algorithm to this problem anyway and hope that we get a reasonably good approximate solution. We now examine the quality of the Greedy Algorithm when used as such a method for approximation. We want to derive bounds for the term

$$f(M) := \min\{\frac{w(T_g)}{w(T_0)} : \quad w : E \to \mathbb{R}_0^+ \}, {}^3$$

where T_g denotes a solution of problem (P) constructed by the Greedy Algorithm and T_0 is an optimal solution for (P). We follow the paper by Korte and Hausmann (1978) in this section; similar results were found independently by Jenkyns (1976).

First we introduce some useful parameters for independence systems. For any subset A of E, the *lower rank* of A is

$$\mathrm{lr}(A) := \min \{|I| : I \subset A, I \in \mathbf{S}, I \cup \{a\} \notin \mathbf{S} \text{ for all } a \in A \backslash I\}.$$

Analogously, we define the *upper rank* of A as

$$\mathrm{ur}(A) := \max \{|I| : I \subset A, I \in \mathbf{S}, I \cup \{a\} \notin \mathbf{S} \text{ for all } a \in A \backslash I\}.$$

Moreover, the *rank quotient* of M is

$$\mathrm{rq}(M) := \min \{\frac{\mathrm{lr}(A)}{\mathrm{ur}(A)} : A \subset E\}.$$

(Here terms $\frac{0}{0}$ might occur; such terms are considered to have value 1.) By Theorem 5.2.1, we then have:

Lemma 5.4.1. *An independence system $M = (E, \mathbf{S})$ is a matroid if and only if $rq(M) = 1$.* □

---

[3] As the Greedy Algorithm might yield different solutions T_g for different orderings of the elements of E (for elements having the same weight), we also have to minimize over all T_g.

The rank quotient indicates how much M differs from a matroid. Below, we will get an interesting estimate for the rank quotient confirming this interpretation. But first, we prove the following theorem due to Jenkyns (1976) and Korte and Hausmann (1978)[4], which shows how the quality of the solution found by the Greedy Algorithm depends on the rank quotient of M.

Theorem 5.4.2. *Let $M = (E, \mathbf{S})$ be an independence system with a weight function $w : E \to \mathbb{R}_0^+$. Moreover, let T_g be a solution of problem (P) found by the Greedy Algorithm and T_0 an optimal solution. Then*

$$rq(M) \leq \frac{w(T_g)}{w(T_0)} \leq 1.$$

Proof. The second inequality is trivial. To prove the first inequality, we introduce the following notation. Suppose the set E is ordered according to decreasing weight, say $E = \{e_1, \ldots, e_m\}$, where

$$w(e_1) \geq w(e_2) \geq \ldots \geq w(e_m).$$

We write

$$E_i := \{e_1, \ldots, e_i\} \quad \text{for } i = 1, \ldots, m.$$

Defining $w(e_{m+1}) := 0$, we get the formulae:

$$w(T_g) = \sum_{i=1}^{m} |T_g \cap E_i|(w(e_i) - w(e_{i+1})) \tag{5.1}$$

$$w(T_0) = \sum_{i=1}^{m} |T_0 \cap E_i|(w(e_i) - w(e_{i+1})). \tag{5.2}$$

As $T_0 \cap E_i$ is an independent subset of E_i, we have $|T_0 \cap E_i| \leq \mathrm{ur}(E_i)$. By definition of the Greedy Algorithm, $T_g \cap E_i$ is a maximal independent subset of E_i, so that $|T_g \cap E_i| \geq \mathrm{lr}(E_i)$ holds. Using these observations, we get

$$|T_g \cap E_i| \geq |T_0 \cap E_i| \cdot \frac{\mathrm{lr}(E_i)}{\mathrm{ur}(E_i)} \geq |T_0 \cap E_i| \, rq(M).$$

Using (5.1) and (5.2) yields

$$
\begin{aligned}
w(T_g) &= \sum_{i=1}^{m} |T_g \cap E_i|(w(e_i) - w(e_{i+1})) \\
&\geq rq(M) \cdot \sum_{i=1}^{m} |T_0 \cap E_i|(w(e_i) - w(e_{i+1})) \\
&= rq(M) \cdot w(T_0). \qquad \square
\end{aligned}
$$

---

[4] The statement of the theorem was conjectured or proved somewhat earlier by various other authors, compare the remarks in Korte and Hausmann (1978).

As w and T_g were chosen arbitrarily in Theorem 5.4.2, we immediately obtain $\mathrm{rq}(M) \leq f(M)$. The following result shows that this bound is best possible, that is, $\mathrm{rq}(M) = f(M)$ holds. Theorems 5.4.2 and 5.4.3 together generalize the characterization of matroids given in Theorem 5.2.1.

Theorem 5.4.3. *Let $M = (E, \mathbf{S})$ be an independence system. Then there exists a weight function $w : E \to \mathbb{R}_0^+$ and a solution T_g for problem (P) found by the Greedy Algorithm such that*

$$\frac{w(T_g)}{w(T_0)} = \mathrm{rq}(M),$$

where T_0 denotes an optimal solution for (P).

Proof. Choose a subset A of E such that

$$\frac{\mathrm{lr}(A)}{\mathrm{ur}(A)} = \mathrm{rq}(M)$$

holds. Moreover, let I_l and I_u, respectively, be maximal independent subsets of A satisfying $|I_l| = \mathrm{lr}(A)$ and $|I_u| = \mathrm{ur}(A)$. Define the weight function w by

$$w(e) := \begin{cases} 1 & \text{for } e \in A, \\ 0 & \text{otherwise} \end{cases}$$

and order the elements $e_1, \ldots, e_m$ of E such that

$$I_l = \{e_1, \ldots, e_{\mathrm{lr}(A)}\}, \quad A \backslash I_l = \{e_{\mathrm{lr}(A)+1}, \ldots, e_{|A|}\}, \quad E \backslash A = \{e_{|A|+1}, \ldots, e_m\}.$$

Then I_l is the solution for (P) found by the Greedy Algorithm (with respect to this order of the elements of E). Moreover, I_u obviously is an optimal solution for (P), so that

$$\frac{w(I_l)}{w(I_u)} = \frac{|I_l|}{|I_u|} = \frac{\mathrm{lr}(A)}{\mathrm{ur}(A)} = \mathrm{rq}(M).$$

$\square$

As Theorems 5.4.2 and 5.4.3 show, the rank quotient of an independence system gives a tight bound for how good the solution found by the Greedy Algorithm approximates the optimal solution of (P), so that it is a measure for the quality of approximation as desired. However, this leaves us with the nontrivial problem of determining this rank quotient for a given independence system M. We give an example where it is possible to determine the rank quotient explicitly.

Theorem 5.4.4. *Let $G = (V, E)$ be a graph and $M = (E, \mathbf{S})$ the independence system defined by the set of all matchings of G (see Exercise 5.1.5). If each connected component of G is isomorphic to a complete graph K_i with $i \leq 3$ or to a star, then $\mathrm{rq}(M) = 1$. In all other cases, $\mathrm{rq}(M) = \frac{1}{2}$.*

Proof. First we show that rq(M) $\geq \frac{1}{2}$, that is,

$$\frac{\mathrm{lr}(A)}{\mathrm{ur}(A)} \geq \frac{1}{2} \qquad \text{for all } A \subset E.$$

Let I_1 and I_2 be two maximal independent subsets of A, that is, two maximal matchings contained in A. Obviously, it is sufficient to show $|I_1| \geq \frac{1}{2}|I_2|$. We define a mapping $\alpha : I_2 \backslash I_1 \to I_1 \backslash I_2$ as follows. Let e be any edge in $I_2 \backslash I_1$. As $I_1 \cup \{e\} \subset A$ and I_1 is a maximal independent subset of A, $I_1 \cup \{e\}$ cannot be a matching. Thus, there exists an edge $\alpha(e) \in I_1$ which has a vertex in common with e. As I_2 is a matching, we cannot have $\alpha(e) \in I_2$, so that we have indeed defined a mapping $\alpha : I_2 \backslash I_1 \to I_1 \backslash I_2$. It is trivial that each edge $e \in I_1 \backslash I_2$ can have a common vertex with at most two edges of $I_2 \backslash I_1$, so that e can have at most two preimages under α. It follows that

$$|I_1 \backslash I_2| \geq |\alpha(I_2 \backslash I_1)| \geq \frac{1}{2}|I_2 \backslash I_1|$$

and hence,

$$|I_1| = |I_1 \backslash I_2| + |I_1 \cap I_2| \geq \frac{1}{2}|I_2 \backslash I_1| + \frac{1}{2}|I_1 \cap I_2| = \frac{1}{2}|I_2|.$$

If the connected components of G are all isomorphic to a graph K_i with $i \leq 3$ or to a star, then obviously $\mathrm{lr}(A) = \mathrm{ur}(A)$ for all $A \subset E$, so that rq(M) $= 1$. Otherwise, G has to contain a subgraph (U, A) isomorphic to a path P_3 of length 3. Then it is clear that $\mathrm{lr}(A) = 1$ and $\mathrm{ur}(A) = 2$, so that rq(M) $\leq \frac{1}{2}$. Together with the converse inequality proved above, this yields the statement of the theorem. $\qquad \square$

We mention a further similar result without proof; the interested reader is referred to Korte and Hausmann (1978).

Result 5.4.5. *Let G be the complete graph on n vertices and $M = (E, \mathbf{S})$ the independence system defined by the set $\mathbf{S}$ of cycles of G. Then*

$$\frac{1}{2} \leq rq(M) \leq \frac{1}{2} + \frac{3}{2n}.$$

$\qquad \square$

Note that the maximal independent sets of M are precisely the Hamiltonian circuits of G. Thus, Result 5.4.5 shows that the Greedy Algorithm can find a good approximation for the optimal solution of the problem to find a Hamiltonian circuit of maximal weight in K_n (for a given weight function $w : E \to \mathbb{R}_0^+$), which is the problem 'opposite' to the TSP (where we look for a Hamiltonian circuit of minimal weight).

The above examples might suggest a rather optimistic view of the Greedy Algorithm as a technique for approximation. The following exercise shows that it is possible to construct a class of independence systems whose rank quotient approaches 0.

Exercise 5.4.6. Let G be the complete directed graph on n vertices, and $M = (E, \mathbf{S})$ the independence system determined by the acyclic directed subgraphs of G, that is,

$$\mathbf{S} = \{D \subset E : D \text{ does not contain any directed cycle}\}.$$

Then $\mathrm{rq}(M) \leq \frac{2}{n}$, so that $\lim_{n \to \infty} \mathrm{rq}(M) = 0$.

Next, we show how to derive an estimate for the rank quotient of an independence system. We need a lemma.

Lemma 5.4.7. *Any independence system $M = (E, \mathbf{S})$ can be represented as the intersection of finitely many matroids on E, that is, there exist a positive integer k and matroids $M_i = (E, \mathbf{S}_i)$ for $i = 1, \ldots, k$ such that*

$$\mathbf{S} = \bigcap_{i=1}^{k} \mathbf{S}_i.$$

Proof. Let $C_1, \ldots, C_k$ be the minimal elements of the set $\{A \subset E : A \notin \mathbf{S}\}$, that is, the circuits of the independence system M. It is easy to see that

$$\mathbf{S} = \bigcap_{i=1}^{k} \mathbf{S}_i, \qquad \text{where } \mathbf{S}_i := \{A \subseteq E : C_i \not\subseteq A\}.$$

We still have to show that all $M_i = (E, \mathbf{S}_i)$ are matroids. So let A be an arbitrary subset of E. If C_i is not a subset of A, then A is independent in M_i, so that A itself is the only maximal independent subset of A in M_i. Now suppose $C_i \subseteq A$. Then, by definition, the maximal independent subsets of A in M_i are the sets of the form $A \backslash \{e\}$ for some $e \in C_i$. Thus, all maximal independent subsets of A have the same cardinality $|A| - 1$ in this case. We have shown that M_i satisfies condition (3) of Theorem 5.2.1, so that M_i is a matroid. $\square$

Theorem 5.4.8. *Let the independence system $M = (E, \mathbf{S})$ be the intersection of the matroids $M_1, \ldots, M_k$ on E. Then we have $\mathrm{rq}(M) \geq \frac{1}{k}$.*

Proof. Let A be any subset of E and I_1, I_2 two maximal independent subsets of A. Obviously, it is sufficient to show that $|I_1| \geq \frac{1}{k}|I_2|$ holds. For $i = 1, \ldots, k$ and $j = 1, 2$, let $I_{i,j}$ be a maximal independent subset (in M_i) of $I_1 \cup I_2$ containing I_j. Suppose there exists an element $e \in I_2 \backslash I_1$ with $e \in I_{i,1} \backslash I_1$ for $i = 1, \ldots, k$, then

$$I_1 \cup \{e\} \subseteq \bigcap_{i=1}^{k} I_{i,1} \in \mathbf{S},$$

contradicting the maximality of I_1. Thus, any element $e \in I_2 \backslash I_1$ can be contained in at most $k - 1$ of the sets $I_{i,1} \backslash I_1$. It follows that

$$\sum_{i=1}^{k} |I_{i,1}| - k|I_1| = \sum_{i=1}^{k} |I_{i,1} \setminus I_1|$$

$$\leq (k-1)|I_2 \setminus I_1| \leq (k-1)|I_2|.$$

As all the M_i are matroids, we have $|I_{i,1}| = |I_{i,2}|$ for $i = 1, \ldots, k$ and hence

$$|I_2| \leq \left(\sum_{i=1}^{k} |I_{i,2}| - k|I_2| \right) + |I_2|$$

$$= \sum_{i=1}^{k} |I_{i,1}| - (k-1)|I_2| \leq k|I_1|,$$

which proves the theorem.   □

It can be shown that, for any natural number k, there exists an independence system for which the bound given in Theorem 5.4.8 is tight. Unfortunately, this is not true for all independence systems, as can be shown using Theorem 5.4.5. The interested reader is referred to Korte and Hausmann (1978).

Example 5.4.9. Let $G = (V, E)$ be a strongly connected directed graph and M the intersection of the graphic matroid $(E, \mathbf{S}_1)$ (that is, $\mathbf{S}_1$ is the set of all forests contained in E) with the head-partition matroid of G. Then the independent sets of maximal cardinality in M are precisely the spanning arborescences of G. (Note that, in this case, the independent sets of maximal cardinality are not necessarily all the bases, that is, all the maximal independent sets of M: For example, we cannot be sure that any arbitrary arborescence can be completed to a spanning arborescence.)

Exercise 5.4.10. Let G be a directed graph. Find three matroids such that each directed Hamiltonian path in G is an independent set of maximal cardinality in their intersection.

As Exercise 5.4.9 shows, the Greedy Algorithm constructs an arborescence whose weight is at least half of the weight of a maximal arborescence. However, we mentioned in Section 4.8 already that a maximal arborescence can be found with complexity $O(|E| \log |V|)$ (using a technique which is considerably more complicated). The following result concerning the intersection of two arbitrary matroids is interesting in this context.

Result 5.4.11. *Suppose the independence system $M(E, \mathbf{S})$ is the intersection of two matroids $M_1 = (E, \mathbf{S}_1)$ and $M_2 = (E, \mathbf{S}_2)$. Moreover, let $w : E \to \mathbb{R}_0^+$ be a weight function on M. If it is possible to check in polynomial time whether a set is independent in M_1 or M_2, respectively, then it is also possible to find an independent set of maximal weight in M in polynomial time.*   □

For a situation as described in Result 5.4.11, we say that the two matroids M_1 and M_2 are given by 'oracles for independence' (which means that it is possible – no matter how – to check whether a given set is independent). Then Result 5.4.11 states that a maximal independent set in M can be found in 'oracle polynomial time' (that is, by using both oracles a polynomial number of times); see Hausmann and Korte (1981) for more on oracles representing matroids and independence systems. Result 5.4.11 is very important in Combinatorial Optimization. We have skipped the proof because the corresponding algorithms (even in the undirected case) as well as the proofs for correctness are rather difficult and use tools from Matroid Theory exceeding the limits of this book. The interested reader should consult the papers by Lawler (1975), Edmonds (1979) and Cunningham (1986), or the books by Lawler (1976) and White (1987). Analogous problems for the intersection of at least three matroids are presumably not solvable in polynomial time, not even in the undirected case.

Problem 5.4.12 (Matroid intersection problem, MIP). There are three given matroids $M_i = (E, \mathbf{S}_i)$ for $i = 1, 2, 3$ and a natural number k. Does there exist a subset A of E such that $|A| \geq k$ and $A \in \mathbf{S}_1 \cap \mathbf{S}_2 \cap \mathbf{S}_3$?

Theorem 5.4.13. *MIP is NP-complete.*

Proof. Obviously, it is sufficient to give some special class of problems in MIP which is NP-complete. Exercise 5.4.10 shows that the question whether a given directed graph contains a directed Hamiltonian path is a special case of MIP. This problem ('directed Hamiltonian path', DHP) is of course NP-complete, as the analogous problem HP for the undirected case is NP-complete by Exercise 2.7.7 and HP can be transformed polynomially to DHP (by substituting the given graph by its complete orientation).   □

Theorem 5.4.13 shows how remarkable the results presented in this chapter really are: Although the problem of determining a maximal (directed) independent set in the intersection of $k \geq 3$ matroids is NP-hard, the Greedy Algorithm gives a polynomial method (which is even rather simple) for finding an approximate solution which differs only by a fixed ratio (which does not depend on the cardinality of the underlying set E) from the optimal solution. We will see in Chapter 14 that this result is by no means trivial, giving an example of an optimization problem for which even the question whether an approximate solution with a fixed ratio of quality exists is NP-hard.

5.5 Minimization in Independence Systems

In this section, we look at the problem of minimization in independence systems, that is, at how to find a maximal independent set of minimal weight.

First we show that this task is simple for matroids, because there, the Greedy Algorithm can treat any arbitrary weight function.

Theorem 5.5.1. *Let* $M = (E, \mathbf{S})$ *be a matroid with weight function* $w : E \to \mathbb{R}$. *Then the Greedy Algorithm 5.1.1 finds an optimal solution for the problem*

(BMAX)   *Maximize* $w(T)$ *such that* T *is a basis of* M.

Proof. The statement of the theorem is correct for non-negative weights by definition. So suppose that negative weights occur. Set

$$C := \max \{-w(e) : e \in E, w(e) < 0\}$$

and consider the weight function $w' : E \to \mathbb{R}_0^+$ defined by

$$w'(e) := w(e) + C \qquad \text{for all } e \in E.$$

As all bases of M have the same cardinality, say k, the weights $w(T)$ and $w'(T)$ differ, for any basis T, only by the constant kC. In particular, any basis of maximal weight for w' also has maximal weight for w. Thus, we can use the Greedy Algorithm to find a basis T of maximal weight for w', and this basis is also a solution for the original problem (BMAX). Now it is clear that the Greedy Algorithm works for w in the same way as for w'. $\square$

Theorem 5.5.2. *Let* $M = (E, \mathbf{S})$ *be a matroid with weight function* $w : E \to \mathbb{R}$. *Then the Greedy Algorithm 5.1.1 finds an optimal solution for the problem*

(BMIN)   *Minimize* $w(T)$ *such that* T *is a basis of* M,

if step (1) in 5.1.1 is replaced by

(1')   *order the elements of* E *according to their weight, say*
       $E = \{e_1, \ldots, e_m\}$ *with* $w(e_1) \leq w(e_2) \leq \ldots \leq w(e_m)$.

Proof. This follows immediately from Theorem 5.5.1 by looking at the weight function $-w$ instead of w. $\square$

As an application, we look at the Greedy Algorithm in the context of duality. Suppose we have a given matroid $M = (E, \mathbf{S})$ with a weight function $w : E \to \mathbb{R}_0^+$. Obviously, a basis B of M has maximal weight if and only if the corresponding cobasis B^* of M^* has minimal weight. Now we use the Greedy Algorithm (as given in Theorem 5.5.2) for determining a basis B^* of M^* having minimal weight. Then, at some point of time during the execution of the algorithm, an element e_k is added to the independent subset T^* constructed so far if $T^* \cup \{e_k\}$ is independent in M^*. Thus, from the point of view of M, e_k is removed from the solution; the solution for the maximization problem in M is precisely the complement of the solution of the minimization problem in M^*. We get the following dual version (formulated in M):

Algorithm 5.5.3 (Dual Greedy Algorithm). Let $(E, \mathbf{S})$ be a matroid with weight function $w : E \to \mathbb{R}_0^+$.

Procedure DUALGREEDY $(G, w; T)$

(1) order the elements of E according to their weight, e.g. $E = \{e_1, \ldots, e_m\}$ with $w(e_1) \le w(e_2) \le \ldots \le w(e_m)$;
(2) $T \leftarrow E$;
(3) **for** $k = 1$ **to** m **do**
(4)   **if** $(E \backslash T) \cup \{e_k\}$ does not contain a cocircuit
        then remove e_k from T **fi**
(5) **od.**

Note that the condition in step (4) is satisfied if and only if $T^* \cup \{e_k\} = (E \backslash T) \cup \{e_k\}$ is independent in M^*, so that the correctness of the Greedy Algorithm immediately yields the following theorem.

Theorem 5.5.4. *The dual Greedy Algorithm computes a basis B of $M = (E, \mathbf{S})$ with maximal weight.* $\square$

Example 5.5.5. Let $M = M(G)$ be the matroid corresponding to a graph G. Then the dual Greedy Algorithm examines the edges of G in the order given by increasing weight. An edge examined at a certain point during the algorithm is removed from T (where, in the beginning, $T = E$) if it does not form a cocycle with the edges already removed, that is, if removing this edge does not destroy the connectedness of the graph (E, T) (or, respectively, if G itself was not connected, if the number of connected components of G is not increased). This special case was already treated by Kruskal (1956).

In the remainder of this section, we look at the question whether the Greedy Algorithm is a useful technique for approximation for problems as in Theorems 5.5.1 and 5.5.2 if $M = (E, \mathbf{S})$ is any independence system (not a matroid). However, even for the maximization problem, the quotient of the weight of a solution found by the Greedy Algorithm and the weight of an optimal solution, which we used as a measure for the quality of approximation before, does not make sense if negative weights occur. Theorem 5.4.2 carries over to the case of arbitrary weight functions if we look at the problem (P) of Section 5.4 (that is, we are not looking for a basis but for an independent set of maximal weight) and terminate the Greedy Algorithm as soon as an element of negative weight would be chosen.

The question whether there is a guarantee for the quality of an approximate solution of the minimization problem

(PMIN)   Minimize $w(A)$ such that A is a maximal
            independent set in $\mathbf{S}$,

where $w : E \to \mathbb{R}_0^+$ is a non-negative weight function, is more interesting.

Here, the reciprocal quotient

$$g(M) := \min \{ \frac{w(T_0)}{w(T_g)} : \quad w : E \to \mathbb{R}_0^+ \}$$

should be used for measuring the quality of a solution found by the Greedy Algorithm (again, T_g denotes a solution found by the Greedy Algorithm and T_0 is an optimal solution for (PMIN)). The matroids are precisely the independence systems with $g(M) = 1$. Unfortunately, no result analogous to Theorem 5.4.2 can be proved, as was already shown by Korte and Hausmann (1978) who gave a trivial series of examples (a path of length two with various weight functions). We give a class of examples due to Reingold and Tarjan (1981), which are particularly interesting.

Example 5.5.6. By G_t we denote the complete graph on 2^t vertices. For each graph G_t, we define a weight function w_t satisfying the triangle inequality as follows. First choose a Hamiltonian circuit C_t (for $t \geq 2$; for $t = 1$, C_1 is the only edge of G_1) in G_t and define w_t on C_t as shown in Figure 5.1; the edges not marked explicitly with their weight all have weight 1. For any other edge $e = uv$ (not occuring in C_t) of G_t, its weight $w_t(e)$ is the distance $d_t(u,v)$ in the network (C_t, w_t). As the largest weight occuring in C_t is precisely the sum of the weights of the other edges of C_t, it is easy to see that w_t indeed satisfies the triangle inequality.

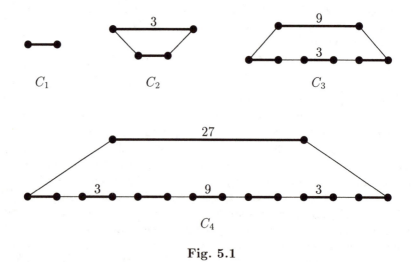

Fig. 5.1

Now consider the problem of finding a maximal matching (that is, a 1-factor) of minimal weight for (G_t, w_t). It is easy to see that the Greedy Algorithm computes, for the cases $t = 1, \ldots, 4$ shown in Figure 5.1, the matchings M_t drawn bold there having weight 1, 4, 14, or 46, respectively (if edges of the same weight are ordered accordingly). It can be seen that, in the general case (that is, for any t), we also get such a 1-factor M_t of G_t of weight

$$w_t(M_t) = 2 \cdot 3^{t-1} - 2^{t-1}.$$

The formula for the weight of M_t can easily be derived from the recursion (which is obvious from Figure 5.1)

$$w_{t+1}(M_{t+1}) = 2w_t(M_t) - 3^{t-1} + 3^t,$$

where $w_1(M_1) = 1$. We leave the details to the reader. On the other hand, it is possible (for $t \geq 2$) to find a 1-factor M'_t of G_t of weight 2^{t-1} consisting of the edges not drawn bold in Figure 5.1, so that $M'_t = C_t \backslash M_t$. Then the quality of the approximation found by the Greedy Algorithm is only

$$\frac{2^{t-1}}{2 \cdot 3^{t-1} - 2^{t-1}} \quad \rightarrow \quad 0 \qquad (\text{for } t \rightarrow \infty).$$

Recall that, according to Theorem 5.4.4, the rank quotient of the independence system $(E_t, \mathbf{S}_t)$ whose independent sets are the matchings in G_t has value 2 for all $t \geq 2$. Nevertheless, as we saw above, the Greedy Algorithm might yield an arbitrarily bad solution for (PMIN).

It was shown by Reingold and Tarjan (1981) that the bound for $\frac{w(T_0)}{w(T_g)}$ we found in Example 5.5.6 is worst possible. For any weight function on the complete graph K_n satisfying the triangle inequality, we have

$$\frac{w(T_g)}{w(T_0)} \leq \left(\frac{3^\theta}{2^{\theta+1} - 1} - 1 \right) \cdot \frac{4}{3} n^{\log \frac{3}{2}},$$

where $\theta = \lceil \log n \rceil - \log n$. For the proof, which is relatively complicated, we refer to the original paper. Determining a 1-factor of minimal weight with respect to a weight function w on a complete graph satisfying the triangle inequality will be a tool for solving the 'Chinese postman problem' in Chapter 13; this problem has interesting practical applications (for example, drawing large graphs with a plotter).

Exercise 5.5.7. Show that it is not possible in Example 5.5.6 to change the weight function w_t such that the quotient M'_t/M_t becomes smaller. Moreover, show that, for an arbitrary weight function (not necessarily satisfying the triangle inequality), it is not possible to give any measure (as a function in n) for the quality of a 1-factor in a complete graph found by the Greedy Algorithm.

5.6 Accessible Set Systems

The problem of generalizing the Greedy Algorithm not only to an indepen-dence system, but even further to any system of sets, or to some ordered structure, has found considerable interest. In this last section of Chapter 5, we look at the possible generalization of the Greedy Algorithm to arbitrary systems of sets. As the methods used in the proofs are rather similar to the methods used before (although more complicated in detail), we skip all the proofs and refer the reader to the references given.

A *set system* is simply a pair $M = (E, \mathbf{S})$, where E is a finite set and $\mathbf{S}$ is a non-empty subset of the power set of E. The elements of $\mathbf{S}$ are called *feasible sets* of M; maximal feasible sets are again called *bases*. As the Greedy Algorithm always chooses single elements and adds them one after the other to the feasible set to be constructed, it does not make sense to look at an arbitrary set system. We have to make sure, at least, that any (maximal) feasible set can be obtained by adding single elements successively to the empty set. Formally, this means requiring that the *accessibility axiom* holds:

> (A)   For any non-empty feasible set $X \in \mathbf{S}$, there exists
> an element $x \in X$ such that $X \backslash \{x\} \in \mathbf{S}$.

In particular, it follows (because $\mathbf{S} \neq \emptyset$) that the empty set is contained in $\mathbf{S}$. A set system M satisfying axiom (A) is called an *accessible set system*. Any independence system is an accessible set system, but axiom (A) is a much weaker condition than the requirement of being closed under inclusion. Now we consider, for any accessible set system M and any weight function $w : E \to \mathbb{R}$, the optimization problem

> (BMAX)   Maximize $w(B)$ such that B is a basis of M.

(BMAX) above generalizes the corresponding problem for independence sys-tems. The following version of the Greedy Algorithm 5.1.1[5] can be applied to accessible set systems.

Algorithm 5.6.1. Let $M = (E, \mathbf{S})$ be an accessible set system and $w : E \to \mathbb{R}$ a weight function.

---

[5] Note that it does not make sense to apply the original Greedy Algorithm if $\mathbf{S}$ is not closed under inclusion: In this case, it might happen that an element x cannot be added to the feasible set T constructed so far (because $T \cup \{x\}$ is not feasible), but it might be allowed to add x at some later point of the algorithm to the set $T \cup A$. If $w(x) > w(y)$ for some $y \in A$, the Greedy Algorithm 5.1.1 would fail in this situation.

Procedure GREEDY $(E, \mathbf{S}, w; T)$

(1) $T \leftarrow \emptyset;\; X \leftarrow E;$
(2) **while** there exists $x \in X$ with $T \cup \{x\} \in \mathbf{S}$ **do**
(3)   choose some $x \in X$ with $T \cup \{x\} \in \mathbf{S}$ and
            $w(x) \geq w(y)$ for all $y \in X$ with $T \cup \{y\} \in \mathbf{S};$
(4) $T \leftarrow T \cup \{x\};\; X \leftarrow X \backslash \{x\}$
(5) **od.**

Now we have to characterize those accessible set systems for which the Greedy Algorithm 5.6.1 always finds an optimal solution for (BMAX). This problem was solved only recently by Helman, Mont and Shapiro (1993). Before describing their result, we look at a special class of accessible set systems introduced by Korte and Lovász (1981).

An accessible set system M satisfying the exchange axiom (2) of Theorem 5.2.1 is called a *greedoid*. Greedoids have been studied intensively and are important in so far as a lot of interesting objects in Combinatorics and Optimization are greedoids. In particular, the so-called 'antimatroids' are greedoids. Antimatroids can be considered a combinatorial abstraction of the notion of convexity (in the same way as matroids are an abstraction of the notion of linear independence), and they play an important role for studying convexity, partially ordered sets and searching processes in Graph Theory. Greedoids occur as well in the context of matchings or of the Gauß elimination technique. We will not go into detail here and recommend the reader to consult the extensive survey by Bjørner and Ziegler (1992) and, for further study, the interesting monograph by Korte, Lovász and Schrader (1991). We emphasize that, unfortunately, the Greedy Algorithm does not find an optimal solution of the problem (BMAX) for all greedoids.[6] However, Korte and Lovász (1984) were able to characterize those greedoids for which the Greedy Algorithm works. A more simple characterization (and some further equivalent conditions) is due to Bryant and Brooksbank (1992):

Result 5.6.2. *Let* $M = (E, \mathbf{S})$ *be a greedoid. Then the Greedy Algorithm 5.6.1 finds an optimal solution of (BMAX) for any weight function* $w : E \to \mathbb{R}$ *if and only if* M *satisfies the following axiom:*

(SE)   *For* $J, K \in \mathbf{S}$ *with* $|J| = |K| + 1$, *there always exists some* $a \in J \backslash K$ *such that* $K \cup \{a\}$ *and* $J \backslash \{a\}$ *are in* $\mathbf{S}$.

$\square$

Condition (SE) is called the *strong exchange axiom*. It is a stronger version of the exchange axiom (2) of Theorem 5.2.1 which is trivially satisfied for any matroid. We need some more preparations to be able to formulate the characterization of those accessible set systems $M = (E, \mathbf{S})$ for which the

---

[6] Characterizing greedoids using the Greedy Algorithm is only possible using certain non-linear objective functions, see Korte, Lovász and Schrader (1991).

Greedy Algorithm computes an optimal solution. For any feasible set A, we define

$$\text{ext}(A) := \{x \in E \backslash A : A \cup \{x\} \in \mathbf{S}\}.$$

Now there are some situations where the Greedy Algorithm does not even construct a basis, but stops with some feasible set which is not maximal. This happens if there exists a basis B and a feasible set $A \subset B$, $A \neq B$, such that $\text{ext}(A) = \emptyset$. In this case, if we define the weight function w by

$$w(x) := \left\{ \begin{array}{ll} 2 & \text{for } x \in A, \\ 1 & \text{for } x \in B \backslash A, \\ 0 & \text{otherwise,} \end{array} \right.$$

then the Greedy Algorithm constructs A, but cannot extend A to the optimal basis B. The accessibility axiom (A) is too weak to prevent such situations, because it merely makes sure that a basis B can be obtained somehow by adding single elements successively to the empty set, but not necessarily by adding elements to some arbitrary feasible subset of B. Thus, we need the following *extensibility axiom*:

(E)   For any basis B and any feasible subset $A \subset B$, $A \neq B$, there exists some $x \in B \backslash A$ with $A \cup \{x\} \in \mathbf{S}$.

This axiom is necessary for the Greedy Algorithm to find an optimal solution in M; note that it is satisfied for all greedoids. We need one more definition. For any set system $M = (E, \mathbf{S})$, define

$$\overline{\mathbf{S}} := \{X \subseteq E : \text{ there is } A \in \mathbf{S} \text{ with } X \subseteq A\}$$

and call $\overline{M} := (E, \overline{\mathbf{S}})$ the *hereditary closure* of M. Now we require that the *closure congruence axiom* holds:

(CC)   For any feasible set A, for all $x, y \in \text{ext}(A)$ and for any subset $X \subseteq E \backslash (A \cup \text{ext}(A))$, $A \cup X \cup \{x\} \in \overline{\mathbf{S}}$ implies $A \cup X \cup \{y\} \in \overline{\mathbf{S}}$.

Exercise 5.6.3. Show that, if the Greedy Algorithms works for an accessible set system $M = (E, \mathbf{S})$, then M satisfies axiom (CC).

It is possible to show that axiom (CC) is independent of the exchange axiom, even if we look at those accessible set systems only which satisfy the extensibility axiom. In fact, there are greedoids not satisfying (CC); on the other hand, independence systems always satisfy (CC), because the only choice for X is $X = \emptyset$. We need one more axiom.

(ME)   The hereditary closure $\overline{M}$ of M is a matroid.

(ME) is called the *matroid embedding axiom*. Now we can state the result of Helman, Mont and Shapiro (1993) announced above.

Result 5.6.4. *Let $M = (E, \mathbf{S})$ be an accessible set system. Then the following statements are equivalent:*

(1) M satisfies axioms (E), (CC) and (ME).

(2) For any weight function $w : E \to \mathbb{R}$, the optimal solutions of (BMAX) are precisely those bases of M which are found by the Greedy Algorithm 5.6.1 (for an appropriate order of the elements of equal weight).

(3) For any weight function $w : E \to \mathbb{R}$, the Greedy Algorithm 5.6.1 yields an optimal solution of (BMAX). □

The reader might try to fill in the missing parts of the proof (this is a more demanding exercise, but can be done using the methods presented above) or look at the original paper, which contains some further interesting results. In particular, Helman, Mont and Shapiro (1993) considered bottleneck problems, that is, problems of the form

(BNP)   Maximize min $\{w(x) : x \in B\}$ such that B is a basis of M,

where $w : E \to \mathbb{R}$ is again a weight function. In particular, the Greedy Algorithm constructs, under conditions equivalent to those of Result 5.6.4, an optimal solution for (BNP). However, this is true even under conditions which are considerably weaker. We introduce one more axiom called the *strong extensibility axiom*:

(SE)   For any basis B and any feasible set A with $|A| < |B|$, there exists $x \in B \backslash A$ with $A \cup \{x\} \in \mathbf{S}$.

Then the following characterization holds:

Result 5.6.5. *Let $M = (E, \mathbf{S})$ be an accessible set system. The Greedy Algorithm 5.6.1 yields, for any weight function $w : E \to \mathbb{R}$, an optimal solution for (BNP) if and only if M satisfies axiom (SE).* □

The Greedy Algorithm for partially ordered set systems was studied by Faigle (1979). He obtained a characterization analogous to Results 5.6.4 and 5.6.5. Further characterizations of related structures by the Greedy Algorithm (or versions modified appropriately) can be found in Faigle (1985), Goecke (1988) and Boyd and Faigle (1990), where ordered languages, greedoids of Gauß elimination and antimatroids are studied, respectively. Finally, there is another important generalization of the notion of matroid, namely the *oriented matroids*. However, we do not consider these structures here and refer the reader to the monographs by Bachem and Kern (1992) and Bjørner, Las Vergnas, Sturmfels, White and Ziegler (1992).

6. Flows

In this chapter, we look at 'flows' in networks: How much can be transported in a network from some 'source' s to some 'sink' t if the 'capacities' of the connections are given? Such a network might be a model for a system of pipelines or a water supply system or for a system of roads. The theory of flows is one of the most important parts of Combinatorial Optimization; it has various applications as well in Mathematics as in other fields. The book by Ford and Fulkerson (1962) 'Flows in Networks', formerly the standard reference, is still worth reading; an extensive treatment is in the recent monograph by Ahuja, Magnanti and Orlin (1993). In Chapter 7, we will see several applications of the theory of flows within Combinatorics, and flows and related notions will appear again and again during the remainder of this book.

6.1 The Theorems of Ford and Fulkerson

In this chapter, we look at networks of the following special kind. Let $G = (V, E)$ be a directed graph with a mapping $c : E \to \mathbb{R}_0^+$; the value $c(e)$ is called the *capacity* of edge e. Moreover, let s and t be two special vertices of G such that t is accessible from s. Then $N = (G, c, s, t)$ is called a *flow network* or a *capacitated network* with *source* s and *sink* t.[1] A *flow* on N is a mapping $f : E \to \mathbb{R}_0^+$ satisfying the following conditions:

(F1) $0 \leq f(e) \leq c(e)$ for each edge e;
(F2) for each vertex $v \neq s, t$, we have that $\displaystyle\sum_{e^+=v} f(e) = \sum_{e^-=v} f(e)$,

where e^- and e^+ denote the start and end vertex of e, respectively.

Thus, the *feasibility condition* (F1) means that, through each edge, there is a non-negative flow which is bounded above by the capacity of the edge. The *flow conservation condition* (F2) means that flows are preserved: at each vertex (except for the source and the sink), the amount that flows in also

---

[1] Some authors require in addition $d_{in}(s) = d_{out}(t) = 0$. We do not need this requirement here; it would also be inconvenient for our investigation of symmetric networks and a network synthesis problem in Chapter 10.

flows out. It is quite obvious that the total flow coming out of s should be the same as the total flow going into t. The following lemma confirms this observation:

Lemma 6.1.1. *Let N be a flow network with flow f. Then*

$$\sum_{e^-=s} f(e) - \sum_{e^+=s} f(e) = \sum_{e^+=t} f(e) - \sum_{e^-=t} f(e).$$

Proof. It is trivial that

$$\sum_{e^-=s} f(e) + \sum_{e^-=t} f(e) + \sum_{v\neq s,t}\sum_{e^-=v} f(e) = \sum_{e} f(e) =$$
$$= \sum_{e^+=s} f(e) + \sum_{e^+=t} f(e) + \sum_{v\neq s,t}\sum_{e^+=v} f(e).$$

Now the statement follows immediately from (F2).   □

The sum of flows occuring in the equation in Lemma 6.1.1 is called the *value* of f and is denoted by $w(f)$. A flow f is called *maximal* if $w(f) \geq w(f')$ for all flows f' on N. The main problem studied in the theory of flows is how to find a maximal flow in a given network. Note that, a priori, it is not entirely obvious that maximal flows exist; however, we will soon see that such flows always have to exist. First, we want to find an upper bound for the value of a flow. We need some definitions. Let $N = (G, c, s, t)$ be a flow network. A *cut* of N is a partition $V = S \cup T$ of the vertex set V of G into two disjoint sets S and T such that $s \in S$ and $t \in T$ (that is, a special case of the cuts of $|G|$ introduced in Section 4.3). The *capacity* of the cut (S, T) is

$$c(S, T) = \sum_{e^-\in S, e^+\in T} c(e),$$

that is, the sum of all capacities of edges e contained in the corresponding cocycle $E(S, T)$ which are oriented from S to T. The cut (S, T) is called *minimal* if, for any cut (S', T'), the condition $c(S, T) \leq c(S', T')$ holds. The following lemma shows that the capacity of a minimal cut is an upper bound on the value of a flow.

Lemma 6.1.2. *Let $N = (G, c, s, t)$ be a flow network, (S, T) a cut and f a flow. Then*

$$w(f) = \sum_{e^-\in S, e^+\in T} f(e) - \sum_{e^+\in S, e^-\in T} f(e),$$

and therefore, in particular, $w(f) \leq c(S, T)$.

Proof. Summing the equation in (F2) over all $v \in S$, we get

$$w(f) = \sum_{v \in S} \left(\sum_{e^- = v} f(e) - \sum_{e^+ = v} f(e) \right) =$$

$$= \sum_{e^- \in S, e^+ \in S} f(e) - \sum_{e^+ \in S, e^- \in S} f(e) + \sum_{e^- \in S, e^+ \in T} f(e) - \sum_{e^+ \in S, e^- \in T} f(e).$$

The first two terms add to 0. Now note that $f(e) \leq c(e)$ holds for edges e with $e^- \in S$ and $e^+ \in T$ and $f(e) \geq 0$ holds for edges e with $e^+ \in S$ and $e^- \in T$. $\square$

In the following we will see that the maximal value of a flow is precisely the minimal capacity of a cut. But first we characterize the maximal flows. We need a definition. Let f be a flow in the network $N = (G, c, s, t)$. An (undirected) path W from s to t is called an *augmenting path* (with respect to f), if, for any forward edge $e \in W$, the condition $f(e) < c(e)$ holds, and for any backward edge $e \in W$, $f(e) > 0$ holds. The following basic theorems are all due to Ford and Fulkerson (1956).

Theorem 6.1.3 (Augmenting Path Theorem). *A flow f on a flow network N is maximal if and only if there is no augmenting path with respect to f.*

Proof. First let f be a maximal flow. Suppose there is an augmenting path W. Let d be the minimum of the values $c(e) - f(e)$ (over all forward edges e in W) and $f(e)$ (over the backward edges in W), respectively. Then, by definition of an augmenting path, d is positive. We define a mapping $f' : E \to \mathbb{R}_0^+$ as follows:

$$f'(e) := \begin{cases} f(e) + d & \text{if } e \text{ is a forward edge in } W, \\ f(e) - d & \text{if } e \text{ is a backward edge in } W, \\ f(e) & \text{otherwise.} \end{cases}$$

Now it is easy to see that f' is a flow on N with value $w(f') = w(f) + d > w(f)$ contradicting the maximality of f.

Conversely, suppose there is no augmenting path in N with respect to f. Let S be the set of all vertices v such that there exists an augmenting path from s to v (including s itself) and $T = V \backslash S$. Then, by hypothesis, (S, T) is a cut of N. Thus, each edge e with $e^- \in S$ and $e^+ \in T$ must be *saturated*, that is, $f(e) = c(e)$ holds. Also, each edge e with $e^- \in T$ and $e^+ \in S$ must be *void*, that is, $f(e) = 0$. But then, by Lemma 6.1.2, $w(f) = c(S, T)$, so that f must be maximal. $\square$

From the above proof, we obtain the following characterization of maximal flows.

Corollary 6.1.4. *A flow f on a flow network N is maximal if and only if the set S of all vertices accessible from s on an augmenting path (with respect to f) is not all of V; if this is the case, then $w(f) = c(S,T)$, where $T := V \backslash S$.* □

Theorem 6.1.5 (Integral Flow Theorem). *Let $N = (G, c, s, t)$ be a flow network where all capacities $c(e)$ are integers. Then there is a maximal flow on N such that all values $f(e)$ are integral.*

Proof. By setting $f_0(e) := 0$ for all e, we can define an integral flow f_0 on N of value 0. If this (trivial) flow is not maximal, then there exists an augmenting path with respect to f_0. The number d appearing in the proof of Theorem 6.1.3 is, in this case, a positive integer, so that it is possible to construct – as shown in the proof of Theorem 6.1.3 – an integral flow f_1 of value d. This technique can be applied iteratively. As the value of the flow is increased in each step by a positive integer and the capacity of a (minimal) cut is an upper bound on the value of the flow (by Lemma 6.1.2), after a finite number of steps we get a flow f for which no augmenting path exists. By Theorem 6.1.3, this flow f is an (integral) maximal flow.   □

Theorem 6.1.6 (Max-Flow Min-Cut Theorem). *The maximal value of a flow on a flow network N is equal to the minimal capacity of a cut in N.*

Proof. If all capacities are integers, the assertion follows from Theorem 6.1.5 and Corollary 6.1.4. The case where all capacities are rational can be reduced to the integer case by multiplying all numbers by their common denominator. Then real-valued capacities can be treated by using a continuity argument, since the set of flows is a compact subset of $\mathbb{R}^{|E|}$ and since $w(f)$ is a continuous function of f. A different (constructive) proof for the real case can be derived from the Theorem of Edmonds and Karp (1972) which will be treated in the next section.   □

Theorem 6.1.6 was proved by Ford and Fulkerson (1956) and independently also by Elias, Feinstein and Shannon (1956). In practice, of course, real capacities do not occur, because a computer can only represent (a finite number of) rational numbers anyway. From now on, we mostly restrict ourselves to integral flows. Sometimes, we also look at networks on directed multigraphs which is not really more general, because parallel edges can be substituted by a single edge whose capacity is the sum of the corresponding capacities of the parallel edges. The remainder of this chapter treats several algorithms for finding a maximal flow. The proof of Theorem 6.1.5 suggests a rough outline of such an algorithm:

(1) $f(e) \leftarrow 0$ for all edges e;
(2) **while** there exists an augmenting path with respect to f **do**
(3)   let $W = (e_1, \ldots, e_n)$ be an augmenting path from s to t;

(4) $d \leftarrow \min(\{c(e_i) - f(e_i) : e_i \text{ forward edge }\}$
                $\cup \{f(e_i) : e_i \text{ backward edge }\});$
(5) $f(e_i) \leftarrow f(e_i) + d$ for each forward edge e_i;
(6) $f(e_i) \leftarrow f(e_i) - d$ for each backward edge e_i;
(7) **od**.

Of course, we still have to specify a technique for finding augmenting paths. We can use a modification of breadth first search (BFS); here edges may be used without considering their orientation as long as they satisfy the condition $f(e) < c(e)$ or $f(e) > 0$, respectively. But as we not only have to find out whether t is accessible from s by an augmenting path, but also have to find the value for d and change the values $f(e)$ accordingly, it is easier to use a labelling technique; this will also allow us to find a minimal cut. The following algorithm is due to Ford and Fulkerson (1957).

Algorithm 6.1.7 (Labelling Algorithm of Ford and Fulkerson). Let $N = (G, c, s, t)$ be a flow network.

Procedure FORDFULK$(N; f, S, T)$

(1) **for** $e \in E$ **do** $f(e) \leftarrow 0$ **od**;
(2) label s with $(-, \infty)$;
(3) **for** $v \in V$ **do** $u(v) \leftarrow$ false; $d(v) \leftarrow \infty$ **od**;
(4) **repeat**
(5)   choose a vertex v which is labelled and satisfies $u(v) =$ false;
(6)   **for** $e \in \{e \in E : e^- = v\}$ **do**
(7)   **if** $w = e^+$ is not labelled **and** $f(e) < c(e)$
(8)   **then** $d(w) \leftarrow \min\{c(e) - f(e), d(v)\}$ and label
                    w with $(v, +, d(w))$ **fi**
(9)   **od**;
(10)   **for** $e \in \{e \in E : e^+ = v\}$ **do**
(11)   **if** $w = e^-$ is not labelled **and** $f(e) > 0$
(12)   **then** $d(w) \leftarrow \min\{f(e), d(v)\}$ and label w with $(v, -, d(w))$
                    fi
(13)   **od**;
(14) $u(v) \leftarrow$ true;
(15)   **if** t is labelled
(16)   **then** let d be the last component of the label of t;
(17) $w \leftarrow t$;
(18)   **while** $w \neq s$ **do**
(19)   find the first component v of the label of w;
(20)   **if** the second component of the label of w is $+$
(21)   **then** set $f(e) \leftarrow f(e) + d$ for edge $e = vw$
(22)   **else** set $f(e) \leftarrow f(e) - d$ for edge $e = wv$
(23)   **fi**;
(24) $w \leftarrow v$

(25)   **od**;
(26)   delete all labels except the one of s;
(27)   **for** $v \in V$ **do** $d(v) \leftarrow \infty$; $u(v) \leftarrow$ false **od**
(28)   **fi**
(29) **until** $u(v) =$ true for all vertices v which are labelled;
(30) let S be the set of vertices which are labelled and $T \leftarrow V \backslash S$.

Using the proofs we gave for Theorems 6.1.3 and 6.1.5, we immediately get the following theorem due to Ford and Fulkerson (1957).

Theorem 6.1.8. *Let N be a network whose capacity function c takes only integral (or rational) values. Then Algorithm 6.1.7 determines a maximal flow f and a minimal cut (S, T), so that $w(f) = c(S, T)$ holds.*   □

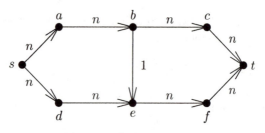

Fig. 6.1 A flow network

The above algorithm might fail for irrational capacities (if vertex v in step (5) is chosen in an unfortunate manner); an example can be found in Ford and Fulkerson (1962), p. 21. In this example, the algorithm not only does not terminate, but it also converges to a value which is only $\frac{1}{4}$ of the maximal possible value of a flow. Moreover, Algorithm 6.1.7 is not polynomial even for integer capacities, because the number of necessary changes of the flow f does not only depend on $|V|$ and $|E|$, but might also depend on c. For example, if we use the paths

$$s \,\text{---}\, a \,\text{---}\, b \,\text{---}\, e \,\text{---}\, f \,\text{---}\, t \qquad \text{and} \qquad s \,\text{---}\, d \,\text{---}\, e \,\text{---}\, b \,\text{---}\, c \,\text{---}\, t$$

alternately as augmenting paths for the network in Figure 6.1 (which the algorithm will do if vertex v in step (5) is chosen accordingly), the value of the flow will only be increased by 1 in each step, so that we need $2n$ iterations. Of course, this can be avoided by choosing the paths appropriately; using

$$s \,\text{---}\, a \,\text{---}\, b \,\text{---}\, c \,\text{---}\, t \qquad \text{and} \qquad s \,\text{---}\, d \,\text{---}\, e \,\text{---}\, f \,\text{---}\, t,$$

we need only two iterations. In the next section, we show how the augmenting paths can be chosen efficiently. There, we also apply the resulting algorithm to an example and show the computations in detail. We close this section with a couple of exercises.

Exercise 6.1.9. Let $N = (G, c, s, t)$ be a flow network where there are restrictions on the capacities of the vertices as well: There is a further mapping $d : V \to \mathbb{R}_0^+$ and the flows f have to satisfy the further restriction

$$\text{(F3)} \qquad \sum_{e^+=v} f(e) \leq d(v) \quad \text{for } v \neq s, t.$$

Reduce this problem to a problem in an appropriate ordinary flow network and generalize Theorem 6.1.6 to flow networks with additional restrictions on the capacities of the vertices (see Ford and Fulkerson (1962), §1.11). A practical application might be an irrigation network where the vertices are pumping stations whose capacity is limited.

Exercise 6.1.10. How can the case of several sources and several sinks be treated?

Exercise 6.1.11. Let $N = (G, c, s, t)$ be a flow network. Show that there is at least one edge e in N such that, if we remove e from N, the maximal value of a flow will decrease, if this value is positive. An edge e is called *most vital* if the maximal value of a flow is decreased by the largest possible value by the removal of e. Is an edge of maximal capacity in a minimal cut necessarily most vital?

Exercise 6.1.12. Let f be a flow in a flow network N. The *support* of f is supp $f = \{e \in E : f(e) \neq 0\}$. A flow f is called *elementary* if supp f is a path. The proof of Theorem 6.1.6 and the Algorithm of Ford and Fulkerson show that there exists a maximal flow which is the sum of elementary flows. Show that not every maximal flow can be represented by such a sum.

Exercise 6.1.13. Modify the process of labelling the vertices in Algorithm 6.1.7 in such a way that the augmenting path chosen always has maximal possible capacity (so that the value of the flow is increased as much as possible). Hint: Use an appropriate variation of the Algorithm of Dijkstra.

6.2 The Algorithm of Edmonds and Karp

As we have seen at the end of the previous section, Algorithm 6.1.7 of Ford and Fulkerson is not polynomial if the vertices v in the labelling process are chosen in an unfortunate way. We now consider a modification of the algorithm due to Edmonds and Karp (1972) for which we can prove a complexity of $O(|V||E|^2)$. As we will see, it is sufficient to use an augmenting path of shortest length (that is, having as few edges as possible) for increasing the flow. To find such a path, we can – similar to the technique used in BFS (Algorithm 3.3.1) – simply modify step (5) of Algorithm 6.1.7 such that the vertex v with $u(v) = $ false which was labelled first is chosen; note that the labelling process is done as in BFS (compare Algorithm 3.3.1). This principle for selecting vertex v is easy to implement: we can order the labelled vertices in a queue (so that some vertex w is appended to the queue when it is labelled in step (8) or (12)). We are now able to prove the following theorem due to Edmonds and Karp (1972).

Theorem 6.2.1. *If step (5) in Algorithm 6.1.7 is replaced by*

(5')   let v be, among all vertices with $u(v) = $ false, the vertex which was labelled first,

then the resulting algorithm has complexity $O(|V||E|^2)$.

Proof. We have already seen that, by replacing step (5) by (5'), the flow f is always increased using an augmenting path of shortest length. Let f_0 (the flow of value 0 defined in step (1)), $f_1, f_2, \ldots, f_k, \ldots$ be the sequence of flows constructed during the algorithm and $x_v(k)$ the shortest length of an augmenting path from s to v with respect to f_k. We prove first that the inequality

$$x_v(k + 1) \geq x_v(k) \quad \text{for all } k \text{ and } v \tag{6.1}$$

holds. So suppose (6.1) does not hold for some pair (v, k); then we may assume that $x_v(k + 1)$ is minimal among the $x_w(k + 1)$ for which (6.1) is violated. Consider the last edge e on a shortest augmenting path from s to v with respect to f_{k+1}. Suppose first that e is a forward edge, so that $e = uv$ for some vertex u. Then we must have $f_{k+1}(e) < c(e)$. Now $x_v(k+1) = x_u(k+1)+1$, so that by the way we chose v, $x_u(k+1) \geq x_u(k)$, and hence $x_v(k+1) \geq x_u(k)+1$. Note that we must have $f_k(e) = c(e)$, because otherwise $x_v(k) \leq x_u(k) + 1$ and $x_v(k + 1) \geq x_v(k)$ in contradiction to our assumption above. This means that e must have been used as a backward edge when f_k was changed to f_{k+1}. As the augmenting path we used for this change had shortest length, it follows that $x_u(k) = x_v(k) + 1$ and $x_v(k + 1) \geq x_v(k) + 2$, a contradiction. The case that e is a backward edge is treated analogously. Moreover, in a similar way, we prove the inequality

$$y_v(k + 1) \geq y_v(k), \tag{6.2}$$

where $y_v(k)$ denotes the length of a shortest augmenting path from v to t with respect to f_k.

When increasing the flow, there is always at least one edge of the augmenting path which is *critical*: The flow through this edge is either increased up to its capacity or is decreased to 0. Let $e = uv$ be a critical edge in the augmenting path with respect to f_k; this path consists of $x_v(k)+y_v(k) = x_u(k)+y_u(k)$ edges. If e is used the next time in some augmenting path (with respect to f_h, say), it has to be used in the opposite direction, that is, if e was a forward edge for f_k, it has to be a backward edge for f_h and vice versa.

Suppose that e was a forward edge for f_k. Then we must have $x_v(k) = x_u(k) + 1$ and $x_u(h) = x_v(h) + 1$. By (6.1) and (6.2), $x_v(h) \geq x_v(k)$ and $y_u(h) \geq y_u(k)$ must hold. It follows that

$$x_u(h) + y_u(h) = x_v(h) + 1 + y_u(h) \geq x_v(k) + 1 + y_u(k) = x_u(k) + y_u(k) + 2.$$

We see that the augmenting path with respect to f_h is at least two edges longer than the augmenting path with respect to f_k. This statement is true as well for the case that e was a backward edge for f_h (exchange the roles of u and v in the above argument). Trivially, no augmenting path can contain more than $|V| - 1$ edges. Thus, each edge can be critical in at most $\frac{|V|-1}{2}$ changes of flow, so that the flow can be changed at most $O(|V||E|)$ times. (In particular, the algorithm terminates even if the capatities are real!) Finding an augmenting path and changing the flow takes only $O(|E|)$ steps, because each edge – as in BFS – is treated at most three times (twice during the labelling process and once when the flow is changed). Thus, we obtain the desired complexity of $O(|V||E|^2)$. $\Box$

As the cardinality of E is between $O(|V|)$ and $O(|V|^2)$, we get immediately:

Corollary 6.2.2. *The Algorithm of Edmonds and Karp has complexity* $O(|V|^3)$ *for sparse (for example planar) graphs and* $O(|V|^5)$ *for dense graphs.* $\Box$

Examples for networks with n vertices and $O(n^2)$ edges for which the Algorithm of Edmonds and Karp really needs $O(n^3)$ changes of the flow are given by Zadeh (1972) and Zadeh (1973b). Thus, the estimates used in the proof of Theorem 6.2.1 are best possible. Of course, this does not mean that there might not be a better algorithm: One possible approach would be to look for algorithms which do not use augmenting paths (we will see examples in Sections 6.4 and 6.6), another might be to combine several changes of flows using augmenting paths in some clever way (see Sections 6.3 and 6.4). However, these techniques are considerably more involved. We mention that Edmonds and Karp (1972) have shown as well that the flow has to be changed at most $O(\log w)$ times (where w is the maximal value of a flow on N) if we always choose an augmenting path of maximal capacity (see Exercise 6.1.13). The number of steps necessary for this method is easy to estimate (although we do not know w in the first place), because w is obviously bounded by

$$W = \min \left\{ \sum_{e^- = s} c(e), \sum_{e^+ = t} c(e) \right\}.$$

Although this technique does not yield a polynomial algorithm (because the bound depends on the capacities as well), it might still be better in concrete cases (for small W), cf. Exercise 6.2.5.

Example 6.2.3. We use the Algorithm of Edmonds and Karp to determine a maximal flow and a minimal cut in the network N given in Figure 6.2. The capacities are given there in parentheses; the numbers without parentheses in the following figures always give the respective values of the flow. We also state the labels which are assigned at the respective stage of the algorithm; when examining the possible labellings coming from some vertex v on forward edges (steps (6) through (9)) and on backward edges (steps (10) through (13)), we consider the vertices w in alphabetical order, so that the course of the algorithm is uniquely determined. The augmenting path used for the construction of the next flow is drawn bold.

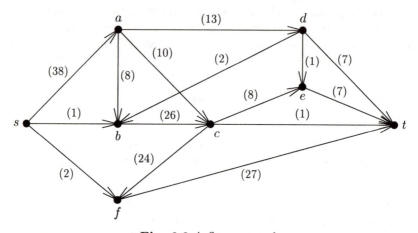

Fig. 6.2 A flow network

We start with the zero flow f_0, that is, $w(f_0) = 0$. The vertices are labelled in the order a, b, f, c, d, t as shown in Figure 6.3; e is not labelled because t is reached before e is considered. Figures 6.3 to 6.12 show how the algorithm works. Note that the last augmenting path uses a backward edge, see Figure 6.11. In Figure 6.12, we have also indicated the minimal cut resulting from the algorithm.

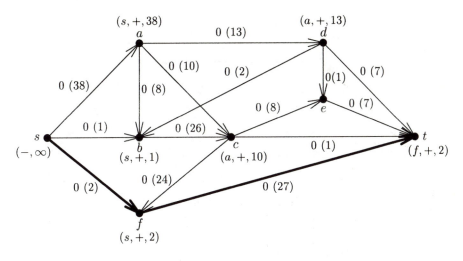

Fig. 6.3 $w(f_0) = 0$

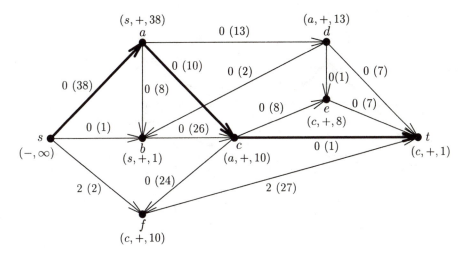

Fig. 6.4 $w(f_1) = 2$

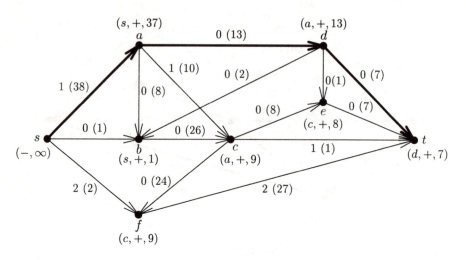

Fig. 6.5 $w(f_2) = 3$

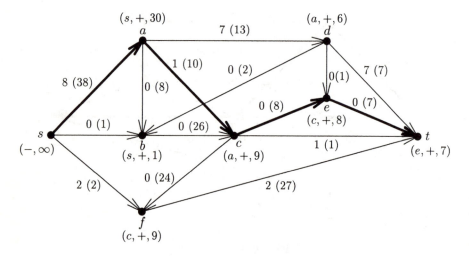

Fig. 6.6 $w(f_3) = 10$

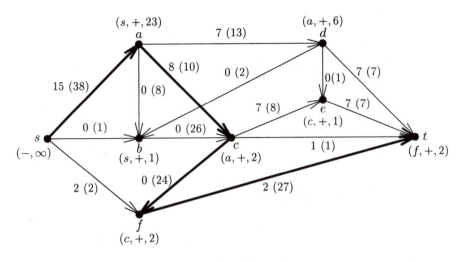

Fig. 6.7 $w(f_4) = 17$

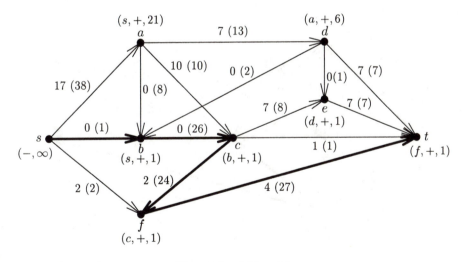

Fig. 6.8 $w(f_5) = 19$

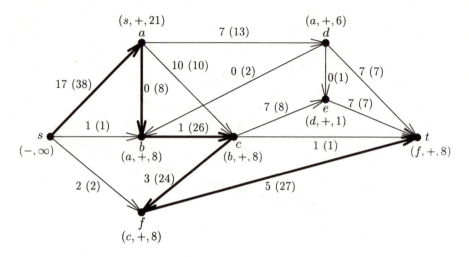

Fig. 6.9 $w(f_6) = 20$

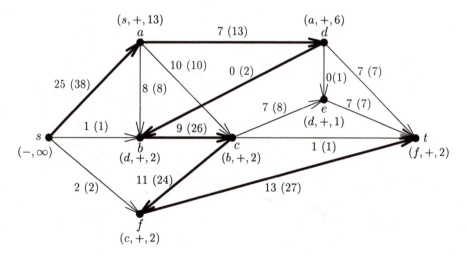

Fig. 6.10 $w(f_7) = 28$

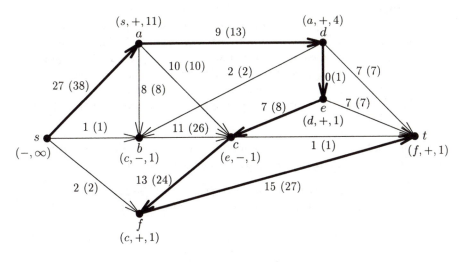

Fig. 6.11 $w(f_8) = 30$

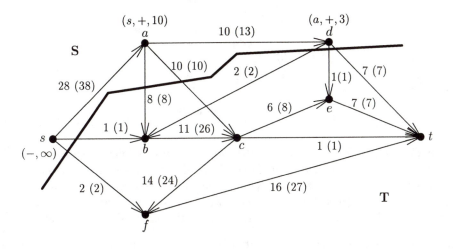

Fig. 6.12 $w(f_9) = 31 = c(S, T)$

It can be shown that, for any flow network, at most $|E|$ changes of the flow (even using just augmenting paths which consist of forward edges only) are sufficient to find the maximal flow; see Lawler (1976), p. 119. However, this result is of no practical interest, because we do not know how to find such paths.

Considering Example 6.2.3 more closely, we see that a lot of the labels are not changed from one iteration to the next. As all the labels are deleted in step (26) after each change of the flow, this means we do a lot of unnecessary calculations. It is possible to obtain algorithms of better complexity by combining the changes of the flow into bigger 'phases'. To do this, a 'blocking flow' is constructed in some appropriate auxiliary network. This subject is treated in Sections 6.3 and 6.4.

Exercise 6.2.4. Determine a maximal flow for the network of Figure 6.2 by always choosing an augmenting path of maximal capacity.

Exercise 6.2.5 (Papadimitriou and Steiglitz (1982)). Apply the Algorithm of Edmonds and Karp to the network shown in Figure 6.13.

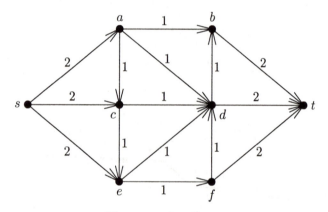

Fig. 6.13 A network

Exercise 6.2.6. Suppose we have determined a maximal flow for a flow network N (using the Algorithm of Edmonds and Karp), and realize afterwards that we used an incorrect capacity for some edge e. Is it possible to use the maximal flow obtained for the problem with the incorrect capacity to solve the corrected problem, or do we have to apply the whole algorithm again?

Exercise 6.2.7. Change the capacity of edge $e = ac$ in the network of Figure 6.2 to $c(e) = 8$ or to $c(e) = 12$, respectively. How does this change the value of a maximal flow? Give a maximal flow for each of these two cases.

Exercise 6.2.8. Change the network of Figure 6.2 as follows: The capacity of edge ac is increased to 12, edge ad gets capacity 16, and the edges de and ct are removed. Determine a maximal flow for the new network.

Exercises 6.2.6 to 6.2.8 show that – if we know a solution of a given problem already – it is possible to change several capacities in the network and find solutions for the corresponding new problems without great effort.

6.3 Layered Networks and Phases

Let $N = (G, c, s, t)$ be a flow network and f a flow for N. Define a second flow network (G', c', s, t) as follows: G' has the same vertex set as G. For each edge $e = uv$ of G with $f(e) < c(e)$, there is an edge $e' = uv$ in G' with $c'(e') = c(e) - f(e)$; for each edge $e = uv$ with $f(e) \neq 0$, G' contains an edge $e'' = vu$ with $c'(e'') = f(e)$.

The labelling process in steps (6) to (9) (or (10) to (13), respectively) in the Algorithm of Ford and Fulkerson uses only those edges e of G for which G' contains an edge e' (or e'', respectively). An augmenting path with respect to f in G corresponds to a directed path from s to t in G'. Thus, we can use G' to decide whether f is maximal and – if it is not – to find an augmenting path. We call $N' = (G', c', s, t)$ the *auxiliary network* with respect to f. The next lemma is clear.

Lemma 6.3.1. *Let $N = (G, c, s, t)$ be a flow network with flow f and N' the corresponding auxiliary network. Then f is maximal if and only if t is not accessible from s in G'.*   □

Example 6.3.2. Consider the flow $f = f_3$ of Example 6.2.3 (see Figure 6.6). The corresponding auxiliary network is given in Figure 6.14.

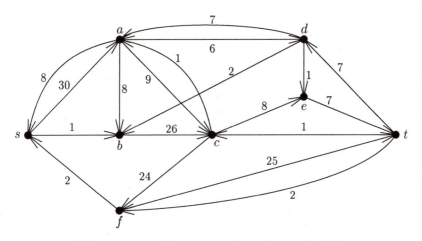

Fig. 6.14 Auxiliary network for Example 6.3.2

It is clear intuitively that a maximal flow in N' can be used to change f when constructing a maximal flow in N. The following two results make this fact more precise.

Lemma 6.3.3. *Let* $N = (G, c, s, t)$ *be a flow network with flow* f *and* N' *the corresponding auxiliary network. Moreover, let* f' *be a flow on* N'. *Then there exists a flow* f'' *of value* $w(f'') = w(f) + w(f')$ *on* N.

Proof. For each edge $e = uv$ of G, let $e' = uv$ and $e'' = vu$. If e' or e'', respectively, is not contained in N', we set $f'(e') = 0$ or $f'(e'') = 0$, respectively. Putting $f'(e) := f'(e') - f'(e'')$, we may interpret f' as a 'flow' on N (where the minus sign in front of $f'(e'')$ comes from the fact that e' and e'' have opposite orientation). This flow satisfies condition (F2), but not necessarily (F1). Obviously, the mapping f'' defined by

$$f''(e) := f(e) + f'(e') - f'(e'')$$

satisfies condition (F2) as well. By definition of N', the conditions $0 \le f'(e') \le c(e) - f(e)$ and $0 \le f'(e'') \le f(e)$ hold for each edge e, so that f'' satisfies (F1) as well. Thus, f'' is a flow which obviously has value $w(f) + w(f')$. □

Theorem 6.3.4. *Let* $N = (G, c, s, t)$ *be a flow network with flow* f *and corresponding auxiliary network* N'. *Denote the value of a maximal flow on* N *and* N' *by* w *and* w', *respectively. Then we have* $w = w' + w(f)$.

Proof. Lemma 6.3.3 implies that $w \ge w' + w(f)$. Now let g be a maximal flow on N, that is, $w(g) = w$. We define a flow g' on N' as follows: For each edge $e = uv$ of G, set

$$g'(e') := g(e) - f(e) \qquad \text{if} \quad g(e) > f(e) \quad \text{and}$$
$$g'(e'') := f(e) - g(e) \qquad \text{if} \quad g(e) < f(e).$$

Note that, under the conditions given above, e' and e'' really are edges of N' and their capacities are large enough to make sure that (F1) holds. For all other edges in N', we define $g' = 0$. It can be seen easily that g' is a flow of value $w(g') = w(g) - w(f)$ on N'. Hence, $w' \ge w - w(f)$ holds as well. □

Exercise 6.3.5. Give an alternative proof for Theorem 6.3.4 by proving that the capacity $c'(S, T)$ of a cut (S, T) in N' is equal to $c(S, T) - w(f)$.

Remark 6.3.6. Note that the graph G' may contain parallel edges even if G itself – as we always assume – does not. This phenomenon occurs when G contains antiparallel edges, say $d = uv$ and $e = vu$: Then G' contains the parallel edges d' and e'' with capacities $c'(d') = c(d) - f(d)$ and $c'(e'') = f(e)$, respectively. For the validity of the preceding proofs (and the subsequent algorithms as stated), it is important that parallel edges of G' are *not* identified (and their capacities added). Indeed, if we identified the edges d' and e'' above into a new edge e^* with capacity $c'(e^*) := c(d) - f(d) + f(e)$, it would no longer be obvious how to distribute a flow value $f'(e^*)$ when defining f'' in the proof of Lemma 6.3.3: We would have to decide which part of $f'(e^*)$ should contribute to $f''(d)$ (with a plus sign) and which part to $f''(e)$ (with a minus sign). Of course, it would always be possible to arrange this in such a manner that a flow f'' satisfying the feasibility condition (F1) arises, but this would require some unpleasant case distinctions. For this reason, we allow G' to contain parallel edges.[2] However, when actually programming an algorithm using auxiliary networks, it might be worthwhile to identify parallel edges of G' and add the necessary case distinctions for distributing the flow on N' during the augmentation step. In this case, one should also simplify things by 'cancelling' flow on pairs of antiparallel edges in such a way that only one edge of such a pair carries a non-zero flow.

We have seen that it is possible to find a maximal flow for our original network N by finding appropriate flows in a series of auxiliary networks $N_1 = N'(f_0)$, $N_2 = N'(f_1), \ldots$ In the Algorithm of Ford and Fulkerson (or Edmonds and Karp, respectively), we basically constructed a new auxiliary network after each change of the flow (using an augmenting path); there, the labelling process corresponded to the task of constructing the auxiliary network. Thus, constructing the auxiliary networks explicitly will only yield a better algorithm if we construct several augmenting paths all at once and determine the new auxiliary network afterwards. We use 'blocking' flows to be able to do so. A flow f is called a *blocking flow* if there does not exist an augmenting path with respect to f consisting of forward edges only. It is trivial that any maximal flow is blocking as well. However, the converse is false: For example, the flow f_8 of Example 6.2.3 (see Figure 6.11) is blocking, but not maximal. The auxiliary networks constructed so far are still too big and complex (consider Example 6.3.2!); thus, we treat an appropriate subnetwork only. The main idea of the algorithm due to Dinic (1970) is to use not only an augmenting path of shortest length, but also to keep an appropriate network $N''(f)$ basically unchanged (with only slight modifications) until there are no more augmenting paths of the same length.

For better motivation, we again consider the Algorithm of Edmonds and Karp (1972). Making step (5) of Algorithm 6.1.7 more precise in step (5') of Theorem 6.2.1 has the effect that the labelling process on the auxiliary network N' is executed as a BFS on G'. In this process, G' is divided into levels or layers of vertices of the same distance to s (see Section 3.3). As we are only interested in finding augmenting paths of shortest length, N' contains a lot of information we do not need. We may omit

---

[2] Alternatively, we could forbid G to contain antiparallel edges; this might be achieved, for instance, by subdividing one edge of an antiparallel pair into two edges.

(i) all vertices $v \neq t$ with $d(s, v) \geq d(s, t)$ and all edges incident with them,
(ii) all edges leading from some vertex in layer j to some vertex in layer $i \leq j$.

The resulting network $N'' = (G'', c'', s, t)$ is called the *layered auxiliary network* with respect to f. Strictly speaking, N'' might only be called a network (as before when speaking of N') if t is accessible from s (this is part of the definition of flow networks), that is, if f was not maximal. The name 'layered' network comes from the fact that G'' is a *layered digraph*: the vertex set V of G'' is the disjoint union of subsets $V_0, \ldots, V_k$ and all edges of G'' have the form uv with $u \in V_i$ and $v \in V_{i+1}$ for some index i.

Example 6.3.7. Consider again the flow $f = f_3$ of Example 6.2.3 and the corresponding auxiliary network N' of Example 6.3.2 (see Figure 6.14). Then the layered auxiliary network N'' is as given in Figure 6.15. Here, the capacities are written in parentheses; the other numbers are the values of a blocking flow g on N'' which is the 'sum' of the three augmenting paths of Figures 6.6, 6.7 and 6.8. Thus, all three paths of length four of Example 6.2.3 can in fact be found in the much more easily understandable network N'' (instead of N'). Note that g is blocking but not maximal: The sequence (s, a, d, e, c, f, t) of vertices forms an augmenting path containing the backward edge ce.

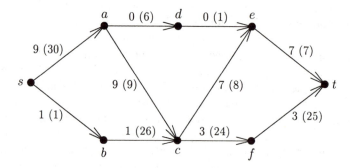

Fig. 6.15 Layered auxiliary network

Even N'' might contain unnecessary elements, for example vertices from which t is not accessible. But as such vertices cannot be determined during the BFS used for constructing N'', we do not bother to find and remove them in general.

Exercise 6.3.8. How could vertices v in N'' from which t is not accessible be removed?

Exercise 6.3.9. Draw N' and N'' for the flow f_7 of Example 6.2.3 (see Figure 6.10) and determine a blocking flow for N''.

We now treat two algorithms for determining maximal flows. Both of them start with a given flow (for example the flow of value zero) and construct a blocking flow in the corresponding layered auxiliary network N'', which is then used to change the flow already known. This technique is repeated until a maximal flow is found. Note that a flow f' of value $w(f')$ on $N''(f)$ may indeed be used to change the original flow f to a flow of value $w(f) + w(f')$, because N'' is a sub-network of N'; thus, we may apply Lemma 6.3.3 and the technique used in its proof.

Exercise 6.3.10. Show that Theorem 6.3.4 does not carry over to $N''(f)$.

We begin, for example, with the zero flow f_0, construct a blocking flow g_0 in $N''(f_0)$, use this flow to change f_0 to a flow f_1 of value $w(g_0)$, construct a blocking flow g_1 in $N''(f_1)$, and so on. The technique terminates as soon as the sink t is not accessible from s in $N''(f_k)$. Then t is not accessible from s in $N'(f_k)$ either, so that, by Lemma 6.3.1, f_k is maximal. We call the construction of a blocking flow g_i and the corresponding change of f_i to f_{i+1} a *phase* of the algorithm. In the next section, we treat the problem of how to find blocking flows. But first, we want to derive an estimate for how many phases are needed and write down an algorithm for constructing the layered auxiliary network.

Lemma 6.3.11. *Let $N = (G, c, s, t)$ be a flow network with flow f and $N''(f)$ the corresponding layered auxiliary network. Moreover, let g be a blocking flow on $N''(f)$, h the flow on N of value $w(f) + w(g)$ constructed from f and g as in Lemma 6.3.3 and $N''(h)$ the layered auxiliary network with respect to h. Then the distance from s to t is larger in $N''(h)$ than in $N''(f)$.*

Proof. It is easy to see that $N''(h)$ is the layered auxiliary network for $N'(f)$ with respect to g. (Note: The analogous statement for $N''(f)$ instead of $N'(f)$ does not hold, as Exercise 6.3.13 below will show.) As g is a blocking flow on $N''(f)$, there is no augmenting path from s to t in $N''(f)$ consisting of forward edges only. If there exists an augmenting path in $N'(f)$ with respect to g (which of course must have value 0 on those edges which are not contained in $N''(f)$), then this path has to contain a backward edge or one of those edges which were omitted during the construction of $N''(f)$. In both cases, the length of this path must be larger than the distance from s to t in $N''(f)$. Thus, the distance from s to t in the layered auxiliary network for $N'(f)$ with respect to g (that is, in $N''(h)$) is indeed larger than the corresponding distance in $N''(f)$. $\square$

Corollary 6.3.12. *Let N be a flow network. Then the construction of a maximal flow on N needs at most $|V| - 1$ phases.*

Proof. Let $f_0, f_1, \ldots, f_k$ be the sequence of flows constructed during the algorithm. Lemma 6.3.11 implies that the distance from s to t in $N''(f_k)$ is at least k larger than this distance in $N''(f_0)$. Thus, the number of phases can be at most $|V| - 1$. $\square$

Exercise 6.3.13. Choose f to be the flow f_3 of Example 6.2.3 and g to be the blocking flow on $N''(f)$ of Example 6.3.7. Draw the layered auxiliary networks with respect to g on $N'(f)$ and on $N''(f)$. What does the flow h determined by f and g on N look like? Convince yourself that $N''(h)$ is indeed equal to the layered auxiliary network with respect to g on $N'(f)$.

The following procedure for constructing the layered auxiliary network $N''(f)$ corresponds to the labelling process in the Algorithm of Ford and Fulkerson with step (5) substituted by (5') (as in Theorem 6.2.1). During the execution of the BFS, the procedure also orders the vertices in layers and omits vertices and edges which are not needed as described in the definition of N''. The Boolean variable max has value true if f is already maximal, that is, if t is not accessible from s, and false otherwise. The variable $d + 1$ contains the number of layers of N''.

Algorithm 6.3.14. Let $N = (G, c, s, t)$ be a flow network with flow f.

Procedure AUXNET $(N, f; N'', \text{max}, d)$

(1) $i \leftarrow 0$, $V_0 \leftarrow \{s\}$, $E'' \leftarrow \emptyset$, $V'' \leftarrow V_0$;
(2) **repeat**
(3) $i \leftarrow i + 1$, $V_i \leftarrow \emptyset$;
(4)   **for** $v \in V_{i-1}$ **do**
(5)   **for** $e \in \{e \in E : e^- = v\}$ **do**
(6)   **if** $u = e^+ \notin V''$ **and** $f(e) < c(e)$
(7)   **then** $e' \leftarrow vu$, $E'' \leftarrow E \cup \{e'\}$, $V_i \leftarrow V_i \cup \{u\}$;
                    $c''(e') \leftarrow c(e) - f(e)$ **fi**
(8)   **od**;
(9)   **for** $e \in \{e \in E : e^+ = v\}$ **do**
(10)   **if** $u = e^- \notin V''$ **and** $f(e) \neq 0$
(11)   **then** $e'' \leftarrow vu$, $E'' \leftarrow E \cup \{e''\}$, $V_i \leftarrow V_i \cup \{u\}$;
                    $c''(e'') \leftarrow f(e)$ **fi**
(12)   **od**
(13)   **od**;
(14)   **if** $t \in V_i$ **then** remove all vertices $v \neq t$ together with all
            edges e satisfying $e^+ = v$ from V_i **fi**;
(15) $V'' \leftarrow V'' \cup V_i$
(16) **until** $t \in V''$ **or** $V_i = \emptyset$;
(17) **if** $t \in V''$ **then** max $\leftarrow$ false; $d \leftarrow i$ **else** max $\leftarrow$ true **fi**.

It is now easy to show the following lemma.

Lemma 6.3.15. *Algorithm 6.3.14 constructs the layered auxiliary network $N'' = (G'', c'', s, t)$ on $G'' = (V'', E'')$ with complexity $O(|E|)$.* □

In the next section, we treat two techniques for constructing a blocking flow g on N''. Let us assume for the moment that we know such a procedure BLOCKFLOW $(N''; g)$ already. Then we can use g for changing f. The following procedure performs this task; it uses the construction given in the proof of Lemma 6.3.3. Note that N'' never contains both e' and e''.

Algorithm 6.3.16. Let $N = (G, c, s, t)$ be a given flow network with flow f and suppose we have already constructed N'' and a blocking flow g.

Procedure AUGMENT$(f, g; f)$

(1) **for** $e \in E$ **do**
(2)   **if** $e' \in E''$ **then** $f(e) \leftarrow f(e) + g(e')$ **fi**;
(3)   **if** $e'' \in E''$ **then** $f(e) \leftarrow f(e) - g(e'')$ **fi**
(4) **od**.

This puts us in a position to formulate an algorithm for determining a maximal flow.

Algorithm 6.3.17. Let $N = (G, c, s, t)$ be a flow network.

Procedure MAXFLOW$(N; f)$

(1) **for** $e \in E$ **do** $f(e) \leftarrow 0$ **od**;
(2) **repeat**
(3)   AUXNET$(N, f; N''$, max,$d)$;
(4)   **if** max = false
(5)   **then** BLOCKFLOW$(N''; g)$; AUGMENT$(f, g; f)$ **fi**
(6) **until** max = true.

The only part we are still missing in the above algorithm is a procedure BLOCKFLOW for determining a blocking flow g on N'', then Algorithm 6.3.17 will construct a maximal flow on N. Each phase of the algorithm has complexity at least $O(|E|)$, because AUGMENT has this complexity. It is quite obvious that BLOCKFLOW will also have complexity at least $O(|E|)$; in fact, the known algorithms have even larger complexity. Altogether, MAXFLOW has – if we denote the complexity of BLOCKFLOW by $k(N)$ – a complexity of $O(|V|k(N))$; note that, by Corollary 6.3.12, the algorithm has at most $O(|V|)$ phases.

Exercise 6.3.18. Modify Algorithm 6.3.17 in such a way that it finds a minimal cut (S, T) as well.

6.4 Constructing Blocking Flows

In this section, we want to fill in the gap left in Algorithm 6.3.17 and give two algorithms for constructing blocking flows. The simpler of the two is due to Dinic (1970); his algorithm constructs (starting with the zero flow) augmenting paths of length d in the layered auxiliary network N'' (where

$d + 1$ is the number of layers) and uses them to change the flow g until t is no longer accessible from s; then g is a blocking flow. It has two advantages compared to the Algorithm of Edmonds and Karp (1972): First, in $N''(f)$, we consider only those paths which consist of forward edges exclusively (as a path containing a backward edge has length at least $d + 2$). Second, when bringing the input data up to date after having changed the flow g, we only have to decrease the capacities of the edges contained in the augmenting path used and omit vertices and edges we do not need anymore. In particular, we do not have to do the whole labelling process again.

Algorithm 6.4.1. Let $N = (G, c, s, t)$ be a layered flow network with layers $V_0, \ldots, V_d$, where all capacities are positive.

Procedure BLOCKFLOW$(N; g)$

(1) **for** $e \in E$ **do** $g(e) \leftarrow 0$ **od**;
(2) **repeat**
(3) $v \leftarrow t$, $a \leftarrow \infty$;
(4)   **for** $i = d$ **downto** 1 **do**
(5)   choose some edge $e_i = uv$;
(6) $a \leftarrow \min \{c(e_i), a\}$, $v \leftarrow u$
(7)   **od**;
(8)   **for** $i = 1$ **to** d **do**
(9) $g(e_i) \leftarrow g(e_i) + a$, $c(e_i) \leftarrow c(e_i) - a$;
(10)   **if** $c(e_i) = 0$ **then** omit e_i from E **fi**
(11)   **od**;
(12)   **for** $i = 1$ **to** d **do**
(13)   **for** $v \in V_i$ **do**
(14)   **if** $d_{in}(v) = 0$
(15)   **then** omit v and all edges e with $e^- = v$
(16)   **fi**
(17)   **od**
(18)   **od**
(19) **until** $t \notin V_d$.

Theorem 6.4.2. *Algorithm 6.4.1 determines a blocking flow on N with complexity $O(|V||E|)$.*

Proof. By definition of a layered auxiliary network, each vertex is accessible from s at the beginning of the algorithm. Thus, there always exists an edge e_i with end vertex v which can be chosen in step (5) (independent of the edges $e_{i+1}, \ldots, e_d$ chosen before), so that the algorithm constructs a path $(e_1, \ldots, e_d)$ from s to t. Moreover, when the iteration (4) to (7) is finished, the variable a contains the capacity a of this path, namely $a = \min \{c(e_i) : i = 1, \ldots, d\}$. In steps (8) to (11), the flow constructed so far (in the first iteration, this is the zero flow) is increased by a along the path and the capacities of the edges $e_1, \ldots, e_d$ are decreased accordingly. Edges whose capacity is decreased to 0 cannot appear on any further augmenting path and are therefore omitted. At the end of the iteration (8) to (11), we have reached t and changed the flow. Before executing the loop (4) to (11) again, we have to check whether t is still accessible from s. More precisely, we have to make sure that, in the modified layered network, any vertex is still accessible from s. This task is done by the loop (12) to (18): It can be shown (using induction on i) that this loop removes exactly those vertices which are not accessible from s as well as all edges beginning in these vertices. If, after the loop, t is still contained in N, the whole process can be repeated. Finally, the algorithm has to terminate after at most $|E|$ changes of the flow g, because, in each iteration, at least one edge is removed, and if all edges are removed, t cannot be in V_d any more. Obviously, each iteration (4) to (16) has complexity $O(|V|)$, which yields complexity $O(|V||E|)$ for the whole algorithm. □

Using the remarks at the end of Section 6.3, we get immediately:

Corollary 6.4.3. *If Algorithm 6.3.17 uses the procedure BLOCKFLOW of Algorithm 6.4.1, the whole algorithm (due to Dinic) calculates, for a given flow network N, a maximal flow with complexity $O(|V|^2|E|)$.* □

Note that the Algorithm of Dinic has a complexity of $O(|V|^4)$ for dense graphs (whereas the Algorithm of Edmonds and Karp needs $O(|V|^5)$ steps). Using a different technique for constructing blocking flows will even reduce the complexity for any graph to $O(|V|^3)$. But first, we look at an example for how the Algorithm of Dinic works.

Example 6.4.4. Consider again the flow $f = f_3$ of Example 6.2.3. The corresponding layered auxiliary network N'' was given in Example 6.3.7 (see Figure 6.15). We apply Algorithm 6.4.1 to N''. If, in step (5), we always choose the edge uv for which u is first in alphabetical order, the algorithm becomes deterministic. First, the path $s — a — c — e — t$ of capacity 7 is constructed. The corresponding flow g_1 is shown in Figure 6.16; the numbers in parentheses give the new capacities (which were changed when the flow was changed). The edge et, which is drawn broken, is removed during this first iteration.

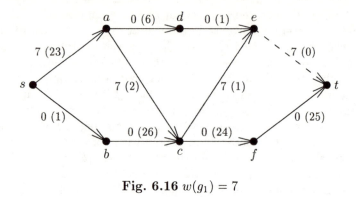

Fig. 6.16 $w(g_1) = 7$

During the next iteration, the algorithm constructs the path $s — a — c — f — t$ in the network of Figure 6.16; it has capacity two. Figure 6.17 shows the new network with the new flow g_2. Edge ac has been removed.

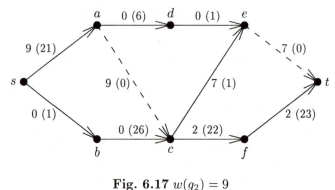

Fig. 6.17 $w(g_2) = 9$

Finally, in the network of Figure 6.17, the next iteration constructs the path $s — b — c — f — t$ of capacity one; we get the flow g_3 as given in Figure 6.18. Also, this iteration removes the edge sb, vertex b and edge bc, then vertex c and the edges ce and cf, vertex f and edge ft, and finally vertex t (see Figure 6.18). As t was removed, g_3 is a blocking flow. (This is the same blocking flow we gave in Figure 6.15.)

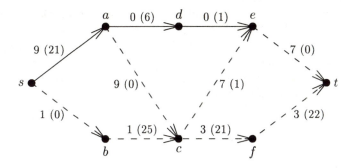

Fig. 6.18 Blocking flow g_3 with $w(g_3) = 10$

Exercise 6.4.5. Use Algorithm 6.4.1 to determine a blocking flow on the layered network shown in Figure 6.19 (taken from Syslo, Deo and Kowalik (1983)).

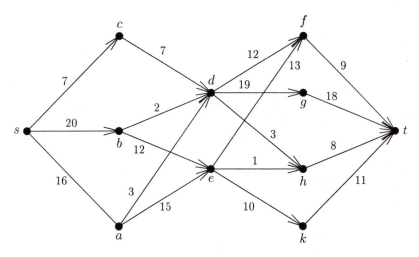

Fig. 6.19 A layered network

We now turn to a different method due to Malhotra, Kumar and Mahaswari (1978) for constructing blocking flows. It has complexity $O(|V|^2)$. This algorithm does not use augmenting paths and tries instead to 'push' as big a flow as possible through the network. We need some notation. Let $N = (G, c, s, t)$ be a layered flow network. For each vertex v, the *flow potential* $p(v)$ is defined by

$$p(v) := \min \{ \sum_{e^- = v} c(e), \sum_{e^+ = v} c(e) \}.$$

That is, $p(v)$ is the maximal value a flow passing through v could possibly have. A vertex u is called a *minimal point* and its flow potential the *minimal potential* if $p(u) \leq p(v)$ holds for all vertices v. It is clear intuitively that it is possible to construct a flow g of value $w(g) = p(u)$ by 'pushing' the flow from u forward to t and 'pulling' it back from u to s. This is the main idea of the following Algorithm of Malhotra, Kumar and Mahaswari (1978) for constructing a blocking flow on N.

Algorithm 6.4.6. Let $N = (G, c, s, t)$ be a given layered flow network with layers $V_1, \ldots V_d$, where all capacities are positive.

Procedure BLOCKMKM $(N; g)$

(1) **for** $e \in E$ **do** $g(e) \leftarrow 0$ **od**;
(2) **for** $v \in V$ **do**
(3)   **if** $v = t$ **then** $p^-(v) \leftarrow \infty$ **else** $p^-(v) \leftarrow \sum_{e^- = v} c(e)$ **fi**
(4)   **if** $v = s$ **then** $p^+(v) \leftarrow \infty$ **else** $p^+(v) \leftarrow \sum_{e^+ = v} c(e)$ **fi**
(5) **od**;
(6) **repeat**
(7)   **for** $v \in V$ **do** $p(v) \leftarrow \min \{p^+(v), p^-(v)\}$ **od**;
(8)   choose a minimal point w;
(9)   PUSH$(w, p(w))$;
(10)   PULL$(w, p(w))$;
(11)   **while** there exists v with $p^+(v) = 0$ or $p^-(v) = 0$ **do**
(12)   **for** $e \in \{e \in E : e^- = v\}$ **do**
(13) $u \leftarrow e^+$, $p^+(u) \leftarrow p^+(u) - c(e)$;
(14)   remove e from E
(15)   **od**;
(16)   **for** $e \in \{e \in E : e^+ = v\}$ **do**
(17) $u \leftarrow e^-$, $p^-(u) \leftarrow p^-(u) - c(e)$;
(18)   remove e from E
(19)   **od**;
(20)   remove v from V
(21)   **od**
(22) **until** $s \notin V$ or $t \notin V$.

Here, PUSH is the following procedure for 'pushing' a flow of value $p(w)$ to t:

Procedure PUSH (y, k)

(1) let Q be a queue with single element y;
(2) **for** $u \in V$ **do** $b(u) \leftarrow 0$ **od**;
(3) $b(y) \leftarrow k$;
(4) **repeat**

(5)   remove the first element v from Q;

(6)   **while** $v \neq t$ **and** $b(v) \neq 0$ **do**

(7)   choose an edge $e = vu$;

(8) $m \leftarrow \min \{c(e), b(v)\}$;

(9) $c(e) \leftarrow c(e) - m,\ g(e) \leftarrow g(e) + m$;

(10) $p^+(u) \leftarrow p^+(u) - m,\ b(u) \leftarrow b(u) + m$;

(11) $p^-(v) \leftarrow p^-(v) - m,\ b(v) \leftarrow b(v) - m$;

(12)   append u to Q;

(13)   **if** $c(e) = 0$ **then** remove e from E **fi**

(14)   **od**

(15) **until** $Q = \emptyset$.

The procedure PULL for 'pulling' a flow of value $p(w)$ to s can be defined analogously; we leave the details to the reader.

Theorem 6.4.7. *Algorithm 6.4.6 constructs a blocking flow g on N with complexity $O(|V|^2)$.*

Proof. We show first that an edge e is removed from E only if there is no augmenting path containing e consisting of forward edges only. This is clear if e is removed in step (14) or (18), because, in this case, $p^+(v) = 0$ or $p^-(v) = 0$, respectively, so that no augmenting path containing v and consisting of forward edges can exist (where $e^- = v$ or $e^+ = v$, respectively). If e is removed in step (13) of procedure PUSH (or, analogously, in procedure PULL), we have $c(e) = 0$ at this point, so that, because of step (9), $g(e)$ has reached the original capacity $c(e)$ and this means that e cannot be used any more as a forward edge. As each iteration of BLOCKMKM removes edges and decreases capacities, an edge which cannot be used as a forward edge with respect to g any more (at the point of the algorithm when it is removed) will not be any useful in the later iterations of the algorithm. Thus, at the end of BLOCKMKM (that is, when s or t have been removed), there does not exist any augmenting path consisting of forward edges, so that g is a blocking flow.

We show that g is a flow by using induction on the number of iterations of the **repeat**-loop (6) to (22). Initially, g is the zero flow. Now suppose that g is a flow at a certain point of the algorithm (after the i-th iteration, say). All vertices v which cannot be used any more (that is, vertices into which no flow can enter or from which no flow can emerge any more) are removed during the **while**-loop (11) to (21) and all edges incident with these vertices are removed as well. Thus, during the next iteration (that is, after the flow potentials have been brought up to date in step (7)), the algorithm chooses a vertex w with minimal potential $p(w) \neq 0$ (because, if $p(w) = 0$, w would have been removed before during the **while**-loop). Next, we have to convince ourselves that the procedure PUSH$(w, p(w))$ really generates a flow of value $p(w)$ from w (as the source) to the sink t. As Q is a queue, the vertices u in PUSH are treated as in a BFS on the layers $V_k, V_{k+1}, \ldots, V_d$ (where $w \in V_k$). During the first iteration of the **repeat**-loop of PUSH, we have $v = w$ and $b(v) = p(w)$; here $b(v)$ contains the value of the flow which has to flow out of v. During the **while**-loop, the flow of value $b(v)$ is distributed between the edges vu having tail v. Here, the capacity of an edge vu is always used entirely, except if $b(v) < c(e)$. In step (9), the capacity of vu is reduced (that is, reduced to 0 in most cases, so that vu will be removed in step (13)) and the value of the flow increased accordingly. Then, in step (11), we have to decrease the value $b(v)$ of the flow which still has to emerge from v by some other edge and increase $b(u)$ accordingly (in step (10)). The flow potentials are changed accordingly. Thus, the value of the flow $b(v)$ we need is distributed between the vertices of the next layer. As we chose w to be a vertex of minimal potential, we always have $b(v) \leq p(w) \leq p(v)$, so that it is always possible to distribute the flow. At the end of procedure PUSH, the flow of value $p(w)$ has reached t because $V_d = \{t\}$. It can be shown analogously that the procedure PULL$(w, p(w))$ constructs a flow of value $p(w)$ from the source s to w (and adds this flow to g), but, of course, PULL does this construction in the opposite direction. We leave the details to the reader.

Each iteration of the **repeat**-loop of BLOCKMKM removes at least one vertex (because the flow potential of the minimal vertex w is decreased to 0 during PUSH and PULL), so that the algorithm terminates after at most $|V| - 1$ iterations. We need an estimate for how often each edge is treated. We need $O(|E|)$ steps in (3) and (4) to find the initial values of p^+ and p^-. As an edge e can be removed only once, e can only appear at most once during the **for**-loops (12) to (19) or in step (13) of PUSH or PULL. On the other hand, when PUSH or PULL are executed, for each vertex v, there is at most one edge treated which, after having been treated, still has capacity $\neq 0$ (that is, which has not been removed). As PUSH and PULL are called at most $|V| - 1$ times, we get at most $O(|V|^2)$ steps for treating these edges. As $O(|V|^2)$ is at least as large as $O(|E|)$, the number of operations we need altogether for treating the edges is $O(|V|^2)$. It is easy to see that all other operations of the algorithm need at most $O(|V|^2)$ steps as well, so that BLOCKMKM indeed has complexity $O(|V|^2)$.   □

The algorithm which results from replacing BLOCKFLOW by BLOCKMKM in Algorithm 6.3.17 is called the *MKM-Algorithm*. Using our remarks at the end of Section 6.3, Theorem 6.4.7 implies:

Theorem 6.4.8. *The MKM-Algorithm constructs a maximal flow for a given flow network N with complexity $O(|V|^3)$.*   □

Example 6.4.9. Consider again the layered auxiliary network of Example 6.3.7. Here, the flow potentials are: $p(s) = 31$, $p(a) = 15$, $p(b) = 1$, $p(c) = 32$, $p(d) = 1$, $p(e) = 7$, $p(f) = 24$, $p(t) = 32$. Vertex b is minimal and, after the first iteration, we get the flow g_1 as given in Figure 6.20; vertex b and edges sb and bc have been removed.

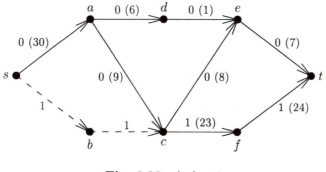

Fig. 6.20 $w(g_1) = 1$

Next, we have flow potentials $p(s) = 30$, $p(a) = 15$, $p(c) = 9$, $p(d) = 1$, $p(e) = 7$, $p(f) = 23$, $p(t) = 31$, so that d is the unique minimal vertex. After the second iteration, we have constructed flow g_2, and d, ad and de have been removed (see Figure 6.21).

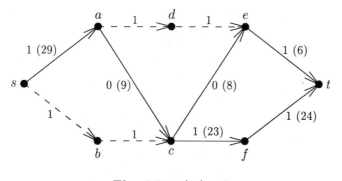

Fig. 6.21 $w(g_2) = 2$

Now $p(s) = 29$, $p(a) = 9$, $p(c) = 9$, $p(e) = 6$, $p(f) = 23$ and $p(t) = 30$. Vertex e is minimal and we get the flow g_3 as shown in Figure 6.22; e, ce and et have been removed.

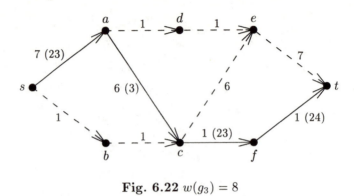

Fig. 6.22 $w(g_3) = 8$

Next, the flow potentials are $p(s) = 23$, $p(a) = 3$, $p(c) = 3$, $p(f) = 23$, $p(t) = 24$. We use the minimal vertex a and construct the flow g_4 which is a blocking flow (see Figure 6.23); all remaining elements of the network have been removed. Note that g_4 differs from the flow we found in Example 6.4.4 ($w(g_4) = 11$).

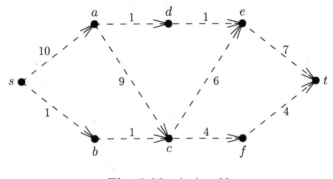

Fig. 6.23 $w(g_4) = 11$

Exercise 6.4.10. Use Algorithm 6.4.6 to find a blocking flow for the layered auxiliary network of Exercise 6.4.5.

We have now seen three different algorithms (which are nowadays considered classical) for constructing maximal flows. For dense graphs (that is, $|E| = O(|V|^2)$), these algorithms have very different complexities. The MKM-Algorithm is, for this case, by far the best one; however, it is also the most complicated one. Further algorithms having complexity $O(|V|^3)$ have been found by Karzanov (1974), Tarjan (1984) and Goldberg and Tarjan (1988); the last of these papers also contains an algorithm of complexity $O(|V||E| \log(|V|^2/|E|))$. We treat the Algorithm of Goldberg and Tarjan in Section 6.6. The approach of Goldberg and Tarjan can also be used to solve the parametrized flow problem (where the capacities of the edges incident with s and t depend monotonously on some real parameter); the complexity will only change by a constant factor, see Gallo, Grigoriades and Tarjan (1989). Cheriyan and Maheshwari (1989) gave a modification of the Algorithm of Goldberg and Tarjan with complexity $O(|V|^2|E|^{\frac{1}{2}})$; we treat this modification in Section 6.6 as well. An algorithm with complexity $O(|V||E| \log |V|)$ is due to Sleator (1980), see also Sleator and Tarjan (1983). In the paper by Ahuja and Orlin (1989), there is an algorithm of complexity $O(|V||E| + |V|^2 \log U)$, where U is the maximum of the capacities $c(e)$ occuring in the problem. Ahuja, Orlin and Tarjan (1989) improved this result a bit further and showed that $\log U$ can be replaced by $(\log U)^{\frac{1}{2}}$ in the above complexity. Cheriyan and Hagerup (1989) proposed a probabilistic algorithm and Alon (1990), King, Rao and Tarjan (1994) and Cheriyan and Hagerup (1995) gave deterministic versions based on this algorithm; for graphs satisfying $|V|(\log |V|)^2 \leq |E| \leq |V|^{\frac{5}{3}} \log |V|$, one obtains a complexity of only $O(|V||E|)$. An algorithm of complexity $O(\frac{|V|^3}{\log |V|})$ can be found in Cheriyan, Hagerup and Mehlhorn (1996). Good surveys over the newer algorithms are the ones by Ahuja, Magnanti and Orlin (1989), Ahuja, Magnanti and Orlin (1991) and Goldberg, Tardos and Tarjan (1990). An extensive monograph on flow theory (and related problems) was written by Ahuja, Magnanti and Orlin (1993). Finally, in a recent paper by Karger (1997), another new idea for solving the max-flow problem was given: Karger proceeds by computing approximately minimal cuts and uses these to compute a maximum flow (thus reversing the usual approach). He shows that his algorithm (which is, however, not of practical interest) has an improved complexity with high probability.

A completely different approach to the problem of finding a maximal flow is to specialize the well-known Simplex Algorithm to flow theory. The algorithm this approach yields is called the 'Network Simplex Algorithm' and is of practical interest; we refer the reader to the books by Chvátal (1983) and Bazaraa, Jarvis and Sherali (1990), and to the papers by Goldfarb and Hao (1990), Goldfarb and Hao (1991) and Goldberg, Grigoriades and Tarjan (1991), where, for the first time, a suitable specification of this method was shown to have polynomial running time.

For planar graphs, it is possible to find a maximal flow with complexity $O(|V|^{\frac{3}{2}} \log |V|)$, see Johnson and Venkatesan (1982). If s and t are in the same area of G, even a complexity of $O(|V| \log |V|)$ is sufficient according to Itai and Shiloach (1979). In the undirected case (that is, in symmetric flow networks, see Section 10.1), the problem can be solved with complexity $O(|V| \log^2 |V|)$, as was shown by Hassin and Johnson (1985). For flow networks on bipartite graphs, fast algorithms can be found in Gusfield, Martel and Fernandez-Baca (1987) and in Ahuja, Orlin, Stein and Tarjan (1994); these algorithms are particularly interesting if one of the two

components of the bipartition is very small compared with the other component. Finally, for comparisons of the efficiency of various flow algorithms, we
refer to Cheung (1980), Galil (1981), Imai (1983), Goldberg and Grigoriades
(1998), Derigs and Meier (1989), Ahuja, Kodialam, Mishra and Orlin (1992)
and the relevant papers in the collection edited by Johnson and McGeoch
(1993).

6.5 Zero-One Flows

In this section, we look at a special case which occurs in many combinatorial
applications of flow theory (these will be treated in the next chapter), namely
integral flows which take the values 0 and 1 only. In that case, the estimates
for the complexity we have obtained so far can be improved; to see this, it is
sufficient to look at the Algorithm of Dinic (1970). We need some terminology.
A *0-1-network* is a flow network $N = (G, c, s, t)$ for which $c(e)$ has values 0
and 1 only. A flow f on a network N is called a *0-1-flow* if f has values 0
and 1 only. The following lemma was proved by Even and Tarjan (1975).

Lemma 6.5.1. *Let $N = (G, c, s, t)$ be a 0-1-network. Then*

$$d(s, t) \leq \frac{2|V|}{\sqrt{M}}, \tag{6.3}$$

*where M is the maximal value of a flow on N. If, in addition, each vertex v
of N except for s and t satisfies at least one of the conditions $d_{in}(v) \leq 1$ or
$d_{out}(v) \leq 1$, then even*

$$d(s, t) \leq 1 + \frac{|V|}{M}. \tag{6.4}$$

Proof. Let D be the maximal distance from s in N and, for $i = 0, \ldots, D$,
let V_i be the set of all vertices $v \in V$ with $d(s, v) = i$. Then, for any $i < d(s, t)$,

$$(S_i, T_i) := (V_0 \cup V_1 \cup \ldots \cup V_i, V_{i+1} \cup \ldots \cup V_D)$$

is a cut. As any edge e with $e^- \in S_i$ and $e^+ \in T_i$ obviously satisfies $e^- \in V_i$
and $e^+ \in V_{i+1}$ and as N is a 0-1-network, Lemma 6.1.2 implies

$$M \leq c(S_i, T_i) \leq |V_i| \cdot |V_{i+1}| \quad \text{for } i = 0, \ldots, d(s, t) - 1.$$

Thus, at least one of the two values $|V_i|$ or $|V_{i+1}|$ has to be at least $\sqrt{M}$, so
that at least half of the layers V_i with $i \leq d(s, t)$ have to contain at least $\sqrt{M}$
vertices. It follows that

$$d(s, t) \frac{\sqrt{M}}{2} \leq |V_0| + \ldots + |V_{d(s,t)}| \leq |V|,$$

and hence (6.3) holds. If N satisfies the additional condition of the lemma, the flow through any vertex obviously can have value at most one, so that we get the stronger inequality

$$M \leq |V_i| \quad \text{for } i = 1, \ldots, d(s,t) - 1.$$

This implies

$$M(d(s,t) - 1) \leq |V_1| + \ldots + |V_{d(s,t)-1}| \leq |V|,$$

which proves (6.4).   □

Using estimates which are a bit more accurate, (6.3) can be improved to $d(s,t) \leq |V|/\sqrt{M}$, but we will not need this improvement for the statements about complexity we want to prove in the following, so that we leave it to the reader as an exercise.

Lemma 6.5.2. *Let $N = (G, c, s, t)$ be a layered 0-1-network. Then the Algorithm of Dinic can be used to determine a blocking flow g on N with complexity $O(|E|)$.*

Proof. It is easy to see that the following modification of Algorithm 6.4.1 finds a blocking flow g for a 0-1-network N.

Procedure BLOCK01FLOW (N, g)

(1) $L \leftarrow \emptyset$;
(2) **for** $v \in V$ **do** $ind(v) \leftarrow 0$ **od**;
(3) **for** $e \in E$ **do** $g(e) \leftarrow 0$; $ind(e^+) \leftarrow ind(e^+) + 1$ **od**;
(4) **repeat**
(5) $v \leftarrow t$;
(6)   **for** $i = d$ **downto** 1 **do**
(7)   choose an edge $e = uv$ and remove e from E;
(8) $ind(v) \leftarrow ind(v) - 1$; $g(e) \leftarrow 1$;
(9)   **if** $ind(v) = 0$
(10)   **then** append v to L;
(11)   **while** $L \neq \emptyset$ **do**
(12)   remove the first vertex v from L;
(13)   **for** $\{e \in E : e^- = v\}$ **do**
(14)   remove e from E; $ind(e^+) \leftarrow ind(e^+) - 1$;
(15)   **if** $ind(e^+) = 0$ **then** append e^+ to L **fi**;
(16)   **od**;
(17)   **od**;
(18)   **fi**;
(19) $v \leftarrow u$;
(20)   **od**;
(21) **until** $ind(t) = 0$.

Obviously, each edge e is treated (and then removed) at most once during the **repeat**-loop in this procedure, so that the complexity of BLOCK01FLOW is $O(|E|)$.   □

Theorem 6.5.3. *Let $N = (G, c, s, t)$ be a 0-1-network. Then the Algorithm of Dinic can be used to compute a maximal 0-1-flow on N with complexity* $O(|V|^{2/3}|E|)$.

Proof. Using Lemma 6.5.2, all we have to show is that the Algorithm of Dinic needs only $O(|V|^{2/3})$ phases for treating a 0-1-network. We denote the maximal value of a flow on N by M. As the value of the flow is increased by at least 1 during each phase of the algorithm, the statement is true for $M \leq |V|^{2/3}$. Now suppose $M > |V|^{2/3}$. Then there is a phase (which is uniquely determined) where the value of the flow is increased to a value larger than $M - |V|^{2/3}$. Let f be the 0-1-flow on N which the algorithm had constructed at the point of time when this phase began; then $w(f) \leq M - |V|^{2/3}$. Hence, $M' = M - w(f) \geq |V|^{\frac{2}{3}}$ for the value M' of a maximal flow on $N'(f)$ (by Theorem 6.3.4). Obviously, N' is a 0-1-network as well, so that the distance $d(s, t)$ from s to t in $N'(f)$ satisfies the inequality

$$d(s, t) \leq \frac{2|V|}{\sqrt{M'}} \leq 2|V|^{2/3}$$

by Lemma 6.5.1. Now we know by Lemma 6.3.11 that the distance between s and t in the corresponding auxiliary network increases in each phase, so that the construction of f could have taken at most $2|V|^{2/3}$ phases. After the phase corresponding to f, we have, by definition of f, that $w(f) > M - |V|^{2/3}$, so that at most $|V|^{2/3}$ phases are necessary to increase the value of the flow step by step until it reaches M. Thus, the number of phases is indeed at most $O(|V|^{2/3})$.   □

Similarly, we get a further improvement of the complexity if the 0-1-network N satisfies the additional condition of Lemma 6.5.1.

Theorem 6.5.4. *Let $N = (G, c, s, t)$ be a 0-1-network. If each vertex $v \neq s, t$ of N satisfies at least one of the conditions $d_{in}(v) \leq 1$ or $d_{out}(v) \leq 1$, then the Algorithm of Dinic can be used to determine a maximal 0-1-flow on N with complexity* $O(|V|^{1/2}|E|)$.

Proof. Using Lemma 6.5.2, it suffices to show that, for 0-1-networks, the Algorithm of Dinic needs at most $O(|V|^{1/2})$ phases. Again, we denote the maximal value of a flow on N by M. We may assume w.l.o.g. that $M > |V|^{1/2}$. Consider the unique phase of the algorithm at the end of which the value of f is larger than $M - |V|^{1/2}$ for the first time. Denote the 0-1-flow on N which the algorithm had constructed when this phase began by f; then $w(f) \leq M - |V|^{1/2}$ and thus $M' = M - w(f) \geq |V|^{1/2}$, where M' is the value of a maximal flow on $N'(f)$ (use Theorem 6.3.4). Obviously, $N'(f)$ is a 0-1-network which likewise satisfies the additional condition of the statement, so that the distance from s to t in $N'(f)$ satisfies the inequality

$$d(s,t) \leq 1 + \frac{|V|}{M'} \leq 1 + |V|^{1/2}$$

by Lemma 6.5.1. As the distance from s to t in the corresponding auxiliary network increases with each phase, the construction of f cannot have taken more than $1 + |V|^{1/2}$ phases. As it cannot take more than $|V|^{1/2}$ additional phases to increase the value of the flow stepwise until it reaches M, the total number of phases can indeed not exceed $O(|V|^{1/2})$.   □

We close this section with a couple of exercises which we will have a closer look at later.

Exercise 6.5.5. A dancing event is attended by m girls and n boys. We want to arrange a dance where as many couples as possible should participate, but only couples who have known each other before are allowed. Formulate this task as a graph theoretical problem.

Exercise 6.5.6. Given a bipartite graph $G = (S \,\dot\cup\, T, E)$, we are looking for a matching (see Exercise 5.1.5) of maximal cardinality on G. Show that this problem is equivalent to finding a maximal 0-1-flow on an appropriate flow network. Moreover, use the algorithms and results of this chapter to design an algorithm for this problem having complexity at most $O(|V|^{5/2})$.

The method for finding a maximal matching given in Exercise 6.5.6 is due basically to Hopcroft and Karp (1973); it was noticed only by Even and Tarjan (1975) that this method actually is a special case of the MAXFLOW-Algorithm. We will meet maximal matchings quite often in this book: the bipartite case will be treated in Section 7.2, the general case will be studied in Chapters 12 and 13.

Exercise 6.5.7. Let $G = (S \,\dot\cup\, T, E)$ be a bipartite graph. Show that the set system $(S, \mathbf{S})$ defined by

$$\mathbf{S} = \{X \subset S : \text{ there exists a matching } M \text{ with } X = \{e^- : e \in M\}\}$$

is a matroid; here e^- means the vertex incident with e which is in S. (Hint: Use the interpretation of a network given in Exercise 6.5.6 for proving condition (3) of Theorem 5.2.1 constructively.) This result is quite interesting, because the set $\mathbf{M}$ of all matchings does not form a matroid on E, see Exercise 5.1.5.

6.6 The Algorithm of Goldberg and Tarjan

This last section of Chapter 6 is devoted to a more recent algorithm for finding maximal flows which is due to Goldberg and Tarjan (1988). The algorithms we have looked at so far construct a maximal flow, starting with the zero flow, by augmenting the flow (either along a single augmenting path or by constructing blocking flows in appropriate auxiliary networks in phases) iteratively. The Algorithm of Goldberg and Tarjan is based on a completely different concept; it uses 'preflows', for which it is allowed that the value of the flow entering a vertex is larger than the flow leaving it. This preflow property is maintained throughout the algorithm; it is only at the very end of the algorithm that the preflow becomes a (maximal) flow. The main idea is to shift flow from vertices with 'excess flow' toward the sink t, if possible, using paths which are not necessarily shortest paths to t, but only momentary estimates for such paths. However, it might occur that excess flow cannot be pushed forward from some vertex v and has to be sent back to the source. We soon make this more precise. Altogether, the algorithm is very intuitive, rather easy to analyze and, without any special tricks, needs a complexity of only $O(|V|^3)$. By using more complicated data structures, it can even be made considerably faster, as remarked already at the end of Section 6.4.

Following Goldberg and Tarjan (1988), we define flows in this section in a formally different (although of course equivalent) way; this notation due to Sleator (1980) will make the presentation of the algorithm a bit easier. First, it is quite convenient to extend the capacity function $c : E \to \mathbb{R}_0^+$ to all of $V \times V$ by defining $c(uv) = 0$ for $(u, v) \notin E$. Now we drop the condition that flows cannot be negative and define a flow $f : V \times V \to \mathbb{R}$ by:

(1) $f(v, w) \leq c(v, w)$ for all $(v, w) \in V \times V$
(2) $f(v, w) = -f(w, v)$ for all $(v, w) \in V \times V$
(3) $\sum_{u \in V} f(u, v) = 0$ for all $v \in V \setminus \{s, t\}$.

The anti-symmetry condition (2) has the effect that it cannot occur that both edges of a pair vw and wv of antiparallel edges[3] of G carry positive flow, a situation we do not need anyway. Moreover, it simplifies the formal description, because we do not have to make a distinction between forward and backward edges anymore. Also, the formulation of the flow conservation condition (3) becomes easier. For an intuitive interpretation, the reader should consider only the non-negative part of the flow function; this part is a flow as defined before (Section 6.1). The reader is asked to convince himself that condition (3) is, because of the antisymmetry of f, equivalent to condition (F2) used before. The definition of the value of a flow is a bit easier now, too:

---

[3] Note that condition (2) also forces G to be *symmetric*: if vw is an edge, wv must also be an edge of G.

$$w(f) := \sum_{v \in V} f(v, t).$$

Next, we define a *preflow* to be a mapping $f : V \times V \to \mathbb{R}$ satisfying conditions (1) and (2) above and the following weaker version of condition (3):

$$(4) \qquad \sum_{u \in V} f(u, v) \geq 0 \qquad \text{for all } v \in V \backslash \{s\}.$$

Using the intuitive interpretation, condition (4) means that, for each vertex $v \neq s$, the flow entering v is at least as large as the flow leaving v. The value

$$e(v) := \sum_{u \in V} f(u, v)$$

is called the *flow excess* in v. The Algorithm of Goldberg and Tarjan (1988) tries to push flow excess from some vertex v with $e(v) > 0$ forward toward t, or, if that is impossible, to let it flow back to s. For this purpose, it uses paths which approximate shortest paths in an auxiliary network (which, however, is not constructed explicitly). The choice of these paths is controlled by a labelling function on the vertex set. We need a description of what usable edges look like (analogous to the auxiliary network used in the classical algorithms). For a given preflow f, we define the *residual capacity* $r_f : V \times V \to \mathbb{R}$ as follows:

$$r_f(v, w) := c(v, w) - f(v, w).$$

If $r_f(v, w) > 0$, we can move some flow through edge vw. In our intuitive interpretation, this means either that this edge vw is not saturated yet (that is, $0 \leq f(v, w) < c(v, w)$) or that wv is a non-void edge (which means $0 < f(w, v) \leq c(w, v)$ and hence $f(v, w) = -f(w, v) < 0 \leq c(v, w)$). Any edge satisfying $r_f(v, w) > 0$ is called a *residual edge*; and the *residual graph*

$$G_f = (V, E_f), \quad \text{where} \quad E_f = \{vw \in E : r_f(v, w) > 0\},$$

corresponding to f does, in fact, take the role of the auxiliary network $N'(f)$ used in the classical algorithms. Now we introduce the labelling function mentioned above. A mapping

$$d : V \to \mathbb{N}_0 \cup \{\infty\}$$

is called a *valid labelling* for a given preflow f if the following two conditions hold:

$$(5) \qquad d(s) = |V|, \quad d(t) = 0$$

$$(6) \qquad d(v) \leq d(w) + 1 \quad \text{for all } vw \in E_f.$$

Now the Algorithm of Goldberg and Tarjan (1988) begins with some suitable preflow and a corresponding valid labelling, for example $d(s) = |V|$, $d(v) = 0$ for all $v \in V \backslash \{s\}$. It executes operations (specified later) for changing the preflow or the labelling d, respectively. However, the labelling always has to remain valid; as mentioned before, it is used to estimate shortest paths in the respective residual graph. More precisely, if $d(v) < |V|$, $d(v)$ is always a lower bound for the distance of v to t in G_f, whereas, for $d(v) > |V|$, t is not accessible from v and $d(v) - |V|$ is a lower bound for the distance from v to s in G_f. As initial values for the preflow we use $f(s,v) = -f(v,s) = c(s,v)$ for all $v \neq s$ and $f(v,w) = 0$ for any $v, w \neq s$. The algorithm terminates if the preflow has become a flow (which is then actually a maximal flow). We need one more notion to be able to write down the algorithm in its general form. A vertex v is called *active* if $v \neq s, t$ and $e(v) > 0$ as well as $d(v) < \infty$ hold.

Algorithm 6.6.1. Let $N = (G, c, s, t)$ be a flow network, where $c : V \times V \to \mathbb{R}_0^+$; that is, for $(v, w) \notin E$ we have $c(v, w) = 0$.

Procedure GOLDBERG $(N; f)$

(1) **for** $(v, w) \in (V \backslash \{s\}) \times (V \backslash \{s\})$ **do** $f(v, w) \leftarrow 0$; $r_f(v, w) \leftarrow c(v, w)$ **od**;
(2) $d(s) \leftarrow |V|$;
(3) **for** $v \in V \backslash \{s\}$ **do**
(4) $f(s, v) \leftarrow c(s, v)$; $r_f(s, v) \leftarrow 0$;
(5) $f(v, s) \leftarrow -c(s, v)$; $r_f(v, s) \leftarrow c(v, s) + c(s, v)$;
(6) $d(v) \leftarrow 0$;
(7) $e(v) \leftarrow c(s, v)$
(8) **od**
(9) **while** there exists an active vertex v **do**
(10)   choose an active vertex v and execute an
           admissible operation for v
(11) **od**.

In (10), one of the following operations may be used:

Procedure PUSH $(N, f, v, w; f)$

(1) $\delta \leftarrow \min(e(v), r_f(v, w))$;
(2) $f(v, w) \leftarrow f(v, w) + \delta$; $f(w, v) \leftarrow f(w, v) - \delta$;
(3) $r_f(v, w) \leftarrow r_f(v, w) - \delta$; $r_f(w, v) \leftarrow r_f(w, v) + \delta$;
(4) $e(v) \leftarrow e(v) - \delta$; $e(w) \leftarrow e(w) + \delta$.

The procedure PUSH is *admissible* if v is active, $r_f(v, w) > 0$ and $d(v) = d(w) + 1$.

Procedure RELABEL $(N, f, v, d; d)$

(1) $d(v) \leftarrow \min \{d(w) + 1 : r_f(v, w) > 0\}$;

The procedure RELABEL is *admissible* if v is active and $r_f(v, w) > 0$ always implies $d(v) \leq d(w)$. [4]

---

[4] The minimum in (1) is defined to be ∞ if there does not exist any w with $r_f(v, w) > 0$. However, we will see that this case cannot occur.

Now we prove a series of lemmas to show finally that Algorithm 6.6.1 constructs, in finitely many steps, a maximal flow on N (in the form given by conditions (1) to (3) at the beginning of this section). It is particularly interesting that the algorithm always works, no matter which active vertices are chosen and which admissible operations are executed in the corresponding **while**-loop. To get good estimates for the complexity, however, we will have to specify appropriate criteria for how those choices are to be made.

We show first that the algorithm is correct under the assumption that it terminates at all. Then we estimate the maximal number of admissible operations executed during the **while**-loop and use this result to show that the algorithm is finite. Our first lemma is a simple but important observation.

Lemma 6.6.2. *Let f be a preflow on N, d a valid labelling on V with respect to f and v an active vertex. Then either a PUSH-operation or a RELABEL-operation is admissible for v.*

Proof. As d is valid, we have $d(v) \leq d(w) + 1$ for all w with $r_f(v, w) > 0$. If PUSH (v, w) is not admissible for any w, we must even have $d(v) \leq d(w)$ for all w with $r_f(v, w) > 0$, as d takes only integer values. But then RELABEL is admissible. □

Lemma 6.6.3. *During the execution of Algorithm 6.6.1, f always is a preflow and d always is a valid labelling (with respect to f).*

Proof. We use induction on the number k of admissible operations already executed. The statement is true for $k = 0$, because f is initialized to be a preflow in steps (1) to (8) and the labelling d defined there is valid for f; this follows from $d(v) = 0$ for $v \neq s$ and the fact that the edges sv have been saturated in step (4). Now suppose the statement holds after k operations have been executed. If the $(k + 1)$-th operation is a PUSH (v, w), f obviously keeps the properties of a preflow; moreover, the labels are not changed. PUSH (v, w) increases the value $f(v, w)$ by $\delta > 0$. If vw is removed from the residual graph G_f, it is obvious that the labelling stays valid. If, on the other hand, wv is added to G_f, d stays valid as well, because PUSH (v, w) was admissible, so that $d(w) = d(v) - 1$ holds. It remains to consider the case that a RELABEL-operation is executed. In this case, RELABEL has to be admissible, so that $d(v) \leq d(w)$ holds for the active vertex v and all vertices w with $r_f(v, w) > 0$. Now $d(v)$ is increased to the minimum of all the $d(w) + 1$, so that the condition $d(v) \leq d(w) + 1$ still holds for all w with $r_f(v, w) > 0$ after this change. All other labels remain unchanged, so that the new labelling d is still valid for f. □

Lemma 6.6.4. *Let f be a preflow on N and d any arbitrary valid (with respect to f) labelling on V. Then t is not accessible from s in the residual graph G_f.*

Proof. Suppose there exists a path

$$W \quad : \quad s = v_0 \text{ --- } v_1 \text{ --- } \ldots \text{ --- } v_m = t$$

in G_f. As d is a valid labelling, we have $d(v_i) \leq d(v_{i+1})+1$ for $i = 0, \ldots, m-1$. It follows that $d(s) \leq d(t)+m < |V|$, because $d(t) = 0$ and the path can have length at most $|V| - 1$. But then d cannot be admissible because $d(s) \neq |V|$. $\quad\square$

Theorem 6.6.5. *If Algorithm 6.6.1 terminates and all labels are finite at the end of the algorithm, then the preflow f constructed is in fact a maximal flow on N.*

Proof. Lemma 6.6.2 implies that the algorithm can terminate only if there are no more active vertices. As all labels are finite, this means that $e(v) = 0$ holds for each vertex $v \neq s, t$. Thus, the preflow constructed in the last step is indeed a flow on N. By Lemma 6.6.4, there is no path from s to t in G_f. But this implies that there is no augmenting path from s to t with respect to f. Thus, the statement follows from Theorem 6.1.3. $\quad\square$

It remains to show that the algorithm terminates and that the labels stay finite. We need two more lemmas.

Lemma 6.6.6. *Let f be a preflow on N. If v is a vertex with positive flow excess $e(v)$, then s is accessible from v in G_f.*

Proof. Denote the set of vertices accessible from v in G_f by S and put $T := V \backslash S$. By definition of S, we have $f(u,w) \leq 0$ for all vertices u, w with $u \in T$ and $w \in S$, because

$$0 = r_f(w,u) = c(w,u) - f(w,u) \geq 0 + f(u,w).$$

Using the antisymmetry of f, we get

$$\sum_{w \in S} e(w) \quad = \quad \sum_{u \in V, w \in S} f(u,w)$$

$$= \quad \sum_{u \in T, w \in S} f(u,w) + \sum_{u,w \in S} f(u,w)$$

$$= \quad \sum_{u \in T, w \in S} f(u,w) \leq 0.$$

By definition of a preflow, we must have $e(w) \geq 0$ for all $w \neq s$. As $e(v) > 0$, the above inequality can hold only if $s \in S$. $\quad\square$

Lemma 6.6.7. *During the execution of Algorithm 6.6.1, we always have $d(v) \leq 2|V| - 1$ for any vertex v.*

Proof. It is clear that the statement holds after the initialization in steps
(1) to (8). The label $d(v)$ of a vertex is changed only during an operation
RELABEL(v) and this operation is admissible only if v is active. In particular,
this means that $v \neq s, t$, so that the statement is trivial for s and t. Moreover,
we must have $e(v) > 0$. Then, by Lemma 6.6.6, there exists a path

$$W \quad : \quad v = v_0 \text{\textemdash} v_1 \text{\textemdash} \ldots \text{\textemdash} v_m = s$$

in the residual graph G_f. As d is a valid labelling, $d(v_i) \leq d(v_{i+1}) + 1$ holds
for $i = 0, \ldots, m - 1$. As W can have length at most $|V| - 1$, it follows that

$$d(v) = d(v_0) \leq d(s) + m \leq d(s) + |V| - 1 = 2|V| - 1. \qquad \square$$

Lemma 6.6.8. *During the execution of Algorithm 6.6.1, at most $2|V| - 1$
RELABEL-operations occur for any given vertex $v \neq s, t$, so that the total
number of RELABEL-operations is at most $(2|V| - 1)(|V| - 2) < 2|V|^2$.*

Proof. Each RELABEL(v)-operation increases $d(v)$. As, by Lemma 6.6.7, $d(v)$
is bounded by $2|V| - 1$ during the whole execution of Algorithm 6.6.1, the
statement follows. $\qquad \square$

To estimate the number of PUSH-operations, we have to distinguish two
cases. A call of PUSH(v, w) is called a *saturating PUSH* if, after the operation,
$r_f(v, w) = 0$ holds (that is, $\delta = r_f(v, w)$ in step (1) of the PUSH) and a *non-
saturating PUSH* otherwise.

Lemma 6.6.9. *During the execution of Algorithm 6.6.1, at most $2|V||E|$
saturating PUSH-operations occur.*

Proof. If a saturating PUSH(v, w) is executed, we must have either $vw \in E$
or $wv \in E$, because otherwise, neither of these two edges could be contained in G_f. Moreover, the condition $d(v) = d(w) + 1$ must be satisfied. After a saturating PUSH(v, w), another PUSH(v, w) can only be executed if a PUSH(w, v) has occurred in between (because, after a saturating
PUSH(v, w), $r_f(v, w) = 0$ holds). But this is possible only if $d(w) = d(v) + 1$
was satisfied at some point in between, so that $d(w)$ must have been increased
by at least 2 before the PUSH(w, v). For the next PUSH(v, w) to be admissible, $d(v)$ must have been increased by at least two, if the PUSH(w, v) was
saturating. On the other hand, $d(v) + d(w) \geq 1$ holds as soon as the first PUSH
from v to w or from w to v is executed. Moreover, $d(v), d(w) \leq 2|V| - 1$ holds
at the end of the algorithm, so that, when the last PUSH-operation involving
v and w is executed, we must have $d(v) + d(w) \leq 4|V| - 3$. Thus, for any edge
$vw \in E$, there can be at most $2|V| - 1$ saturating PUSH-operations between
v and w; this means that the total number of saturating PUSH-operations
cannot exceed $(2|V| - 1)|E|$. $\qquad \square$

Lemma 6.6.10. *During the execution of Algorithm 6.6.1, there are at most* $4|V|^2|E|$ *nonsaturating PUSH-operations.*

Proof. Consider the function

$$\Phi := \sum_{v \text{ active}} d(v)$$

and look at the values it takes during the execution of Algorithm 6.6.1. (Such a function is usually called a *potential.*) First, after the initialization, $\Phi = 0$ and at the end of the algorithm, $\Phi = 0$ again. Any nonsaturating PUSH(v, w) decreases Φ by at least one, because then $r_f(v, w) > e(v)$, so that v becomes inactive, whereas the vertex w which might have become active by the PUSH must satisfy $d(w) = d(v) - 1$ (because the PUSH must have been admissible). Any saturating PUSH(v, w) increases Φ by at most $2|V| - 1$, because the vertex w which might have become active by this PUSH-operation must satisfy $d(w) \le 2|V| - 1$ by Lemma 6.6.7. During the whole algorithm, the saturating PUSH-operations can increase Φ by at most $2(2|V| - 1)|V||E|$, by Lemma 6.6.9 and the RELABEL-operations can increase Φ by at most $(2|V| - 1)(|V| - 2)$ by Lemma 6.6.7. As the value by which Φ is increased during the whole algorithm must be the same as the value by which it is decreased again, we get the upper bound

$$(2|V| - 1)(2|V||E| + |V| - 2) \le 4|V|^2|E|$$

for the total number of nonsaturating PUSH-operations. Note that G is connected, so that $|E| \ge |V| - 1$.   □

Theorem 6.6.11. *Algorithm 6.6.1 terminates after at most* $O(|V|^2|E|)$ *admissible operations.*

Proof. This follows immediately from the preceding lemmas.   □

The precise amount of time Algorithm 6.6.1 needs depends on how the admissible operations are implemented and in which order they are applied in the **while**-loop. In any case, the running time will be polynomial. We treat two variants which allow estimates of the complexity which are particularly good. The two variants differ only in the way an active vertex v is chosen; both use the obvious strategy not to change v unneccessarily, but to keep v until either $e(v) = 0$ or all edges incident with v have already been used for a PUSH(v, w) (as far as this is possible) and a RELABEL(v) has been executed afterwards. To do this, we need to keep adjacency lists A_v; moreover, for each vertex v, there always is a distinguished *current edge*. Initially, this edge is always the first edge of A_v; we assume A_v to have a fixed order. The active vertices are kept in a queue Q. As preflows are asymmetric, we may view G as being undirected; for each edge $e = \{v, w\} \in E$, there are capacities $c(v, w)$

and $c(w, v)$ assigned to e. In the following algorithm, the active vertices are chosen according to the rule 'first in first out', which explains the name of the algorithm.

Algorithm 6.6.12 (FIFO Preflow Push Algorithm). Let $N = (G, c, s, t)$ be a flow network, where G is a graph given by adjacency lists A_v. Moreover, Q is a queue and rel a Boolean variable.

Procedure FIFOFLOW $(N; f)$

(1) **for** $(v, w) \in (V \backslash \{s\}) \times (V \backslash \{s\})$ **do** $f(v, w) \leftarrow 0$; $r_f(v, w) \leftarrow c(v, w)$ **od**;
(2) $d(s) \leftarrow |V|$; $Q \leftarrow \emptyset$;
(3) **for** $v \in V \backslash \{s\}$ **do**
(4) $f(s, v) \leftarrow c(s, v)$; $r_f(s, v) \leftarrow 0$;
(5) $f(v, s) \leftarrow -c(s, v)$; $r_f(v, s) \leftarrow c(v, s) + c(s, v)$;
(6) $d(v) \leftarrow 0$;
(7) $e(v) \leftarrow c(s, v)$
(8)   **if** $e(v) > 0$ **and** $v \neq t$ **then** append v to Q **fi**
(9) **od**
(10) **while** $Q \neq \emptyset$ **do**
(11)   remove the first vertex v from Q;
(12)   select the first edge in A_v as the current edge;
(13)   rel $\leftarrow$ false;
(14)   **repeat**
(15)   let vw be the current edge in A_v;
(16)   **if** $r_f(v, w) > 0$ **and** $d(v) = d(w) + 1$
(17)   **then** PUSH $(N, f, v, w; f)$;
(18)   **if** $w \notin Q$ **and** $w \neq s, t$ **then** append w to Q **fi**
(19)   **fi**
(20)   **if** $e(v) > 0$ **then**
(21)   **if** vw is not the last edge in A_v
(22)   **then** choose the next edge in A_v as current edge
(23)   **else** RELABEL $(N, f, v, d; d)$; rel $\leftarrow$ true;
(24)   **fi**
(25)   **fi**
(26)   **until** $e(v) = 0$ **or** rel = true;
(27)   **if** $e(v) > 0$ **then** append v to Q **fi**
(28) **od**.

It is easy to see that Algorithm 6.6.12 is indeed a special case of Algorithm 6.6.1. Thus, the algorithm terminates after a finite number of steps with a maximal flow on N. The following theorem due to Goldberg and Tarjan (1988) gives its complexity.

Theorem 6.6.13. *Algorithm 6.6.12 determines a maximal flow on N with complexity $O(|V|^3)$.*

Proof. Obviously, the initialization in steps (1) to (9) has complexity $O(|E|)$. In each RELABEL(v)-operation, the edges contained in the adjacency list A_v are examined once; here, any vertex v can occur at most $(2|V| - 1)$ times by Lemma 6.6.8. Thus, the adjacency list A_v of v is examined at most $(4|V| - 1)$ times during the whole algorithm: once during each of the $2|V| - 1$ RELABEL-operations, once before each relabeling (at the time when the current edge runs through A_v and the possible PUSH-operations from v are executed) and once after the last relabeling. Each PUSH-operation needs only $O(1)$ steps. Thus, we get a total complexity of $O(|V||A_v|)$ plus O(number of PUSH(v,w)) operations for the operations concerning vertex v. By summing over all vertices, we get a complexity of $O(|V||E|)$ plus O(number of all PUSH-operations). In view of Lemma 6.6.9, it remains to improve the bound of $O(|V|^2|E|)$ for the number of nonsaturating PUSH-operations given in Lemma 6.6.10 to $O(|V|^3)$.

For this purpose, we divide the execution of the algorithm into phases (which, in the original literature, are called 'passes over Q' which is a bit misleading): phase 1 consists of the execution of the **repeat**-loop for those vertices which were originally appended to Q, that is, when Q was initialized in step (8). If phase i is defined, phase $i + 1$ consists of the execution of the **repeat**-loop for those vertices which were appended to Q during phase i. The **repeat**-loop is terminated for v as soon as a nonsaturating PUSH(v,w) is executed (see step (26)). During each phase, at most $O(|V|)$ vertices v are removed from Q, so that there are at most $O(|V|)$ nonsaturating PUSH-operations during each phase. Thus, all we have to show is that there can be at most $O(|V|^2)$ phases.

We define a potential Φ, similar to what we did in the proof of Lemma 6.6.10, which depends on how far the algorithm has been executed. Let Φ be the maximal value of all labels $d(v)$ of all active vertices v. Consider how Φ changes during some phase. If there are no RELABEL-operations during this phase, then, for each active vertex v, flow excess is moved to vertices w which have a smaller label. Thus, Φ has to decrease during such a phase. On the other hand, if Φ remains unchanged or increases during a phase, at least one label must have been increased. By Lemma 6.6.7, $d(v)$ can be increased to at most $2|V| - 1$ for any vertex $v \neq s, t$. Thus, the total increase of Φ during the execution of the whole algorithm can be at most $O(|V|^2)$. By Lemma 6.6.8, there can also be at most $O(|V|^2)$ RELABEL-operations. As $\Phi = 0$ holds at the beginning as well as at the end of the algorithm, there can be at most $O(|V|^2)$ phases.   □

Examples which show that the FIFO-algorithm might indeed need $O(|V|^3)$ steps were constructed by Cheriyan and Maheshwari (1989). The second variant of Algorithm 6.6.1 which we present now always chooses an active vertex which has the maximal label of all the active vertices. For implementation, we use a priority queue with priority function d instead of an ordinary queue Q. This variant was suggested by Goldberg and Tarjan (1988) as well.

Algorithm 6.6.14 (Highest Label Preflow Push Algorithm). Let $N = (G, c, s, t)$ be a given flow network, where G is a graph given by adjacency lists A_v. Moreover, let Q be a priority queue with priority function d and rel a Boolean variable.

Procedure HLFLOW $(N; f)$

(1) **for** $(v, w) \in (V\backslash\{s\}) \times (V\backslash\{s\})$ **do** $f(v, w) \leftarrow 0$; $r_f(v, w) \leftarrow c(v, w)$ **od**;
(2) $d(s) \leftarrow |V|$; $Q \leftarrow \emptyset$;
(3) **for** $v \in V\backslash\{s\}$ **do**
(4) $f(s, v) \leftarrow c(s, v)$; $r_f(s, v) \leftarrow 0$;
(5) $f(v, s) \leftarrow -c(s, v)$; $r_f(v, s) \leftarrow c(v, s) + c(s, v)$;
(6) $d(v) \leftarrow 0$;
(7) $e(v) \leftarrow c(s, v)$
(8)   **if** $e(v) > 0$ **and** $v \neq t$ **then** insert v into Q with priority $d(v)$ **fi**;
(9) **od**
(10) **while** $Q \neq \emptyset$ **do**
(11)   remove a vertex v of highest priority $d(v)$ from Q;
(12)   select the first edge in A_v as the current edge;
(13)   rel $\leftarrow$ false;
(14)   **repeat**
(15)   let vw be the current edge in A_v;
(16)   **if** $r_f(v, w) > 0$ **and** $d(v) = d(w) + 1$ **then**
(17)   PUSH $(N, f, v, w; f)$;
(18)   **if** $w \notin Q$ **and** $w \neq s, t$ **then** insert w into Q
                    with priority $d(w)$ **fi**
(19)   **fi**
(20)   **if** $e(v) > 0$ **then**
(21)   **if** vw is not the last edge in A_v
(22)   **then** choose the next edge in A_v as current edge;
(23)   **else** RELABEL $(N, f, v, d; d)$; rel $\leftarrow$ true
(24)   **fi**
(25)   **fi**
(26)   **until** $e(v) = 0$ **or** rel = true;
(27)   **if** $e(v) > 0$ **then** insert v into Q with priority $d(v)$ **fi**;
(28) **od**.

The complexity of this algorithm was given as $O(|V|^3)$ by Goldberg and Tarjan (1988); their estimate was improved by Cheriyan and Maheshwari (1989) as follows.

Theorem 6.6.15. *Algorithm 6.6.14 determines a maximal flow on N with complexity $O(|V|^2 |E|^{\frac{1}{2}})$.*

Proof.[5] Similar to the proof of Theorem 6.6.13, the main problem is to find a bound for the number of nonsaturating PUSH-operations; all other estimates can be done analogously. Note that $O(|V||E|)$ (that is, the bound for the saturating PUSH-operations) is dominated by $O(|V|^2|E|^{\frac{1}{2}})$. As in the proof of Theorem 6.6.13, we divide the algorithm into phases, but this time, a phase consists of all operations executed between two consecutive RELABEL-operations. The *length* l_i of the i-th phase is defined as the difference between d_{max} at the beginning and at the end of the phase, where d_{max} denotes the maximal label $d(v)$ of all active vertices v. (Note that d_{max} decreases monotonously during a phase; immediately after the end of the phase, when a RELABEL-operation is executed, d_{max} increases again.) First, we claim that the sum of the lengths l_i of all phases is at most $O(|V|^2)$. To see this, it is sufficient to show that the increase of d_{max} during the whole algorithm may be at most $O(|V|^2)$. But this follows immediately from Lemma 6.6.7, because, for each vertex v, the label $d(v)$ increases monotonously and is bounded by $2|V| - 1$.

The basic idea of the proof is to partition the nonsaturating PUSH-operations in some clever way. We call a nonsaturating PUSH(u, v)-operation *special* (in the original paper, it is called 'non-zeroing') if it is the first PUSH-operation on edge uv after a RELABEL(u)-operation. Now consider a non-saturating, non-special PUSH-operation PUSH(z, w). We try to construct (in reverse order) a directed path T_w with end vertex w which consists entirely of edges for which the last nonsaturating PUSH-operation executed was a non-special one. Suppose we have reached a vertex $u \neq w$ and the last edge we constructed for T_w is uv. This means that the last PUSH(u, v) was a non-saturating, non-special PUSH. Before this PUSH-operation was executed, we had $e(u) > 0$. Consider the last PUSH-operation PUSH(y, u) executed before this PUSH(u, v). If there is no such PUSH-operation, the construction of T_w is terminated. (This case occurs if and only if the whole flow excess in u comes directly from s, that is, if it was assigned to u during initialization.) If this PUSH(y, u) was saturating or special, we terminate the construction of T_w at vertex u as well; otherwise we substitute u by y and continue analogously. It is easy to see that T_w is indeed a path: no cycle can occur during the construction, because the PUSH-operations move flow only towards vertices which have lower labels, so that, for a cycle to arise, there must have been a RELABEL for one of the vertices used. But this is not possible by our way of construction. We call the sequence of nonsaturating PUSH-operations corresponding to such a path T_w a *trajectory* with *originating edge* xy, where xy is the last edge encountered during the construction of T_w for which a saturating or a special PUSH has been executed. Note that this edge is not a part of T_w. In the exceptional case mentioned above, the originating edge of T_w is the edge su.

---

[5] The proof of Theorem 6.6.15 is comparatively involved and may be skipped at first reading.

We want to show that all non-special nonsaturating PUSH-operations can be partitioned into such trajectories. We even prove a somewhat stronger statement (which we need later): Two trajectories containing PUSH-operations on edges which are current simultaneously cannot have any vertices (except the end vertices) in common. We may assume w.l.o.g. that the two trajectories correspond to paths T_w and $T_{w'}$, for which (at a certain point of the algorithm) both $e(w) > 0$ and $e(w') > 0$ hold. Let xy and $x'y'$, respectively, be the originating edges of the two trajectories. Suppose u is a common vertex contained in both trajectories, where $u \neq y, y', w, w'$. We may also choose u to be the last such vertex. Let uv and uv' be the edges occuring in T_w and $T_{w'}$, respectively. Now suppose that $\mathrm{PUSH}(u, v)$ was executed before $\mathrm{PUSH}(u, v')$ (note that $v \neq v'$ by the choice of u). Then $\mathrm{PUSH}(u, v')$ can only have been executed after some flow excess was moved to u again by some $\mathrm{PUSH}(z, u)$-operation. But then, the condition $d(z) = d(u) + 1$ must have been satisfied, which means that there must have been a $\mathrm{RELABEL}(z)$-operation executed before (note that the active vertex is always a vertex having a maximal label and u was already active before z). Thus, the $\mathrm{PUSH}(z, u)$-operation was a special PUSH and the construction of $T_{w'}$ should have been terminated at vertex u with originating edge zu, contradicting the choice of u. It follows that two trajectories containing PUSH-operations on edges which are current simultaneously cannot have any vertices in common (except the end vertices). It is now clear that any two trajectories are always disjoint.

Let us call a trajectory *short* if it consists of at most K operations; here, K is a parameter whose value we will fix later in an optimal way. As the originating edge of any trajectory comes from a saturating or a special PUSH-operation (or, in the exceptional case, from the initialization of the preflow), the number of short trajectories is bounded by $O(|V||E|)$: By Lemma 6.6.9, there are at most $O(|V||E|)$ saturating PUSH-operations; moreover, there can be at most $O(|V||E|)$ special PUSH-operations, because there are at most $O(|V|)$ RELABEL-operations per vertex by Lemma 6.6.8 (and a $\mathrm{PUSH}(u, v)$ can only be special (by definition) if it was the first PUSH on uv after a $\mathrm{RELABEL}(u)$). Thus, all the short trajectories together may contain up to $O(K|V||E|)$ nonsaturating PUSH-operations.

Now we have to examine the *long* trajectories, that is, those trajectories containing more than K operations. As any two trajectories containing PUSH-operations on edges which are current simultaneously cannot contain any common vertices (except the end vertices), there are, at any point of the algorithm, at most $\frac{|V|}{K}$ long trajectories which contain a PUSH-operation current at this point. In particular, for any phase of the algorithm, there are at most $\frac{|V|}{K}$ long trajectories meeting this phase. By definition, there are no RELABEL-operations during any phase and $\mathrm{PUSH}(u, v)$ can only be executed for $d(u) = d(v) + 1$, so that, in a phase of length l_i, there can be only l_i nonsaturating PUSH-operations for each trajectory. Recall that l_i is the difference between the values of d_{max} at the beginning and at the end of phase i; thus, if PUSH-operations have been executed on a path of length c during phase i, the maximal label must have been decreased by c at least. As the sum of all lengths l_i – see above – is $O(|V|^2)$, all the long trajectories together may contain at most $O(|V|^3/K)$ nonsaturating PUSH-operations.

Thus, altogether, the algorithm needs at most $O(K|V||E|) + O(|V|^3/K)$ nonsaturating PUSH-operations. Now we get the optimal bound on the complexity by 'balancing' these two terms, that is, by choosing K in such a way that $K|V||E| = |V|^3/K$. Thus, $K = |V||E|^{-\frac{1}{2}}$, which yields the complexity given in the statement of the theorem. $\qquad\square$

Balancing techniques as in the proof above are a popular and very useful tool when analyzing the complexity of algorithms. Cheriyan and Maheshwari (1989) have shown as well that the bound in Theorem 6.6.15 is best possible: There exist families of networks for which Algorithm 6.6.14 indeed needs $O(|V|^2|E|^{\frac{1}{2}})$ steps. From the practical point of view, Algorithm 6.6.14 is at the moment probably the best known method for determining maximal flows; see the empirical studies mentioned at the end of Section 6.4.

Example 6.6.16. We apply Algorithm 6.6.14 to the flow network of Figure 6.2 (see Example 6.2.3). Where a choice has to be made, we use alphabetical order as usual. We always show several operations summarized in one figure, namely at least one RELABEL-operation together with the PUSH-operations following it (that is, one phase); sometimes we even put two or three shorter phases together. This makes the illustration somewhat shorter. We do not draw pairs of antiparallel edges and put in those edges only whose flow is non-negative (as explained at the beginning of this section); this makes the figures simpler and easier to understand. Moreover, we give the capacities only in the first figure (after initialization) in parentheses. Thus, the numbers in the following figures always give the values as they are after the last operation executed. The number written on some edge e is the value $f(e)$ of the current preflow f; a (new) value coming from a saturating PUSH-operation is framed, whereas other new values (coming from a nonsaturating PUSH-operation) have a circle. Moreover, the vertices v are labelled with the pair $(d(v), e(v))$, that is, the valid label and the flow excess in v are given. For the vertices s and t, only the (unchanging) valid label is given; these vertices are never active by definition. With each figure, we also list the RELABEL- and nonsaturating PUSH-operations executed and the queue Q containing the active vertices (as it is after all those operations have been executed). Note that the maximal flow constructed by HLFLOW given in Figure 6.31 differs from the maximal flow of Figure 6.12: the edge ct does not carry any flow and the value of the flow on the edges cf and ft is larger accordingly.

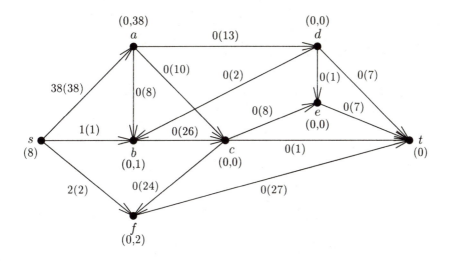

Fig. 6.24 Initialization: $Q = (a, b, f)$

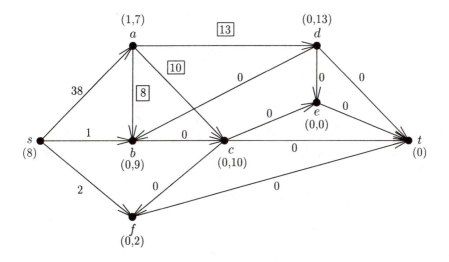

Fig. 6.25 RELABEL(a), $Q = (a, b, c, d, f)$

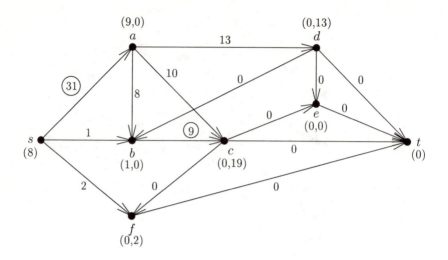

Fig. 6.26 RELABEL(a), PUSH(a, s), RELABEL(b), PUSH(b, c),
$$Q = (c, d, f)$$

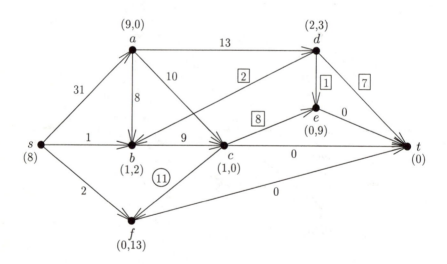

Fig. 6.27 RELABEL(c), PUSH(c, f), RELABEL(d), RELABEL(d),
$$Q = (d, b, e, f)$$

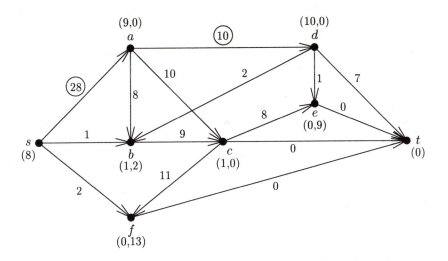

Fig. 6.28 RELABEL(d), PUSH(d,a), PUSH(a,s), $Q = (b,e,f)$

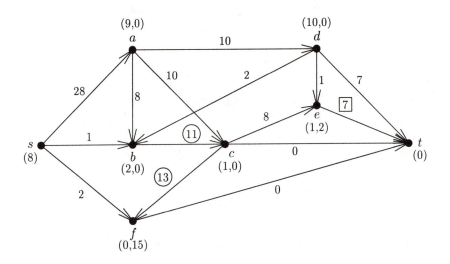

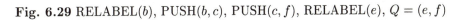

Fig. 6.29 RELABEL(b), PUSH(b,c), PUSH(c,f), RELABEL(e), $Q = (e,f)$

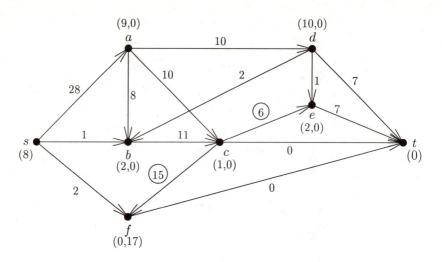

Fig. 6.30 RELABEL(e), PUSH(e,c), PUSH(c,f), $Q = (f)$

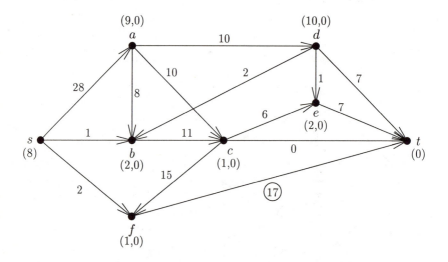

Fig. 6.31 RELABEL(f), PUSH(f,t), $Q = \emptyset$

Exercise 6.6.17. Apply Algorithm 6.6.12 to the flow network of Figure 6.2 (where a choice has to be made, always use alphabetical order) and compare the number of RELABEL- and PUSH-operations necessary with the corresponding numbers for Algorithm 6.6.14 of Example 6.6.16.

For a discussion of the implementation of PUSH- and RELABEL-algorithms, see Cherkassky and Goldberg (1995).

7. Applications in Combinatorics

In this chapter, we use the theorems of Ford and Fulkerson about maximal flows to prove some central theorems of Combinatorics. In particular, Transversal Theory can be developed from the theory of flows on networks; this approach was first suggested in the book by Ford and Fulkerson (1962) and is also used in the survey by Jungnickel (1986). Compared with the usual approach of taking the Marriage Theorem of Hall (1935) – which we treat in Section 7.3 – as the starting point of Transversal Theory (as in the book by Mirsky (1971b)), our way of proceeding has the advantage that we get algorithms for constructing the respective objects simultaneously, for example by specializing the Algorithm of Dinic (1970) in an appropriate way. We will study disjoint paths in graphs, matchings in bipartite graphs, transversals, combinatorics of matrices, partitions of directed graphs, partially ordered sets, parallelisms and the Supply-Demand-Theorem.

7.1 Disjoint Paths: The Theorem of Menger

The theorems treated in this section may be considered as variations of one of the most popular results of Graph Theory, namely of the Theorem of Menger (1927). All these theorems deal with the number of disjoint paths joining two vertices of a graph or a directed graph, respectively. There are two possible definitions of what 'disjoint' means here. Let G be a given (directed) graph and s and t two vertices of G. Then a set of (directed) paths in G with start vertex s and end vertex t is called *arc disjoint* or *vertex disjoint*, respectively, if no two of these paths have an edge or a vertex $v \neq s, t$, respectively, in common. A subset A of E is called an *arc separator* for s and t if any (directed) path from s to t must contain some edge from A. A subset X of $V \setminus \{s, t\}$ is called a *vertex separator* for s and t if any (directed) path from s to t meets X in some vertex. The following theorem, although quite similar to the original Theorem of Menger (1927), was published much later by Ford and Fulkerson (1956) and Elias, Feinstein and Shannon (1956).

Theorem 7.1.1. *Let G be a (directed) graph and s and t two vertices of G. Then the maximal number of (directed) edge disjoint paths from s to t is equal to the minimal cardinality of an edge separator for s and t.*

Proof. Let G be a directed graph and denote the network on G where each edge has capacity $c(e) = 1$ by N. If t is not accessible from s, the statement is trivial. So suppose that t is accessible from s. Obviously, any k arc disjoint directed paths from s to t yield a flow f of value k by defining $f(e) = 1$ if e occurs in one of the paths and $f(e) = 0$ otherwise. Conversely, as the proof of Theorem 6.1.5 shows, we can construct a maximal flow (of integral value k', where $k' \geq k$) on N beginning with the zero flow by using k' augmenting paths of capacity 1. However, these paths are not necessarily directed, as backward edges are allowed. We claim that, in this case, it is always possible to find k' augmenting paths without backward edges as well. So suppose $e = uv$ is a backward edge occuring in the path W; then there has to exist a path W' which was constructed before W and which contained e as a forward edge. Thus, the paths W and W' have to form

$$ W = s \xrightarrow{\quad W_1 \quad} v \xrightarrow{\quad e \quad} u \xrightarrow{\quad W_2 \quad} t $$

and

$$ W' = s \xrightarrow{\quad W_1' \quad} u \xrightarrow{\quad e \quad} v \xrightarrow{\quad W_2' \quad} t. $$

Then we may substitute the paths W and W' by the paths $W_1 W_2'$ and $W_1' W_2$ and thus eliminate edge e. We may assume that e is the backward edge which occurred first, then W_1, W_2' and W_1' contain forward edges only (whereas W_2 might still contain backward edges, of course). Repeating this construction as often as needed, we obtain k' augmenting paths consisting of forward edges only; these paths are directed paths from s to t in G. Any two augmenting paths consisting of forward edges have to be arc disjoint (because of their capacity), so that $k' \leq k$ and hence $k = k'$.

Thus, we have shown that the maximal number of arc disjoint paths from s to t in G is equal to the maximal value of a flow on N and hence, by Theorem 6.1.6, to the capacity of a minimal cut in N. It remains to show that the minimal cardinality of an edge separator for s and t is equal to the capacity of a minimal cut in N. Obviously, any cut (S, T) in N yields an edge separator $A = \{e : e^- \in S, e^+ \in T\}$ of cardinality $c(S, T)$. Conversely, let A be a given minimal arc separator for s and t. Denote the set of those vertices v which are accessible from s by a directed path containing no edges of A by S_A and let $T_A = V \backslash S_A$. Then (S_A, T_A) is a cut in N. Looking at the definition of the sets S_A and T_A, it is clear that any edge e with $e^- \in S_A$ and $e^+ \in T_A$ has to be contained in A. As A is minimal, A consists of exactly these edges and is therefore induced by a cut. This proves the theorem for the directed case.

Now let G be a graph. We reduce this case to the directed case treated above by considering the complete orientation $\overrightarrow{G}$ of G. Obviously, a system of arc disjoint paths in G induces a corresponding system of arc disjoint directed paths in $\overrightarrow{G}$. The converse is true as well if the arc disjoint directed paths in $\overrightarrow{G}$ do not contain any pair of antiparallel edges. But such a pair of edges can be eliminated similar to the elimination of backward edges in the first part of the proof. Now let k be the maximal number of arc disjoint directed paths in G and hence also in $\overrightarrow{G}$. Then there exists an arc separator $\overrightarrow{A}$ in $\overrightarrow{G}$ of cardinality k; the corresponding set of edges in G is an arc separator for s and t in G of cardinality $\leq k$. But the minimal cardinality of an arc separator for s and t trivially has to be at least as large as the maximal number of disjoint paths from s to t, proving the assertion. □

The proof of Theorem 7.1.1 shows that we can use the Algorithm of Dinic to construct a maximal 0-1-flow (of value k, say) and then find k arc disjoint paths from s to t. The algorithm has to be modified for this task so that it immediately eliminates a backward edge whenever such an edge occurs. The reader should provide such a modification and convince himself that this does not increase the complexity of the algorithm. We get the following result.

Corollary 7.1.2. *Let G be a (directed) graph and s and t two vertices of G. Then the maximal number of (directed) arc disjoint paths from s to t (and a system of such paths) can be determined with complexity $O(|V|^{2/3}|E|)$.*

Proof. Use Theorems 7.1.1 and 6.5.3. □

The following result can be proved using methods similar to those used in the proof of Theorem 7.1.1.

Exercise 7.1.3. Show that it is possible, for any flow network, to construct a maximal flow using augmenting paths consisting of forward edges only. Apply this result to the flow network of Example 6.2.3.

We turn to vertex disjoint paths now. The result analogous to Theorem 7.1.1 is the following well-known Theorem of Menger (1927).

Theorem 7.1.4. *Let G be a (directed) graph and s and t any two non-adjacent vertices of G. Then the maximal number of vertex disjoint paths from s to t is equal to the minimal cardinality of a vertex separator for s and t.*

Proof. We reduce the statement to Theorem 7.1.1. Let G be a directed graph; the undirected case can be treated analogously. We define a directed graph G' as follows: The vertices of G' are s, t, and, for any vertex $v \neq s, t$ of G, two vertices v' and v''. For any edge sv or vt in G, G' contains an edge sv' or $v''t$, respectively, and for any edge uv (where $u, v \neq s, t$) in G, G' contains an edge $u''v'$. Finally, G' also contains all the edges of the form $v'v''$ (for any vertex $v \neq s, t$ of G). It is easy to see that vertex disjoint paths in G correspond to arc disjoint paths in G'. By Theorem 7.1.1, the maximal number of vertex disjoint paths from s to t in G is equal to the minimal cardinality of an arc separator for s and t in G'. Such a set of edges could, of course, contain edges not of the form $v'v''$ (which correspond to the vertices in G). But, if some edge $u''v'$ occurs in an arc separator, it can be substituted by $u'u''$ and the new set of edges will still be an arc separator. Thus, we may restrict our considerations to arc separators in G' which contain edges of the form $v'v''$ only; these arc separators in G' correspond immediately to the vertex separators in G. □

Corollary 7.1.5. *Let G be a (directed) graph and s and t two non-adjacent vertices of G. Then the maximal number of vertex disjoint (directed) paths from s to t (and a system of such paths) can be determined with complexity $O(|V|^{1/2}|E|)$.*

Proof. We may assume w.l.o.g. that any vertex of G is accessible from s. Then the directed graph G' constructed in the proof of Theorem 7.1.4 still has $O(|V|)$ vertices and $O(|E|)$ edges. The statement follows using similar arguments as in the proof of Corollary 7.1.2 and the fact that the network defined on G' (having capacity 1 for all edges) satisfies the condition of Theorem 6.5.4. □

The existence of disjoint paths plays an important role for questions of network reliability: If there are k disjoint paths from s to t, the connection between s and t can still be maintained even if $k - 1$ edges (or $k - 1$ vertices, respectively) fail. Such considerations are important for computer networks, for example[1]. Therefore, it suggests itself to measure the strenghth of connectivity of a connected graph by the number of vertex disjoint paths between any two given vertices. The Theorem of Menger leads to the following definition of the *connectivity $\kappa(G)$* of a graph $G = (V, E)$. If G is a complete graph K_n, then $\kappa(G) = n - 1$; otherwise

$$\kappa(G) = \min \{|T| : T \subset V \text{ and } G\backslash T \text{ is not connected}\}.$$

G is called *k-connected* if $\kappa(G) \geq k$. We return to questions of connectivity in Chapter 11, and only mention three exercises here.

Exercise 7.1.6 (Whitney (1932a)). Show that a graph G is k-connected if and only if any two vertices of G are connected by at least k vertex disjoint paths. (Hint: Note that the Theorem of Menger only applies to non-adjacent vertices s and t.)

Exercise 7.1.7. Show that a planar graph can be at most 5-connected. (Hint: Look at Exercise 1.5.13.) Moreover, find a 4-connected planar graph on six vertices, show that a 5-connected planar graph has at least 12 vertices and give an example on 12 vertices.

---

[1] For more on network reliability, we recommend the book by Colbourn (1987).

Exercise 7.1.8. Let S and T be two disjoint subsets of the vertex set V of a graph $G = (V, E)$. Show that the minimal cardinality of a vertex separator X for S and T (that is, any path from some vertex in S to some vertex in T has to contain some vertex in X) is equal to the maximal number of paths from S to T such that no two of these paths have any vertex in common (not even one of the end vertices!).

7.2 Matchings: The Theorem of König

Recall that a *matching* in a graph G is a set M of edges no two of which have a vertex in common. In this section, we consider matchings in bipartite graphs only and postpone the general case until Chapter 12. The following result was already proved in Exercise 6.5.6.

Theorem 7.2.1. *Let G be a bipartite graph. Then a matching of maximal cardinality in G can be determined with complexity $O(|V|^{\frac{1}{2}})$.*   □

Unfortunately, it has become common usage to call a matching of maximal cardinality a *maximal matching*. This is unfortunate insofar as the term 'maximal' suggests that a such matching cannot be extended to a matching of larger cardinality; however, this property does not imply that the matching has maximal cardinality, as the example in Figure 7.1 shows.

Exercise 7.2.2. Let G be any arbitrary (not necessarily bipartite) graph. Suppose the cardinality of a maximal matching in G is k. Find a lower bound for the number of edges of a matching which cannot be extended.

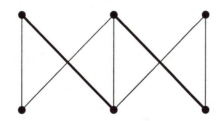

Fig. 7.1 A matching which cannot be extended

Theorem 7.2.1 is a special case of Corollary 7.1.5. To see this, let $G = (S \mathbin{\dot\cup} T, E)$ be the given bipartite graph. We define a new graph H which has, in addition to the vertices of G, two new vertices s and t and whose edges are the edges of G plus all edges sx for $x \in S$ and yt for $y \in T$. Obviously, the edges of a matching K in G correspond to vertex disjoint paths from s to t in H (associating the path $s \text{———} x \text{———} y \text{———} t$ to edge

xy in G, where $x \in S$ and $y \in T$). Of course, for determining a maximal matching in practice, we should not use Corollary 7.1.5 (and the graphs used there) but work with H itself as described in the solution of Exercise 6.5.6.

Now we apply Theorem 7.1.4 to the graph H defined above and consider what this means for G. We have seen already that vertex disjoint paths in H correspond to matchings in G. A vertex separator for s and t in H just is a set X of vertices in G such that each edge of G has at least one of its end vertices in X, that is, X is a vertex cover for G. This yields the following result due to König (1931) and Egerváry (1931).

Theorem 7.2.3. *The maximal cardinality of a matching in a bipartite graph G is equal to the minimal cardinality of a vertex cover for G.*   □

Theorem 7.2.3 is often stated in the language of matrices, see Theorem 7.4.1. Obviously, the maximal cardinality of a matching in a bipartite graph $G = (S \mathbin{\dot{\cup}} T, E)$ is bounded by $\min\{|S|, |T|\}$. A matching of this cardinality is called a *complete matching*. The following Theorem of Hall (1935) characterizes the bipartite graphs which have a complete matching. This theorem is likewise often stated in another language, see Theorem 7.3.1.

Theorem 7.2.4. *Let $G = (S \mathbin{\dot{\cup}} T, E)$ be a bipartite graph with $|S| \geq |T|$. For $J \subset T$, let $\Gamma(J)$ be the set of all vertices $s \in S$ such that there exists an edge st with $t \in J$. Then G has a complete matching if and only if the following condition is satisfied:*

$$(H) \qquad |\Gamma(J)| \geq |J| \qquad \text{for all } J \subset T.$$

Proof. Condition (H) is necessary: Let M be a complete matching of G and J a subset of T. Let $E(J)$ be the set of edges contained in M which are incident with a vertex in J. Then the end vertices of the edges in $E(J)$ which are contained in S form a subset of cardinality $|J|$ of $\Gamma(J)$. Conversely, suppose that condition (H) is satisfied and that the maximal cardinality of a matching in G is less than $|T|$. Then, by Theorem 7.2.3, there exists a vertex cover $X = S' \cup T'$ with $S' \subset S$ and $T' \subset T$ such that $|S'| + |T'| < |T|$. But then the end vertices u of those edges uv for which v is one of the $|T| - |T'|$ vertices in $T \backslash T'$ are all contained in S', so that

$$|\Gamma(T \backslash T')| \leq |S'| < |T| - |T'| = |T \backslash T'|,$$

a contradiction.   □

For $|S| = |T|$, a complete matching is precisely a 1-factor of G; in this case, we also talk of a *perfect matching*. An important consequence of Theorem 7.2.4 is the following sufficient condition for the existence of a perfect matching. We need one more definition: A *regular bipartite graph* is a bipartite graph $G = (S \mathbin{\dot{\cup}} T, E)$ such that all vertices have the same degree $\neq 0$. Note that this implies in particular that $|S| = |T|$.

Corollary 7.2.5. *Let $G = (S \cup T, E)$ be a regular bipartite graph. Then G has a perfect matching.*

Proof. By Theorem 7.2.4, it is sufficient to show that G satisfies condition (H). Let r be the degree of the vertices of G. If J is a k-subset of T, there are exactly kr edges of the form st with $t \in J$ and $s \in S$. As any vertex of S is incident with exactly r edges, these kr edges have to be incident with at least k distinct vertices in S. □

Corollary 7.2.6. *A bipartite graph G has a 1-factorization if and only if it is regular.*

Proof. It is obvious that the regularity of G is necessary. Corollary 7.2.5 implies that this condition is sufficient as well. □

Exercise 7.2.7. Show that an r-regular graph in general does not have a 1-factorization, even if it has an even number of vertices.

The following – somewhat surprising – application of Corollary 7.2.6 is due to Petersen (1891).

Theorem 7.2.8. *Any $2k$-regular graph (where $k \neq 0$) has a 2-factorization.*

Proof. Let G be a $2k$-regular graph and assume w.l.o.g. that G is connected. By Theorem 1.3.1, G contains an Euler tour C. Let H be an orientation of G such that C is a directed Euler tour for H. Now we define a regular bipartite graph G' as follows: For any vertex v of H, let G' have two vertices v' and v'' and for any edge uv of H, let G' contain an edge $u'v''$. Then each vertex of G' has degree k. By Corollary 7.2.6, G' has a 1-factorization. It is easy to see that each 1-factor of G' corresponds to a 2-factor of G, so that we get a 2-factorization for G. □

We close this section with some exercises concerning factorizations:

Exercise 7.2.9. Let G be a graph on $3n$ vertices. A 2-factor of G is called a *triangle factor* or a $\triangle$-*factor* if it is the disjoint union of n circles of length 3. Show that the graph K_{6n} can be decomposed into one $\triangle$-factor and $6n - 3$ 1-factors. (Hint: View the vertex set as the union of three sets R, S, T of cardinality $2n$ and consider regular bipartite graphs on any two of these sets. Furthermore, use Exercise 1.1.2.)

$\triangle$-factors are used in Finite Geometry; for example, Exercise 7.2.9 is used by Jungnickel and Lenz (1987) for constructing certain 'linear spaces'. The general problem of decomposing K_{6n} into c $\triangle$-factors and d 1-factors was studied by Rees (1987). It is always possible to decompose K_{6n} into a 1-factor and $3n - 1$ $\triangle$-factors yielding a so-called 'near-Kirkman triple system'; see Baker and Wilson (1977) and Huang, Mendelsohn and Rosa (1982).

The most popular problem in this context is the case of 'Kirkman triple systems', which are decompositions of K_{6n+3} into $\triangle$-factors. The name comes from a famous problem in recreational mathematics, namely 'Kirkman's School Girl Problem' which was posed by Kirkman (1850): 'Fifteen young ladies in a school walk out three abreast for seven days in succession; it is required to arrange them daily, so that no two will walk twice abreast.' If we represent the school girls by 15 vertices and join two of them by an edge if they walk abreast, then a daily arrangement corresponds to a $\triangle$-factor of K_{15}; the seven $\triangle$-factors for the seven days then form a decomposition into $\triangle$-factors. A solution of this problem is given in Figure 7.2, where only one $\triangle$-factor is drawn. The other $\triangle$-factors of the decomposition are obtained by rotating the given factor around vertex ∞ such that the set $\{p_0, \ldots, p_6\}$ is left invariant; there are seven possibilities to do so (including the identity mapping). The general problem of decomposing the graph K_{6n+3} into $\triangle$-factors was only solved 120 years later by Ray-Chaudhuri and Wilson (1971); see also Beth, Jungnickel and Lenz (1998), §IX.6.

Exercise 7.2.10. Decompose the graph K_9 into $\triangle$-factors. (Hint: There is no 'cyclic' decomposition as in Figure 7.2.)

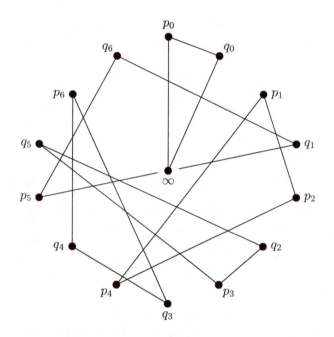

Fig. 7.2 Kirkman's school girl problem

Exercise 7.2.11. Decompose the graph K_{6n-2} into 3-factors. (Hint: Use Theorem 7.2.8.)

Readers interested in seeing more results on 1-factorizations and graph decompositions in general should consult the monographs by Bosák (1990) and Wallis (1997).

7.3 Partial Transversals: The Marriage Theorem

This section presents the basic theory of transversals. We begin with some definitions: Let $\mathbf{A} = (A_1, \ldots, A_n)$ be a family of subsets of a (finite) set S. Then any family $(a_1, \ldots, a_n)$ with $a_j \in A_j$ for $j = 1, \ldots, n$ is called a *system of representatives* for $\mathbf{A}$. If, moreover, $a_i \neq a_j$ holds for any $i \neq j$, then $(a_1, \ldots, a_n)$ is called a *system of distinct representatives*, short SDR, for $\mathbf{A}$; the underlying set $\{a_1, \ldots, a_n\}$ is then called a *transversal* of $\mathbf{A}$.[2] Let us construct a bipartite graph G with vertex set $S \cup T$, where $T = \{1, \ldots, n\}$, which has an edge st whenever $s \in A_t$. Then, for $J \subset T$, the set $\Gamma(J)$ defined in Theorem 7.2.4 is the union of all sets A_t with $t \in J$. As a perfect matching of G then is the same as an SDR for $\mathbf{A}$, Theorem 7.2.4 yields immediately:

Theorem 7.3.1 (Marriage Theorem). *Let $\mathbf{A} = (A_1, \ldots, A_n)$ be a family of subsets of a finite set S. Then $\mathbf{A}$ has a transversal if and only if the following condition is satisfied:*

$$(H') \qquad |\bigcup_{j \in J} A_j| \geq |J| \quad \text{for all} \quad J \subset \{1, \ldots, n\}.$$

$\square$

This theorem was proved by Hall (1935) using the language of set families, which is, of course, equivalent to the terminology used for bipartite graphs. The name *Marriage Theorem* is due to the following interpretation of the theorem: Let S be a set of girls and view the index set T as a set of boys; any set A_t is the set of girls which boy t would be willing to marry. Then the Marriage Theorem gives a necessary and sufficient condition for when it is possible to arrange marriages such that each boy marries some girl of his choice. Of course, the roles of boys and girls can be exchanged. For more symmetry, it is also possible to assume that $|S| = |T|$ and put only those girls in A_t which are actually prepared to accept a proposal from boy t. Then the marriage theorem becomes a statement about the possibility that all boys

---

[2] For an intuitive interpretation, we might think of the A_i as certain groups of people who each send a representative a_i into a committee. Then the SDR property means that no committee member is allowed to represent more than one group and the transversal $\{a_1, \ldots, a_n\}$ just is the committee. Another interpretation is given below.

and girls get a partner of their choice. Thus condition (H') can be put into everyday language as follows: If nobody is too fastidious in his/her choice, there is someone for everybody!

The Marriage Theorem is often considered to be the root of Transversal Theory, which then appears as a sequence of specializations and applications of this theorem. In particular, the Theorems of König, Menger and Ford and Fulkerson can be derived from the Marriage Theorem. The book by Mirsky (1971b) uses this approach. We give two exercises pointing in that direction.

Exercise 7.3.2. Give a direct proof for Theorem 7.3.1 using induction on n. (Hint: Use a case distinction depending on the existence of a *critical subfamily* of $\mathbf{A}$, that is, a subfamily $(A_j)_{j \in J}$ with $|\bigcup_{j \in J} A_j| = |J|$.)

Exercise 7.3.3. Derive Theorem 7.2.3 from Theorem 7.3.1.

We use the Marriage Theorem to prove some further results from Transversal Theory. We need some definitions. An SDR for a subfamily $(A_j)_{j \in J}$ of $\mathbf{A} = (A_1, \ldots, A_n)$ is called a *partial SDR* for $\mathbf{A}$; the underlying set $\{a_j : j \in J\}$ is called a *partial transversal* of $\mathbf{A}$. The Marriage Theorem only distinguishes between families of sets having a transversal and those not having one. A finer measure for how 'representable' a family of sets is is the *transversal index* $t(\mathbf{A})$, that is, the maximal cardinality of a partial transversal of $\mathbf{A}$. The *deficiency* of a partial transversal of cardinality k is the number $n - k$; hence, the transversal index is n minus the minimal deficiency of a partial transversal. The following condition for the existence of a partial transversal with a given deficiency due to Ore (1955) can be derived easily from the Marriage Theorem.

Theorem 7.3.4 (Deficiency Version of the Marriage Theorem). *Let* $\mathbf{A} = (A_1, \ldots, A_n)$ *be a family of subsets of a finite set* S. *Then* $\mathbf{A}$ *has a partial transversal of cardinality* k *(that is, with deficiency $n - k$) if and only if*

$$\left| \bigcup_{j \in J} A_j \right| \geq |J| + k - n \quad \text{for all} \quad J \subset \{1, \ldots, n\}. \tag{7.1}$$

Proof. Let D be an arbitrary set disjoint to S and having cardinality $d = n - k$. Define a family $\mathbf{A}' = (A'_1, \ldots, A'_n)$ of subsets of $S \cup D$ by putting $A'_i := A_i \cup D$. By Theorem 7.3.1, $\mathbf{A}'$ has a transversal if and only if condition (H) holds for $\mathbf{A}'$, that is, if and only if (7.1) holds for $\mathbf{A}$. Now any transversal of $\mathbf{A}'$ yields, by omitting the elements of D it contains, a partial transversal for $\mathbf{A}$ of cardinality at least k. Conversely, any partial transversal of cardinality k of $\mathbf{A}$ can be extended to a transversal of $\mathbf{A}'$ by adding the elements of D. $\square$

Corollary 7.3.5. *The minimal deficiency of a partial transversal of* **A** *is*

$$d(\mathbf{A}) = \ max\ \{|J| - |\bigcup_{j \in J} A_j| : J \subset \{1, \ldots, n\}\}$$

and the transversal index is $t(\mathbf{A}) = n - d(\mathbf{A})$.   □

Exercise 7.3.6. Translate Corollary 7.3.5 into the language of bipartite graphs.

Theorem 7.3.7. *Let* $\mathbf{A} = (A_1, \ldots, A_n)$ *be a family of subsets of a finite set* S. *Then a subset* X *of* S *is a partial transversal of* **A** *if and only if the following condition holds:*

$$|\bigcup_{j \in J} A_j \cap X| \geq |J| + |X| - n \quad for\ all\quad J \subset \{1, \ldots, n\}. \qquad (7.2)$$

Proof. Obviously, X is a partial transversal of **A** if and only if X is a partial transversal of $\mathbf{A}' := (A_i \cap X)_{i=1,\ldots,n}$, that is, if $\mathbf{A}'$ has a partial transversal of cardinality $|X|$. The statement then follows from Theorem 7.3.4.   □

The partial transversals characterized in the theorem above are the independent sets of a matroid, as was shown by Edmonds and Fulkerson (1965).

Theorem 7.3.8. *Let* $\mathbf{A} = (A_1, \ldots, A_n)$ *be a family of subsets of a finite set* S *and let* **S** *be the set of partial transversals of* **A**. *Then* $(S, \mathbf{S})$ *is a matroid.*

Proof. Consider the bipartite graph G corresponding to **A** defined at the beginning of this section. Then the partial transversals of **A** are precisely the subsets of the form $\{e^- : e \in M\}$ of S, where M is a matching of G. That reduces the statement to Exercise 6.5.7.   □

The matroids described in Theorem 7.3.8 are called *transversal matroids*. Theorems 7.3.8 and 5.2.5 together immediately yield the following result (a constructive proof for this result was given in the solution for Exercise 6.5.7).

Corollary 7.3.9. *Let* **A** *be a family of subsets of a finite set* S. *If* **A** *has a transversal, then any partial transversal of* **A** *can be extended to a transversal.*
□

Corollary 7.3.9 is generally attributed to Hoffman and Kuhn (1956). But Hall (1956) should also be mentioned in this context; he gave the first algorithm for determining an SDR, and this algorithm yields a constructive proof for Corollary 7.3.9. However, the solution for Exercise 6.5.7 given in the appendix yields a simpler proof; the Algorithm of Hall is much harder to understand than the determination of a maximal partial SDR (that is, more precisely, of a maximal matching in the corresponding bipartite graph) using network flows.

A more general version of Theorem 7.3.8 using matchings in arbitrary graphs for constructing matroids was proved by Edmonds and Fulkerson (1965); we present this theorem in Section 12.5. The following exercise can be solved using Theorem 7.3.8.

Exercise 7.3.10. Let $E = A_1 \cup \ldots \cup A_k$ be a partition of a finite set E. Moreover, let $d_1, \ldots, d_k$ be positive integers. Then $(E, \mathbf{S})$ is a matroid, where

$$\mathbf{S} = \{X \subset E : |X \cap A_i| \leq d_i \text{ for } i = 1, \ldots, k\}.$$

The matroids defined in Exercise 7.3.10 are called *partition matroids*. If we choose E to be the edge set of a directed graph G and A_i $(i = 1, \ldots, |V|)$ as the set of all edges with end vertex i, and set $d_1 = \ldots = d_{|V|} = 1$, we get the head-partition matroid of Theorem 5.1.3.

We derive some further results from the Marriage Theorem, beginning with the following strengthening of Corollary 7.3.9 due to Mendelsohn and Dulmage (1958).

Theorem 7.3.11. *Let* $\mathbf{A} = (A_1, \ldots, A_n)$ *be a family of subsets of a finite set* S. *Moreover, let* $\mathbf{A}'$ *be a subfamily of* $\mathbf{A}$ *and* S' *a subset of* S. *Then the following statements are equivalent:*

(1) $\mathbf{A}'$ *has a transversal and* S' *is a partial transversal of* $\mathbf{A}$.
(2) *There exists a subset* S'' *of* S *containing* S' *and a subfamily* $\mathbf{A}''$ *of* $\mathbf{A}$ *containing* $\mathbf{A}'$ *such that* S'' *is a transversal of* $\mathbf{A}''$.

Proof. It is trivial that (1) follows from (2). So suppose that (1) holds. Set $m := |S|$ and assume $\mathbf{A}' = (A_1, \ldots, A_k)$. Let D be an arbitrary set of cardinality n which is disjoint to S. Consider the family $\mathbf{B}$ consisting of the sets

$$A_1, \ldots, A_k, A_{k+1} \cup D, \ldots, A_n \cup D \text{ and } m \text{ times the set } (S \backslash S') \cup D.$$

Now suppose that $\mathbf{B}$ has a transversal. As $\mathbf{B}$ consists of $m + n$ subsets of the set $S \cup D$ having $m + n$ elements, this transversal has to be $S \cup D$ itself. Thus, S is a transversal of a subfamily of $\mathbf{B}$ which contains all the sets $A_1, \ldots, A_k$, some of the sets $A_{k+1} \cup D, \ldots, A_n \cup D$ and some copies of $(S \backslash S') \cup D$. If we delete all those elements representing copies of $(S \backslash S') \cup D$ from S, we get a subset S'' of S containing S' which is a transversal for a subfamily of $\mathbf{A}$ containing $\mathbf{A}'$.

It remains to show that the family $\mathbf{B}$ defined above satisfies condition (H') of the Marriage Theorem. This condition is

$$\left| \left(\bigcup_{j \in J} A_j \right) \cup \left(\bigcup_{j \in K} A_j \cup D \right) \cup \left(\bigcup_{i=1}^{c} (S \backslash S') \cup D \right) \right| \geq |J| + |K| + c \qquad (7.3)$$

for all $J \subset \{1, \ldots, k\}$, $K \subset \{k + 1, \ldots, n\}$ and $c \in \{0, \ldots, m\}$. First consider the case $c = 0$. If $K = \emptyset$, (7.3) follows from condition (H') for $\mathbf{A}'$ which is satisfied by hypothesis (because $\mathbf{A}'$ has a transversal). If $K \neq \emptyset$, the union of sets on the left hand side contains the set D having n elements, so that (7.3) is satisfied because $n \geq |J| + |K|$. Now let $c \neq 0$, say $c = m$. As D and S are disjoint, (7.3) becomes

$$\left| \bigcup_{j \in J} A_j \cup (S \setminus S') \right| \geq |J| + m - n \quad \text{for } J \subset \{1, \dots, n\}. \tag{7.4}$$

But

$$\left| \bigcup_{j \in J} A_j \cup (S \setminus S') \right| = m - |S'| + \left| \left(\bigcup_{j \in J} A_j \right) \cap S' \right|,$$

so that (7.4) is equivalent to

$$\left| \left(\bigcup_{j \in J} A_j \right) \cap S' \right| \geq |J| + |S'| - n.$$

This condition is satisfied by Theorem 7.3.7, because S' is a partial transversal of $\mathbf{A}$ by hypothesis. $\qquad \square$

Now we translate Theorem 7.3.11 into the language of bipartite graphs, because there the symmetry of this result (between subsets of S and subfamilies of $\mathbf{A}$) is more apparent. Let M be a matching in a graph $G = (V, E)$. We say that M *covers* a subset X of V if each vertex of X is incident with some edge of M. Now we get the following result equivalent to 7.3.11.

Corollary 7.3.12. *Let $G = (S \mathbin{\dot\cup} T, E)$ be a bipartite graph, S' a subset of S and T' a subset of T. If there exist two matchings covering S' and T', respectively, then there also exists a matching covering $S' \cup T'$.*

Proof. Apply Theorem 7.3.11 to the family $\mathbf{A} = (A_t)_{t \in T}$ of subsets of S which corresponds to G. $\qquad \square$

An intuitive proof of Corollary 7.3.12 (as well as an interesting interpretation of this result) can be found in Lawler (1976), §5.4.

Exercise 7.3.13. Let $\mathbf{A} = (A_t)_{t \in T}$ be a finite family of subsets of a finite set S. Show that $\mathbf{A}$ induces a matroid on T as well.

The following result due to Hall (1935) is a further application of the Marriage Theorem. It gives a criterion for when two families of sets have a common system of representatives.

Theorem 7.3.14. *Let* $\mathbf{A} = (A_1, \ldots, A_n)$ *and* $\mathbf{B} = (B_1, \ldots, B_n)$ *be two families of subsets of a finite set* S. *Then* $\mathbf{A}$ *and* $\mathbf{B}$ *have a common system of representatives if and only if the following condition holds:*

$$|\{i : B_i \cap (\bigcup_{j \in J} A_j) \neq \emptyset\}| \geq |J| \quad \text{for all } J \subset \{1, \ldots, n\}. \tag{7.5}$$

Proof. $\mathbf{A}$ and $\mathbf{B}$ have a common system of representatives if and only if there is a permutation π of $\{1, \ldots, n\}$ such that $A_i \cap B_{\pi(i)} \neq \emptyset$ (for $i = 1, \ldots, n$). Define the family $\mathbf{C} = (C_1, \ldots, C_n)$ by $C_j := \{i : A_j \cap B_i \neq \emptyset\}$, then the condition above reduces to the existence of a transversal of $\mathbf{C}$. It is now easy to see that condition (H') for $\mathbf{C}$ is equivalent to (7.5), so that the assertion follows from Theorem 7.3.1. □

The following two results due to van der Waerden (1927) and Miller (1910), respectively, are easy consequences of Theorem 7.3.14.

Corollary 7.3.15. *Let* $M = A_1 \dot{\cup} \ldots \dot{\cup} A_n = B_1 \dot{\cup} \ldots \dot{\cup} B_n$ *be two partitions of a finite set* M *into subsets of cardinality* k. *Then* $(A_1, \ldots, A_n)$ *and* $(B_1, \ldots, B_n)$ *have a common transversal.* □

Corollary 7.3.16. *Let* H *be a subgroup of the finite group* G. *Then the families of right and left cosets of* H *in* G, *respectively, have a common system of representatives.* □

Theorems 7.3.4, 7.3.7, 7.3.11 and 7.3.14 could all be proved by applying the Marriage Theorem to some appropriate family of sets. Therefore, the Marriage Theorem is a 'self-strenghtening' result; this was pointed out first by Mirsky (1969a). A further result which can be proved in this way is left to the reader as an exercise; it is due to Halmos and Vaughan (1950).

Exercise 7.3.17 (Harem Theorem). Let $\mathbf{A} = (A_1, \ldots, A_n)$ be a family of subsets of a finite set S and $(p_1, \ldots, p_n)$ a family of positive integers. Show that a family of pairwise disjoint sets

$$(X_1, \ldots, X_n) \text{ with } X_i \subset A_i \quad \text{and} \quad |X_i| = p_i \quad \text{for } i = 1, \ldots, n$$

exists if and only if the following condition holds:

$$|\bigcup_{i \in J} A_i| \geq \sum_{i \in J} p_i \quad \text{for all } J \subset \{1, \ldots, n\}.$$

We close this section with some remarks. Network Flow Theory can be used to prove many further results about (partial) transversals and systems of representatives; we refer to Ford and Fulkerson (1958b) and Ford and Fulkerson (1962). In particular, it is possible to derive a criterion for when two families of sets have a common transversal. However, this result follows more easily from a generalization of the Marriage Theorem for matroids (which is a statement about the existence of transversals which are independent in the matroid) due to Rado (1942). It turns out that the theory of matroids is a natural structural setting for Transversal Theory; we refer to the books by Mirsky (1971b) and Welsh (1976) as well as to the survey by Mirsky (1969b), which is well worth reading, and to Mirsky and Perfect (1967).

7.4 Combinatorics of Matrices

This section treats some combinatorial theorems about matrices. We begin by translating Theorem 7.2.3 into the terminology of matrices. Let $A = (a_{ij})$ ($i = 1, \ldots, m$, $j = 1, \ldots, n$) be a matrix where a certain subset of the *cells* (i, j) is marked as *admissible* (usually, these are those cells (i, j) for which $a_{ij} \neq 0$). A set C of cells is called *independent* if no two cells of C lie in the same *line*, that is, row or column, of A. The *term rank* or *scatter number* $\rho(A)$ is the maximal cardinality of an independent set of admissible cells of A. Corresponding to A, we construct a bipartite graph G with vertex set $S \cup T$, where $S = \{1, \ldots, m\}$ and $T = \{1', \ldots, n'\}$, and where G contains an edge st' if and only if cell (s, t) is admissible. Then the matchings of G correspond to the independent sets of admissible cells of A; moreover, vertex covers of G correspond to those sets of lines of A which contain admissible cells only. Hence Theorem 7.2.3 translates into the following result.

Theorem 7.4.1. *The term rank $\rho(A)$ of a matrix A is equal to the minimal number of lines of A which contain all the admissible cells of A.* $\square$

From now on, we restrict our attention to square matrices. We want to derive a criterion due to Frobenius (1912) which tells us when all terms in the sum representation of the determinant of a matrix are equal to 0. Again, we need some definitions. If A is an $(n \times n)$−matrix, any set of n independent cells is called a *diagonal*. A diagonal is called a *non-zero diagonal* or a *positive diagonal*, respectively, if each of its cells has entry $\neq 0$ or > 0, respectively. The *width* of an $(r \times s)$-matrix is $r + s$. Now we mark the cells having entry $\neq 0$ as admissible and define a bipartite graph G corresponding to A (as we did above). Then a non-zero diagonal of A corresponds to a perfect matching of G. We get the following result equivalent to Theorem 7.2.4.

Lemma 7.4.2. *Let A be a square matrix of order n. Then A has a non-zero diagonal if and only if the non-zero entries of any k columns of A belong to at least k different rows.* $\square$

Theorem 7.4.3. *There is at least one entry 0 in any diagonal of an $(n \times n)$-matrix A if and only if A contains a zero submatrix of width $n + 1$.*

Proof. Lemma 7.4.2 states that any diagonal has some entry 0 if and only if there are k columns of A such that all their non-zero entries are contained in $r < k$ rows. Then these k columns have entry 0 in all the remaining $n - r > n - k$ rows, so that they yield a zero submatrix of width $n - r + k \geq n + 1$. □

Note that the diagonals of A correspond precisely to the terms in the sum representation of the determinant of A, so that Theorem 7.4.3 gives the criterion mentioned above. Next, we consider an important class of matrices which always have a positive diagonal. An $(n \times n)$-matrix having non-negative real entries is called *doubly stochastic* if the sum of all entries in a line is 1 for each line of A. The next three results are due to König (1916).

Lemma 7.4.4. *Any doubly stochastic matrix has a positive diagonal.*

Proof. For doubly stochastic matrices, a positive diagonal is the same as a non-zero diagonal. Thus, we may apply Lemma 7.4.2. Now suppose that all non-zero entries of a given set of k columns belong to $r < k$ rows. Denote the matrix determined by these k columns and r rows by B. Then the sum of all entries of B is $= k$ (when added by columns) as well as $\leq r$ (when added by rows), a contradiction. □

We will see that there is a close relationship between doubly stochastic matrices and *permutation matrices*, that is, square matrices which have exactly one entry 1 in each row and column (and all other entries 0).

Theorem 7.4.5 (Decomposition Theorem). *Let A be an $(n \times n)$-matrix with non-negative real entries such that all line sums are equal to s. Then A is a linear combination of permutation matrices with positive real coefficients.*[3]

Proof. Dividing all entries of A by s yields a doubly stochastic matrix A'. Lemma 7.4.4 states that A' (and hence A) has a positive diagonal D. Let P be the permutation matrix corresponding to D (that is, P has entry 1 in the cells of D) and let c be the minimum of the entries in D. Then $B := A - cP$ is a matrix with non-negative real entries and constant line sums as well. But B has at least one more entry 0 than A, so that the assertion follows using induction. □

Corollary 7.4.6 (Lemma of König). *Let A be a square matrix with entries 0 and 1 such that the sum of the entries in each line is k. Then A is the sum of k permutation matrices.*

Proof. The assertion follows immediately from the proof of Theorem 7.4.5, because in this case we always have $c = 1$. □

---

[3] A strong generalization of Theorem 7.4.5 was proved by Lewandowski, Liu and Liu (1986).

The Lemma of König (which the reader should compare with Corollary 7.2.5) and some generalizations of this result are important tools in Finite Geometry, more precisely for the recursive construction of incidence structures, see for example Jungnickel (1979b). A further immediate consequence of Theorem 7.4.5 is the following classical result due to Birkhoff (1946). Recall that, in a real vector space, the *convex hull* of vectors $x_1, \ldots, x_n$ is the set of all linear combinations $x_1 c_1 + \ldots + x_n c_n$ with non-negative coefficients c_i satisfying $c_1 + \ldots + c_n = 1$.

Theorem 7.4.7. *The convex hull of the permutation matrices in $\mathbb{R}^{(n,n)}$ is the set of doubly stochastic matrices.* $\qquad\Box$

More theorems from Combinatorial Matrix Theory can be found in the books by Mirsky (1971b) and Ford and Fulkerson (1962). We mention the following strengthening of Lemma 7.4.4 due to Marcus and Minc (1965) without proof.

Result 7.4.8. *Any doubly stochastic matrix $A = (a_{ij})$ of order n has a diagonal such that the product of the entries of this diagonal is at least n^{-n}.* $\Box$

Looking at the matrix having all entries $1/n$ shows that the bound of Result 7.4.8 is best possible. Summing the products of the entries of a diagonal D over all diagonals gives the *permanent* per A of A; this function differs from the determinant of A only by the sign of the terms in the sum. It was conjectured by van der Waerden (1926) that even per $A \geq n!/n^n$ holds for any doubly stochastic matrix A (with equality for the matrix having all entries $1/n$). This conjecture was open for more than 50 years and was proved only by Egoritsjev (1981) and Falikman (1981); their result is of some interest for the questions we treat here, because it implies the following result.

Theorem 7.4.9. *Let G be a regular bipartite graph with n vertices of degree k. Then there are at least $\frac{n! k^n}{n^n}$ perfect matchings in G.*

Proof. Let A be the 0-1-matrix corresponding to G (that is, $a_{ij} = 1$ if and only if ij is an edge of G). Then the perfect matchings of G correspond to the positive diagonals of A. As $\frac{1}{k} A$ is a doubly stochastic matrix, we have per$(\frac{1}{k} A) \geq \frac{n!}{n^n}$. Now each diagonal of $\frac{1}{k} A$ has product 0 or $\frac{1}{k^n}$, so that there have to be at least $\frac{n! k^n}{n^n}$ positive diagonals of A. $\qquad\Box$

For a proof of van der Waerden's conjecture, we refer the reader – besides the original papers mentioned above – to Knuth (1981), Hall (1986), Minc (1988) and van Lint and Wilson (1992). The permanent plays an important role for determining the number of SDR's of a family of sets in general (or for determining the number of complete matchings of a bipartite graph, respectively), see Mirsky (1971b), Hall (1986) and Minc (1978). Theorem 7.4.9 and its generalizations (see Exercise 7.4.14) are interesting tools in Finite Geometry as well, compare Jungnickel (1979a), Jungnickel (1979b).

We mention two optimization problems for matrices.

Example 7.4.10 (Bottleneck Assignment Problem). Suppose there is a given $(n \times n)$-matrix $A = (a_{ij})$ with non-negative real entries. We are looking for a diagonal of A such that the minimum of its entries is maximal. A possible interpretation of this abstract problem is as follows. We want to assign workers to jobs at an assembly line; the a_{ij} are a measure for the efficiency of worker i when doing job j. Then the minimum of the entries in a diagonal D is a measure for the efficiency which the assignment of workers to jobs according to D would yield. This problem can be solved using the methods described above as follows: Start with some arbitrary diagonal D whose minimal entry is m, say. Now we choose all cells (i, j) with $a_{ij} > m$ as admissible. Then, obviously, there is some diagonal D' whose minimal entry m' is larger than m if and only if there is an admissible diagonal for A. This can be checked with complexity $O(|V|^{5/2})$ by determining the cardinality of a maximal matching in the corresponding bipartite graph G. Note that the problem will be solved after at most $O(n^2)$ such steps.[4]

The following famous problem can be treated in a similar way; we study it extensively in Chapter 13.

Example 7.4.11 (Assignment Problem). Let A be a given square matrix with non-negative real entries. We look for a diagonal of A for which the sum of its entries is maximal (or minimal). We could interpret this problem again as finding an assignment of workers to jobs or machines (which are, this time, independent of each other), where the entries of A give the value of the goods produced (or the amount of time needed for a given number of goods to be produced).

As we will see in Chapter 13, the Assignment Problem can be solved with complexity $O(n^3)$. The 'Hungarian Algorithm' of Kuhn (1955) which is often used for this task is based on finding maximal matchings in an appropriate bipartite graph. We close this section with some exercises.

Exercise 7.4.12. Translate Corollary 7.4.6 into the terminology of bipartite graphs.

Exercise 7.4.13 (Marcus and Ree (1959)). Let A be a doubly stochastic matrix of order n. Then A has a diagonal whose entries have sum at least 1. (Hint: Use Result 7.4.8 and the inequality between the arithmetic mean and the geometric mean.)

Exercise 7.4.14 (Jungnickel (1979a)). Let A be a 0-1-matrix having row sums tr and column sums $\leq r$. Then A is the sum of r matrices A_i having row

---

[4] This problem was generalized by Gabow and Tarjan (1988), who also gave an algorithm with complexity $O((|V| \log |V|)^{1/2}|E|)$. For our classical special case, this yields a complexity of $O((\log |V|)^{1/2}|V|^{5/2})$.

sums t and column sums ≤ 1. (Hint: Use induction on r by determining an appropriate transversal for the family of sets which, for $i = 1, \ldots, m$, contains t copies of each of the sets $T_i := \{j \in \{1, \ldots, n\} : a_{ij} = 1\}$, where A is an $(m \times n)$-matrix.)

Exercise 7.4.15. Let A be a 0-1-matrix with maximal line sum r. Show that A is the sum of r 0-1-matrices with maximal line sum 1. (Hint: Translate the statement into the language of bipartite graphs and use Corollary 7.3.12 for a proof by induction.)

Exercise 7.4.16 (Farahat and Mirsky (1960)). Show that the subspace of $\mathbb{R}^{(n,n)}$ generated by the permutation matrices has dimension $n^2 - 2n + 2$ (see Theorem 7.4.7).

7.5 Dissections: The Theorem of Dilworth

In this section we deal with decomposition theorems for directed graphs and partially ordered sets, respectively. Again, we begin with a definition: Let G be a (directed) graph. A subset X of the vertex set of G is called *independent* or *stable* if no two vertices of X are connected by an edge. The maximal possible cardinality $\alpha(G)$ of such an independent set of G is called the *independence number* of G. (Note that, analogously, the matchings in a graph are precisely the 'independent' sets of edges; the maximal cardinality of a matching is therefore often denoted by $\alpha'(G)$.)

Obviously, the complement of an independent set of G is a vertex cover of G. Denoting the minimal possible cardinality of a vertex cover of G by $\beta(G)$, the following lemma is clear.

Lemma 7.5.1. *Let $G = (V, E)$ be a (directed) graph. Then*

$$\alpha(G) + \beta(G) = |V|.$$

$\square$

From now on, let G always be a directed graph. A *dissection* of G is a set of directed paths in G such that the sets of vertices on these paths form a partition of the vertex set V of G. We denote the minimal possible number of paths contained in such a dissection by Δ. Then we have the following theorem due to Dilworth (1950).

Theorem 7.5.2. *Let G be a transitive acyclic directed graph. Then the maximal cardinality α of an independent set of vertices of G is equal to the minimal number Δ of paths in a dissection of G.*

Proof. As G is transitive, any directed path can meet any independent set in at most one vertex; this implies $\alpha \leq \Delta$. The converse inequality can be reduced to Theorem 7.2.3, a method of proof introduced by Fulkerson (1956). We substitute each vertex v of G by two vertices v', v'' and construct a bipartite graph H with vertex set $V' \ \dot\cup \ V''$, where H contains an edge $v'w''$ if and only if vw is an edge of G. First, we show that any matching M of cardinality k of H can be used to construct a dissection of G into $n - k$ (where $n = |V|$) paths. So let $\{v_i'w_i'' : i = 1, \ldots, k\}$ be a matching in H. Then $v_1w_1, \ldots, v_kw_k$ are edges of G such that the vertices $v_1, \ldots, v_k$ and the vertices $w_1, \ldots, w_k$ are pairwise distinct. However, $v_i = w_j$ is possible; in this case, we can put the paths v_iw_i and v_jw_j together to form a path $v_j \;—\; w_j = v_i \;—\; w_i$. By continuing in this manner (that is, joining paths having the same start or end vertex), we finally obtain c paths whose vertex sets are pairwise disjoint. Suppose these paths have lengths $x_1, \ldots, x_c$. The remaining $n - ((x_1 + 1) + \ldots + (x_c + 1))$ vertices are then partitioned into (trivial) paths of length 0. Altogether, this yields a dissection of G into $n - (x_1 + \ldots + x_c) = n - k$ paths. In particular, we may choose a maximal matching of H, that is, $k = \alpha'(G)$. By Theorem 7.2.3, we have $\alpha'(H) = \beta(H) \geq \beta(G)$ and, by Lemma 7.5.1, $\alpha(G) = n - \beta(G)$. Thus, G can be dissected into $n - \alpha'(H) \leq \alpha(G)$ paths, so that $\Delta \leq \alpha$ holds. $\square$

Dilworth gave his theorem using the terminology of partially ordered sets. Let $(M, \leq)$ be a partially ordered set and G the corresponding (transitive and acyclic) directed graph, see Example 2.6.1. Then directed paths in G correspond to *chains* in M, that is, to subsets of M which are linearly ordered with respect to $\leq$ (this means that, for any two elements a, b of this subset, either $a \leq b$ or $b \leq a$). The independent sets in G correspond to *antichains* of M; these are subsets of M such that, for any two distinct elements a, b, neither $a \leq b$ nor $b \leq a$ holds. Then Theorem 7.5.2 translates into the following result.

Theorem 7.5.3 (Theorem of Dilworth). *Let $(M, \leq)$ be a partially ordered set. Then the maximal cardinality of an antichain of M is equal to the minimal number of chains into which M can be partitioned.* $\square$

The number described in Theorem 7.5.3 is called the *Dilworth number* of $(M, \leq)$. Before drawing some conclusions from Theorem 7.5.3, we have a closer look at the proof of Theorem 7.5.2. Obviously, the inequality $\Delta \leq \alpha$ carries over to any acyclic directed graph. (Note that the converse inequality does not hold for this more general case, as the example in Figure 7.3 shows.) Gallai and Milgram (1960) showed that the graph does not even have to be acyclic for this inequality to hold; however, there is no proof known for this result which uses the methods of Network Flow Theory (or matchings).

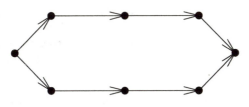

Fig. 7.3 A digraph with $\alpha = 4$ and $\Delta = 2$

We leave the proof of the following result to the reader as a more difficult exercise.

Exercise 7.5.4. Prove the following Theorem of Gallai and Milgram (1960): For any directed graph G, the inequality $\Delta \le \alpha$ holds. (Hint: Look at a minimal counterexample.)

Exercise 7.5.5. Prove the following Theorem of Redéi (1934): Any tournament contains a Hamiltonian path, where a *tournament* is an orientation of K_n. The name can be explained by looking at a kind of competition where there is no draw, as tennis, for example. If each player (or team) plays against any other player (or team) and an edge oriented as ij means that player i won against player j, an orientation of K_n indeed represents the outcome of a tournament.

As announced above, we now consider some consequences of Theorem 7.5.3.

Corollary 7.5.6. *Let $(M, \le)$ be a partially ordered set with at least $rs + 1$ elements. Then M contains a chain of cardinality $r + 1$ or an antichain of cardinality $s + 1$.*

Proof. If M does not contain an antichain of cardinality $s + 1$, then M can be partitioned into s chains by Theorem 7.5.3. At least one of these chains has to contain at least $r + 1$ elements.   □

Corollary 7.5.6 yields a simple proof for the following result originally proved by Erdös and Szekeres (1935).

Theorem 7.5.7. *Any sequence of real numbers of length $n \ge r^2 + 1$ contains a monotonous subsequence of length $r + 1$.*

Proof. Let $(a_i)_{i=1,\ldots,n}$ be the given sequence. Set

$$M = \{(i, a_i) : i = 1, \ldots, n\}$$

and define a partial ordering $\le$ on M by

$$(i, a_i) \le (j, a_j) \quad \Longleftrightarrow \quad i \le j \text{ and } a_i \le a_j.$$

Now suppose that M contains an antichain with $r + 1$ elements and let $i_1 < i_2 < \ldots < i_{r+1}$ be the first coordinates of these elements. Then the corresponding second coordinates form a strictly decreasing subsequence of length $r + 1$. If there is no such antichain, M has to contain a chain of length $r + 1$ by Corollary 7.5.6; here, the second coordinates form an increasing subsequence of length $r + 1$. □

The following well-known result of Sperner (1928) has become the starting-point for various further studies of partially ordered sets (called 'Sperner Theory', see the survey of Greene and Kleitman (1978) as well as Griggs (1988) and the monograph by Engel (1997)). It can also be proved by using the Theorem of Dilworth.

Theorem 7.5.8 (Sperner's Lemma). *Let the power set 2^M of a finite set M be partially ordered with respect to inclusion; then the maximal cardinality of an antichain is $\binom{n}{\lfloor n/2 \rfloor}$, where $n = |M|$.*

Proof. Obviously, the subsets of cardinality $\lfloor n/2 \rfloor$ form an antichain of the above cardinality. To show that there is no antichain having more elements, consider the directed graph G with vertex set 2^M corresponding to $(2^M, \subseteq)$. By Theorem 7.5.2, it suffices to partition G into $\binom{n}{\lfloor n/2 \rfloor}$ directed paths. Now the vertex set of G is partitioned in a natural way into $n + 1$ sets of vertices having the same cardinality. Consider the bipartite graph G_k induced by G on the subsets of M of cardinality k and $k + 1$, respectively. We claim that each of the G_k contains a complete matching. Obviously, we may assume $k + 1 \leq n/2$. Note that any j k-subsets of M are incident with $j(n - k)$ edges in G_k. As each $(k + 1)$-subset is on exactly $k + 1 \leq n/2$ edges in G_k, these $j(n - k)$ edges have to be incident with at least $\frac{j(n-k)}{k+1} \geq j$ distinct $(k + 1)$-subsets. Thus, by Theorem 7.2.4, G_k has a complete matching. Finally, the complete matchings of the bipartite graphs G_k ($k = 0, \ldots, n - 1$) can be 'joined' to form the desired directed paths in G. □

A further interesting application of Theorem 7.5.2 treating distributive lattices was given by Dilworth (1950); for this so-called 'Coding Theorem' of Dilworth we refer to Aigner (1997). We give two more exercises.

Exercise 7.5.9 (Mirsky (1971a)). Let $(M, \leq)$ be a partially ordered set. Show that the maximal cardinality of a chain in M is equal to the minimal number of antichains into which M can be partitioned. (This result is 'dual' to the Theorem of Dilworth, but its proof is much easier than the proof of Theorem 7.5.2. Hint: Consider the set of maximal elements.)

Exercise 7.5.10. Use the Theorem of Dilworth to derive the Marriage Theorem.

We remark that the proof of Theorem 7.5.2 due to Fulkerson (1956) which we gave above is also interesting from an algorithmic point of view, because it allows to calculate the Dilworth number of G by determining a maximal matching in the bipartite graph H (because $\Delta = n - \alpha'(H)$). Thus, Theorem 7.5.2 implies the following result.

Corollary 7.5.11. *Let* $G = (M, E)$ *be a given transitive acyclic directed graph (or a partially ordered set* $(M, \leq)$, *respectively). Then the maximal cardinality of an independent set of vertices in* G *(that is, the minimal number of paths in a dissection of* G *or the Dilworth number of* $(M, \leq)$, *respectively) can be calculated with complexity* $O(|M|^{5/2})$. □

The proof of the Theorem of Gallai and Milgram (1960), on the contrary, is not applicable algorithmically – compare the solution for Exercise 7.5.4. As this theorem is stronger than the Theorem of Dilworth and even admits a relatively easy proof, it would be interesting from the algorithmic point of view to find a proof using the theory of flows or reduce the general case to the special case of acyclic directed graphs. However, there is no such proof known yet.

7.6 Parallelisms: The Theorem of Baranyai

This section treats an application of the Integral Flow Theorem 6.1.5 in Finite Geometry, namely the Theorem of Baranyai (1975) about parallelisms. Let X be a given finite set of cardinality n, say. We denote the set of t-subsets of X by $\binom{X}{t}$. A *parallelism* of $\binom{X}{t}$ is a partition of $\binom{X}{t}$ whose classes are themselves partitions of X; the classes are called *parallel classes*. Such a parallelism satisfies the Euclidean axiom for parallels: For any point $x \in X$ and any t-subset Y of X, there is exactly one t-subset Y' parallel to Y (that is, contained in the same parallel class as Y) such that $x \in Y'$. Obviously, such a parallelism can exist only if t is a divisor of n. It was already conjectured by Sylvester that this condition is sufficient as well. For $t = 3$, the conjecture was proved by Peltesohn (1936); the general case was solved only by Baranyai (1975). His main idea was to use induction on n; however, it is easy to see that this approach requires a statement which is much stronger than Sylvester's conjecture (we explain this later). In fact, Baranyai proved the following result.

Theorem 7.6.1. *Let* X *be a set with* n *elements and* $A = (a_{ij})$ $(i = 1, \ldots, r; j = 1, \ldots, s)$ *a matrix over* $\mathbb{Z}_0^+$. *Moreover, let* $t_1, \ldots, t_r$ *be integers such that* $0 \leq t_i \leq n$ *for* $i = 1, \ldots, r$. *Then there exist subsets* A_{ij} *of the power set* 2^X *of* X *with cardinality* a_{ij} *satisfying the conditions*

(1) for any i, $\{A_{i1}, \ldots, A_{is}\}$ *is a partition of* $\binom{X}{t_i}$,

(2) for any j, $A_{1j} \cup \ldots \cup A_{rj}$ is a partition of X

if and only if A satisfies the conditions

(3) $a_{i1} + \ldots + a_{is} = \binom{n}{t_i}$ for $i = 1, \ldots, r$,
(4) $t_1 a_{1j} + \ldots t_r a_{rj} = n$ for $j = 1, \ldots, s$.

Proof. Trivially, conditions (1) and (2) imply (3) and (4). So suppose conversely that (3) and (4) are satisfied; we have to construct appropriate sets A_{ij}. We do this using induction on n; the induction basis $n = 1$ is trivial. So let $n \neq 1$ and suppose the statement has already been proved for $n-1$. We sketch the idea of the proof first: Suppose we had already found the desired sets A_{ij}. Then, removing some point $x_0 \in X$ from all subsets of X for each i would yield partitions of $\binom{X'}{t_i}$ and $\binom{X'}{t_i-1}$, where $X' := X \setminus \{x_0\}$. Note that x_0 would be removed, for fixed j, from exactly one of the A_{ij}. We want to invert this procedure, which is easier said than done.

We define a network $N = (G, c, q, u)$ as follows: G has vertices q (the source), u (the sink) and $x_1, \ldots, x_r$ and $y_1, \ldots, y_s$. The edges of G are all the qx_i (with capacity $c(qx_i) = \binom{n-1}{t_i-1}$), all the $y_j u$ (with capacity 1) and all the $x_i y_j$ (with capacity 1 or 0 depending on whether $a_{ij} \neq 0$ or $a_{ij} = 0$). Now let f be a flow on N, then f can have value at most $c(y_1 u) + \ldots + c(y_s u) = s$. We show that a (rational) flow having this value exists. Note

$$c(qx_1) + \ldots + c(qx_r) = \binom{n-1}{t_1-1} + \ldots + \binom{n-1}{t_r-1} = s;$$

this follows from

$$\sum_{j=1}^{s} (t_1 a_{1j} + \ldots + t_r a_{rj}) = ns = \sum_{i=1}^{r} t_i \binom{n}{t_i} = n \sum_{i=1}^{r} \binom{n-1}{t_i-1},$$

which in turn is a consequence of (3) and (4). Now we define f by

$$f(qx_i) := \binom{n-1}{t_i-1}, \quad f(y_j u) := 1 \quad \text{and} \quad f(x_i y_j) := \frac{t_i a_{ij}}{n}$$

(for $i = 1, \ldots, r$, $j = 1, \ldots, s$). Condition (4) yields $\frac{t_i a_{ij}}{n} \leq 1 = c(x_i y_j)$ (for $a_{ij} \neq 0$). Moreover, if f is a flow at all, then f obviously has value $w(f) = s$. This means we have to check the validity of condition (F2) for f:

$$\sum_{e^- = x_i} f(e) = \sum_{j=1}^{s} f(x_i y_j) = \sum_{j=1}^{s} \frac{t_i a_{ij}}{n} = \binom{n}{t_i} \frac{t_i}{n} = \binom{n-1}{t_i-1} = f(qx_i)$$

and

$$\sum_{e^+ = y_j} f(e) = \sum_{i=1}^{r} f(x_i y_j) = \sum_{i=1}^{r} \frac{t_i a_{ij}}{n} = 1 = f(y_j u),$$

which follows from (3) and (4), respectively. Thus, f is indeed a maximal flow on N. Now, by Theorem 6.1.5, there also exists a maximal *integral* flow f' on N; this flow obviously has to have the form

$$f'(qx_i) = f(qx_i) = \binom{n-1}{t_i - 1}, f'(y_j u) = f(y_j u) = 1, f'(x_i y_j) =: e_{ij} \in \{0, 1\}$$

(for $i = 1, \ldots, r$, $j = 1, \ldots, s$). Here, the e_{ij} have to satisfy the following conditions (because of (F2)):

$$(5) \quad e_{i1} + \ldots + e_{is} = \binom{n-1}{t_i - 1} \qquad \text{for } i = 1, \ldots, r$$

and

$$(6) \quad e_{1j} + \ldots + e_{rj} = 1 \qquad \text{for } j = 1, \ldots s.$$

Now we define

$$t_i' := \begin{cases} t_i & \text{for } i = 1, \ldots r \\ t_{i-r} - 1 & \text{for } i = r+1, \ldots 2r \end{cases}$$

and

$$a_{ij}' := \begin{cases} a_{ij} - e_{ij} & \text{for } i = 1, \ldots, r \\ e_{i-r, j} & \text{for } i = r+1, \ldots 2r \end{cases}$$

for $j = 1, \ldots s$. The condition $0 \leq t_i' \leq n-1$ holds except if $t_i = n$ or $t_{i-r} = 0$. But these two cases are trivial and may be excluded without loss of generality, because they correspond to partitions of $\{X\}$ and $\{\emptyset\}$. Next, we want to show that the t_i' and the matrix $A' = (a_{ij}')$ satisfy conditions (3) and (4) for $n-1$ instead of n; note $a_{ij}' \geq 0$ for all i, j. This follows from (5) and (6):

$$a_{i1}' + \ldots + a_{is}' = (a_{i1} + \ldots + a_{is}) - (e_{i1} + \ldots + e_{is}) = \binom{n}{t_i} - \binom{n-1}{t_i - 1} = \binom{n-1}{t_i'}$$

(for $i = 1, \ldots r$) and

$$a_{i1}' + \ldots + a_{is}' = e_{i-r,1} + \ldots + e_{i-r,s} = \binom{n-1}{t_{i-r} - 1} = \binom{n-1}{t_i'}$$

(for $i = r+1, \ldots 2r$) as well as

$$\begin{aligned} a_{1j}' t_1' + \ldots + a_{2r,j}' t_{2r}' &= ((a_{1j} - e_{1j})t_1 + \ldots + (a_{rj} - e_{rj})t_r) + \\ &\qquad + (e_{1j}(t_1 - 1) + \ldots + e_{rj}(t_r - 1)) \\ &= (a_{1j}t_1 + \ldots + a_{rj}t_r) - (e_{1j} + \ldots + e_{rj}) = n - 1 \end{aligned}$$

(for $j = 1, \ldots, s$). Thus, by induction hypothesis, there exist subsets A_{ij}' (for $i = 1, \ldots, 2r$ and $j = 1, \ldots, s$) of $2^{X'}$ satisfying conditions analogous to (1) and (2). For any j, exactly one of the sets $A_{r+1,j}', \ldots, A_{2r,j}'$ is non-empty because of (6). Then this subset contains exactly one $(t_i - 1)$-set, say X_j. We define

$$A_{ij} := \begin{cases} A'_{ij} & \text{for } e_{ij} = 0 \\ A'_{ij} \cup \{X_j \cup \{x_0\}\} & \text{for } e_{ij} = 1 \end{cases}$$

(for $i = 1, \ldots, r$, $j = 1, \ldots, s$). It remains to show that these sets A_{ij} satisfy conditions (1) and (2). Trivially, A_{ij} has cardinality a_{ij}. Moreover, for fixed i, $\{A_{i1}, \ldots, A_{is}\}$ is a partition of $\binom{X}{t_i}$: Suppose Y is any arbitrary t_i-subset of X not containing x_0. Then Y occurs in exactly one of the sets A'_{ij}. If Y contains x_0, then $Y' = Y \setminus \{x_0\}$ occurs in exactly one of the sets $A'_{r+1,j}, \ldots, A'_{2r,j}$, say in $A'_{i+r,j}$; then Y occurs in A_{ij}. This proves that (1) holds. Finally, for any j, the set $A'_{1j} \cup \ldots \cup A'_{2r,j}$ is a partition of X'; and as x_0 was added to exactly one of these sets (namely to X_j), condition (2) has to be satisfied as well. □

If we set $r = 1$, $t_1 = t$, $s = \binom{n-1}{t-1}$ and $a_{1j} = \frac{n}{t}$ (for all j) in Theorem 7.6.1, we get the conjecture of Sylvester mentioned at the beginning of this section.

Corollary 7.6.2. *Let X be a set with n elements and t a positive integer. Then $\binom{X}{t}$ has a parallelism if and only if t is a divisor of n.*   □

The proof of Theorem 7.6.1 yields a technique for constructing a parallelism of $\binom{X}{t}$ recursively. However, this technique would not be very efficient because the number of rows of the matrix A doubles with each iteration, so that the complexity is exponential. If $t = 2$, a parallelism is the same as a 1-factorization of the complete graph on X; for this case, an explicit solution was given in Exercise 1.1.2. Beth (1974) gave parallelisms for $t = 3$ and appropriate values of n (using finite fields); see also Beth, Jungnickel and Lenz (1998), §VIII.8. No such series of parallelisms are known for larger values of t. The interesting monograph by Cameron (1976) about parallelisms of complete designs (those are exactly the parallelisms defined here) should be mentioned in this context. Also, we remark that in Finite Geometry, parallelisms are studied for several other kinds of incidence structures, for example in Kirkman's school girl problem (see Section 7.2); we refer the reader to Beth, Jungnickel and Lenz (1998).

7.7 Supply and Demand: The Theorem of Gale and Ryser

In the last section of this chapter, we consider a further application of Network Flow Theory in Optimization, namely the Supply and Demand Problem. Let (G, c) be a network and X and Y disjoint subsets of the vertex set V. The elements x of X are to be sources and the vertices y in Y are interpreted as sinks. With any source x, we associate a *supply* $a(x)$ and with each sink y we associate a *demand* $b(y)$ (thinking of a company producing a product and people who want to buy it). Now we look for a *feasible flow* on (G, c), that is, a mapping $f : E \to \mathbb{R}_0^+$ satisfying the following conditions:

(ZF 1) $0 \leq f(e) \leq c(e)$ for all $e \in E$;

(ZF 2) $\displaystyle\sum_{e^- = x} f(e) - \sum_{e^+ = x} f(e) \leq a(x)$ for all $x \in X$;

(ZF 3) $\displaystyle\sum_{e^+ = y} f(e) - \sum_{e^- = y} f(e) \geq b(y)$ for all $y \in Y$;

(ZF 4) $\displaystyle\sum_{e^+ = v} f(e) = \sum_{e^- = v} f(e)$ for all $v \in V \backslash (X \cup Y)$.

Thus, the amount of flow coming out of a source cannot be larger than the corresponding supply $a(x)$ and the amount of flow going into a sink has to be at least as large as the corresponding demand $b(y)$. For all other vertices (sometimes called *intermediate nodes* or *transshipment nodes*), the amount of flow going into that node has to be the same as the flow coming out of it; this is analogous to condition (F2).

We show how to reduce the existence problem for feasible flows to our usual flows. To this end, we add two new vertices to G, namely the source s and the sink t, and we also add all edges sx (for $x \in X$) with capacity $c(sx) = a(x)$ and all edges yt (for $y \in Y$) with capacity $c(yt) = b(y)$. We get a new network N and it is easy to see that the original problem admits a feasible flow if and only if there exists a flow on N which saturates all edges yt, that is, if the maximal value of a flow on N is equal to the sum w of the demands $b(y)$. Using Theorem 6.1.6, this means that there exists a feasible flow if and only if any cut in N has capacity at least w. As any cut in N has the form $(S \cup \{s\}, T \cup \{t\})$ (where (S, T) is a cut[5] in G), we get the condition

$$c(S \cup \{s\}, T \cup \{t\}) = c(S, T) + \sum_{x \in X \cap T} a(x) + \sum_{y \in Y \cap S} b(y) \geq \sum_{y \in Y} b(y).$$

This proves the following result of Gale (1957).

Theorem 7.7.1 (Supply-Demand-Theorem). *For a given Supply and Demand Problem (G, c, X, Y, a, b), there exists a feasible flow if and only if the following condition is satisfied:*

$$c(S, T) \geq \sum_{y \in Y \cap T} b(y) - \sum_{x \in X \cap T} a(x) \quad \text{for any cut } (S, T). \qquad \Box \qquad (7.6)$$

We use Theorem 7.7.1 to derive necessary and sufficient conditions for the existence of a bipartite graph G with vertex set $V = S \dot\cup T$ and given degree sequences $(p_1, \ldots, p_m)$ for the vertices in S and $(q_1, \ldots, q_n)$ for the vertices in T. We may assume $q_1 \geq q_2 \geq \ldots \geq q_n$ (we will see that this assumption is quite useful). An obvious necessary condition for the existence of such a graph is $p_1 + \ldots + p_m = q_1 + \ldots + q_n$; however, this condition is not sufficient.

---

[5] In contrast to our former definition, $S = \emptyset$ or $T = \emptyset$ are allowed here.

Exercise 7.7.2. Show that there is no bipartite graph with degree sequences $(5, 4, 4, 2, 1)$ and $(5, 4, 4, 2, 1)$.

The following theorem of Gale (1957) and Ryser (1957) gives the desired conditions:

Theorem 7.7.3. *Let $(p_1, \ldots, p_m)$ and $(q_1, \ldots, q_n)$ be two sequences of non-negative integers satisfying the conditions $q_1 \geq q_2 \geq \ldots \geq q_n$ and $p_1 + \ldots + p_m = q_1 + \ldots + q_n$. Then there exists a bipartite graph G with vertex set $V = X \cup Y$ and degree sequences $(p_1, \ldots, p_m)$ on X and $(q_1, \ldots, q_n)$ on Y if and only if the following condition holds:*

$$\sum_{i=1}^{m} min(p_i, k) \geq \sum_{j=1}^{k} q_j \quad for \ k = 1, \ldots, n. \tag{7.7}$$

Proof. Let $X = \{x_1, \ldots, x_m\}$ and $Y = \{y_1, \ldots, y_n\}$. We define a Supply and Demand Problem as follows. The network (G, c) contains all edges $x_i y_j$ with capacity $c(x_i y_j) = 1$. Moreover, with x_i we associate the supply $a(x_i) = p_i$ and with y_j we associate the demand $b(y_j) = q_j$. Obviously, the existence of a feasible flow for (G, c) is equivalent to the existence of a bipartite graph with vertex set $V = X \cup Y$ having the given degree sequences (the edges with non-zero flow in the network are precisely the edges of G). Thus, we have to show that condition (7.6) of Theorem 7.7.1 is equivalent to (7.7).

For any subset U of V, put $U' = \{i : x_i \in U\}$ and $U'' = \{j : y_j \in U\}$. Then, by definition of c, we have $c(S, T) = |S'||T''|$, where $T := V \backslash S$. First, suppose there exists a feasible flow. Then (7.6) implies

$$|S'||T''| \geq \sum_{j \in T''} q_j - \sum_{i \in T'} p_i \quad for \ all \ S \subset V. \tag{7.8}$$

Choosing $S = \{x_i : p_i > k\} \cup \{y_{k+1}, \ldots, y_n\}$, (7.8) becomes

$$k \ |\{i : p_i > k\}| \geq \sum_{j=1}^{k} q_j - \sum_{p_i \leq k} p_i;$$

however, for $p_i \leq k$, we have $p_i = min(p_i, k)$ and, for $p_i > k$, we have $k = min(p_i, k)$; this gives condition (7.7).

Conversely, suppose that condition (7.7) is satisfied and let S be an arbitrary subset of V. Then the cut (S, T), where $T = V \backslash S$, satisfies (with $k := |T''|$):

$$c(S, T) = \sum_{i \in S'} k \geq \sum_{i \in S'} min(p_i, k) \geq \sum_{j=1}^{k} q_j - \sum_{i \in T'} min(p_i, k)$$

$$\geq \sum_{j \in T''} q_j - \sum_{i \in T'} p_i = \sum_{y \in Y \cap T} b(y) - \sum_{x \in X \cap T} a(x).$$

Thus, (7.7) also implies (7.6). $\square$

Theorem 7.7.3 was stated and proved by Ryser (1957) in the language of 0-1-matrices; we show how to translate the statement of Theorem 7.7.3 into Ryser's theorem. With any bipartite graph $G = (X \cup Y, E)$, we associate, as usual, a matrix $M = (m_{xy})(x \in X, y \in Y)$ such that $m_{xy} = 1$ if $xy \in E$ and $m_{xy} = 0$ otherwise. Conversely, any 0-1-matrix yields a bipartite graph. Then the degree sequence on X corresponds to the sequence of row sums of M and the degree sequence on Y corresponds to the sequence of column sums of M. In this way, Theorem 7.7.3 can be stated as a criterion for the existence of a 0-1-matrix with given row and column sums:

Theorem 7.7.4. *Let $(p_1, \ldots, p_m)$ and $(q_1, \ldots, q_n)$ be two sequences of non-negative integers satisfying the conditions $q_1 \geq q_2 \geq \ldots \geq q_n$ and $q_1 + \ldots + q_n = p_1 + \ldots + p_m$. Then there exists a 0-1-matrix of size $(m \times n)$ with row sums $(p_1, \ldots, p_m)$ and column sums $(q_1, \ldots, q_n)$ if and only if condition (7.6) of Theorem 7.7.3 holds.* $\square$

A different proof of Theorems 7.7.3 and 7.7.4 using methods of Transversal Theory can be found, for example, in Mirsky (1971b).

Exercise 7.7.5. Suppose there is a given Supply and Demand Problem, where the functions c, a and b are integral. If there exists a feasible flow, is there an integral feasible flow as well?

8. Colourings

This chapter treats a subject occurring quite often in Graph Theory, namely colourings. First, we show the relationship between colourings and partial orderings (as studied in Section 7.5) and mention 'perfect' graphs. Then we prove the two main theorems about colourings of vertices and edges (namely the Theorems of Brooks and Vizing). Finally, we consider edge colourings of Cayley graphs; these are graphs which are defined using groups. We will barely scractch the surface of a vast area in this chapter; for a detailed study of colouring problems we refer the reader to the monograph by Jensen and Toft (1995).

8.1 Comparability Graphs and Interval Graphs

We apply the results of Section 7.5 to two classes of graphs which are particularly interesting. The first of these two classes shows a further way of interpreting partial orderings in a graph theoretical way. Let $(M, \leq)$ be a partially ordered set. We define a graph G with vertex set M by choosing all those sets $\{x, y\}$ (where $x \neq y$) as edges of G for which x and y are *comparable*, that is, for which $x \leq y$ or $y \leq x$ holds. Any such graph G is called a *comparability graph*. Thus, a graph G is a comparability graph if and only if it has a transitive orientation. It it possible to check with complexity $O(|V|^{5/2})$ whether some given graph is a comparability graph, and such a graph can then be oriented with complexity $O(|V|^2)$, see Spinrad (1985).

We need some more definitions. A *colouring* of a graph $G = (V, E)$ assigns a 'colour' to each of its vertices such that adjacent vertices always have different colour. The *chromatic number* $\chi(G)$ is the minimal number of colours needed in a colouring of G.[1]

---

[1] The *Four Colour Theorem* (formerly the famous *Four Colour Conjecture* or *4CC*) states that any planar graph has chromatic number $\chi \leq 4$. This conjecture was finally proved by Appel and Haken (1977a), Appel and Haken (1977b) with the help of a computer. For a simplified proof, see Robertson, Sanders, Seymour and Thomas (1997); this also provides an independent verification. (There was some controversy about the validity of the Appel-Haken proof, because of its extraordinary length and complexity as well as the huge amount of computer time needed for establishing the result.) The book

Example 8.1.1. A graph G has chromatic number 2 if and only if its vertex set can be partitioned into two subsets S and T such that no edge has both end vertices in either S or T. Thus, the graphs G with $\chi(G) = 2$ are precisely the (non-empty) bipartite graphs.

We need two more notations. The maximal cardinality of a clique in a graph G is denoted by $\omega(G)$. The *clique partition number* $\theta(G)$ is the minimal number of cliques in a partition of the vertex set of G into cliques. There are some connections between the independence number α and the parameters ω, θ and χ of a graph G and its complementary graph $\overline{G}$ which are easy to see.

Lemma 8.1.2. *For any graph G, the following equalities and inequalities hold:*

$$\chi(G) \geq \omega(G); \quad \alpha(G) \leq \theta(G); \quad \alpha(G) = \omega(\overline{G}); \quad \theta(G) = \chi(\overline{G}).$$

Proof. The first inequality holds because the vertices of a clique obviously have to have different colours. Noting that any two vertices of an independent set have to be in different cliques yields the second inequality. Now observe that independent sets in G are precisely the cliques in $\overline{G}$ and that a colouring is equivalent to a partition of the vertex set into independent sets. □

Theorem 8.1.3. *Let G be a comparability graph or the complement of such a graph. Then $\alpha(G) = \theta(G)$ and $\omega(G) = \chi(G)$.*

Proof. Let G be a comparability graph. Then the cliques in G are precisely the chains of the corresponding partially ordered set $(M, \leq)$ and the independent sets in G are the antichains of $(M, \leq)$. Theorem 7.5.3 now implies $\alpha(G) = \theta(G)$ and Exercise 7.5.9 yields $\omega(G) = \chi(G)$. The statement for $\overline{G}$ then follows using Lemma 8.1.2. □

We have a closer look at the complements of comparability graphs. Let $M_1, \ldots, M_n$ be intervals of real numbers and G the graph on $\{1, \ldots, n\}$ whose edges are precisely the sets $\{i, j\}$ with $M_i \cap M_j \neq \emptyset$. Any such graph is called an *interval graph*.

Lemma 8.1.4. *Any interval graph is the complement of a comparability graph.*

Proof. Let $M_1, \ldots, M_n$ be intervals of real numbers and G the corresponding interval graph. We define a partial ordering $\leq$ on $\{1, \ldots, n\}$ by

$$i < j \quad :\Leftrightarrow \quad x < y \quad \text{for all } x \in M_i \text{ and all } y \in M_j.$$

Obviously, $\{i, j\}$ is an edge in the comparability graph corresponding to $\leq$ if and only if $M_i \cap M_j = \emptyset$, that is, if $\{i, j\}$ is not an edge of G. □

---

by Aigner (1984), which is worth reading, develops Graph Theory motivated by the Four Colour Conjecture and the attempts to solve it.

Exercise 8.1.5. Show that any interval graph is *triangulated*: Any cycle of length at least 4 has a *chord*, that is, an edge of G which connects two non-consecutive vertices of the cycle.

Conversely, Gilmore and Hoffman (1964) showed that any triangulated graph whose complement is a comparability graph has to be an interval graph. The same authors (and, independently, Ghouila-Houri (1962)) proved that a graph G is a comparability graph if and only if any closed trail (not necessarily a cycle) $(v_0, v_1, \ldots, v_{2n}, v_{2n+1} = v_0)$ of odd length has a chord of the form $v_i v_{i+2}$. Proofs for these results can also be found in Berge (1973), Chapter 16. Further characterizations are given in Gallai (1967). The paper by Fishburn (1985) contains more about interval graphs; applications in Biology were treated by Mirkin and Rodin (1984). Booth and Lueker (1976) as well as Korte and Möhring (1989) give algorithms for recognizing interval graphs.

Corollary 8.1.6. *Let G be an interval graph or the complement of such a graph. Then $\alpha(G) = \theta(G)$ and $\omega(G) = \chi(G)$.*   □

Example 8.1.7. We meet interval graphs in practical applications: The intervals are given by the points of time a certain job is begun and finished. A colouring of such a graph with as few colours as possible then corresponds to an optimal assignment of the jobs to (as few as possible) workers or teams of workers. A colouring is given by a partition of the corresponding comparability graph (that is, of the complement of the given interval graph) into as few cliques as possible, that is, using the Theorem of Dilworth, by a partition of the corresponding partial ordering into chains (compare the proof of 8.1.4). We mentioned at the end of Section 7.5 that this can be done using a flow network. An explicit algorithm avoiding the use of flows can be found in Ford and Fulkerson (1962), §II.9.

Comparability graphs and interval graphs are special cases of an important class of graphs we now introduce briefly. A graph G is called *perfect* if the condition $\alpha(H) = \theta(H)$ holds for any induced subgraph H of G. Equivalently, G is perfect if the condition $\omega(H) = \chi(H)$ holds for any induced subgraph H. The fact that these two conditions are equivalent was first conjectured by Berge and then proved by Lovász (1972) ('Perfect Graph Theorem'); a proof can also be found in Berge (1973). Using Lemma 8.1.2, this result can also be formulated as follows: The complement of a perfect graph is perfect as well. Obviously, any induced subgraph of a comparability graph is again a comparability graph, so that we can summarize the results of this section as follows.

Theorem 8.1.8. *Comparability graphs, interval graphs and the complements of such graphs are perfect.*   □

Exercise 8.1.9. Show that bipartite graphs are perfect.

More about perfect graphs can be found in Berge (1973), Chapter 16; for example, it is shown that any triangulated graph is perfect. The 'strong perfect graph conjecture' of Berge is still unsolved: A graph is perfect if and only if neither G nor $\overline{G}$ contain a cycle of odd length ≥ 5 as an induced subgraph. Note that determining α, θ, ω and χ is an NP-hard problem for graphs in general, thus, it is quite likely that no good algorithm exists for this problem (see Garey and Johnson (1979)). However, all these parameters can be found in polynomial time for perfect graphs, see Grötschel, Lovász and Schrijver (1984), so that perfect graphs are particularly interesting from an algorithmic point of view as well. This result and further interesting papers can be found in Volume 21 of Annals of Discrete Mathematics (Berge and Chvátal (1984)), which is devoted entirely to perfect graphs; see also Golumbic (1980) and Chapter 9 of Grötschel, Lovász and Schrijver (1993). Grötschel, Lovász and Schrijver (1993)

8.2 Colourings

In this section we prove some basic results about the chromatic number $\chi(G)$ of a graph G. Let us first consider the following simple algorithm for colouring a graph. Given an ordering $v_1, \ldots, v_n$ of the vertices of G, we colour the vertices one by one, always using the smallest possible colour, where the colours are given by the numbers $1, 2, \ldots$. Clearly, this algorithm is a version of the Greedy Algorithm.

Algorithm 8.2.1. Let $G = (V, E)$ be a graph given by adjacency lists A_i and $\mathbf{v} = (v_1, \ldots, v_n)$ an ordering of the vertices of G. The algorithm constructs a colouring f of G with colours $1, 2, \ldots$.

Procedure COLOUR $(G, \mathbf{v}; f)$.

(1) $f(v_1) \leftarrow 1$;
(2) **for** $i = 2$ **to** n **do**
(3) $f(v_i) \leftarrow \min \{ j : f(v_h) \neq j$ for all $h = 1, \ldots, i - 1$ with $h \in A_i \}$
(4) **od.**

Lemma 8.2.2. *For any graph* G, $\chi(G) \leq \Delta(G) + 1$, *where* $\Delta(G)$ *is the maximal degree of* G.

Proof. Let $v_1, \ldots, v_n$ be any ordering of the vertices of G. As vertex v_i can have at most $\Delta(G)$ adjacent predecessors when it is coloured in step (3) of Algorithm 8.2.1, there are at most $\Delta(G)$ colours v_i cannot be coloured with, so that $f(v_i) \leq \Delta(G) + 1$. □

Example 8.2.3. There are graphs for which equality holds in Lemma 8.2.2. Obviously, we have $\chi(K_n) = n = \Delta(K_n) + 1$ and, for C_{2n+1} a cycle of length $2n + 1$, $\chi(C_{2n+1}) = 3 = \Delta(C_{2n+1}) + 1$. On the other hand, $\chi(C_{2n}) = 2 = \Delta(C_{2n})$.

Using an appropriate ordering of the vertices, we can prove the following stronger bound.

Lemma 8.2.4. *For any graph G,*

$$\chi(G) \leq 1 + \ max \ \{\delta(H) : H \text{ is an induced subgraph of } G\},$$

where $\delta(H)$ denotes the minimal degree of H.

Proof. Denote the maximum defined in the above statement by k, then $k \geq \delta(G)$ by hypothesis. Therefore, we may choose a vertex v_n with deg $v_n \leq k$. Now look at the induced subgraph $H = H_{n-1} := G\backslash v_n$ and choose a vertex v_{n-1} having at most degree k in H. We continue in this manner until we get a graph H_1 consisting of only one vertex (namely vertex v_1). Now we use the ordering $v_1, \ldots, v_n$ we just found and apply Algorithm 8.2.1. Then each vertex v_i has at most k adjacent predecessors, because deg $v_i \leq k$ holds in H_i. Thus, Algorithm 8.2.1 needs at most $k + 1$ colours for colouring G. □

Lemma 8.2.4 is interesting mainly because of the following corollary.

Corollary 8.2.5. *If G is connected and not regular, we have $\chi(G) \leq \Delta(G)$.*

Proof. Write $k = \Delta(G)$ and suppose $\chi(G) > k$. Then, by Lemma 8.2.4, G must have an induced subgraph H with $\delta(H) = k$. But, as k is the maximal degree in G, H must be a k-regular subgraph which is not connected to any vertex outside of H. Now G is connected by hypothesis, so that we must have $G = H$ and G has to be k-regular. □

Our next result is the most important one of this section. It is due to Brooks (1941) and states that, with only the trivial exceptions already mentioned, $\chi(G) \leq \Delta(G)$ for any graph G.

Theorem 8.2.6 (Theorem of Brooks). *Let G be a connected graph. If G is neither a complete graph K_n nor a cycle C_{2n+1} of odd length, then $\chi(G) \leq \Delta(G)$ holds.*

Proof. Using Corollary 8.2.5, we may assume that G is regular of degree $k = \Delta(G)$. Now $k = 2$ means that G is a cycle and we know the chromatic number of a cycle (see Example 8.2.3). So let $k \geq 3$. First suppose that G is not 2-connected. Then there exists a vertex v such that $H := G\backslash v$ is not connected (see Section 7.1). Let $V_1, \ldots, V_k$ be the connected components of H. Using induction on the number of vertices, we may assume that it is possible to colour the subgraph of G induced on $V_i \cup \{v\}$ with k colours. Then G can obviously be coloured using k colours as well. Thus, we can now turn to the case where G is 2-connected.

The statement will be proved if we can show that there exist three vertices v_1, v_2 and v_n such that G contains the edges v_1v_n and v_2v_n, whereas v_1 and

v_2 are not adjacent, and such that the graph $H := G \backslash \{v_1, v_2\}$ is connected. Suppose we have already found such vertices; then we may order the remaining vertices as follows: For any i with $n - 1 \geq i \geq 3$, we choose (in decreasing order, that is, beginning with $i = n-1$) a vertex v_i in $V \backslash \{v_1, v_2, v_{i+1}, \ldots, v_n\}$ adjacent to at least one of the vertices $v_{i+1}, \ldots, v_n$ (this is possible because of the connectedness of H). Now, if we apply Algorithm 8.2.1 using this ordering of the vertices, we first get $f(v_1) = f(v_2) = 1$ because v_1 and v_2 are not adjacent. Furthermore, any vertex v_i with $3 \leq i \leq n - 1$ has at most $k - 1$ adjacent predecessors, because v_i is adjacent to at least one vertex v_j with $j > i$. Finally, v_n is adjacent to the vertices v_1 and v_2 which have the same colour. Therefore, the algorithm needs at most k colours.

We still have to show that G contains vertices v_1, v_2 and v_n satisfying the above conditions. First suppose that G is even 3-connected. We choose any vertex for v_n. Note that the set $\Gamma(v_n)$ of vertices adjacent to v_n has to contain two non-adjacent vertices v_1 and v_2. (Otherwise the $k + 1$ vertices in $\Gamma(v_n) \cup \{v_n\}$ form a complete graph K_{k+1} and, because of the connectedness and the k-regularity of G, this graph would have to be G itself, which contradicts the hypothesis of the theorem.) As G is 3-connected, H must still be connected. Now turn to the case where G is 2-connected but not 3-connected. Here, we may choose a vertex separator $\{v, v_n\}$. Let $V_1, \ldots V_k$ be the connected components of $G \backslash \{v, v_n\}$ and define $G_i := G|(V_i \cup \{v, v_n\})$. Then the graphs G_i are connected; moreover, v_n has to have some neighbour $\neq v$ in each of the G_i (because otherwise $G \backslash v$ would not be connected). Now we choose two neighbours $v_1 \in G_1$ and $v_2 \in G_2$ of v_n such that $v_1, v_2 \neq v$. Then v_1 and v_2 are not adjacent and $H := G \backslash \{v_1, v_2\}$ is still connected which is seen as follows. Let x be any vertex of H. Then it is sufficient to show that v is still accessible from x in H. Now G is 2-connected, so that there are two vertex disjoint paths from x to v in G by Theorem 7.1.4, and obviously H has to contain at least one such path. This shows that H is connected and concludes the proof of the theorem. □

We make some remarks about the Theorem of Brooks: The bound $\chi(G) \leq \Delta(G)$ may be arbitrarily bad, as the example of the bipartite graphs shows (here $\chi(G) = 2$ and $\Delta(G)$ can take any value ≥ 2). Determining $\chi(G)$ is an NP-hard problem, see Karp (1972). If $P \neq NP$ holds, then there is not even a polynomial algorithm producing an approximate solution which always needs less than $2\chi(G)$ colours, see Garey and Johnson (1976). However, Turner (1988) gave an algorithm of complexity $O(|V| + |E| \log k)$ which, with probability almost 1, colours any given k-colourable graph with k colours.

In the context of colourings, there are two important conjectures concerning the structure of k-colourable graphs. The first one, which is due to Hadwiger (1943), is one of the most famous open problems of Graph Theory. *Hadwiger's Conjecture* states that, if $\chi(G) \geq n$, then G contains a subgraph contractible to K_n. This conjecture has been proved for $n \leq 6$; for $n \leq 4$, the proof can be found in Theorem 5.13 of Aigner (1984). By a result of

Wagner (1960), the case $n = 5$ is equivalent to the Four Colour Conjecture and is therefore proved as well. Finally, the case $n = 6$ was established by Robertson, Seymour and Thomas (1993). The general case remains open; see Toft (1996) for a recent survey of Hadwiger's conjecture. The other important conjecture due to Hajós (1961) sounds similar but is in fact stronger. *Hajós' Conjecture* states that any graph with $\chi(G) \geq n$ contains a subdivision of K_n. However, Catlin (1979) found a counterexample for $n = 8$ (and hence for all $n \geq 8$), so that this conjecture is false in general. (Note that a subdivision of K_n can be contracted to K_n.) For $n \leq 4$, Hajós' conjecture is true (see Aigner (1984)), for $n = 5, 6, 7$ it is still open.

For more profound studies of the chromatic number, algebraic tools, such as the chromatic polynomial, are needed. This is one of the central subjects of Algebraic Combinatorics; we refer the interested reader to Godsil (1993) or Tutte (1984).

8.3 Edge Colourings

In this section we treat *edge colourings*; this means we assign a 'colour' to each edge such that any two edges having a vertex in common have distinct colours. The smallest possible number of colours needed for an edge colouring of a graph G is called the *chromatic index* or the *edge chromatic number* $\chi'(G)$. Note that $\chi'(G)$ is the chromatic number $\chi(L(G))$ of the line graph of G. The counterpart of the Theorem of Brooks about colourings is the Theorem of Vizing (1964). However, the bound for $\chi(G)$ in the Theorem of Brooks could be arbitrarily bad, whereas the Theorem of Vizing asserts that $\chi'(G)$ can only take one of two possible values, namely $\Delta(G)$ or $\Delta(G) + 1$.

Exercise 8.3.1. Show $\chi'(G) = \Delta(G)$ for any bipartite graph G. (Hint: Use Exercise 7.4.15.)

Theorem 8.3.2 (Theorem of Vizing). *For   any   graph G,   either* $\chi'(G) = \Delta(G)$ *or* $\chi'(G) = \Delta(G) + 1$ *holds.*

Proof. The inequality $\chi'(G) \geq \Delta(G)$ is obvious. Using induction on $|E|$, we show that $\chi'(G) \leq \Delta(G) + 1$. The induction basis is trivial. So assume that $G \backslash e_1$ (where $e_1 = uv_1$ is any edge of G) has already been coloured using $\Delta(G) + 1$ colours; we are going to use this colouring of $G \backslash e_1$ to construct a colouring of G. We need a notation. For any two colours α and β, let $G(\alpha, \beta)$ be the subgraph of G whose edges are precisely those edges of G which have colour α or β. Obviously, the connected components of $G(\alpha, \beta)$ are paths or cycles of even length whose edges are by turns coloured with α and β. Note that permuting the two colours α and β in one (or more) of the connected components of $G(\alpha, \beta)$ yields a valid colouring again.

As any vertex v of G has degree at most $\Delta(G)$, there is at least one colour γ 'missing' at vertex v in the colouring of $G \backslash e_1$ (that is, none of the edges incident with v has colour γ). If the same colour is missing at u and at v_1, we may assign this colour to edge e_1. Now suppose that this is not the case, so that colour α is missing at vertex u and colour $\beta_1 \neq \alpha$ is missing at v_1. Also, we may assume that some edge incident with v_1 is coloured with α and some edge $e_2 = uv_2$ is coloured with β_1. We change the given colouring as follows: We assign colour β_1 to edge e_1 and leave edge e_2 without a colour for the moment. If colour α is missing at v_2, we may colour e_2 with α. So suppose that α is assigned to some edge incident with v_2. If u, v_1 and v_2 are not in the same connected component of $G(\alpha, \beta_1)$, we can exchange the colours α and β_1 in the component containing v_2, so that colour α is then missing at v_2 (and α is still missing at u) and we may assign colour α to e_2. Otherwise, u, v_1 and v_2 are contained in the same connected component of $G(\alpha, \beta_1)$, which means that there is a path from u to v_2 alternately coloured with α and β_1. This path together with the (not yet coloured) edge e_2 forms a cycle, see Figure 8.1.

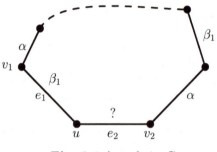

Fig. 8.1 A cycle in G

Now suppose that colour $\beta_2 \neq \beta_1$ is missing at v_2. We may also assume w.l.o.g. that this colour occurs at vertex u (otherwise we might assign β_2 to edge e_2 and get a valid colouring); let $e_3 = uv_3$ be the edge coloured with β_2. We change the given colouring as follows: Assign colour β_2 to edge e_2 and leave edge e_3 without a colour for the moment. As before, we may assume that colour α occurs at vertex v_3 and that u, v_2 and v_3 lie in the same connected component of $G(\alpha, \beta_2)$ (otherwise, it would be possible to find a colour for e_2 and finish the colouring as above). Thus, there is a path from u to v_3 coloured in turns with α and β_2 and this path together with the (not yet coloured) edge e_3 forms a cycle. We have now found two 'alternating' cycles as shown in Figure 8.2. Continuing this procedure of changing the colouring analogously to what we did above, we have to reach some vertex v_k adjacent to u such that edge $e_k = uv_k$ is not yet coloured, and we have one of the following cases: Either some colour $\beta_k \neq \beta_{k-1}$ is missing at v_k and this colour is also missing at u; in this case, e_k may be assigned this colour.

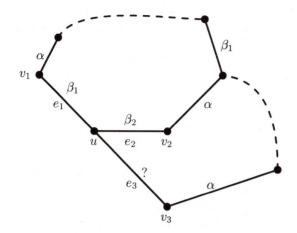

Fig. 8.2 Two cycles in G

Or, some colour β_i with $i \leq k - 2$ is missing at v_k. (Note that one of these alternatives has to occur at some point, because we can find at most deg $u \leq \Delta(G)$ neighbours of u.) As before, u, v_i and v_{i-1} are contained in the same connected component of $G(\alpha, \beta_i)$. This component is a path W from u to v_{i+1} alternately coloured with α and β_i and this path does not contain v_k (because colour β_i is missing at v_k). Thus, the component C of $G(\alpha, \beta_i)$ containing v_k is disjoint to W (see Figure 8.3). Now, after having exchanged colours α and β_i in C, we may assign colour α to e_k. $\Box$

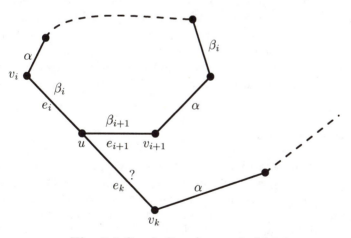

Fig. 8.3 Concluding the proof of 8.3.2

A short proof for a generalization of the Theorem of Vizing, which in particular provides an alternative proof of Theorem 8.3.2 as well, can be found in Berge and Fournier (1991).

As we saw in Exercise 8.3.1, bipartite graphs always have chromatic index $\chi'(G) = \Delta(G)$. The following statement about regular graphs is a consequence of the Theorem of Vizing.

Corollary 8.3.3. *Let G be a k-regular graph with n vertices. If n is odd, then $\chi'(G) = k + 1$. If n is even, then $\chi'(G) = k$ holds if and only if G has a 1-factorization.*

Proof. Let n be odd, say $n = 2m + 1$. Then any colour can be assigned to at most m edges. But as G contains $\frac{(2m+1)k}{2} > mk$ edges, we cannot have $\chi'(G) = k$, so that, by Theorem 8.3.2, $\chi'(G) = k + 1$. Now let n be even, say $n = 2m$. Then it can be shown analogously that $\chi'(G) = k$ holds if and only if each colour is assigned to exactly m edges. But this is equivalent to the fact that the colour classes of edges form a 1-factorization.   □

The book by Yap (1986) contains an extensive discussion of edge colourings. Even though the Theorem of Vizing states that the chromatic index $\chi'(G)$ can only take two possible values, determining $\chi'(G)$ is an NP-hard problem. Holyer (1981) proved that this is true even if G is 3-regular. For the bipartite case (where $\chi'(G) = \Delta(G)$), there are fast algorithms (see for example Gabow and Kariv (1982) or Cole and Hopcroft (1982)); their complexity is $O(|E| \log |E|)$. For the general case, an algorithm can be found in Hochbaum, Nishizeki and Shmoys (1986). If the colouring we are looking for does not have to be the optimal one, but might be slightly worse, the proof of Vizing's Theorem given above yields an algorithm which finds an edge colouring using $\Delta(G) + 1$ colours with complexity $O(|V||E|)$. Shannon (1949) proved that multigraphs have chromatic index $\chi'(G) \leq \frac{3\Delta(G)}{2}$. More recent results in this direction can be found for example in Anderson (1977) and Hilton and Jackson (1987), where the following result is proved: If all edges occuring more than once in G form a matching, we still have $\chi'(G) \leq \Delta(G)+1$.

8.4 Cayley Graphs

This section is devoted to a class of graphs having an automorphism group which makes them particularly interesting. A graph $G = (V, E)$ is called a *Cayley graph* if it has an automorphism group H which operates regularly (or 'sharply transitive') on V. In other words: For any two vertices v and w, there is exactly one automorphism h in H which maps v to $v^h = w$.[2] (Note that we do not require $H = \text{Aut } G$; H is some subgroup of Aut G!) There

---

[2] We denote the image of a vertex v under some automorphism h by v^h; this is common usage in Algebra as well as in Finite Geometry.

are two reasons for studying these graphs in this section. First, we want to say something about automorphisms of graphs at least for one example and second, this leads to an interesting application of the Theorem of Vizing.

In the literature, Cayley graphs are mostly defined by a description in the terminology of Group Theory. Let H be some (finite) group (written multiplicatively) with unit element 1 and let S be a subset of H having the following properties:

$$1 \notin S \quad \text{and} \quad S = S^{-1} := \{s^{-1} : s \in S\}. \tag{8.1}$$

Then we define a graph $G = G(H, S)$ with vertex set $V = H$ and edge set $E = E(H, S) = \{\{x, y\} : xy^{-1} \in S\}$. Note that this really yields a graph because $xy^{-1} \in S$ is equivalent to $yx^{-1} \in S^{-1}$ and $S = S^{-1}$ holds by (8.1). Now H operates on G by right translation (that is, $h \in H$ maps x to $x^h := xh$) and we see that G is a Cayley graph with respect to H (note that $h \in H$ maps an edge $\{x, y\}$ to the edge $\{xh, yh\}$, because $xy^{-1} \in S$ is equivalent to $(xh)(yh)^{-1} \in S$). In fact, any Cayley graph can be written in this form.

Lemma 8.4.1. *A graph $G = (V, E)$ is a Cayley graph with respect to the automorphism group H if and only if G is isomorphic to a graph of the form $G(H, S)$.*

Proof. We have already seen above that any graph of the form $G(H, S)$ is a Cayley graph with respect to H. Conversely, suppose G is a Cayley graph with respect to H. Choose an arbitrary vertex c in G to be the 'base vertex' and identify any vertex v with the unique element h of H for which $c^h = v$ holds. In particular, c is then identified with the unit element 1. Now we define S by $S := \{h \in H : \{1, h\} \in E\}$. If $\{x, y\}$ is any edge of G, then $\{xy^{-1}, 1\} = \{xy^{-1}, yy^{-1}\}$ is an edge as well, because H is an automorphism group of G and $h \in H$ maps a vertex $z = 1^z$ to $zh = (1^z)^h$. Thus, $\{x, y\} \in E$ is equivalent to $xy^{-1} \in S$. Now if $\{1, h\}$ is an edge, then $\{h^{-1}, 1\}$ is an edge as well, so that $S = S^{-1}$. As G does not contain any loops, $1 \notin S$ is also satisfied and G is isomorphic to $G(H, S)$. $\qquad\square$

Our next lemma gives the connected components of a Cayley graph $G(H, S)$.

Lemma 8.4.2. *The connected components of $G = G(H, S)$ are the right cosets of the subgroup U of H generated by S.*

Proof. By definition of a Cayley graph, $\{x_i, x_{i+1}\}$ is an edge if and only if $s_i = x_i x_{i+1}^{-1} \in S$ (for $i = 1, \ldots, m - 1$). Therefore, $(x_1, \ldots, x_m)$ is a sequence of vertices corresponding to a walk in G if and only if $x_1 x_m^{-1} = s_1 \ldots s_{m-1}$ is an element of U, that is, if $x_1 \in U x_m$ holds. $\qquad\square$

Consider the question when the chromatic index of a Cayley graph $G(H, S)$ is equal to $\Delta(G)$. Note that a Cayley graph $G(H, S)$ is always regular. Corollary 8.3.3 and Lemma 8.4.2 imply that a necessary condition for $\chi'(G) = \Delta(G)$

is that the subgroup U of G generated by S has even order; then an edge colouring using $\Delta(G)$ colours is the same as a 1-factorization of G. As we will see, there are some indications that these conditions might be sufficient as well.

Conjecture 8.4.3. A Cayley graph $G(H, S)$ has a 1-factorization if and only if the subgroup U of H generated by S has even order.

A Theorem by Stern and Lenz (1980) shows that this conjecture holds for *cyclic* graphs (these are Cayley graphs $G(H, S)$ for which the group H is a cyclic group). Later, Stong (1985) – who apparently was not aware of the paper of Stern and Lenz – obtained stronger results; we present the most important ones. The proof we give is a variant of the proofs given by Stern and Lenz or Stong, respectively; all known proofs rely heavily on the Theorem of Vizing. The following theorem gives a general construction for 1-factorizations in certain Cayley graphs, which we will use to prove Conjecture 8.4.3 for three classes of groups.[3]

Theorem 8.4.4. *Let $G = G(H, S)$ be a Cayley graph and suppose that the group H has a normal subgroup N of index 2.[4] Then G has a 1-factorization if S satisfies one of the following two conditions:*

(1) $G^* = G(N, S \cap N)$ has a 1-factorization.
(2) $S \backslash N$ contains an element d such that $s \in S \cap N$ always implies $dsd^{-1} \in S \cap N$.

Proof. If (1) holds, we may assume w.l.o.g. that S is not contained in N, so that we can choose some arbitrary element $d \in S \backslash N$; and if (2) holds, let d be the element described in the statement. Then $H \backslash N = dN = Nd$. Consider the cocycle C in G defined by the cut (N, dN), that is, $C = \{\{x, y\} \in E : x \in N \text{ and } y \in dN\}$. As the subgroup N of H operates regularly as well on N as on dN (by right translation), it is obvious that the orbits of N on C are 1-factors, say $F_1, \ldots, F_r$. We may assume $F_1 = \{\{n, dn\} : n \in N\}$, because $n(dn)^{-1}$ is in S. Deleting the remaining F_i $(i = 2, \ldots, r)$ from G yields a regular graph G'. If we delete F_1 as well, we get a disconnected graph G'' which is the disjoint union of the two isomorphic graphs $G^* = G(N, S \cap N)$ and G^*d induced by G on N and $dN = Nd$, respectively. (Here G^*d denotes the image of G^* under right translation with d.) Now it is sufficient to find a 1-factorization of G' or of G''. If condition

---

[3] For the (elementary) statements and definitions concerning groups which we use in the remainder of this section, we refer the reader to Huppert (1967) or Suzuki (1982).

[4] This condition holds for large classes of groups: It is sufficient that all elements of odd order form a normal subgroup of H. For example, this is true if the 2-Sylow subgroups of H are cyclic. A simple ad hoc proof of this statement is given in Lemma X.12.1 of Beth, Jungnickel and Lenz (1998). For a stronger result in this direction, we refer to Satz IV.2.8 in Huppert (1967).

(1) is satisfied, G^* (and hence also G^*d) has a 1-factorization which yields a 1-factorization of G''.

So suppose that condition (2) is satisfied. We denote the degree of the vertices of the regular graph G^* (and hence also of G^*d) by t, then G' is $(t+1)$-regular. Using the Theorem of Vizing, we can colour the edges of G^* with $t+1$ colours. Note that the mapping $n \to dn$ induces an isomorphism from G^* to G^*d: $\{m,n\}$ is an edge of G^* if and only if $mn^{-1} \in S \cap N$ holds, that is – because of (2) –, if $d(mn^{-1})d^{-1} = (dm)(dn)^{-1} \in S \cap N$. Now this is equivalent to $\{dm, dn\}$ being an edge of G and hence also of G^*d. We use this isomorphism to define an edge colouring of G^*d with $t+1$ colours: an edge $\{dm, dn\}$ of G^*d is assigned the same colour the edge $\{m,n\}$ of G^* has. As both G^* and G^*d are t-regular, there is exactly one colour $c(v)$ missing at each of the vertices v of G'. By construction, we have $c(n) = c(dn)$ for all $n \in N$. Thus, we can colour the edge $\{n, dn\}$ of F_1 using colour $c(n)$ (for any n), so that we get an edge colouring of G' with $t+1$ colours. This edge colouring is equivalent to the desired 1-factorization of G'.   □

We can now prove Conjecture 8.4.3 for three large classes of groups.

Theorem 8.4.5. *Let H be an abelian group, a 2-group or a generalized dihedral group. Then the Cayley graph $G = G(H,S)$ has a 1-factorization if and only if the subgroup u of H generated by S has even order.*

Proof. If H is a 2-group (that is, $|H| = 2^a$ for some a), then H has a normal subgroup N of index 2. Using induction on a, we may assume that we know a 1-factorization for $G(N, S \cap N)$ already. Then condition (1) of Theorem 8.4.4 holds, so that G itself has a 1-factorization. Now suppose that H is abelian. We may assume w.l.o.g. that G is connected, that is, $H = U$ holds and that H has even order. Again, H has a normal subgroup of index 2. As G is connected, there exists an element $d \in S \backslash N$. Now condition (2) of Theorem 8.4.4 is satisfied because H is abelian, so that G has a 1-factorization. Finally, suppose that H is a generalized dihedral group. Then H has even order $2n$ and is the semi-direct product of an abelian[5] group N of order n with the cyclic group of order 2 (which we write multiplicatively as $\{1, b\}$ here); moreover, the relation $bab = a^{-1}$ holds for all $a \in N$. As any subgroup of H is either abelian or a generalized dihedral group again, we may assume w.l.o.g. that G is connected, that is, $H = U$. Again, there exists an element $d \in S \backslash N$, say $d = ba$ with $a \in N$. Then $s \in S \cap N$ always implies $dsd^{-1} = (ba)s(a^{-1}b) = bsb = s^{-1} \in S \cap N$, so that condition (2) of Theorem 8.4.4 holds and G has a 1-factorization.   □

Unfortunately, the results we know so far do not suffice to prove Conjecture 8.4.3 for, say, all nilpotent groups. However, the conjecture is true for this

---

[5] The classical dihedral groups are the ones where N is cyclic, see for example I.9.15 in Huppert (1967). The generalized dihedral groups play an important role in reflection geometry, see Bachmann (1989).

case if S is a minimal generating set for H, see Stong (1985). Theorem 8.4.5 implies that the Petersen graph is not a Cayley graph, because we showed in Exercise 7.2.7 that it does not have a 1-factorization and the only groups of order 10 are the cyclic group and the dihedral group.

Cayley graphs have found much interest; in particular, the conjecture of Lovász (1970a) stating that any connected Cayley graph contains a Hamiltonian cycle has been examined by many authors. The conjecture is still open, although it has been proved for several classes of groups. In particular, the conjecture is true for all abelian groups. A proof of this result as well as more on Cayley graphs and automorphism groups of graphs can be found in the interesting book by Yap (1986). It is also of interest to examine the strongly regular Cayley graphs; a nice survey of this subject is given by Ma (1994). We conclude this section with a basic exercise regarding this topic.

Exercise 8.4.6. Prove that a Cayley graph $G(H, S)$ is strongly regular with parameters (v, k, λ, μ) if and only if the following conditions are satisfied:

(1) $|H| = v$, $|S| = k$.
(2) The list of quotients cd^{-1} with $c, d \in S$ and $c \neq d$ contains each element $h \neq 1$ of H either λ or μ times, depending on whether or not h belongs to S.

The set S is then called a *partial difference set* (since H is usually written additively in this context so that (2) turns into a condition on differences).

9. Circulations

In Chapter 6, we introduced the simplest kind of flow problems (namely the determination of maximal flows in a network); in Chapter 7, we studied the various applications of this theory. The present chapter treats generalizations of the flows we worked with so far. For example, it occurs quite often that, for some network, there are lower bounds on the capacities of the edges or a cost function on the edges given as well. To solve this kind of problem, it makes sense to remove the exceptional role of the vertices s and t and to require that the condition of flow preservation (F2) of Chapter 6 holds for each vertex in the network including s and t. Doing this, we obtain the notion of 'circulation' on a directed graph. As we will see, there are various new possibilites for applying this new notion. Not all of these can be treated using the theory of maximal flows we presented above; however, the methods of Chapter 6 are a central tool for the more general case.

9.1 Circulations and Flows

We begin by giving a formal definition for what a circulation is, then show the connection between them and the flows treated in Chapter 6 and give a couple of applications. Let $G = (V, E)$ be a directed graph; in most cases, we assume that G is connected (w.l.o.g.). A mapping $f : E \to \mathbb{R}$ is called a *circulation* on G if it satisfies the preservation condition

$$(Z1) \quad \sum_{e^+=v} f(e) = \sum_{e^-=v} f(e) \quad \text{for all vertices } v.$$

Moreover, let $b : E \to \mathbb{R}$ and $c : E \to \mathbb{R}$ be two given mappings with $b(e) \le c(e)$ for all $e \in E$; b and c are called *capacity constraints*. Then a circulation f is called *feasible* or *legal* if

$$(Z2) \quad b(e) \le f(e) \le c(e) \quad \text{for each edge } e.$$

Finally, let $\gamma : E \to \mathbb{R}$ be a further mapping called *cost function*. Then the *cost* of a circulation f is defined as

$$\gamma(f) := \sum_{e \in E} \gamma(e) f(e).$$

A feasible circulation f is called *optimal* or *minimum cost circulation* if $\gamma(f) \leq \gamma(g)$ holds for any feasible circulation g.

We convince ourselves that the flows introduced in Chapter 6 are basically a special kind of circulations.

Example 9.1.1 (Max-Flow Problem). Let $N = (G, c, s, t)$ be a flow network with a flow f of value $w(f)$. Let G' be the directed graph we get by adding the edge $r = ts$ to the digraph G. We extend the mappings c and f to G' as follows:

$$c(r) := \infty^1 \quad \text{and} \quad f(r) := w(f).$$

Then f is a circulation on G' by (F2) and Lemma 6.1.1. Setting $b(e) = 0$ for all edges e of G', f is even feasible. Conversely, any feasible circulation f' on G' obviously yields a flow of value $f(r)$ on G. The edge r is often called the *return arc* of N. We still have to describe the maximal flows on N in our new terminology. We define a cost function on G' by

$$\gamma(r) := -1 \quad \text{and} \quad \gamma(e) := 0 \quad \text{otherwise.}$$

Then a flow f on N is maximal if and only if the corresponding circulation has minimal cost; that is, using the cost function defined above, maximal flows on N correspond to optimal circulations on G'.

It is quite evident that, by removing the exceptional role of s and t, it is possible to treat circulations in a much more elegant manner than flows. For example, all circulations on a directed graph G' obviously form a vector space; we make use of this observation in Section 9.3. Moreover, the fact that circulations are a much more general concept enables us to solve a large number of additional problems. We present some of them.

Example 9.1.2 (flows with a lower bound on the capacities). Let $N = (G, c, s, t)$ be a flow network and $b : E \to \mathbb{R}$ an additional mapping satisfying the condition $b(e) \leq c(e)$ for all edges e. We look for a maximal flow f on N which satisfies the condition

$$(F1') \quad b(e) \leq f(e) \leq c(e) \text{ for all } e \in E.$$

instead of condition (F1) of Chapter 6. We use the same transformation as in Example 9.1.1: we add the return arc r (with $c(r) = \infty$) and define γ as before. Moreover, we extend the given function b to G' by setting $b(r) = 0$. Then the maximal flow we are looking for corresponds to an optimal circulation on G' again. However, note that the problem might well be unsolvable, because there might not be any feasible circulations. We give an example for this situation in Figure 9.1 (each edge e is labelled with $b(e)$ and $c(e)$).

---

[1] As usual, ∞ means a sufficiently large number, for example $\sum_{e^- = s} c(e)$.

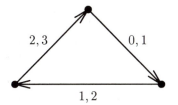

Fig. 9.1 A directed graph not admitting any feasible circulation

Example 9.1.3 (Minimum Cost Flow Problem). Let $N = (G, c, s, t)$ be a given flow network with a cost function $\gamma : E \to \mathbb{R}$. The cost of a flow f is defined – analogous to circulations – as $\gamma(f) = \sum \gamma(e)f(e)$, so that $\gamma(e)$ is the cost caused by one unit of flow flowing through edge e. Suppose that the maximal value of a flow through N is w, then we are looking for a flow of value w having minimal cost. To formulate this problem in the terminology of circulations, we introduce the return arc $r = ts$ again and define $c(r) = b(r) = w$ and $\gamma(r) = 0$. If there is a lower bound b on the capacities in N (as in Example 9.1.2), we have declared all mappings we need. Otherwise we define $b(e) = 0$ for all edges of G. Now any feasible circulation corresponds to a flow of value w (because $b(r) = c(r) = w$). As $\gamma(r) = 0$, an optimal circulation then is the extension of an *optimal flow*, that is, of a flow with minimal cost.

Example 9.1.4 (Assignment Problem). We show that the Assignment Problem of Example 7.4.11 can be reduced to Example 9.1.3. So let $A = (a_{ij})$ be a given $(n \times n)$-matrix with non-negative real entries; we are looking for a diagonal of A such that the sum of the entries of this diagonal is minimal. We construct a bipartite directed graph on vertex set $S \mathbin{\dot{\cup}} T$, where S and T are both n-sets, and add two more vertices s and t. The graph has all the (s, x), all the (x, y) and all the (y, t) (with $x \in S$ and $y \in T$) as edges and all edges have capacity $c(e) = 1$. We define the cost function by $\gamma(s, x) = \gamma(y, t) = 0$ and $\gamma(x, y) = a_{xy}$. Then any integral flow of value n having minimal cost gives a solution for our problem.

As the diagonals of A correspond to the complete matchings of the bipartite graph on $S \mathbin{\dot{\cup}} T$, the Assignment Problem can also be formulated as a problem of weighted matchings; we look at the problem from this point of view in Chapter 13. At the end of the present chapter, we mention some generalizations of the Assignment Problem. We show next that even the determination of shortest paths can be formulated as a problem of circulations.

Example 9.1.5 (Shortest Path Problem). Let G be a network where $\gamma(e)$ is the length of edge e; we are looking for a shortest path from s to t. Interpreting γ as the cost function and assigning capacity $c(e) = 1$ to each edge, a shortest path from s to t is the same as an integral flow of value 1 having minimal cost, so that the problem is a special case of 9.1.3. Of course, problems concerning paths are not solved this way in practice; on the contrary, determining shortest paths is used as a tool for constructing optimal circulations.

Exercise 9.1.6. Let G be a connected mixed multigraph where each vertex is incident with an even number of edges. Reduce the question whether an Euler tour exists in G (note that, in such a tour, all directed edges have to be used according to their direction!) to the determination of a feasible circulation in an appropriate directed graph (compare Ford and Fulkerson (1962)).

Exercise 9.1.7 (Caterer Problem). The owner of some restaurant needs fresh napkins every day, say he needs $r_1, \ldots, r_N$ fresh napkins for N consecutive days. He can either buy new napkins (paying some price α for each napkin) or use washed ones; here, the laundry service offers two possibilities: a fast service (the napkins are returned clean after m days and each costs β) and a normal service (taking n days at a price of δ for each napkin). All napkins have to be bought before the first day. Formulate the task of supplying the needed napkins at the lowest possible cost as a special case of 9.1.3. This problem had its origin in the practical task of either servicing or buying new engines for airplanes (compare Ford and Fulkerson (1962), §III.8).

9.2 Feasible Circulations

As the problems presented in the previous section show, it is a basic problem to find a feasible circulation for a given directed graph G with capacity constraints b and c (or to show, respectively, that no such circulation on G exists). This problem can be solved using the methods of Chapter 6 by introducing an appropriate flow network; this technique was originally suggested by Ford and Fulkerson (1962) and can be found, for example, in Berge and Ghouila-Houri (1962). To make the presentation a bit easier technically, we assume that $b(e) \geq 0$ holds for each edge e; the general case can be treated similarly (compare Exercise 9.2.3). The above condition is satisfied in most applications anyway, as the examples of the previous section show.

Let G be a directed graph with non-negative capacity constraints b and c. We add two vertices s and t and all edges of the form sv or vt to G (where v is a vertex of G) and denote the resulting larger directed graph by H.

Moreover, we define a capacity function c' on H by

(1) $c'(e) := c(e) - b(e)$ if e is an edge of G;
(2) $c'(sv) := \sum\limits_{e^+ = v} b(e)$ for any vertex v of G;

(3) $c'(vt) := \sum\limits_{e^- = v} b(e)$ for any vertex v of G.

Thus we get a flow network $N = (H, c', s, t)$. Obviously, $c'(e) \geq 0$ holds for each edge e of H, so that the methods of Chapter 6 can be used to determine a maximal flow on N; say f' is such a flow. Trivially, f' can have value at most

$$W := \sum_v c'(sv) = \sum_e b(e) = \sum_v c'(vt).$$

Moreover, $w(f') = W$ can hold if and only if any edge of H starting at s (and any edge of H ending at t) is saturated by f', that is, $f'(sv) = c'(sv)$ and $f'(vt) = c'(vt)$ hold. We show that there exists a feasible circulation on G if and only if f' indeed has value W.

Theorem 9.2.1. *Let G be a directed graph with non-negative capacity constraints b and c and $N = (H, c', s, t)$ the flow network described above. Then there exists a feasible circulation on G if and only if the maximal value of a flow on N is $W = \sum b(e)$.*

Proof. First let f' be a flow of value $w(f') = W$ on N. We define f on G by

$$f(e) = f'(e) + b(e) \quad \text{for each edge } e \text{ of } G. \tag{9.1}$$

As f' satisfies the condition $0 \leq f'(e) \leq c'(e) = c(e) - b(e)$, it follows immediately that (Z2) holds for f. Thus, if we show that f satisfies (Z1) as well, then f is the desired feasible circulation on G. So let v be any vertex of G. As f' is a flow on N, (F2) implies

$$f'(sv) + \sum_{e^+ = v} f'(e) = f'(vt) + \sum_{e^- = v} f'(e). \tag{9.2}$$

As $w(f') = W$, all edges of H incident with s or t are saturated, so that

$$f'(sv) = \sum_{e^+ = v} b(e) \quad \text{and} \quad f'(vt) = \sum_{e^- = v} b(e). \tag{9.3}$$

Now (9.1) and (9.2) imply

$$\sum_{e^+ = v} f(e) = \sum_{e^- = v} f(e). \tag{9.4}$$

Conversely, let f be a feasible circulation on G. Then we can define a mapping f' on the edge set of H using (9.1) and (9.3). As f is feasible, we have $0 \leq f'(e) \leq c'(e)$ for each edge e of G. For edges sv or vt, respectively, $c'(sv) = f'(sv)$ or $c'(vt) = f'(vt)$ hold by construction. All edges incident with s are therefore saturated, so that $w(f') = W$. It is clear that f' is indeed a flow, because (9.1), (9.3) and (9.4) imply (9.2). $\qquad\square$

Example 9.2.2. Let G be the directed graph given in Figure 9.2 with capacity constraints b and c.

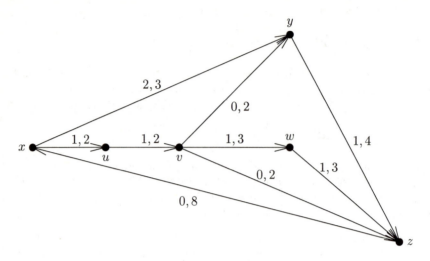

Fig 9.2 A directed graph with capacity constraints

We are looking for a feasible flow from x to z, that is, for a feasible circulation on G (where we take the edge zx as return arc). By Theorem 9.2.1, we have to examine the flow network N shown in Figure 9.3. We could use one of the algorithms of Chapter 6 to do this, but, for this simple example, it is also sufficient to have a good look at the network. We know that all edges incident with s or t have to be saturated if there exists a feasible circulation at all. Thus, we define the value of the flow on these edges to be equal to the capacity. (The values of f' are printed bold in Figure 9.3.) Then (F2) is satisfied automatically for the vertices u, v and w. As (F2) has to hold for x as well, we set $f'(zx) = 3$; then it is obvious that $f'(yz) = 1$ satisfies (F2) for y and z as well.

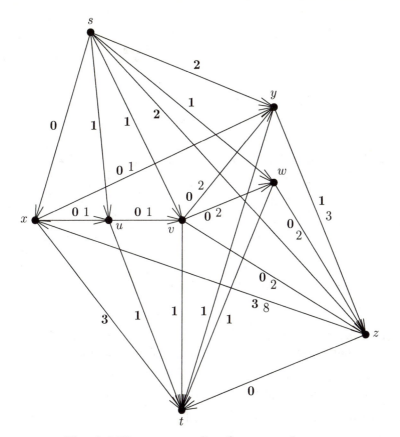

Fig. 9.3 The corresponding flow network

Thus, we get the feasible circulation f on G given in Figure 9.4. f can be interpreted as a feasible flow from x to z having value $w(f) = 3$. However, this is not a maximal feasible flow from x to z yet: we can increase the value of the flow to 3 on the path $x \text{ --- } y \text{ --- } z$ and to 2 on the path $x \text{ --- } u \text{ --- } v \text{ --- } w \text{ --- } z$. We get a flow of value 5; this is the maximal possible value of a flow because of the capacities of the edges xy and xu.

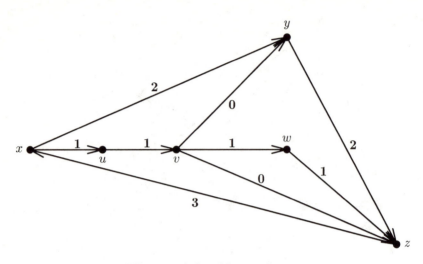

Fig. 9.4 A feasible circulation

Exercise 9.2.3. Modify the construction of the flow network N for Theorem 9.2.1 such that it can treat negative lower capacity constraints $b(e)$ as well.

The proof of Theorem 9.2.1 yields (using Exercise 9.2.3) an algorithm for constructing feasible circulations.

Algorithm 9.2.4. Let G be a directed graph with capacity constraints b and c.

Procedure LEGCIRC $(G, b, c;$ legal, $f)$

(1) $V' \leftarrow V \cup \{s, t\}$, $E' \leftarrow E \cup \{sv : v \in V\} \cup \{vt : v \in V\}$;
(2) **for** $e \in E$ **do** $c'(e) \leftarrow c(e) - b(e)$ **od**;
(3) **for** $v \in V$ **do** $c'(sv) \leftarrow \sum\limits_{\substack{e^+=v \\ b(e)>0}} b(e) - \sum\limits_{\substack{e^-=v \\ b(e)<0}} b(e)$;

$$c'(vt) \leftarrow \sum\limits_{\substack{e^-=v \\ b(e)>0}} b(e) - \sum\limits_{\substack{e^+=v \\ b(e)<0}} b(e) \ \textbf{od};$$

(4) $H \leftarrow (V', E')$, $N \leftarrow (H, c', s, t)$;
(5) MAXFLOW $(N; f')$;
(6) **if** $f'(sv) = c'(sv)$ for all $v \in V$ **then** legal $\leftarrow$ true **else** legal $\leftarrow$ false **fi**;
(7) **if** legal=true **then**
(8)   **for** $e \in E$ **do** $f(e) \leftarrow f'(e) + b(e)$ **od**
(9) **fi**.

Corollary 9.2.5. *Algorithm 9.2.4 decides with complexity $O(|V|^3)$ whether there exists a feasible circulation on G and, if possible, constructs such a circulation.*

Proof. Theorem 9.2.1 and Exercise 9.2.3 imply that the algorithm is correct. As the network N has $O(|V|)$ vertices, a maximal flow f' on N can be constructed with complexity $O(|V|^3)$ by Theorem 6.4.8, if we use the MKM-Algorithm in MAXFLOW. All the remaining operations of Algorithm 9.2.4 have complexity $O(|E|)$. $\square$

Of course, we may as well use some other algorithm instead of MAXFLOW in Algorithm 9.2.4 for finding a maximal flow on N; however, that means we also get a different complexity. Using the results of Section 6.6, it is possible, for example, to reach a complexity of $O(|V|^2|E|^{1/2})$.

Exercise 9.2.6. Describe an algorithm which decides whether a given flow network with lower capacity constraint b has a feasible flow and, if possible, constructs a maximal feasible flow. What complexity could such an algorithm have?

Note that there exists a completely different algorithm for constructing a feasible circulation. We begin with any circulation (for example $f = 0$) and change this circulation successively until we get a feasible circulation (or until we realize that no such circulation exists, respectively). We refer the reader to Ford and Fulkerson (1962), §11.3. The algorithm described there has the disadvantage that it is not possible to give a polynomial bound for the complexity, even for integral capacity constraints b and c, because the complexity depends on the values b and c take.

Next we give a criterion for the existence of a feasible circulation which may be considered a generalization of the Max-Flow Min-Cut Theorem 6.1.6. We need some notations. Let G be a directed graph with non-negative capacity constraints b and c. A *cut* of G is a partition $V = S \,\dot\cup\, T$ of the vertex set of G (analogous to Section 4.3). The *capacity* of the cut (S, T) is given by

$$c(S, T) := \sum_{\substack{e^- \in S \\ e^+ \in T}} c(e) - \sum_{\substack{e^+ \in S \\ e^- \in T}} b(e).$$

Now consider the flow network $N = (H, c', s, t)$ constructed on G as in Theorem 9.2.1. Then (S', T') is a cut of N (where $S' = S \cup \{s\}$ and $T' = T \cup \{t\}$) of capacity

$$c'(S', T') = \sum_{\substack{e^- \in S' \\ e^+ \in T'}} c'(e),$$

where e runs through all the edges of H. By definition of c', we get the following identity, where the sums now run over the edges e of G only.

$$\begin{aligned}
c'(S', T') &= \sum_{v \in T} c'(sv) + \sum_{v \in S} c'(vt) + \sum_{\substack{e^- \in S \\ e^+ \in T}} c'(e) \\
&= \sum_{e^+ \in T} b(e) + \sum_{e^- \in S} b(e) + \sum_{\substack{e^- \in S \\ e^+ \in T}} (c(e) - b(e))
\end{aligned}$$

$$= \sum_{\substack{e^- \in S \\ e^+ \in T}} c(e) - \sum_{\substack{e^+ \in S \\ e^- \in T}} b(e) + \sum_e b(e)$$

$$= c(S,T) + W.$$

Note that any cut (S', T') of N can be derived from a cut (S, T) of G in this way. Now, by Theorem 9.2.1, there exists a feasible circulation on G if and only if the maximal value of a flow on N is equal to W and Theorem 6.1.6 yields that the maximal value of a flow on N is the minimal capacity of a cut (S', T'). Thus, we get the condition $c'(S', T') \geq W$ for all (S', T'), that is, $c(S, T) \geq 0$ for all cuts (S, T) of G. We have proved the following theorem due to Hoffman (1960).

Theorem 9.2.7 (Circulation Theorem). *Let G be a directed graph with non-negative capacity constraints b and c. Then there exists a feasible circulation on G if and only if any cut (S, T) of G has non-negative capacity, that is, if*

$$\sum_{\substack{e^- \in S \\ e^+ \in T}} c(e) \geq \sum_{\substack{e^+ \in S \\ e^- \in T}} b(e)$$

holds for any cut (S, T) of G.   □

We use Theorem 9.2.7 to determine the maximal value of a feasible flow on a flow network $N = (G, c, s, t)$ with lower capacity constraint b (compare Example 9.1.2 and Exercise 9.2.6). Again, we add the return arc $r = ts$ to G and set $b(r) = v$, $c(r) = \infty$. Then the feasible circulations correspond to feasible flows on N of value $\geq v$. According to Theorem 9.2.7, such a circulation exists if the condition $c(S, T) \geq 0$ holds for any cut (S, T) of G. If $t \in S$ and $s \in T$, the term $c(r) = \infty$ occurs in $c(S, T)$, so that the condition clearly holds for those cuts. If $s \in S$ and $t \in T$, the term $-b(r) = -v$ occurs in $c(S, T)$ and this yields the condition

$$\sum_{\substack{e^- \in S \\ e^+ \in T}} c(e) - \sum_{\substack{e^+ \in S \\ e^- \in T}} b(e) \geq v.$$

In all other cases (that is, for $s, t \in S$ or $s, t \in T$), we get conditions which imply that feasible flows on N exist independently of the value of the flow, because the return arc r does not occur in the sum for $c(S, T)$. Thus, we get the maximal value for a flow – if there exists a feasible flow on N in the first place – if v is the minimal capacity of an 'ordinary' cut of N (that is, a cut with $s \in S$ and $t \in T$). Here, of course, we have to define the capacity $c(S, T)$ as before as

$$c(S, T) := \sum_{\substack{e^- \in S \\ e^+ \in T}} c(e) - \sum_{\substack{e^+ \in S \\ e^- \in T}} b(e).$$

Theorem 9.2.8. *Let $N = (G, c, s, t)$ be a flow network with non-negative lower capacity constraint b. If there exists a feasible flow f on N (that is, a flow with $b(e) \leq f(e) \leq c(e)$ for all edges e), then the maximal value of such a flow is equal to the minimum of the capacities $c(S, T)$ of all cuts (S, T). A necessary and sufficient condition for the existence of a feasible flow on N is that $c(X, Y) \geq 0$ for all partitions $V = X \cup Y$ with $t \notin X$ or $s \notin Y$.*   □

If we look at Theorem 9.2.8 for ordinary flows (that is, where $b = 0$), the existence of feasible flows is trivial. The capacity $c(S, T)$ of a cut then is the same as the capacity defined in Chapter 6 and Theorem 9.2.8 becomes the Max-Flow Min-Cut Theorem 6.1.6.

Exercise 9.2.9. Let G be a mixed multigraph. Find necessary and sufficient conditions for the existence of an Euler tour in G (compare Exercise 9.1.6).

Exercise 9.2.10. Let $N = (G, c, s, t)$ be a flow network with non-negative lower capacity constraint b. Describe a technique for determining a minimal feasible flow on N. Which complexity could such a technique have? (Note that this problem was irrelevant for the flows we treated in Chapter 6, because the zero flow always was a trivial minimal feasible flow.) Moreover, find a description for the value of such a minimal feasible flow analogous to Theorem 9.2.8.

Exercise 9.2.11. Let G be a connected directed graph with capacity constraints b and c, where $b(e)$ is always positive and $c(e) = \infty$ for all edges e. Show that G has a feasible circulation if and only if any edge is contained in a directed cycle. Give a criterion for the existence of a feasible flow on a network $N(G, c, s, t)$ with $c(e) = \infty$ for all e and a positive lower capacity constraint b.

Feasible circulations on undirected (and mixed) graphs were studied by Seymour (1979) and Arkin and Papadimitriou (1986), respectively.

9.3 Elementary Circulations

In the present and the following section, we look at the problem how to 'decompose' a given circulation into circulations which are 'as simple as possible'. The results we get will be used when we study three algorithms for determining optimal circulations in Sections 9.5 to 9.8. We begin by translating the notion of a circulation into the terminology of Linear Algebra. Let G be a (not necessarily connected) directed graph with incidence matrix A (see Section 4.2), say with vertex set $V = \{1, \ldots, n\}$ and edge set $E = \{e_1, \ldots, e_m\}$. Any mapping $f : E \to \mathbb{R}$ induces a vector $\mathbf{f}$ in $\mathbb{R}^m$, namely

$$\mathbf{f} := (f(e_1), f(e_2), \ldots, f(e_m)).$$

It is easy to see that a flow f satisfies condition (Z1) if and only if $Af^T = 0$, because the i-th row of A has entry $+1$ (or -1, respectively) in those columns j for which edge e_j has end vertex (or start vertex) i. We have shown the following lemma.

Lemma 9.3.1. *Let G be a directed graph with incidence matrix A. Then $f : E \to \mathbb{R}$ is a circulation if and only if $Af^T = 0$.*   □

Thus, the circulations are precisely the mappings in the kernel of the linear mapping from $\mathbb{R}^m$ to $\mathbb{R}^n$ corresponding to the matrix A. These mappings form a vector space of dimension $m - \text{rank } A$. Now Theorem 4.2.4 implies that rank $A = n - p$, where p is the number of connected components of G.

Corollary 9.3.2. *Let G be a directed graph with incidence matrix A. Then the circulations on G form a vector space of dimension $\nu(G) = m - n + p$ (where m, n and p denote the number of edges, vertices and connected components of G, respectively).*   □

The number $\nu(G)$ is called the *cyclomatic number* of G; we will see soon where this name comes from.

Corollary 9.3.3. *Let f be a circulation on the directed graph G. If G is a tree, we have $f = 0$.*

Proof. As G is a tree, we have $p = 1$ and $m = n - 1$, so that $\nu(G) = 0$.   □

The next exercise yields a further proof for Corollary 9.3.3.

Exercise 9.3.4. Let (S, T) be a cut of G and f a circulation on G.

a) Show that $f(S, T) = f(T, S)$, where

$$f(S, T) = \sum_{\substack{e^- \in S \\ e^+ \in T}} f(e).$$

b) Show (without using algebraic tools) that the support of a circulation (compare Exercise 6.1.12) does not contain any bridges.

We are looking for 'natural' bases for the vector space of circulations on G. A circulation $f \neq 0$ is called *elementary* if its support is minimal with respect to inclusion, that is, if there is no circulation $g \neq 0$ such that the support of g is contained in, but not equal to, the support of f. The following theorem shows that elementary circulations correspond to cycles.

Theorem 9.3.5. *Let G be a directed graph and f a circulation on G. Then f is elementary if and only if the support of f is a (not necessarily directed) cycle of G. For any cycle of G, there exists an elementary circulation.*

Proof. We show first that, for any cycle $K = (e_1, \ldots, e_k)$, there exists an elementary circulation f_K having support K. We set $f_K(e) = 0$ for all edges $e \notin K$ and $f_K(e_i) = +1$ or -1, respectively (for $i = 1, \ldots, k$), depending on whether e_i is a forward or a backward edge of K. It is immediate that f_K is a circulation on G. (This is merely the first part of the proof of Theorem 4.2.3 put into different words.) Now let g be a circulation whose support is strictly contained in the support of f. We may assume w.l.o.g. that $g(e_k) = 0$. As K is a cycle, the edges $e_1, \ldots, e_{k-1}$ are a forest, so that Corollary 9.3.3 implies that $g = 0$. Hence, f_K is elementary. Conversely, let f be any elementary circulation on G. As $f \neq 0$, the support of f has to contain a closed trail and hence a cycle K. As there exists a circulation having support K and as f is elementary by hypothesis, the support of f has to be K itself. $\square$

The next theorem shows that the cyclomatic number of G is equal to the maximal number of 'linearly independent cycles' of G.

Theorem 9.3.6. *Let G be a directed graph having n vertices, m edges and p connected components. Then there exists a basis of the vector space Z of circulations on G consisting of $\nu(G) = m - n + p$ elementary circulations.*

Proof. It suffices to show the statement for each connected component of G, so that we may assume w.l.o.g. $p = 1$, that is, G is connected. Let T be a spanning tree of $|G|$. For each edge e of $|G|\backslash T$, let $C_T(e)$ be the unique cycle of $|G|$ containing e and edges of T only (compare Section 4.3). By Theorem 9.3.5, there exists an elementary circulation f_e on G having support $C_T(e)$. It remains to show that the f_e form a basis of Z. As there are exactly $m - n + 1$ edges e in $|G|\backslash T$, all we have to show (by Corollary 9.3.2) is that the f_e are linearly independent. However, this is clear because the support of f_e contains exactly one edge, namely e, outside of T. $\square$

Exercise 9.3.7. Write some arbitrary circulation on G explicitly as a linear combination of the elementary circulations f_e of the proof of 9.3.6.

Theorem 9.3.6 shows why the vector space Z of circulations on G is also called the *cycle space* of G^2. Horton (1987) showed that a basis of Z having smallest weight (where weights are assigned to the edges of G) can be found with complexity $O(|V||E|^3)$; in the undirected case, at most $\frac{3(n-1)(n-2)}{2}$ edges are needed. However, determining a basis of Z having smallest weight and consisting of fundamental cycles (that is, a basis as given in the proof of 9.3.6) is an NP-hard problem according to Deo, Prabhu and Krishnamoorthy (1982).

---

[2] The cycle space of a graph is a special case of a more general construction assigning certain modules to any 'geometry'; see Ghinelli and Jungnickel (1990) and the references given there.

Exercise 9.3.8. Let G be a directed graph having n vertices, m edges and p connected components. Let A be the incidence matrix of G and $q : V \to \mathbb{R}$ a mapping which we call a *potential*. We define $\delta q : E \to \mathbb{R}$ by

$$\delta(xy) := q(y) - q(x) \quad \text{for any edge } xy.$$

Any mapping of the form δq is called a *potential difference* (the terminology comes from electricity networks). Show the following results (which are analogous to our results about circulations):

a) The potential differences form a vector space P corresponding to the space generated by the rows of A. Determine dim P.
b) For any cocycle of G, there exists a potential difference having this cocycle as support.
c) If G is connected, use a spanning tree T for constructing a basis of P (Hint: Compare Lemma 4.3.2).

The vector space P is called the *cocycle space* or *bond space* of G (note that cocycles are also called *bonds*).

9.4 Minty's Painting Lemma

We saw in Theorem 9.3.6 that any circulation on a directed graph G can be written as a sum of elementary circulations. We strengthen this result by showing that non-negative circulations can be written as linear combinations of non-negative elementary circulations with positive coefficients. First, we prove a lemma due to Minty (1966) about colourings which will be very useful in other contexts as well.

Theorem 9.4.1 (Painting Lemma). *Let G be a directed graph whose edges are coloured arbitrarily with the colours black, red and green; edges without colour are allowed as well. Moreover, let e_0 be a black edge of G. Then one and only one of the following statements is true:*

(1) There exists a cycle K containing e_0 which contains no edges without colour; moreover, all black edges of K have the same orientation as e_0 and all green edges have opposite orientation.

(2) There exists a cocycle C containing e_0 not containing any red edges; moreover, all black edges of C have the same orientation as e_0 and all green edges have opposite orientation.

Proof. Let $e_0 = ts$. We label the vertices of G beginning with s according to the following rules:

(a) s is labelled.
(b) Suppose v is already labelled. A vertex u not yet labelled becomes labelled if and only if there exists a black edge or a red edge vu or a red edge or a green edge uv.

The labelling process terminates if no further vertices can be labelled according to rule (b). This may happen in two possible ways:

Case 1: Vertex t has been labelled. Then rule (b) implies that there exists a path from s to t which contains no edges without colour and for which each black edge is a forward edge and each green edge is a backward edge. Adding edge $e_0 = ts$ then yields a cycle as in statement (1).

Case 2: Vertex t has not been labelled. Then let S be the set of all vertices which have been labelled, that is, we have $s \in S$ and $t \in V \backslash S$. Let C be the cocycle of G corresponding to the cut $(S, V \backslash S)$. Then, by rule (b), there are no red edges in C, as well as no black edges with start vertex in S, and no green edges with end vertex in S (otherwise it would be possible to label a vertex of $V \backslash S$). C is a cocycle as described in statement (2).

It remains to show that statements (1) and (2) cannot hold simultaneously. So suppose C is a cocycle as in (2) and K is a cycle as described in (1). As C and K both contain e_0, K has to contain one further edge of C, because s and t are in different parts of the cut defining C; suppose $e_1 \in K \cap C$. Now e_1 cannot be red or black because of (2) (note that e_1 is oriented in the opposite direction as e_0). Thus, e_1 is either green or does not have any colour. But as e_1 has the same orientation as e_0 in the cycle K, K cannot satisfy (1). $\square$

Colouring all edges of G black yields an interesting corollary. We need a notation. Let C be the cocycle corresponding to the cut (S, T). C is called a *directed cocycle* or a *cocircuit* if all edges of C have the same orientation (from S to T, say).

Corollary 9.4.2. *Any edge of a directed graph is either contained in a directed cycle or in a directed cocycle.* $\square$

Our next theorem is the theorem about non-negative circulations mentioned above.

Theorem 9.4.3. *Let G be a directed graph and $f \neq 0$ a circulation on G. Then f is non-negative (that is, $f(e) \geq 0$ for all edges e) if and only if f can be represented as $f = \lambda_1 f_1 + \ldots + \lambda_k f_k$, where the f_i are non-negative elementary circulations and the λ_i are positive numbers.*

Proof. It is trivial that the condition given above is sufficient. Conversely, let $f \neq 0$ be a non-negative circulation on G and let G' be the sub-digraph of G defined by the support of f. As f satisfies condition (Z1), G' cannot contain a directed cocycle. Thus, by Corollary 9.4.2, G' contains a directed cycle K_1. Let f_1 be the elementary circulation corresponding to K_1; that is, $f_1(e) = 1$ for all edges e in K_1 and $f_1(e) = 0$ otherwise. Define $\lambda_1 := \min \{f(e) : e \in K_1\} > 0$ and $g := f - \lambda_1 f_1$. Then g is a non-negative circulation on G as well. If $g = 0$, we are done; otherwise the support of g

contains at least one edge less than the support of f, so that the assertion follows by induction.   □

Corollary 9.4.4. *Let* $N = (G, c, s, t)$ *be a flow network. Then any flow can be written as a sum of elementary flows and non-negative elementary circulations.*

Proof. Let G' be the graph we obtain by adding the return arc $r = ts$ to G (as in Example 9.1.1). We have already seen that any flow f can be extended to a circulation on G' by defining $f(r) := w(f)$. As flows are non-negative by definition, this circulation is non-negative as well. Now the assertion follows from Theorem 9.4.3; note that all those elementary circulations f_i on G' whose support contains r yield elementary flows on N.   □

It was shown in Exercise 6.1.12 that we cannot avoid using elementary circulations as well in Corollary 9.4.4. We can now write the (constructive) proof of Minty's Painting Lemma as an algorithm which constructs, given any colouring of a directed graph with the colours black, red and green, a cycle K or a cocycle C, respectively, as described in Theorem 9.4.1. The Boolean variable 'cycle' has value 'true' if and only if the algorithm constructs a cycle.

Algorithm 9.4.5. Let G be a directed graph and F a partial colouring of the edges of G with the colours black, red and green; moreover, let e_0 be a black edge of G.

Procedure MINTY $(G, F, e_0;$ cycle, $K, C)$

(1) **for** $v \in V$ **do** $u(v) \leftarrow$ false **od**;
(2) $s \leftarrow e_0^+$; $t \leftarrow e_0^-$; $K \leftarrow \emptyset$; $C \leftarrow \emptyset$; $A \leftarrow \emptyset$;
(3) label s with $(-, -)$ and set $A \leftarrow A \cup \{s\}$;
(4) **repeat**
(5)   choose a labelled vertex v with $u(v) =$ false;
(6)   **for** $e \in \{e \in E : e^- = v\}$ **do**
(7)   **if** $w = e^+$ is not labelled **and** $F(e) =$ red **or** $F(e) =$ black
(8)   **then** label w with $(v, +)$; $A \leftarrow A \cup \{w\}$ **fi**
(9)   **od**;
(10)   **for** $e \in \{e \in E : e^+ = v\}$ **do**
(11)   **if** $w = e^-$ is not labelled **and** $F(e) =$ red **or** $F(e) =$ green
(12)   **then** label w with $(v, -)$; $A \leftarrow A \cup \{w\}$ **fi**
(13)   **od**;
(14) $u(v) \leftarrow$ true;
(15) **until** t is labelled **or** $u(v) =$ true for all $v \in A$;
(16) **if** t is labelled
(17) **then** cycle $\leftarrow$ true, $K \leftarrow K \cup \{e_0\}$, $w \leftarrow t$;
(18)   **while** $w \neq s$ **do**
(19)   find the first component v of the label of w;
(20)   **if** the second component of the label of w is $+$

(21)   **then** $e \leftarrow vw$ **else** $e \leftarrow wv$ **fi**;
(22) $K \leftarrow K \cup \{e\}$; $w \leftarrow v$
(23)   **od**;
(24) **else** cycle $\leftarrow$ false; $C \leftarrow \{e \in E : e^- \in A, e^+ \in V \backslash A$ or
$$e^+ \in A, e^- \in V \backslash A\}$$
(25) **fi**.

Theorem 9.4.6. *Algorithm 9.4.5 constructs a cycle or a cocycle of G, respectively, as described in Theorem 9.4.1. It has complexity $O(|E|)$.*

Proof. The assertion follows immediately from Theorem 9.4.1.   □

Example 9.4.7. We show that Algorithm 6.1.7 of Ford and Fulkerson (1957) is basically a special case of Algorithm 9.4.5. We choose e_0 to be the return arc $r = ts$ (compare Example 9.1.1), which is coloured black. The remaining edges e are coloured as follows: black if e is void, green if e is saturated and red otherwise. The reader should convince herself that case (1) of the Painting Lemma then yields an augmenting path from s to t, whereas in case (2) no such path exists. The cocycle the algorithm constructs in this case corresponds to a (minimal) cut of N whose capacity is equal to the value of the (maximal) flow f.

Analogous to Chapter 6, it is useful in step (5) of Algorithm 9.4.5 to choose the vertex v with $u(v) =$ false which was labelled first; then, in case (1), we get a shortest path from s to t, that is, a cycle K of shortest length. To do so, the labelled vertices are again put into a queue.

9.5 The Algorithm of Klein

The next sections treat three algorithms for constructing optimal circulations. We begin with an algorithm due to Klein (1967) which is particularly simple. During this algorithm, we have to examine an appropriate auxiliary digraph and find out whether it contains cycles of negative length; to do so, we use Algorithm 3.9.1 (NEGACYCLE).

Algorithm 9.5.1. Let G be a directed graph with capacity constraints b and c and a cost function γ. The algorithm finds out whether there exists a feasible circulation; if this is the case, an optimal circulation is constructed.

Procedure KLEIN $(G, b, c, \gamma;$ legal, $f)$

(1) LEGCIRC $(G, b, c;$ legal, $f)$;
(2) **if** legal $=$ true **then repeat**
(3) $E' \leftarrow \emptyset$;
(4)   **for** $e = uv \in E$ **do**
(5)   **if** $f(e) < c(e)$

(6)   then $E' \leftarrow E' \cup \{e\}$; $tp(e) \leftarrow 1$; $c'(e) \leftarrow c(e) - f(e)$;
              $w(e) \leftarrow \gamma(e)$ fi;
(7)   if $b(e) < f(e)$
(8)   then $e' \leftarrow vu$; $E' \leftarrow E' \cup \{e'\}$; $tp(e') \leftarrow 2$;
              $c'(e') \leftarrow f(e) - b(e)$; $w(e') \leftarrow -\gamma(e)$
(9)   fi
(10)   od;
(11) $H \leftarrow (V, E')$;
(12)   NEGACYCLE $(H, w; d, p, \text{neg}, K)$;
(13)   if neg = true
(14)   then $\delta \leftarrow \min \{c'(e) : e \in K\}$;
(15)   for $e \in K$ do
(16)   if $tp(e) = 1$ then $f(e) \leftarrow f(e) + \delta$
                  else $f(e) \leftarrow f(e) - \delta$ fi
(17)   od
(18)   fi
(19)   until neg = false
(20) fi.

We have to check whether Algorithm 9.5.1 is correct and find out its complexity. First, we show that the algorithm terminates if and only if the circulation f constructed so far is optimal. Step (19) has the effect that the algorithm terminates only if there is no cycle of negative length in the auxiliary digraph H corresponding to f. Thus, we have to prove the following lemma.

Lemma 9.5.2. *Let G be a directed graph with capacity constraints b and c and a cost function γ. Moreover, let f be a feasible circulation on G. Then f is optimal if and only if the auxiliary network (H, w) constructed in steps (3) to (11) of Algorithm 9.5.1 does not contain any directed cycle of negative length.*

Proof. It is obvious that the condition given in the assertion is necessary, because if (H, w) contains a directed cycle K of negative length, then it is possible to change the present feasible circulation f as in steps (14) to (17) such that we get a new feasible circulation with smaller cost. Note that the cost is changed by the following amount:

$$\delta\left(\sum_{\substack{e \in K \\ tp(e) = 1}} \gamma(e) - \sum_{\substack{e \in K \\ tp(e) = 2}} \gamma(e)\right) = \delta\left(\sum_{e \in K} w(e)\right) < 0.$$

Now assume conversely that the condition of the theorem is satisfied. We have to show that this implies $\gamma(g) \geq \gamma(f)$ for any feasible circulation g. For this purpose, consider the circulation $g - f$. This circulation induces a circulation on H as follows: If $c(e) \geq f(e) > g(e) \geq b(e)$, we define (with

$e = uv$ and $e' = vu$) $h(e') := f(e) - g(e)$; if $c(e) \geq g(e) > f(e) \geq b(e)$, we set $h(e) := g(e) - f(e)$. For all other edges of H, $h(e) := 0$. Then h is a non-negative circulation on H, so that, by Theorem 9.4.3, there exist elementary circulations $h_1, \ldots, h_k$ and positive numbers $\lambda_1, \ldots, \lambda_k$ with $h = \lambda_1 h_1 + \ldots + \lambda_k h_k$. It follows that

$$\gamma(g) - \gamma(f) = w(h) = \lambda_1 w(h_1) + \ldots + \lambda_k w(h_k) \geq 0,$$

because, by our hypothesis, (H, w) does not contain any directed cycles of negative length. (Here $w(h)$ denotes the cost of the circulation h on H with respect to the cost function w.) Thus, $\gamma(g) \geq \gamma(f)$ holds indeed. □

In step (1) of Algorithm 9.5.1, a feasible circulation – if one exists – is constructed by LEGCIRC (see Corollary 9.2.5); if no such circulation exists, the algorithm terminates (because legal = false). We have seen that each iteration of the **repeat**-loop changes the present feasible circulation such that the new feasible circulation has smaller cost; we leave the details to the reader. It remains to answer the question under which conditions the algorithm is sure to terminate (so that, by Lemma 9.5.2, it has constructed an optimal circulation). We assume first that b and c are integral. Then the feasible circulation constructed first is integral as well, because MAXFLOW (and hence LEGCIRC) constructs, for integral capacity constraints, an integral maximal flow (compare Theorem 6.1.5). Therefore, the capacity function c' on E' defined in steps (4) to (10) is integral, too, so that δ is integral (see step (14)). It follows by induction that each feasible circulation constructed during the algorithm is integral. We have seen that changing the present circulation f in step (16) according to a cycle K of negative length decreases the cost (see the proof of Lemma 9.5.2) by $\delta w(K)$. Thus, if we assume γ to be integral as well, the cost is decreased with each iteration of the **repeat**-loop by a positive integer. As

$$\sum_{\substack{e \\ \gamma(e) > 0}} \gamma(e)b(e) + \sum_{\substack{e \\ \gamma(e) < 0}} \gamma(e)c(e)$$

is a lower bound for $\gamma(f)$ for any feasible circulation f on G, this means that the algorithm has to terminate as soon as this bound is achieved. The same arguments can be used for rational values of b, c and γ (they can be multiplied with their main denominator).

Theorem 9.5.3. *Let G be a directed graph with rational capacity constraints b and c and a rational cost function γ. Then Algorithm 9.5.1 determines an optimal circulation f on G. If b, c and γ are integral, f is integral as well.* □

Calling LEGCIRC in Algorithm 9.5.1 has complexity $O(|V|^3)$ by Corollary 9.2.5. Moreover, each iteration of the **repeat**-loop has complexity $O(|V|^3)$, because NEGACYCLE has this complexity by Theorem 3.9.2. Unfortunately, the whole algorithm is not polynomial, because the number of iterations depends on the values of the functions b, c and γ. However, the algorithm becomes polynomial if the cycles of negative length are chosen appropriately, as Goldberg and Tarjan (1989) showed. We look at this variation of Algorithm 9.5.1 in Section 9.10.

Exercise 9.5.4. Give an upper bound for the number of iterations of the **repeat**-loop in Algorithm 9.5.1 if the functions b, c and γ are integral.

The most popular classical algorithm for determining an optimal circulation is not the Algorithm of Klein (1967) presented here, but the so-called 'out-of-kilter'-Algorithm due to Fulkerson (1961) and Minty (1960). However, this algorithm is considerably more complicated than the technique shown above; a main tool is the Painting Lemma of Section 9.4. We refer the interested reader to Ford and Fulkerson (1962), Lawler (1976) or Gondran and Minoux (1984) for a presentation of the out-of-kilter-Algorithm. This algorithm is not polynomial either; its complexity depends on the capacity constraints as well. However, it could be considered polynomial in some sense by taking the capacities into the calculation of the size of the input data (logarithmically, which means that, for a natural number z, we take $\log_2 z$ as the measure for the size of z). Edmonds and Karp (1972) showed that, using an appropriate scaling, a complexity of $O(|E|^2 p)$ can be obtained, where $p = \log_2 C$ and C is the maximum of the capacities $c(e)$. Barahona and Tardos (1989) give an algorithm which is particularly simple and, in this weaker sense, polynomial as well. It is based on Theorem 7.5.2 and an idea of Weintraub (1974) and it uses several cycles of negative length simultaneously during each iteration. The first algorithm which is polynomial in our sense[3] was given by Tardos (1985). The complexity of his algorithm is $O(|E|^2 T \log|E|)$, where T is the complexity of the MAXFLOW-Algorithm used. His result was improved and varied several times; we refer the interested reader to Fujishige (1986), Galil and Tardos (1988), Goldberg and Tarjan (1990), Goldberg and Tarjan (1989), Gabow and Tarjan (1989), Ahuja, Goldberg, Orlin and Tarjan (1992) and Orlin (1993). Altogether, it is possible at least to reach a complexity of $O(|V|^4 \log|V|)$. The Algorithm of Goldberg and Tarjan (1990) will be presented in Section 9.8; its complexity is $O(|V|^3 |E| \log|V|)$.

---

[3] Algorithms which are polynomial in our sense (that is, their complexity is independent of the capacity constraints and the cost function) are often called 'strongly polynomial' in the literature. For this property, all numbers occuring during the algorithm have to be polynomial in the total size of the input data. This is trivially true if the algorithm contains additions, subtractions, comparisons and multiplications or divisions by a constant factor only. We call algorithms which are polynomial in $|E|$, $|V|$ and the logarithm of the size of the input data 'weakly polynomial'

9.6 The Algorithm of Busacker and Gowen

In this section, we consider the special case where the lower capacity constraint on G is always 0. In this case, the circulation of value 0 is feasible. If we assume that G does not contain any directed cycles of negative length (with respect to γ), the zero circulation is even optimal. Distinguishing the edge ts as the return arc, the zero flow is a flow of minimal cost on the flow network $(G \backslash ts, c, s, t)$. We solve the Minimum Cost Flow Problem of Example 9.1.3 by constructing flows of minimal cost with increasing values beginning with the zero flow. This can be done by using a path of minimal cost for augmenting the flow. The corresponding algorithm is due to Busacker and Gowen (1961).

The Algorithm of Busacker and Gowen is basically the same as the Algorithm of Ford and Fulkerson of Section 6.1. Each change of the flow is done using an augmenting path of minimal cost. To determine such a path, the auxiliary network introduced at the beginning of Section 6.3 is used. So let $N = (G, c, s, t)$ be a flow network with cost function γ which does not contain any cycles of negative length. Moreover, let f be an *optimal flow* of value $w(f) = w$ on N (that is, f has minimal cost $\gamma(f)$ of all flows of value w). Now consider the auxiliary network $N' = (G', c', s, t)$ with respect to f and define a cost function γ' on N' as follows. For each edge $e = uv$ of G with $f(e) < c(e)$, we assign cost $\gamma'(e') := \gamma(e)$ to edge $e' = uv$ of G' (where $c'(e') = c(e) - f(e)$); for each edge $e = uv$ of G with $f(e) > 0$, edge $e'' = vu$ of G' is assigned cost $\gamma'(e'') := -\gamma(e)$ (with $c'(e'') = f(e)$). If we add the return arc $r = ts$ with capacity constraints $b(r) = c(r) := w$ to N as well as to N' (and $b(e) := 0$ for all other edges e) and set $f(r) := w$, then f is an optimal circulation and N' is the auxiliary network corresponding to this circulation (with $c'(r) := 0$). As f is optimal, N' does not contain any directed cycles of negative length according to Lemma 9.5.2. Therefore, it is possible (if w is not yet the maximal value of a flow on N) to find an augmenting path of minimal cost among all augmenting paths from s to t in N' (using the Algorithm of Floyd-Warshall of Section 3.8, for example). Suppose W is such a path and denote the capacity of W by δ. We use W for constructing a flow f' on N of value $w(f') = w + \delta$ (analogous to Algorithm 6.1.7) and claim that f' is an optimal flow of this value.

Considering f' and f as circulations, $f' - f$ is a circulation whose support is a cycle K containing the return arc r having minimal cost (with respect to γ', where $\gamma'(r) = 0$). Thus, $f' - f = \delta f_K$, where f_K is the elementary circulation corresponding to the cycle K (as in Theorem 9.3.5). Now suppose that g is any flow of value $w + \delta$ on N (or the corresponding circulation, respectively). Analogous to the proof of Lemma 9.5.2, we can show that $g - f$ induces a non-negative circulation h on N' (more precisely, on G' with the return arc r added). By Theorem 9.4.3, we can write h as a linear combination $h = \lambda_1 h_1 + \ldots + \lambda_k h_k$ of non-negative elementary circulations on N' with positive coefficients λ_i. We may assume that the h_i are ordered such that the supports of $h_1, \ldots, h_p$ contain the return arc r, whereas the supports of $h_{p+1}, \ldots, h_k$ do not. As g and f' have the same value, we have that $\lambda_1 + \ldots + \lambda_p = w(h) = w(g) - w(f) = w(f') - w(f) = \delta$. Moreover, $\gamma'(h_i) \geq \gamma'(f_K)$ for $i = 1, \ldots, p$, because K is a cycle of minimal cost containing r. Finally, we know that $\gamma'(h_i) \geq 0$ for $i = p + 1, \ldots, k$, because – as remarked above – there are no directed cycles of negative cost with respect to γ'. Thus,

$$
\begin{aligned}
\gamma'(g) - \gamma'(f) = \gamma'(h) &= \lambda_1 \gamma'(h_1) + \ldots + \lambda_k \gamma'(h_k) \\
&\geq (\lambda_1 + \ldots + \lambda_p)\gamma'(f_K) = \gamma'(f') - \gamma'(f),
\end{aligned}
$$

which implies immediately that $\gamma'(g) \geq \gamma'(f')$. We have proved the following lemma.

Lemma 9.6.1. *Let $N = (G, c, s, t)$ be a flow network with cost function γ and suppose there are no directed cycles of negative cost with respect to γ. Moreover, let f be an optimal flow of value w on N and W an augmenting path of minimal cost in the auxiliary network $N' = (G', c', s, t)$ with respect to the cost function γ' defined above. If f' is the flow we obtain by augmenting f using W (with capacity δ), then f' is an optimal flow of value $w + \delta$. If c, f and γ are integral, then so is f'.* □

Lemma 9.6.1 shows that the following algorithm is correct. As the algorithm is basically just a variation of the Algorithm of Ford and Fulkerson, we give an informal description only; the reader should be able to write down a detailed version without difficulty.

Algorithm 9.6.2. Let $N = (G, c, s, t)$ be a flow network, where the capacity function c is integral, and let γ be a cost function such that G does not contain any directed cycles having negative cost. The algorithm constructs an integral optimal flow of value v on N.

Procedure OPTFLOW $(G, c, s, t, \gamma, v; f, \text{sol})$

(1) **for** $e \in E$ **do** $f(e) \leftarrow 0$ **od**;
(2) sol $\leftarrow$ true, val $\leftarrow 0$;
(3) **while** sol = true **and** val < v **do**
(4)   construct the auxiliary network $N' = (G', c', s, t)$ with cost function γ';
(5)   **if** t is not accessible from s in G'
(6)   **then** sol $\leftarrow$ false
(7)   **else** determine a shortest path W from s to t in (G', γ');
(8) $\delta \leftarrow \min \{c'(e) : e \in W\}$; $\delta' \leftarrow \min(\delta, v - \text{val})$; val $\leftarrow$ val $+\delta'$;
(9)   augment f along W by δ'
(10)   **fi**
(11) **od.**

The Boolean variable sol states whether the problem has a solution, that is, whether there exists a flow of value v on N. If sol has value true at the end of the algorithm, then f is an optimal flow of value v. Note that at most v iterations of the **while**-loop are needed because the value val of the flow is increased by at least 1 during each iteration. Constructing N' and augmenting f needs $O(|E|)$ steps in each iteration. A shortest path with respect to γ could be determined, for example, using the Algorithm of Floyd-Warshall of Section 3.8 with complexity $O(|V|^3)$, so that we get a total (non-polynomial) complexity of $O(|V|^3 v)$ for Algorithm 9.6.2. If we assume that γ is non-negative, we may use the Algorithm of Dijkstra instead of the Algorithm of Floyd-Warshall for determining a shortest path from s to t in (G', γ') in the first iteration; this takes $O(|V|^2)$ steps only. However, during the following iterations, negative values of γ' do always occur (for backward edges). We now describe a trick due to Edmonds and Karp (1972) which allows us to use the Algorithm of Dijkstra in spite of the negative values of γ'; we substitute γ' be an appropriate non-negative auxiliary function γ^*.

Let f be an optimal flow on N of value w. Suppose we have already determined an augmenting path W of shortest length from s to t in (G', γ') and all distances $d'(s, x)$ in (G', γ'). (We mentioned already that this is possible with complexity $O(|V|^2)$ for $f = 0$ using the Algorithm of Dijkstra.) We denote the augmented (using W) optimal flow by f', the auxiliary network corresponding to f' by $N'' = (G'', c'', s, t)$ (this differs from our notation of Chapter 6) and the new cost function by γ''. What we want is to determine a shortest path W' from s to t in (G'', γ'') and all distances $d''(s, x)$ in (G'', γ''). For this purpose, we substitute $\gamma''(e)$ for each edge $e = uv$ of G'' by

$$\gamma^*(e) := \gamma''(e) + d'(s, u) - d'(s, v) \tag{9.5}$$

and denote the distances in (G'', γ^*) by $d^*(s, x)$. Now (9.5) implies for any path X from s to x in G''

$$\gamma^*(X) = \gamma''(X) - d'(s, x),$$

so that a shortest path from s to t in G'' with respect to γ^* is a shortest path with respect to γ'' as well. Moreover, the distances

$$d''(s, x) = d^*(s, x) + d'(s, x)$$

with respect to γ'' can be calculated easily from those with respect to γ^*. Thus, we can use (G'', γ^*) in the algorithm instead of (G'', γ''), which is very useful because γ^* is non-negative. To show this, let $e = uv$ be any edge of G''. If e is not contained in the augmenting path W used for constructing f' or if e is a forward edge of W, then e is an edge of G' as well. In this case, $\gamma''(e) = \gamma'(e)$ and hence (by definition of the distance), $d'(s, u) + \gamma'(e) \geq d'(s, v)$, that is, $\gamma^*(e) \geq 0$. Now if $e = uv$ is a backward edge in W, then $e' = vu$ is an edge of G' and by definition of the distance, $d'(s, u) = d'(s, v) + \gamma'(e')$ holds, because W is a path of shortest length with respect to γ'. Now

$\gamma''(e) = -\gamma'(e')$ implies that $\gamma^*(e) = 0$ in this case. Thus, γ^* is indeed non-negative. Therefore, we may use the Algorithm of Dijkstra for (G'', γ^*) and determine the distances and a shortest augmenting path W' with complexity $O(|V|^2)$ and $O(|E| \log |V|)$, respectively (compare Theorems 3.6.2 and 3.6.7, respectively). We get the following result due to Edmonds and Karp (1972).

Theorem 9.6.3. *Let $N = (G, c, s, t)$ be a flow network with integral capacity function c and non-negative cost function γ. Then Algorithm 9.6.2 can be used to determine an optimal flow of value v with complexity $O(v|V|^2)$ or $O(v|E| \log |V|)$, respectively.* ☐

In Section 10.5, we apply Algorithm 9.6.2 to an example. A particular advantage of the algorithm is that it allows to construct optimal flows for all possible values recursively. We denote the cost of an optimal flow of value v on N by $\gamma(v)$. Then Algorithm 9.6.2 can be used to find the *cost curve* of N, that is, the function $v \to \gamma(v)$.

Exercise 9.6.4. Find the properties of the cost curve of $N = (G, c, s, t)$, where the cost function γ is non-negative and the capacity function c is integral. In particular, show that the cost curve is *convex*, that is

$$\gamma(\lambda v + (1 - \lambda)v') \le \lambda\gamma(v) + (1 - \lambda)\gamma(v')$$

for all v, v' and all λ with $0 \le \lambda \le 1$.

Exercise 9.6.5. Discuss the complexity of the Assignment Problem 9.1.4.

9.7 Potentials and ε-Optimality

This section provides the necessary basics for treating the polynomial Algorithm of Goldberg and Tarjan (1990) for determining optimal circulations in the following sections. Similar to Section 6.6, we introduce a presentation of circulations which is a bit different from what we used before, but which will cause some technical simplifications (see footnote to Theorem 9.7.4). As it is not quite as obvious as it was for flow networks that the new notation is equivalent to the old definitions, we show the necessary transformations in detail.

Construction 9.7.1. Let $G = (V, E)$ be a directed graph with capacity constraints b and c. Our first step is to substitute all pairs of antiparallel edges by a single edge (having any of the two possible orientations). So suppose

$$e' = uv \qquad \text{and} \qquad e'' = vu$$

are two antiparallel edges in G. We substitute e' and e'' by the edge $e = uv$ with capacity constraints

$$b(e) := b(e') - c(e'') \qquad \text{and} \qquad c(e) := c(e') - b(e'').$$

This definition makes sense because $b(e') \leq c(e')$ and $b(e'') \leq c(e'')$ immediately imply $b(e) \leq c(e)$. If f is any feasible circulation for $N = (G, b, c)$, then f is still feasible after the above transformation of N if we define

$$f(e) := f(e') - f(e'').$$

Now suppose conversely that f is a feasible circulation on the transformed network N', that is,

$$b(e') - c(e'') \leq f(e) \leq c(e') - b(e'') \tag{9.6}$$

holds for the new edge e. We have to distribute $f(e)$ into two parts $f(e')$ and $f(e'')$ such that f is also feasible in the original network. Thus, we look for values x and y in the equation

$$f(e) = x - y$$

such that the inequalities

$$b(e') \leq x \leq c(e') \quad \text{and} \quad b(e'') \leq y = x - f(e) \leq c(e'')$$

hold. This is equivalent to

$$\max \{b(e'), b(e'') + f(e)\} \leq x \leq \min \{c(e'), c(e'') + f(e)\}.$$

It is easy to see that it is indeed possible to choose x appropriately; this follows immediately from (9.6). (A similar argument shows that we do not need parallel edges; indeed, we always excluded them when we looked at flows and circulations.)

Thus, we may now assume that $N = (G, b, c)$ does not contain any pair of antiparallel edges. In our second step, we make G and f 'symmetric', that is, we reintroduce antiparallel edges. For any edge $e = uv$, we add the antiparallel edge $e' = vu$ and define b, c and f by

$$b(e') := -c(e), \qquad c(e') := -b(e), \qquad f(e') := -f(e).$$

Then f is a feasible circulation for the new symmetric network, because

$$b(e) \leq f(e) \leq c(e)$$

implies immediately that

$$-c(e) \leq -f(e) \leq -b(e).$$

We see that we do not need to state lower bounds explicitly any more, because

$$-f(e) = f(e') \leq c(e') = -b(e)$$

automatically yields the lower bound $b(e) \leq f(e)$. For convenience, we extend the definition of c and f to all of $V \times V$ by defining the values of c and f as 0 for all pairs (u, v) which are not edges in G. Then the compatibility condition (Z2) for f is written as

$$(1) \qquad f(u, v) = -f(v, u) \qquad \text{for all } (u, v) \in V \times V$$

and

$$(2) \qquad f(u, v) \leq c(u, v) \qquad \text{for all } (u, v) \in V \times V.$$

Analogous to Section 6.6, we set

$$e(v) = e_f(v) := \sum_{u \in V} f(u, v);$$

then the flow conservation condition (Z1) is written as

$$(3) \qquad e_f(v) = 0 \qquad \text{for all } v \in V. \qquad \qquad \Box$$

From now on, we restrict our attention to networks $N = (G, c)$, where $c : V \times V \to \mathbb{R}$ is an arbitrary[4] mapping. A (feasible) *circulation* on N is a mapping $f : V \times V \to \mathbb{R}$ satisfying conditions (1), (2) and (3). A mapping which satisfies conditions (1) and (2) only is called a *pseudoflow* on N. We still have to define a cost function $\gamma : V \times V \to \mathbb{R}$ to be able to consider optimality at all. Now the antisymmetry conditions for circulations force us to require γ to satisfy the corresponding condition

$$(4) \qquad \gamma(u, v) = -\gamma(v, u) \qquad \text{for all } (u, v) \in V \times V.$$

Then the cost of a pseudoflow f is given by

$$(5) \qquad \gamma(f) := \frac{1}{2} \sum_{(u,v)} \gamma(u, v) f(u, v).$$

The factor $1/2$ is necessary because the symmetry we require has the consequence that the cost of the flow is counted twice for each edge uv of the original directed graph G in the above sum; to see this, note that $\gamma(u, v) f(u, v) = \gamma(v, u) f(v, u)$. An optimal pseudoflow (or an optimal circulation, respectively) is a pseudoflow (or a circulation) of minimal cost. This finishes the transformation of our usual circulations to the definition of circulations used by Goldberg and Tarjan (1990).[5]

Analogous to Section 6.6, we define a residual graph G_f (with respect to a given pseudoflow f); if f is a circulation, this graph corresponds to the

---

[4] Of course, c is not completely arbitrary: We must have $-c(v, u) \leq c(u, v)$, because otherwise, there are no feasible circulations on N.

[5] For an intuitive interpretation of the 'new' circulations, consider only its positive part on a network without antiparallel edges.

auxiliary network used in Section 9.5. For a given pseudoflow f, we define the *residual capacity* $r_f : V \times V \to \mathbb{R}$ by

$$r_f(v, w) := c(v, w) - f(v, w).$$

If $r_f(v, w) > 0$, edge (v, w) can be used to move some more flow: in our intuitive interpretation, this means that (u, v) is a non-saturated edge. Any edge with $r_f(v, w) > 0$ is called a *residual edge*; the *residual graph* $G_f = (V, E_f)$ with respect to f, where $E_f = \{(v, w) \in V \times V : r_f(v, w) > 0\}$, corresponds to the auxiliary network introduced in the classical approaches.

Exercise 9.7.2. Find a procedure RESIDUAL for constructing the residual graph.

We prove a further optimality criterion for circulations. We need a definition and a lemma first. A *potential* or a *price function* on the vertex set V is an arbitrary mapping $p : V \to \mathbb{R}$. For a given potential p and a given cost function γ, the *reduced cost* γ_p are defined by

$$(6) \qquad \gamma_p(u, v) := \gamma(u, v) + p(u) - p(v).$$

The following lemma is proved easily just by verifying the calculations.

Lemma 9.7.3. *Let (G, c) be a network with cost function γ and p a potential on V. Then, for any directed path W in G with start vertex u and end vertex v,*

$$\gamma_p(W) = \gamma(W) + p(u) - p(v)$$

holds. In particular, for any directed cycle K in G, we have

$$\gamma_p(K) = \gamma(K). \qquad \square$$

The second statement of the lemma, namely that the reduced cost of a directed cycle is equal to the original cost of that cycle, is particularly important for us. We need it to prove the following theorem.

Theorem 9.7.4. *Let $N = (G, c)$ be a network with cost function γ and let f be a circulation on N. Then the following statements are equivalent:*

(a) f is optimal.
(b) The residual graph G_f does not contain any directed cycles of negative length (with respect to γ).
(c) There exists a potential p on V such that $\gamma_p(u, v) \geq 0$ for all $uv \in E_f$.

(d) There exists a potential p on V which satisfies the condition

$$\gamma_p(u,v) < 0 \Rightarrow f(u,v) = c(u,v).^6$$

for all $(u,v) \in V \times V$.

Proof. Conditions (a) and (b) are equivalent by Lemma 9.5.2. Moreover, conditions (c) and (d) are obviously equivalent if we consider the definition of the residual graph G_f. Thus, it is sufficient to show that conditions (b) and (c) are equivalent. First, let p be a potential satisfying condition (c). Then it is trivial that all cycles in G_f have non-negative length with respect to the reduced cost γ_p. By Lemma 9.7.3, the analogous condition holds for γ, that is, (b) is satisfied.

Now suppose conversely that condition (b) holds. We construct an auxiliary graph H_f by adding a new vertex s and all edges sv for $v \in V$ to G_f. By construction, s is a root of H_f. We extend γ to H_f by defining $\gamma(sv) := 0$ for all $v \in V$. As G_f (and hence H_f) does not contain any cycles of negative length, Theorem 3.4.6 yields that there exists an SP-tree T with root s for H_f. We define a potential p by $p(v) := d_T(s,v)$, where $d_T(s,v)$ denotes the distance of s from v in the network (T,γ). Then, by Exercise 3.4.5, the condition

$$d_T(s,v) \leq d_T(s,u) + \gamma(u,v)$$

holds for all edges $uv \in G_f$, so that

$$\gamma_p(u,v) = \gamma(u,v) + p(u) - p(v) \geq 0 \quad \text{for all } uv \in G_f.$$

Thus, the potential p defined above satisfies condition (c).   □

The basic idea of the Algorithm of Goldberg and Tarjan (1990) is to construct a sequence of circulations on (G,c) (improving with each step) which are 'almost optimal'. Theorem 9.7.4 suggests the following weakening of the notion of optimality: A circulation (or, more general, a pseudoflow) f is called ε-*optimal* if there exists a potential p on V satisfying the condition

$$(7) \quad \gamma_p(u,v) \geq -\varepsilon \quad \text{for all } uv \in G_f,$$

---

[6] The optimality criterion for potentials is one example for how the different way of description used in this section simplifies the technical details of our presentation. Of course, an analogous criterion can be proved using the standard notation for a network (G,b,c). However, we need three conditions which have to be satisfied for all edges $uv \in E$, namely (compare Ahuja, Magnanti and Orlin (1993), p.330):
a) $f(u,v) = b(u,v) \Rightarrow c_p(u,v) \geq 0$,
b) $f(u,v) = c(u,v) \Rightarrow c_p(u,v) \leq 0$,
c) $b(u,v) < f(u,v) < c(u,v) \Rightarrow c_p(u,v) = 0$.
These conditions are called *complementary slackness conditions*; they are a special case of the corresponding conditions used in Linear Programming. Note that the potentials $p(v)$ correspond to the dual variables if the problem of determining an optimal circulation is written as a linear program.

where $\varepsilon \geq 0$ is any real number. Obviously, (7) can be written as

(7′) $\gamma_p(u, v) < -\varepsilon \Rightarrow uv \notin G_f$ for all $(u, v) \in V \times V$.

The following simple result shows how important the notion of ε-optimality is (at least for integral cost functions). It states that it is sufficient to determine an almost optimal circulation.

Theorem 9.7.5. Let $N = (G, c)$ be a network with an integral cost function $\gamma : V \times V \to \mathbb{Z}$. Moreover, let $\varepsilon > 0$ be a real number satisfying the condition $\varepsilon |V| < 1$. Then any ε-optimal circulation on N is already optimal.

Proof. Let p be a potential satisfying condition (7) and suppose K is a directed cycle in G_f. Then Lemma 9.7.3 implies

$$\gamma(K) = \gamma_p(K) \geq -|K|\varepsilon \geq -|V|\varepsilon > -1.$$

As γ is integral, we have $\gamma(K) \geq 0$. Thus, (G_f, γ) does not contain any directed cycles of negative length, so that f is optimal by Theorem 9.7.4. $\square$

Next, we need a method for checking whether a given circulation is ε-optimal and, if it is, for constructing a corresponding potential satisfying condition (7). This can be done with similar arguments as in the proof of Theorem 9.7.4; the corresponding result is true even for pseudoflows.

Theorem 9.7.6. Let f be a pseudoflow on the network $N = (G, c)$ with cost function γ. For $\varepsilon > 0$, we define the function $\gamma^{(\varepsilon)}$ by

$$\gamma^{(\varepsilon)}(u, v) := \gamma(u, v) + \varepsilon \quad \text{for all } (u, v) \in V \times V.$$

Then f is ε-optimal if and only if the network $(G_f, \gamma^{(\varepsilon)})$ does not contain any directed cycles of negative length.

Proof. We define the graph H_f as in the proof of Theorem 9.7.4. Note that the directed cycles in H_f are precisely the same as in G_f, because s has indegree 0. We extend $\gamma^{(\varepsilon)}$ to H_f by defining $\gamma^{(\varepsilon)}(sv) := 0$ for all $v \in V$, so that we can check the condition given in the statement for H_f (instead of G_f). First suppose that f is ε-optimal with respect to the potential p and let K be a directed cycle in G_f. Then Lemma 9.7.3 implies $\gamma(K) = \gamma_p(K) \geq -|K|\varepsilon$ and hence

$$\gamma^{(\varepsilon)}(K) = \gamma(K) + |K|\varepsilon \geq 0.$$

Thus, $(G_f, \gamma^{(\epsilon)})$ does not contain any directed cycles of negative length. Conversely, suppose that this condition holds. Analogous to the proof of Theorem 9.7.4, we can choose an SP-tree T for $(H_f, \gamma^{(\varepsilon)})$ and define the potential p by $p(v) := d_T(s, v)$. It follows that

$$\gamma_p^{(\varepsilon)}(u, v) \geq 0, \quad \text{that is,} \quad \gamma_p(u, v) \geq -\varepsilon$$

for all $(u, v) \in G_f$. $\square$

The proof of Theorem 9.7.6 shows the validity of the following corollary, which allows us to construct the corresponding potential p satisfying condition (7) for any ε-optimal circulation with complexity $O(|V||E|)$ (using Exercise 3.9.3).

Corollary 9.7.7. *Let f be an ε-optimal pseudoflow on $N = (G, c)$ with respect to the cost function γ. Moreover, let T be an SP-tree with root s in the auxiliary graph H_f with respect to $\gamma^{(\varepsilon)}$. Then the potential p defined by*

$$p(v) := d_T(s, v)$$

satisfies condition (7). □

Exercise 9.7.8. Write down a procedure POTENTIAL explicitly which determines a potential as in Corollary 9.7.7 with complexity $O(|V||E|)$.

Note that any pseudoflow f – and hence any circulation – on (G, c) is ε-optimal (with respect to γ) for some appropriate value of ε. For example, if ε is the maximum C of all values $|\gamma(u, v)|$ and the potential p is the zero potential, f is always ε-optimal. Thus, the problem is how to find the smallest ε such that a given pseudoflow f is still ε-optimal; in this case, we call f an ε-*tight* pseudoflow. We need one more notation to be able to state a characterization for ε-tight pseudoflows. Let (H, w) be a network. For any directed cycle K in H,

$$m(K) := \frac{w(K)}{|K|}$$

is called the *mean weight* of K.[7] Moreover,

$$\mu(H, w) := \min\{m(K) : K \text{ directed cycle in } (H, w)\}$$

is called the *minimum cycle mean*.

Theorem 9.7.9. *Let f be a pseudoflow on (G, c) which is not optimal with respect to the cost function γ. Then f is ε-tight, where $\varepsilon := \mu(G_f, \gamma)$.*

Proof. Let K be a directed cycle in G_f and suppose ε is the real number for which f is ε-tight. Then Theorem 9.7.6 implies (using the notation of Theorem 9.7.6)

$$\gamma^{(\varepsilon)}(K) = \gamma(K) + |K|\varepsilon \geq 0,$$

that is,

$$m(K) = \frac{\gamma(K)}{|K|} \geq -\varepsilon.$$

As this is true for any directed cycle K, we have

$$\mu := \mu(G_f, \gamma) \geq -\varepsilon, \quad \text{that is,} \quad \varepsilon \geq -\mu.$$

---

[7] In our context, the names 'mean cost' or 'mean length' would make more sense; however, we do not intend to deviate from common usage.

Conversely, for any directed cycle K,

$$m(K) = \frac{\gamma(K)}{|K|} \geq \mu$$

holds by definition. It follows that

$$\gamma^{(-\mu)}(K) = \gamma(K) - |K|\mu \geq 0.$$

Using Theorem 9.7.6 again, f is at least $(-\mu)$-optimal, so that $\varepsilon \leq -\mu$. Hence $\varepsilon = -\mu$. $\qquad\square$

It remains to answer the question how the minimum cycle mean could be determined. Karp (1978) showed that this can be done with complexity $O(|V||E|)$, the same complexity as for determining an SP-tree or checking whether a directed cycle of negative length exists (see 3.9.3). Note that determining $\mu(H, w)$ also answers the question whether a cycle of negative length exists. The technique used by Karp (1978) is based on the following characterization of $\mu(H, w)$.

Theorem 9.7.10. *Let (H, w) be a network on the directed graph $H = (V, E)$ with root s and suppose H contains directed cycles. For any vertex v and any positive integer k let $F_k(v)$ denote the minimal length of a directed walk from s to v with exactly k edges; if such a walk does not exist, we define $F_k(v) = \infty$. Then*

$$\mu(H, w) = \min_{v \in V} \max \left\{ \frac{F_n(v) - F_k(v)}{n - k} : k = 1, \ldots, n - 1 \right\},$$

where $n = |V|$.

Proof. We prove the above identity first for the special case that $\mu(H, w) = 0$. Then (H, w) does not contain any directed cycles of negative length, so that the shortest length of a path from s to v is equal to the shortest length of a walk from s to v. Therefore,

$$F_n(v) \geq d(s, v) = \min \{F_k(v) : k = 1, \ldots, n - 1\},$$

and hence

$$F_n(v) - d(s, v) = \max \{F_n(v) - F_k(v) : k = 1, \ldots, n - 1\} \geq 0$$

and

$$\max \left\{ \frac{F_n(v) - F_k(v)}{n - k} : k = 1, \ldots, n - 1 \right\} \geq 0.$$

We see that it suffices to show that there exists a vertex v with $F_n(v) = d(s, v)$. Let K be any cycle of weight 0 and u a vertex in K; moreover, let W be a path of length $d(s, u)$ from s to u. Then, if we append K to W once or several times, we always get a shortest walk W' (of length $d(s, u)$)

from s to u. Note that any part W'' of W' beginning in s with end vertex v, say, has to be a shortest walk from s to v. It is obvious that we may choose v in such a way that W'' consists of exactly n edges; this vertex v then satisfies $F_n(v) = d(s, v)$.

It remains to consider the case $\mu(H, w) = \mu \neq 0$. We substitute the weight function w by the function w' defined by

$$w'(uv) := w(uv) - \mu \qquad \text{for all } uv \in E.$$

Then any cycle K in H satisfies

$$w'(K) = w(K) - |K|\mu,$$

so that

$$m'(K) = m(K) - \mu.$$

Thus, the minimum cycle mean for directed cycles is reduced by μ; it follows that $\mu(H, w') = 0$. This means we may apply our above considerations to (H, w'), so that

$$\mu(H, w') = 0 = \min_{v \in V} \ \max \ \{\frac{F_n'(v) - F_k'(v)}{n - k} : k = 1, \ldots, n - 1\}.$$

Obviously, any walk W in H satisfies

$$w'(W) = w(W) - |W|\mu,$$

so that $F_l'(v) = F_l(v) - l\mu$. This implies

$$\frac{F_n'(v) - F_k'(v)}{n - k} = \frac{(F_n(v) - n\mu) - (F_k(v) - k\mu)}{n - k} = \frac{F_n(v) - F_k(v)}{n - k} - \mu$$

and the statement of the theorem follows. $\qquad \qquad \square$

Corollary 9.7.11. *Let H be any connected directed graph with weight function $w : E \to \mathbb{R}$. Then $\mu(H, w)$ can be determined with complexity $O(|V||E|)$.*

Proof. If H is acyclic (which can be checked with complexity $O(|E|)$ by Theorem 2.6.6), we have $\mu(H, w) = \infty$. Otherwise we may, if necessary, add a root s to H (as we did in the proof of Theorem 9.7.4) without introducing any new directed cycles. Then Theorem 9.7.10 may be applied to the new graph. The values $F_k(v)$ can be calculated recursively using the initial values

$$F_0(s) = 0, \quad F_0(v) = \infty \quad \text{for } v \neq s$$

and the identity

$$F_k(v) = \ \min \ \{F_{k-1}(u) + w(uv) : uv \in E\};$$

this obviously takes $O(|V||E|)$ steps. Having calculated all the $F_k(v)$, $\mu(H, w)$ can be determined by $O(|V|^2)$ comparisons (by Theorem 9.7.9). As H is connected, $|V|$ is dominated by $|E|$ and the assertion follows. $\qquad \square$

Exercise 9.7.12. Write down a procedure MEANCYCLE having the properties described in Corollary 9.7.11. The procedure should (without increasing the complexity) also be able to construct a cycle explicitly which has the minimum cycle mean as its mean weight.

A further algorithm for determining $\mu(H, w)$ was given by Orlin and Ahuja (1992); their algorithm has a complexity of $O(|V|^{1/2}|E| \log (|V|C))$, where C is the maximum of the absolute values $|\gamma(u, v)|$. Young, Tarjan and Orlin (1991) designed another efficient algorithm; experiments with random graphs suggest that its average complexity is $O(|E| + |V| \log|V|)$. We summarize the results about circulations obtained so far.

Theorem 9.7.13. Let f be a circulation on the network $N = (G, c)$ with cost function γ. Then the number ε for which f is ε-tight can be determined with complexity $O(|V||E|)$.

Proof. We calculate $\mu = \mu(G_f, \gamma)$; this can be done with the desired complexity by Corollary 9.7.11. If $\mu \geq 0$, G_f does not contain any directed cycles of negative length with respect to γ, so that f is optimal by Theorem 9.7.4 and hence $\varepsilon = 0$. Otherwise $\mu < 0$ and f is not optimal. But then $\varepsilon = -\mu$ by Theorem 9.7.9. $\square$

Theorem 9.7.13 allows us to determine an optimal measure for the quality of any given circulation on N. As mentioned above, the method of Goldberg and Tarjan (1990) is based on finding a sequence of ε-optimal circulations for decreasing ε and finally applying Theorem 9.7.5 (in the integral case). We present their algorithm in the next section.

Exercise 9.7.14. Write down a procedure TIGHT explicitly which determines the number ε of Theorem 9.7.13 with complexity $O(|V||E|)$.

9.8 Determining Optimal Circulations by Successive Approximation

In this section, we present a generic version of the polynomial Algorithm of Goldberg and Tarjan (1990) for determining optimal circulations which is based on the ideas treated in the previous section. We assume that we have already designed an auxiliary procedure REFINE which constructs from an ε-optimal circulation f with corresponding potential p a circulation f' with corresponding potential p' for $\varepsilon' = \varepsilon/2$. An efficient version of REFINE will be derived in the next section. We always assume that the network we deal with does not have any antiparallel edges; we may do this w.l.o.g. because of the considerations of the beginning of the last section.

Algorithm 9.8.1. Let $N = (G_0, b, c)$ be a network with cost function γ, where $G_0 = (V, E_0)$ is a directed graph without any pairs of antiparallel edges. The algorithm constructs (if possible) an optimal circulation f_0 on N.

Procedure OPTCIRC $(G_0, b, c, \gamma;$ legal, $f_0)$

(1) LEGCIRC $(G_0, b, c;$ legal, $f)$
(2) **if** legal $=$ true **then**
(3) $E \leftarrow E_0$;
(4)   **for** $uv \in E_0$ **do**
(5) $E \leftarrow E \cup \{vu\};\ f(v, u) \leftarrow -f(u, v)$;
(6) $\gamma(v, u) \leftarrow -\gamma(u, v);\ c(v, u) \leftarrow -b(u, v)$
(7)   **od**;
(8) $G \leftarrow (V, E)$;
(9)   TIGHT $(G, c, \gamma, f; \varepsilon)$
(10)   **while** $\varepsilon > 0$ **do**
(11)   POTENTIAL $(G, c, \gamma, f, \varepsilon; p)$;
(12)   REFINE $(G, c, \gamma, f, \varepsilon, p; f)$;
(13)   TIGHT $(G, c, \gamma, f; \varepsilon)$
(14)   **od**;
(15) $f_0 \leftarrow f|E_0$;
(16) **fi**.

Theorem 9.8.2. *Let $N = (G_0, b, c)$ be a network with an integral cost function γ, where $G_0 = (V, E_0)$ is a directed graph without any pairs of antiparallel edges. Moreover, suppose that REFINE is a procedure which constructs from an ε-optimal circulation f with corresponding potential p an $\varepsilon/2$-optimal circulation and its corresponding potential. Then Algorithm 9.8.1 constructs an optimal circulation f_0 on N (if there are any feasible circulations at all) with complexity $O(\log(|V|C))$, where*

$$ C := \ max \ \{|\gamma(e)| : e \in E_0\}. $$

Proof. By Corollary 9.2.5, step (1) of the algorithm constructs (if possible) a feasible circulation f on N. Steps (3) to (8) determine, as in Construction 9.7.1, the symmetric version (G, c) of the network (G_0, b, c) as well as the corresponding versions of the functions f and γ. In step (9), the procedure TIGHT calculates the value of ε for which f is ε-tight. If $\varepsilon > 0$, that is, f is not yet optimal, the algorithm determines a corresponding potential p for f, improves f to an $\varepsilon/2$-optimal circulation f' and determines the precise value of ε' for which f' is ε'-tight. All this is done during the **while**-loop (10) to (14) and this **while**-loop terminates only if $\varepsilon' = 0$, that is, f' is an optimal circulation. As ε is decreased with each iteration of the loop by at least a factor of $1/2$ (note that $\varepsilon' < \varepsilon/2$ is possible!) and the initial circulation f is trivially C-optimal (this was already mentioned in Section 9.7), an ε-optimal circulation f for $\varepsilon < 1/|V|$ is found after at most $O(\log(|V|C))$ iterations. Theorem 9.7.5 then yields that f is already optimal, so that $\varepsilon = 0$ and the **while**-loop is terminated. Finally, in step (15), f_0 is assigned the values of the optimal circulation f (on (G, c)) restricted to the original network.   □

In the remainder of this section, we show that Algorithm 9.8.1 terminates even if γ is not necessarily integral (after $O(|E| \log |V|)$ iterations). This requires some work still; we begin by showing that the value $f(e)$ for those edges e where the reduced cost $\gamma_p(e)$ (with respect to the potential p corresponding to f) is considerably larger than ε (where f is ε-tight) cannot be changed any more in subsequent iterations.

Theorem 9.8.3. *Let f be an ε-optimal circulation with corresponding potential p on a network $N = (G, c)$ with cost function γ. Moreover, suppose that $\varepsilon > 0$ and that*

$$|\gamma_p(u, v)| \geq |V|(\varepsilon + \delta)$$

holds for some edge uv and a constant $\delta \geq 0$. Then any δ-optimal circulation g satisfies $g(u, v) = f(u, v)$.

Proof. Because of the antisymmetry of f and γ, we may assume that $\gamma_p(u, v) \geq 0$. So let g be any circulation with $g(u, v) \neq f(u, v)$. Our hypothesis yields that $\gamma_p(u, v) > \varepsilon$, that is, $\gamma_p(v, u) < -\varepsilon$. Then the definition of ε-optimality implies

$$f(u, v) = -f(v, u) = -c(v, u).$$

Therefore, $g(u, v) \neq f(u, v)$ and

$$g(u, v) = -g(v, u) \geq -c(v, u)$$

together imply that $g(u, v) > f(u, v)$. We show that g cannot be δ-optimal. For this purpose, we look at the directed graph $G^>$ on vertex set V with edge set

$$E^> := \{xy \in E : g(x, y) > f(x, y)\}.$$

Obviously, $G^>$ is a subdigraph of G_f containing edge uv. We show first that $G^>$ contains a directed cycle containing uv. Consider the directed graph H whose edges are all those edges e of G_f satisfying

$$h(e) := g(e) - f(e) \neq 0.$$

We colour the edges of H either black or green depending on whether $h(e) > 0$ or $h(e) < 0$. The antisymmetry condition implies that an edge $e = xy$ is black if and only if the antiparallel edge $e' = yx$ is green. Now we apply the Painting Lemma (Theorem 9.4.1): There exists either a cycle K or a cocycle C containing $e_0 := uv$ such that all black edges of this cycle (or cocycle, respectively) have the same orientation as e_0, whereas all green edges are oriented in the opposite direction. In the first case, any green edge occuring in K can be substituted by the corresponding antiparallel edge, so that we get a directed cycle in $G^>$ containing e_0. The second case leads to a contradiction: Let (S, T) be the cut of H corresponding to C. By Exercise 9.3.4, we have that $h(S,T) = h(T,S)$. However, the properties of C given in the painting lemma (and $e_0 \in C$) imply that $h(S,T) > 0$ and $h(T,S) < 0$. Thus, this case is not possible, so that a directed cycle K containing uv has to exist in $G^>$ as desired. All edges of K are contained in G_f, which implies (using Lemma 9.7.3 and the definition of ε-optimality) that

$$\begin{aligned} \gamma(K) &= \gamma_p(K) \geq \gamma_p(u,v) - (|K| - 1)\varepsilon \\ &\geq |V|(\varepsilon + \delta) - (|V| - 1)\varepsilon > |V|\delta \geq |K|\delta \end{aligned}$$

holds. Now let $\overline{K}$ be the cycle of G which we obtain by inverting the orientation of all edges of K. Then $\overline{K}$ is contained in $G^<$, where $G^<$ is the subdigraph having edge set

$$E^< := \{xy \in E : g(x,y) < f(x,y)\},$$

so that $G^<$ is contained in the residual graph G_g. The antisymmetry of γ implies

$$\gamma(\overline{K}) = -\gamma(K) < -|K|\delta = -|\overline{K}|\delta$$

and hence

$$\gamma^{(\delta)}(\overline{K}) = \gamma(\overline{K}) + \delta|\overline{K}| < 0.$$

Now g cannot be δ-optimal by Theorem 9.7.6. $\square$

We call an edge uv ε-*fixed* if the value $f(u,v)$ is the same for all ε-optimal circulations f on (G,c) with respect to γ.

Corollary 9.8.4. *Let f be an ε-optimal circulation with corresponding potential p on (G,c) with respect to cost function γ, where $\varepsilon > 0$. Then any edge uv with*

$$|\gamma_p(u,v)| \geq 2|V|\varepsilon$$

is ε-fixed. $\square$

Lemma 9.8.5. *Let f be an ε-tight circulation with $\varepsilon \neq 0$ on the network $N = (G,c)$ with respect to cost function γ and potential p. Moreover, let K be a directed cycle of minimum cycle mean in the residual graph G_f. Then*

$$\gamma_p(u,v) = -\varepsilon \quad \text{for all } uv \in K.$$

Proof. By hypothesis, we have

$$\gamma_p(u,v) \geq -\varepsilon \quad \text{for all } uv \in E_f. \tag{9.7}$$

On the other hand, $\mu(G_f,\gamma) = -\varepsilon$ by Theorem 9.7.9; note that this number is negative because $\varepsilon \neq 0$. Then, by Lemma 9.7.3,

$$\frac{1}{|K|}\sum_{uv \in K}\gamma_p(u,v) = \frac{1}{|K|}\sum_{uv \in K}\gamma(u,v) = m(K) = -\varepsilon.$$

Now (9.7) immediately implies the assertion. $\square$

Lemma 9.8.6. *Let $N = (G, c)$ be a network with cost function γ. For $\varepsilon > 0$, let F_ε denote the set of all ε-fixed edges in G. If there exists an ε-tight circulation f, then, for any non-negative constant δ with $2\delta|V| \leq \varepsilon$, the set F_ε is a proper subset of F_δ.*

Proof. It is trivial that $F_\varepsilon \subseteq F_\delta$. Thus, we have to find some edge which is δ-fixed but not ε-fixed. As f is an ε-tight circulation, there exists a directed cycle K in the residual graph G_f of mean weight $m(K) = -\varepsilon$ (with respect to γ) by Theorem 9.7.9. Thus, we may increase f along K by a sufficiently small amount and get a new feasible circulation f'. We want to show that f' is ε-optimal as well, which implies that the edges of K cannot be contained in F_ε. So let p be a potential corresponding to f, then $\gamma_p(u, v) \geq -\varepsilon$ holds for all edges uv in G_f. The only edges uv of $G_{f'}$ which are not necessarily contained in G_f as well are those edges for which vu is contained in K (note that at least the cycle having opposite orientation to K has to be contained in $G_{f'}$!). These edges satisfy (because $vu \in G_f$ and by Lemma 9.8.5)

$$\gamma_p(u, v) = -\gamma_p(v, u) = \varepsilon > 0,$$

so that f' is ε-optimal with respect to potential p.

Next, we show that at least one edge of K is contained in F_δ. Let g be any δ-optimal circulation with corresponding potential p'. By the choice of K, we have

$$\gamma_{p'}(K) = \gamma_p(K) = \gamma(K) = -|K|\varepsilon;$$

we used Lemma 9.7.3 again. Therefore, K has to contain an edge uv with

$$\gamma_{p'}(u, v) \leq -\varepsilon \leq -2|V|\delta.$$

Thus, $|\gamma_{p'}(u, v)| \geq 2|V|\delta$, so that, by Corollary 9.8.4, uv is contained in F_δ. $\square$

Theorem 9.8.7. *If there exists any feasible circulation on N, Algorithm 9.8.1 determines an optimal circulation on N in $O(|E| \log|V|)$ iterations of the **while**-loop, assuming that REFINE satisfies the requirements of Theorem 9.8.2.*

Proof. Let f be an ε-optimal circulation calculated at some point of the algorithm. By our assumptions with respect to REFINE, we need at most $O(\log |V|)$ iterations to construct a δ-tight circulation f' from f for some δ with $\delta \leq \varepsilon/2|V|$. If $\delta = 0$, the algorithm terminates. Otherwise, the set F_δ of δ-fixed edges contains at least one more edge than F_ε. Now the algorithm has to terminate for sure if *all* edges are δ-fixed, which takes at most $O(|E| \log |V|)$ iterations. $\square$

Note that Algorithm 9.8.1 terminates earlier in general, because, in most cases, not all edges are 0-fixed: It is very well possible that there are several different optimal circulations. In the next section, we show that the auxiliary procedure REFINE can be executed in $O(|V|^3)$ steps. The above results then yield the following theorem proved by Goldberg and Tarjan (1990).

Theorem 9.8.8. *Let $N = (G, b, c)$ be a network with cost function γ. Then Algorithm 9.8.1 determines an optimal circulation on N with complexity $O(|E||V|^3 \log |V|)$. If γ is integral and $C = max\,\{|\gamma(u, v)| : uv \in E\}$, the complexity is bounded by $O(|V|^3 \log (|V|C))$ as well.* $\square$

If G is not a dense graph, the complexity may be improved by using intricate data structures; Goldberg and Tarjan (1990) gave a version of REFINE which needs only $O(|V||E| \log (|V|^2/|E|))$ steps.

9.9 A Polynomial Procedure REFINE

We still have to describe the auxiliary procedure REFINE with complexity $O(|V|^3)$ which was used in the last section. This procedure due to Goldberg and Tarjan (1990) is very similar to Algorithm 6.6.1 of Goldberg and Tarjan (1988) for determining a maximal flow on a flow network; even the proofs are similar. As in Section 6.6, we first give a rather general version where the auxiliary operations used can be chosen in any arbitrary order. Afterwards, an appropriate way of choosing these operations will lead to a comparatively good complexity. Again, we call a vertex v *active* if its flow excess (defined as usual) $e(v)$ satisfies the condition $e(v) > 0$ with respect to f.

Algorithm 9.9.1. Let (G, c) be a network as described in 9.7.1 with cost function γ. Moreover, let f be an ε-optimal circulation with corresponding potential p. The algorithm determines an $\varepsilon/2$-optimal circulation and the corresponding potential.

Procedure REFINE $(G, c, \gamma, f, \varepsilon, p; f)$

(1) $\varepsilon \leftarrow \varepsilon/2$;
(2) **for** $uv \in E$ **do**
(3) $\gamma_p(u, v) \leftarrow \gamma(u, v) + p(u) - p(v)$;
(4)   **if** $\gamma_p(u, v) < 0$
(5)   **then** $f(u, v) \leftarrow c(u, v)$; $f(v, u) \leftarrow -c(u, v)$;
(6) $r_f(u, v) \leftarrow 0$; $r_f(v, u) \leftarrow c(v, u) - f(v, u)$
(7)   **fi**
(8) **od**;
(9) **for** $v \in V$ **do** $e(v) \leftarrow \sum_u f(u, v)$ **od**;
(10) **while** there exist admissible operations **do**
(11)   choose some admissible operation and execute it
(12) **od**.

Here the possible admissible operations are:

Procedure PUSH($f, v, w; f$)

(1) $\delta \leftarrow$ min $(e(v), r_f(v, w))$;
(2) $f(v, w) \leftarrow f(v, w) + \delta$; $f(w, v) \leftarrow f(w, v) - \delta$;
(3) $r_f(v, w) \leftarrow r_f(v, w) - \delta$; $r_f(w, v) \leftarrow r_f(w, v) + \delta$;
(4) $e(v) \leftarrow e(v) - \delta$; $e(w) \leftarrow e(w) + \delta$.

PUSH is *admissible* if v is active and $r_f(v, w) > 0$ and $\gamma_p(v, w) < 0$ hold.

Procedure RELABEL $(f, v, p; f, p)$

(1) $\Delta \leftarrow \varepsilon+$ min $\{\gamma_p(v, w) : r_f(v, w) > 0\}$;
(2) $p(v) \leftarrow p(v) - \Delta$;
(3) **for** $w \in V \backslash \{v\}$ **do**
(4) $\gamma_p(v, w) \leftarrow \gamma_p(v, w) - \Delta$; $\gamma_p(w, v) \leftarrow -\gamma_p(v, w)$
(5) **od.**

RELABEL is *admissible* if v is active and $r_f(v, w) > 0$ always implies $\gamma_p(v, w) \geq 0$. Alternatively, we could describe the modification of the value $p(v)$ in RELABEL by the command

$$p(v) \leftarrow \text{ max } \{p(w) - \gamma(v, w) - \varepsilon : r_f(v, w) > 0\}$$

(as in the original paper).

We show first (as in Section 6.6) that Algorithm 9.9.1 is correct, assuming that it terminates. The following lemma is similar to Lemma 6.6.2 and equally obvious.

Lemma 9.9.2. *Let f be an ε-optimal pseudoflow on (G, c) with respect to cost function γ and corresponding potential p. Moreover, let v be an active vertex. Then either RELABEL(v) is admissible or there is an edge vw for which PUSH(v, w) is admissible.*   □

Lemma 9.9.3. *Let f be an ε-optimal pseudoflow on (G, c) with respect to cost function γ and corresponding potential p. Moreover, let v be an active vertex. Then the changed flow after a PUSH-operation on some edge vw is still ε-optimal. A RELABEL(v)-operation decreases $p(v)$ by at least ε; again, the flow is still ε-optimal after the RELABEL-operation.*

Proof. To prove the first statement, note that a PUSH(v, w) does not change the reduced cost of edges which occur already in G_f. If edge wv is added to G_f by the PUSH(v, w), the conditions for the admissibility of a PUSH-operation yield that $\gamma_p(v, w) < 0$, so that $\gamma_p(w, v) > 0$ and the new residual edge wv satisfies the condition for ε-optimality.

Now consider a RELABEL(v)-operation. If this operation is admissible, we must have $\gamma_p(v, w) \geq 0$ for all $vw \in E_f$, so that

$$p(v) \geq p(w) - \gamma(v, w) \quad \text{for all } vw \in E_f$$

holds before the RELABEL is executed. This implies for the changed value $p'(v)$ of the potential after the RELABEL:

$$p'(v) = \max \{p(w) - \gamma(v, w) - \varepsilon : vw \in E_f\} \leq p(v) - \varepsilon.$$

Therefore, $p(v)$ is decreased by at least ε during the RELABEL(v)-operation. The only edges whose reduced cost is changed by a RELABEL(v) are the edges which are incident with v. For any edge of the form wv, $\gamma_p(w, v)$ is increased by at least ε; trivially, this does not change the ε-optimality. Now consider a residual edge of the form vw. By definition of $p'(v)$, such an edge satisfies

$$p'(v) \geq p(w) - \gamma(v, w) - \varepsilon$$

and hence

$$\gamma_{p'}(v, w) = \gamma(v, w) + p'(v) - p(w) \geq -\varepsilon,$$

so that the condition for ε-optimality holds in this case as well.   □

Theorem 9.9.4. *If Algorithm 9.9.1 terminates, the pseudoflow f it constructed is an $\varepsilon/2$-optimal circulation.*

Proof. Note that the pseudoflow f constructed during the initialization (2) to (8) is even 0-optimal by definition, so that it is for sure $\varepsilon/2$-optimal (because all edges with negative reduced cost are saturated). Now Lemma 9.9.3 states that the flow keeps the property of $\varepsilon/2$-optimality during the whole algorithm. However, because of Lemma 9.9.2, the algorithm can terminate only if there is no active vertex any more. But this means that $e(v) \leq 0$ holds for all vertices v, so that

$$\sum_v e(v) = \sum_{u,v} f(u, v) = 0$$

implies that $e(v) = 0$ for all vertices v. Therefore, the $\varepsilon/2$-optimal pseudoflow which was constructed during the last iteration of the algorithm is indeed a circulation.   □

To show that Algorithm 9.9.1 terminates, we have to find an upper bound for the number of admissible operations executed during the algorithm. As in Section 6.6, we distinguish *saturating* PUSH-operations (those with $\delta = r_f(v, w)$) and *non-saturating* PUSH-operations. We begin by analyzing the RELABEL-operations. The following important lemma is analogous to Lemma 6.6.6.

Lemma 9.9.5. *Let f be a pseudoflow and g a circulation on (G, c). For any vertex v with $e_f(v) > 0$, there exists a vertex w with $e_f(w) > 0$ and a sequence of pairwise distinct vertices $v = v_0, v_1, \ldots, v_{k-1}, v_k = w$ with $v_i v_{i+1} \in E_f$ and $v_{i+1} v_i \in E_g$ for $i = 0, \ldots, k - 1$.*

Proof. We define the directed graphs $G^>$ and $G^<$ as in the proof of Theorem 9.8.3; then $G^>$ is a subdigraph of G_f and $G^<$ is a subdigraph of G_g. Moreover, we have

$$xy \in E^> \Leftrightarrow yx \in E^<,$$

because pseudoflows are antisymmetric. Thus, it is sufficient to show that a (directed) path

$$W \quad : \quad v_0 = v \text{------} v_1 \text{------} \ldots \text{------} v_k$$

with $e_f(v_k) < 0$ exists in $G^>$. Denote the set of vertices which are accessible from v in $G^>$ by S and set $\overline{S} := V \backslash S$. (The set $\overline{S}$ might be empty.) For any pair (x, y) of vertices with $x \in S$ and $y \in \overline{S}$, we have $g(x, y) \leq f(x, y)$ by definition. Now, as g is a circulation and f and g are antisymmetric,

$$
\begin{aligned}
0 &= \sum_{y \in \overline{S}} e_g(y) = \sum_{x \in V, y \in \overline{S}} g(x, y) \\
&= \sum_{x \in S, y \in \overline{S}} g(x, y) \leq \sum_{x \in S, y \in \overline{S}} f(x, y) \\
&= \sum_{x \in S, y \in V} f(x, y) = - \sum_{x \in S, y \in V} f(y, x) = - \sum_{x \in S} e_f(x).
\end{aligned}
$$

However, $v \in S$ and $e_f(v) > 0$. Therefore, S has to contain a vertex w with $e_f(w) < 0$, which proves the statement. □

Lemma 9.9.6. *At most $3|V|$ RELABEL(v)-operations are executed during Algorithm 9.9.1 for any given vertex v. Thus, there are at most $O(|V|^2)$ RELABEL-operations during the whole execution of the algorithm.*

Proof. Note that the values of the potential can only decrease during the execution of REFINE, see Lemma 9.9.3. Now let f be an ε-optimal pseudoflow with corresponding potential p as it was at a point of the algorithm immediately after a RELABEL(v)-operation. Then $e_f(v) > 0$. In this proof, we denote the original ε-optimal circulation and the corresponding potential (the input parameters of REFINE) by g and q. Now we apply Lemma 9.9.5, that is, there exists a vertex w with $e_f(w) < 0$ and a directed path

$$W \quad : \quad v = v_0 \text{------} v_1 \text{------} \ldots \text{------} v_{k-1} \text{------} v_k = w$$

with $v_i v_{i+1} \in E_f$ and $v_{i+1} v_i \in E_g$ for $i = 0, \ldots, k-1$. Then the $\varepsilon/2$-optimality of f implies (using Lemma 9.7.3)

$$-\frac{\varepsilon k}{2} \leq \sum_{i=0}^{k-1} \gamma_p(v_i, v_{i+1}) = p(v) - p(w) + \sum_{i=0}^{k-1} \gamma(v_i, v_{i+1});$$

analogously, the ε-optimality of the original circulation g gives the condition

$$-\varepsilon k \leq \sum_{i=0}^{k-1} \gamma_q(v_{i+1}, v_i) = q(w) - q(v) + \sum_{i=0}^{k-1} \gamma(v_{i+1}, v_i).$$

Adding these two inequalities, the antisymmetry of the cost function implies

$$-\frac{3\varepsilon k}{2} \leq p(v) - p(w) + q(w) - q(v).$$

Now we show that $p(w) = q(w)$: RELABEL can only be applied for vertices with positive flow excess, so that the original value $q(w)$ of the potential for a vertex w with $e_f(w) < 0$ cannot have changed unless the flow excess had become positive at some point. However, a vertex which has positive flow excess at some point can never again get negative flow excess because of (1) in PUSH. Thus, we have indeed $p(w) = q(w)$, because $e_f(w) < 0$. We get

$$p(v) \geq q(v) - \frac{3\varepsilon k}{2} \geq q(v) - \frac{3\varepsilon |V|}{2}.$$

Now Lemma 9.9.3 states that each RELABEL(v)-operation decreases the original value $q(v)$ of the potential by at least $\varepsilon/2$, so that (for a given vertex v) there cannot be more than $3|V|$ such operations. □

We can now also treat the saturating PUSH-operations.

Lemma 9.9.7. *There are at most $O(|V||E|)$ saturating PUSH-operations during the execution of Algorithm 9.9.1.*

Proof. Consider the saturating PUSH-operations for a given edge vw. After such a PUSH(v, w) has been executed, we have $r_f(v, w) = 0$, so that a further PUSH on vw is possible only if a PUSH(w, v) is executed first. Now the saturating PUSH(v, w) was admissible only if $\gamma_p(v, w) < 0$, whereas a PUSH(w, v) requires the converse condition

$$\gamma_p(w, v) < 0, \quad \text{that is,} \quad \gamma_p(v, w) > 0.$$

Thus, there always has to be a RELABEL(v)-operation between two saturating PUSH-operations on vw, because that is the only way

$$\gamma_p(v, w) = \gamma(v, w) + p(v) - p(w)$$

could have been decreased. Now, by Lemma 9.9.6, there can be at most $O(|V|)$ saturating PUSH-operations on any edge vw during the execution of Algorithm 9.9.1. □

The non-saturating PUSH-operations are, similar to Section 6.6, the crucial part in the complexity of REFINE. We need a lemma to be able to analyze how many non-saturating PUSH-operations are executed. We call the edges vw of the residual graph G_f which have negative reduced cost $\gamma_p(v, w)$ *admissible edges* and denote the subdigraph of G_f which contains only the admissible edges the *admissible graph* $G_A = G_A(f)$.

Lemma 9.9.8. *The admissible graph G_A is acyclic during the whole execution of Algorithm 9.9.1.*

Proof. As mentioned in the proof of Theorem 9.9.4, the pseudoflow f constructed during the initialization (2) to (8) is even 0-optimal, so that the corresponding graph G_A is empty and trivially acyclic. Now a PUSH(v, w) can only be executed if $\gamma_p(v, w) < 0$, so that $\gamma_p(w, v) > 0$. Therefore, the antiparallel edge wv, which is perhaps added to G_f, is definitely not added to G_A. Hence PUSH-operations do not add edges to G_A, so that G_A stays acyclic. Now consider a RELABEL(v)-operation. Before this operation is executed, we have $\gamma_p(u, v) \geq -\varepsilon/2$ for all $uv \in G_f$. As we saw in Lemma 9.9.3, RELABEL(v) decreases $p(v)$ by at least $\varepsilon/2$, so that, after the RELABEL(v), $\gamma_p(u, v) \geq 0$ holds. Therefore, G_A does not contain any edges with end vertex v and G_A is still acyclic after the RELABEL(v). □

Similar to Section 6.6, we could now find an upper bound for the number of non-saturating PUSH-operations. However, as we proceed by giving the admissible operations a particularly efficient order, we leave the general result to the reader as an exercise.

Exercise 9.9.9. Show that at most $O(|V|^2|E|)$ non-saturating PUSH-operations are executed during Algorithm 9.9.1. (Hint: Consider the function $\Phi = \sum\limits_{v \text{ active}} \Phi(v)$, where $\Phi(v)$ is the number of vertices which are accessible from v in the admissible graph G_A.)

We present a special version of REFINE due to Goldberg and Tarjan (1990) called 'first-active'-method. It is similar to the highest-distance-method of Section 6.6. Again, we keep adjacency lists A_v and distinguish, for each vertex v, a *current edge*; initially, this is always the first edge of A_v. Moreover, the vertices are kept topologically sorted during the whole algorithm, that is, we keep a topological sorting of V with respect to the admissible graph G_A in a list L. As G_A is initially empty, the vertices can be added arbitrarily to L during the initialization. Furthermore, we need a *current vertex*; this is always the vertex for which we want to execute the next PUSH(v, w) or, if this is not possible, a RELABEL(v). Immediately after a RELABEL(v), v is deleted from L and inserted again at the beginning of L. As v has indegree 0 at this point (see the proof of Lemma 9.9.8), this makes sure that L is still a topological sorting with respect to G_A. In this case, v stays the current vertex. If v becomes inactive without a RELABEL(v) having been executed, the next vertex in L becomes the current vertex. As L contains a topological sorting of G_A, there can be no active vertex in L before v. We get the following algorithm.

Algorithm 9.9.10 (First Active Method). Let (G, c) be a network with cost function γ as described in Section 9.7. Moreover, let f be an ε-optimal circulation with corresponding potential p. G is given by adjacency lists A_v. Moreover, L is a list and rel a Boolean variable.

Procedure FAREFINE $(G, c, \gamma, f, \varepsilon, p; f)$

(1) $\varepsilon \leftarrow \varepsilon/2$;
(2) **for** $uv \in E$ **do**
(3) $\gamma_p(u, v) \leftarrow \gamma(u, v) + p(u) - p(v)$;
(4)   **if** $\gamma_p(u, v) < 0$
(5)   **then** $f(u, v) \leftarrow c(u, v)$, $f(v, u) \leftarrow -c(u, v)$
(6) $r_f(u, v) \leftarrow 0$, $e_f(v, u) \leftarrow c(v, u) - f(v, u)$
(7)   **fi**
(8) **od**;
(9) **for** $v \in V$ **do** $e(v) \leftarrow \sum_u f(u, v)$ **od**;

(10) $L \leftarrow V$;
(11) let v be the first vertex in L;
(12) **while** there exists an active vertex **do**
(13)   **if** $e(v) > 0$
(14)   **then** rel $\leftarrow$ false;
(15)   **repeat**
(16)   let vw be the current edge in A_v;
(17)   **if** $r_f(v, w) > 0$ **and** $\gamma_p(v, w) < 0$
(18)   **then** PUSH$(f, v, w; f)$;
(19)   **fi**
(20)   **if** $e(v) > 0$ **then**
(21)   **if** vw is not the last edge in A_v
(22)   **then** choose the next edge in A_v as current edge
(23)   **else** RELABEL$(f, v, p; f, p)$; rel $\leftarrow$ true;
(24)   choose the next edge in A_v as current edge
(25)   **fi**
(26)   **fi**
(27)   **until** $e(v) = 0$ **or** rel $=$ true;
(28)   **if** $e(v) = 0$
(29)   **then** substitute v by the next vertex in L
(30)   **else** move v to the beginning of L
(31)   **fi**
(32)   **else** substitute v by the next vertex in L
(33)   **fi**
(34) **od**.

Theorem 9.9.11. *Algorithm 9.9.10 constructs an $\varepsilon/2$-optimal circulation f on (G, c) with complexity $O(|V|^3)$.*

Proof. As Algorithm 9.9.10 is a special version of Algorithm 9.9.1, Theorem 9.9.4 implies that it is correct, provided that it terminates. By Lemma 9.9.6, there are at most $O(|V|^2)$ RELABEL-operations during the execution of the algorithm; each of them needs at most $O(|V|)$ steps. Moreover, by Lemma 9.9.7, there are at most $O(|V||E|)$ saturating PUSH-operations each of which takes only $O(1)$ steps. It is therefore sufficient to show that there are at most $O(|V|^3)$ non-saturating PUSH-operations during the whole algorithm. As we saw already, the list L contains a topological sorting of the vertices with respect to the admissible graph G_A at each point of the algorithm. Now we call the sequence of operations between two RELABEL-operations (as well as the sequence of operations from the beginning of the algorithm until the first RELABEL-operation and the sequence of operations after the last RE-LABEL until the algorithm terminates) a phase. Thus, Lemma 9.9.6 implies that there are at most $O(|V|^2)$ phases during the execution of the algorithm. At the beginning of each phase, v is always the first vertex of L (initially because of (11), later because of (30)). Of course, the algorithm can examine at most all the $|V|$ vertices of L before the next RELABEL-operation is executed (or the algorithm terminates). However, for each vertex, there can be at most one non-saturating PUSH-operation, because then $e(v) = 0$ and v is replaced by the next vertex of L. This yields the bound of at most $O(|V|)$ non-saturating PUSH-operations during each phase. □

Using the procedure FAREFINE above in Algorithm 9.8.1 (instead of RE-FINE), we get an algorithm which constructs an optimal circulation for a given network with the complexity stated in Theorem 9.8.8.

9.10 The Algorithm of Klein II

In this section, we return to the Algorithm of Klein (1967) and show that an appropriate special version of the algorithm is polynomial; this result is due to Goldberg and Tarjan (1989). The complexity of this version of the Algorithm of Klein is worse than the complexity given in Theorem 9.8.7, but it has the advantage of being particularly simple and intuitive.

First consider what a specialization of the Algorithm of Klein to flow networks as in Chapter 6 would look like. As in Example 9.1.1, we add the return arc $r = ts$ to the flow network $N = (G, c, s, t)$, assign cost $\gamma(r) = -1$ and $\gamma(e) = 0$ for all other edges e and consider the corresponding problem of finding an optimal circulation. Then a flow f of value w on N corresponds to a circulation f' on $G' := G \cup \{r\}$ with cost $-w(f)$. Now let (H, w) be the auxiliary network with respect to f' (as constructed in Algorithm 9.5.1). Obviously, the only cycles of negative length are cycles containing the return arc; however, these cycles correspond precisely to the augmenting paths in G with respect to f (that is, to paths from s to t in the auxiliary network $N'(f)$, see Section 6.3). It is now easy to see that, in this special case, the Algorithm of Klein is simply the Algorithm 6.1.7 of Ford and Fulkerson for determining a maximal flow. In particular, the Algorithm of Klein is not polynomial even if all functions are integral (this was shown in Section 6.1).

However, we showed in Section 6.2 that the Algorithm of Ford and Fulkerson becomes polynomial if the augmenting paths are chosen in a clever way. Edmonds and Karp (1972) proposed to choose an augmenting path W of shortest length in $N'(f)$. All we have to do is to transfer this strategy to the equivalent problem for circulations. As already mentioned, W corresponds to a cycle K of negative length in (H, w). Now any such cycle has length $w(K) = -1$, but the length $|W|$ of W is reflected in the mean weight $m(K)$ of K, because

$$m(K) = \frac{w(K)}{|K|} = -\frac{1}{|W| + 1}.$$

Thus, an augmenting path of shortest length in $N'(f)$ corresponds to a cycle with minimum cycle mean $\mu(H, w)$. This motivates the approach used by Goldberg and Tarjan (1989): they proposed to use a (negative) cycle of minimum cycle mean for changing the present circulation f. Such a cycle can be determined efficiently by the method of Karp (1978) described in Section 9.7. The resulting algorithm is indeed polynomial.

Algorithm 9.10.1 (Minimum Mean Cycle-Canceling Algorithm).
Let G be a directed graph with capacity constraints b and c and a cost function γ. The algorithm finds out whether an admissible circulation exists; if this is the case, it constructs an optimal circulation.

Procedure MMCC $(G, b, c, \gamma;$ legal, $f)$

(1) LEGCIRC $(G, b, c, \gamma;$ legal, $f)$;
(2) **if** legal $=$ true **then repeat**
(3) $E' \leftarrow \emptyset$;
(4)   **for** $e = uv \in E$ **do**
(5)   **if** $f(e) < c(e)$
(6)   **then** $E' \leftarrow E' \cup \{e\}$; $tp(e) \leftarrow 1$; $c'(e) \leftarrow c(e) - f(e)$;
             $w(e) \leftarrow \gamma(e)$ **fi**;
(7)   **if** $b(e) < f(e)$
(8)   **then** $e' \leftarrow vu$; $E' \leftarrow E' \cup \{e'\}$; $tp(e') \leftarrow 2$;
             $c'(e') \leftarrow f(e) - b(e)$; $w(e') \leftarrow -\gamma(e)$
(9)   **fi**
(10)   **od**;
(11) $H \leftarrow (V, E')$;
(12)   MEANCYCLE $(H, w; \mu, K,$ acyclic$)$

(13)   **if** acyclic $=$ false **and** $\mu < 0$
(14)   **then** $\delta \leftarrow$ min $\{c'(e) : e \in K\}$;
(15)   **for** $e \in K$ **do**
(16)   **if** $tp(e) = 1$ **then** $f(e) \leftarrow f(e) + \delta$
                          else $f(e) \leftarrow f(e) - \delta$ **fi**
(17)   **od**
(18)   **fi**
(19)   **until** acyclic $=$ true **or** $\mu \geq 0$
(20) **fi**.

The procedure MEANCYCLE used above is the algorithm described in Exercise 9.7.12. In the following, if f is changed along K (in step (14) to (17) above), we say that K is *cancelled*.

The rest of this section is devoted to showing that Algorithm 9.10.1 is indeed polynomial. We now think of the original network (G_0, b, c) and the corresponding circulations as being in the form (G, c) described in Section 9.7 and Algorithm 9.8.1, respectively. Then we can use the results of Sections 9.7 and 9.8. Even though the MMCC-Algorithm does *not* use the technique of successive approximation, we still need the theory of ε-optimality for analyzing it.

We saw in Section 9.7 that any circulation f is ε-tight for some appropriate $\varepsilon \geq 0$; we denote this number by $\varepsilon(f)$. The following lemma shows that changing f along a cycle of minimum cycle mean does at least not increase the parameter $\varepsilon(f)$.

Lemma 9.10.2. *Let f be an ε-tight circulation on (G, c) with respect to the cost function γ, where $\varepsilon > 0$. Moreover, let K be a directed cycle of minimum cycle mean in the residual graph G_f. Then the circulation g obtained by cancelling K satisfies $\varepsilon(g) \leq \varepsilon(f) = \varepsilon$.*

Proof. Let p be a potential corresponding to f. Then, by Lemma 9.8.5,

$$\gamma_p(u, v) = -\varepsilon \qquad \text{for all } uv \in K. \tag{9.8}$$

We get the residual graph G_g from G_f by deleting some edges of K and adding some edges which are antiparallel to edges of K. Now (9.8) implies for edges $uv \in K$ that

$$\gamma_p(v, u) = -\gamma_p(u, v) = \varepsilon > 0,$$

so that the condition $\gamma_p(u, v) \geq -\varepsilon$ holds for all edges uv in G_g as well and g is ε-optimal (with respect to the potential p). Therefore, $\varepsilon(g) \leq \varepsilon = \varepsilon(f)$. $\square$

Now it might be possible that cancelling K does not change $\varepsilon(f)$, that is, $\varepsilon(g) = \varepsilon(f)$ in Lemma 9.10.2. However, the next lemma shows that this cannot occur too often.

Lemma 9.10.3. *Let f be a circulation on (G, c) which is ε-tight with respect to the cost function γ. Suppose g is a circulation obtained from f by cancelling $|E|$ cycles of minimum cycle mean as in Algorithm 9.10.1. Then*

$$\varepsilon(g) \leq (1 - \frac{1}{|V|})\varepsilon.$$

Proof. Let p be a potential corresponding to f, that is,

$$\gamma_p(u, v) \geq -\varepsilon \qquad \text{for all } uv \in E_f.$$

As we saw in the proof of Lemma 9.10.2, all edges added to G_f when cancelling a cycle of minimum cycle mean have positive reduced cost $\gamma_p(u, v)$. On the other hand, at least one edge e (for which the minimum in step (14) of Algorithm 9.10.1 is achieved) is deleted from G_f. Now we distinguish two cases; note that p always remains the original potential.

Case 1: All the $|E|$ cycles which were cancelled to obtain g consist of edges e with $\gamma_p(e) < 0$ only. Then all the edges added to G_f by those cancellations have positive reduced cost. As at least one edge with negative reduced cost is deleted with each cancellation, all the remaining edges in the residual graph must have non-negative reduced cost after $|E|$ cancellations. Therefore, g is optimal, that is, $\varepsilon(g) = 0$ and the assertion holds.

Case 2: At least one of the cycles cancelled contains some edge with non-negative reduced cost with respect to p. Let K be the cycle with this property which was cancelled first. Then, before K was cancelled, all edges e added to G_f had positive reduced cost $\gamma_p(e)$. Therefore,

$$\gamma_p(e) \geq -\varepsilon \quad \text{for all } e \in K \quad \text{and} \quad \gamma_p(u, v) \geq 0 \quad \text{for some edge } uv \in K.$$

It follows that

$$m(K) \quad = \quad \frac{1}{|K|} \sum_{e \in K} \gamma(e) = \frac{1}{|K|} \sum_{e \in K} \gamma_p(e)$$

$$\geq \quad \frac{-(|K| - 1)\varepsilon}{|K|} \geq -(1 - \frac{1}{|V|})\varepsilon.$$

Let h be the circulation which had been constructed directly before K was cancelled. Then

$$\mu(G_h, \gamma) = m(K) \geq -(1 - \frac{1}{|V|})\varepsilon$$

and therefore (using Theorem 9.7.9)

$$\varepsilon(h) = -\mu(G_h, \gamma) \leq (1 - \frac{1}{|V|})\varepsilon.$$

Applying Lemma 9.10.2 iteratively shows that $\varepsilon(g) \leq \varepsilon(h)$, which implies the assertion. □

We need one more simple lemma.

Lemma 9.10.4. *Let m be a positive integer and $(y_k)_{k\in\mathbb{N}}$ a sequence of non-negative real numbers satisfying the condition*

$$y_{k+1} \leq (1 - \frac{1}{m})y_k \quad \text{for all } k \in \mathbb{N}.$$

Then

$$y_{k+m} \leq \frac{1}{2}y_k \quad \text{for all } k \in \mathbb{N}.$$

Proof. By hypothesis, we always have

$$y_k \geq y_{k+1} + \frac{1}{m-1} \cdot y_{k+1},$$

so that recursively

$$
\begin{aligned}
y_k &\geq y_{k+1} + \frac{y_{k+1}}{m-1} \\
&\geq (y_{k+2} + \frac{y_{k+2}}{m-1}) + \frac{y_{k+1}}{m-1} \geq y_{k+2} + \frac{2y_{k+2}}{m-1} \\
&\geq \cdots \geq y_{k+m} + \frac{m y_{k+m}}{m-1} \geq 2y_{k+m}. \qquad \square
\end{aligned}
$$

Theorem 9.10.5. *Algorithm 9.10.1 finds an optimal circulation on (G, b, c) after $O(|V||E|^2 \log|V|)$ iterations.*

Proof. Set $k := |V||E|\lceil \log |V| + 1\rceil$ and divide the iterations of Algorithm 9.10.1 into phases of k subsequent cancellations. We show that, during each phase where the algorithm does not yet terminate, at least one more edge of G becomes ε-fixed (for some appropriate ε). This yields the assertion, because the algorithm has to terminate at the point when all edges have become ε-fixed.

Now let f_0 and f_k be the circulations constructed directly before the first cancellation and directly after the last cancellation of some phase, respectively. Set $\varepsilon := \varepsilon(f_0)$ and $\varepsilon' := \varepsilon(f_k)$ and let p be a potential corresponding to f_k, that is,

$$\gamma_p(v, w) \geq -\varepsilon' \quad \text{for all } vw \in G_{f_k}.$$

Lemma 9.10.3 states that any $|E|$ subsequent cancellations decrease $\varepsilon(f)$ by at least a factor of $1 - \frac{1}{|V|}$ and Lemma 9.10.4 then implies that any $|V||E|$ subsequent cancellations decrease $\varepsilon(f)$ by at least a factor of $1/2$. Therefore,

$$\varepsilon' \leq \varepsilon \cdot (\frac{1}{2})^{\lceil \log|V|+1\rceil} \leq \frac{\varepsilon}{2|V|},$$

so that

$$-\varepsilon \leq -2|V|\varepsilon'. \tag{9.9}$$

Now let K be the cycle which is cancelled first during that phase (that is, f_0 is changed using K). Then, by Theorem 9.7.9,

$$m(K) = -\varepsilon \text{ in } (G_{f_0}, \gamma).$$

Now Lemma 9.7.3 immediately implies

$$m(K) = -\varepsilon \text{ in } (G_{f_0}, \gamma_p),$$

so that K has to contain an edge uv with $\gamma_p(u, v) \leq -\varepsilon$. Using (9.9) then yields

$$\gamma_p(u, v) \leq -2|V|\varepsilon',$$

so that uv is ε'-fixed by Corollary 9.8.4. On the other hand, uv was not ε-fixed, because uv is contained in the cycle K which was cancelled when f_0 was changed. Therefore, at least one further edge becomes δ-fixed (for some appropriate δ) during each phase. $\square$

Exercise 9.10.6. Show that Algorithm 9.10.1 terminates after $O(|V||E| \log (|V|C))$ iterations if the cost function γ is integral, where

$$C := \max \{|\gamma(u, v)| : uv \in E\}.$$

Using Exercise 9.7.12, Theorem 9.10.5 and Exercise 9.10.6 now yields the following result.

Theorem 9.10.7. *Algorithm 9.10.1 determines an optimal circulation on* (G, b, c) *with complexity* $O(|V|^2|E|^3 \log |V|)$. *If* γ *is integral, the complexity is bounded by* $O(|V|^2|E|^2 \log (|V|C))$ *as well.* $\square$

A detailed examination of the number of cancellations necessary in Algorithm 9.10.1 can be found in Radzik and Goldberg (1991). Using appropriate data structures and making some changes in the way the negative cycles are chosen, the bounds of Theorem 9.10.7 can be improved; a variation of the Algorithm of Klein having complexity $O(|V||E|^2 (\log |V|)^2)$ was obtained by Goldberg and Tarjan (1989). Ervolina and McCormick (1993) gave two polynomial algorithms which work with cancellations of cuts; these algorithms are (in the context of Linear Programming) dual to the above algorithms where cycles are cancelled.

9.11 Some Further Problems

At the end of this chapter, we mention some further problems which can be treated using optimal circulations or optimal flows, respectively. We also mention some generalizations of the problems treated so far; however, we have to refer to the literature for more information on these problems.

Example 9.11.1 (Transshipment Problem). Let $G = (V, E)$ be a directed graph with a non-negative capacity function $c : E \to \mathbb{R}$ and a non-negative cost function $\gamma : E \to \mathbb{R}$. Moreover, let X and Y be disjoint subsets of V; we call the elements of X sources and the elements of Y sinks (as in Section 7.7). Again we associate with each source x a supply $a(x)$ and with each sink y a demand $b(y)$ (where the functions a and b are non-negative). We want to find – as in the Supply and Demand-Problem of Section 7.7 – a feasible flow[8] on (G, c), that is, a mapping $f : E \to \mathbb{R}$ satisfying conditions (ZF 1) to (ZF 4) of Section 7.7. Moreover, we want to find an *optimal flow* among all feasible flows, that is, a flow of minimal cost with respect to γ. The Transshipment Problem is the weighted version of the Supply and Demand-Problem. Again, we add a new source s and a new sink t as well as all edges sx with capacity $c(sx) := a(x)$ and all edges yt with $c(yt) := b(y)$. Moreover, we extend the cost function γ by defining $\gamma(sx) := 0$ and $\gamma(yt) := 0$. Then an optimal flow on the resulting flow network N of value $\sum b(y)$ is a solution for our problem. To find such a solution, we could use the Algorithm of Busacker and Gowen (1961) of Section 9.6, for example.

Example 9.11.2 (Transportation Problem). A Transshipment Problem where $V = X \,\dot\cup\, Y$ holds is called a *Transportation Problem*. In this problem, there are no *intermediate nodes*, so that any vertex of V is either a source or a sink. If G is the complete bipartite graph on $X \,\dot\cup\, Y$, the problem is called *Hitchcock Problem*, see Hitchcock (1941). Note that the Assignment Problem of Example 9.1.4 is a special Hitchcock Problem: it is the case where $|X| = |Y|$ and all capacities as well as the values $a(x)$ and $b(y)$ are equal to 1.

We have seen that the Hitchcock Problem is a very special case of the problem of finding optimal flows on a flow network. Conversely, it can be shown that the general problem of finding optimal flows can be transformed to a Hitchcock Problem (even without capacity constraints) on an appropriate bipartite graph, see Lawler (1976) §4.14, for example.

It should be mentioned that the Transshipment Problem (with or without capacity constraints) is often solved in practice with a special version of the Simplex Algorithm of Linear Programming, namely the so-called Network Simplex Algorithm. A very good presentation of this method can be found in part III of the book of Chvátal (1983); this book is recommendable in general.[9] Although the Network Simplex Method is rather bad if applied to certain pathological networks (see Zadeh (1973a)), it is spectacularly successful in practice. As Chvátal (1983) puts it: 'It takes just a few minutes

---

[8] Sometimes, there are upper bounds on the capacities of the edges given as well.

[9] The author of the present book thinks that the most intuitive way to become aquainted with problems of Combinatorial Optimization is the presentation in a Graph Theory context; however, the Theory of Linear Programming is indispensable for further study.

to solve a typical problem with thousands of nodes and tens of thousands of arcs; even problems ten times as large are solved routinely.' Meanwhile, polynomial variants of the Network Simplex Method have been found, see Orlin, Plotkin and Tardos (1993).

Finally, we mention some generalizations of the flow problems treated in this book. In Section 10.2, we consider 'multiterminal'-problems, that is, problems where we want to find maximal values of flow between any two vertices (s, t); in most cases, the graph underlying these networks is undirected.

More about the following three generalizations can be found in Ford and Fulkerson (1962), Gondran and Minoux (1984) and Ahuja, Magnanti and Orlin (1993). For some practical problems, it makes sense to consider flows with gains or losses, that is, the quantity of flow entering an edge at vertex u is changed by a factor m_u while passing through that edge. This might be a model for transactions handled in foreign currency (Grötschel (1985) §8.2 shows a real world example where flows with gains occur) or for losses in a water supply system due to evaporation. A weakly polynomial algorithm for this problem can be found in Goldberg, Plotkin and Tardos (1991). Furthermore, one may consider networks on which different flows occur simultaneously without intermingling ('multicommodity flows'); a polynomial algorithm for this problem was given by Tardos (1986). Finally, dynamic flows are examined, where a time for passing is assigned to the edges; this is definitely interesting for traffic networks. This problem can be reduced to flows in the usual sense, see Ford and Fulkerson (1958a) as well as Ford and Fulkerson (1962). We also mention Lomonosov (1985) for 'multicommodity flows'. A collection of papers concerning network problems can be found in the special edition vol. 13 nos. 2 and 3 of Discrete Applied Mathematics, see Klingman and Philipps (1986).

It is beyond the scope of this book to show how real problems of Operations Research are modelled as network problems. However, putting real world facts into a model is an extremely important (and by no means trivial) task and it has to be accomplished before any of the mathematical algorithms we present here can be applied. We recommend the monograph of Glover, Klingman and Phillips (1992) for more about this subject and the references given there for further concrete case studies. Jarah, Yu, Krishnamurthy and Rakshit (1993) show an interesting new application; they give two models for making decisions between delays and cancellations of flights (when planes cannot be used as planned). In particular, a Minimum Cost-Flow-Problem is solved in this context using the Algorithm of Busacker and Gowen.

10. Synthesis of Networks

Up to now, we have only considered flows or circulations, respectively, for a given network. However, the converse question is very interesting, too: For given conditions on the flow, construct a network (with as little effort as possible) on which such a flow would be possible. On the one hand, we consider the case where all edges can be built with the same cost and we are looking for an undirected network with lower bounds on the maximal values of a flow between any two vertices. We analyze such 'symmetric networks' via 'equivalent flow trees' and 'equivalent cut trees'. This technique has an interesting application for the construction of certain communication networks; this is discussed in Section 10.4. On the other hand, we look at the question of how to increase the maximal value of the flow for a given flow network by increasing the capacities of some edges as economically as possible.

10.1 Symmetric Networks

Let $G = (V, E)$ be an (undirected) graph with a non-negative capacity function $c : E \to \mathbb{R}$. Then $N = (G, c)$ is called a *symmetrical network*.[1] If we want to treat N in the usual way, we can substitute G by its complete orientation $\vec{G}$ and define c accordingly; note that then $c(xy) = c(yx)$ for any edge xy. If we assume that G is connected (that is, $\vec{G}$ is strongly connected), then, for any pair s, t of vertices of G with $s \neq t$, $N_{st} = (\vec{G}, c, s, t)$ defines a flow network as introduced in Section 6.1. We denote the maximal value of a flow on N_{st} by $w(s, t)$. Note that w is a symmetric function as well: we always have $w(s, t) = w(t, s)$. We call w the *flow function* of the symmetric network N. For the sake of simplicity, we define $w(x, x) = 0$ (for all x). In Section 10.3, we will consider the construction of symmetric networks for a given flow function. In the present section, we study the more basic question which symmetric functions w can occur as flow functions. The following theorem due to Gomory and Hu (1961) gives a very elegant characterization.

---

[1] Note that this notation has nothing to do with the alternative notation we used for a flow in Section 6.6.

Theorem 10.1.1. *Let V be a set with n elements and $w : V \times V \to \mathbb{R}_0^+$ a symmetric function. There exists a symmetric network $N = (G, c)$ on an appropriate connected graph $G = (V, E)$ (with vertex set V) having flow function w if and only if, for any three distinct elements x, y, z of V, the following inequality holds:*

$$w(x, y) \geq \min \{w(x, z), w(z, y)\} \tag{10.1}$$

Proof. First suppose that $N = (G, c)$ is any symmetric network on the vertex set V and let x, y, z be any three elements of V. Then, by Theorem 6.1.6, there exists a cut (S, T) with $x \in S$ and $y \in T$ such that $w(x, y) = c(S, T)$. If z is contained in S, it follows that $w(z, y) \leq c(S, T) = w(x, y)$ by Lemma 6.1.2; if z is in T, we have $w(x, z) \leq c(S, T) = w(x, y)$. Thus, condition (10.1) is satisfied for any flow function w.

Conversely, let w be a symmetric function satisfying (10.1). We consider the complete graph K on V with weight function w and choose a maximal spanning tree T of (K, w), see Section 4.5. By Theorem 4.5.3, for any pair (x, y) of vertices, the unique path from x to y in T is a path of maximal capacity (with respect to w); we denote this capacity by $q(x, y)$. Obviously, we have $q(x, y) \geq w(x, y)$, because the edge xy is also a path from x to y. Using induction, (10.1) implies

$$w(x_1, x_k) \geq \min \{w(x_1, x_2), \ldots, w(x_{k-1}, x_k)\} \tag{10.2}$$

for any $k \geq 3$ and any k vertices $x_1, \ldots, x_k$. If we choose the vertices on a path of maximal capacity from x to y for $x_1, \ldots, x_k$, then (10.2) implies $w(x, y) \geq q(x, y)$, and equality holds. Now set $c(e) := w(u, v)$ for any edge $e = uv$ of T and choose $G = T$ and $N = (T, c)$. As the path from x to y in T is uniquely determined, the maximal value of a flow from x to y in N is equal to the capacity $q(x, y) = w(x, y)$ of that path. Therefore, w is the flow function of the symmetric network (T, c).   □

Corollary 10.1.2. *Any flow function on a symmetric network can also be realized on a tree. If the symmetric network N is defined on n vertices, the flow function on N takes at most $n - 1$ distinct values.*

Proof. The first statement follows from the proof of Theorem 10.1.1. The second statement is clear because a tree on n vertices has only $n - 1$ edges, so that at most $n - 1$ distinct weights (and hence at most $n - 1$ distinct capacities) can occur.   □

The following consequence of Theorem 10.1.1 will be used in the next section.

Corollary 10.1.3. *Let N be a symmetric network with flow function w. Then, for any three distinct vertices x, y, z of N, the smallest two of the three values*

$$w(x, y), \quad w(x, z) \quad and \quad w(y, z)$$

are equal.

Proof. This follows immediately from condition (10.1) of Theorem 10.1.1, which implies that it is impossible that the two inequalities

$$w(x,y) < w(x,z) \quad \text{and} \quad w(x,y) < w(y,z)$$

hold simultaneously. □

Exercise 10.1.4. Let $N = (G,c)$ be a symmetric network with flow function w, where G is a complete graph. Show that a spanning tree T of G is an equivalent flow tree for N if and only if T is a maximal spanning tree for the network (G,w). Here, a tree T is called an *equivalent flow tree* for N if the flow function of the symmetric network $(T, w|T)$ is equal to w.

Exercise 10.1.5. Show that any flow function can even be realized on a path and give such a realization for the symmetric network of Figure 10.1. (Hint: Consider a pair (x, y) of vertices such that $w(x, y)$ is maximal and use induction on the number n of vertices.)

Fig 10.1 A symmetric network on a tree

In general, the conditions on a flow for which we want to construct a symmetric network may not satisfy condition (10.1) of Theorem 10.1.1. This leads to the following definitions. Let $r : V \times V \to \mathbb{R}_0^+$ be an arbitrary symmetric function. A network $N = (G, c)$ on a connected graph $G = (V, E)$ on V is called *feasible* for r if all $x, y \in V$ satisfy the condition $w(x, y) \geq r(x, y)$. A *minimal* network for r is a feasible network such that

$$c(E) := \sum_{e \in E} c(e)$$

is minimal among all feasible networks, that is, we require the sum of all capacities (of the edges we have to 'build') to be minimal. This makes sense if the cost of building an edge e depends linearly on the capacity $c(e)$ and if this cost is independent of the choice of e. However, at least the second assumption is not always realistic: in traffic networks, for example, the cost of building an edge depends on the area it crosses and on the distance between the start and the end vertex. Thus, a cost function of the form $\sum \gamma(e)c(e)$ would be more useful. It is possible to treat this case as well (see Gomory and Hu (1962)), but, of course, with a lot more effort. The special case we consider here has a solution which is particularly elegant; we describe this solution in Section 10.3. But first, we have a closer look at analyzing symmetric networks and the synthesis of equivalent flow trees.

10.2 Synthesis of Equivalent Flow Trees

In this section, we analyze a given symmetric network, that is, we determine its flow function. As we can calculate the value of the flow between two given vertices with complexity $O(|V|^3)$ by Theorem 6.4.8 (or Theorem 6.6.13, respectively) and the number of pairs of vertices is only $|V|(|V|-1)/2$, the flow function can be determined with a complexity of at most $O(|V|^5)$. However, Corollary 10.1.2 states that there are at most $|V|-1$ distinct values of the flow, so that it might not be necessary to calculate the value of the flow for each pair of vertices with one of the usual algorithms. Indeed, Gomory and Hu (1961) showed that it suffices to calculate $|V|-1$ values of the flow (most of which can even be found using smaller networks which have been derived from N by 'condensing'); we get a complexity of $O(|V|^4)$ for determining the flow function. A detailed description of this rather complicated algorithm can be found in §IV.3 of Ford and Fulkerson (1962). We present a technique which is considerably simpler due to Gusfield (1990). This technique works with calculating only $|V|-1$ values of the flow as well.

So let $N = (G, c)$ be a symmetric network with flow function w, where $G = (V, E)$. As we saw in the proof of Theorem 10.1.1, there exists a spanning tree T on V and a weight function $w : T \to \mathbb{R}_0^+$ such that the capacity of the path from x to y is equal to the value $w(x, y)$ of the flow function for all pairs $x, y \in V$. This means that T is an equivalent flow tree for N.[2] We present the Algorithm of Gusfield (1990) below in a rather concise and informal way. The algorithm uses the determination of a minimal cut (S, T) for a flow network (G, c, s, t). Such a cut can be found by applying a labelling procedure (see Corollary 6.1.4) after a maximal flow has been found. More precisely, this task can be done using the procedure AUXNET modified according to

---

[2] Using this rather sloppy notation (that is, using the same symbol w for the weight function on T as well as for the flow function on N) is justified because we have $w(x, y) = w(e)$ for each edge $e = xy$ of T.

Exercise 6.3.18 with complexity $O(|E|)$. Therefore, we can use any algorithm for determining maximal flows in Gusfield's Algorithm for finding the desired cuts.

Algorithm 10.2.1. Let $N = (G, c)$ be a symmetric network on $G = (V, E)$, where $V = \{1, \ldots, n\}$. The algorithm determines an equivalent flow tree (B, w). It also calculates the function $p(i)$ which, for $i \neq 1$, gives the predecessor of i on a path from vertex 1 to vertex i in B. Thus, B consists of the edges $\{p(i), i\}$ for $i = 2, \ldots, n$.

Procedure FLOWTREE $(G, c; B, w)$

(1) $B \leftarrow \emptyset$;
(2) **for** $i = 2$ **to** n **do** $p(i) \leftarrow 1$ **od**;
(3) **for** $s = 2$ **to** n **do**
(4) $t \leftarrow p(s)$;
(5)   calculate a minimal cut (S, T) and the value w of a maximal flow in the flow network (G, c, s, t);
(6) $B \leftarrow B \cup \{st\}$; $w(s, t) \leftarrow w$;
(7)   **for** $i = s + 1$ **to** n **do**
(8)   **if** $i \in S$ **and** $p(i) = t$ **then** $p(i) \leftarrow s$ **fi**
(9)   **od**
(10) **od**.

Note that the function p in the procedure FLOWTREE defines a spanning tree B on V at any point of the algorithm. B is initialized in step (2) as a star with center 1. During the s-th iteration, B is a tree for which all vertices $i \geq s$ are leaves; the value $p(i)$ gives, for $i \geq s$, the unique neighbour of i in the tree B. The neighbour is chosen as the sink t and a minimal cut (S, T) for the network with source s and sink t is calculated. Next, edge st is assigned the maximal value of a flow from s to t as weight $w = c(S, T)$. The next task (steps (7) to (9)) is to cut off from t all leaves $i > s$ which are contained in S and whose unique neighbour $p(i)$ in B is vertex t as well and connect these vertices as leaves to s. Before proving that B is indeed an equivalent flow tree (with respect to the given weight function) at the end of the algorithm, we give an example.

Example 10.2.2. Consider the network of Figure 10.2, where the numbers written on the edges state the capacities.

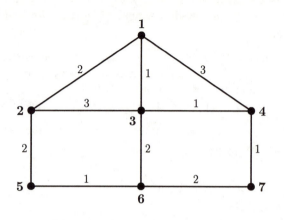

Fig 10.2 A symmetric network

Figure 10.3 shows the star with center 1 constructed during the initialization and the tree resulting from the iteration for $s = 2$. Note that, during this iteration, $t = 1$ and $w(s,t) = 5 = c(S,T)$ for the cut $S = \{2,3,5,6,7\}$ and $T = \{1,4\}$. (In this simple example, the values of the flow and a minimal cut can always be found by inspection of the graph.)

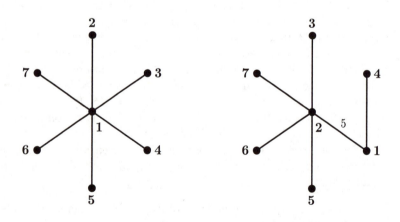

Fig. 10.3 Initialization and iteration $s = 2$

Now the leaves $3,5,6$ and 7 are cut from $t = 1$ and connected to $s = 2$ instead, and edge $\{1,2\}$ is assigned weight 5. During the next iteration, $s = 3$, $t = 2$ and $w(S,T) = 6 = c(S,T)$ with $S = \{1,3,4,6,7\}$ and $T = \{2,5\}$. The leaves 6 and 7 are cut off from $t = 2$ and connected to $s = 3$; edge $\{2,3\}$ is assigned weight 6. This yields the tree on the left hand side of Figure 10.4. This tree is not changed during the two subsequent iterations, but two more edges are assigned their weights. For $s = 4$, we have $t = 1$ and $w(s,t) = 5 = c(S,T)$ with $S = \{4\}$, $T = \{1,2,3,5,6,7\}$; and for $s = 5$, we have $t = 2$ and $w(s,t) = 3 = c(S,T)$ with $S = \{5\}$ and $T = \{1,2,3,4,6,7\}$. The next iteration yields a new tree: For $s = 6$ and $t = 3$, we get $w(s,t) = 4 = c(S,T)$ for $S = \{6,7\}$ and $T = \{1,2,3,4,5\}$. Therefore, vertex 7 is cut off from vertex 3 and connected to vertex 6; this yields the tree on the right hand side of Figure 10.4. This tree remains unchanged during the last iteration: for $s = 7$, we have $t = 6$, $w(s,t) = 3 = c(S,T)$ with $S = \{7\}$ and $T = \{1,2,3,4,5,6\}$. It is easy to check that this last tree is indeed an equivalent flow tree.

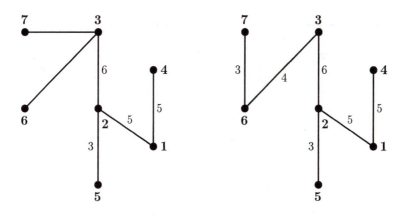

Fig. 10.4 Iterations $s = 3, 4, 5$ and $s = 6, 7$

To show that Algorithm 10.2.1 is correct, we need some preliminaries. The following lemma is due to Gomory and Hu (1961).

Lemma 10.2.3. *Let $N = (G, c)$ be a symmetric network and (X, Y) a min-imal (x,y)-cut[3] for two vertices x and y of G. Moreover, let u and v be two vertices in X and (U, V) a minimal (u,v)-cut. If $y \in U$, then $(U \cup Y, V \cap X)$ is a minimal (u,v)-cut as well; otherwise (that is, if $y \in V$) $(U \cap X, V \cup Y)$ is a minimal (u,v)-cut.*

Proof. We may assume that the four sets

$$P := X \cap U, \quad Q := Y \cap U, \quad R := X \cap V \quad \text{and} \quad S := Y \cap V$$

are all non-empty; otherwise the statement of the lemma is trivial. (For ex-ample, for $Q = \emptyset$, we have $U \cap X = U$ and $V \cup Y = V$.) In this situation, we

---

[3] that is, a minimal cut in the flow network (G, c, x, y).

call (X, Y) and (U, V) *crossing cuts*. Thus, our goal is to construct a minimal (u, v)-cut (U', V') such that (X, Y) and (U', V') are *non-crossing* cuts. Figure 10.5 shows the situation as in the statement of the lemma for the two possible cases for y. Using symmetry arguments, it suffices to consider one of these two cases, for example the case $y \in Q$. (It is insignificant whether $x \in U$ or $x \in V$.)

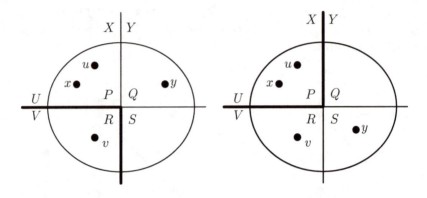

Fig. 10.5 Concerning Lemma 10.2.3

As $(P \cup R \cup S, Q)$ is an (x, y)-cut and (X, Y) is a minimal (x, y)-cut, we have

$$
\begin{aligned}
c(P, Q) + c(P, S) + c(R, Q) + c(R, S) &= c(X, Y) \\
&\leq c(P \cup R \cup S, Q) \\
&= c(P, Q) + c(R, Q) + c(S, Q)
\end{aligned}
$$

and therefore

$$c(P, S) + c(R, S) \leq c(S, Q).$$

Using the trivial inequality $c(P, S) \geq 0$, we get

$$c(R, S) \leq c(S, Q),$$

so that

$$
\begin{aligned}
c(P \cup Q \cup S, R) &= c(P, R) + c(Q, R) + c(S, R) \\
&\leq c(P, R) + c(Q, R) + c(Q, S) + c(P, S) = c(U, V);
\end{aligned}
$$

we used the symmetry of c here. As (U, V) is a minimal (u, v)-cut, $(P \cup Q \cup S, R) = (U \cup Y, V \cap X)$ has to be a minimal (u, v)-cut as well. $\square$

Corollary 10.2.4. *Under the assumptions of Lemma 10.2.3, there always exists a minimal (u,v)-cut (U',V') with $U \cap X = U' \cap X$ such that (X,Y) and (U',V') are non-crossing cuts.* $\square$

We now turn to analyzing the procedure FLOWTREE. We assume that, in each iteration, the edge $\{s,t\}$ which is assigned its weight $w(s,t)$ in step (6) is oriented from s to t. Then the tree B generated by the algorithm is oriented such that, for each edge st of B, $s > t$ holds. Moreover, all directed paths in B are oriented towards vertex 1, that is, B has opposite orientation than an arborescence with root 1. For the tree of Example 10.2.2, the orientation is shown in Figure 10.6.

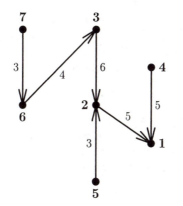

Fig 10.6 Oriented flow tree for Example 10.2.2

Lemma 10.2.5. *Let B be a directed tree generated by Algorithm 10.2.1 for a symmetric network $N = (G,c)$. Moreover, let $W = W_{ij}$ be a directed path in B with start vertex i and end vertex j and kj a (directed) edge in B such that $k \leq h$ holds for each vertex $h \neq j$ on W. Then, at the point of the algorithm when a minimal (k,j)-cut $C = (K,J)$ is constructed, i is adjacent to j (in the tree constructed by the algorithm at that point). Moreover, $i \in K$ holds if and only if k is a vertex on W.*

Proof. After initialization, each vertex $h \neq 1$ is a leaf and has 1 as its unique neighbour. Vertex h stays a leaf until iteration h. The neighbour of h can change (from u to v, for example) only if $s = v$ and $t = u$ in some iteration. It is easy to see that the directed path W_{h1} from h to 1 in the tree B consists precisely of those vertices which were the unique neighbour of h at some point during the first h iterations of the algorithm. Now the path W_{ij} is part of the path W_{i1}, so that i, while it was still a leaf, must have been adjacent to j at some point of time before iteration i was executed. If the neighbour of i was changed afterwards, this can only have happened during iteration $s = h$

(where $t = j$) for the predecessor h of j on W_{ij}. However, $k \leq h$ holds by hypothesis, so that i must have been adjacent to j during iteration $s = k$, that is, when the (k, j)-cut (K, J) was calculated. Now if k is a vertex on the path W (that is, $k = h$ is the predecessor of j on W), then i must have been contained in K, because otherwise it would not have been cut off from j. Conversely, if $i \in K$, then i is indeed cut off from j and connected to k in step (8) of the algorithm, so that $k \in W$ as asserted.   □

Theorem 10.2.6. *Algorithm 10.2.1 determines an equivalent flow tree for any symmetric network N.*

Proof. We introduce some notation first. For any two vertices x and y, W_{xy} denotes the unique path from x to y in the tree B determined by Algorithm 10.2.1. Note that, in general, W_{xy} is not a directed path. Moreover, for any path W in B, the capacity of W in the network (B, w) is denoted by $k(W)$, that is, $k(W)$ is the minimum of the values $w(xy)$ for all edges $xy \in W$. Thus, the statement of the theorem is equivalent to

$$k(W_{xy}) = w(x, y) \quad \text{for all } x, y \in V, \tag{10.3}$$

where w is the flow function on N, as usual. For any edge $xy \in B$ (with $x > y$), let (S_{xy}, T_{xy}) be the minimal (x, y)-cut which the algorithm calculates in step (5) of iteration $s = x$ (with $t = y$); we always assume $x \in S_{xy}$ and $y \in T_{xy}$. To prove (10.3), we distinguish four cases. Note that $k(W_{xy}) \leq w(x, y)$ holds by Theorem 10.1.1.

Case 1: xy is an edge of B, so that $x > y$. Then (10.3) holds trivially, because edge xy has been assigned the value $w(x, y)$ as weight in step (6) of iteration $s = x$.

Case 2: W_{xy} is a directed path from x to y, so that $x > y$ holds again. We use induction on the length l of the path W_{xy}. The induction basis $(l = 1)$ was proved in Case 1. So let $l \geq 2$ and suppose v is the immediate predecessor of y on W_{xy}. Consider the cut (S_{vy}, T_{vy}). By Lemma 10.2.5, $x \in S_{vy}$. Now Lemma 6.1.2 implies $w(x, y) \leq c(S_{vy}, T_{vy}) = w(v, y)$. By induction hypothesis, $w(x, v) = k(W_{xv})$, so that

$$k(W_{xy}) = \min\{k(W_{xv}), w(v, y)\} = \min\{w(x, v), w(v, y)\}.$$

Now if we had $w(x, y) > k(W_{xy})$, Corollary 10.1.3 would imply

$$w(x, y) > k(W_{xy}) = w(x, v) = w(v, y),$$

contradicting $w(x, y) \leq w(v, y)$ above.

Case 3: W_{yx} is a directed path. This case can be treated analogous to Case 2.

Case 4: Neither W_{xy} nor W_{yx} is a directed path. Let z be the first common vertex of the directed paths W_{x1} and W_{y1}. Then W_{xy} is the union of the two directed paths W_{xz} and W_{yz}. Denote the predecessors of z on W_{xz} and W_{yz} by x' and y', respectively. We may assume w.l.o.g that $x' < y'$, so that the cut $(S_{x'z}, T_{x'z})$ is calculated at an earlier point than the cut $(S_{y'z}, T_{y'z})$. Then the cases treated above imply

$$w(x, z) = k(W_{xz}) \quad \text{and} \quad w(y, z) = k(W_{yz}),$$

so that

$$k(W_{xy}) = \min \{w(x, z), w(y, z)\}.$$

Now suppose that $w(x, y) > k(W_{xy})$ holds. Then Corollary 10.1.3 yields

$$k(W_{xy}) = w(x, z) = w(y, z).$$

Therefore, W_{xz} contains some edge of weight $k(W_{xy})$; we choose $e = uv$ to be the last edge on the directed path W_{xz} having this weight. Applying Lemma 10.2.5 to the path W_{xv}, we get $x \in S_{uv}$. As we assumed that $w(x, y) > k(W_{xy})$, we must also have $y \in S_{uv}$, because otherwise

$$w(x, y) \le c(S_{uv}, T_{uv}) = w(u, v) = k(W_{xy}),$$

a contradiction. Applying Lemma 10.2.5 to the path W_{yz}, we also get $y \notin S_{x'z}$. This shows in particular (because $y \in S_{uv}$) that $uv \ne x'z$. Again by Lemma 10.2.5 (applied to the paths W_{xz}, W_{uz} and W_{vz}), it follows that u, v and x are all contained in $S_{x'z}$. Thus, the situation looks as shown in Figure 10.7; the positions of u, v, x and y in one of the four quarters are uniquely determined, whereas there are two possibilities for x' and z. Depending on whether $z \in Q$ or $z \in S$ holds, either $(R, P \cup Q \cup S)$ or $(P, Q \cup R \cup S)$ is a minimal (u, v)-cut by Lemma 10.2.3; this yields the two cases of Figure 10.7. We denote this cut by (U, V).

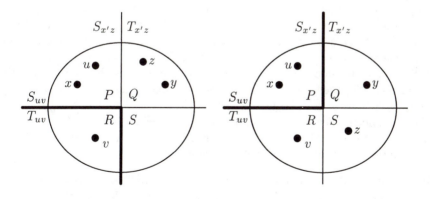

Fig. 10.7 Case 4

First consider the case $z \in Q$. Then the cut (U, V) separates the vertices z and v, so that

$$w(v, z) \leq c(U, V) = c(S_{uv}, T_{uv}) = w(u, v) = k(W_{xy}).$$

On the other hand, as the path W_{vz} is directed, it follows that $w(v, z) = k(W_{vz})$. By the choice of e, we must have $k(W_{vz}) > k(W_{xy})$, contradicting the inequality above. Therefore, this case cannot occur and z must be in S. Now the cut (U, V) separates the vertices x and y and we get

$$w(x, y) \leq c(U, V) = c(S_{uv}, T_{uv}) = w(u, v) = k(W_{xy}),$$

that is, $w(x, y) = k(W_{xy})$.   □

Corollary 10.2.7. *Let N be a symmetric network on $G = (V, E)$. Then an equivalent flow tree for N can be determined with complexity $O(|V|^3 |E|^{1/2})$.*

Proof. The statement follows immediately from Theorems 6.6.15 and 10.2.6, if we use Algorithm 6.6.14 for determining a maximal flow and (as mentioned at the beginning of this section) a minimal cut in step (5) of procedure FLOWTREE.   □

10.3 Synthesizing Minimal Networks

As announced at the end of Section 10.1, we now show how to find a minimal feasible network (N, c) on V for realizing a given symmetric function r as request function. The construction method described below is due to Gomory and Hu (1961). First consider the complete graph K on V with weight function r. Any maximal spanning tree T for K is called a *dominant requirement tree* for r. Such a tree T could be determined using the Algorithm of Prim (Algorithm 4.4.3 modified for maximal spanning trees as in Section 4.5), for example, with a complexity of $O(|V|^2)$. Next, T is partitioned into uniform trees (where a graph with a weight function is called *uniform* if all edges have the same weight) as follows. Suppose m is the minimal weight occuring in T, then the tree containing the same edges as T, but each edge with weight m, is a uniform tree. Now delete all edges of weight $r(e) = m$ from T and replace the weight $r(e)$ of all other edges by $r(e) - m > 0$. The result is a forest on V; the trees contained in this forest are then partitioned into uniform trees using the same procedure as above.

Example 10.3.1. Let K be the graph of Figure 10.8 (where edges of weight $r(e) = 0$ are not drawn). The edges drawn bold form a dominant requirement tree T. Note that T is not uniquely determined: edge gh of T could be substituted by edge bg, for example. This tree can be partitioned into uniform trees $U_1, \ldots, U_6$ as shown in Figure 10.9.

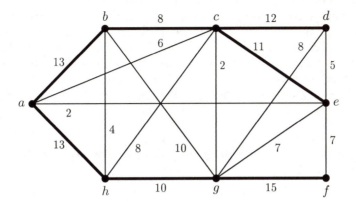

Fig. 10.8 A dominating tree

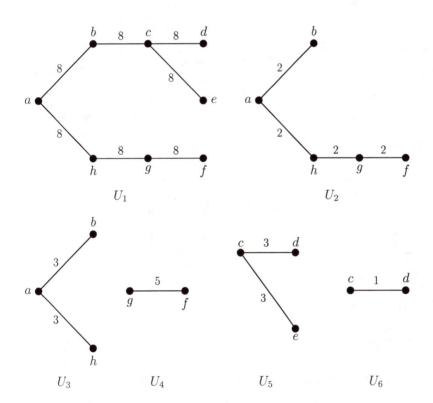

Fig. 10.9 Partitioning T into uniform trees

Now suppose the dominant requirement tree T has been partitioned into the uniform trees $U_1, \ldots, U_k$. For each tree U_i containing at least three vertices, we form a cycle C_i on the vertices of U_i (in any arbitrary order); each edge in this cycle is assigned weight $u_i/2$, where u_i is the weight of the edges in U_i. Trees U_i consisting of one edge only are kept as C_i with unchanged weight. Now consider the graph $G = (V, E)$ whose edge set is the union of the edge sets of $C_1, \ldots, C_k$, where parallel edges are merged to form one edge with weight the sum of the individual weights.

Example 10.3.2. For the partition of Figure 10.9, we may get the cycles $C_1, \ldots, C_6$ shown in Figure 10.10 and the symmetric network (G, c) shown in Figure 10.11.

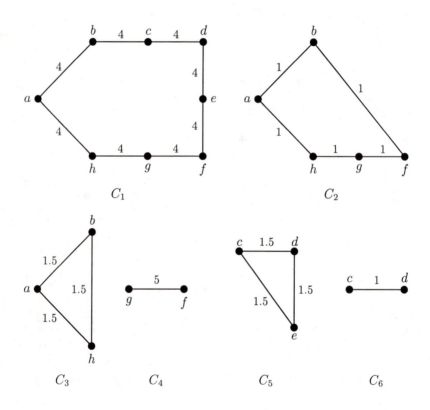

Fig. 10.10 The cycles corresponding to the trees of Figure 10.9

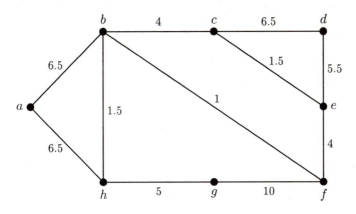

Fig. 10.11 The corresponding symmetric network

We now show that the symmetric network (G, c) thus constructed is a minimal feasible network for r. We prove first that N is feasible for r; we want to do so by verifying the following condition:

$$w(u, v) \geq r(u, v) \quad \text{for any edge } uv \text{ of } T. \tag{10.4}$$

It is obvious that this condition is at least necessary. On the other hand, for any two vertices x and y, the unique path in T from x to y is a path of maximal capacity in K by Theorem 4.5.3, so that condition (10.4) implies that $w(x, y) \geq r(x, y)$ holds for all x and y: If W is the path of maximal capacity, (10.2) in the proof of Theorem 10.1.1 implies

$$w(x, y) \geq \min \{w(u, v) : uv \text{ an edge of } W\} \geq \min \{r(u, v) : uv \in W\}$$
$$\geq r(x, y),$$

because xy is a path of capacity $r(x, y)$ in K (and (10.4) holds). It is quite obvious that (10.4) is satisfied for the symmetric network (G, c) defined above. For each cycle C_i, between any two vertices u and v of C_i, a flow of value u_i can be realized. If we add, for a given edge uv of T, the flows of those C_i for which U_i contains both u and v, we get a flow of value

$$\sum_{\substack{i \\ u, v \in U_i}} u_i = r(u, v).$$

It remains to show that N is a minimal network for r. For any vertex x, we define

$$u(x) := \max \{r(x, y) : y \neq x\},$$

that is, $u(x)$ is the maximal value of flow required in x. As $(x, V \backslash x)$ is a cut (for simplicity, we omit the parentheses from now on), Theorem 6.1.6 yields, for any symmetric network $N' = (G', c')$ which is feasible for r,

$$c'(x, V \backslash x) \geq u(x);$$

summing this over all vertices x gives

$$\sum_{x, y \in V} c'(x, y) \geq \sum_{x \in V} u(x) =: u(V) \tag{10.5}$$

(where $c'(x, y) = 0$ for edges xy not contained in G'). Therefore, the sum of all capacities in N' is at least $u(V)/2$. Now we claim that equality in (10.5) holds for the network N constructed above; then, of course, N is minimal. We define a function u' on V by

$$u'(x) := \max \{r(x, y) : xy \text{ an edge in } T\};$$

then it is trivial that $u'(x) \leq u(x)$ for all x.[4] By construction of N, $c(x, V \backslash x) = u'(x)$ holds for any vertex x, so that in N

$$\sum_{x, y \in V} c(x, y) = \sum_{x \in V} u'(x) \leq u(V).$$

Thus, for $N' = N$, equality holds in (10.5).

Now what about the complexity of this procedure? The dominant requirement tree can be determined using the Algorithm of Prim which needs $O(|V|^2)$ steps, by Theorem 4.4.4. Then T can be partitioned into uniform trees in $O(|V|^2)$ steps as well (because there are at most $|V| - 1$ distinct weights) and the network (G, c) can also be constructed from the uniform trees in $O(|V|^2)$ steps. This proves the following result of Gomory and Hu (1961).

Theorem 10.3.3. *Let r be a given symmetric function on V (the values of r are requirements on the values of the flow). Then it is possible to determine a minimal feasible symmetric network for r with complexity $O(|V|^2)$.* $\qquad\square$

We will not write down the algorithm described above in a formal way. As there are many different choices for the dominant requirement tree T and the order of the vertices in each of the cycles C_i, there are many different minimal networks for r. It is possible to make one more distinction between all these networks, although this further property might still be satisfied by several networks. A minimal network for r is called *dominating* if its flow function w satisfies the condition

$$w(x, y) \geq w'(x, y) \text{ for the flow function } w' \text{ of any minimal network } N' \text{ for } r.$$

It was proved by Gomory and Hu (1961) that such networks exist.

---

[4] It is possible to show (by applying the Algorithm of Prim, for example) that even $u(x) = u'(x)$ holds for all x. However, we do not need this for our proof.

Theorem 10.3.4. *For any symmetric function r of flow requirements on V, there exists a dominating minimal network for r.*

Proof. We change the given weight function r on K as follows:

$$s(x, y) := \min \{u(x), u(y)\},$$

where u is defined by $u(x) := \max \{r(x, y) : y \neq x\}$, as before. The following inequalities show that $u(x) = \max \{s(x, y) : y \neq x\}$ holds as well:

$$
\begin{aligned}
u(x) &\geq & \max \{s(x, y) : y \neq x\} &= \max \{\min(u(x), u(y)) : y \neq x\} \\
&\geq & \max \{ \min(u(x), r(x, y)) : y \neq x\} \\
&= & \max \{r(x, y) : y \neq x\} &= u(x).
\end{aligned}
$$

Now we construct a minimal feasible network N for s. As

$$r(x, y) \leq \min (u(x), u(y)) = s(x, y)$$

holds for all x and y, N is then also feasible for r. In N, all flow requirements have to be satisfied with equality, that is, $w(x, y) = s(x, y)$ holds for all x and y. Otherwise, there would exist x, y with $w(x, y) > s(x, y)$ and (w.l.o.g.) $u(x) \leq u(y)$, so that Lemma 6.1.2 would imply

$$c(x, V \backslash x) \geq w(x, y) > s(x, y) = u(x).$$

As N is minimal for s, this contradicts the fact that a minimal network has to satisfy inequality (10.5) with equality (as we found out in the proof of Theorem 10.3.3). As the function u is the same for r and s, N has to be a minimal feasible network for r as well.

Finally, let N' be any minimal network for r (with capacity function c' and flow function w'). Moreover, let x and y be any two vertices in V. Suppose $s(x, y) = w(x, y) < w'(x, y)$ and w.l.o.g. $s(x, y) = u(x) \leq u(y)$. Applying Lemma 6.1.2 once more yields

$$c'(x, V \backslash x) \geq w'(x, y) > w(x, y) = u(x),$$

so that we cannot have equality in (10.5) for N'. This contradicts the minimality of N' and finishes the proof.   □

A dominating network is distinguished among all minimal networks for r by the fact that the values of the flow are as large as possible for any two vertices (and the cost is as small as possible). Any further increase of the value of the flow would mean that the sum of the capacities has to be increased as well (and therefore the cost would increase). We treat this problem in Section 10.5.

Exercise 10.3.5. Determine a dominating feasible network N for Example 10.3.1 and show that there are pairs x, y of vertices for which the value of the flow on N is larger than the flow value in the minimal network of Figure 10.11 (by giving an example).

A more general problem of synthesizing a flow network was treated by Gomory and Hu (1964). The problem we studied above is the special case of their problem where, at any point of time, there is only one single request for flow (for a unique pair of vertices); this case is called 'complete time-sharing' or 'multi-terminal network flow'. The other extremal case occurs if all requests r have to be satisfied simultaneously; this leads to the 'multi-commodity flows' already mentioned at the end of Chapter 9 (see Gondran and Minoux (1984) and Ford and Fulkerson (1958c)). Gomory and Hu (1964) also treat the case where the requests for flow are time-dependent.

10.4 Cut Trees

In this section we consider a strenghtening of the notion of equivalent flow trees introduced in Section 10.2 and present an interesting application to the construction of certain communication networks. The material of this section will not be needed later, so the reader is free to skip this section.

Let $N = (G, c)$ be a symmetric network with flow function w. An equivalent flow tree B for N is called a *cut tree* for N if, for any two vertices x and y of N, the cut (U, V) determined by an edge $e = uv$ of minimal weight $w(u, v)$ on the path W_{xy} from x to y in B is always a minimal (x, y)-cut. It is easy to see that, in order to show that some equivalent flow tree is a cut tree, it suffices to verify the above condition for all edges $xy \in B$. The following example shows that an equivalent flow tree for N is not always a cut tree.

Example 10.4.1. Consider the symmetric network N of Example 10.2.2 and the equivalent flow tree B constructed there (that is, the tree on the right hand side of Figure 10.4). Then the condition for a cut tree is satisfied for almost all edges of B, the only exception being the edge $e = \{2, 3\}$. The cut corresponding to e is $S = \{3, 6, 7\}$, $T = \{1, 2, 4, 5\}$ with capacity $c(S, T) = 7$, but $w(2, 3) = 6$. However, modifying B slightly (we will see soon where this modification comes from) yields the cut tree B' for N shown in Figure 10.12.

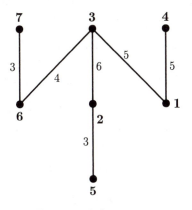

Fig. 10.12 A cut tree

The method given by Gomory and Hu (1961) does in fact always construct not only an equivalent flow tree, but a cut tree. However, an appropriate version of the simpler Algorithm 10.2.1 can be used for this purpose as well (this version yields the cut tree given in Example 10.4.1).

Algorithm 10.4.2. Let $N = (G, c)$ be a symmetric network on $G = (V, E)$, where $V = \{1, \ldots, n\}$. The algorithm determines a cut tree (B, w). The additional function $p(i)$ contains, for a vertex $i \neq 1$, the predecessor of i on a path from vertex 1 to i in B, so that B consists of the edges $\{p(i), i\}$ for $i = 2, \ldots, n$.

Procedure CUTTREE $(G, c; B, w)$

(1) $B \leftarrow \emptyset$;
(2) **for** $i = 2$ **to** n **do** $p(i) \leftarrow 1$ **od**;
(3) **for** $s = 2$ **to** n **do**
(4) $t \leftarrow p(s)$;
(5)   determine a minimal cut (S, T) and the value w of a maximal flow in the flow network (G, c, s, t);
(6) $f(s) \leftarrow w$;
(7)   **for** $i = 1$ **to** n **do**
(8)   **if** $i \in S \backslash \{s\}$ **and** $p(i) = t$ **then** $p(i) \leftarrow s$ **fi**
(9)   **od**
(10)   **if** $p(t) \in S$ **then** $p(s) \leftarrow p(t)$; $p(t) \leftarrow s$; $f(s) \leftarrow f(t)$; $f(t) \leftarrow w$ **fi**
(11) **od**
(12) **for** $i = 2$ **to** n **do**
(13) $w(i, p(i)) \leftarrow f(i)$;
(14) $B \leftarrow B \cup \{\{i, p(i)\}\}$
(15) **od**.

The main difference between Algorithms 10.2.1 and 10.4.2 is that, during iteration s of the above algorithm, not only vertices $i > s$ which are in S are cut off from t and connected to s, but this is done for vertices $i < s$ as well. In that case, the weight of an edge it which was removed has to be transferred to the new edge is. Moreover, the tree B does not 'grow' by adding one edge after the other (as in Algorithm 10.2.1, step (6)), but it might happen that edges $\{s, p(s)\}$ already constructed are changed again. This explains why the procedure CUTTREE appears to be a bit more involved. For a proof of the following result due to Gusfield (1990), we refer to the original paper because of its length and technical complexity.

Theorem 10.4.3. *Let $N = (G, c)$ be a symmetric network. Then Algorithm 10.4.2 constructs a cut tree for N. By using Algorithm 6.6.14 in step (5), one may achieve a complexity of $O(|V|^3 |E|^{1/2})$.*   □

A further algorithm for constructing $|V| - 1$ cuts corresponding to a cut tree was designed by Cheng and Hu (1992); their algorithm allows to use any symmetric cost function (not necessarily the capacity) for constructing the cuts. Gusfield and Naor (1991) studied related problems.

Next, we use cut trees for treating Problem 4.7.9 (Optimum Communication Spanning Tree). As already mentioned in Section 4.7, this problem is NP-complete. However, Hu (1974) was able to give an efficient solution for the special case where all edge weights are equal. We formulate this special case explicitly.

Problem 10.4.4 (Optimum Requirement Spanning Tree). Let G be a complete graph on the vertex set V and $r : V \times V \to \mathbb{R}_0^+$ a request function. We look for a spanning tree T for G such that the sum

$$\sum_{\substack{u, v \in V \\ u \neq v}} d(u, v) \cdot r(u, v) =: \gamma(T)$$

is minimal. Here $d(u, v)$ denotes the distance of u and v in the tree T.

The technique Hu (1974) used for solving Problem 10.4.4 includes finding a cut tree for an appropriate symmetric network. For this purpose, the pair $N = (G, r)$ of Problem 10.4.4 is considered as a symmetric network on G with capacity function r. We have the following lemma.

Lemma 10.4.5. *Let G be a complete graph with vertex set V and $r : V \times V \to \mathbb{R}_0^+$ a request function. Consider the symmetric network $N = (G, r)$. Then, for any spanning tree T of G,*

$$\gamma(T) = \sum_{e \in T} c(S_T(e)),$$

where $S_T(e)$ denotes the cut of G determined by $e \in T$ (as in Section 4.3) and $c(S_T(e))$ is the capacity of the cut $S_T(e)$ in N.

Proof. The cost $\gamma(T)$ can be written as follows

$$\gamma(T) = \sum_{e \in T} \sum_{\substack{u, v \in V \\ u \neq v \\ e \in W_{uv}}} r(u,v),$$

where W_{uv} is the path from u to v in T. Thus, we have to show that

$$\sum_{\substack{u, v \in V \\ u \neq v \\ e \in W_{uv}}} r(u,v) = c(S_T(e)).$$

However, this is clear because the path W_{uv} in T contains the edge e if and only if u and v are contained in different components of the cut $S_T(e)$. $\square$

We need the preceding lemma to prove the following result of Hu (1974); the proof we present is considerably simpler than the one given in the original paper.

Theorem 10.4.6. *Let G be a complete graph with vertex set V and $r : V \times V \to \mathbb{R}_0^+$ a request function. Then any cut tree T for the symmetric network $N = (G, r)$ is a solution of Problem 10.4.4.*

Proof. Let w be the flow function on N. As we saw in Exercise 10.1.4, any maximal spanning tree B for (G, w) is an equivalent flow tree for N. We denote the weight all of these trees have by β and show first that

$$\gamma(T) \geq \beta \tag{10.6}$$

holds for any spanning tree T of G. Consider the weight function w' on T defined by

$$w'(u, v) := c(S_T(e)) \quad \text{for all } e = uv \in T.$$

We extend w' to the flow function of the symmetric network (T, w'); then we know, as before, that T is a maximal spanning tree for the network (G, w'). Now (10.6) follows if we can show that

$$w(x, y) \leq w'(x, y) \quad \text{for all } x, y \in V. \tag{10.7}$$

So let x and y be any two vertices and $e = uv$ an edge of minimal weight (with respect to w') on the path W_{xy} from x to y in T. Then, as $S_T(e)$ is an (x, y)-cut, we have indeed

$$w'(x, y) = w'(u, v) = c(S_T(e)) \geq w(x, y).$$

Thus, to solve Problem 10.4.4, we may restrict our attention to equivalent flow trees B for N. But, for any such tree B,

$$\gamma(B) = \sum_{e \in B} c(S_B(e)) \geq \sum_{e=uv \in B} w(u,v) = w(B) = \beta,$$

because $S_B(u,v)$ is a (u,v)-cut. Now equality holds above if and only if $S_B(u,v)$ is a minimal (u,v)-cut for all $uv \in B$, that is, if B is a cut tree for N. $\qquad \square$

Theorems 10.4.3 and 10.4.6 imply immediately:

Corollary 10.4.7. *Problem 10.4.4 can be solved with complexity* $O(|V|^3|E|^{1/2})$ *using Algorithm 10.4.2.* $\qquad \square$

Example 10.4.8. Interpreting the capacity function of the symmetric network N on $V = \{1, \ldots, 7\}$ of Figure 10.8 as request function for the complete graph K_V (where, of course, we set $r(u,v) = 0$ for edges which are not contained in N), the spanning tree T of Figure 10.12 solves Problem 10.4.4 for this request function. The weights given in that figure are the capacities of the cuts $S_T(e)$ and we have

$$\gamma(T) = \sum_{e \in T} c(S_T(e)) = 26.$$

For comparison, the equivalent flow tree B of Figure 10.4 (found by the simpler Algorithm 10.2.1) has cost

$$\gamma(B) = \sum_{e \in B} c(S_B(e)) = 27,$$

so that B is indeed not an optimal solution of Problem 10.4.4.

Exercise 10.4.9 (Hu (1974)). Determine an optimal solution for Problem 10.4.4 for $V = \{1, \ldots, 6\}$ and the following values of the request function: $r(1,2) = 10$, $r(1,6) = 8$, $r(2,3) = 4$, $r(2,5) = 2$, $r(2,6) = 3$, $r(3,4) = 5$, $r(3,5) = 4$, $r(3,6) = 2$, $r(4,5) = 7$, $r(4,6) = 2$, $r(5,6) = 3$.

10.5 Increasing the Capacities

In the final section of the present chapter, we treat the question how the maximal value of a flow on a flow network $N = (G, c, s, t)$ can be increased as economically as possible. Our problem is: How should the capacities of the edges be increased if we want to increase the maximal value w of a flow on N by k units? We assume that the cost for increasing the capacity of an edge e by $d(e)$ units is proportional to $d(e)$.

So let $N = (G, c, s, t)$ be a flow network with an integral capacity function c and let $\delta : E \to \mathbb{N}$ be some mapping. For any $v \in \mathbb{N}$, we look for a mapping $d = d_v : E \to \mathbb{N}_0$ such that the network $(G, c + d, s, t)$ allows a flow of value v and the sum

$$z(v) := \sum_{e \in E} d(e)\delta(e)$$

is minimal. Thus, the cost for realizing a flow of value v on N (by increasing the capacities of the connections which exist already) is at least $z(v)$. For a given v, the function d_v then specifies how the capacities are to be increased in an optimal way. Of course, the problem of finding the maximal possible flow value for a given budget b can be solved using the same approach: we have to find the largest value of v such that $z(v) \leq b$. (In general, the bound b is not achieved with equality, because we assumed the capacities to be integral, but equality can be obtained by interpolation.) The problem described above (called the *Parametric Budget Problem*) was treated first by Fulkerson (1959). Our technique for solving this problem uses the Algorithm of Busacker and Gowen (1961) of Section 9.6 and is somewhat simpler than Fulkerson's method.

We define a directed graph H on the vertex set V of N as follows. Any edge e of G is contained in H as well with capacity $c'(e) = c(e)$ and cost $\gamma(e) = 0$. Moreover, for each edge $e = uv$ of G, H also contains a parallel edge $e' = uv$ with capacity $c'(e') = \infty$ and cost $\gamma(e') = \delta(e)$. (We can avoid parallel edges by subdividing e'.) Then our problem is obviously solved by an optimal flow f of value v on the flow network $N' = (H, c', s, t)$ with respect to the cost function γ. As f is optimal, $f(e') \neq 0$ can hold only if e is saturated already, that is, if $f(e) = c'(e)$. The function d_v is then determined by $d_v(e) := f(e')$. Thus, it is possible to calculate d_v and $z(v)$ for any positive integer v using the Algorithm of Busacker and Gowen. It is obvious that $z(v) = 0$ for $v \leq w$ (in this case, we do not have to increase any capacities!), so that we can start the algorithm as given in 9.6.2 with a maximal flow f on N instead of the zero flow.

Example 10.5.1. Consider again the flow network N of Example 6.2.3, see Figure 10.13, where we state the capacities in parentheses and the cost in brackets. In 6.2.3, we calculated a maximal flow f of value $w = 31$ (see Figure 6.12); for the convenience of the reader, we show this flow again in Figure 10.14. The minimal cut (S, T) corresponding to f is drawn in Figure 10.14 as well. Now we use f as the initial flow in the Algorithm of Busacker and Gowen. We have to imagine G as being extended to H, that is, for each edge e of G, we have to add a parallel edge e' with capacity ∞ and cost $\delta(e)$. We proceed by constructing the auxiliary network N^* corresponding to f. As this network is (because of the parallel edges and the backward edges) quite complicated already, we omit edges which are not important for us because they are not contained in any path of minimal cost from s to t in N^*. More precisely, we omit

(i) edges with end vertex s or start vertex t;
(ii) edges e' for which e is not yet saturated;
(iii) edges leading from T to S (vertices in S can be reached from s by a path of cost 0, so that we want to direct our path from S to T, not reversely);

(iv) edges e which are saturated.

The interesting part of N^* is shown in Figure 10.15, where a path W of minimal cost from s to t is drawn bold. In this figure, the numbers without parentheses give the cost and the numbers in parentheses state the capacities in N^*. The path W has cost 2 and capacity 10. Thus, we may increase the existing maximal flow of value $w = 31$ by ε with cost 2ε to a flow of value $v = 31 + \varepsilon$ (where $\varepsilon = 1, \ldots, 10$). The flow g of value 41 obtained for $\varepsilon = 10$ is shown in Figure 10.16; the edge ac whose capacity was increased is drawn bold. If any further increase of the value of the flow is desired, it is possible to continue accordingly using the Algorithm of Busacker and Gowen. If the budget b is given, this procedure terminates as soon as $z(v) > b$.

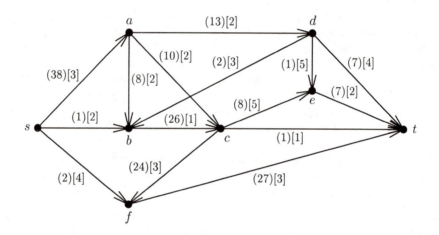

Fig. 10.13 Flow network with cost for capacity increase

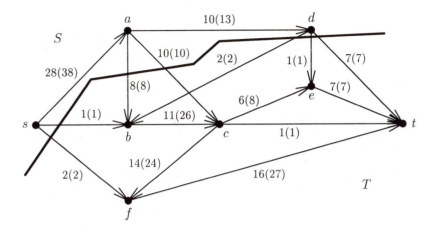

Fig. 10.14 Maximal flow and minimal cut on N

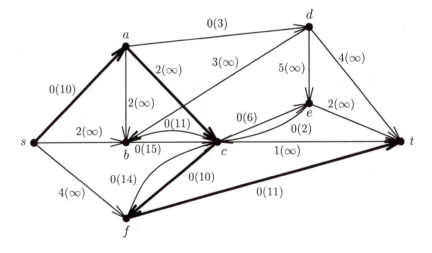

Fig. 10.15 A path of minimal cost in N^*

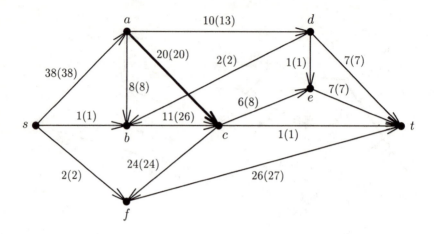

Fig. 10.16 An optimal flow of value 41

Exercise 10.5.2. Determine the cost function $z(v)$ for all v for the flow network of Example 10.5.1. (Hint: Two more steps of Algorithm 9.6.2 are needed.)

It is clear by Exercise 9.6.4 that the cost function $z(v)$ is always a piecewise linear, monotonously increasing, convex function. Moreover, we need at most $|E|$ iterations of the Algorithm of Busacker and Gowen to determine $z(v)$ for all v, because that is the latest possible point where we can reach a path of minimal cost from s to t which has infinite capacity.

A survey of various problems and algorithms concerning the design of networks for communication or transport purposes can be found in Magnanti and Wong (1984).

11. Connectivity

In the first chapter, we defined what 'connected' and 'strongly connected' means; we also introduced the notion of k-connectivity in Chapter 7. The Algorithm of Moore (BFS) we presented in Chapter 3 is an efficient method for determining the connected components of a graph. Now, in the present chapter, we mainly treat algorithmic questions concerning k-connectivity and strong connectivity for directed graphs. We develop a further strategy for searching (besides BFS), namely 'Depth First Search'. This chapter also contains various theoretical results, for example characterizations of 2-connected graphs and of edge connectivity.

11.1 k-Connected Graphs for $k \geq 2$

In Section 7.1, we defined the connectivity $\kappa(G)$ and what k-connected means. Now we introduce a further notation: For any two vertices s and t of a graph G, the number $\kappa(s,t)$ denotes the maximal number of vertex disjoint paths from s to t in G. Then the Theorem of Menger (1927) given in Section 7.1 states that, for non-adjacent vertices s and t, the number $\kappa(s,t)$ is equal to the minimal cardinality of a vertex separator for s and t. The following important result of Whitney (1932a) was already proved in Exercise 7.1.6.

Theorem 11.1.1 (Theorem of Whitney). *A graph G is k-connected if and only if $\kappa(s,t) \geq k$ for any two vertices s and t of G, that is,*

$$\kappa(G) = \min \{\kappa(s,t) : s,t \in V\}.$$

$\square$

Exercise 11.1.2. a) Determine $\kappa(K_{m,n})$.
b) Show that a k-connected graph on n vertices contains at least $\lceil \frac{kn}{2} \rceil$ edges. (Note that Harary (1962) showed that this bound is tight.)

Exercise 11.1.3. Let G be a k-connected graph and T a set of k vertices of G. Then, for any vertex $s \notin T$, there exists a set of k paths with start vertex s and end vertex in T which are pairwise vertex disjoint (except for s).

Before looking at the problem of how to determine the connectivity for a given graph, we apply Exercise 11.1.3 to the existence problem for Hamiltonian circuits; the following sufficient condition was found by Chvátal and Erdös (1972).

Theorem 11.1.4. *Let G be a k-connected graph, where $k \geq 2$. If $\alpha(G) \leq k$, then G is Hamiltonian.*

Proof. As G is 2-connected, G has to contain cycles. (We leave it as an exercise here to prove this statement; or see Theorem 11.3.1.) Let K be a cycle of maximal length m. Then we must have $m \geq k$, because otherwise, Exercise 11.1.3 applied to the vertex set of K together with $k - m$ additional vertices (as set T) and any arbitrary vertex $s \notin T$ would yield a cycle of length $> m$. Now suppose K is not a Hamiltonian circuit, then there exists a vertex $s \notin K$. Again by Exercise 11.1.3, there exist k paths W_i $(i = 1, \ldots, k)$ with start vertex s and end vertex t_i on K which are pairwise disjoint except for s. Moreover, we may assume that t_i is the only vertex W_i has in common with K. Now consider K as a directed cycle (oriented in any direction) and denote the successor of t_i on K by u_i. If s is adjacent to one of the vertices u_i, we may substitute the edge $t_i u_i$ of K by the path from t_i to s followed by the edge $s u_i$. This yields a cycle of length $> m$ and contradicts our assumption that K is a cycle of maximal length. Thus, s cannot be adjacent to any of the vertices u_i. As $\alpha(G) \leq k$, the $(k + 1)$-set $\{s, u_1, \ldots, u_k\}$ cannot be independent, so that G contains an edge of the form $u_i u_j$. Then, by substituting the edges $t_i u_i$ and $t_j u_j$ of K by the edge $u_i u_j$ and the paths from s to t_i and from s to t_j, we get a cycle of length $> m$ again, a contradiction. It follows that K has to be a Hamiltonian circuit. □

Corollary 11.1.5. *If the closure $[G]$ of a graph G satisfies the condition $\alpha([G]) \leq \kappa([G])$, G is Hamiltonian.*

Proof. This follows immediately from Theorems 1.4.1 and 11.1.4. □

Exercise 11.1.6. Show that Theorem 11.1.4 is best possible by constructing (for all κ) a graph G with $\alpha(G) = \kappa(G) + 1$ which is not Hamiltonian.

Now we turn to the question which complexity a technique for determining the connectivity of a given graph could have. By Theorem 11.1.1, it suffices to determine the maximal number of vertex disjoint paths between any two vertices of G. Corollary 7.1.5 states that this can be done for any pair of vertices with complexity $O(|V|^{1/2}|E|)$, so that we have a total complexity of $O(|V|^{5/2}|E|)$. If G is not a complete graph, we have to examine non-adjacent pairs of vertices only (we will see this in the proof of Theorem 11.1.9). We present a simple algorithm due to Even and Tarjan (1975) whose complexity is a little better.

Exercise 11.1.7. Design an algorithm for determining the maximal value of a flow on a 0-1-network (MAX01FLOW) and an algorithm for calculating the maximal number of vertex disjoint paths in a (directed) graph between two given vertices s and t (PATHNR). Hint: Use the results of Sections 6.5 and 7.1.

Algorithm 11.1.8. Let $G = (V, E)$ be a graph on n vertices. The algorithm calculates the connectivity of G.

Procedure KAPPA $(G;$ kappa)

(1) $n \leftarrow |V|$, $k \leftarrow 0$, $y \leftarrow n - 1$, $S \leftarrow V$;
(2)   **repeat**
(3)   choose $v \in S$ and remove v from S;
(4)   **for** $w \in S \backslash A_v$ **do** PATHNR$(G, v, w; x)$;
            $y \leftarrow \min \{y, x\}$ **od**;
(5) $k \leftarrow k + 1$
(6)   **until** $k > y$;
(7)   kappa $\leftarrow y$
(8) **fi.**

Theorem 11.1.9. *Let* $G = (V, E)$ *be a connected graph. Then Algorithm 11.1.8 calculates the connectivity of* G *with complexity* $O(|V|^{1/2}|E|^2)$.

Proof. Note that, if G is a complete graph K_n, the algorithm terminates after having removed all n vertices and yields kappa $= y = n - 1$. Now look at the case where G is not complete. During the **repeat**-loop, vertices $v_1, v_2, \ldots, v_k$ are chosen successively until the minimum γ of all values $\kappa(v_i, w)$ (where w runs through the vertices which are not adjacent to v_i) is less than k; then we have $k \geq \gamma + 1 \geq \kappa(G) + 1$. By definition, there exists a vertex separator T for G of cardinality $\kappa(G)$. As $k \geq \kappa(G) + 1$, there is at least one vertex $v_i \notin T$. Now $G \backslash T$ is not connected, so that there exists a vertex v in $G \backslash T$ such that any path from v to v_i meets the set T. In particular, v_i and v cannot be adjacent and $\gamma \leq \kappa(v_i, v) \leq \kappa(G)$, so that $\gamma = \kappa(G)$. This shows that the algorithm is correct. It has complexity $O(\kappa(G)|V|^{3/2}|E|)$ because, during each of the $\kappa(G)$ iterations of the **repeat**-loop, the procedure PATHNR is called $O(|V|)$ times, and each of these calls has complexity $O(|V|^{1/2}|E|)$. Now $\kappa(G) \leq \deg v$ for any vertex v. Using the equality $\sum \deg v = 2|E|$, we get

$$\kappa(G) \leq \min \{\deg v : v \in V\} \leq 2 \frac{|E|}{|V|},$$

which yields the complexity $O(|V|^{1/2}|E|^2)$ as asserted. $\qquad \square$

As we have seen, it takes a considerable amount of work to determine the exact value of $\kappa(G)$. Therefore, one is often satisfied with checking whether G is (at least) k-connected. For $k = 1$, this can be done with complexity $O(|E|)$ using the Algorithm of Moore, see Section 3.3. For $k = 2$, we give an algorithm in Section 11.3 which is due to Tarjan (1972) and has complexity $O(|E|)$ as well. Even for $k = 3$, it is possible to achieve a complexity of $O(|E|)$, although with considerable effort, see Hopcroft and Tarjan (1973). Even (1977) gave an algorithm for the case $k \leq |V|^{1/2}$ having complexity $O(k|V||E|)$ (see also Even (1979), p. 129); in particular, for fixed k, it is possible to check with complexity $O(|V||E|)$ whether a graph is k-connected. The problem of checking whether a given graph is k-connected is also treated in Galil (1980); an unusual approach for this task is given in Linial, Lovász and Widgerson (1988). For the purpose of designing communication networks it is of interest to find a k-connected subgraph of minimal weight in a directed complete graph; for this problem, we refer to Bienstock, Brickell and Monma (1990) and the references given there.

11.2 Depth First Search

The searching technique for graphs we treat in this section will be used repeatedly throughout the present chapter. While the BFS in Algorithm 3.3.1 examines a graph G in a 'breadth first' fashion (that is, vertices which have larger distance to the start vertex s are examined later than those with smaller distance to s), the alternative method 'depth first search' follows paths as far as possible: from a vertex v already treated, we proceed to any vertex w adjacent to v which was not yet treated and, after having examined w, continue to look for the next 'unlabelled vertex' directly from w. Thus, we construct a maximal path starting at some initial vertex s. Tremaux (see Lucas (1882)) knew this idea already; it was used to study mazes (see Tarry (1895)). The following version is taken from the fundamental paper of Tarjan (1972).

Algorithm 11.2.1 (depth first search, DFS). Let $G = (V, E)$ be a graph and s a vertex of G.

Procedure DFS $(G, s; nr, p)$

(1) **for** $v \in V$ **do** $nr(v) \leftarrow 0$; $p(v) \leftarrow 0$ **od**;
(2) **for** $e \in E$ **do** $u(e) \leftarrow$ false **od**;
(3) $i \leftarrow 1$; $v \leftarrow s$; $nr(s) \leftarrow 1$;
(4) **repeat**
(5)   **while** there exists $w \in A_v$ with $u(vw) =$ false **do**
(6)   choose some $w \in A_v$ with $u(vw) =$ false; $u(vw) \leftarrow$ true;
(7)   **if** $nr(w) = 0$ **then** $p(w) \leftarrow v$; $i \leftarrow i + 1$; $nr(w) \leftarrow i$;
                $v \leftarrow w$ **fi**
(8)   **od**;
(9) $v \leftarrow p(v)$
(10) **until** $v = s$ **and** $u(sw) =$ true for all $w \in A_s$.

The algorithm labels the vertices with a number nr according to the order in which they are reached; $p(w)$ is the vertex from which w was accessed.

Theorem 11.2.2. *Each edge in the connected component of s is used exactly once in each direction during the execution of Algorithm 11.2.1. Thus, if G is connected, Algorithm 11.2.1 has complexity $O(|E|)$.*

Proof. First, we give a precise formulation of what we mean by 'using an edge in some direction' by showing that the DFS constructs a walk in G beginning in s. In step (6), an edge $e = vw$ (initially $v = s$) is used from v to w; if $nr(w) = 0$, v is replaced by w. If $nr(w) \neq 0$, e is used immediately in the opposite direction from w to v and the algorithm proceeds (if possible) with another edge incident with v which was not used yet. If there is no such edge any more (that is, all edges incident with v have been used at least once), the edge $p(v)v$ (which was used to reach v) is used in the opposite direction and v is replaced by $p(v)$. Thus, the algorithm indeed constructs a walk in G.

Now we show that no edge can be used twice in the same direction (so that the walk is in fact a trail in $\overrightarrow{G}$). Suppose this claim is false, then there is an edge $e = vw$ which is used twice in the same direction. We may assume w.l.o.g that e is the first such edge and that e is used from v to w. As each edge is labelled 'true' in step (6) when it is used first, $u(e)$ must have value true when e is used the second time. Thus, e must be used the second time when step (9) is executed. But then we must have $w = p(v)$ and (because of the condition in (5)) all edges incident with v have to be labelled with 'true' already. Thus, with $d = \deg v$, the walk must have left v (at least) d times before e is used the second time. This means that the walk must have arrived at v at least $d + 1$ times, so that some edge of the form uv must have been used twice from u to v before, a contradiction.

It remains to show that each edge of G is used in both possible directions (we may assume G to be connected). Let S be the set of all vertices v for which each edge incident with v is used in both directions. First, the above considerations show that the algorithm terminates. At that point, the algorithm must have reached a vertex v with $p(v) = 0$ such that there is no edge incident with v which is labelled with 'false' (because of (10)). This can only happen for $v = s$ and it also implies that all edges incident with s must have been used from s to some other vertex. But then all these deg s edges must also have been used to reach s from some other vertex (because none of them was used twice in the same direction). This means $s \in S$. We claim that $S = V$. Suppose that our claim is wrong. As G is connected, there exist edges connecting S to $V \backslash S$. Let $e = vw$ be the edge with $v \in S$ and $w \in V \backslash S$ which is used first during the algorithm. Note that any edge connecting some vertex of S and some vertex of $V \backslash S$ is used in both directions by definition of S. As we reach vertex w for the first time when we use e from v to w, $nr(w) = 0$ at that point of time. Then, in step (7), we set $v = p(w)$ and e is labelled 'true'. Now we can only use e again according to step (9), that is, from w to v. At that point, all edges incident with w must have been labelled 'true'. As each edge incident with w can only be used at most once in each direction, each of these edges must have been used in both directions, so that $w \in S$, a contradiction.   □

Theorem 11.2.2 shows that the DFS is indeed a possible strategy for finding the exit of a maze (if it is possible to label 'edges' – that is, 'paths' in the maze – which have been used already), see Exercise 11.2.6. In the next section, we use a refined version of the DFS for studying 2-connected graphs. The application below is somewhat simpler.

Theorem 11.2.3. *Let G be a connected graph and s a vertex of G. Let T denote the directed graph on V whose edges are precisely the $p(v)v$, where $p(v)$ has been determined by $DFS(G, s; nr, p)$. Then T is a spanning arborescence for G with root s.*

Proof. As each vertex v of G is reached for the first time during the DFS via the edge $p(v)v$, $|T|$ is obviously connected. More precisely, the sequence $v = v_0, v_1, v_2, \ldots$ with $v_{i+1} = p(v_i)$ for $v_i \neq s$ yields a path from s to v in T. Thus, s is a root of T. Moreover, T contains exactly $|V| - 1$ edges (for s, $p(s) = 0$ is not a vertex of G), so that $|T|$ is a tree by Theorem 1.2.8.   □

Theorem 11.2.3 states that we can – similar to the BFS of Section 3.3 – use Algorithm 11.2.1 to check (with complexity $O(|E|)$) whether a given graph G is connected and, if it is, find a spanning arborescence with root s. The edges $p(v)v$ contained in this arborescence are called *tree edges* and the other edges *back edges*. The next result explains this terminology.

Lemma 11.2.4. *Let G be a connected graph and T a spanning arborescence of G determined by the DFS. Moreover, let $e = uv$ be a back edge of G (with respect to T). Then u is an ancestor or a descendant of v in T, where a vertex u is called an ancestor or a descendant of v, respectively, if there exists a directed path from u to v in T (or a directed path from v to u, respectively).*

Proof. We may assume w.l.o.g. that $nr(v) < nr(u)$, that is, u is reached at a later point of time during the DFS than v. As all edges incident with v are labelled 'true' according to step (5) before the algorithm stops to examine these edges, e has to be treated at this point as well. As u is not a direct descendant of v (because otherwise $v = p(u)$ and uv would be a tree edge), u must have been labelled before e was examined. This means that u is an indirect descendant of v.   □

Example 11.2.5. Consider the graph G of Figure 11.1 (which is the undirected version of the directed graph given in Figure 3.3) and execute a DFS beginning in s. To make the algorithm deterministic, we choose the edges in step (6) according to alphabetical order of their end vertices. Then the vertices are reached in the following order: s, a, b, c, d, e, f, g. After that, the algorithm 'backtracks' from g to f, to e and then to d. Now h is reached and the algorithm backtracks to d, c, b and a and finally to s. The directed tree T constructed by the DFS is shown in Figure 11.2. The BFS Algorithm of Section 3.3, in comparison, treats the vertices in the order $s, a, b, c, d, e, f, h, g$; the corresponding tree T' was given in Figure 3.5. Note that the distance $d(s, x)$ in T' is equal to the corresponding distance in G, whereas this is not true in T: here vertex g has distance 7 from s (the maximal distance from s occurring in T). This shows that the DFS indeed tries to reach the 'depth' of the graph.

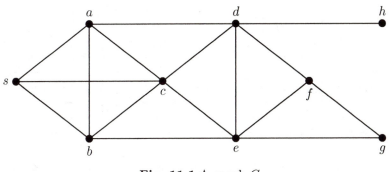

Fig. 11.1 A graph G

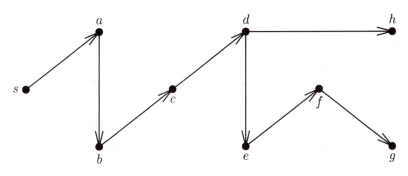

Fig. 11.2 DFS tree for G

Exercise 11.2.6. Describe a maze by an appropriate graph and use this construction to find a path through the maze of Figure 11.3 by a DFS. (This task is somewhat lengthy, but very instructive!)

Fig. 11.3 A maze

11.3 2-Connected Graphs

A *cut point* or *articulation point* of a graph G is a vertex v such that $G \backslash v$ has more connected components than G. According to the definition of Section 7.1, a connected graph with at least three vertices which does not contain any cut points is 2-connected. A connected graph containing cut points is called *separable*. The maximal induced subgraphs of a graph G which are not separable are called the *blocks* or *biconnected components* of G. Note that the blocks of a graph do not form a partition of its vertex set V in general. For example, the graph of Figure 11.1 has blocks $\{s, a, b, c, d, e, f, g\}$ and $\{d, h\}$. If c is a cut point of a connected graph G, then $V \backslash c$ can be partitioned into sets $V_1 \overset{.}{\cup} \ldots \overset{.}{\cup} V_k$ such that two vertices a and b are in the same part of the partition if and only if they are connected by a path not containing c. Therefore, no block can contain vertices from more than one of the V_i; in particular, two blocks intersect in at most one vertex (and this vertex has to be a cut point). Another useful observation is that any cycle has to be contained in a block. We give some conditions equivalent to 2-connectedness due to Whitney (1932b).

Theorem 11.3.1. *Let G be a graph with at least 3 vertices which does not contain any isolated vertices. Then the following conditions are equivalent:*

(1) G is 2-connected.
(2) For any two vertices of G, there exists a cycle containing both of them.
(3) For any vertex v and any edge e of G, there exists a cycle containing both v and e.
(4) For any two edges of G, there exists a cycle containing both of them.
(5) For any two vertices x and y and any edge e of G, there exists a path from x to y containing e.
(6) For any three vertices x, y, z of G, there exists a path from x to y containing z.
(7) For any three vertices x, y, z of G, there exists a path from x to y not containing z.

Proof.

(1) $\Leftrightarrow$ (2) :   If G is 2-connected, Theorem 11.1.1 implies that any two vertices are connected by two vertex disjoint paths; the union of these paths yields the desired cycle containing both vertices. Conversely, a graph satisfying condition (2) obviously cannot contain any cut points.

(1) $\Rightarrow$ (3) :   Let $e = uw$; we may assume w.l.o.g. that $v \neq u, w$. We subdivide e by a new vertex x, that is, we substitute e by the edges ux and xw (compare Section 1.5) to get a new graph G'. As G satisfies (2) as well, G' cannot contain any cut points, that is, G' is 2-connected as well. This also implies that G' satisfies (2). Therefore, there is a cycle containing v and x in G'; then the corresponding cycle in G has to contain v and e.

(3) $\Rightarrow$ (2) :   Let u and v be two vertices of G. As G does not contain any isolated vertices, there exists an edge e incident with u. If (3) holds, there exists a cycle containing e and v; this cycle also contains u and v.

(1) $\Rightarrow$ (4) :   Similar to '(1) $\Rightarrow$ (3)'.

(4) $\Rightarrow$ (2) :   Similar to '(3) $\Rightarrow$ (2)'.

(1) $\Rightarrow$ (5) :   Let G' be the graph we get by adding an edge $e' = xy$ to G (if x and y are not adjacent in G in the first place). Obviously G' is 2-connected as well, so that (4) implies that there is a cycle in G' containing e and e'. Removing e' from this cycle yields the desired path in G.

(5) $\Rightarrow$ (6) :   Choose an edge e incident with z. Then, by (5), there is a path from x to y containing e (and then z as well, of course).

(6) $\Rightarrow$ (7) :   As (6) holds for any three vertices of G, there exists a path from x to z containing y. The first part of this path (the part from x to y) is the desired path.

(7) $\Rightarrow$ (1) :   If (7) holds, G can obviously not contain any cut points. $\square$

Exercise 11.3.2. Let G be a connected graph with at least two vertices. Show that G contains at least two vertices which are not cut points. Is this bound tight?

Exercise 11.3.3 (Gallai (1964)). For any graph G, we define the *block-cutpoint graph* $bc(G)$ as follows. The vertices of $bc(G)$ are the blocks and the cut points of G, and a block B and a cut point c of G are adjacent in $bc(G)$ if and only if c is contained in B. Show that the following statements hold.

a) If G is connected, $bc(G)$ is a tree.

b) For any vertex v, let $b(v)$ denote the number of blocks containing v, and $b(G)$ the number of blocks of G. If G has precisely p connected components, we have

$$b(G) = p + \sum_v (b(v) - 1).$$

c) Let $c(B)$ be the number of cut points contained in block B and $c(G)$ the number of all cut points of G. Then

$$c(G) = p + \sum_B (c(B) - 1).$$

d) $b(G) \geq c(G) + 1$.

Exercise 11.3.4 (Ramachandra Rao (1968)). Let G be a connected graph with r cut points. Show that G has at most $\binom{n-r}{2} + r$ edges and construct a graph where this bound is tight. (Hint: Use the number k of blocks of G and Exercise 11.3.3 d); also, derive a formula for the sum of the cardinalities of the blocks from 11.3.3 b)).

For the remainder of this section, let G be a connected graph. Suppose we have constructed a spanning arborescence T for G with root s by a DFS (compare Theorem 11.2.3). We use the functions nr and p occuring in the DFS for determining the cut points of G (and hence the blocks). Moreover, we introduce an additional function L (for 'low point'): For a given vertex v, consider all vertices u which are accessible from v by a path (which might be the empty path) consisting of a directed path in T followed by at most one back edge. Then $L(v)$ is the minimum of the values $nr(u)$ for all these vertices u.

Example 11.3.5. Let G be the graph of Example 11.2.5 (see Figure 11.1). In Figure 11.4, the vertices of G are labelled with the numbers they are assigned during the DFS; the numbers in parentheses are the values of the function L. The edges of the tree constructed by the DFS are drawn bold. (For calculating the values $L(i)$, note that it works best to begin with the leaves of the tree, that is, to treat the vertices in the order according to decreasing DFS numbers. In Algorithm 11.3.8, we will see how the function L may be calculated during the DFS.)

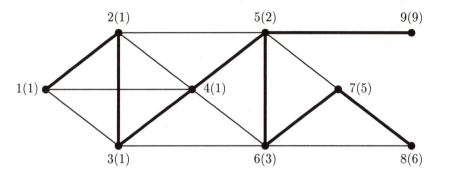

Fig. 11.4 Labels assigned during the DFS and function L

The following result of Tarjan (1972) shows why the function L is important.

Lemma 11.3.6. *Let G be a connected graph, s a vertex of G and T the spanning arborescence of G determined by $DFS(G, s; nr, p)$ (see Theorem 11.2.3). Moreover, let u be a vertex of G not equal to s. Then u is a cut point if and only if there is a tree edge $e = uv$ such that $L(v) \geq nr(u)$ (where L is the function defined above).*

Proof. First suppose that u is a cut point of G. Then we can partition $V \backslash u$ into $V_1 \cup \ldots \cup V_k$ (where $k \geq 2$) such that, for $i \neq j$, all paths connecting a vertex of V_i with a vertex of V_j have to contain u. We may assume w.l.o.g. that $s \in V_1$. Let $e = uv$ be the first tree edge for which $v \notin V_1$ holds, say $v \in V_2$. As there are no edges connecting a vertex of V_2 with a vertex of $V \backslash (V_2 \cup \{u\})$ and as all vertices which are accessible from v by tree edges are again in V_2 (and are therefore reached at a later point of the algorithm than u), it follows that $L(v) \geq nr(u)$.

Conversely, let $e = uv$ be a tree edge with $L(v) \geq nr(u)$. Denote the set of all vertices on the path from s to u in T by S (including s, but not u) and let T' be the part of T having root v, that is, T' consists of the descendants of v. By Lemma 11.2.4, there cannot be an edge connecting a vertex of T' with a vertex of $V \backslash (S \cup T' \cup \{u\})$. Moreover, there are no edges of the form xy with $x \in T'$ and $y \in S$, because such an edge would be a back edge, so that $L(v) \leq nr(y) < nr(u)$ (because of the path from v to x in T' followed by the edge xy), a contradiction. Therefore, each path connecting a vertex in T' with a vertex in S has to contain u, so that u is a cut point. $\square$

Lemma 11.3.7. *Under the same assumptions as in Lemma 11.3.6, s is a cut point if and only if s is on at least two tree edges.*

Proof. First, let s be a cut point and $V_1 \,\dot\cup \ldots \dot\cup\, V_k$ (with $k \geq 2$) a partition of $V \backslash s$ such that any path from a vertex of V_i to a vertex of V_j (for $i \neq j$) has to contain s. Let $e = sv$ be the first tree edge (with $v \in V_1$, say). Then all the vertices not in V_1 are not accessible from v in T, so that s has to be incident with at least one further tree edge.

Conversely, let sv and sw be tree edges and T' the part of T which has root v. By Lemma 11.2.4, there are no edges connecting a vertex of T' to a vertex in $V \backslash (T' \cup \{s\})$. As the set $V \backslash (T' \cup \{s\})$ is non-empty by hypothesis (it contains w), s is a cut point.   □.

In Example 11.3.5, obviously, the only cut point is vertex 5, in agreement with Lemmas 11.3.6 and 11.3.7. We want to design a version of the DFS which simultaneously calculates the function L and determines the cut points and the blocks of G. First consider how L could be calculated. We set $L(v) := nr(v)$ when v is reached for the first time. If v is a leaf of T, the definition of L implies

$$L(v) = \min \{nr(u) : u = v \text{ or } vu \text{ is a back edge in } G\}, \qquad (11.1)$$

so that we replace $L(v)$ by $\min \{L(v), nr(u)\}$ as soon as the algorithm uses a back edge vu (that is, as soon as $nr(u) \neq 0$ during the examination of vu in step (6) or (7) of the DFS). When the algorithm backtracks from v to $p(v)$ in step (9), all back edges have been examined, so that $L(v)$ has obtained its correct value (11.1). Similarly, if v is not a leaf, we have

$$L(v) = \min (\{nr(u) : u = v \text{ or } vu \text{ a back edge }\} \cup \{L(u) : vu \text{ a tree edge}\}).$$
$$(11.2)$$

Thus, if v is not a leaf, the only difference is that we have to replace $L(v)$ by $\min \{L(v), L(u)\}$ as soon as a tree edge vu is used (that is, as soon as this edge is used for the second time from u to v, because, at that point, the examination of u is finished and $L(u)$ has its correct value; this can be shown by induction).

Now we are in a position to state the Algorithm of Tarjan (1972). It is advantageous to use a *stack* S for determining the blocks. A stack is a list where elements are appended at the end and removed at the end as well ('last in - first out') (in contrast to a *queue* where elements are appended at the end, but removed at the beginning ('first in - first out')). For a more detailed discussion of these data structures (as well as for possible implementations), we refer to Aho, Hopcroft and Ullman (1974), Aho, Hopcroft and Ullman (1983) and Corman, Leiserson and Rivest (1990). The reader should note that Algorithm 11.3.8 has precisely the same structure as the DFS Algorithm 11.2.1 (and therefore also the same complexity $O(|E|)$).

Algorithm 11.3.8. Let G be a connected graph and s a vertex of G. The algorithm determines the set C of cut points of G and the blocks of G (in particular, the number k of blocks of G).

Procedure BLOCKCUT $(G, s; C, k)$

(1) **for** $v \in V$ **do** $nr(v) \leftarrow 0$; $p(v) \leftarrow 0$ **od**;
(2) **for** $e \in E$ **do** $u(e) \leftarrow$ false **od**;
(3) $i \leftarrow 1$; $v \leftarrow s$; $nr(s) \leftarrow 1$; $C \leftarrow \emptyset$; $k \leftarrow 0$; $L(s) \leftarrow 1$;
(4) create a stack S with single element s;
(5) **repeat**
(6)   **while** there exists $w \in A_v$ with $u(vw) =$ false **do**
(7)   choose some $w \in A_v$ with $u(vw) =$ false; $u(vw) \leftarrow$ true;
(8)   **if** $nr(w) = 0$
(9)   **then** $p(w) \leftarrow v$; $i \leftarrow i + 1$; $nr(w) \leftarrow i$;
                 $L(w) \leftarrow i$; append w to S; $v \leftarrow w$
(10)   **else** $L(v) \leftarrow \min \{L(v), nr(w)\}$
(11)   **fi**
(12)   **od**;
(13)   **if** $p(v) \neq s$
(14)   **then if** $L(v) < nr(p(v))$
(15)   **then** $L(p(v)) \leftarrow \min \{L(p(v)), L(v)\}$
(16)   **else** $C \leftarrow C \cup \{p(v)\}$; $k \leftarrow k + 1$;
(17)   create a list B_k containing all vertices of S up to v
                 (including v) and remove these vertices from S;
                 append $p(v)$ to B_k
(18)   **fi**
(19)   **else if** there exists $w \in A_s$ with $u(sw) =$ false **then** $C \leftarrow C \cup \{s\}$
             fi;
(20) $k \leftarrow k + 1$; create a list B_k containing all vertices of S
             up to v (including v) and remove these vertices from S;
             append s to B_k
(21)   **fi**;
(22) $v \leftarrow p(v)$
(23) **until** $p(v) = 0$ **and** $u(vw) =$ true for all $w \in A_v$.

Theorem 11.3.9. *Algorithm 11.3.8 determines the cut points and the blocks of a connected graph G with complexity $O(|E|)$.*

Proof. As in the original DFS, each edge is used exactly once in each direction (see Theorem 11.2.2) and for each edge, a constant number of steps is executed. Therefore, it is clear that Algorithm 11.3.8 has complexity $O(|E|)$. The considerations above show that $L(v)$ has the correct value (11.1) or (11.2) respectively, as soon as the algorithm has finished examining vertex v (because the condition in step (6) is no longer satisfied). A formal proof of this fact could be given using induction on $nr(v)$ (in decreasing order). Note that the edge vw chosen in step (7) is a back edge if and only if $nr(w) \neq 0$ holds and that the tree edge $p(v)v$ is used in step (15) for updating the value of $L(p(v))$ after $L(v)$ has been determined (unless this updating is redundant because of $L(v) \geq nr(p(v)) \geq L(p(v))$). It remains to show that the cut points and the blocks are determined correctly. After the algorithm has finished examining vertex v (according to the condition in (6)), it is checked in (14) or (19) whether $p(v)$ is a cut point. First suppose that $p(v) \neq s$. Then, if the condition in (14) is satisfied, the (correct) value of $L(v)$ is used to update $L(p(v))$ (as explained above); otherwise, $p(v)$ is a cut point by Lemma 11.3.6. In that case, $p(v)$ is added to the set C of cut points in step (16). The vertices in S up to v (including v) are descendants of v in T (where T is the arborescence determined by the DFS). Now these vertices are not necessarily all the descendants of v, because it is possible that descendants of cut points were removed earlier; there might have been cut points among these vertices. However, it can be shown by induction that no proper descendants of such cut points are contained in S any more. (The induction basis – for leaves of T – is clear.) Therefore, the set B_k of step (17) is indeed a block. Now let $p(v) = s$. Then, if the condition in step (19) holds, s is a cut point by Lemma 11.3.7. It can be shown as above that B_k is a block of G. In particular, s is added to C if and only if, at the point of time when $p(v) = s$ occured for the first time, not all the edges incident with s were treated yet. In both cases, v is replaced at this point by its predecessor $p(v)$. Lemmas 11.3.6 and 11.3.7 also imply that all cut points have been found when the algorithm terminates (that is, after all the edges have been used in both directions).   □

Exercise 11.3.10. Execute Algorithm 11.3.8 for the graph of Figure 11.5. If there are choices to be made, use alphabetical order.

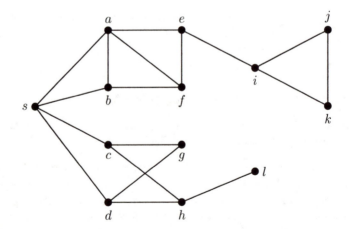

Fig. 11.5 A connected graph G

11.4 Depth First Search for Directed Graphs

In this section we show how the DFS (Algorithm 11.2.1) is performed for a directed graph G. For this purpose, all edges vw are to be interpreted as directed from v to w (in step (5) of the algorithm, for example). In all other respects, the algorithm is executed as before, so that the only difference compared to the undirected case is that we can use edges with $u(e) = $ false in one direction only (namely in forward direction). Even if G is connected, it might happen in general that we do not reach all vertices of G, that is, some vertices are not labelled by nr. More precisely, DFS($G, s; nr, p$) reaches all those vertices which are accessible from s by a directed path. We often assume that these are all the vertices of G; otherwise, DFS may be executed again for a vertex s' not accessible from s, etc. Then Theorem 11.2.2 is still valid basically: all those edges whose start vertex is accessible from s are used exactly once in each direction. Edges of the form $p(v)v$ are again called *tree edges*. If all vertices of G are accessible from s, the tree edges form a spanning arborescence of G with root s again (as in Theorem 11.2.3). In the general case, we get a directed spanning forest. As all proofs are analogous to the proofs of Section 11.2, we omit them. The following theorem summarizes our above considerations.

Theorem 11.4.1. *Let G be a directed graph and s a vertex of G. Moreover, let S be the set of vertices of G which are accessible from s. Then DFS($G, s; nr, p$) reaches precisely the vertices of S (that is, $nr(v) \neq 0$ if and only if $v \in S$), and the tree edges $p(v)v$ form a spanning arborescence on S. The complexity of the algorithm is $O(|E|)$.*   □

In the undirected case, there were only tree edges and back edges (the latter connecting a vertex and one of its ancestors), see Lemma 11.2.4. For a directed graph, we have to distinguish three kinds of edges beside the tree edges:

(1) *Forward edges*: these are edges of the form $e = vu$ such that u is a descendant of v (but not $v = p(u)$). In this case, we have $nr(u) > nr(v)$.

(2) *Back edges*: these are edges of the form $e = vu$ such that u is an ancestor of v; here, $nr(u) < nr(v)$.

(3) *Cross edges*: these are edges of the form $e = vu$ such that u is neither an ancestor nor a descendant of v. In particular, each edge connecting two distinct directed trees (if not all vertices of G are accessible from s) is a cross edge. But cross edges may also exist within a single directed tree; in that case, we have $nr(u) < nr(v)$.

Example 11.4.2. Let G be the directed graph shown in Figure 11.6. The result the DFS yields for G (executed from a and f) is drawn in Figure 11.7 (choices are made in alphabetical order as usual). Tree edges are drawn bold, cross edges broken, all other edges are in 'normal' print. The only back edge is eb.

Exercise 11.4.3. Let u and v be two vertices in a tree found by the DFS and suppose $nr(u) > nr(v)$. Show that, if $e = vu$ is an edge of G, e is indeed a forward edge.

Exercise 11.4.4. Let G be a directed graph and $T_1, \ldots, T_k$ a directed spanning forest found by executing the DFS on G several times. Show that G is acyclic if and only if G does not contain any back edges.

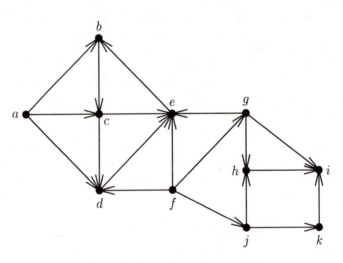

Fig. 11.6 A directed graph G

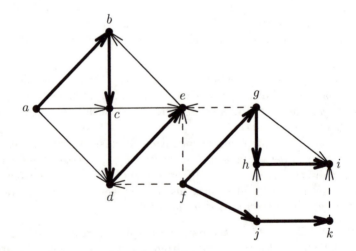

Figure 11.7 The result of a DFS on G

11.5 Strongly Connected Directed Graphs

Analogous to the notion of blocks in a graph, any maximal strongly connected induced subdigraph of a directed graph G (or its vertex set, respectively) is called a *strong component* of G. For example, the vertices b, c, d, e of the directed graph shown in Figure 11.6 form a strong component; all other strong components of this graph contain only a single element. Our first result gives some obvious equivalent conditions for strong connectedness.

Theorem 11.5.1. *Let G be a directed graph with at least three vertices which does not contain any isolated vertices. Then the following conditions are equivalent.*

(1) G is strongly connected.

(2) For any two vertices of G, there exists a directed closed walk containing both of them.

(3) For any vertex v and any edge e of G, there exists a directed closed walk containing v and e.

(4) For any two edges of G, there exists a directed closed walk containing both of them.

(5) For any two vertices x and y and any edge e of G, there exists a directed walk from x to y containing e.

(6) For any three vertices x, y, z of G, there exists a directed walk from x to y containing z.

Proof. The statements are clear (look at the definition of strong connectedness). □

Exercise 11.5.2. The reader will have noticed that the properties stated in Theorem 11.5.1 are mostly analogous to those of Theorem 11.3.1; however, it uses walks instead of cycles or paths, respectively. Show by giving counterexamples that

(a) the analogous statement to (7) of Theorem 11.3.1 does not hold,

(b) that the statements of Theorem 11.5.1 do not hold if we replace walks by cycles or paths, respectively.

We mention that, for a strongly connected directed graph G, $|G|$ is not necessarily 2-connected. On the other hand, a 2-connected graph cannot contain any bridges and is therefore orientable by the Theorem of Robbins (Theorem 1.6.2).

Exercise 11.5.3. Let G be a connected directed graph. Show that G is strongly connected if and only if any edge of G is contained in a directed cycle. (This implies that the criterion for the existence of a feasible circulation given in Exercise 9.2.11 can be replaced by 'G is strongly connected'.)

We want to give an algorithm for determining the strong components of a directed graph G. This algorithm is taken from the book of Aho, Hopcroft and Ullman (1983); it consists of executing the DFS both for G and for the directed graph having opposite orientation. A further algorithm for this task was given by Tarjan (1972); his algorithm requires to execute the DFS only once, but needs – similar to Algorithm 11.3.8 – the function $L(v)$. Tarjan's algorithm can also be found in Even (1979), §3.4. The basic concept of the algorithm we give below is considerably simpler; as both techniques have the same complexity, we have chosen the one which is easier to present and to explain. We have to modify the DFS Algorithm a little, because we need a second labelling $Nr(v)$ of the vertices; these numbers give the order in which the examination of the vertices is finished.

Algorithm 11.5.4. Let $G = (V, E)$ be a directed graph and s a root of G.

Procedure DFSM $(G, s; nr, Nr, p)$

(1) **for** $v \in V$ **do** $nr(v) \leftarrow 0$; $Nr(v) \leftarrow 0$; $p(v) \leftarrow 0$ **od**;
(2) **for** $e \in E$ **do** $u(e) \leftarrow$ false **od**;
(3) $i \leftarrow 1$; $j \leftarrow 0$; $v \leftarrow s$; $nr(s) \leftarrow 1$; $Nr(s) \leftarrow |V|$;
(4) **repeat**
(5)   **while** there exists $w \in A_v$ with $u(vw) =$ false **do**
(6)   choose some $w \in A_v$ with $u(vw) =$ false; $u(vw) \leftarrow$ true;
(7)   **if** $nr(w) = 0$ **then** $p(w) \leftarrow v$; $i \leftarrow i + 1$; $nr(w) \leftarrow i$;
            $v \leftarrow w$ **fi**
(8)   **od**;
(9) $j \leftarrow j + 1$; $Nr(v) \leftarrow j$; $v \leftarrow p(v)$
(10) **until** $v = s$ **and** $u(sw) =$ true for each $w \in A_s$.

Using this procedure, we can write down the Algorithm of Aho, Hopcroft and Ullman (1983) for determining the strong components of G. We assume w.l.o.g. that each vertex of G is accessible from s.

Algorithm 11.5.5. Let G be a directed graph and s a root of G. The algorithm determines the strong components of G.

Procedure STRONGCOMP $(G, s; k)$

(1) DFSM $(G, s; nr, Nr, p)$; $k \leftarrow 0$;
(2) let H be the graph we obtain by reversing the orientation of all edges of G;[1]
(3) **repeat**
(4)   choose the vertex r in H for which $Nr(r)$ is maximal;
(5) $k \leftarrow k + 1$; DFS$(H, r; nr', p')$; $C_k \leftarrow \{v \in H : nr'(v) \neq 0\}$;

---

[1] This means replacing each edge uv of G by vu.

(6)   remove all vertices of C_k and all the edges incident with them from H;[2]

(7) **until** the vertex set of H is empty.

Theorem 11.5.6. *Let G be a directed graph with root s. Then Algorithm 11.5.5 calculates the strong components $C_1, \ldots, C_k$ of G with complexity $O(|E|)$.*

Proof. The statement about the complexity is clear. We have to show that the directed forest on the vertex sets $C_1, \ldots, C_k$ determined by the second DFS during the **repeat**-loop indeed consists of the strong components of G. Let v and w be two vertices in the same strong component of G, that is, there exist directed paths from v to w and from w to v in G (and then obviously in H as well). We may suppose that v is reached before w during the DFS on H. Moreover, let T_i be the directed tree containing v, and x the root of T_i. As w is accessible from v in H and was not examined before, w has to be contained in T_i as well (Theorem 11.4.1 implies that w is reached during the execution of the DFS with root x). Conversely, we have to show that any two vertices v and w contained in the same directed tree T_i (on C_i) are contained in the same strong component. Again, let x be the root of T_i and suppose w.l.o.g. $v \neq x$. As v is a descendant of x in T_i, there exists a directed path from x to v in H, which corresponds to a directed path from v to x in G. Now v was not yet examined when the DFS on H with root x began, so that we have $Nr(v) < Nr(x)$ because of (4). Therefore, the examination of v was finished earlier than the examination of x during the DFS on G (step (9) of Algorithm 11.5.4). But as x is accessible from v in G, v cannot have been reached earlier than x during the DFS on G. This means that the whole examination of v was done during the examination of x, that is, v has to be a descendant of x in the spanning tree T for G. Therefore, there is a directed path from x to v in G as well and x and v are contained in the same strong component. Analogously, w has to be contained in the same strong component. $\qquad\square$

Example 11.5.7. We apply Algorithm 11.5.5 to the directed graph G of Figure 11.6. As a is not a root of G, we have to modify the algorithm slightly or apply it twice (from a and from f). Figure 11.8 shows the directed graph H and the result of the DFS on G modified according to 11.5.4. All edges of H have orientation opposite to the orientation they have in G; the numbers stated are the values $Nr(v)$ calculated by DFSM on G (executed from a and from f). The cross edges connecting the two directed trees are omitted. In Figure 11.9, the strong components as determined by Algorithm 11.5.5 are drawn; to make the figures simpler, we left out all the edges connecting distinct strong components. Note that a DFS on H using a different order of the start vertices (beginning in e, for example) would yield an incorrect result.

---

[2] The resulting directed graph is still denoted by H.

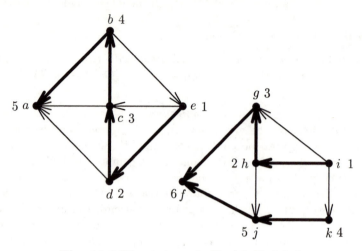

Fig. 11.8 Directed graph H with Nr-labels

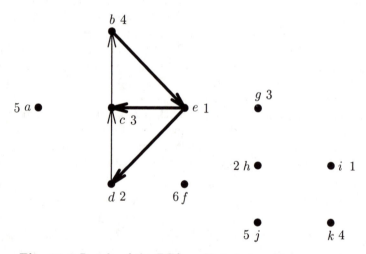

Fig. 11.9 Result of the DFS on H and strong components

Exercise 11.5.8. Determine the strong components of the directed graph of Figure 3.3.

Exercise 11.5.9. Give a definition for the term 'strongly k-connected' for directed graphs and investigate whether the main results of Section 11.1 carry over.

Exercise 11.5.10. Let $C_1, \ldots, C_k$ be the strong components of a directed graph G. We define a directed graph G', the *condensation* of G, as follows: the vertices of G' are $C_1, \ldots, C_k$ and $C_i C_j$ is an edge of G' if and only if there exists an edge uv in G with $u \in C_i$ and $v \in C_j$. Show that G' is acyclic and determine G' for the directed graph of Figure 3.3 (compare Exercise 11.5.8).

11.6 Edge Connectivity

At the end of this chapter we consider notions of connectivity arising from replacing vertex separators and vertex disjoint paths by edge separators and edge disjoint paths. Let G be a (directed) graph and u and v two vertices of G. By $\lambda(u, v)$ we denote the minimal cardinality of an edge separator for u and v. By Theorem 7.1.1, $\lambda(u, v)$ is also the maximal number of edge disjoint (directed) paths from u to v. The *edge connectivity* $\lambda(G)$ is defined as

$$\lambda(G) := \min \{\lambda(u, v) : u, v \in V\}.$$

G is called *m-fold edge connected*[3] if $\lambda(G) \geq m$. Moreover, $\delta(G)$ denotes the minimal degree (or the minimum of all $d_{in}(v)$ and all $d_{out}(v)$, respectively) of all vertices of G. The following simple result is due to Whitney (1932a).

Theorem 11.6.1. *Let G be a (directed) graph. Then*

$$\kappa(G) \leq \lambda(G) \leq \delta(G).$$

Proof. We consider the undirected case; the directed case can be treated similarly. Let v be a vertex with deg $v = \delta(G)$. Removing all edges incident with v obviously yields a disconnected graph, so that $\lambda(G) \leq \delta(G)$. If $\lambda(G) = 1$, G contains a bridge $e = uv$. Then G cannot be 2-connected, because removing u from G yields either a K_1 or a disconnected graph. If $\lambda(G) = k \geq 2$, removing $k - 1$ edges $e_2, \ldots, e_k$ of an edge separator from G results in a graph H containing a bridge $e_1 = uv$. Therefore, if we remove from G one of the end vertices of each of the e_i distinct from u and v (for $i = 2, \ldots, k$), we get either a disconnected graph or a graph where e_1 is a bridge (so that removing u makes the graph disconnected). In any case, $\kappa(G) \leq k = \lambda(G)$. $\square$

The graph of Figure 11.10 shows that the inequalities of Theorem 11.6.1 might be proper inequalities. The construction underlying this graph can be generalized considerably.

Exercise 11.6.2 (Chartrand and Harary (1968)). For given numbers k, d and m with $0 < k \leq m \leq d$, find a graph with $\kappa(G) = k$, $\lambda(G) = m$ and $\delta(G) = d$. (Hint: Distinguish the cases $k = d$ and $k \neq d$.)

---

[3] Some authors use the terms 'line connectivity' and 'line connected' instead.

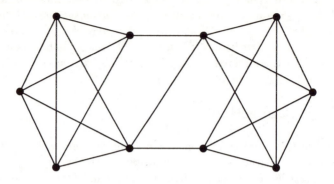

Fig. 11.10 A graph with $\kappa = 2$, $\lambda = 3$ and $\delta = 4$

Exercise 11.6.3 (Chartrand (1966)). Let G be a graph with n vertices. Show that $\lambda(G) = \delta(G)$ holds if $\delta(G) \geq n/2$. Is this bound tight?

The following lemma due to Schnorr (1979) is useful for determining $\lambda(G)$ because it allows to determine min $\{\lambda(u, v) : u, v \in V\}$ by calculating $\lambda(u, v)$ for relatively few pairs u, v.

Lemma 11.6.4. *Let G be a (directed) graph with vertex set $V = \{v_1, \ldots, v_n\}$. Writing $v_{n+1} := v_1$, we have*

$$\lambda(G) = \min \{\lambda(v_i, v_{i+1}) : i = 1, \ldots, n\}.$$

Proof. Let u and v be vertices of G such that $\lambda(G) = \lambda(u, v)$ (such vertices exist by definition); moreover, let T be an edge separator of cardinality $\lambda(u, v)$ for u and v. Denote the set of all vertices w for which there is a (directed) path from u to w not containing any edge of T by X; similarly, the set of all vertices w for which any directed path from u to w contains some edge from T is called Y. Then (X, Y) is a cut of G and obviously $u \in X$, $v \in Y$. Now T is an edge separator for x and y for any pair x, y of vertices with $x \in X$ and $y \in Y$, because otherwise, there would be a path from u to y not containing any edges from T. Therefore, we have $|T| = \lambda(G) \leq \lambda(x, y) \leq |T|$, that is, $\lambda(x, y) = \lambda(G)$. Obviously, there must be an index i such that $v_i \in X$ and $v_{i+1} \in Y$, so that $\lambda(G) = \lambda(v_i, v_{i+1})$ holds for this i. □

The reader is invited to show why an analogous argument for vertex separators does not work. By Corollary 7.1.2, each $\lambda(u, v)$ can be determined with complexity $O(|V|^{2/3}|E|)$. Then Lemma 11.6.4 immediately yields the following result.

Theorem 11.6.5. *The edge connectivity $\lambda(G)$ of a (directed) graph G can be determined with complexity $O(|V|^{5/3}|E|)$.* □

Putting in a little more effort, the edge connectivity of a (directed) graph can even be determined with complexity $O(|V||E|)$, see Matula (1987) and Mansour and Schieber (1989). Finally, we mention two interesting results concerning edge connectivity; proofs can be found in the original papers by Edmonds (1973) and Even, Garey and Tarjan (1977), or in Even (1979) §6.3.

Result 11.6.6. *Let G be a directed graph and u a vertex of G. We set $k := min \{\lambda(u,v) : v \neq u\}$. Then there are k edge disjoint directed spanning trees of G with root u.*   □

Result 11.6.7. *Let G be a directed graph with $\lambda(G) \geq k$. For any two vertices u and v and for any m with $0 \leq m \leq k$, there are m directed paths from u to v and $k-m$ directed paths from v to u, all of which are edge disjoint.* □

We refer to Chapter 1 of Bollobas (1978) for a treatment of extremal cases; a typical problem of this sort is the determination of the common structure of 2-connected graphs for which removing any edge destroys the 2-connectedness.

12. Matchings

This chapter is devoted to the problem of finding maximal matchings in arbitrary graphs; the bipartite case was treated in Section 7.2. Contrary to the bipartite case, the general case cannot be reduced immediately to a flow problem. However, we will see that the notion of an augmenting path can be modified appropriately. Kocay and Stone (1993) and Kocay and Stone (1995) showed that matchings can be treated in the context of Flow Theory by introducing special networks and flows satisfying certain symmetry conditions. Subsequently, Fremuth-Paeger and Jungnickel (1998a, 1998b, 1998c, 1998d, 1998e) provided a general theory based on this approach, including efficient algorithms. We will not present this rather involved theory because it would take up too much space, and refer the reader to the original sources instead.

We emphasize again that a maximal matching is a matching of maximal cardinality and that a matching which cannot be extended any more does by no means have to be maximal (see Section 7.2). The graphs for which any non-extendable matching is maximal were characterized by Meng (1974). A solution which is algorithmically satisfying (that is, it can be checked in polynomial time whether a graph is 'equi-matchable') was given by Lesk, Plummer and Pulleyblank (1984).

12.1 The 1-Factor Theorem

It is trivial that any matching of a graph $G = (V, E)$ can have at most $|V|/2$ elements. Such a matching exists if and only if $|V|$ is even and G has a 1-factor. As in the bipartite case, a 1-factor is also called a *perfect matching* of G. In this section, we prove the 1-Factor Theorem of Tutte (1947) which characterizes the graphs having a perfect matching. This result is a generalization of the Marriage Theorem 7.3.1 of Hall (1935).

Let $G = (V, E)$ be a graph. For a subset S of V, $p(S)$ denotes the number of connected components of odd cardinality in the graph $G\backslash S$. If G has a perfect matching K, then at least one vertex of each *odd component* (that is, each connected component of odd cardinality) has to be incident with an edge of K whose other vertex is contained in S. Therefore, we must have $p(S) \leq |S|$. The 1-Factor Theorem of Tutte (1947) states that this necessary

condition for the existence of a perfect matching is sufficient as well. We give
a short proof due to Anderson (1971).

Theorem 12.1.1 (1-Factor Theorem). *Let $G = (V, E)$ be a graph. G has
a perfect matching if and only if the following condition holds:*

$$(T) \qquad p(S) \leq |S| \qquad \text{for any subset } S \text{ of } V,$$

where $p(S)$ denotes the number of odd components of $G \backslash S$.

Proof. As we saw above, condition (T) is necessary. Now suppose conversely
that condition (T) is satisfied. For $S = \emptyset$, (T) implies that $|V|$ is even, say
$|V| = 2n$. We use induction on n; the case $n = 1$ is trivial. Obviously, for any
subset S of V,

$$p(S) \equiv |S| \pmod 2. \tag{12.1}$$

We distinguish two cases.

Case 1: We have $p(S) < |S|$ for all subsets S with $2 \leq |S| \leq 2n$. Then (12.1)
implies that even $p(S) \leq |S| - 2$. Choose some edge $e = uv$ of G and consider
the graph $H = G \backslash A$, where $A = \{u, v\}$. For any subset S of $V \backslash A$, let $p'(S)$
be the number of odd components of $H \backslash S$. Now, if such a set S satisfies the
condition $p'(S) > |S|$, it follows that

$$p(S \cup A) = p'(S) > |S| = |S \cup A| - 2,$$

so that $p(S \cup A) \geq |S \cup A|$ because of (12.1), which contradicts our hypothesis.
Therefore, we always have $p'(S) \leq |S|$, that is, H satisfies condition (T).
Therefore, by the induction hypothesis, H has a perfect matching K. Then
$K \cup \{e\}$ is a perfect matching of G.

Case 2: There exist subsets S of V with $p(S) = |S| \geq 2$. Choose a maximal
subset R with this property. Then each component of $G \backslash R$ has to be odd:
Suppose C were an even component, then we could add a vertex a of C to
R and get a further odd component which contradicts the maximality of R.
Let R' be the set of all (odd) components of $H := G \backslash R$. Moreover, denote
the bipartite graph with vertex set $R \cup R'$ for which a vertex r in R and a
component C in R' are adjacent if and only if there is an edge rc in G with
$c \in C$ by B. We show that B has a maximal matching by verifying condition
(H) of Theorem 7.2.4 for the bipartite graph B. Let J be a set of (odd)
components of H and T the set of vertices in R which are adjacent to some
component in J. Now condition (T) for G implies that

$$|J| = p(T) \leq |T|,$$

so that (H) holds for B. Thus, by Theorem 7.2.4, it is possible to choose a
vertex x from each component and associate it with a vertex y_x in R such
that $x y_x$ always is an edge in G and the y_x are pairwise distinct. This yields

a matching K of G. It remains to show that, for each component C (with vertex x chosen above), the induced graph G_C on the vertex set $C \setminus x$ has a perfect matching K_C. Then the union of K and all these matchings K_C is a perfect matching of G. Thus, we have to verify condition (T) for G_C. For a subset W of $C \setminus x$, let $p_C(W)$ be the number of odd components of $G_C \setminus W$. If $p_C(W) > |W|$ holds for such a subset W, (12.1) implies that $p_C(W) \geq |W| + 2$, so that

$$p(W \cup R \cup \{x\}) = p_C(W) + p(R) - 1 \geq |W| + |R| + 1 = |W \cup R \cup \{x\}|.$$

However, this contradicts the maximality of R. Therefore, (T) holds for G_C. $\square$

Exercise 12.1.2. Let $G = (S \mathbin{\dot\cup} T, E)$ be a bipartite graph with $|S| = |T|$. Show that condition (T) for the existence of a perfect matching in G reduces to condition (H) of Theorem 7.2.4 in this case.

Exercise 12.1.3 (Petersen (1891)). Let G be a 3-regular graph without bridges. Show that G has a perfect matching. Does any 3-regular graph containing bridges have a perfect matching as well? Does any 3-regular graph without bridges have a factorization?

Next we present a 'deficiency' version of Theorem 12.1.1 (analogous to the deficiency version of the Marriage Theorem in Section 7.3) due to Berge (1958). Let K be a matching in the graph $G = (V, E)$. Then a vertex v which is not incident with any edge in K is called *exposed* with respect to K; a vertex incident with some edge of K is *saturated*.

Theorem 12.1.4. Let $G = (V, E)$ be a graph. G has a matching with precisely d exposed vertices if and only if the following condition holds:

$$d \equiv |V| \ (mod \ 2) \quad and \quad p(S) \leq |S| + d \ for \ all \ S \subset V. \tag{12.2}$$

Proof. We define an auxiliary graph H as follows. Add a d-element set D with $D \cap V = \emptyset$ to the vertex set V of G and all edges of the form vw with $v \in V$ and $w \in D$ to E. It is now easy to see that G has a matching with precisely d exposed vertices if and only if H has a perfect matching. Therefore, we have to show that (12.2) is equivalent to the existence of a perfect matching of H. For any subset X of $V \cup D$, let $p'(X)$ denote the number of odd components of $H \setminus X$. Then obviously $p'(S \cup D) = p(S)$ for all $S \subset V$. If H has a perfect matching, then condition (T) for H implies immediately

$$p(S) = p'(S \cup D) \leq |S \cup D| = |S| + d \text{ for all } S \subset V.$$

Moreover, if H has a perfect matching, $|V| + d$ has to be even, so that (12.2) is necessary. Now suppose conversely that (12.2) is satisfied. By Theorem 12.1.1, we have to show that the following condition holds:

$$p'(X) \leq |X| \text{ for all } X \subset V \cup D. \tag{12.3}$$

If D is not contained in X, then $H \backslash X$ is connected by the construction of H, so that (12.3) is obviously satisfied for $X \neq \emptyset$. For $X = \emptyset$, (12.3) holds because $|V \cup D| = |V| + d$ is an even number by hypothesis. Now suppose $D \subset X$, say $X = S \cup D$ for some $S \subset V$. Then (12.2) implies

$$p'(X) = p(S) \leq |S| + d = |X|,$$

so that (12.3) is satisfied for this case as well. □

Corollary 12.1.5. *Let $G = (V, E)$ be a graph and K a maximal matching of G. Then there are precisely*

$$d = \ max \ \{p(S) - |S| : S \subset V\}$$

exposed vertices and K contains precisely $\frac{|V|-d}{2}$ edges.

Proof. The statement follows immediately from Theorem 12.1.4 and the fact that $|V| \equiv p(S) + |S| \equiv p(S) - |S| \pmod 2$ holds. □

12.2 Augmenting Paths

In this section we present a method how to use 'augmenting paths', if a matching K in a graph $G = (V, E)$ is given, for finding a matching K' of larger cardinality. Let us consider the bipartite case again. In the solution of Exercise 6.5.6, we determined a maximal matching of G by looking for a maximal flow on the 0-1-network (on the directed graph H) described there. We show how the augmenting paths occurring during this process can be described within G. Let K be a matching of cardinality k in G and f the corresponding 0-1-flow (as in the solution of Exercise 6.5.6). Then an augmenting path looks as follows:

$$s \text{ —— } v_1 \text{ —— } v_2 \text{ —— } \ldots \text{ —— } v_{2n-1} \text{ —— } v_{2n} \text{ —— } t,$$

where v_1 and v_{2n} are vertices which are not incident with any saturated edge and where the edges $v_{2i}v_{2i+1}$ are backward edges (that is, they are saturated). In other words: the vertices v_1 and v_{2n} are exposed with respect to K and the edges $v_{2i}v_{2i+1}$ are contained in K. Thus, an augmenting path has the form illustrated in Figure 12.1. The edges contained in the matching K are drawn bold.

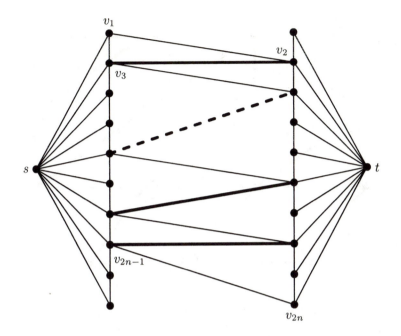

Fig. 12.1 An augmenting path

Analogous to the bipartite case, we now define augmenting paths for graphs in general. Let K be a matching in any graph $G = (V, E)$. An *alternating path* with respect to K is a path W whose edges are by turns contained in K and not contained in K. An alternating path W is called an *augmenting path* if its start and end vertex are distinct exposed vertices.

Example 12.2.1. The edges drawn bold in the graph G shown in Figure 12.2 form a matching K. The vertices a, f and y are exposed with respect to K and the sequences (a, b, c, d, e, f) and (a, b, c, u, v, w, x, y) define augmenting paths W and W', respectively. Interchanging the roles of edges and nonedges of K on the path W', for example (that is, formally, substituting K by $K \oplus W'$, where $\oplus$ denotes the symmetric difference), yields the matching K' of cardinality $|K| + 1$ given in Figure 12.3. K' is obviously a maximal matching of G, as any matching can have at most $|V|/2$ edges.

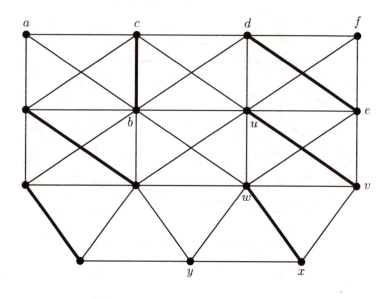

Fig. 12.2 Graph G with matching K

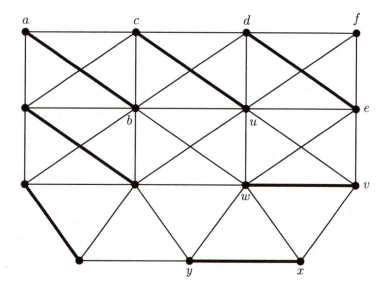

Fig. 12.3 Matching $K' = K \oplus W'$

Motivated by Example 12.2.1, we prove the following fundamental theorem due to Berge (1957).

Theorem 12.2.2 (Augmenting Path Theorem). *A matching K in a graph $G = (V, E)$ is maximal if and only if there is no augmenting path with respect to K in G.*

Proof. We assume first that K is maximal. If there exists an augmenting path W in G, we may – as in Example 12.2.1 – substitute K by $K' = K \oplus W$. Then K' is a matching of cardinality $|K| + 1$, a contradiction. Conversely, suppose that K is not maximal. We show the existence of an augmenting path with respect to K. Let K' be a maximal matching. Consider the subgraph H of G determined by the edges in $K \oplus K'$. Any vertex of H has degree at most 2 and any vertex v having degree 2 has to be incident with precisely one edge of K and one edge of K'. Therefore, any connected component of H consisting of more than one vertex has to be either a cycle of even length (where edges of K and K' alternate) or a path formed by such an alternating sequence of edges. As K' contains more edges than K, there exists at least one such path whose first and last edge is an edge of K'. This path is an augmenting path with respect to K, because its end vertices are obviously exposed. □

This theorem is the basis of almost all known algorithms for determining maximal matchings in arbitrary graphs. The basic idea is clear: Starting with a given matching (the empty one, for example, or just any edge), we try to find an augmenting path (with respect to the present matching) and use it to enlarge the matching until no such paths exist any more. Thus, what we need is an efficient technique for finding augmenting paths (note that the number of paths in a graph in general grows exponentially with the size of the graph). Any such path has to start at an exposed vertex, so that we could use a variation of the BFS starting with an exposed vertex. We show first that any exposed vertex has to be examined at most once.

Lemma 12.2.3. *Let G be a graph, K a matching in G and u an exposed vertex with respect to K. Moreover, let W be an augmenting path and $K' = K \oplus W$. If there is no augmenting path with respect to K starting at u, then there is no augmenting path with respect to K' starting at u either.*

Proof. Let v and w be the end vertices of W; then, by hypothesis, $u \neq v, w$. Suppose there exists an augmenting path W' with respect to K' starting at u. If W and W' have no common vertex, then W' is an augmenting path with respect to K as well, which contradicts our assumption. So let u' be the first vertex on W' which is contained in W as well and let e be the unique edge of K' incident with u'. Then u' divides the path W into two parts. One of these parts does not contain e; let us call this part W_1. Moreover, we denote the part of W' from u to u' by W_1'. Then W_1 and W_1' together form an augmenting path with respect to K starting at u (see Figure 12.4)[1], a contradiction. □

---

[1] The edges of K' are drawn bold in Figure 12.4; note that $K' \cap W_1' = K \cap W_1'$ and $K' \cap W_1 \subset K \oplus W_1$.

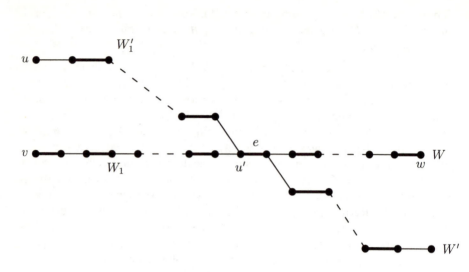

Fig. 12.4 Proof of Lemma 12.2.3

Now suppose we have some algorithm for constructing a maximal matching by using augmenting paths for enlarging the matching step by step. Then each iteration of the algorithm in which an augmenting path is determined and used for changing the present matching is called a *phase* of the algorithm. The following result is an immediate consequence of Lemma 12.2.3.

Corollary 12.2.4. *If, during some phase of the construction of a maximal matching, there is no augmenting path starting from an exposed vertex u, then there is no such path in any of the later phases either.* □

Exercise 12.2.5. Let G be a connected graph such that any matching in G can be extended to a perfect matching; such a graph is called *randomly matchable*. Show that the only graphs on $2n$ vertices having this property are the graphs $K_{n,n}$ and K_{2n} (cf. Sumner (1979) and Lesk, Plummer and Pulleyblank (1984)). (Hint: Show first that G has to be 2-connected. If G is bipartite and contains non-adjacent vertices s and t which are in different parts of the bipartition of G, consider a path (of odd length) from s to t and construct a matching whose only exposed vertices are s and t. If G is not bipartite, show first that any vertex is contained in a cycle of odd length. Then prove that any two vertices are connected by a path of odd length and proceed as in the bipartite case.)

Exercise 12.2.6. Let G be a graph with $2n$ vertices such that either $\deg v \geq n$ holds for any vertex v or $|E| \geq \frac{1}{2}(2n - 1)(2n - 2) + 2$. Show that G has a perfect matching; then find a generalization of this result.

12.3 Alternating Trees and Flowers

The first polynomial algorithm for determining maximal matchings was discovered by Edmonds (1965b). He used – as almost all known algorithms treating this problem – augmenting paths, that is, his algorithm is based on Theorem 12.2.2. Edmonds gave a complexity of $O(|V|^4)$ for his algorithm (which he did not state in an explicit formal way); however, Gabow (1976) and Lawler (1976) showed that implementing the algorithm appropriately reduces the complexity to $O(|V|^3)$ only. We present such a version of the Algorithm of Edmonds in Section 12.4. The best algorithm for finding a maximal matching known at present is a generalization of the technique presented by Hopcroft and Karp (1973) which is due to Micali and Vazirani (1980); as in the bipartite case (compare Theorem 7.2.1), this algorithm has (for general graphs!) a complexity of $O(|V|^{1/2}|E|)$. An extensive discussion of this algorithm was given by Peterson and Loui (1988), but the first formal correctness proof appeared only 14 years after the algorithm had been discovered, see Vazirani (1994). Empirical studies concerning implementations and quality of various algorithms for determining maximal matchings can be found in Derigs and Heske (1980) and Ball and Derigs (1983). More recent advances concerning implementation questions can be found in the monograph edited by Johnson and McGeoch (1993).

Although we could use the empty matching to initialize the construction of a maximal matching via augmenting paths, it is obviously better in practice to determine a reasonably large initial matching in a heuristic manner. In most cases, this reduces the number of phases the algorithm needs considerably. We show a simple method for finding such an initial matching; it is a variation of the Greedy Algorithm.

Algorithm 12.3.1. Let $G = (V, E)$ be a graph with vertex set $V = \{1, \ldots, n\}$. The algorithm constructs a matching K (which is not extendable) described by an array 'mate' as follows: for $ij \in K$, mate$(i) = j$ and mate$(j) = i$, whereas for exposed vertices k, mate$(k) = 0$. The variable nrex denotes the number of exposed vertices with respect to K.

Procedure INMATCH$(G;$ mate, nrex$)$

(1) nrex $\leftarrow n$;
(2) **for** $i = 1$ **to** n **do** mate$(i) \leftarrow 0$ **od**;
(3) **for** $k = 1$ **to** $n - 1$ **do**
(4)   **if** mate$(k) = 0$ **and** there exists $j \in A_k$ with mate$(j) = 0$
(5)   **then** choose $j \in A_k$ with mate$(j) = 0$;
(6)   mate$(j) \leftarrow k$; mate$(k) \leftarrow j$; nrex $\leftarrow$ nrex -2
(7)   **fi**
(8) **od**.

Let K be a matching in G. For any saturated vertex v, we call the vertex u such that $uv \in K$ the *mate* of v (as in Algorithm 12.3.1 above). Our next problem is to design a technique for finding augmenting paths; this problem turns out to be more difficult than it appears at first sight.

We begin by choosing an exposed vertex r (with respect to K) of G. If there exists an exposed vertex s adjacent to r, we can extend K immediately by simply adding the edge rs. Of course, this case cannot occur if K was constructed by Algorithm 12.3.1. Otherwise, we take r as the start vertex for a BFS and put all vertices $a_1, \ldots, a_p$ adjacent to r in the first layer; note that all these vertices are saturated. As we are looking for augmenting (that is, in particular, alternating) paths, we put only the vertices $b_i = \mathrm{mate}(a_i)$ in the second layer. The next layer consists of all vertices $c_1, \ldots, c_q$ which are adjacent to one of the b_i and where the connecting edge is not contained in K. We continue this process analogously; as we will see below, certain difficulties arise. If there is some exposed vertex in one of the layers 3, 5, 7 etc., we have found an augmenting path. This motivates the following definition: A tree T with root r contained in the graph G is called an *alternating tree* if r is an exposed vertex and any path beginning in r is an alternating path. The vertices in layers 0, 2, 4, ... are called *outer vertices*, the ones in layers 1, 3, 5, ... are *inner vertices* of T.[2] Thus, an alternating tree has a form similar to the tree shown in Figure 12.5 (where edges of K are drawn bold).

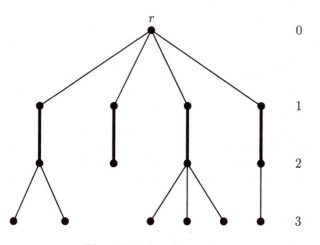

Fig. 12.5 An alternating tree

We construct an alternating tree with root r until either we find an exposed inner vertex (and an augmenting path) or we find out that no such vertex exists. Suppose layer $2i - 1$ is constructed already. If no vertex in this layer is exposed, layer $2i$ can be constructed simply by adding, for each vertex v of layer $2i - 1$, the vertex $w = \mathrm{mate}(v)$ and the edge vw to T. However, there might be difficulties when constructing the next layer of inner vertices.

---

[2] Some authors use the notation *even vertex* or *odd vertex* instead.

Let x be a vertex in layer $2i$ and $y \neq \text{mate}(x)$ a vertex adjacent to x. Then there are four possible cases.

Case 1: y is exposed (and not yet contained in T). Then – as we saw above – we have found an augmenting path.

Case 2: y is not exposed and neither y nor $\text{mate}(y)$ are contained in T. Then we put y in layer $2i + 1$ (and $\text{mate}(y)$ in layer $2i + 2$).

Case 3: y is already contained in T as an inner vertex. Then adding y and edge xy to T would yield a cycle of even length in T (see Figure 12.6). However, we do not need such an edge (at least at this point), because we have already found an alternating path from r to the inner vertex y.

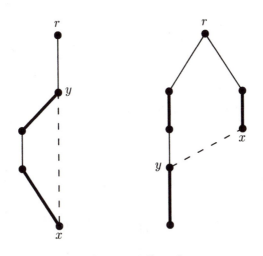

Fig. 12.6 Case 3

Case 4: y is already contained in T as an outer vertex. Then adding the edge xy to T would yield a cycle of odd length $2k + 1$ in T; k edges of this cycle are contained in K (see Figure 12.7). Such cycles are called *blossoms*; these blossoms (which of course do not occur in the bipartite case) cause the difficulties mentioned above. Edges forming a blossom with the tree constructed so far cannot be ignored. For example, consider the blossom shown in Figure 12.8. Each of the vertices a, b, c, d, e, f could occur as an outer or as an inner vertex on an alternating path beginning in r: a is an inner vertex with respect to (r, a) and an outer vertex with respect to (r, b, d, e, f, c, a). Now, if there exists an edge ax such that x is exposed, (r, b, d, e, f, c, a, x) will be an augmenting path. If we simply omit the edge fc when constructing T, it is possible that we will not find any augmenting path in T (this happens, for example, for the graph G of Figure 12.8), even though such a path exists.

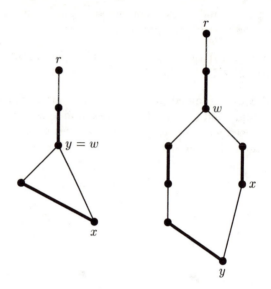

Fig. 12.7 Case 4

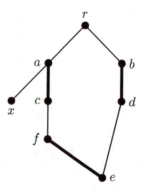

Fig. 12.8 A blossom

An obvious way to proceed would be to use all vertices of a blossom both as inner and as outer vertices, so that we cannot miss an augmenting path which uses part of a blossom. Pape and Conradt (1980) proposed to split up each blossom into two alternating paths, such that the vertices of a blossom appear twice in the alternating tree T (they appear as inner and as outer vertices). The graph of Figure 12.8 yields the alternating tree of Figure 12.9, which indeed contains the augmenting path from x to r.

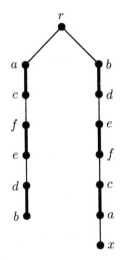

Fig. 12.9 Alternating tree corresponding to the graph of Figure 12.8

When using this construction, it is not allowed, of course, to add some vertex z as an inner point if mate(z) is already contained in the tree T as a predecessor of the outer point x which is examined at present. Otherwise, for example, the (incorrect) 'augmenting path' (r, a, b, c, d, b, a, s) would be constructed for the graph of Figure 12.10.

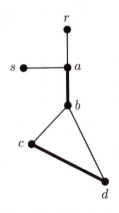

Fig 12.10 A graph without augmenting paths

But even if this condition is observed (which could be done by keeping a predecessor function during the process), problems remain. It might happen that an edge xy which was left out earlier according to case 3 (that is, an edge closing a cycle of even length) is needed at a later point because it is also contained in a blossom. For example, look at the graph G shown in Figure 12.11.[3] Constructing an alternating tree starting at vertex r, where we examine the outer vertices in the order $r, 2, 4, 6, 5, 3$, yields the tree T of Figure 12.12.

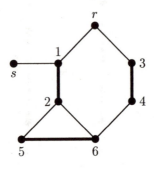

Fig. 12.11 A graph G

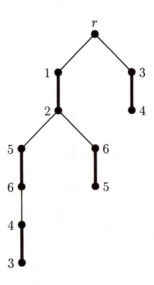

Fig. 12.12 Alternating tree corresponding to the graph of Figure 12.11

---

[3] This example is due to Dr. C. Fremuth-Paeger.

We see that the only augmenting path $(r, 4, 6, 5, 2, 1, s)$ in G is missed, because edge $\{4, 6\}$ is ignored at the point of time when vertex 4 is examined, so that vertex 1 is not added as an outer vertex. Note that this path would be found if we began constructing the tree at vertex s. However, by 'duplicating' G, it is easy to construct a graph in which the only augmenting path (between r and r') is not found by the process described above (for an appropriate ordering of the adjacency lists), see Figure 12.13.[4]

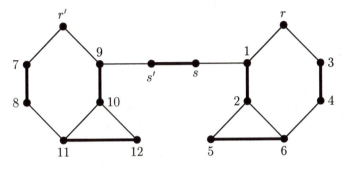

Fig. 12.13 A graph with a unique augmenting path

The difficulties discussed above are avoided in the Algorithm of Edmonds (1965b); his algorithm 'shrinks' blossoms to a single vertex. At a later point of the algorithm, blossoms which were shrunk before are 'expanded' again. We treat this process in the next section.

In the bipartite case, the naive method of constructing an alternating tree works, because no cycles of odd length occur. Therefore, there are no blossoms and it is clear for any vertex whether it is to be added as an inner or as an outer vertex. If $V = S \dot{\cup} S'$ and $r \in S$ (w.l.o.g.), then obviously all vertices of S accessible from r have to be outer vertices and all accessible vertices of S' have to be inner vertices. Therefore, there exists an augmenting path starting at vertex r if and only if the corresponding alternating tree contains an exposed inner vertex. Below, we give an algorithm for constructing a maximal matching using this technique. Even though its complexity is worse than the complexity of Theorem 7.2.1, it is desirable to have a technique (which is still quite good) which is independent from Flow Theory. Moreover, this

---

[4] These observations and the example of Figure 12.13 show that the algorithm given in Pape and Conradt (1980), which is also treated in Syslo, Deo and Kowalik (1983) (and in the first two German editions of this book as well), is not correct. The reason is that there might be links between blossoms and cycles of even length treated earlier during the procedure. In particular, the statement of Exercise 3-72 in Syslo, Deo and Kowalik (1983) that edges xy closing a cycle of even length (as described in case 3) may be ignored is wrong.

algorithm will be the basis of the Hungarian Algorithm treated in Chapter 13.

Algorithm 12.3.2. Let $G = (V, E)$ be a bipartite graph with bipartition $V = S \,\dot\cup\, S'$, where $S = \{1, \ldots, n\}$ and $S' = \{1', \ldots, m'\}$ with $n \leq m$. The algorithm constructs a maximal matching K described by an array mate. The function $p(y)$ gives, for $y \in S'$, the vertex in S from which y was accessed.

Procedure BIPMATCH $(G;$ mate, nrex$)$

(1) INMATCH $(G;$ mate, nrex$)$;
(2) $r \leftarrow 0$;
(3) **while** nrex ≥ 2 **and** $r < n$ **do**
(4) $r \leftarrow r + 1$;
(5)   **if** mate$(r) = 0$
(6)   **then for** $i = 1$ **to** m **do** $p(i') \leftarrow 0$ **od**;
(7) $Q \leftarrow \emptyset$; append r to Q; aug $\leftarrow$ false;
(8)   **while** aug $=$ false **and** $Q \neq \emptyset$ **do**
(9)   remove the first vertex x of Q;
(10)   **if** there exists $y \in A_x$ with mate$(y) = 0$
(11)   **then** choose such a y;
(12)   **while** $x \neq r$ **do**
(13)   mate$(y) \leftarrow x$; next $\leftarrow$ mate(x); mate$(x) \leftarrow y$;
(14) $y \leftarrow$ next; $x \leftarrow p(y)$
(15)   **od**;
(16)   mate$(y) \leftarrow x$; mate$(x) \leftarrow y$; nrex $\leftarrow$ nrex-2;
                     aug $\leftarrow$ true
(17)   **else for** $y \in A_x$ **do**
(18)   **if** $p(y) = 0$ **then** $p(y) \leftarrow x$; append mate(y) to Q **fi**
(19)   **od**
(20)   **fi**
(21)   **od**
(22)   **fi**
(23) **od.**

Of course, it is also possible to use the empty matching as initialization; simply replace (1) and (2) by

(1') **for** $v \in V$ **do** mate$(x) \leftarrow 0$ **od**;
(2') $r \leftarrow 0$; nrex $\leftarrow n$;

We leave it to the reader to convince herself that the following theorem holds.

Theorem 12.3.3. *Let $G = (V, E)$ be a bipartite graph with $V = S \,\dot\cup\, S'$. Then Algorithm 12.3.2 determines a maximal matching of G with complexity $O(|V||E|)$.* $\square$

An algorithm for determining a maximal matching of a bipartite graph which does not use augmenting paths was given by Balinsky and Gonzales (1991). Their algorithm has complexity $O(|V||E|)$.

12.4 The Algorithm of Edmonds

In this section, we present an algorithm for constructing maximal matchings due to Edmonds (1965b). From now on, $G = (V, E)$ is always a connected graph with a given matching K. We begin by constructing an alternating tree T with root r as described in the previous section. Vertices are added to T at most once and edges xy closing a cycle of even length are ignored (case 3 above). As soon as we meet an edge xy closing a blossom B (case 4 above, see Figure 12.7), we interrupt the construction of T to 'shrink' the blossom B. We describe this operation formally as a *contraction* of G with respect to B. We define a graph G/B as follows:

- The vertex set of G/B is $V/B := (V\backslash B) \cup \{b\}$, where b is a new vertex (that is, $b \notin V$ is a new symbol).
- The edge set E/B of G/B is derived from E by removing all edges $uv \in E$ with $u \in B$ or $v \in B$ and adding an edge ub for all those $u \in V\backslash B$ which are adjacent in G to at least one vertex of B.[5]

To distinguish it from the original vertices, the new vertex b is called a *pseudo node* of G/B. Now we have to consider the effect shrinking some blossom B has on the construction of T. Note that the matching K of G induces in a trivial way a matching K/B of G/B. At the point of the algorithm where an edge xy closing a blossom B is examined, only two vertices of B have been found yet (namely x and y). The whole blossom can be determined by following the paths from x and y to the root r in T; the first common vertex w of these two paths is called the *base* of B. Note that w is an outer point of T. Thus, the blossom B is the union of the two paths W_{wx} and W_{wy} from the base w to the vertices x and y, respectively. Omitting these two paths from T and replacing the base w by the pseudo node b, we get an alternating tree T/B for G/B (with respect to the matching K/B). We proceed with our construction in G/B and the next outer vertex we examine is the pseudo node b. Of course, there might be further blossoms. Let us give an example to illustrate how the procedure described above works.

Example 12.4.1. Let G be the graph of Figure 12.14. Starting at vertex $r = 17$, we construct the alternating tree T of Figure 12.15. We examine outer vertices in the order in which they were reached (that is, as a sort of BFS) and use increasing order for the adjacency lists. Note that the edge

---

[5] Note that G/B is the result of a sequence of elementary contractions (see Section 1.5) for the edges contained in the blossom B.

$\{6,3\}$ is ignored (according to case 3) when the outer vertex 6 is examined, because it closes a cycle of even length. Similarly, the edge $\{8,9\}$ is ignored when vertex 8 is examined.

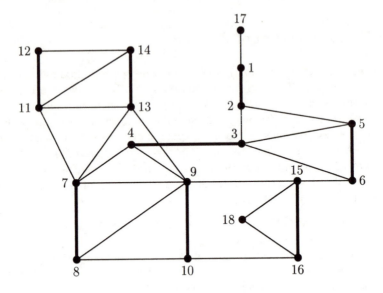

Fig. 12.14 A graph G with matching K

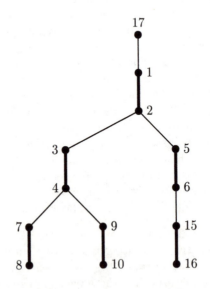

Fig. 12.15 Alternating tree T in G

The edge $\{8, 10\}$ closes the blossom $B = \{4, 7, 8, 9, 10\}$. This blossom has base 4 and is contracted to a pseudo node b; we obtain the graph $G' := G/B$ and the corresponding alternating tree T/B shown in Figure 12.16.

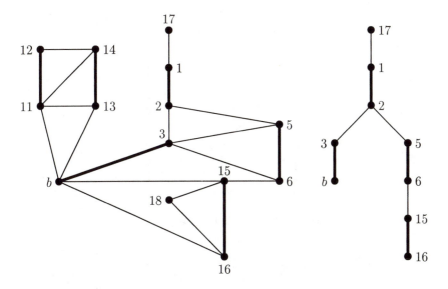

Fig. 12.16 Contracted graph G/B with alternating tree T/B

Continuing the construction with the outer vertex b (which is nearest to the root $r = 17$), we get the alternating tree T' of Figure 12.17. Edge $\{b, 15\}$ is ignored according to case 3, because it closes a cycle of even length, but edge $\{b, 16\}$ closes a further blossom $B' = \{b, 2, 3, 5, 6, 15, 16\}$ which has base 2. B' is contracted to a new pseudo node b'. Note that pseudo nodes can contain other pseudo nodes which were constructed earlier. The result is the graph $G'' := G'/B'$ and the corresponding tree T'/B' of Figure 12.18.

When the outer vertex b' is examined, we find the exposed vertex 18 and the augmenting path

$$W'' \quad : \quad 18\text{------}b'\text{------}1\text{------}17$$

in G''. We use this path to determine an augmenting path W in G. For this purpose, we trace W in opposite direction from vertex 18 back to the root 17 of T''. The first vertex we reach is the pseudo node b'; this means that there is at least one vertex p in G' adjacent to 18 which is contained in the blossom B'. In fact, there are two such vertices, namely 15 and 16. We choose one of them, say $p = 15$. In the blossom B', $p = 15$ is incident with a unique edge in $K' := K/B$, namely the edge $e = \{15, 16\}$. We trace the path from 15 to 16 and continue in B' until we reach the base 2 of B'.

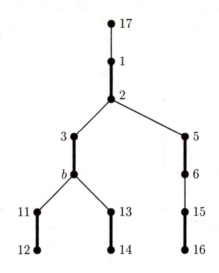

Fig. 12.17 Alternating tree T' for G'

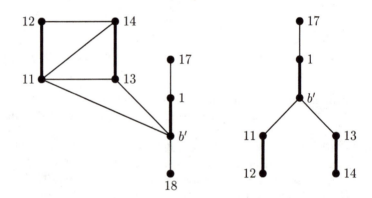

Fig. 12.18 Contracted graph G'/B' with alternating tree T'/B'

We have now constructed from the augmenting path W'' in G'' the augmenting path

$$W'   :   18 \text{——} 15 \text{——} 16 \text{——} b \text{——} 3 \text{——} 2 \text{——} 1 \text{——} 17$$

in G'. Now tracing W' backwards from vertex 18 to 17 in T', we meet the pseudo node b. Vertex 16 (the immediate predecessor of b on W') has to be adjacent to at least one vertex in the blossom B; this vertex is 10. The unique edge of K incident with 10 is $\{10, 9\}$, so that we follow the blossom B from 10 to 9 and on to the base 4. This yields the augmenting path

W : 18——15——16——10——9——4——3——2——1——17

in the original graph G. Augmenting our initial matching K using this augmenting path, we get the perfect matching shown in Figure 12.19.

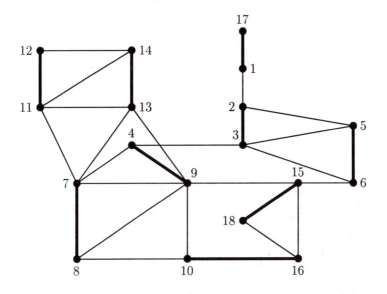

Fig. 12.19 Perfect matching in G

Exercise 12.4.2. Use the method described in Example 12.4.1 to enlarge the matching shown in the graph of Figure 12.11. Use vertex r as the root of the alternating tree; if choices have to be made, use the vertices according to increasing labels.

The Algorithm of Edmonds generalizes the method described in Example 12.4.1. Before stating his algorithm explicitly, we consider the question why this shrinking process for blossoms always works. It is sufficient to show that the graph $G' := G/B$ resulting from contracting the first blossom B contains an augmenting path starting at vertex r (or b, respectively) if and only if the original graph contains such a path. Note that, if $r \in B$, the start vertex r has to be replaced by the pseudo node b in G'. The rest is clear by induction. We split up the statement we want to prove into the two following lemmas.

Lemma 12.4.3. *Let G be a connected graph with a matching K and r an exposed vertex with respect to K. Suppose that, during the construction of an alternating tree T with root r (according to the rules described above), the first blossom B is found when edge $e = xy$ is examined (where x is the outer vertex which the algorithm examines at this point of time and y is an outer vertex of T as well). Let w be the base of the blossom B and denote the* *contracted graph, where B was replaced by the pseudo node b, by $G' := G/B$. If G contains an augmenting path with respect to K starting at r, then G' contains an augmenting path with respect to the induced matching $K' := K/B$ with start vertex r (or b, respectively, if $r \in B$).*

Proof. Let W be an augmenting path in G with respect to K starting at vertex r and suppose the end vertex of W is s. As all vertices in W are saturated except for r and s, we may assume w.l.o.g. that r and s are the only exposed vertices of G. (Otherwise, we may remove all further exposed vertices and the edges incident with them from G.) If W and B do not have any vertices in common, the statement is obvious, because then W is an augmenting path in G' with respect to K' as well. If W and B are not disjoint, we distinguish two cases.

Case 1: The root r is contained in the blossom B, that is, r is the base of B. We trace W from r to s. Let q be the first vertex of W which is not contained in B and p its predecessor on W (that is, the last vertex of W contained in B; note that it is possible that $p = r$). Now the edge pq is not contained in B. Denote the part of W from r to p by W_1 and the part from q to s by W_2 (see Figure 12.20). Then

$$W' := b \underline{\hspace{1cm}} q \xrightarrow{W_2} s$$

is an augmenting path in G' with respect to K'.

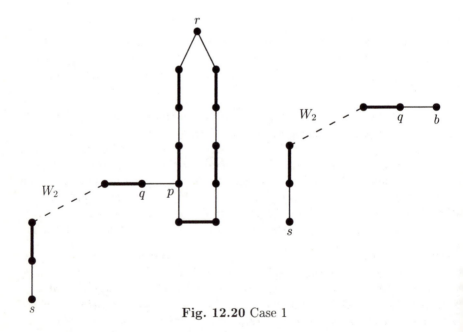

Fig. 12.20 Case 1

Case 2: The root r of T is not contained in the blossom B; then the base of B is an outer vertex $w \neq r$. Denote the alternating path of even length from r to w in T by P; P is often called the *stem* of the blossom B. In this case, it is not quite obvious how the augmenting path W with respect to K passes through the blossom B (there might be several distinct paths in T starting in r). We use a trick which allows us to reduce this case to case 1. We replace K by the matching $K_1 := K \oplus P$ which has the same cardinality as K. Now w and s are the only exposed vertices with respect to K_1, so that the blossom B (which has not been changed) has base w if we begin constructing an alternating tree at vertex w (see Figure 12.21), so that the situation is as in case 1 (with respect to K_1). As there exists an augmenting path in G with respect to K, K was not maximal. Therefore, K_1 is not maximal either and there exists an augmenting path W_1 with respect to K_1 in G. According to case 1, there exists an augmenting path W_1' in G' with respect to K_1/B, so that the matching K_1/B is not maximal. It follows that the matching K/B of G' (which has the same cardinality as the matching K_1/B) is not maximal either and there must be an augmenting path in G' with respect to K/B. As r and s are the only exposed vertices in G', the statement follows. $\square$

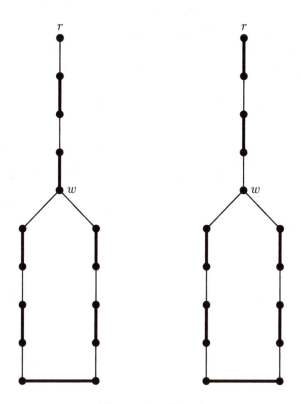

Fig. 12.21 Case 2

Lemma 12.4.4. *Let G be a connected graph with a matching K and suppose r is an exposed vertex with respect to K. Moreover, let B be a blossom with basis w and $G' := G/B$ the contracted graph where B was replaced by the pseudo node b. If G' contains an augmenting path with respect to $K' = K/B$ starting at r (or starting at b, if $r \in B$, respectively), then there exists an augmenting path in G with respect to K starting at r.*

Proof. If the augmenting path W' in G' does not contain the pseudo node b, then W' is a path in G as well and the statement is clear. So suppose $b \in W'$. We consider the case $r \notin B$ only; the case $r \in B$ is analogous (in fact, even simpler). Let w be the base of B. First suppose that the distance from r to b in W' is even. Then W' has the form

$$W' = r \xrightarrow{\;\;P_1\;\;} p \text{——} b \text{——} q \xrightarrow{\;\;P_3\;\;} s,$$

where P_1 is the part of W' from r to $p := \text{mate}(b)$. Now q must be adjacent to a vertex q' of B. Denote the alternating path of even length in B from w to q' by P_2 (if $w = q'$, we have $P_2 = \emptyset$), then

$$W = r \xrightarrow{\;\;P_1\;\;} p \text{——} w \xrightarrow{\;\;P_2\;\;} q' \text{——} q \xrightarrow{\;\;P_3\;\;} s$$

is an augmenting path in G with respect to K, where P_3 denotes the same part of W' from q to s as above (see Fig 12.22). Now if the distance from r to b in W' is odd, the distance from s to b in W' has to be even. Then, by exchanging the roles of r and s, we may proceed analogously. (This case may indeed occur, as the solution for Exercise 12.4.2 shows.)   □

The following exercise shows that the condition that the blossom must have been found during the construction of the alternating tree is necessary in Lemma 12.4.3 (whereas no such condition is needed for Lemma 12.4.4).

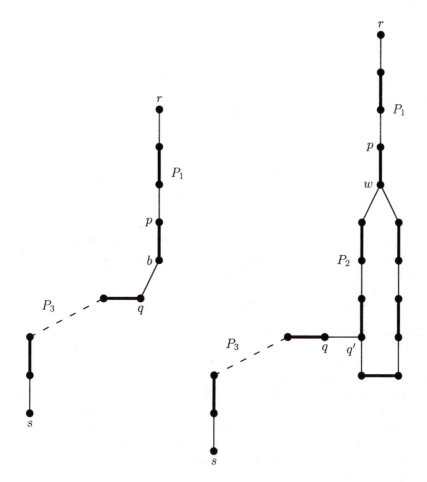

Fig. 12.22 Proof of Lemma 12.4.4

Exercise 12.4.5. Consider the graph G with the matching K shown in Figure 12.23. Obviously, G contains a unique blossom. Show that the contracted graph G' does not contain an augmenting path with respect to K', even though G contains such a path (with respect to K).

Fig. 12.23 Graph with a blossom

Now we state a version of the Algorithm of Edmonds (1965b) illustrated in Example 12.4.1. However, in this version, the graph will not be contracted explicitly if a blossom B is found (this would require rather involved update operations), but the vertices in B are labelled as 'inactive'; this is done by a Boolean function $a(v)$ (for all v).

Algorithm 12.4.6 (Algorithm of Edmonds). Let $G = (V, E)$ be a graph with $V = \{1, \ldots, n\}$ given by adjacency lists A_v. The algorithm constructs a maximal matching of G described by an array mate and determines the number of exposed vertices in G.

The main procedure MAXMATCH uses (in addition to the procedure INMATCH given in Algorithm 12.3.1 which determines the initial matching) three auxiliary procedures BLOSSOM, CONTRACT and AUGMENT. These three procedures are described after MAXMATCH in a less formal way. In MAXMATCH, the function $d(y)$ contains, for a vertex y, its position in the present alternating tree T (with root r): vertices which are not in the tree yet have $d(y) = -1$; for all other vertices, $d(y)$ is the distance between y and the root r in T. In particular, vertices y for which $d(y)$ is odd are inner vertices and if $d(y)$ is even, then y is an outer vertex. The outer vertices are kept in a priority queue Q whose priority function is the distance from the root r in T (that is, the function d). The construction of the alternating tree is always continued from the first active vertex of Q. Initially, all vertices are active. Vertices become inactive if they are contained in a blossom which is contracted. The examination of the neighbours of an outer vertex x is done as described in Section 12.3 and a blossom is contracted as soon as it is found. The two Boolean variables aug and cont are used to control the loop: we have aug = false until an augmenting path is found; during the examination of an outer vertex x, cont has value false until a blossom is found (and contracted). As we need the adjacency lists A_v of G later to 'expand' the augmenting paths, these lists may not be changed during the algorithm. We use new adjacency lists $CA(v)$ for describing the contracted graphs.

Procedure MAXMATCH $(G;$ mate, nrex)

(1) INMATCH$(G;$ mate, nrex);
(2) $r \leftarrow 0$;
(3) **while** nrex ≥ 2 **and** $r < n$ **do**
(4) $r \leftarrow r + 1$;
(5)   **if** mate$(r) = 0$
(6)   **then** $Q \leftarrow \emptyset$, aug $\leftarrow$ false, $m \leftarrow 0$;
(7)   **for** $v \in V$ **do**
(8) $p(v) \leftarrow 0$, $d(v) \leftarrow -1$, $a(v) \leftarrow$ true;
(9) $CA(v) \leftarrow A_v$
(10)   **od**;
(11) $d(r) \leftarrow 0$; append r to Q;
(12)   **while** aug=false **and** $Q \neq \emptyset$ **do**
(13)   remove the first vertex x of Q;
(14)   **if** $a(x) =$ true
(15)   **then** cont $\leftarrow$ false
(16)   **for** $y \in CA(x)$ **do** $u(y) \leftarrow$ false **od**;
(17)   **repeat**
(18)   choose $y \in CA(x)$ with $u(y) =$ false; $u(y) \leftarrow$ true;
(19)   **if** $a(y) =$ true
(20)   **then if** $d(y) \equiv 0 \pmod 2$
(21)   **then** $m \leftarrow m + 1$;
(22)   BLOSSOM $(x, y; B(m), w(m))$;
(23)   CONTRACT $(B(m), m, w)$;
(24)   **else if** $d(y) = -1$
(25)   **then if** mate$(y) = 0$
(26)   **then** AUGMENT(x, y)
(27)   **else** $z \leftarrow$ mate(y);
(28) $p(y) \leftarrow x$; $d(y) \leftarrow d(x) + 1$;
(29) $p(z) \leftarrow y$; $d(z) \leftarrow d(y) + 1$;
(30)   insert z with priority $d(z)$ into Q;
(31)   **fi**
(32)   **fi**
(33)   **fi**
(34)   **fi**
(35)   **until** $u(y) =$ true for all $y \in CA(v)$ **or** aug = true
                        or cont = true
(36)   **fi**
(37)   **od**
(38)   **fi**
(39) **od**.

The following procedure BLOSSOM constructs a blossom B with root w. This procedure is called by MAXMATCH if, during the examination of an outer vertex x, a further outer vertex y is found in $CA(x)$ (according to case 4 in Section 12.3).

Procedure BLOSSOM $(x, y; B, w)$

(1) $W \leftarrow \{x\}$; $W' \leftarrow \{y\}$; $u \leftarrow x$; $v \leftarrow y$;
(2) **repeat**
(3) $W \leftarrow W \cup \{p(u)\}$; $u \leftarrow p(u)$
(4) **until** $p(u) = r$;
(5) **repeat**
(6) $W' \leftarrow W' \cup \{p(v)\}$; $v \leftarrow p(v)$
(7) **until** $v = r$;
(8) $S \leftarrow W \cap W'$;
(9) let w be the element of S for which $d(w) \geq d(z)$ for all $z \in S$;
(10) $B \leftarrow ((W \cup W') \backslash S) \cup \{w\}$.

The procedure CONTRACT is used for contracting a blossom B. As mentioned above, the vertices of B are not really removed from the graph, but are only labelled as inactive. Also, the adjacency lists $CA(v)$ for the contracted graph are updated.

Procedure CONTRACT (B, m, w)

(1) $b \leftarrow n + m$; $a(b) \leftarrow$ true;
(2) $p(b) \leftarrow p(w)$; $d(b) \leftarrow d(w)$; mate$(b) \leftarrow$ mate(w);
(3) insert b into Q with priority $d(b)$;
(4) $CA(b) \leftarrow \bigcup_{z \in B} CA(z)$;
(5) **for** $z \in CA(b)$ **do** $CA(z) \leftarrow CA(z) \cup \{b\}$ **od**;
(6) **for** $z \in B$ **do** $a(z) \leftarrow$ false **od**;
(7) **for** $z \in CA(b)$ **do**
(8)   **if** $a(z) =$ true **and** $p(z) \in B$
(9)   **then** $d(z) \leftarrow d(b) + 1$; $p(z) \leftarrow b$;
(10) $d(\text{mate}(z)) \leftarrow d(z) + 1$;
(11)   **fi**
(12) **od**
(13) cont $\leftarrow$ true.

The procedure AUGMENT stated below serves to construct an augmenting path and to change the matching K accordingly if an exposed vertex y was found during the construction of the alternating tree T (that is, during the examination of a vertex x in the queue Q).

Procedure AUGMENT (x, y)

(1) $W \leftarrow \{y, x\}; v \leftarrow x;$
(2) **repeat**
(3) $\qquad W \leftarrow W \cup \{p(v)\}; v \leftarrow p(v)$
(4) **until** $p(v) = r;$
(5) **while** there exists $b \in W$ with $b > n$ **do**
(6) $\qquad$ choose the largest $b \in W$ with $b > n;$
(7) $\qquad B \leftarrow B(b - n); w \leftarrow w(b - n); z \leftarrow \text{mate}(w);$
(8) $\qquad$ let q be the neighbour of b on W which is $\neq z;$
(9) $\qquad$ choose some $q' \in B \cap CA(q);$
(10) $\qquad$ determine the alternating path B' of even length in B
$\qquad\qquad$ from w to $q';$
(11) $\qquad$ replace b by w in $W;$
(12) $\qquad$ insert B' into W between w and q
(13) **od**;
(14) $u \leftarrow y; v \leftarrow x;$
(15) **while** $v \neq r$ **do**
(16) $\qquad z \leftarrow \text{mate}(v); \text{mate}(v) \leftarrow u; \text{mate}(u) \leftarrow v;$
(17) $\qquad u \leftarrow z;$ let v be the successor of z on W
(18) **od**
(19) $\text{mate}(v) \leftarrow u; \text{mate}(u) \leftarrow v;$
(20) $\text{nrex} \leftarrow \text{nrex} -2; \text{aug} \leftarrow \text{true}.$

Theorem 12.4.7. *Let $G = (V, E)$ be a connected graph. Then Algorithm 12.4.6 determines a maximal matching of G. If the auxiliary procedures BLOSSOM, CONTRACT and AUGMENT are implemented appropriately, the algorithm has a complexity of $O(|V|^3)$.*

Proof. The detailed discussion above where we derived the algorithm (in the present and the previous section) shows that Algorithm 12.4.6 is correct. However, we summarize the main points once more. After constructing an initial matching K (during the procedure INMATCH) described by the array mate, the outer **while**-loop in MAXMATCH contains the search for an augmenting path with respect to K with start vertex r (by constructing an alternating tree T with root r). Obviously, this search can only be successful if there are still at least two exposed vertices, that is, if $\text{nrex} \geq 2$. Moreover, we may restrict the examination of exposed vertices r as start vertices for an augmenting path to $r \leq n - 1$, because an augmenting path with start vertex n would have been found earlier when its end vertex was used as the root of an alternating tree. It follows from Theorem 12.2.2 and Lemma 12.2.3 that it is sufficient to examine each exposed vertex at most once as the root of an alternating tree.

As already mentioned, the outer vertices of T are kept in the priority queue Q and examined according to a BFS (if they are active). During the inner **while**-loop, the first active vertex x from Q is chosen (as long as this is possible and no augmenting path has been found yet) and, by examining the vertices adjacent to x, the construction of the tree T is continued. Choosing x according to the priority function $d(x)$ makes sure that the construction of T is always continued from a vertex which is as near as possible to the root r (as in a BFS). We need the priority function $d(x)$ because contractions of blossoms may change the distances in the present tree T: A new pseudo node b is, in general, nearer to the root than other active vertices which were in the tree before. Inner vertices y are ignored during this examination of the vertices adjacent to x by the conditions in step (20) and (24), respectively (because, in that case, the edge xy would close a cycle of even length and y would already be accessible from r in T by an alternating path of odd length). Note that the function $d(y)$ is used to distinguish whether y is already contained in T (in that case, $d(y) > 0$ is the distance between r and y) or y has not been added to the tree yet (then $d(y) = -1$).

If the condition $d(y) \equiv 0 \pmod 2$ holds in step (20) (that is, y is already contained in T as an outer vertex), then the edge xy closes a blossom B. According to Lemmas 12.4.3 and 12.4.4, we may then continue with the contracted graph G/B instead of G, because G contains an augmenting path with respect to K if and only if such a path exists in G/B with respect to the induced matching K/B. The first step in replacing G by G/B is to construct the blossom B by calling the procedure BLOSSOM in step (22). BLOSSOM uses the predecessor function $p(v)$ (that is, $p(v)$ is the predecessor of v on the path from the root r to v in T) to determine the paths W and W' from x and y, respectively, to the root r. Then the intersection S of W and W' is the stem of the blossom. As the function d gives the distance of a vertex from the root r of T, the base w of B is precisely the vertex of S for which d has the maximal value. Therefore, the blossom B is indeed $((W \cup W')\backslash S) \cup \{w\}$ as stated in step (10) of BLOSSOM and the procedure indeed constructs the blossom B as well as its base w.

Now, in step (23) of MAXMATCH, the procedure CONTRACT is called to replace the graph G by the contracted graph G/B and change K and T accordingly. The pseudo node b used to signify B is numbered as $b := n + m$, where m is a counter containing the number of blossoms already found. Thus, the pseudo nodes are precisely those vertices b for which $b > n$. Steps (1) to (3) of CONTRACT label b as an active vertex, insert b into Q and replace the basis w and all other vertices of B by b in T. To do this, the predecessor of b is defined to be $p(w)$ and the distance of b from r is set to $d(w)$. We need the induced matching K/B as well, so that mate(b) is defined to be mate(w). Steps (4) to (6) contain the implicit contraction: all vertices of B are labelled as inactive and all vertices adjacent to some vertex of B are made neighbours of b by putting them into $CA(b)$. In steps (7) to (12), T is updated to T/B by defining b to be the predecessor of all active vertices z whose predecessor $p(z)$ was some vertex in B and defining the distance of these vertices to the root r to be $d(b) + 1$. The same is done for the corresponding outer vertices mate(z).

Finally, the variable cont is given value true, so that, back in MAXMATCH, the examination of vertex x (which is not active any more) is stopped, and the construction of T is continued with the active vertex in Q which has highest priority (that is, smallest distance from r).

If a vertex y is not yet contained in the tree when edge xy is examined (that is, $d(y) = -1$ still), it is checked in step (25) whether y is an exposed vertex. If it is not, the vertices y (as an inner vertex) and $z := \text{mate}(y)$ (as an outer vertex) are added to the tree T by appending the path x ——— y ——— z at x and defining the distances of y and z to r accordingly. Finally, if y is exposed, procedure AUGMENT is called to enlarge the matching K of G. Steps (1) to (4) of AUGMENT construct an augmenting path W with respect to the present matching K' which is induced by K in the graph G' (the – maybe several times – contracted graph). During the first while-loop, the pseudo nodes on this path (which are distinguished by the property $b > n$) are 'expanded' in decreasing order, that is, the pseudo nodes which were constructed first are expanded last. To execute such an 'expansion', the neighbour $q \neq \text{mate}(b)$ of b is determined and the edge $\{b, q\}$ on W is substituted by the alternating path (of even length) from the base w of the corresponding blossom to the vertex $q' \in B$ adjacent to q (see the proof of Lemma 12.4.4). Thus, when the first while-loop is terminated, W is an augmenting path in G with respect to K. We view this path as being oriented from y to the root r. The second while-loop augments the matching K according to this path by changing the function mate accordingly. In step (20), the number of exposed vertices is decreased by 2 and the variable aug is assigned value true, so that, back in MAXMATCH, the construction of the tree T is stopped according to step (12) or (35), respectively. Then the outer while-loop of MAXMATCH begins again with the next exposed vertex r.

The repeat-loop in MAXMATCH (which contains the search for an exposed outer vertex from a fixed vertex x) is terminated according to step (35) if a contraction or an augmentation has been performed or if all vertices y adjacent to x (and active at this point of time) were examined. The inner while-loop terminates if either an augmenting path was found or if Q is empty; in the latter case the construction of T is terminated without succeeding in finding an augmenting path. Note that, in this case, we have constructed an alternating tree T' for a (in general, contracted) graph G' in which all blossoms found during the construction beginning in r were contracted. Therefore, if there is no augmenting path with start vertex r in G', there is no such path in G either (by Lemma 12.4.4). In both cases, the algorithm continues with the next exposed vertex as the root of an alternating tree. This process continues until the outer while-loop is terminated (as discussed above) and the matching K is maximal.

It remains to consider the complexity of MAXMATCH. It is trivial that there are at most $O(|V|)$ iterations of the outer while-loop. Thus, we have to show that the process of constructing an alternating tree with root r (that is, one phase) can be executed in $O(|V|^2)$ steps, provided that the auxiliary procedures are implemented appropriately. Each blossom contains at least three vertices and each vertex can be contracted (that is, be labelled as inactive) at most once, so that there can be at most $O(|V|)$ contractions. To be more accurate, at most $|V|/2$ pseudo nodes occur during the inner **while**-loop, which means that there are at most $O(|V|)$ iterations of the inner **while**-loop. At the point of the algorithm where the vertices y adjacent to x are examined during the **repeat**-loop, at most $O(|V|)$ edges are treated, so that this whole process can take at most $O(|V|^2)$ steps, not counting the complexity of the auxiliary procedures BLOSSOM, CONTRACT and AUGMENT. It is easy to show that one call of BLOSSOM takes at most $O(|V|)$ steps and as there are at most $O(|V|)$ calls of BLOSSOM, these operations contribute at most $O(|V|^2)$ steps as well.

We show next that all the calls of CONTRACT together need at most $O(|V|^2)$ steps if step (4) is implemented appropriately. The construction of the adjacency list of the pseudo node b is the only operation of CONTRACT whose complexity is not quite obvious. It is possible to execute this construction by a labelling process: Initially, all vertices are not labelled. Next, we label all vertices occurring in one of the adjacency lists of the vertices contained in B. Finally, we define $CA(b)$ to be the set of all the labelled vertices. This method takes (for each blossom B) $O(|V|)$ steps plus the number of steps we need for examining the adjacency lists of the vertices of B. But as there are only $O(|V|)$ vertices which might occur in one of the blossoms and have to be examined, these operations (added over all calls of CONTRACT) cannot take more than $O(|V|^2)$ steps.

Finally, we have to convince ourselves that an eventual call of AUGMENT has complexity at most $O(|V|^2)$. Obviously, there are at most $O(|V|)$ iterations of the first **while**-loop. All operations during this loop can be executed in $O(|V|)$ steps, except the determination of a vertex $q' \in CA(q)$ in step (9) and the determination of an alternating path from w to q' in step (10) during the 'expansion' of a pseudo node b to a blossom B. However, the first of these two operations can be implemented by a labelling process (where we begin by labelling the vertices in $CA(s)$, say) having complexity $O(|V|)$. The second operation can also be done in $O(|V|)$ steps if we store the blossom B in BLOSSOM not simply as a set, but as a doubly linked list. (Note that all we have to do is trace B from q' in the direction given by mate(q') until we reach the base w.) Therefore, AUGMENT has complexity $O(|V|^2)$ as well.

As we have seen, each iteration of the outer **while**-loop of MAXMATCH needs (assuming that the auxiliary procedures CONTRACT and AUGMENT are implemented appropriately) at most $O(|V|^2)$ steps, so that the total complexity of MAXMATCH is $O(|V|^3)$. $\qquad\qquad\square$

It should be mentioned that implementing the procedures for determining a maximal matching as described above is in fact a rather cumbersome task. To close this section, we give one more exercise.

Exercise 12.4.8. Let G be a bipartite graph with vertex set $V = S \stackrel{.}{\cup} T$, where $S = \{1, \ldots, n\}$ and $T = \{1', \ldots, n'\}$. G is called *symmetric* if the existence of an edge ij' in G always implies that ji' is also an edge of G. A matching of G is called *symmetric* if K does not contain any edge of the form ii' and, for each edge $ij' \in K$, the edge ji' is contained in K as well. How could a maximal symmetric matching in a symmetric bipartite graph be determined?

12.5 Matching Matroids

In this section we present the generalization of Theorem 7.3.8 due to Edmonds and Fulkerson (1965) which was announced already in Section 7.3.

Theorem 12.5.1. *Let $G = (V, E)$ be a graph and $\mathbf{S}$ the set of all those subsets of V which are given by the vertices covered by some matching in G. Then $(V, \mathbf{S})$ is a matroid.*

Proof. Let A and A' be two independent subsets of V with $|A| = |A'| + 1$ and suppose that K and K' are matchings in G which meet the vertices in A and A', respectively. If there exists a vertex $a \in A \backslash A'$ such that K' meets $A' \cup \{a\}$, then condition (2) of Theorem 5.2.1 is trivially satisfied. Otherwise let X be the symmetric difference of K and K'. Then X has to consist of alternating cycles and alternating paths (as in the proof of Theorem 12.2.2), that is, of cycles and paths in which edges of K and K' appear alternatingly. As $|A \backslash A'| = |A' \backslash A| + 1$, X has to contain a path W connecting a vertex $x \in A \backslash A'$ to a vertex $y \notin A'$. Then $K' \oplus W$ is a matching meeting $A' \cup \{x\}$. Therefore, condition (2) of Theorem 5.2.1 is always satisfied and $(V, \mathbf{S})$ is a matroid.   □

For any matroid $(M, \mathbf{S})$ and any subset N of M, the *restriction* $(N, \mathbf{S}|N)$, where $\mathbf{S}|N = \{A \subset N : A \in \mathbf{S}\}$, is a matroid as well, so that Theorem 12.5.1 immediately implies the following result.

Corollary 12.5.2. *Let $G = (V, E)$ be a graph and W a subset of V. Moreover, let $\mathbf{S}$ be the set of all subsets of W consisting of vertices covered by some matching of G. Then $(W, \mathbf{S})$ is a matroid.*   □

The matroids described in Corollary 12.5.2 are called *matching matroids*.

Exercise 12.5.3. Derive Theorem 7.3.8 from Corollary 12.5.2.

Exercise 12.5.4. Let G be a graph and A some subset of V. Show that, if there exists a matching K meeting all vertices in A, then there exists a maximal matching meeting A as well. (In particular, any vertex of G which is not isolated is contained in some maximal matching.)

We close this chapter with some remarks. Even though we know an efficient algorithm for determining a matching of maximal cardinality, determining a non-extendable matching of minimal cardinality is an NP-hard problem (even for planar or bipartite graphs, and even for maximal degree ≤ 3). This result was proved in an unpublished manuscript by Yannakakis and Gavril (1978), see also Garey and Johnson (1979).

The notion of a matching can be generalized as follows. Let $G = (V, E)$ be a graph with $V = \{1, \ldots, n\}$ and $f : V \to \mathbb{N}_0$ a mapping. A subgraph of G with $\deg(v) = f(v)$ for $v = 1, \ldots, n$ is called an f-*factor* of G. Tutte generalized his 1-Factor Theorem 12.1.1 to a necessary and sufficient condition for the existence of an f-factor, see Tutte (1952). His general theorem can be derived from the 1-Factor Theorem, see Tutte (1954). Anstee (1985) gave an algorithmic proof of Tutte's theorem which allows to determine an f-factor with complexity $O(n^3)$ (or show that no such factor exists, respectively). The question of existence of f-factors can also be treated using special networks in the framework of Flow Theory, see Kocay and Stone (1993) and Fremuth-Paeger and Jungnickel (1998a, 1998b, 1998c, 1998d, 1998e). Further generalizations (where the degrees of the vertices are restricted by upper and lower bounds) can be found in Lovász (1970b) and Anstee (1985). Many further results concerning matchings as well as an extensive bibliography are contained in the detailed monograph 'Matching Theory' by Lovász and Plummer (1986).

13. Weighted Matchings

In the previous chapter, we studied matchings of maximal cardinality ('cardinality matching'). The present chapter is devoted to weighted matchings, in particular to the problem of how to determine a matching of maximal weight in some network (G, w) ('weighted matching'). In the bipartite case, this problem is equivalent to the 'assignment problem' (see Example 9.1.4), so that the methods introduced in Chapter 9 can be applied. However, we give a further algorithm for the bipartite case, the 'Hungarian Algorithm', which is one of the most popular and most important combinatorial algorithms. We proceed by showing the connection to the Theory of Linear Programming, which we need to understand why the approach used in the Hungarian Algorithm is successful (this is due to the particularly simple structure of the corresponding polytope and to the total unimodularity of the incidence matrix of a bipartite graph). In this context, it will also become clear why the determination of maximal (weighted) matchings is much more difficult for arbitrary graphs than for bipartite graphs and which significance the blossoms have. It makes no sense to describe an algorithm for this problem without introducing more of the Theory of Linear Programming, and for this reason, no such algorithm is included in this book. However, we show two interesting applications of weighted matchings, namely the Chinese Postman Problem (featuring a postman who is looking for the optimal route for delivering his mail) and the determination of shortest paths for the case that edges of negative weight occur. Finally, we say something about matchings with certain additional conditions (as they appear quite often in practice) ('exact matching'); we will see that such problems are inherently more difficult.

13.1 The Bipartite Case

Let $G = (V, E)$ be a bipartite graph with weight function $w : E \to \mathbb{R}$. The weight $w(K)$ of a matching K of G is defined, as usual, as

$$w(K) := \sum_{e \in K} w(e).$$

A matching K is called a *maximal weighted matching* if $w(K) \geq w(K')$ holds for every matching K' of G. Obviously, a maximal weighted matching does not contain any edges of negative weight. Thus, such edges may as well be omitted from the graph and we may assume that w is non-negative. But even under this assumption, a maximal weighted matching is not necessarily also a matching of maximal cardinality. However, if we extend G to a complete bipartite graph by adding all missing edges e with weight $w(e) = 0$, we may always assume that a matching of maximal weight is a complete matching. Therefore, we restrict our considerations to complete matchings. We can even achieve $|S| = |T|$ by adding the appropriate number of vertices to the smaller of the two sets and introducing edges of weight 0 again. We see that it is sufficient to treat the problem of determining a perfect matching of maximal weight in a complete bipartite graph $K_{n,n}$. We call such a matching an *optimal matching* of $(K_{n,n}, w)$.[1]

So let $w : E \to \mathbb{R}_0^+$ be a weight function for the graph $K_{n,n}$. Suppose the maximal weight of all edges is C. We define the *cost* of a perfect matching K by

$$\gamma(K) := \sum_{e \in K} \gamma(e),$$

where the cost $\gamma(e)$ of an edge e is defined by $\gamma(e) := C - w(e)$. Then the optimal matchings are obviously precisely the perfect matchings of minimal cost. Thus, determining an optimal matching in G with respect to the weight function w is equivalent to solving the Assignment Problem for the matrix $A = (C - w(ij))$, and this is a special case of the minimum cost flow problem (compare Examples 9.1.3 and 9.1.4). All we have to do is to find an optimal flow of value n in the flow network described in 9.1.4. This can be done using the Algorithm of Busacker and Gowen (1961) which yields a complexity of $O(n^3)$.

Theorem 13.1.1. *Let w be a non-negative weight function for $K_{n,n}$. Then an optimal matching can be determined with complexity $O(n^3)$.*   □

Exercise 13.1.2. Design a procedure OPTMATCH for finding an optimal matching in $K_{n,n}$ (for a non-negative weight function) which has complexity $O(n^3)$.

The complexity $O(n^3)$ stated above is, in fact, the best known result for positive weight functions on complete bipartite graphs $K_{n,n}$. It is possible to determine a matching of maximal weight for some non-complete bipartite graphs with a smaller complexity; this follows, for example, from Theorem 9.6.3, using the same method as described above (see also Tarjan (1983), p. 114). The best known complexity for determining an optimal matching in

---

[1] To determine a perfect matching of maximal weight in a bipartite graph containing edges of negative weight, we can add a sufficiently large constant to all weights first and thus reduce this case to the case of a non-negative weight function. Finally, the problem of finding a perfect matching of minimal weight can be treated by replacing w by $-w$.

a bipartite graph is $O(|V||E| + |V|^2 \log |V|)$, see Fredman and Tarjan (1987). Gabow and Tarjan (1989) and Orlin and Ahuja (1992) gave algorithms of complexity $O(|V|^{1/2}|E| \log (|V|C))$. A polynomial version of the Network Simplex Algorithm for the Assignment Problem can be found in Ahuja and Orlin (1992).

13.2 The Hungarian Algorithm

In this section, we present a further algorithm for determining an optimal matching for a bipartite graph with complexity $O(n^3)$. This algorithm is due to Kuhn (1955) and Kuhn (1956) and is based on ideas of König and Egerváry, so that Kuhn named it the 'Hungarian Algorithm'. This algorithm does not yield a better complexity than the bound of Theorem 13.1.1, but it is presented here because it is one of the most popular and most important algorithms in Combinatorics. We also use this algorithm to illustrate the connections between Matching Theory and Linear Programming in the next section.

So let G be the complete bipartite graph $K_{n,n}$ with vertex set $V = S \cup T$, where $S = \{1, \ldots, n\}$ and $T = \{1', \ldots, n'\}$. Moreover, we have a non-negative weight function w described by the matrix $W = (w_{ij})$ (so that w_{ij} is the weight of the edge $\{i, j'\}$). A pair of real vectors $\mathbf{u} = (u_1, \ldots, u_n)$ and $\mathbf{v} = (v_1, \ldots, v_n)$ is called a *feasible node weighting* if

$$u_i + v_j \geq w_{ij} \quad \text{for all } i, j = 1, \ldots, n \tag{13.1}$$

holds. The set of all feasible node weightings $(\mathbf{u}, \mathbf{v})$ is denoted by $\mathbf{Z}$. Moreover, let M be the weight of an optimal matching in G.

Lemma 13.2.1. *For any feasible node weighting* $(\mathbf{u}, \mathbf{v})$ *and for any perfect matching of* G, *we have*

$$w(K) \leq M \leq \sum_{i=1}^{n} (u_i + v_i). \tag{13.2}$$

Proof. The statement follows immediately by summing (13.1) over all edges of the matching K. □

If we can find a feasible node weighting $(\mathbf{u}, \mathbf{v})$ and a matching K such that equality holds in (13.2), then this matching has to be optimal. The feasible node weightings are important because it is always possible to achieve equality in (13.2); the Hungarian Algorithm will give a constructive proof for this fact. (This approach is not a trick appearing out of nowhere; we will see its theoretical background in the next section.)

Let us characterize the case of equality in (13.2). For a given feasible node weighting $(\mathbf{u}, \mathbf{v})$, we define the subgraph $H_{\mathbf{u},\mathbf{v}}$ on vertex set V whose edges are precisely those ij' for which $u_i + v_j = w_{ij}$ holds. $H_{\mathbf{u},\mathbf{v}}$ is called the *equality subgraph* for $(\mathbf{u}, \mathbf{v})$.

Lemma 13.2.2. *Let $H = H_{\mathbf{u},\mathbf{v}}$ be the equality subgraph for $(\mathbf{u}, \mathbf{v}) \in \mathbf{Z}$. Then*

$$\sum_{i=1}^{n}(u_i + v_i) = M$$

holds if and only if H has a perfect matching. In this case, every perfect matching of H is an optimal matching of G.

Proof. First assume that $\sum(u_i + v_i) = M$ holds. Suppose that H does not contain any perfect matching. For $J \subset S$, $\Gamma(J)$ denotes, as usual, the set of all vertices $j' \in T$ adjacent to some vertex $i \in J$. By Theorem 7.2.4, there exists a subset J of S with $|\Gamma(J)| < |J|$. (Note that we exchanged the roles of S and T compared to 7.2.4.) Set $\delta := \min\{u_i + v_j - w_{ij} : i \in J, j' \notin \Gamma(J)\}$ and define $(\mathbf{u}', \mathbf{v}')$ as follows:

$$u_i' := \begin{cases} u_i - \delta & \text{for } i \in J \\ u_i & \text{for } i \notin J \end{cases} \quad \text{and} \quad v_j' := \begin{cases} v_j + \delta & \text{for } j' \in \Gamma(J) \\ v_j & \text{for } j' \notin \Gamma(J). \end{cases}$$

Then $(\mathbf{u}', \mathbf{v}')$ is a feasible node weighting as well: The condition $u_i' + v_j' \geq w_{ij}$ might only be violated for $i \in J$ and $j' \notin \Gamma(J)$. But in this case $\delta \leq u_i + v_j - w_{ij}$, so that $w_{ij} \leq (u_i - \delta) + v_j = u_i' + v_j'$. We now obtain a contradiction:

$$M \leq \sum(u_i' + v_j') = \sum(u_i + v_j) - \delta|J| + \delta|\Gamma(J)| = M - \delta(|J| - |\Gamma(J)|) < M.$$

Conversely, suppose that H contains a perfect matching K. Then, for any edge of K, equality holds in (13.1), so that summation of (13.1) over all edges of K immediately yields equality in (13.2). This shows also that every perfect matching of H is an optimal matching of G.   □

The Hungarian Algorithm starts with any feasible node weighting $(\mathbf{u}, \mathbf{v}) \in \mathbf{Z}$, say with $v_1 = \ldots = v_n = 0$ and $u_i = \max\{w_{ij} : j = 1, \ldots, n\}$ (for $i = 1, \ldots, n$). If the corresponding equality subgraph contains a perfect matching, our problem is solved. Otherwise, the algorithm determines a subset J of S with $|\Gamma(J)| < |J|$ and changes the feasible node weighting $(\mathbf{u}, \mathbf{v})$ as in the proof of Lemma 13.2.2. This decreases the sum $\sum(u_i + v_i)$ and yields at least one new edge ij' with $i \in J$ and $j' \notin \Gamma(J)$ (with respect to $H_{\mathbf{u},\mathbf{v}}$) which is contained in the new equality subgraph $H_{\mathbf{u}',\mathbf{v}'}$. This procedure is repeated until the partial matching in H can be extended. Finally, we get a graph H containing a perfect matching K which is an optimal matching of G as well. For extending the matchings and for changing $(\mathbf{u}, \mathbf{v})$, we use an alternating tree (appropriately labelled) in H. In the following algorithm, we keep a variable δ_j for each $j' \in T$ which may be viewed as a 'potential': δ_j is the present minimal value of $u_i + v_j - w_{ij}$. Moreover, $p(j)$ denotes the vertex i for which this minimal value was obtained first.

Algorithm 13.2.3 (Hungarian Algorithm). Let G be a complete bipartite graph with vertex set $V = S \,\dot\cup\, T$, where $S = \{1, \ldots, n\}$ and $T = \{1', \ldots, n'\}$. Moreover, each edge ij' of G has a non-negative weight w_{ij}. The algorithm determines an optimal matching in G which is described (as in Chapter 12) by an array 'mate'. (Note that Q denotes a set, not a queue, in what follows.)

Procedure HUNGARIAN $(n, w;$ mate$)$

(1) **for** $v \in V$ **do** mate$(v) \leftarrow 0$ **od**;
(2) **for** $i = 1$ **to** n **do** $u_i \leftarrow \max \{w_{ij} : j = 1, \ldots, n\}$; $v_i \leftarrow 0$ **od**;
(3) nrex $\leftarrow n$;
(4) **while** nrex $\neq 0$ **do**
(5)   **for** $i = 1$ **to** n **do** $m(i) \leftarrow$ false; $p(i) \leftarrow 0$; $\delta_i \leftarrow \infty$ **od**;
(6)   aug $\leftarrow$ false; $Q \leftarrow \{i \in S : \text{mate}(i) = 0\}$;
(7)   **repeat**
(8)   remove some arbitrary vertex i from Q; $m(i) \leftarrow$ true; $j \leftarrow 1$;
(9)   **while** aug $=$ false **and** $j \leq n$ **do**
(10)   **if** mate$(i) \neq j'$
(11)   **then if** $u_i + v_j - w_{ij} < \delta_j$
(12)   **then** $\delta_j \leftarrow u_i + v_j - w_{ij}$; $p(j) \leftarrow i$;
(13)   **if** $\delta_j = 0$
(14)   **then if** mate$(j') = 0$
(15)   **then** AUGMENT (mate, p, j'; mate);
(16)   aug $\leftarrow$ true; nrex $\leftarrow$ nrex -1
(17)   **else** $Q \leftarrow Q \cup \{\,\text{mate}(j')\}$
(18)   **fi**
(19)   **fi**
(20)   **fi**
(21)   **fi**;
(22) $j \leftarrow j + 1$
(23)   **od**;
(24)   **if** aug $=$ false **and** $Q = \emptyset$
(25)   **then** $J \leftarrow \{i \in S : m(i) = \text{true}\}$; $K \leftarrow \{j' \in T; \delta_j = 0\}$;
(26) $\delta \leftarrow \min \{\delta_j : j' \in T \backslash K\}$;
(27)   **for** $i \in J$ **do** $u_i \leftarrow u_i - \delta$ **od**;
(28)   **for** $j' \in K$ **do** $v_j \leftarrow v_j + \delta$ **od**;
(29)   **for** $j' \in T \backslash K$ **do** $\delta_j \leftarrow \delta_j - \delta$ **od**;
(30) $X \leftarrow \{j' \in T \backslash K : \delta_j = 0\}$;
(31)   **if** mate$(j') \neq 0$ for all $j' \in X$
(32)   **then for** $j' \in X$ **do** $Q \leftarrow Q \cup \{\text{mate}(j')\}$ **od**
(33)   **else** choose $j' \in X$ with mate$(j') = 0$;
(34)   AUGMENT (mate, p, j'; mate);
(35)   aug $\leftarrow$ true; nrex $\leftarrow$ nrex $- 1$
(36)   **fi**

(37)   **fi**
(38)   **until** aug = true
(39) **od**.

Procedure AUGMENT (mate, p, j'; mate)

(1) **repeat**
(2) $i \leftarrow p(j)$; mate(j') $\leftarrow i$; next $\leftarrow$ mate(i); mate(i) $\leftarrow j'$;
(3)   **if** next $\neq 0$ **then** $j' \leftarrow$ next **fi**
(4) **until** next $=0$.

Theorem 13.2.4. *Algorithm 13.2.3 determines an optimal matching of G with complexity $O(n^3)$.*

Proof. We call all the operations executed during one iteration of the **while**-loop (4) to (39) a *phase*. First, we show by induction on the phases that the array mate always defines a matching in the equality subgraph $H_{\mathbf{u},\mathbf{v}}$. This is true at the beginning of the algorithm because of step (1). Now suppose it is true at the beginning of some phase. During the **repeat**-loop, an alternating forest (that is, the disjoint union of alternating trees) B is constructed in $H_{\mathbf{u},\mathbf{v}}$. The outer vertices of this forest are those vertices i in S for which $m(i) =$ true and the inner vertices of B are the vertices $j' \in T$ for which $\delta_j = 0$. As soon as the condition in (14) holds, we have found an augmenting path with end vertex j' in B; in that case, the present matching in $H_{\mathbf{u},\mathbf{v}}$ is extended by one edge by AUGMENT. As B is contained in $H_{\mathbf{u},\mathbf{v}}$, the extended matching is contained in $H_{\mathbf{u},\mathbf{v}}$ as well.

Up to now, we assumed that the condition in (24) is not satisfied. If this condition holds during the **repeat**-loop, we must have reached $Q = \emptyset$ without finding an augmenting path in B. If this is the case, subsets J of S and K of T are defined in (25) such that (in the terminology of the proof of Lemma 13.2.2) $K = \Gamma(J)$: In step (8), all vertices which were an element of Q at some point were examined, so that, during the **while**-loop (9) to (23), all vertices in $\Gamma(J)$ were labelled with some vertex $i = p(j)$ and δ_j was set to 0. Note that the vertices in $\Gamma(J)$ are precisely those vertices j' for which $u_i + v_j = w_{ij}$ holds for some $i \in J$ and that, for any vertex j' of K, the vertex mate(j') is contained in J because of (17) and (8). As J contains all the exposed vertices as well (because of (6)), we must have $|\Gamma(J)| < |J|$. Therefore, it makes sense to proceed by changing the feasible node weighting $(\mathbf{u}, \mathbf{v})$ as in the proof of Lemma 13.2.2 and, by doing so, decrease the sum $\sum (u_i + v_i)$. This is done in steps (26) to (28); we denote the changed vectors (for the moment) by $\mathbf{u}'$ and $\mathbf{v}'$, respectively. Now (27) and (28) imply for each edge ij' of $H_{\mathbf{u},\mathbf{v}}$ with $i \in J$ and $j' \in K$

$$u_i' + v_j' = (u_i - \delta) + (v_j + \delta) = w_{ij} \quad (\text{because } ij' \in H_{\mathbf{u},\mathbf{v}}),$$

so that all such edges of $H_{\mathbf{u},\mathbf{v}}$ are contained in $H_{\mathbf{u}',\mathbf{v}'}$ as well. Moreover, the condition $u_i' + v_j' \geq w_{ij}$ still holds for all i and j (this can be seen as in the proof of Lemma 13.2.2). By (27), when changing $\mathbf{u}$ to $\mathbf{u}'$, the potential δ_j is decreased by δ for all $j' \in T \backslash K$; this is done in step (29). Now the way we defined δ implies that this produces at least one $j' \in T \backslash K$ for which $\delta_{j'} = 0$. Therefore, $H_{\mathbf{u}',\mathbf{v}'}$ contains at least one edge ij' with $i \in J$ and $j' \notin K$, that is, an edge leaving J which was not contained in $H_{\mathbf{u},\mathbf{v}}$.[2] In step (30), all vertices $j' \notin K$ with $\delta_j = 0$ are put together into the set X. If there exists a vertex $j' \in X$ which is exposed, we have found an augmenting path in $H_{\mathbf{u}',\mathbf{v}'}$ and the present matching can be extended by AUGMENT (in steps (33) to (35)). Otherwise, the vertex mate(j') can be added to the alternating forest B for each $j' \in X$. Then Q is not empty any more (according to (32)) and the construction of B can be continued in the **repeat**-loop. Note that the set $K = \Gamma(J)$ becomes larger by at least one element with each execution of steps (25) to (37), so that an exposed vertex must have been found after having changed $(\mathbf{u}, \mathbf{v})$ at most n times. This shows also that each phase terminates with aug $=$ true and that the matching is extended during each phase. Obviously, there are exactly n phases. As changing the feasible node weighting $(\mathbf{u}, \mathbf{v})$ and executing the procedure AUGMENT both have complexity $O(n)$, these parts of a phase need at most $O(n^2)$ steps. Any vertex is inserted into Q and examined in the inner **while**-loop at most once during each phase. The inner **while**-loop has complexity $O(n)$, so that the algorithm consists of n phases of complexity $O(n^2)$, which yields a total complexity of $O(n^3)$ as asserted. $\square$

Note that each phase of Algorithm 13.2.3 basically is an application of Algorithm 12.3.2 to the equality subgraph $H_{\mathbf{u},\mathbf{v}}$. Thus, the determination of an optimal matching can be reduced to the problem of 'cardinality matching'. It happens quite often that the weighted version of some optimization problem can be reduced to several applications of the unweighted version; this is also the basic idea of the 'out-of-kilter'-Algorithm for determining an optimal circulation mentioned in Chapter 9.

Example 13.2.5. We use Algorithm 13.2.3 for determining an optimal matching of the graph $(K_{5,5}, w)$, where the weight function w is given by the following matrix $W = (w_{ij})$:

---

[2] Note that, in general, $H_{\mathbf{u}',\mathbf{v}'}$ does not contain $H_{\mathbf{u},\mathbf{v}}$ (we will see this in Example 13.2.5), because there may be edges ij' with $i \notin J$ and $j' \in K$ which are left out of $H_{\mathbf{u},\mathbf{v}}$. However, this does not cause any problems because all vertices $j' \in K$ are saturated by the matching constructed so far; as mentioned above, mate(j') is defined for all $j' \in K$ (and is contained in J). Therefore, $H_{\mathbf{u}',\mathbf{v}'}$ still contains the present matching.

$$
\begin{pmatrix}
3 & 8 & 9 & 1 & 6 \\
1 & 4 & 1 & 5 & 5 \\
7 & 2 & 7 & 9 & 2 \\
3 & 1 & 6 & 8 & 8 \\
2 & 6 & 3 & 6 & 2
\end{pmatrix}
\quad
\begin{matrix}
9 \\ 5 \\ 9 \\ 8 \\ 6
\end{matrix}
$$

$$
0 \quad 0 \quad 0 \quad 0 \quad 0 \qquad \mathbf{v/u}
$$

The numbers on the right hand side of and below the matrix are the u_i and the v_j, respectively, which the algorithm uses as initial values according to step (2) of Algorithm 13.2.3. To make the execution of the algorithm deterministic, we always choose the smallest element of Q in step (8). Then, in the first phase, $i = 1$. We obtain the following values of δ_j and $p(j)$:

$$
\begin{array}{ccccc c}
1' & 2' & 3' & 4' & 5' & j' \\
6 & 1 & 0 & \infty & \infty & \delta_j \\
1 & 1 & 1 & - & - & p(j).
\end{array}
$$

Vertex $3'$ is exposed, so that $\{1, 3'\}$ is chosen as the first edge of the matching. During the second phase, $i = 2$ is chosen and edge $\{2, 4'\}$ is added to the matching. During the third phase, $Q = \{3, 4, 5\}$, so that initially, $i = 3$ and

$$
\begin{array}{ccccc c}
1' & 2' & 3' & 4' & 5' & j' \\
2 & 7 & 2 & 0 & 7 & \delta_j \\
3 & 3 & 3 & 3 & 3 & p(j).
\end{array}
$$

As vertex $4'$ is saturated already, mate$(4') = 2$ is added to Q. Then $i = 2$ is removed from Q in step (8) and we get

$$
\begin{array}{ccccc c}
2 & 1 & 2 & 0 & 0 & \delta_j \\
3 & 2 & 3 & 3 & 2 & p(j).
\end{array}
$$

Now vertex $5'$ is exposed and AUGMENT yields the new matching consisting of the edges $\{2, 5'\}$, $\{3, 4'\}$ and $\{1, 3'\}$ (because we had $p(5) = 2$, mate$(2) = 4'$, $p(4) = 3$ and mate$(3) = 0$ before). During the fourth phase, $Q = \{4, 5\}$, that is, $i = 4$ and

$$
\begin{array}{ccccc c}
5 & 7 & 2 & 0 & 0 & \delta_j \\
4 & 4 & 4 & 4 & 4 & p(j).
\end{array}
$$

As the vertices $4'$ and $5'$ are both saturated, their mates 3 and 2 are inserted into Q. We obtain, for $i = 2$, $i = 3$ and $i = 5$ in step (8), the following values for δ_j and $p(j)$ (in the given order):

$$
i = 2: \quad
\begin{array}{ccccc}
4 & 1 & 2 & 0 & 0 \\
2 & 2 & 4 & 4 & 4
\end{array}
$$

$$
i = 3: \quad
\begin{array}{ccccc}
2 & 1 & 2 & 0 & 0 \\
3 & 2 & 4 & 4 & 4
\end{array}
$$

$$
i = 5: \quad
\begin{array}{ccccc}
2 & 0 & 2 & 0 & 0 \\
3 & 5 & 4 & 4 & 4.
\end{array}
$$

Vertex $2'$ is exposed; as $p(2) = 5$ is exposed as well, edge $\{5, 2'\}$ is added to the matching. We have now constructed the matching

$$K = \{\{1, 3'\}, \{2, 5'\}, \{3, 4'\}, \{5, 2'\}\}$$

in the equality subgraph $H_{\mathbf{u}, \mathbf{v}}$, see Figure 13.1.

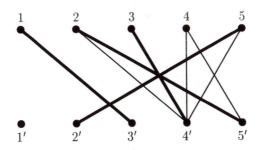

Fig. 13.1 Equality subgraph with a matching

During the fifth phase, we first have $Q = \{4\}$, so that $i = 4$ and the values of δ_j and $p(j)$ are

$$
\begin{array}{ccccc}
5 & 7 & 2 & 0 & 0 \\
4 & 4 & 4 & 4 & 4.
\end{array}
$$

Similar to the preceding phase, 2 and 3 are inserted into Q. Then the values of δ_j and $p(j)$ are changed for $i = 2$ and $i = 3$ as follows:

$$
i = 2: \quad
\begin{array}{ccccc}
4 & 1 & 2 & 0 & 0 \\
2 & 2 & 4 & 4 & 4
\end{array}
$$

$$
i = 3: \quad
\begin{array}{ccccc}
2 & 1 & 2 & 0 & 0 \\
3 & 2 & 4 & 4 & 4.
\end{array}
$$

Now we have $Q = \emptyset$ for the first time and the feasible node weighting $(\mathbf{u}, \mathbf{v})$ is changed according to steps (27) and (28). We obtain (with $J = \{2, 3, 4\}$, $K = \{4', 5'\}$ and $\delta = 1$)

$$
\begin{array}{c}
\left(
\begin{array}{ccccc}
3 & 8 & 9 & 1 & 6 \\
1 & 4 & 1 & 5 & 5 \\
7 & 2 & 7 & 9 & 2 \\
3 & 1 & 6 & 8 & 8 \\
2 & 6 & 3 & 6 & 2
\end{array}
\right)
\quad
\begin{array}{c}
9 \\
4 \\
8 \\
7 \\
6
\end{array}
\\[4pt]
\begin{array}{ccccc}
0 & 0 & 0 & 1 & 1
\end{array}
\qquad \mathbf{v}/\mathbf{u}
\end{array}
$$

and the new equality subgraph given in Figure 13.2. Note that edge $\{5, 4'\}$ was removed from and edge $\{2, 2'\}$ was added to the new equality subgraph.

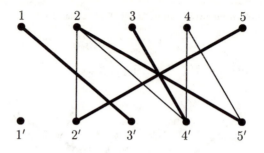

Fig. 13.2 Second equality subgraph

Now the δ_j are changed in step (29) as follows:

$$\begin{array}{ccccc} 1 & 0 & 1 & 0 & 0 \\ 3 & 2 & 4 & 4 & 4. \end{array}$$

Then $X = \{2'\}$ and as $2'$ is not exposed and mate$(2') = 5$, vertex 5 is inserted into Q. We get with $i = 5$:

$$\begin{array}{ccccc} 1 & 0 & 1 & 0 & 0 \\ 3 & 2 & 4 & 4 & 4. \end{array}$$

Again, $Q = \emptyset$. This time, the feasible node weighting $(\mathbf{u}, \mathbf{v})$ is changed to (where $J = \{2, 3, 4, 5\}$, $K = \{2', 4', 5'\}$ and $\delta = 1$)

$$\begin{pmatrix} 3 & 8 & \mathbf{9} & 1 & 6 \\ 1 & 4 & 1 & 5 & \mathbf{5} \\ \mathbf{7} & 2 & 7 & 9 & 2 \\ 3 & 1 & 6 & \mathbf{8} & 8 \\ 2 & \mathbf{6} & 3 & 6 & 2 \end{pmatrix} \quad \begin{array}{c} 9 \\ 3 \\ 7 \\ 6 \\ 5 \end{array}$$

$$\begin{array}{ccccc} 0 & 1 & 0 & 2 & 2 \end{array} \quad \mathbf{v}/\mathbf{u}.$$

The new equality subgraph is shown in Figure 13.3; this time, three edges have been added and none removed. Figure 13.3 also shows the final perfect matching.

The δ_j are then changed to

$$\begin{array}{ccccc} 0 & 0 & 0 & 0 & 0 \\ 3 & 2 & 4 & 4 & 4. \end{array}$$

Now we have $X = \{1', 3'\}$, and as vertex $1'$ is exposed, the matching can be extended. With $p(1) = 3$, mate$(3) = 4'$, $p(4) = 4$ and mate$(4) = 0$ we obtain the optimal matching $\{\{1, 3'\}, \{2, 5'\}, \{3, 1'\}, \{4, 4'\}, \{5, 2'\}\}$. The corresponding entries are printed bold in the above matrix. The sum of the weights of this matching is 35, which is – as it should be – equal to $\sum (u_i + v_i)$ for the feasible node weighting $(\mathbf{u}, \mathbf{v})$ given there.

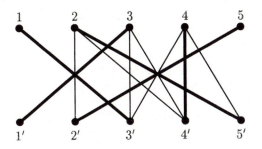

Fig. 13.3 Third equality subgraph with perfect matching

Exercise 13.2.6. Determine an optimal matching of $K_{9,9}$ with respect to the following weight matrix

$$\begin{pmatrix} 0 & 31 & 24 & 80 & 62 & 39 & 24 & 41 & 42 \\ 31 & 0 & 0 & 34 & 54 & 5 & 51 & 45 & 61 \\ 24 & 0 & 0 & 31 & 32 & 59 & 28 & 44 & 25 \\ 80 & 34 & 31 & 0 & 65 & 45 & 25 & 44 & 47 \\ 62 & 54 & 32 & 65 & 0 & 38 & 48 & 66 & 68 \\ 39 & 5 & 59 & 45 & 38 & 0 & 8 & 25 & 18 \\ 24 & 51 & 28 & 25 & 48 & 8 & 0 & 71 & 66 \\ 41 & 45 & 44 & 44 & 66 & 25 & 71 & 0 & 69 \\ 42 & 61 & 25 & 47 & 68 & 18 & 66 & 69 & 0 \end{pmatrix}$$

(Hint: Even though the matrix is quite big, the algorithm works rather fast. The first four phases are almost trivial.)

Analyzing Algorithm 13.2.3 again, the reader might realize that the proof works even for non-negative weights from an arbitrarily ordered abelian group. (This remark seems to be due to Lüneburg.) Recall that an abelian group G is called *ordered* if there is a partial ordering $\leq$ defined on its underlying set such that

$$x \leq y \qquad \Longleftrightarrow \qquad x + z \leq y + z$$

holds for all $x, y, z \in G$. As, for example, $(\mathbb{R}^+, \cdot)$ is ordered, Algorithm 13.2.3 can also be used (for weights ≥ 1) to determine a matching for which the product of the weights is maximal. More generally, the 'Algebraic Assignment Problem' is the problem of finding a perfect matching of maximal (or minimal) weight where the weights come from an ordered commutative monoid (compare Section 3.10). For this problem, we refer to Zimmermann (1981) and to Burkard, Hahn and Zimmermann (1977).

Exercise 13.2.7. Show that the Bottleneck Assignment Problem (see Example 7.4.10) is a special case of the Algebraic Assignment Problem. (We refer to Lawler (1976), §5.7 and to Gabow and Tarjan (1988) for the Bottleneck Assignment Problem.)

Exercise 13.2.8. Determine a *product-optimal* matching for the graph $K_{5,5}$ with respect to the weight matrix of Example 13.2.5, that is, a perfect matching for which the product of its weights is maximal. (Hint: Apply the Hungarian Algorithm within the group $(\mathbb{Q}^+, \cdot)$. Note that the 'zero' of this group is 1 and that the 'positive' elements of this group are the numbers ≥ 1.)

Exercise 13.2.9. Consider the problem of finding a product-optimal matching of $K_{n,n}$ with respect to a weight matrix all of whose entries are positive integers. Show that this problem is equivalent to determining an optimal matching with respect to some other appropriate weight matrix. Would it be better in practice to use this transformation and then apply Algorithm 13.2.3 directly?

Exercise 13.2.10. Is every optimal matching also product-optimal?

13.3 Matchings, Linear Programs and Polytopes

The Hungarian Algorithm presented in the previous section is a very elegant and efficient technique for determining an optimal matching in a weighted bipartite graph; it is even good for being executed manually. And it has one more advantage: it allows to check the correctness of the result after execution; for this purpose, we only have to check at the end of the algorithm whether the vectors **u** and **v** are a feasible node weighting and the weight of the matching is equal to $\sum(u_i + v_i)$. If (and only if) this is the case, the matching is indeed optimal (see Lemma 13.2.2).

However, we did not give any motivation for considering feasible node weightings in the previous section. In fact, it is not pure coincidence that this technique works and moreover, that it allows such an easy check of the correctness of the result. To understand this, we have to appeal to the Theory of Linear Programming (although this is avoided as far as possible in this book). As mentioned earlier, this theory is absolutely necessary for a deeper treatment of Combinatorial Optimization. Therefore, we now make an excursion into Linear Programming, even though the material presented here will not be used much in the remainder of this book.

A *Linear Programming Problem*, or short *LP*, is an optimization problem of the following kind. We want to maximize (or minimize) a (linear) *objective function* with respect to some given side constraints which have the form of linear equalities or inequalities. Put into a formula, this looks as follows.

(LP) Maximize $x_1 c_1 + \ldots + x_n c_n$

subject to the constraints $a_{i1}x_1 + \ldots + a_{in}x_n \leq b_i$ $(i = 1, \ldots, m)$.

In most cases, the variables x_i have to satisfy $x_i \geq 0$ for $i = 1, \ldots, n$ as well. (Note that any equality can be substituted by two inequalities.) Writing $A = (a_{ij})$, $\mathbf{x} = (x_1, \ldots, x_n)$ and $\mathbf{c} = (c_1, \ldots, c_n)$, we get a shorter form of (LP):

$$(LP') \quad \text{Maximize } \mathbf{c}\mathbf{x}^T \text{ subject to } A\mathbf{x}^T \leq \mathbf{b}^T \text{ and } \mathbf{x} \geq \mathbf{0}.$$

For our purposes, A, $\mathbf{b}$ and $\mathbf{c}$ are integral, but we allow $\mathbf{x}$ to have real values. Indeed, the solutions of (LP) are in general not integral but rational. Adding the condition '$\mathbf{x}$ integral' to the LP, we get the corresponding *Integer Linear Programming Problem*, short *ILP*.[3] If we even require $\mathbf{x}$ to satisfy $x_i \in \{0, 1\}$ for $i = 1, \ldots, n$, we have a *zero-one linear program* or *ZOLP*. Most of the interesting problems of Combinatorial Optimization can be formulated as a ZOLP; this is true in particular for optimal matchings.

Example 13.3.1. Let $G = (V, E)$ be a complete bipartite graph with a non-negative weight function w. Then the optimal matchings of G are precisely the solutions of the following ZOLP:

$$\text{Maximize} \quad \sum_{e \in E} w(e)x_e$$

$$\text{subject to } x_e \geq 0 \text{ for all } e \in E \quad \text{and} \quad \sum_{e \in \delta(v)} x_e = 1 \quad \text{for all } v \in V,$$

where $\delta(v)$ denotes the set of edges incident with vertex v. An edge e is contained in the corresponding perfect matching if and only if $x_e = 1$. The inequalities above make sure that any solution $\mathbf{x}$ indeed corresponds to a perfect matching. In this case, the vectors $\mathbf{x}$ satisfying the constraints (that is, the *admissible* vectors) are the same for the ZOLP and the corresponding ILP. Using the incidence matrix A of G, we can write the ZOLP shorter as

---

[3] Note that the problem SAT treated in Section 2.7 can be considered as a special case of the problem ILP of Integer Linear Programming, see e.g. Papadimitriou and Steiglitz (1982), Chapter 13. This implies that ILP is NP-complete and therefore it is likely that it cannot be solved in polynomial time. However, the problem LP of Linear Programming is polynomial, as the Ellipsoid-Algorithm (which is useless for practical purposes) of Khachiyan (1979) shows; see also Papadimitriou and Steiglitz (1982), Chapter 7. A further polynomial algorithm for LP, which is of practical importance as well, is due to Karmarkar (1984). A nice presentation of the questions concerning complexity of LP (including a detailed description of the Algorithm of Karmarkar) can be found in Bazaraa, Jarvis and Sherali (1990); the reader will also find further references to the literature there. The original paper of Karmarkar entailed many studies and variations of his algorithm. The Algorithm of Karmarkar can be understood best in the context of Non-Linear Programming; a variation based on a 'barrier function' is described in Chapter 9.5 of Bazaraa, Sherali and Shetty (1993). A very good discussion of the so-called 'path-following methods' can be found in Gonzaga (1992) which includes a detailed reference list as well; we also recommend the first part of the monograph on 'interior point methods' edited by Terlaky (1996).

$$\text{Maximize } \mathbf{wx}^T \text{ subject to } Ax^T = \mathbf{1}^T \text{ and } \mathbf{x} \geq \mathbf{0}, \qquad (13.3)$$

where $\mathbf{x} = (x_e)_{e \in E}$.

Exercise 13.3.2. (a) Describe the problem of finding an optimal integral circulation on a network (G, b, c) as an ILP.
(b) Describe the problem of finding a maximal spanning tree for a network (G, w) as a ZOLP. Is this an interesting approach to the problem?

To be able to apply the Theory of Linear Programming, we have to transform the ILP of Example 13.3.1 into an ordinary LP. Some geometric considerations will be useful here. If the set of all admissible real vectors $\mathbf{x}$ (that is, those vectors in $\mathbb{R}^n$ which satisfy the inequalities of an LP) for a given LP is not empty, but bounded, then all these vectors form a *polytope* in $\mathbb{R}^n$, that is, the convex hull (see Section 7.4) of a finite number of vectors in $\mathbb{R}^n$. It is well-known that the solution of the LP then is a vector corresponding to a *vertex* of the polytope; here, the vertices of the polytope can be defined as those points for which some appropriate objective function takes its unique maximum over the polytope. It is now clear that the incidence vectors of perfect matchings K of G are vertices of the polytope in $\mathbb{R}^E$ defined by the inequalities (or equalities, respectively) given in Example 13.3.1. If all the vertices of the polytope corresponded to such matchings, then the ZOLP of Example 13.3.1 would be equivalent to the corresponding LP and could be solved – at least on principle – with one of the known algorithms for Linear Programs.[4] Fortunately, this is indeed the case, as the following result of Hoffman and Kruskal (1956) implies (see Papadimitriou and Steiglitz (1982), Theorem 13.1, for example).

Result 13.3.3. *Let A be an integral matrix. If A is totally unimodular, then the vertices of the polytope $\{\mathbf{x} : A\mathbf{x}^T = \mathbf{b}^T, \mathbf{x} \geq \mathbf{0}\}$ are integral for any integral vector $\mathbf{b}$.* □

As we may assume G to be bipartite, the incidence matrix A of G is totally unimodular by Exercise 4.2.12. Then Result 13.3.3 implies immediately that all vertices of the polytope defined by the LP of Example 13.3.1 are indeed integral (and therefore are incidence vectors of perfect matchings of G).

Theorem 13.3.4. *Let A be the incidence matrix of a complete bipartite graph G. Then $\mathbf{P} = \{\mathbf{x} : A\mathbf{x}^T = \mathbf{1}^T, \mathbf{x} \geq \mathbf{0}\}$ is a polytope whose vertices are precisely the incidence vectors of perfect matchings of G. Therefore, the optimal matchings are precisely those solutions of the LP described in Example 13.3.1 which correspond to vertices of $\mathbf{P}$ (for a given objective function).* □

---

[4] However, this is not a very efficient approach in practice because the LP considered is 'degenerate' to a high degree.

Theorem 13.3.4 is interesting, but it does not explain yet why the feasible node weightings of the previous section work so efficiently. For this purpose, we need the notion of 'duality'. For any Linear Program

$$(LP) \qquad \text{Maximize } \mathbf{cx}^T \text{ subject to } A\mathbf{x}^T \leq \mathbf{b}^T \text{ and } \mathbf{x} \geq \mathbf{0},$$

the *dual LP* is

$$(LPD) \qquad \text{Minimize } \mathbf{by}^T \text{ subject to } A^T\mathbf{y}^T \geq \mathbf{c}^T \text{ and } \mathbf{y} \geq \mathbf{0},$$

where $\mathbf{y} = (y_1, \ldots, y_m)$. Then the following theorem holds.

Result 13.3.5 (Strong Duality Theorem). *Let* $\mathbf{x}$ *be an admissible vector for (LP) and* $\mathbf{y}$ *an admissible vector for (LPD). Then* $\mathbf{cx}^T \leq \mathbf{by}^T$ *with equality if and only if* $\mathbf{x}$ *and* $\mathbf{y}$ *are (optimal) solutions of (LP) and (LPD), respectively.* □

Example 13.3.6. Consider the situation of Example 13.3.1. As w is non-negative, we may consider the LP

$$\text{Maximize } \mathbf{wx}^T \text{ subject to } A\mathbf{x}^T \leq \mathbf{1}^T \text{ and } \mathbf{x} \geq \mathbf{0} \qquad (13.4)$$

instead of the original LP given there (the LP (13.4) yields a polytope with integral vertices as well, see Papadimitriou and Steiglitz (1982), Theorem 13.2). The dual program then is

$$\text{Minimize } \mathbf{1y}^T \text{ subject to } A^T\mathbf{y}^T \geq \mathbf{w}^T \text{ and } \mathbf{y} \geq \mathbf{0}, \qquad (13.5)$$

where $\mathbf{y} = (y_v)_{v \in V}$. Using (for $G = K_{n,n}$) variables $u_1, \ldots, u_n$ and $v_1, \ldots, v_n$ (corresponding to the partition $V = S \cup T$ of the vertex set of G) instead of the y_v, (13.5) can be written as

$$\text{Minimize } \sum_{i=1}^n (u_i + v_i) \quad \text{subject to} \quad u_i, v_i \geq 0 \quad (i = 1, \ldots, n) \text{ and}$$
$$u_i + v_j \geq w_{i,j} \quad (i, j = 1, \ldots, n). \qquad (13.6)$$

We see that the admissible vectors $\mathbf{y}$ for the LP dual to (13.4) correspond precisely to the feasible node weightings $(\mathbf{u}, \mathbf{v})$ in $\mathbb{R}^n$. Result 13.3.5 yields that any (perfect) matching K of G and any feasible node weighting $(\mathbf{u}, \mathbf{v})$ satisfy the condition $\sum(u_i + v_i) \geq w(K)$ (Lemma 13.2.1) and that a matching is optimal if and only if equality holds (Lemma 13.2.2). Now we see why the basic idea of the Hungarian Algorithm works. We might also guess that the problem of finding optimal matchings in the non-bipartite case will be considerably harder, because the incidence matrix of G will not be totally unimodular any more (by Exercise 4.2.12), so that the approach using Linear Programming does not work as easily as before. This problem will be considered in the next section. Note that Network Flow Theory (and the theory of circulations, respectively) can be treated in a similar way (see Exercise 13.3.2), because the incidence matrix of a directed graph always is totally unimodular by Theorem 4.2.5. In particular, Lemma 6.1.2 and Theorem 6.1.6 (Max-Flow Min-Cut) can be derived from Result 13.3.5, see e.g. Papadimitriou and Steiglitz (1982), Section 6.1.

We hope that the material of this section has convinced the reader that the Theory of Linear Programming is well worth studying, even if one is interested mainly in algorithms concerning graph theoretical problems. (However, in my opinion, the first approach to Combinatorial Optimization should be via Graph Theory, because it is more intuitive.) We recommend the books of Papadimitriou and Steiglitz (1982), Chvátal (1983), Schrijver (1986) and Nemhauser and Wolsey (1988) for further study.

Let us close this section with some remarks. The Hungarian Algorithm shows that we can restrict our attention to feasible node weightings having integral entries. This is not pure coincidence, but comes from the fact that, if A is totally unimodular, so is A^T, so that the dual program (13.5) for the original program (13.4) of Example 13.3.6 also leads to a polytope with integral vertices. We saw that the Hungarian Algorithm calculates a solution of the linear program (13.4) and the solution of the dual program (13.5) simultaneously. Thus, the Hungarian Algorithm can be viewed as a special case of the 'Primal-Dual' Algorithm of Dantzig, Ford and Fulkerson (1956), which does the same for any linear program (LP) and its dual program (LPD); see Papadimitriou and Steiglitz (1982), for example. Moreover, the Algorithms of Dijkstra and of Ford and Fulkerson as well as the 'out-of-kilter'-Algorithm mentioned in Chapter 9 are special cases of the Primal-Dual Algorithm as well.

We state a result of Hoffman (1974) and Edmonds and Giles (1977) which shows that the vertices of a polytope are integral even under weaker conditions than the total unimodularity of the matrix A.

Result 13.3.7 (Total Dual Integrality Theorem). *If the dual program (LPD) has an (optimal) integral solution for every objective function* $\mathbf{c}$ *of (LP), then the polytope* $\mathbf{P} = \{\mathbf{x} : A\mathbf{x}^T \leq \mathbf{b}^T, \mathbf{x}^T \geq \mathbf{0}\}$ *has integral vertices.*
$\square$

Linear programs having the property described in Result 13.3.7 are called *totally dual integral*. Finally, we refer the reader to four interesting surveys which treat the questions considered in this section more thoroughly, namely Hoffman (1979) (for the role of unimodularity in combinatorial applications of linear inequalities), Lovász (1979) (about integral programs in Graph Theory), and Edmonds and Giles (1984) and Schrijver (1984) about total dual integrality.

13.4 The General Case

This section treats optimal matchings in arbitrary graphs and the corresponding Linear Programs without giving any proofs. Let $G = (V, E)$ be a complete graph K_{2n} with a non-negative weight function w.[5] As in Example 13.3.1, the optimal matchings of (G, w) are precisely the solutions of the integral linear program

$$\text{Maximize } \mathbf{wx}^T \text{ subject to } A\mathbf{x}^T = \mathbf{1}^T \text{ and } \mathbf{x} \geq \mathbf{0}, \qquad (13.7)$$

where $\mathbf{x} = (x_e)_{e \in E}$ and A is the incidence matrix of G. However, A is not totally unimodular by Exercise 4.2.12, so that the methods used in the previous section cannot be transferred immediately. Indeed, the linear program corresponding to (13.7) could have rational solutions; in other words, the corresponding polytope may have vertices which are not integral. A simple example is due to Edmonds (1967a).

Example 13.4.1. Consider the graph $G = K_6$ with the weights shown in Figure 13.4; edges which are not drawn have weight 0. It can be checked easily that the matching K of weight $w(M) = 18$ drawn bold in Figure 13.4 is optimal. On the other hand, the rational values for x_e shown in Figure 13.5 yield $\mathbf{wx}^T = 19$ (which is also the solution of the corresponding linear program).

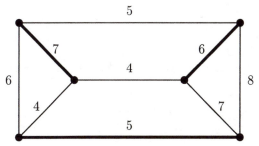

Fig. 13.4 An optimal matching

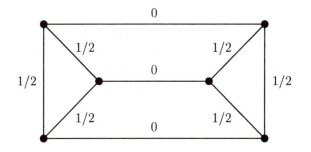

Fig. 13.5 A rational solution which is better

---

[5] It can be seen similar to Section 13.1 that determining a matching of maximal weight (as well as determining a perfect matching of maximal weight or a perfect matching of minimal weight) in a non-bipartite graph can be reduced to the problem of determining an optimal matching in a graph K_{2n}.

One possible way to avoid this unpleasant situation would be to cut off the non-integral vertices of the polytope $\mathbf{P}' := \{\mathbf{x} : A\mathbf{x}^T = \mathbf{1}^T, \mathbf{x} \geq \mathbf{0}\}$ by adding some further inequalities; this approach is common in Integral Linear Programming ('cutting plane algorithms'), see Papadimitriou and Steiglitz (1982), Chapter 14. Thus, we add appropriate inequalities until the system of linear inequalities corresponds to a polytope which is the convex hull of the incidence vectors of the perfect matchings of G, that is, of the solutions of the ILP (13.7) for an appropriate function w. The following result of Edmonds (1965a) shows how this approach works.

Result 13.4.2. *Let $G = (V, E)$ be a graph with an even number of vertices. Then the convex hull $P = P(G)$ of the incidence vectors of the perfect matchings of G is the polytope described by*

$$A\mathbf{x}^T = \mathbf{1}^T, \quad \mathbf{x} \geq \mathbf{0} \qquad and$$

$$\sum_{e \in E|S} x_e \leq \frac{|S|-1}{2} \text{ for any subset } S \text{ of } V \text{ of odd cardinality.}$$

$$(13.8)$$
$\square$

It is clear that the incidence vectors of perfect matchings satisfy (13.8). Result 13.4.2 states that any vector in $\mathbb{R}^E$ satisfying (13.8) is a convex combination of perfect matchings.

Corollary 13.4.3. *Let G be a complete graph K_{2n} with incidence matrix A. Then, for any non-negative weight function w, the linear program*

$$Maximize \ \mathbf{w}\mathbf{x}^T \ subject \ to \ (13.8) \qquad (13.9)$$

has an integral solution (and this solution is the incidence vector $\mathbf{x}$ of an optimal matching of (G, w)). $\square$

The proof Edmonds (1965a) gave for Result 13.4.2 is constructive (that is, algorithmical). Result 13.4.2 can also be derived from the following result of Cunningham and Marsh (1978) together with Result 13.3.7.

Result 13.4.4. *Let $G = (V, E)$ be a graph with incidence matrix A. Then the system of inequalities*

$$A\mathbf{x}^T \leq \mathbf{1}^T, \quad \mathbf{x} \geq \mathbf{0} \qquad and$$

$$\sum_{e \in E|S} x_e \leq \frac{|S|-1}{2} \text{ for any subset } S \text{ of } V \text{ of odd cardinality}$$

$$(13.10)$$

is totally dual integral. $\square$

This result was originally proved algorithmically as well. Short combinatorial proofs of Results 13.4.2 and 13.4.4 can be found in Schrijver (1983b) and Schrijver (1983a). It is now clear that we can – similar to the bipartite case – substitute the ILP (13.7) by the LP (13.9) and use an appropriate special version of the Primal-Dual Algorithm to solve it. In fact, the algorithms most frequently used in practice work with this approach. In particular, this is true for the first solution of the ILP (13.7) which was given by Edmonds (1965a); it has complexity $O(n^4)$. Gabow (1976) and Lawler (1976) showed that the complexity of this algorithm can be improved to $O(n^3)$. A different algorithm of complexity $O(n^3)$ was given by Cunningham and Marsh (1978). The fastest algorithms known for determining a matching of maximal weight in an arbitrary graph have complexity $O(|V||E| + |V|^2 \log|V|)$ (as in the bipartite case), see Gabow (1990). A further fast algorithm (which takes the maximal size of the weights into account) is due to Gabow and Tarjan (1991). An algorithm treating the (interesting) special case where the weight function on a graph K_{2n} is given by the distance of $2n$ vertices in a plane was given by Vaidya (1989); his algorithm has complexity $O(n^{5/2} (\log n)^4)$.

All the algorithms for determining an optimal matching in K_{2n} mentioned above are considerably more involved than the algorithms for the bipartite case. This is not surprising if we consider the additional inequalities needed in (13.8) for subsets of odd cardinality (and, associated with this, the possibility that blossoms occur). As it seems almost impossible to give a sufficient motivation for an algorithm which does not explicitly use the methods of Linear Programming, we do not treat any algorithm for the determination of optimal matchings in arbitrary graphs at all; this would exceed the scope of the present book. However, we state the following result for later use.

Result 13.4.5. *It is possible to determine an optimal matching in K_{2n} with respect to a given non-negative weight function w with complexity $O(n^3)$.* $\square$

For a proof of the above result, we refer to Lawler (1976) or Ball and Derigs (1983). In the book by Papadimitriou and Steiglitz (1982), a technique of complexity $O(n^4)$ is derived from the Primal-Dual Algorithm. An algorithm which does not use Linear Programming explicitly (and which is therefore less motivated) can be found in Gondran and Minoux (1984). Finally, we recommend the monograph by Derigs (1988).

We close this section with some remarks. The inequalities (13.10) define the 'matching-polytope' $\mathbf{K}(G)$ of the graph G, whereas (13.8) describes the 'perfect-matching-polytope' $\mathbf{P}(G)$. These polytopes are the convex hulls of the incidence vectors of the matchings (or the perfect matchings, respectively) of G. Now what would the *linear* span of these vectors in $\mathbb{R}^E$ be? This question is trivial for $\mathbf{K}(G)$: here, any edge alone forms a matching in G, so that the linear span is all of $\mathbb{R}^E$. However, this problem is interesting (and difficult) for $\mathbf{P}(G)$; a solution can be found in Edmonds, Lovász and Pulleyblank (1982). Lovász (1985) asked the question what the *lattice* generated by the incidence vectors of the perfect matchings in $\mathbb{Z}^E$ (that is, the set of integral linear combinations of these vectors) would be and derived interesting partial results. We give two exercises on this subject.

Exercise 13.4.6. Transfer Corollary 7.2.6 to regular bipartite multigraphs.

Exercise 13.4.7 (Lovász (1985)). Let G be a bipartite graph, $\mathbf{L}(G)$ the lattice in $\mathbb{Z}^E$ generated by the incidence vectors of the perfect matchings of G and $\mathbf{H}(G)$ the linear span of $\mathbf{L}(G)$ in $\mathbb{R}^E$. Show that $\mathbf{L}(G) = \mathbf{H}(G) \cap \mathbb{Z}^E$. (Hint: Use Exercise 13.4.6.)

The statement of Exercise 13.4.7 is not true for arbitrary graphs, as was shown by Lovász (1985); the Petersen graph is a counterexample. The general case is treated in Lovász (1987). Related problems can be found in Jungnickel and Leclerc (1988), Jungnickel and Leclerc (1989) and Rieder (1991), where the lattices corresponding to the '2-matchings' of a graph or to the bases of a matroid, respectively, are examined.

For some applications (where n is very large), even the fast algorithms for determining an optimal matching with complexity $O(n^3)$ mentioned above are not fast enough. If that is the case, approximation techniques are often used in practice. In general, these techniques do not find an optimal solution, but they have the advantage of being much faster. We refer the interested reader to Avis (1978), Avis (1983) and to Grigoriadis and Kalantari (1988). An interesting possibility (alternative to using heuristics) for large values of n is to use appropriate LP-relaxations, to solve minimal perfect matchings on appropriate sparse subgraphs or to use post-optimizations methods. We refer to Grötschel and Holland (1985) and to Derigs and Metz (1991), where the authors report that minimal perfect matchings for K_{1000} were found in 10 to 15 seconds (using an IBM 4361 machine). The best practical method at present seems to be the one of Applegate and Cook (1993).

13.5 The Chinese Postman

This section is devoted to an interesting application of the determination of optimal matchings in K_{2n}. The following problem is due to Kwan (1962); it concerns a postman, which is the reason why it is nowadays generally known as the 'Chinese Postman Problem' (CPP). A postman has to deliver the mail for a certain (connected) system of streets. Of course, he would like to choose his tour such that the total distance he has to walk is minimal.

Problem 13.5.1 (Chinese Postman Problem, CPP). Let $G = (V, E)$ be a connected graph and $w : E \to \mathbb{R}_0^+$ a length function on G. We want to find a closed walk C of minimal length $w(C)$ which contains each edge of G at least once.

If G is Eulerian, the solution of the problem is trivial: Any Euler tour C is a solution of CPP of weight $w(E)$. By Theorem 1.3.1, G is Eulerian if and only if each vertex of G has even degree and, by Example 2.5.2, an Euler tour C can then be constructed with complexity $O(|E|)$.

If G is not Eulerian, we use the following approach. Let X be the set of all vertices of G with odd degree. We add a set E' of edges to G such that the following three conditions are satisfied:

(a) Any edge e' of E' is parallel to some edge e in E; we extend w to E' by defining $w(e') := w(e)$.

(b) In $G' = (V, E')$, the vertices of odd degree are precisely the vertices in X.

(c) $w(E')$ is minimal (that is, $w(E') \leq w(E'')$ for any E'' satisfying (a) and (b)).

Then $(V, E \cup E')$ is an Eulerian multigraph containing an Euler tour C, and this Euler tour induces a closed walk of minimal length $w(E) + w(E')$ in G. It is quite obvious that any solution of CPP can be described in this way.

We state – rather informally – the Algorithm of Edmonds and Johnson (1993) for solving the CPP. Note that $|X|$ is even by Lemma 1.1.1.

Algorithm 13.5.2. Let $G = (V, E)$ be a connected graph with a length function $w : E \to \mathbb{R}_0^+$.

Procedure CPP $(G, w; C)$

(1) $X \leftarrow \{v \in V : \deg v \text{ is odd}\}$;

(2) Determine $d(x, y)$ for all $x, y \in X$;

(3) Let H be the complete graph on X with weight function $d(x, y)$. Determine a perfect matching K of minimal weight for (H, d).

(4) Determine a shortest path W_{xy} from x to y in G and, for each edge in W_{xy}, add a parallel edge to G (for all $xy \in K$). Let G' be the multigraph thus defined.

(5) Determine an Euler tour C' in G' and substitute each edge of C' which is not contained in G by the corresponding parallel edge in G. Let C be the closed walk thus defined in G.

Step (2) can be done by Algorithm 3.8.1; however, if $|X|$ is small, it might be better to execute Algorithm 3.6.6 of Dijkstra several times. Determining shortest paths explicitly in step (4) can be done easily by appropriate modifications of the algorithms already mentioned (see Exercise 3.8.3 and 3.6.3, respectively). For the worst case, steps (2) and (4) need a complexity of $O(|V|^3)$. Step (3) can be executed with complexity $O(|X|^3)$ by Result 13.4.5; note that determining a perfect matching of minimal weight is equivalent to determining an optimal matching for a different weight function (defined appropriately), see Section 13.1. Finally, step (5) has complexity $O(|E'|)$ by Example 2.5.2; this yields a total complexity of $O(|V|^3)$.

However, it remains to show that the algorithm works correctly. It is clear that the construction in step (4) adds, for any matching K of H, a set E' of edges to G which satisfies conditions (a) and (b) above, and that the closed walk in G we get by this construction has length $w(E) + d(K)$ (where $d(K)$ is the weight of K with respect to d). Therefore, it is reasonable to choose a matching K of minimal weight in step (3). However, it is not clear immediately that there cannot be some other set E' of edges leading to a solution of smaller weight (found by some other construction method). We need a lemma.

Lemma 13.5.3. *Let $G = (V, E)$ be a connected graph with length function $w : E \to \mathbb{R}_0^+$. Moreover, let H be the complete graph on a subset X of V of even cardinality; the edges of H are assigned weight $d(x, y)$ (that is, the distance between x and y in G with respect to w). Then, for any perfect matching K of H having minimal weight and for any subset E_0 of E for which any two vertices of X have the same distance in G and in (V, E_0), the inequality $d(K) \leq w(E_0)$ holds.*

Proof. Let K be a perfect matching with minimal weight in H, say $K = \{x_1 y_1, \ldots, x_n y_n\}$. Then $d(K) = d(x_1, y_1) + \ldots + d(x_n, y_n)$. Moreover, let W_i be a shortest path from x_i to y_i in (V, E_0) for $i = 1, \ldots, n$. Then, by hypothesis, $w(W_i) = d(x_i, y_i)$. We claim that no edge e with $w(e) \neq 0$ can be contained in more than one of the paths W_i; if we prove this claim, the assertion of the lemma follows. Suppose our claim were wrong, then we may assume w.l.o.g. that

$$W_1 = x_1 \xrightarrow{\ W_1'\ } u \xrightarrow{\ e\ } v \xrightarrow{\ W_1''\ } y_1 \quad \text{and} \quad W_2 = x_2 \xrightarrow{\ W_2'\ } u \xrightarrow{\ e\ } v \xrightarrow{\ W_2''\ } y_2,$$

which implies

$$
\begin{aligned}
d(x_1, y_1) + d(x_2, y_2) &= d(x_1, u) + w(e) + d(v, y_1) + d(x_2, u) + w(e) + d(v, y_2) \\
&> d(x_1, u) + d(u, x_2) + d(y_1, v) + d(v, y_2) \\
&\geq d(x_1, x_2) + d(y_1, y_2).
\end{aligned}
$$

But then substituting $x_1 y_1$ and $x_2 y_2$ by $x_1 x_2$ and $y_1 y_2$ in K would yield a perfect matching of smaller weight, a contradiction.   □

Theorem 13.5.4. *Algorithm 13.5.2 calculates a solution of the CPP with complexity $O(|V|^3)$.*

Proof. We have seen already that Algorithm 13.5.2 yields a closed walk of length $w(E) + d(K)$ containing each edge of G; here, $d(K)$ is the minimal weight of a perfect matching of (H, d). Conversely, suppose that E' is an arbitrary set of edges satisfying conditions (a) to (c). Then E' induces a closed walk of weight $w(E) + w(E')$ containing all edges of G. We have to show that $w(E') \geq d(K)$. Suppose Z is a connected component of (V, E')

containing at least two vertices. Then we must have $Z \cap X \neq \emptyset$, because otherwise, we could omit all edges of E' which are contained in Z and the remaining set of edges would still satisfy (a) and (b). As X is the set of vertices of (V, E') with odd degree, $|Z \cap X|$ has to be even by Lemma 1.1.1. Thus, the connected components of (V, E') induce a partition $X_1, \ldots, X_k$ of X into sets of even cardinality such that any two vertices in X_i are connected by a path in E'. Let $x, y \in X_i$ and W_{xy} the path from x to y in E'. Then W_{xy} must be a shortest path from x to y in G: otherwise, the edges of W_{xy} could be substituted by the edges of a shortest path from x to y and this would yield a set E'' of edges satisfying (a) and (b) and $w(E'') < w(E')$. Now, trivially, W_{xy} is also a shortest path from x to y in (V, E'). Denote the connected component of (V, E') corresponding to X_i by Z_i and let E'_i be the set of edges of E' which have both end vertices in Z_i. Moreover, let H_i be the complete graph on Z_i with weights $d(x, y)$ (where d is the distance function in G or in (Z_i, E'_i), respectively). Then, for any perfect matching K_i of minimal weight in H_i, Lemma 13.5.3 yields $d(K_i) \leq w(E'_i)$. Obviously, $K_1 \cup \ldots \cup K_k$ is a perfect matching of H, and $E' = E'_1 \cup \ldots \cup E'_k$. We get the desired inequality

$$w(E') = w(E'_1) + \ldots + w(E'_k) \geq d(K_1) + \ldots + d(K_k) \geq d(K).$$

$\square$

Example 13.5.5. Let G be the graph of Figure 13.6. Then $X = \{x, y, z, w\}$ and we get the complete graph H shown in Figure 13.7. The edges xw and yz form a perfect matching of minimal weight of H; the corresponding paths are (x, a, w) and (y, x, z). Substituting the corresponding edges in G by two parallel edges, we get the multigraph G' of Figure 13.8. Now it is easy to find an Euler tour in G', for example $(x, y, b, w, c, z, x, y, a, x, a, w, a, z, x)$ of length $30 + 4 = 34$.

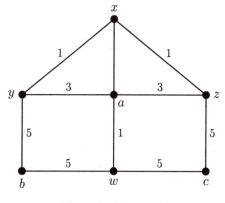

Fig. 13.6 A graph

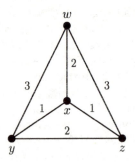

Fig. 13.7 The complete graph H

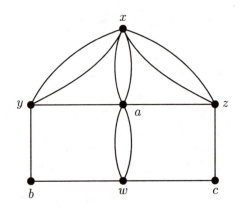

Fig. 13.8 The corresponding Eulerian multigraph

The following exercise treats the directed version of the CPP.

Exercise 13.5.6 (Edmonds and Johnson (1973)). Let G be a directed graph with a non-negative length function w. We want to find a directed closed walk of minimal length containing each edge of G at least once. (Hint: Reduce this problem to the problem of determining an optimal circulation.)

Theorem 13.5.4 and Exercise 13.5.6 (together with an appropriate algorithm for determining an optimal circulation) show that there are good algorithms for the CPP for directed graphs as well as for undirected graphs. In contrast, the CPP for mixed graphs is NP-complete, so that most likely there is no polynomial solution, see Papadimitriou (1976) or Garey and Johnson (1979), see Nobert and Picard (1996) for a cutting plane algorithm for the mixed CCP. Some applications of the CPP were discussed in Barahona (1990).

13.6 Matchings and Shortest Paths

We show in this section that the theory of matchings has interesting applications for the problem of determining shortest paths. In particular, it is possible to use matchings for finding shortest paths in a network on an (undirected) graph without cycles of negative length. We remind the reader that our usual transformation to the directed case (that is, substituting a graph G by its complete orientation $\overrightarrow{G}$) does not work here, because an edge $e = \{u, v\}$ of negative weight $w(e)$ in (G, w) would yield a directed cycle $u \relbar\joinrel\relbar v \relbar\joinrel\relbar u$ of negative length $2w(e)$ in $(\overrightarrow{G}, w)$; but the algorithms given in Chapter 3 require the graph not to contain such cycles. We describe a solution of this path problem below; it is due to Edmonds (1967a).

The first step is to transform the given problem to the problem of determining an f-factor in an appropriate auxiliary graph; this problem was already mentioned at the end of Section 12.5. In our case, the only values $f(v)$ will take are 1 and 2; however, the auxiliary graph might contain loops. A loop $\{v, v\}$ adds 2 to the degree $\deg(v)$ of a vertex v. From now on, we call a path from s to t an $\{s, t\}$-path.

Lemma 13.6.1. *Let $N = (G, w)$ be a network on a graph $G = (V, E)$ with respect to a weight function $w : E \to \mathbb{R}$, and let s and t be two vertices of G. Let G' be the graph which results from adding, for any vertex $v \neq s, t$, the loop $\{v, v\}$ to G. The weight function w is extended to G' by $w(v, v) = 0$. Then there is a one-to-one correspondence between $\{s, t\}$-paths in G and f-factors in G', where f is given by*

$$f(s) = f(t) = 1 \quad and \quad f(v) = 2 \text{ for all } v \neq s, t. \tag{13.11}$$

The weights of an $\{s, t\}$-path W and the corresponding f-factor F are equal. In particular, the problem of determining a shortest $\{s, t\}$-path in (G, w) is equivalent to determining a minimal f-factor in (G', w).

Proof. Suppose W is an $\{s, t\}$-path in G and put

$$F := W \cup \{\{v, v\} : v \text{ is not contained in } W\}.$$

Then it is easy to see that F is an f-factor for G', because the loop $\{v, v\}$ increases the degree of v in F to 2 if v has degree 0 in W (that is, v is not contained in W). Conversely, let F be an f-factor for G'. We look for an $\{s, t\}$-path W. Note that any vertex v for which $\{v, v\} \in F$ cannot be contained in W. As s has degree 1 in F, there is exactly one edge sv_1 in F. Now v_1 has degree 2 in F, so that there exists precisely one further edge in F incident with v_1, say $v_1 v_2$. Continuing in this manner, we construct the edge sequence of a path W with start vertex s in G. As the only other vertex of degree 1 in F is t, t must be the end vertex of W. It is clear by (13.11) that $w(F) = w(W)$. $\qquad\square$

Next we show how to reduce the determination of a (minimal) f-factor for the special case where $f(v) \in \{1, 2\}$ to the determination of a (minimal) perfect matching in an appropriate auxiliary graph whose size is polynomial in the size of the original graph. As already mentioned in Section 12.5, the general existence problem for arbitrary f-factors can be reduced to the general existence problem for perfect matchings, see Tutte (1954).

Lemma 13.6.2. *Let* $G = (V, E)$ *be a graph (where loops are allowed) and* $f : V \to \mathbb{N}$ *a function with* $f(v) \in \{1, 2\}$ *for all* $v \in V$. *Then the* f-*factors of* G *correspond to perfect matchings of an appropriate auxiliary graph* H *with at most* $5|E|$ *edges and at most* $2|V| + 2|E|$ *vertices. If there is a weight function* $w : E \to \mathbb{R}$ *on* G, *a weight function* w *on* H *can be defined in such a way that the weight* $w(F)$ *of an* f-*factor* F *is always equal to the weight* $w(K)$ *of the corresponding perfect matching.*

Proof. The desired transformation consists of two steps. First, the given f-factor problem for G is transformed to an equivalent problem for an auxiliary graph H'. In H', each edge is incident with at least one vertex v for which $f(v) = 1$. So let $e = uv \in E$ be an edge with $u \neq v$ and $f(u) = f(v) = 2$. We subdivide e by introducing two new vertices u_e, v_e and substitute edge e by the path

$$W_e = u \text{——} u_e \text{——} v_e \text{——} v.$$

Moreover, f is extended by the definition

$$f(u_e) := 1 =: f(v_e).$$

Executing this operation for all edges $e = uv$ with $f(u) = f(v) = 2$ and $u \neq v$, we get a graph H'. Now let F be an f-factor in G. Then F yields an f-factor F' in H' as follows: we substitute each edge $e = uv \in F$ with $f(u) = f(v) = 2$ and $u \neq v$ by the edges uu_e and vv_e and add for each edge $e = uv$ with $f(u) = f(v) = 2$ and $u \neq v$ which is not in F the edge $u_e v_e$ to F'. Conversely, any f-factor in H' corresponds to an f-factor in G. The weights of corresponding f-factors F and F' are equal if we define, for each edge $e = uv$ with $f(u) = f(v) = 2$ and $u \neq v$, the weights of the edges on W_e as

$$w(uu_e) := \frac{w(e)}{2} =: w(vv_e) \quad \text{and} \quad w(u_e v_e) := 0.$$

In the second step of the transformation, we define a graph H which results from H' by 'dividing' each vertex v with $f(v) = 2$ into two vertices. That means we substitute any vertex v of H' with $f(v) = 2$ (note that this can hold only for 'old' vertices, that is, vertices which were contained in G) by two vertices v' and v''; moreover, each edge incident with v (that is, each edge $e = uv$ with $u \neq v$) is substituted by two edges $e' = uv'$ and $e'' = uv''$. These operations, which yield the graph H, are well-defined because of the transformations performed in the first step (note that H' does not contain any edges $e = uv$ with $f(u) = f(v) = 2$ and $u \neq v$). Finally, any loop

$\{v, v\}$ with $f(v) = 2$ is substituted by the edge $v'v''$. It is now easy to see that the f-factors F' of H' correspond to the perfect matchings K of H. Note that at most one of the two 'parts' of a 'divided' edge $e = uv$ (with $f(v) = 2$) can be contained in a perfect matching K of H, because we must have $f(u) = 1$ in that case. However, this correspondence between f-factors and perfect matchings is not bijective in general: If F' contains two edges $e_1 = u_1v$ and $e_2 = u_2v$ (where $f(v) = 2$ and $f(u_1) = f(u_2) = 1$), K might contain either u_1v' and u_2v'' or u_1v'' and u_2v'. Thus, in general, there are several perfect matchings of H which correspond to the same f-factor of H'. It is clear, however, that the weights of corresponding f-factors and perfect matchings are equal if we define for 'divided' edges e' and e''

$$w(e') := w(e) =: w(e'').$$

$\square$

By executing the transformations of Lemmas 13.6.1 and 13.6.2 successively, we get the desired reduction of the determination of a shortest path between two vertices s and t in an (undirected) network (G, w) without cycles of negative length to the determination of a perfect matching of minimal weight in an appropriate auxiliary graph H (with respect to an appropriate weight function). As the number of vertices of H is linear in the number of vertices of G, Result 13.4.5 yields the following conclusion.

Result 13.6.3. *Let $G = (V, E)$ be a graph with a weight function $w : E \to \mathbb{R}$ and s and t two vertices of G. If the network $N = (G, w)$ does not contain any cycles of negative length, a shortest path from s to t in N can be determined with complexity $O(|V|^3)$.* $\square$

Example 13.6.4. Consider the network (G, w) of Figure 13.9. The path

$$W = s \text{---} c \text{---} b \text{---} t$$

of length $w(W) = 0$ (drawn bold in Figure 13.9) corresponds to the f-factor

$$F = \{\{a, a\}, sc, cb, bt\}$$

of weight $w(F) = 0$ in the graph G' of Figure 13.10. F is drawn bold there as well. Here, $f(a) = f(b) = f(c) = 2$ and $f(s) = f(t) = 1$.

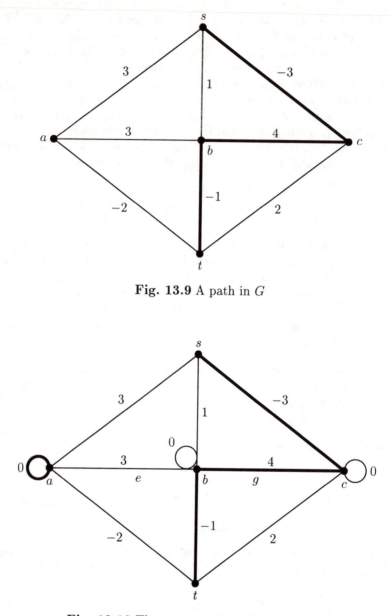

Fig. 13.9 A path in G

Fig. 13.10 The corresponding f-factor in G'

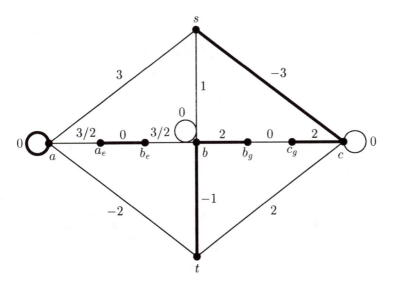

Fig. 13.11 The corresponding f-factor in H'

In the first step, that is, in the transformations of Lemma 13.6.2, where H' is constructed, the edges $e = ab$ and $g = bc$ are divided into paths of length 3. We obtain the auxiliary graph H' with the f-factor

$$F' = \{\{a, a\}, sc, cc_g, bb_g, bt, a_e b_e\}$$

corresponding to F; F' has weight $w(F') = 0$. Figure 13.11 shows H' and F', where F' is drawn bold. We have $f(a) = f(b) = f(c) = 2$ and $f(v) = 1$ for all other vertices v.

Finally, in the second step of the transformation, the three vertices a, b, c with $f(a) = f(b) = f(c) = 2$ are divided into two vertices. This yields the graph H of Figure 13.12 and the perfect matching

$$K = \{aa', sc', c''c_g, b''b_g, b't, a_e b_e\}$$

(again drawn bold) of weight $w(K) = 0$ corresponding to the f-factor F'.

Exercise 13.6.5. Determine an $\{s, t\}$-path of shortest length as well as the corresponding f-factors and a corresponding perfect matching of minimal weight for the network of Example 13.6.4.

Exercise 13.6.6. Discuss the transformation method given above for the case that (G, w) contains cycles of negative length.

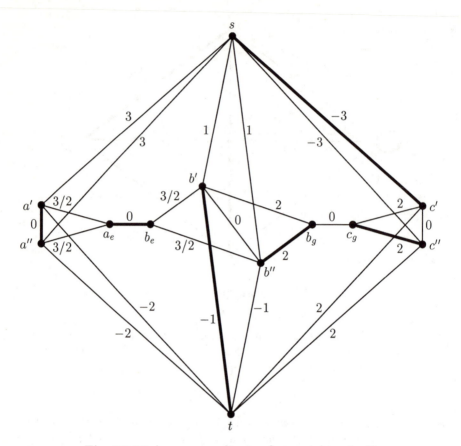

Fig. 13.12 A corresponding perfect matching in H

For a network (G, w) on a directed graph G which does not contain any directed cycles of negative length, the problem of determining a shortest directed path from s to t can be transformed to the problem of determining a perfect matching of minimal weight in a bipartite graph (that is, to the Assignment Problem). This result is due to Hoffman and Markowitz (1963); see also Ahuja, Magnanti and Orlin (1993), Chapter 12.7. As we presented two efficient algorithms for determining shortest paths in this case in Chapter 3 already, we do not present this transformation here. In practice, the converse approach is used quite often, that is, the Assignment Problem is solved using the SP-problem as an auxiliary procedure (without negative weights).

At the end of this section, we solve a further problem concerning shortest paths using the theory of matchings; this example is taken from the lecture notes of Grötschel (1985). Let $N = (G, w)$ be a network on a graph G, where w is a non-negative weight function. We call a path W in G *odd* if the number of edges W contains is odd (that is, W has odd length in the graph theoretical sense). We want to find a shortest odd path between two given vertices s and t. This problem can be reduced to determining a perfect matching of minimal weight in an appropriate auxiliary graph G' which results from G by 'dividing' vertices again. More precisely, each vertex $v \neq s, t$ of G is substituted by two vertices v' and v''. Moreover, for each such vertex, an edge $v'v''$ of weight $w(v'v'') := 0$ is added to E. Any edge sv or tv of G is substituted by an edge sv' or tv', respectively, and any edge uv with $u, v \neq s, t$ is replaced by two edges $u'v'$ and $u''v''$. Then we have the following result; the proof uses similar arguments as the proofs of Lemmas 13.6.1 and 13.6.2 and is left to the reader as an exercise.

Theorem 13.6.7. *Let $N = (G, w)$ be a network on a graph G with respect to a non-negative weight function w. Moreover, let s and t be two vertices of G and G' the auxiliary graph described above. Then the odd $\{s, t\}$-paths W in G correspond bijectively to the perfect matchings K in G' and the length of W is equal to the weight of the matching K corresponding to W under this bijection. In particular, the shortest odd $\{s, t\}$-paths correspond bijectively to the perfect matchings of minimal weight in G'.* □

Example 13.6.8. Let (G, w) be the network of Figure 13.13, where all edges $e \in E$ have weight $w(e) = 1$.

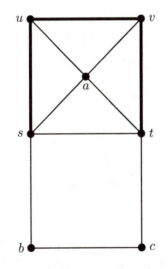

Fig. 13.13 A path of odd length in G

Then the $\{s, t\}$-path

$$W = s \longrightarrow u \longrightarrow v \longrightarrow t$$

(drawn bold in Figure 13.13) of length 3 corresponds to the perfect matching

$$K = \{su', u''v'', v't, a'a'', b'b'', c'c''\}$$

in the auxiliary graph G', see Figure 13.14.

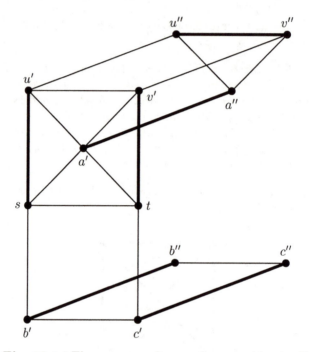

Fig. 13.14 The corresponding perfect matching in G'

Exercise 13.6.9. Find a transformation similar to the one used in Theorem 13.6.7 which allows to find a shortest even $\{s, t\}$-path in (G, w) and apply this transformation to Example 13.6.8.

13.7 Further Problems Concerning Matchings

In this final section of the present chapter, we briefly mention some further problems connected with matchings. First we look at problems with side constraints. Such problems occur in practice, for example, when planning the schedules for bus drivers, school time tables or even when analyzing bio-medical pictures, see Ball (1985), Even, Itai and Shamir (1976) and

Itai and Rodeh (1978). We restrict our attention to rather simple (or at least seemingly simple) types of side constraints.

Problem 13.7.1 (Restricted Perfect Matching, RPM). Let $G = (V, E)$ be a graph, $E_1, \ldots, E_k$ subsets of E and $b_1, \ldots, b_k$ positive integers. Does there exist a perfect matching M of G satisfying the conditions

$$|K \cap E_i| \leq b_i \quad \text{for} \quad i = 1, \ldots, k? \qquad (13.12)$$

(If we want to specify the number k of constraints, we also write RPMk.)

Exercise 13.7.2 (Itai and Rodeh (1978)). Show that RPM1 can be solved with complexity $O(|V|^3)$. (Hint: Reduce the problem to the determination of an optimal matching for the complete graph H on V for an appropriate weight function.)

In contrast to the result of Exercise 13.7.2, the general problem RPM (that is, without restrictions on k) is supposedly not solvable in polynomial time, because Itai, Rodeh and Tanimota (1978) proved that this problem is NP-complete. The following problem is very interesting in this context.

Problem 13.7.3 (Exact Perfect Matching, EPM). Let G be a graph, R a subset of the edge set E and b a positive integer. Does there exist a perfect matching M of G with $|K \cap R| = b$?

Exercise 13.7.4. Show that EPM is a special case of RPM2.

It is still unknown whether EPM (and RPM2, for that matter) has a polynomial solution. Barahona and Pulleyblank (1987) were able to show that the problem is polynomial at least for planar graphs; the algorithm they gave is based on a result of Kasteleyn (1967) which allows to determine the number of perfect matchings in a planar graph. However, Papadimitriou and Yannakakis (1982) conjectured that EPM is NP-complete for arbitrary graphs (that is, there is probably no efficient solution). A good survey of the questions mentioned here (and some special cases which can be solved efficiently) can be found in Leclerc (1986); more information about EPM and various other problems with side constraints is contained in Leclerc (1987).

Finally, we mention a further interesting optimality criterion for perfect matchings, namely *stable matchings*. In the bipartite case, the following nice interpretation is used quite often ('Stable Marriage Problem'). Suppose there are n women and n men. Each of these persons makes up a ranking list of the n persons of the other sex. We want to find a perfect matching (which may be interpreted as a series of marriages) such that there is no unmarried couple consisting of a man and a woman who would both prefer each other to the partners they are married to. Thus, in our formal model, we have a weight function w on the complete orientation of $K_{n,n}$ such that the n edges having vertex v as tail are assigned a permutation of the numbers $1, \ldots, n$ as weights. The perfect matching M we are looking for should have the following property. If xy is an edge not contained in M and xy' and $x'y$ are edges of M, then at least one of the inequalities $w(xy') < w(xy)$ and $w(x'y) < w(xy)$ holds. Gale and Shepley (1962) showed that, for any n and any w, such a stable matching exists; a 'good' solution can be determined with complexity $O(n^2)$, see Wilson (1972), Gusfield (1987) and Irving, Leather and Gusfield (1987). Determining the number of all solutions, however, is an NP-hard problem, see Irving and Leather (1986). The analogous problem for the complete graph K_{2n} (known as the 'stable roommates problem') is more difficult; for example, it cannot be solved for all choices of n and w. Irving (1985) gave an algorithm which decides with complexity $O(n^2)$ whether there exists a solution and, in that case, finds it, see also Gusfield (1988). We recommend the good monograph of Gusfield and Irving (1989) for further study of this type of problems; a nice recent exposition is due to Balinski and Ratier (1997).

14. A Hard Problem: The TSP

Up to now, we designed algorithms only for those optimization problems which allow an efficient (that is, polynomial) solution. This chapter is devoted to NP-complete problems; we use the Travelling Salesman Problem introduced in Chapter 1 and shown to be NP-complete in Chapter 2 as the standard example. We saw in Chapter 2 that NP-complete problems are a class of problems for which no good algorithms are known and it is quite likely even that no such algorithms exist. Now we consider the question how such 'hard' problems might be handled. Possible approaches include approximation techniques, heuristics, relaxations, post-optimization, local optimums, complete enumeration and several more. We explain all the techniques by using the TSP which can serve as a paradigm for a difficult problem.

At the end of this chapter, we briefly mention a very important approach to solving such problems, namely polyhedral combinatorics; going more into detail would exceed the limits of this book. Finally, we present a list of NP-complete problems which were mentioned throughout this book or are closely related to the subjects treated here.

14.1 The Problem

We remind the reader of the problem as it was posed in Section 1.4. We define the TSP formally as follows.

Problem 14.1.1 (Travelling Salesman Problem, TSP). Let $w : E \to \mathbb{R}^+$ be a weight function on the complete graph K_n. We want to find a cyclic permutation $(1, \pi(1), \ldots, \pi^{n-1}(1))$ of the vertex set $\{1, \ldots, n\}$ such that

$$w(\pi) := \sum_{i=1}^{n} w(\{i, \pi(i)\})$$

is minimal. We call any cyclic permutation π of $\{1, \ldots, n\}$ and the corresponding Hamiltonian cycle

$$1 \underline{\quad} \pi(1) \underline{\quad} \ldots \underline{\quad} \pi^{n-1}(1) \underline{\quad} 1$$

in K_n a *tour*; if $w(\pi)$ is minimal among all tours, π is called an *optimal tour*. The weights of the edges are – as in Section 1.4 – given in a matrix W.

We use the following example introduced in Section 1.4 to illustrate the various methods for finding a 'good' solution of the TSP, which are the subject of the present chapter.

Example 14.1.2. Determine an optimal tour for

	Aa	Ba	Be	Du	Fr	Ha	Mu	Nu	St
Aa	0	57	64	8	26	49	64	47	46
Ba	57	0	88	54	34	83	37	43	27
Be	64	88	0	57	56	29	60	44	63
Du	8	54	57	0	23	43	63	44	41
Fr	26	34	56	23	0	50	40	22	20
Ha	49	83	29	43	50	0	80	63	70
Mu	64	37	60	63	40	80	0	17	22
Nu	47	43	44	44	22	63	17	0	19
St	46	27	63	41	20	70	22	19	0

We saw in Theorem 2.7.5 that the TSP is NP-complete, so that we cannot expect to find an efficient algorithm for solving it. Nevertheless, this problem is important in practice and techniques for solving instances of considerable size are needed.

Indeed, there are diverse applications of the TSP which do not resemble the original 'travelling salesman' interpretation at all. For example, the machines in a production plant have to be prepared successively for n production processes. If $W = (w_{ij})$ is the matrix containing the setup costs, the problem of finding an ordering for the production processes such that the total setup cost is minimal can be interpreted as a TSP. Several further interesting applications can be found in Lenstra and Rinnooy Kan (1975) and in Lawler, Lenstra, Rinnooy Kan and Shmoys (1985), Chapter 2. A practical case study which demonstrates the relevance of approximation techniques for solving the TSP for some partial tasks in the production of computers and which is particularly interesting is contained in Grötschel, Jünger and Reinelt (1991). A further impressive example for applying the TSP in X-ray-cristallography (where dramatic savings in the amount of time a measuring process takes were achieved) is described in Bland and Shallcross (1989).

We will see that our above example is of a rather special structure because the weights satisfy the triangle inequality $w_{ik} \leq w_{ij} + w_{jk}$. Of course, this is true whenever the weights stand for distances in the plane or in a graph, or, more general, whenever W corresponds to a metric space (compare Section 3.2). However, the triangle inequality is not always necessarily satisfied. We use the following terminology.

Problem 14.1.3 (Metric Travelling Salesman Problem, ΔTSP). Let $W = (w_{ij})$ be a symmetric matrix describing a TSP. If W satisfies the triangle inequality

$$w_{ik} \leq w_{ij} + w_{jk} \qquad \text{for all} \quad i, j, k = 1, \ldots, n,$$

we call the TSP *metric*.

We will see in Section 14.3 that the general TSP and the metric TSP are quite different: For the metric TSP, there always exists a 'good' approximation algorithm, whereas this is most likely not the case for the general TSP. We mention some variations of the TSP.

Problem 14.1.4 (Asymmetric Travelling Salesman Problem, ATSP). Instead of K_n, we consider the complete directed graph $\overrightarrow{K}_n$ on n vertices, that is, we allow the weight matrix W to be non-symmetric (with entries 0 on the main diagonal). The *asymmetric* TSP contains the usual TSP as a special case and is therefore NP-hard as well.

Example 14.1.5. We drop the condition of Problem 14.1.1 that the travelling salesman should visit each city exactly once, so that we now consider not only Hamiltonian circuits, but any closed walk containing each vertex of K_n at least once. If the TSP considered is metric, an optimal tour is still an optimal solution. However, this is not true in general, as the example of Figure 14.1 shows.

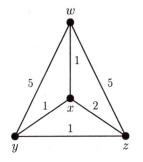

Fig. 14.1 A TSP for $n = 4$

In the above graph, (w, x, y, z, x, w) is a shortest closed walk (of length 6), but the shortest tour (w, x, y, z, w) has length 8. Now a matrix W not satisfying the triangle inequality can be considered as a matrix of lengths in K_n and be used to calculate the matrix $D = (d_{ij})$ of distances (this may be done, for example, with the Algorithm of Floyd and Warshall of Section 3.8). Then D defines a metric TSP and it is easy to see that the optimal closed walks (in the general sense) with respect to W correspond to the optimal tours with respect to D. Thus, the problem described here, although seemingly more general, is in fact just a special case of the metric TSP.

It is also possible to consider any arbitrary connected graph G with some length function w instead of K_n. Then it is not clear immediately whether a tour exists at all; we have to check first whether G is Hamiltonian. As we proved in Section 2.8, this problem (HC) is NP-complete as well.

14.2 Lower Bounds: Relaxations

In practice, it will often be necessary (especially if it is true that there is no polynomial algorithm for the TSP) to construct an approximate solution (which is as good as possible) instead of an optimal tour. For example, if we have a method to find a solution which is at most 2 % worse than the optimal tour, this will suffice for most practical applications (note that data – distances, for example – contain errors in measurement anyway). However, to be able to show that a solution is 'almost optimal', we need lower bounds for the length of a tour. Such bounds may be determined by *relaxation*: Instead of the original problem $\mathbf{P}$, we consider a problem $\mathbf{P}'$ containing $\mathbf{P}$ (which is obtained by weakening some of the conditions defining $\mathbf{P}$). Then, for minimization problems, the weight $w(\mathbf{P}')$ of an optimal solution for $\mathbf{P}'$ is a lower bound for the weight $w(\mathbf{P})$ of an optimal solution for $\mathbf{P}$. Of course, we want $w(\mathbf{P}')$ to be an approximation for $w(\mathbf{P})$ which is as good as possible; moreover, the problem $\mathbf{P}'$ should be solvable efficiently. It turns out that these two properties we want $\mathbf{P}'$ to have usually contradict each other. Moreover, for a lot of problems, it is often not possible to predict the quality of the approximation theoretically, so that we have to use empirical methods. We explain how relaxation works for some examples. Here, $\mathbf{P}$ is always a TSP on the complete graph K_n described by a weight matrix $W = (w_{ij})$.

A. The Assignment Relaxation

We use the Assignment Problem AP (see 7.4.11 and Chapter 13) for $\mathbf{P}'$, that is, we want to find a permutation π of $\{1, \ldots, n\}$ such that $w_{1,\pi(1)} + \ldots + w_{n,\pi(n)}$ is minimal. In particular, we have to examine all cyclic permutations π and, for these permutations, the sum above is equal to the length of the tour determined by π. Therefore, the TSP is indeed relaxable to AP. It is also comparatively easy to determine an optimal solution $w(\text{AP})$: the Hungarian Algorithm of Section 13.2 has complexity $O(n^3)$. Note that the Hungarian Algorithm determines a maximal weighted matching, whereas we want to find a perfect matching of minimal weight for $K_{n,n}$ (with respect to W); the necessary transformation of one problem to the other was described in Section 13.1. Moreover, we cannot use the matrix W as it is, because the entries $w_{ii} = 0$ would yield the identity as an optimal solution (and $w(\text{AP}) = 0$). As we are not interested in permutations with fixed points for the TSP, we set $w_{ii} = \infty$ for all i. In practice, this is done by using a number M (instead of

∞) which is sufficiently large, for example $M = \max \{w_{ij} : i, j = 1, \ldots, n\}$. This modification makes sure that an optimal solution of AP is a permutation without fixed points. If, by coincidence, we get a cyclic permutation as the optimal solution of AP, this permutation is a solution of the TSP as well. However, in general, there is no reason why an optimal solution of AP should be a cyclic permutation. Nevertheless, $w(\text{AP})$ is quite a good approximation for $w(\text{TSP})$ in practice. Balas and Toth considered random instances for values of n between 40 and 100 and got an average of 82 % of $w(\text{TSP})$ for $w(\text{AP})$ (see Lawler, Lenstra, Rinnooy Kan and Shmoys (1985), Ch. 10). That the assignment relaxation has such good approximation properties may be explained by the fact that the cyclic permutations form quite a big part of all permutations without fixed points. The number of permutations without fixed points in S_n is about $n!/e$ (see Hall (1986), for example), so that there is about one cyclic permutation among n/e fixed point free permutations. However, it turns out that $w(\text{AP})$ is not such a good bound for Example 14.1.2.

Example 14.2.1. Consider the TSP of Example 14.1.2, where we replace the diagonal entries 0 in W by 88 (the maximum of the w_{ij}) to get the matrix W' for an AP. To reduce this AP to the determination of a maximal weighted matching, we consider the matrix $W'' = (88 - w'_{ij})$ instead of W' (as described in Section 13.1) and apply the Hungarian Algorithm to W''. Then W'' is the matrix considered in Exercise 13.2.6. A maximal weighted matching has value 603 (see the solution of 13.2.6). Any optimal matching for W'' is a solution of the AP, so that $w(\text{AP})= 9 \times 88 - 603 = 189$. We get the bound $w(\text{TSP}) \geq 189$.

Exercise 14.2.2. Balas and Toth examined the assignment relaxation also for the ATSP and obtained, for 400 problems randomly chosen for n between 50 and 250, that $w(\text{AP})$ was on average 99, 2 % of $w(\text{ATSP})$. How might one explain that the approximation is much better in the asymmetric case?

B. The MST Relaxation

We use the problem MST of determining a minimal spanning tree of K_n (with respect to W) as $\mathbf{P}'$. Of course, a tour is not a tree, but if we omit any edge from a tour, we get a special spanning tree (namely a Hamiltonian path). Therefore, $w(\text{MST}) \leq w(\text{TSP})$. An optimal solution for MST can be determined using the Algorithm of Prim which has complexity $O(n^2)$ (Theorem 4.4.4). We will see later that this type of relaxation is rather good for the ΔTSP, whereas not much can be said for the general TSP; let us see how this relaxation works for our example.

Example 14.2.3. For the TSP of Example 14.1.2, we obtain the minimal spanning tree T shown in Figure 14.2 with $w(T) = 186$. This bound is a bit worse than the bound of Example 14.2.1, but determining a minimal spanning tree is also much easier than solving an AP. Moreover, something is lost by leaving out the weight of one of the edges of the tour. This disadvantage will be overcome with the next type of relaxation due to Held and Karp (1970).

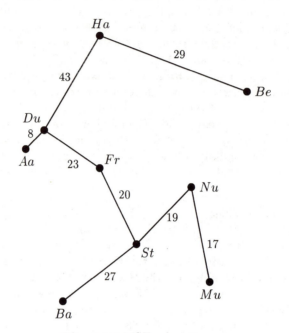

Fig. 14.2 MST relaxation

C. The 1-Tree Relaxation

Suppose we have to solve a TSP on K_n with vertex set $\{1, \ldots, n\}$. A 1-*tree* is a spanning tree on $\{2, \ldots, n\}$ together with two edges incident with vertex 1. Obviously, any tour is a special 1-tree, so that $w(\text{M1T}) \leq w(\text{TSP})$, where M1T denotes the problem of determining a minimal 1-tree. Note that it is easy to solve M1T by determining a minimal spanning tree for $\{2, \ldots, n\}$ and then adding those two edges incident with 1 which have smallest weight. This can be done with complexity $O(n^2)$ by Theorem 4.4.4. Of course, the result depends on the choice of vertex 1. It is also possible to solve a M1T for each of the n vertices, which yields a complexity of $O(n^3)$.

Example 14.2.4. We choose vertex Be of Example 14.1.2 as 1; this choice is motivated by the fact that the sum of the two smallest edge weights is maximal for this vertex. We obtain the 1-tree B of Figure 14.3 (which is the minimal spanning tree of Figure 14.2 with edge $BeNu$ added). It follows that $w(\text{TSP}) \geq w(B) = 186 + 44 = 230$.

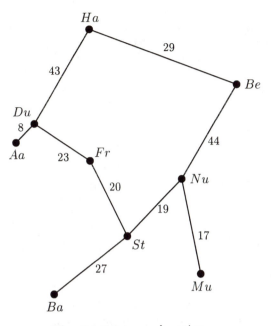

Fig. 14.3 1-tree relaxation

Exercise 14.2.5. Determine a minimal 1-tree for the TSP of Example 14.1.2 for the other possible choices of vertex 1.

Balas and Toth calculated the 1-tree relaxation as well during their examination of the assignment relaxation. On average, $w(\text{M1T})$ was only 63 % of $w(\text{TSP})$, which is much worse than $w(\text{AP})$. This can be explained by the fact that the number of 1-trees is much larger than the number of fixpoint-free permutations.

Exercise 14.2.6. Determine the number of 1-trees of K_n. (Hint: Recall Corollary 1.2.11.)

In the next subsection, we will see that 1-trees together with 'penalty-functions' yield much better results.

Exercise 14.2.7. For a vertex i, let $s(i)$ and $s'(i)$ denote the smallest and second smallest weight, respectively, of an edge incident with i. Show that $w(\text{TSP}) \geq \frac{1}{2} \sum (s(i) + s'(i))$ and calculate this bound for Example 14.1.2.

A variation of the 1-tree relaxation (where only those 1-trees are considered where the degree of the vertices in an independent set is fixed at value 2) was examined by Leclerc and Rendl (1989).

D. The LP Relaxation

For the sake of completeness, we mention the relationship of the TSP with Linear Programming. Analogous to Example 13.3.1, the assignment relaxation of the TSP can be described by the following ZOLP:

Minimize $\sum_{i,j=1}^{n} w_{ij}x_{ij}$ subject to $x_{ij} \in \{0,1\}$ as well as

$$\sum_{j=1}^{n} x_{ij} = 1 \quad \text{and} \quad \sum_{i=1}^{n} x_{ij} = 1.$$
(14.1)

Then the admissible matrices (x_{ij}) correspond precisely to the permutations in S_n. To restrict the possible solutions to tours, that is, to fixed point free cyclic permutations, we add the following inequalities ('subtour elimination constraints'):

$$\sum_{i,j \in S} x_{ij} \leq |S| - 1 \quad \text{for all} \quad S \subset \{1,\ldots,n\}.$$
(14.2)

The inequalities (14.2) indeed have the effect that the path corresponding to the permutation has to leave the subset S, so that no cycles of length $\neq n$ can occur. Let Q be the polytope defined by the admissible solutions of (14.1) and (14.2) (that is, by the tours among the (x_{ij})). In principle, it is possible to describe Q by a system of linear inequalities and solve the corresponding LP.[1] Unfortunately, the inequalities given in (14.1) and (14.2) do not suffice; we do not even know the whole set of necessary inequalities, although large classes (for example the 'clique tree inequalities') are known (see Lawler, Lenstra, Rinnooy Kan and Shmoys (1985), Ch.8 as well as Naddef (1990) and Balas and Fischetti (1993)). As there is an exponential number of inequalities even in (14.2) only, the system (14.1) together with some further (cleverly chosen) inequalities is used for LP relaxation in most cases. This means that, in general, a whole sequence of LP relaxations is solved and the inequalities which are added in the next step are chosen depending on the deficiencies of the solutions calculated before (values $\neq 0,1$ or subtours). The most successful algorithms for solving large instances of the TSP use this technique, see for example Lawler, Lenstra, Rinnooy Kan and Shmoys (1985), Ch. 9, as well as Grötschel and Holland (1991) and Padberg and Rinaldi (1987). Finally, we refer to Padberg and Sung (1991), where the quality of several formulations of the TSP as a linear program is examined.

---

[1] The polytope Q is the convex hull of the incidence vectors of tours and, therefore, its vertices are 0-1-vectors (by definition). Leaving out the restriction $x_{ij} \in \{0,1\}$, the inequalities (14.1) and (14.2) define a polytope Q' containing Q which has rational vertices as well. Thus, all vertices of Q' which are not 0-1-vectors have to be 'cut off' by appropriate further inequalities.

14.3 Lower Bounds: Subgradient Optimization

In this section, we show how the lower bounds obtained by 1-tree relaxation can be improved considerably by using so-called 'penalty-functions'. This method was introduced by Held and Karp (1970), Held and Karp (1971) and used successfully for solving large instances of the TSP. The basic idea is rather simple: We choose some vector $\mathbf{p} = (p_1, \ldots, p_n)$ in $\mathbb{R}^n$ and substitute the weights w_{ij} of the given TSP by transformed weights

$$w'_{ij} := w_{ij} + p_i + p_j \quad (i, j = 1, \ldots, n; \ i \neq j). \tag{14.3}$$

Denoting the weight of a tour π with respect to the w'_{ij} by $w'(\pi)$, we have

$$w'(\pi) = w(\pi) + 2(p_1 + \ldots + p_n) \quad \text{for any tour } \pi; \tag{14.4}$$

in particular, any tour which is optimal for W is also optimal for W'. On the other hand, the weight of a 1-tree cannot be transformed simply by adding the constant $2(p_1 + \ldots + p_n)$. In fact, if B is a 1-tree,

$$w'(B) = w(B) + (\deg_B(1)p_1 + \ldots + \deg_B(n)p_n). \tag{14.5}$$

Then the difference between the weight of some tour and the weight of some 1-tree (which we want to be as small as possible) is

$$w'(\pi) - w'(B) = (w(\pi) - w(B)) - ((\deg_B(1) - 2)p_1 + \ldots + (\deg_B(n) - 2)p_n). \tag{14.6}$$

Thus, if the term

$$d_B(\mathbf{p}) = (\deg_B(1) - 2)p_1 + \ldots + (\deg_B(n) - 2)p_n \tag{14.7}$$

is positive for all 1-trees, we can improve the lower bound $w(\text{M1T})$ of the 1-tree relaxation with respect to W if we determine a minimal 1-tree with respect to W', because the gap between $w(\text{TSP})$ and $w(\text{M1T})$ becomes smaller according to (14.6). We show below how this works for Example 14.1.2. Of course, it is not clear how such a vector $\mathbf{p}$ can be found (if one exists at all). We try the following simple strategy. Calculate a minimal 1-tree B_0 (with respect to W) and choose $p_i := c$ (where c is some positive constant) if vertex i has degree at least 3 in B_0 (that is, the degree of vertex i is too large compared to a tour) and $p_i := -c$ if i has degree 1 (that is, deg i is too small), and $p_i := 0$ otherwise. In other words, the non-zero coordinates of $\mathbf{p}$ are a kind of *penalty* for the vertices not having the right degree in B_0. Furthermore, we have to choose the value of c. It is possible to try $c = 1$; however, in our example, we just use the most advantageous value without explaining where it comes from.

Example 14.3.1. Let B_0 be the minimal 1-tree shown in Figure 14.3 (found in Example 14.2.4 for the TSP of Example 14.1.2). Then the degree of the vertices Aa, Ba and Mu is too small, whereas the degree of Du, Nu and St is too large. We choose $c = 3$ and get $\mathbf{p} = (-3, -3, 0, 3, 0, 0, -3, 3, 3)$. This yields the following transformed weight matrix W':

	Aa	Ba	Be	Du	Fr	Ha	Mu	Nu	St
Aa	0	51	61	8	23	46	58	47	46
Ba	51	0	85	54	31	80	31	43	27
Be	61	85	0	60	56	29	57	47	66
Du	8	54	60	0	26	46	63	50	47
Fr	23	31	56	26	0	50	37	25	23
Ha	46	80	29	46	50	0	77	66	73
Mu	58	31	57	63	37	77	0	17	22
Nu	47	43	47	50	25	66	17	0	25
St	46	27	66	47	23	73	22	25	0

We obtain the minimal 1-tree B_1 (with respect to W') of Figure 14.4 with $w'(B_1) = 242$.

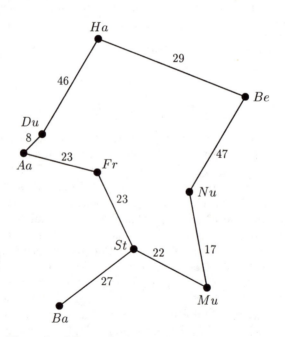

Fig. 14.4 Minimal 1-tree with respect to W'

Again, we chose vertex Be as 1. Instead of edge $DuHa$, we could also have used edge $AaHa$; then, we would have obtained a different minimal 1-tree in which vertices Aa and Du have degree $\neq 2$ as well. For that reason, we prefer the tree B_1 above. Note that the lengths of tours do not change for our choice of **p** because of (14.4). We have now improved the bound of Example 14.2.4 to $w(\text{TSP}) \geq 242$. The vertices of B_1 which do not have the correct degree 2 are Ba and St. We choose $c = 4$ and $\mathbf{p} = (0, -4, 0, 0, 0, 0, 0, 0, 4)$, which yields the following weight matrix W''.

	Aa	Ba	Be	Du	Fr	Ha	Mu	Nu	St
Aa	0	47	61	8	23	46	58	47	50
Ba	47	0	81	50	27	76	27	39	27
Be	61	81	0	60	56	29	57	47	70
Du	8	50	60	0	26	46	63	50	51
Fr	23	27	56	26	0	50	37	25	27
Ha	46	76	29	46	50	0	77	66	77
Mu	58	27	57	63	37	77	0	17	26
Nu	47	39	47	50	25	66	17	0	29
St	50	27	70	51	27	77	26	29	0

Using $Be = 1$ yields the minimal 1-tree B_2 (with respect to W'') of weight $w''(B_2) = 248$ shown in Figure 14.5.

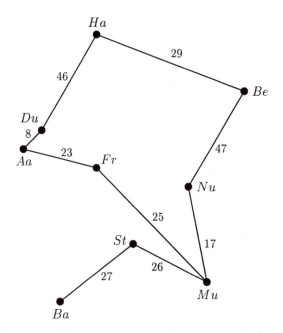

Fig. 14.5 Minimal 1-tree with respect to W''

Looking at the degrees, we see that it is better to use edge $BaSt$ and not one of the edges $BaMu$ or $BaFr$. Now Ba and Mu are the vertices having degree $\neq 2$ in B_2. We choose $c = 1$ and $\mathbf{p} = (0, -1, 0, 0, 0, 0, 1, 0, 0)$ and leave it to the reader to find the weight matrix W^* and convince himself that this yields the minimal 1-tree B_3 of weight $w^*(B_3) = 250$ shown in Figure 14.6. All tours still have the same weight with respect to w^* as they have with respect to w (because of (14.4)). As B_3 is a tour (all vertices have degree 2!), we have now (coincidentally) *solved* our TSP of Example 14.1.2 instead of just approximating a solution: The tour $(Aa, Du, Ha, Be, Nu, Mu, St, Ba, Fr, Aa)$ is optimal and $w(\text{TSP}) = 250$.

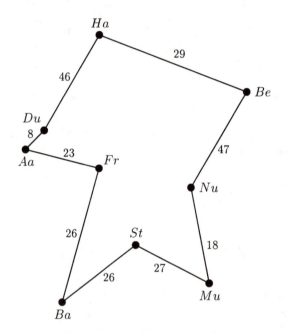

Fig. 14.6 Minimal 1-tree with respect to W^* ($=$ optimal tour)

In general, we have to choose the vector $\mathbf{p}$ as 'advantageous' as possible (maybe in several steps). As a tour which is optimal with respect to w is also optimal with respect to w' (where w' is defined as in (14.3)), we want to make the gap $d(\mathbf{p})$ between the length $w'(\text{TSP})$ of an optimal tour and the weight $w'(B)$ of a minimal 1-tree B as small as possible. (14.5) and (14.6) yield

$$d(\mathbf{p}) = w(\text{TSP}) - \min\ \{w(B) + d_B(\mathbf{p}) : B \text{ a 1-tree}\},$$

so that, if we want to minimize $d(\mathbf{p})$, we have to determine

$$(L) \qquad L(w) = \max\ \{\ \min\{w(B) + d_B(\mathbf{p}) : B \text{ a 1-tree}\} : \mathbf{p} \in \mathbb{R}^n\ \}.$$

In general, we will not end up with $L(w) = w(\text{TSP})$: it is very well possible that no choice of $\mathbf{p}$ yields a minimal 1-tree which is already a tour; an example for this situation can be found in Held and Karp (1970). But the lower bound for $w(\text{TSP})$ given by (L) is particularly good; Volgenant and Jonker (1982) report that the values of $L(w)$ are on average more than 99 % of $w(\text{TSP})$. An interesting theoretical examination of the Held-Karp technique can be found in Shmoys and Williamson (1990).

Of course, solving (L) is a much more complicated problem than the original 1-tree relaxation. There are various approaches to this problem; the vectors $\mathbf{p}$ are called *subgradients* here. These subgradients can be used for solving (L) recursively; this yields a technique (for an appropriate choice of the step widths c) which is sure to converge to $L(w)$. However, it is unpredictable how many steps will be needed, so that the process is often terminated in practice as soon as the improvement of the values is rather small. The problem (L) is a special case of a much more general method which is used quite often for problems of Integral Linear Programming, namely the so-called *Lagrange relaxation*; we refer to Shapiro (1979) and Fisher (1981). The *subgradient optimization* is one out of several possibilities to solve Lagrange relaxations; it is described in detail, together with other methods, in Shor (1985) (see also Held, Wolfe and Crowder (1974)).

Appropriate relaxations are very important for finding the optimal solution of a TSP, because they form an essential part of the 'branch-and-bound' techniques. We present an example for such a technique in Section 14.8. We refer to Volgenant and Jonker (1982) and to Chapter 10 of Lawler, Lenstra, Rinnooy Kan and Shmoys (1985). Further methods for finding lower bounds can be found in Carpaneto, Fischetti and Toth (1989), for example.

14.4 Algorithms for Approximation

The preceding two sections treated the problem of finding lower bounds for the length of an optimal tour, so that it is now natural to ask for upper bounds. It would be nice to have an algorithm (of small complexity, if possible) for constructing a tour which is always a good approximation of the optimal solution. We need a definition to be able to give a precise formulation of this task. Let $\mathbf{P}$ be an optimization problem and $\mathbf{A}$ an algorithm which calculates, for any instance E of $\mathbf{P}$, an admissible (but not necessarily optimal) solution. We denote the weights of an optimal solution and of the solution constructed by $\mathbf{A}$ by $w(E)$ and $w_{\mathbf{A}}(E)$, respectively. If the inequality

$$|w_{\mathbf{A}}(E) - w(E)| \le \varepsilon w(E) \tag{14.8}$$

holds for any instance E, we call $\mathbf{A}$ an *ε-approximative algorithm* for $\mathbf{P}$. Then a 1-approximative algorithm, for example (if such an algorithm exists), always yields a tour which is at most twice as long as an optimal tour. For a given NP-complete problem, we might now try to find at least a polynomial ε-approximative algorithm (for ε as small as possible). Unfortunately, this is often as difficult as solving the original problem. In particular, this is the case for the TSP, as the following result of Sahni and Gonzales (1976) shows.

Theorem 14.4.1. *If there exists an ε-approximative polynomial algorithm for the TSP, then $P = NP$.*

Proof. Suppose $\mathbf{A}$ is an ε-approximative algorithm for the TSP. We show that this implies that there exists a polynomial algorithm for determining a Hamiltonian cycle, so that the assertion follows from Theorem 2.7.4. The proof is similar to the proof of Theorem 2.7.5. Let $G = (V, E)$ be a connected graph; consider the complete graph K_V on V with weights

$$w_{ij} := \begin{cases} 1 & \text{for } ij \in E \\ 2 + \varepsilon|V| & \text{otherwise.} \end{cases}$$

If the algorithm $\mathbf{A}$ is able to determine a tour of weight $n := |V|$, then obviously G has a Hamiltonian cycle. Conversely, suppose that G contains a Hamiltonian cycle. Then the corresponding tour has weight n and is trivially optimal. As $\mathbf{A}$ is an ε-approximative algorithm, $\mathbf{A}$ yields a tour π of weight $w(\pi) \leq (1 + \varepsilon)n$. If this tour contained an edge $e \notin E$, it would have weight $w(\pi) \geq (n - 1) + (2 + \varepsilon n) = (1 + \varepsilon)n + 1$. Therefore, the tour determined by $\mathbf{A}$ induces a Hamiltonian cycle in G and has in fact weight n. Therefore, G has a Hamiltonian cycle if and only if $\mathbf{A}$ constructs a tour of weight n, so that there would be a polynomial algorithm for HC. $\square$

It is trivial that a statement analogous to Theorem 14.4.1 holds for the ATSP. However, the situation is much better for the metric TSP. We need some terminology. Let K_n be the complete graph on $V = \{1, \ldots, n\}$. Then any connected Eulerian multigraph on V is called a *spanning Eulerian multigraph* for K_n.

Lemma 14.4.2. *Let W be the weight matrix of a ΔTSP on K_n and G a spanning Eulerian multigraph for K_n. Then it is possible to construct a tour π with $w(\pi) \leq w(E)$ with complexity $O(|E|)$ (where E is the edge set of G).*

Proof. By Example 2.5.3, it is possible to determine an Euler tour K of G with complexity $O(|E|)$. Suppose $(i_1, P_1, i_2, P_2, \ldots, i_n, P_n, i_1)$ is the sequence of vertices corresponding to K, where $(i_1, \ldots, i_n)$ is a permutation of $\{1, \ldots, n\}$ and the $P_1, \ldots, P_n$ are (possibly empty) sequences on $\{1, \ldots, n\}$. Then $(i_1, \ldots, i_n, i_1)$ is a tour and

$$w(\pi) = \sum_{j=1}^{n} w_{i_j i_{j+1}} \leq w(E) \quad (\text{where } i_{n+1} := i_1)$$

holds because the sum of the weights of all edges in any path from x to y is always an upper bound for w_{xy} (using the triangle inequality), and each edge occurs exactly once in the Euler tour K. □

We now construct approximative algorithms for the metric TSP based on constructing spanning Eulerian multigraphs of small weight. The easiest method is to double the edges of a minimal spanning tree; this yields the following well-known algorithm.

Algorithm 14.4.3 (Tree Algorithm). Let $W = (w_{ij})$ be the weight matrix of a ΔTSP on K_n.

(1) Determine a minimal spanning tree T of K_n (with respect to W).
(2) Let G be the multigraph which results from doubling all edges of T.
(3) Determine an Euler tour K for G.
(4) Choose a tour contained in K.

Step (1) can be executed by the Algorithm of Prim in $O(n^2)$ steps (Theorem 4.4.4) and the procedure EULER of Chapter 2 can be used for step (3). Step (2) and step (4) (which is executed as sketched in the proof of Lemma 14.4.2) have complexity $O(n)$. By Lemma 14.4.2, we obtain a tour π of weight $w(\pi) \leq 2w(T)$; the MST relaxation of Section 14.2 shows that any tour has weight at least $w(T)$. Therefore, $w(\pi)$ is at most twice the weight of an optimal tour. Hence we have the following result:

Theorem 14.4.4. *Algorithm 14.4.3 is a 1-approximative algorithm of complexity* $O(n^2)$ *for* ΔTSP. □

Example 14.4.5. Consider Example 14.1.2 again. We saw in Example 14.2.3 that the MST relaxation yields a minimal spanning tree T of weight $w(T) = 186$ (see Figure 14.2). A possible Euler tour is

$$(Aa, Du, Ha, Be, Ha, Du, Fr, St, Ba, St, Nu, Mu, Nu, St, Fr, Du, Aa),$$

which contains the tour

$$(Aa, Du, Ha, Be, Fr, St, Ba, Nu, Mu, Aa)$$

of length 307 (see Figure 14.7).

Theorem 14.4.4 states that, in the above example, we obtain a tour of length ≤ 372, and it is just good luck that the solution was in fact much better. It is quite possible that Algorithm 14.4.3 constructs a tour whose weight is close to $2w(\text{TSP})$, see Chapter 5 in Lawler, Lenstra, Rinnooy Kan and Shmoys (1985), for example. The difference between the length of the tour of Example 14.4.5 and the optimal tour of Example 14.3.1 is less than 23 %. The following $\frac{1}{2}$-approximative algorithm, which is a bit more involved, is due to Christofides (1976).

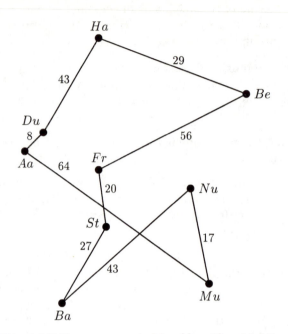

Fig. 14.7 Tour constructed by Algorithm 14.4.3

Algorithm 14.4.6 (Christofides Algorithm). Let $W = (w_{ij})$ be the weight matrix of a ΔTSP on K_n.

(1) Determine a minimal spanning tree T of K_n (with respect to W).
(2) Let X be the set of those vertices which have odd degree in T.
(3) Let H be the complete graph on X with the restriction of W as weight function. Determine a perfect matching K of minimal weight in H.
(4) Let G be the multigraph which results from adding the edges of K to T. Determine an Euler tour C of G.
(5) Choose a tour contained in C.

Theorem 14.4.7. *Algorithm 14.4.6 is a $\frac{1}{2}$-approximative algorithm of complexity $O(n^3)$ for ΔTSP.*

Proof. Besides the procedures used in Algorithm 14.4.3 already, Algorithm 14.4.6 has to determine a perfect matching of minimal weight. This can be done with complexity $O(n^3)$ by Result 13.4.5, so that the total complexity is $O(n^3)$. As G is Eulerian by Theorem 1.3.1, the inequality $w(\pi) \leq w(E) = w(T) + w(K)$ holds by Lemma 14.4.2 for the tour π determined in step (5). Thus, we have to find a bound for $w(K)$. Let $(i_1, i_2, \ldots, i_{2m})$ (where $|X| = 2m$) be the vertices of X in the order in which they occur in some optimal tour σ. Consider the matchings

$$K_1 := \{i_1 i_2, i_3 i_4, \ldots, i_{2m-1} i_{2m}\} \quad \text{and} \quad K_2 := \{i_2 i_3, i_4 i_5, \ldots, i_{2m} i_1\}$$

of H. The triangle inequality for W implies

$$\begin{aligned} w(\sigma) &\geq w_{i_1 i_2} + w_{i_2 i_3} + \ldots + w_{i_{2m-1} i_{2m}} + w_{i_{2m} i_1} \\ &= w(K_1) + w(K_2) \geq 2w(K), \end{aligned}$$

because K is a perfect matching of minimal weight. Thus,

$$w(K) \leq \frac{w(\text{TSP})}{2} \quad \text{as well as} \quad w(T) \leq w(\text{TSP})$$

(by the MST relaxation), so that $w(\pi) \leq \frac{3w(\text{TSP})}{2}$. □

Example 14.4.8. Consider again Example 14.1.2 and the minimal spanning tree T with weight $w(T) = 186$ of Example 14.2.3. The set of vertices of odd degree is $X = \{Aa, Be, Du, St, Ba, Mu\}$. We have to find a perfect matching of minimal weight with respect to the following matrix:

	Aa	Ba	Be	Du	Mu	St
Aa	–	57	64	8	64	46
Ba	57	–	88	54	37	27
Be	64	88	–	57	60	63
Du	8	54	57	–	63	41
Mu	64	37	60	63	–	22
St	46	27	63	41	22	–

By inspection, we obtain $K = \{AaDu, BeMu, BaSt\}$ of weight $w(K) = 95$. Adding the edges of K to T yields an Eulerian multigraph of weight 281 and the Euler tour

$$(Be, Mu, Nu, St, Ba, St, Fr, Du, Aa, Du, Ha, Be).$$

The tour $(Be, Mu, Nu, St, Ba, Fr, Du, Aa, Ha, Be)$ contained in this Euler tour has weight 266 (see Figure 14.8), which is only 6 % more than the optimal value of 250.

The bound of Theorem 14.4.7 is best possible: There are examples where the Christofides Algorithm constructs a tour π for which $\frac{w(\pi)}{w(\text{TSP})}$ is arbitrarily close to $\frac{3}{2}$; see Cornuejols and Nemhauser (1978). However, Theorem 14.4.7 shows that the MST relaxation is pretty good for the ΔTSP (as was mentioned in Section 14.2 already), because it always yields a tour of weight at most $3/2 \, w(\text{TSP})$.

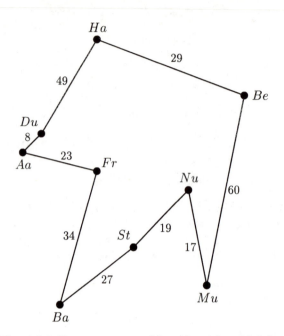

Fig. 14.8 Tour constructed by Algorithm 14.4.6

The Algorithm of Christofides is the best known approximative algorithm for the ΔTSP known so far. We do not know whether there exists an ε-approximative polynomial algorithm for the ΔTSP for some $\varepsilon < 1/2$. A priori, it is conceivable that such an algorithm exists for each $\varepsilon > 0$; such a family of algorithms is called an *approximation scheme*. However, P $\neq$ NP implies that there cannot be a *fully polynomial* approximation scheme for the ΔTSP, that is, a family of ε-approximative algorithms such that their complexity always is polynomial in n and $1/\varepsilon$; see Theorem 6 in Chapter 5 of Lawler, Lenstra, Rinnooy Kan and Shmoys (1985). A couple of years ago, Arora, Lund, Motwani, Sudan and Szegedy (1992) were able to show that, if P $\neq$ NP, there cannot be any approximation scheme for the ΔTSP. This result is true even if the only weights occurring are 1 and 2. Papadimitriou and Yannakakis (1993) gave a 1/6-approximative algorithm for this special case of the ΔTSP (which is of particular interest and occurs in the proof of Theorem 2.7.5). Some other important problems are even more difficult to handle than the ΔTSP. For example, the existence of a polynomial ε-approximative algorithm for determining a maximal clique (for some given $\varepsilon > 0$) implies already that P $=$ NP, see Arora and Safra (1992). For even stronger results in this direction, see Zuckerman (1996). These results use an interesting new idea from Theoretical Computer Science called 'transparent proofs', see Babai, Fortnow and Lund (1991) and Babai, Fortnow, Levin and Szegedy (1991), for example.

To close this section, we use the basic idea of Algorithm 14.4.3 to prove the simple bound for the ratio between the weight of a minimal Steiner tree and a minimal spanning tree which we mentioned in Section 4.6.

Theorem 14.4.9. *Let* $v_1, \ldots, v_n$ *be* n *points in the Euclidean plane. If* S *is a minimal Steiner tree and* T *a minimal spanning tree for these* n *points, then* $w(T) \leq 2w(S)$ *(where the weight of an edge* uv *is the Euclidean distance between* u *and* v *).*

Proof. Consider the ΔTSP on $V = \{v_1, \ldots, v_n\}$ for the Euclidean distance as weight function. As in Algorithm 14.4.3, we double the edges of a minimal Steiner tree S for $v_1, \ldots, v_n$ and determine an Euler tour K for the resulting Eulerian multigraph (V, E). As S contains the vertices $v_1, \ldots, v_n$ (and perhaps some Steiner points), it is possible to choose a tour π contained in K. Then it can be shown as in Lemma 14.4.2 that

$$w(\pi) \leq w(E) = 2w(S).$$

But this implies immediately

$$w(T) \leq w(\text{TSP}) \leq w(\pi) \leq 2w(S).$$

$\square$

Note that the proof of Theorem 14.4.9 (which is due to E.F. Moore, see Gilbert and Pollak (1968)) remains valid for the Steiner problem in an arbitrary metric space.

14.5 Upper Bounds: Heuristics

We saw in Theorem 14.4.1 that we cannot expect to find good approximative algorithms for the general TSP. Still, we want to solve some given TSP as well as possible. After having found lower bounds for $w(\text{TSP})$ in Sections 14.2 and 14.3, we now consider the problem of finding upper bounds. Of course, any tour yields an upper bound, but a tour chosen randomly cannot be expected to give a very good bound. Therefore, we are left with heuristics. These heuristics might (if P $\neq$ NP) produce rather bad bounds, too, but there is reason to hope for a useful result. We can also try to improve the tour constructed by heuristic methods; this problem is treated in the next section.

The so-called *insertion algorithms* are used quite often. Such an algorithm first chooses any city x_1 as a starting point for the tour to be constructed. Then a city x_2 is chosen – using some criterion still to be specified – and added to the partial tour constructed so far. We obtain a partial tour (x_1, x_2, x_1). This procedure is repeated until we have a tour $(x_1, \ldots, x_n, \ldots, x_1)$; the present tour of length k is extended to a tour of length $k + 1$ by adding one more city in the k-th step. The k-th step consists of two tasks:

(1) choosing the city to be added and
(2) finding the point of the partial tour where the city chosen in (1) is to be inserted.

There are various possibilities for the criterion which is used for choosing the city in (1): arbitrary choice, choose the city which has maximal (or minimal) distance to the cities already chosen, choose the city which is 'cheapest' to add, etc. We also have to fix a criterion for step (2); here, an obvious strategy is to insert the city at the point of the partial tour where this causes the least possible additional cost.

We describe an algorithm which works pretty well in practice, although there are no bounds known for its quality, not even for the metric case. In step (1), we always choose the city of maximal distance from the partial tour constructed so far. This might appear strange at first glance, but there is a good reason behind it: As all the cities have to appear in the tour anyway, it is best to plan the raw outline of the tour first by taking all those cities into account which are far apart. Afterwards, the cities which are 'nearer' are used to fix the details of the tour; this does not increase the cost that much any more. Thus, in step (1), we choose the city y which has maximal distance from the partial tour $(x_1, \ldots, x_k, \ldots, x_1)$, where the distance of y from the partial tour is defined as $d(y) = \min \{w_{y,x_1}, \ldots, w_{y,x_k}\}$. Then, in step (2), the city y chosen in (1) is inserted between two consecutive cities x_i and x_j (where indices are modulo k) in the partial tour such that the cost

$$c(i, j) = w_{x_i,y} + w_{y,x_j} - w_{x_i,x_j}$$

is minimal. In the following algorithm, distances are stored in an array denoted by d.

Algorithm 14.5.1 (Farthest Insertion). Let $W = (w_{ij})$ be the weight matrix of a TSP on K_n. Moreover, s is a vertex of K_n (the starting point of the tour T to be constructed).

Procedure FARIN $(W, s; T)$

(1) $T \leftarrow (s, s)$, $K \leftarrow \{ss\}$, $w \leftarrow 0$;
(2) **for** $u = 1$ **to** n **do** $d(u) \leftarrow w_{su}$ **od**;
(3) **for** $i = 1$ **to** $n - 1$ **do**
(4)   choose j with $d(j) = \max \{d(u) : u = 1, \ldots, n\}$;
(5)   **for** $e = xy \in K$ **do** $c(e) \leftarrow w_{xj} + w_{jy} - w_{xy}$ **od**;
(6)   choose an edge $f \in K$ with $c(f) = \min \{c(e) : e \in K\}$, say $f = uv$;
(7)   insert j between u and v in T;

(8) $K \leftarrow (K \backslash \{f\}) \cup \{uj, jv\}$, $w \leftarrow w + c(f)$, $d(j) \leftarrow 0$;
(9)   **for** $x \in \{1, \ldots, n\} \backslash T$ **do** $d(x) \leftarrow \min \{d(x), w_{jx}\}$
(10) **od**.

The following theorem is easy to prove.

Theorem 14.5.2. *Algorithm 14.5.1 constructs a tour T of weight $w(T) = w$ with complexity $O(n^2)$.* $\qquad\qquad\square$

Example 14.5.3. Consider again the TSP of Example 14.1.2; we choose vertex $s = Fr$ as starting point. We always state the distances in the form of a vector with 9 components (the distances to $Aa, \ldots, St$ in this order); first we have $(26, 34, 56, 23, 0, 50, 40, 22, 20)$. The vertex of maximal distance is Be with $d(Be) = 56$. Thus the partial tour for $i = 1$ is $T = (Fr, Be, Fr)$ of length 112. Now the distances in the next iteration are $(26, 34, 0, 23, 0, 29, 40, 22, 20)$; this yields $j = Mu$, $d(Mu) = 40$ and $T = (Fr, Be, Mu, Fr)$ with $w = 156$. For $i = 3$, the distances are $(26, 34, 0, 23, 0, 29, 0, 17, 20)$, so that $j = Ba$ and $T = (Fr, Be, Mu, Ba, Fr)$ of length $w = 187$. In the fourth iteration, $d = (26, 0, 0, 23, 0, 29, 0, 17, 20)$. Inserting $j = Ha$ at the 'point of least cost' yields $T = (Fr, Ha, Be, Mu, Ba, Fr)$ and $w = 210$. For $i = 5$, we obtain $(26, 0, 0, 23, 0, 0, 0, 17, 20)$, $j = Aa$ and $T = (Fr, Aa, Ha, Be, Mu, Ba, Fr)$ of length $w = 235$. The sixth iteration with distances $(0, 0, 0, 8, 0, 0, 0, 17, 20)$ yields $j = St$, $T = (Fr, Aa, Ha, Be, Mu, St, Ba, Fr)$ and $w = 247$. For $i = 7$, we have $j = Nu$ and $T = (Fr, Aa, Ha, Be, Nu, Mu, St, Ba, Fr)$ of length $w = 248$. Finally, $j = Du$ and the final tour

$$T = (Fr, Aa, Du, Ha, Be, Nu, Mu, St, Ba, Fr)$$

has length $w = 250$ (see Figure 14.9). This means that FARIN has found the optimal tour of Example 14.3.1 (see Figure 14.6).

Exercise 14.5.4 (Nearest Insertion). Consider the procedure NEARIN which results from replacing step (4) of Algorithm 14.5.1 by

(4')   choose j with $d(j) = \min \{d(u) : u = 1, \ldots, n, u \notin T\}$

and use it to calculate a tour for the TSP of Example 14.1.2.

Several insertion algorithms are examined in the paper by Rosenkrantz, Stearns and Lewis (1997). More results about heuristics (concerning subjects such as statements about the quality in the metric case, empirical results and probabilistic analysis) can be found in Chapters 5 to 7 of Lawler, Lenstra, Rinnooy Kan and Shmoys (1985).

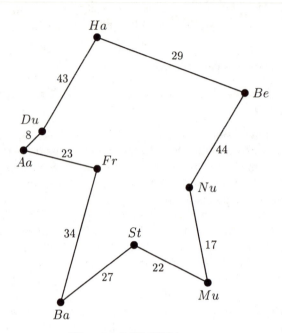

Fig. 14.9 FARIN-tour

14.6 Upper Bounds: Post-Optimization

Having chosen a tour (arbitrarily or by heuristics), the next step is to try to improve this tour if possible, that is, to use *post-optimization*. This means we consider sets of somehow 'adjacent' solutions and look for a 'local optimum'. More formally: Suppose **F** is the set of all admissible solutions for a given optimization problem (for the TSP, **F** is the set of all tours). A *neighbourhood* is a mapping $N : \mathbf{F} \to 2^{\mathbf{F}}$ which maps each $f \in \mathbf{F}$ to its 'neighbourhood' $N(f)$. We call a technique using the determination of local optima in neighbourhoods a *local search algorithm*. Lin (1965) proposed the following neighbourhoods for a TSP on K_n with weight matrix $W = (w_{ij})$. Let f be a tour and $k \in \{2, \ldots, n\}$. Then the neighbourhood $N_k(f)$ is the set of all tours g which can be obtained from f by removing k edges and then adding k (not necessarily distinct) edges again. The neighbourhood $N_k(f)$ is called the *k-change neighbourhood*. Any tour f which has minimal weight of all tours in its neighbourhood $N_k(f)$ is called *k-optimal*. We can now describe a class of local search algorithms for the TSP.

Algorithm 14.6.1 (k-Opt). Let $W = (w_{ij})$ be the weight matrix of a TSP on K_n.

(1) Choose an initial tour f.
(2) **while** there exists $g \in N_k(f)$ with $w(g) < w(f)$ **do**
(3)   choose $g \in N_k(f)$ with $w(g) < w(f)$;
(4) $f \leftarrow g$
(5) **od**.

Of course, this algorithm gives only a rough outline of what tasks have to be performed; it leaves several problems (including the concrete implementation) open. First, we have to decide how the initial tour should be chosen (arbitrarily or using one of the heuristics of Section 14.5). Also, there might be several possibilities for selecting a tour g in step (3); two standard strategies are to choose the first one encountered (*first improvement*) or a g of minimal weight in $N_k(f)$ (*steepest descent*). We could also execute the algorithm several times using different first tours; in that case, it makes sense to choose the initial tours randomly. The most important problem is how to fix the value of k. For large k (that is, larger neighbourhoods), the algorithm yields a better approximation, but the complexity will grow as well.[2] In practice, the value $k = 3$ proposed by Lin (1965) seems to work best. We restrict ourselves to the simpler case $k = 2$ and examine this case in detail.

Let f be a tour described by its set of edges $f = \{e_1, \ldots, e_n\}$, where

$$x_1 \xrightarrow{e_1} x_2 \xrightarrow{e_2} \ldots \xrightarrow{e_{n-1}} x_n \xrightarrow{e_n} x_1$$

is the corresponding Hamiltonian cycle. Then the tours g contained in $N_2(f)$ can be found as follows. Remove any two edges e_i and e_j from f and connect the resulting two paths by inserting two edges e_i' and e_j'. We are interested in the case $f \neq g$ only; note that e_i and e_j should not have a vertex in common, so that this determines e_i' and e_j' uniquely (see Figure 14.10).

Any neighbourhood $N_2(f)$ contains precisely $n(n-3)/2$ tours $g \neq f$. For any such tour g, we define

$$\delta(g) := w(f) - w(g) = w(e_i) + w(e_j) - w(e_i') - w(e_j'). \tag{14.9}$$

Then $\delta(g)$ is a measure for how much better the tour g is compared to the tour f. We set $\delta := \max \{\delta(g) : g \in N_2(f)\}$ and, if $\delta > 0$, replace f by some tour g with $\delta(g) = \delta$. Otherwise, that is, if $\delta \leq 0$, f is already 2-optimal and the algorithm 2-opt is terminated. As we choose g by 'steepest descent', each iteration has complexity $O(n^2)$; the number of iterations is unknown. With these specifications, Algorithm 14.6.1 becomes the following algorithm due to Croes (1958).

---

[2] Obviously, k-opt has – using 'steepest descent' – complexity $O(n^k)$ for each iteration of the **while**-loop; nothing can be said about the number of iterations needed.

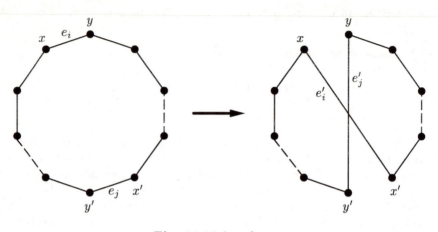

Fig. 14.10 2-exchange

Algorithm 14.6.2 (2-Opt). Let $W = (w_{ij})$ be the weight matrix of a TSP on K_n and suppose f is a tour with edge set $\{e_1, \ldots, e_n\}$.

Procedure 2-OPT $(W, f; f)$

(1) **repeat**
(2) $\delta \leftarrow 0, g \leftarrow f$;
(3)   **for** $h \in N_2(f)$ **do**
(4)   **if** $\delta(h) > \delta$ **then** $g \leftarrow h; \delta \leftarrow \delta(h)$ **fi**
(5)   **od**;
(6) $f \leftarrow g$;
(7) **until** $\delta = 0$.

Note that Algorithm 14.6.2 has to terminate with a 2-optimal tour g, because each time step (4) is executed (that is, the present tour is replaced by a better tour), the length of the present tour is decreased and this can obviously be done only a finite number of times. However, this does not mean at all that the solution the algorithm finds has to be optimal. It is possible that the algorithm gets stuck in a 'bad' neighbourhood. Therefore, it is common practice to execute 2-OPT (and other local search algorithms) several times for distinct initial tours.

Example 14.6.3. Consider again the TSP of Example 14.1.2 and choose the tour of weight 266 constructed by the Christofides-Algorithm in Example 14.4.8 for f (see Figure 14.8). During the first iteration of 2-OPT, the edges $BeMu$ and $NuSt$ are substituted by $BeNu$ and $MuSt$; this yields the tour $(Be, Nu, Mu, St, Ba, Fr, Du, Aa, Ha, Be)$ of length 253. The second iteration of 2-OPT exchanges edges $FrDu$ and $AaHa$ for $FrAa$ and $DuHa$. The resulting tour is the tour of length 250 shown in Figure 14.9 which was at that point found by the procedure FARIN; it is 2-optimal (and even optimal, as we know from Section 14.3).

Exercise 14.6.4. Apply 2-OPT to the tour of Example 14.4.5 (see Figure 14.7).

For faster execution, it might make sense to use the first tour g which is better than f in k-opt ('first improvement'). When solving a metric TSP, it make sense to consider not all possible substitutions of edges, but restrict the algorithm to edges being 'near by'. Or (1976) gave a variation of 3-opt which examines only a small portion of all possible edge substitutions, so that it needs much less time for execution, but still yields good results. The basic idea is to try first to insert three consecutive cities of f between two other cities; if this improves the tour, the corresponding substitution of edges is done immediately. If no more improvements can be achieved by using three consecutive cities, the algorithm continues by considering pairs of consecutive cities, and so on. A report about practical experiments with 2-OPT for large instances (up to a million cities) of the Euclidean TSP (where the distances are given by the Euclidean distance between n points in the plane) can be found in Bentley (1990).

An algorithm designed by Lin and Kernighan (1973) has proved to be very efficient in practice; however, this algorithm is also much more involved. It uses variable values for k and decides during each iteration how many edges are to be substituted. For this purpose, the algorithm contains a number of tests to check, after r edges have been substituted already, whether it makes sense to exchange a further edge (this is done until certain conditions are satisfied). However, there are examples for which the Lin-Kernighan-Algorithm needs exponentially many steps, see Papadimitriou (1992). Meanwhile, new heuristics have been proposed (for instance, 'threshold accepting', 'tabu search' and the 'great deluge algorithm'); they often yield results of surprising quality and use relatively little computer time, see Dueck and Scheuer (1990), Fiechter (1994) and Dueck (1993). The approach via genetic algorithms and evolution programs is interesting as well, see Chapter 10 in Michalewicz (1992) and the references given there, in particular Mühlenbein, Gorges-Schleuter and Krämer (1988). Unfortunately, it is impossible to prove any theoretic statements about the quality of these algorithms.

Thus, the general approach to the TSP consists of two steps: First, an initial tour is constructed using some heuristic (as in Section 14.5); insertion algorithms are usually used for this task. Second, a local search algorithm is used to improve the present tour. Simultaneously, lower bounds are calculated (using the Algorithm of Held and Karp of Section 14.3 or LP-relaxation) to be able to judge how good the approximation is. Even for large instances of several hundred cities, it is nowadays usually possible to reduce the gap between the solution found and the optimal value to 1 % or less. Of course, it is possible to construct degenerate examples for which the above techniques yield arbitrarily bad results, see Papadimitriou and Steiglitz (1978), but practical examples can be solved quite well. Golden and Stewart presented and analyzed a new composite heuristic in Chapter 7 of Lawler, Lenstra, Rinnooy Kan and Shmoys (1985) which seems to behave particularly well. Finally, we recommend the recent monograph on local search techniques edited by Aarts and Lenstra (1997).

14.7 Exact Neighbourhoods

We saw in the previous section how neighbourhoods are used for determining locally optimal solutions (for hard problems). Using this approach, we hope that the locally optimal solution (or the best of several of these) is pretty good globally as well; of course we would like it best if any local optimum were optimal for the whole problem already. This leads to the following definition: Let F be the set of admissible solutions of some optimization problem. A neighbourhood $N : F \to 2^F$ is called an *exact neighbourhood* if any locally optimal solution is already a global optimum. Our above experiences with the TSP suggest, however, that this idea is not very helpful for this problem. Before examining exact neighbourhoods for the TSP, we give an example for a (polynomial) problem where exact neighbourhoods are helpful, namely the determination of a minimal spanning tree.

Example 14.7.1. Let $G = (V, E)$ be a connected graph with weight function $w : E \to \mathbb{R}$. We define a neighbourhood N as follows. For a given spanning tree T of G, $N(T)$ consists of precisely those spanning trees T' which result from T by adding some edge e and then removing an edge (distinct from e) from the cycle $C_T(e)$ (see Section 4.3). The results of Section 4.3 imply that this neighbourhood is exact; it suffices to verify condition (4.1) of Theorem 4.3.1 for the (global) optimality of a given locally optimal tree T. If condition (4.1) is not satisfied, then it is possible to find an edge $e \in E \backslash T$ and an edge f in $C_T(e)$ such that $w(e) < w(f)$. Adding e and removing f from T then yields a tree $T' \in N(T)$ with $w(T') < w(T)$; this contradicts the local optimality of T. Note that this argument is just the first part of the proof of Theorem 4.3.1. Therefore, Theorem 4.3.1 may be interpreted as a proof for the fact that the neighbourhood N is exact. Note that the Algorithms of Kruskal and Prim of Section 4.4 work basically because this neighbourhood is exact.

Example 14.7.1 suggests the following strategy for solving optimization problems:

(1) Find an exact neighbourhood N.
(2) Find an efficient algorithm for examining $N(f)$ for any admissible solution f; that is, the algorithm should be able to recognize whether f is locally (and, therefore, also globally) optimal and, if this is not the case, improve f to a better solution f'.

Of course, it is not clear how good a search algorithm based on (1) and (2) would be, because in general it is unknown how many neighbourhoods $N(f)$ have to be examined until a (local) optimum is found. However, taking our experiences with the TSP into account, we would be satisfied already with an exact neighbourhood and a polynomial algorithm for examining this neighbourhood. (It can be shown that not even the huge neighbourhood N_{n-3} of Section 14.6 is exact.) But we will see that even this would only be possible if P = NP. The proof of this statement requires some effort. We begin by showing that the following problem is NP-complete.

Problem 14.7.2 (Restricted Hamiltonian Cycle, RHC). Let G be a graph with a Hamiltonian path. Does G contain a Hamiltonian cycle as well?

Even though this problem sounds somewhat simpler than HC, it is just as difficult: Knowing a Hamiltonian path does not help at all when searching for a Hamiltonian cycle, as the following result due to Papadimitriou and Steiglitz (1977) shows.

Theorem 14.7.3. *RHC is NP-complete.*

Proof. As HC is NP-complete by Theorem 2.7.4, it is sufficient to transform HC polynomially to RHC. To do this, we use the auxiliary graph D (for 'diamond') shown in Figure 14.11. Let $G = (V, E)$ be a connected graph. We substitute each vertex v of G by a diamond D_v and, by adding edges appropriately, construct a graph G' which always contains a Hamiltonian path and which contains a Hamiltonian cycle if and only if G has a Hamiltonian cycle. As G' has eight times the number of edges G has, this is a polynomial transformation of HC to RHC. We construct G' in such a way that each diamond D_v can only be accessed from $G' \backslash D_v$ by one of the vertices labelled as N, S, W and E in Figure 14.11.

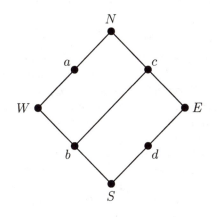

Fig. 14.11 a diamond D

We claim that any Hamiltonian cycle of G' has to pass through the diamond using one of the paths shown in Figure 14.12 (we call these two possibilities 'North-South'- and 'West-East'-method, respectively). Suppose K is a Hamiltonian cycle of G' accessing the diamond D_v at vertex N. Then K has to contain vertex a next (otherwise a would not be contained in K at all because deg $a = 2$). The next vertex of K is W and K cannot leave D_v in W, because otherwise either d or b and c would not be contained in K. Therefore, K contains b, c, E, d and S in this order; this yields the North-South-method. It can be seen analogously that a Hamiltonian cycle entering D_v in W can only pass through D_v by the West-East-method.

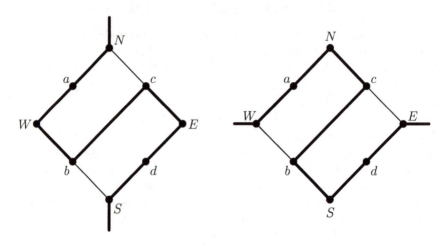

North-South-method   West-East-method

Fig. 14.12 Hamiltonian paths through D

We may assume w.l.o.g. $V = \{1, \dots, n\}$. Now the n copies D_v of D forming the vertex set of G' are connected by the following edges: $S_1 N_2, S_2 N_3, \dots, S_{n-1} N_n$. These edges make sure that G' contains a Hamiltonian path, namely the North-South method of D_1 followed by $S_1 N_2$, followed by the North-South-method of D_2, etc. (see Figure 14.13).

Moreover, G' contains, for each edge ij of G, the edges $W_i E_j$ and $W_j E_i$. Then, if G contains a Hamiltonian cycle K, G' contains a Hamiltonian cycle K' induced by K: The diamonds in G' are visited in the same order as K visits the vertices of G and each diamond is passed through using the West-East-method. Conversely, suppose that G' has a Hamiltonian cycle K'. Then K' cannot access any of the diamonds D_i in N_i or S_i, because otherwise K' would have to pass through all of the diamonds using the North-South-method.

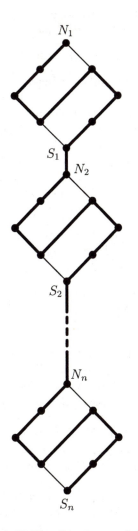

Fig. 14.13 Hamiltonian path for G'

This would yield the Hamiltonian path W of G' shown in Figure 14.13, but this path cannot be extended to a cycle because G' does not contain the edge $N_1 S_n$. Therefore, K' has to pass through all the diamonds by the West-East-method, so that K' obviously induces a Hamiltonian cycle K in G. □

We use Theorem 14.7.3 to show that the following problem is NP-complete as well; this result is likewise due to Papadimitriou and Steiglitz (1977).

Problem 14.7.4 (TSP Suboptimality). Suppose we are given a TSP and a tour. Is this tour suboptimal, that is, does there exist a shorter tour?

Theorem 14.7.5. *TSP Suboptimality is NP-complete.*

Proof. By Theorem 14.7.3, it is sufficient to transform the problem RHC to the problem TSP suboptimality. Let G be a graph on vertex set $V = \{1, \ldots, n\}$ and P a Hamiltonian path for G. Consider the TSP on K_n with weight matrix $W = (w_{ij})$ as in the proof of Theorem 2.7.5. Then the Hamiltonian path P can be extended to a tour π of length $w(\pi) \leq (n-1) + 2 = n + 1$; if we even have a tour of length n, then G contains a Hamiltonian cycle. On the other hand, G contains a Hamiltonian cycle if and only if the tour above is not optimal. Thus, if TSP suboptimality is solvable in polynomial time, then so is RHC. □

Corollary 14.7.6. *If there exists an exact neighbourhood N for the TSP such that there is a polynomial algorithm for deciding whether a given tour T is (locally) optimal, then $P = NP$.*

Proof. Such an algorithm would be able to decide TSP suboptimality in polynomial time. Thus, the statement follows from Theorem 14.7.5. □

Note that the statement of Corollary 14.7.6 is stronger than just the NP-completeness of the TSP. If P ≠ NP, then TSP is not solvable in polynomial time by Theorem 2.7.5, so that no algorithm basing on a polynomial local search process (for an exact neighbourhood) could yield a solution after a polynomial number of iterations. However, there still might be an exact neighbourhood and a polynomial algorithm which examines local optimality and, if possible, constructs a better tour, but which might need more than a polynomial number of iterations. Corollary 14.7.6 excludes even this possibility.

Thus, by Corollary 14.7.6, a neighbourhood for the TSP cannot be exact if it allows a polynomial algorithm for checking local optimality (always assuming that P ≠ NP). In particular, this is true for the neighbourhoods N_k (for fixed k), because they allow an algorithm of complexity $O(n^k)$. The following exercise shows that a local search algorithm based on a neighbourhood which can be examined in polynomial time cannot be ε-approximative (not even if we allow more than a polynomial number of iterations).

Exercise 14.7.7 (Papadimitriou and Steiglitz (1977)). Let N be a neighbourhood for the TSP which allows a polynomial algorithm **A** for examining whether a given tour is locally optimal. Moreover, let **A'** be the local search algorithm based on **A** (as in Section 14.6). Suppose that **A'** is ε-approximative for some appropriate ε. Show that this implies (without any conditions on the number of iterations) already that P = NP. (Hint: Show, as in Theorem 14.4.1, that otherwise HC would be solvable in polynomial time.

Why does $\mathbf{A}'$ need only a polynomial number of iterations for the instances of the TSP described there?)

Even though the above considerations show that we cannot expect to have any guarantee for the quality of the results of the algorithms described above (3-OPT, for example), these algorithms still work quite well in practice. The following exercise can be solved using similar methods.

Exercise 14.7.8. Show that the following problem is NP-complete: Decide whether a given edge ij occurs in an optimal tour (for some instance of the TSP).

14.8 Optimal Solutions: Branch and Bound

This section is devoted to the problem of finding optimal solutions of the TSP. All the known techniques basically amount to analyzing all possible solutions; this is not surprising because the TSP is an NP-complete problem. However, it is possible to find an optimal solution without too much effort by using some tricks (and hoping for some good luck). We use Example 14.1.2 again to illustrate this. The method we use is called *branch and bound*. In each step, the set of all possible solutions is split up into two or more subsets which are represented by branches in a decision tree. For the TSP, an obvious criterion for dividing all tours into subsets is whether they contain a given edge or not. But using a decision tree only makes sense if we calculate lower bounds for the weight of all solutions in the respective subtrees in each step (using an appropriate relaxation) and compare them with some known upper bound. Then, all the branches of the tree where the upper bound is smaller than the lower bound for this branch may be left out of further consideration, so that quite often a large number of tours can be excluded. Of course, the quality of this method depends on the relaxation and on the branching criteria used; it can only be judged heuristically.

We describe one of the oldest branch and bound techniques which is due to Little, Murty, Sweeney and Karel (1963). The algorithm was designed to treat the ATSP, but, of course, it also works for the special case of the TSP. It is not particularly efficient, but easy to understand and to illustrate. Our purpose is to show how branch and bound algorithms work in principle; we refer the reader to Chapter 10 of Lawler, Lenstra, Rinnooy Kan and Shmoys (1985) for a survey of the more recent versions which work with more complicated relaxations and branching criteria. The name 'branch and bound' originates from the paper of Little, Murty, Sweeney and Karel above.

Let $W = (w_{ij})$ be the weight matrix of a given TSP on K_n. We choose the diagonal entries w_{ii} as ∞ (as we did for the assignment relaxation); this can be interpreted as forbidding to use the loops ii. For calculating the lower bounds, we transform the weight matrix similar to what we did in Section 14.3. For some given row (or column) of W, we subtract some positive number d from all the entries such that the resulting matrix W' still has all entries non-negative. Considering tours as Hamiltonian cycles (or as permutations), each tour corresponds to a diagonal of the matrix W (we saw this already when we treated the assignment relaxation). Therefore, any tour has to contain some entry of the respective row (or column) and has smaller weight with respect to W' than it has with respect to W. In particular, the optimal tours for W are the same as for W'. We continue this process until we get a matrix W'' having at least one entry 0 in each row and each column; such a matrix is called *reduced*. Using induction, it follows that the optimal tours for W are the same as for W'' and that the weight of each tour is s units smaller with respect to W'' than it is with respect to W (where s is the sum of all the numbers subtracted during the construction of W''). Therefore, s has to be a lower bound for the weight of all tours (with respect to W). Note that the weight matrices resulting from the above construction are not symmetric any more (in contrast to the transformations used in Section 14.3).

Consider the TSP of 14.1.2 again. Substituting the diagonal entries 0 by ∞ and subtracting, for each row of the matrix, the minimum of the entries of this row, we get the following matrix.

	Aa	Ba	Be	Du	Fr	Ha	Mu	Nu	St
Aa	0	49	56	0	18	41	56	39	38
Ba	30	∞	61	27	7	56	10	16	0
Be	35	59	∞	28	27	0	31	15	34
Du	0	46	49	∞	15	35	55	36	33
Fr	6	14	36	3	∞	30	20	2	0
Ha	20	54	0	14	21	∞	51	34	41
Mu	47	20	43	46	23	63	∞	0	5
Nu	30	26	27	27	5	46	0	∞	2
St	27	8	44	22	1	51	3	0	∞

We treat the columns of the above matrix in the same manner and obtain the reduced matrix W':

	Aa	Ba	Be	Du	Fr	Ha	Mu	Nu	St
Aa	∞	41	56	0	17	41	56	39	38
Ba	30	∞	61	27	6	56	10	16	0
Be	35	51	∞	28	26	0	31	15	34
Du	0	38	49	∞	14	35	55	36	33
Fr	6	6	36	3	∞	30	20	2	0
Ha	20	46	0	14	20	∞	51	34	41
Mu	47	12	43	46	22	63	∞	0	5
Nu	30	18	27	27	4	46	0	∞	2
St	27	0	44	22	0	51	3	0	∞

W'

The sum of all the numbers subtracted is $s = 8 + 27 + 29 + 8 + 20 + 29 + 17 + 17 + 19 + 8 + 1 = 183$, so that each tour has weight at least 183 (with respect to W). Of course, we found better bounds before, for example 230 using 1-tree relaxation in Example 14.2.4, but this does not help us in the present context.

Next, we have to choose an edge ij to split up the set of solutions (note that we have to use directed edges ij here!). Tours not containing ij can then be described by the weight matrix M resulting from W' by substituting the (i,j)-entry by ∞. As we want to obtain a larger value for the lower bound s, we should obviously choose some edge for which the corresponding entry in W' is 0 (and is in fact the only entry 0 in its row and column), so that the matrix M can be reduced further. Also, it is obvious that we should use the entry 0 for which M can be reduced by the largest possible number. In our example, this is the edge $BeHa$; here, M can be reduced by $30 + 15 = 45$. Thus, the first part of the decision tree looks as follows.

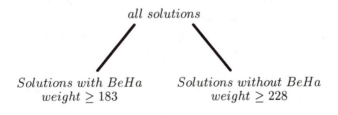

all solutions

Solutions with $BeHa$
weight ≥ 183

Solutions without $BeHa$
weight ≥ 228

From Example 14.5.3, we know a tour of weight 250. Our further considerations should confirm that this tour is optimal, as we know already from Section 14.3. But this tour does not help us to exclude one of the branches of the decision tree yet. Of course, this is to be expected, because the known solution of weight 250 contains the edge $HaBe$ (for an appropriate orientation) and therefore has to occur in the right branch of the decision tree. However, our original TSP was symmetric, so that it suffices to consider the right branch of the tree. For any tour containing edge $BeHa$, there is a corresponding tour of the same weight not containing $BeHa$ (namely the tour having reverse orientation). Thus, W' can be replaced by the following weight matrix M.

	Aa	Ba	Be	Du	Fr	Ha	Mu	Nu	St
Aa	∞	41	56	0	17	11	56	39	38
Ba	30	∞	61	27	6	26	10	16	0
Be	20	36	∞	13	11	∞	16	0	19
Du	0	38	49	∞	14	5	55	36	33
Fr	6	6	36	3	∞	0	20	2	0
Ha	20	46	0	14	20	∞	51	34	41
Mu	47	12	43	46	22	33	∞	0	5
Nu	30	18	27	27	4	16	0	∞	2
St	27	0	44	22	0	21	3	0	∞

M

Again, we use the entry 0 of M which allows the largest possible further reduction when replaced by ∞ for splitting up the set of possible solutions. This time, that is the entry (Ha, Be); the possible reduction amounts to $14 + 27 = 41$. Now the part of the decision tree which belongs to tours containing neither $HaBe$ nor $BeHa$ has a lower bound of 269, so that this branch can be ignored because of the known tour of weight 250. In other words: any optimal tour for the TSP of Example 14.1.2 has to contain edge $HaBe$. This fact is not surprising really, because $HaBe$ is the shortest edge incident with Be (and all the other edges are considerably longer). Now all tours we still have to consider contain $HaBe$, so that none of these tours contains a further edge beginning in Ha or ending in Be and we may omit row Ha and column Be from our matrix M. In the next step, we use the (Aa, Du)-entry of the resulting 8×8-matrix. For tours not containing edge $AaDu$, we may replace this entry by ∞ and reduce the resulting matrix by $11 + 3 = 14$. This yields the following matrix A.

	Aa	Ba	Du	Fr	Ha	Mu	Nu	St
Aa	∞	30	∞	6	0	45	28	27
Ba	30	∞	24	6	26	10	16	0
Be	20	36	10	11	∞	16	0	19
Du	0	38	∞	14	5	55	36	33
Fr	6	6	0	∞	0	20	2	0
Mu	47	12	43	22	33	∞	0	5
Nu	30	18	24	4	16	0	∞	2
St	27	0	19	0	21	3	0	∞

A

A yields a lower bound of 242. We will consider A later and first examine those tours which contain edge $AaDu$. For these tours, row Aa and column Du may be omitted from M. Moreover, edge $DuAa$ cannot occur any more, so that the corresponding entry may be replaced by ∞. The resulting matrix can be reduced further: 6 can be subtracted in column Aa and 5 can be subtracted in row Du. This yields the matrix M' and a new lower bound of 239.

$$
\begin{array}{c}
\\
\\
\\
M'
\end{array}
\begin{array}{c}
\\
Ba \\
Be \\
Du \\
Fr \\
Mu \\
Nu \\
St
\end{array}
\begin{array}{ccccccc}
Aa & Ba & Fr & Ha & Mu & Nu & St \\
24 & \infty & 6 & 26 & 10 & 16 & 0 \\
14 & 36 & 11 & \infty & 16 & 0 & 19 \\
\infty & 33 & 9 & 0 & 50 & 31 & 28 \\
0 & 6 & \infty & 0 & 20 & 2 & 0 \\
41 & 12 & 22 & 33 & \infty & 0 & 5 \\
24 & 18 & 4 & 16 & 0 & \infty & 2 \\
21 & 0 & 0 & 21 & 3 & 0 & \infty
\end{array}
$$

Consider tours not containing edge $FrAa$ next. Then the entry corresponding to $FrAa$ may be substituted by ∞, so that the matrix can be reduced by 14. That yields a new lower bound of 253, so that this branch of the decision tree can be ignored (because we know a tour of weight 250). Therefore, we may restrict our attention to tours containing edge $FrAa$. We omit row Fr and column Aa from M'. As our tour now contains edges $FrAa$ and $AaDu$, the edge $DuFr$ cannot occur; we replace the corresponding entry by ∞. The resulting matrix M'' looks as follows.

$$
\begin{array}{c}
\\
\\
M''
\end{array}
\begin{array}{c}
\\
Ba \\
Be \\
Du \\
Mu \\
Nu \\
St
\end{array}
\begin{array}{cccccc}
Ba & Fr & Ha & Mu & Nu & St \\
\infty & 6 & 26 & 10 & 16 & 0 \\
36 & 11 & \infty & 16 & 0 & 19 \\
33 & \infty & 0 & 50 & 31 & 28 \\
12 & 22 & 33 & \infty & 0 & 5 \\
18 & 4 & 16 & 0 & \infty & 2 \\
0 & 0 & 21 & 3 & 0 & \infty
\end{array}
$$

The corresponding lower bound is still 239. Considering tours without edge $DuHa$ yields a lower bound of 283, so that we can restrict our attention to tours containing $DuHa$. We discard row Du and column Ha. Moreover, the tours considered now contain the path (Fr, Aa, Du, Ha, Be), so that the entry corresponding to edge $BeFr$ has to be substituted by ∞. In the next step, we find that the tour has to contain edge $BeNu$, because, without

$BeNu$, we get a lower bound of $239 + 16 = 255$. This means we can also leave out edge $NuFr$; replacing the corresponding entry by ∞ has the effect that we can subtract 5 in row Mu. Now our lower bound is 244 and we have the following matrix.

$$
\begin{array}{c}
 \\
Ba \\
Mu \\
Nu \\
St
\end{array}
\begin{array}{cccc}
Ba & Fr & Mu & St \\
\left(\begin{array}{cccc}
\infty & 6 & 10 & 0 \\
7 & 17 & \infty & 0 \\
18 & \infty & 0 & 2 \\
0 & 0 & 3 & \infty
\end{array} \right)
\end{array}
$$

We may now insert edge $MuSt$ into our tour, because, for tours not containing $MuSt$, we get a lower bound of 251. Next we omit row Mu and column St and replace the (St, Mu)-entry by ∞. Subtracting 6 in row Ba, we get a lower bound of 250, and this means we are finished. Continuing the procedure accordingly would yield the additional edges $StBa$, $BaFr$ and $NuMu$, that is, we get the optimal tour $(Fr, Aa, Du, Ha, Be, Nu, Mu, St, Ba, Fr)$ of length 250 already known. Thus, we could have obtained this tour without heuristic methods by executing a sort of DFS on the decision tree and always choosing the branch with the smallest lower bound for continuing the process. However, it is possible that we discover only at a later point of the decision tree that we could have ignored some earlier branches.

It remains to consider the case represented by the matrix A above. Suppose the tour did not contain edge $DuAa$, then the matrix could be reduced by $5 + 6$, which yields a lower bound of 253. Therefore, we insert edge $DuAa$ into our tour and discard row Du and column Aa from A. Next, we see that an optimal tour in this branch of the tree has to contain $BeNu$, because otherwise we get a lower bound of 252. Now we may omit row Be and column Nu and replace the (Ha, Nu)-entry by ∞ (because $HaBe$ and $BeNu$ are contained in the tour). Having done this, we subtract 5 in row Mu, which yields a lower bound of 247 and the matrix A' below.

$$
A'
\begin{array}{c}
 \\
Aa \\
Ba \\
Fr \\
Mu \\
Nu \\
St
\end{array}
\begin{array}{cccccc}
Ba & Du & Fr & Ha & Mu & St \\
\left(\begin{array}{cccccc}
30 & \infty & 6 & 0 & 45 & 27 \\
\infty & 24 & 6 & 26 & 10 & 0 \\
6 & 0 & \infty & 0 & 20 & 0 \\
7 & 38 & 17 & 28 & \infty & 0 \\
18 & 24 & 4 & \infty & 0 & 2 \\
0 & 19 & 0 & 21 & 3 & \infty
\end{array} \right)
\end{array}
$$

Next we insert edge $FrDu$ (leaving out this edge would increase the lower bound by 19 to 266), cancel row Fr and column Du and replace the (Aa, Fr)-entry by ∞. That yields edge (Aa, Ha) (otherwise we get a lower bound of 295) and we can replace the (Nu, Fr)-entry by ∞. Now edge (Mu, St) has to be contained in the tour and the (St, Mu)-entry is changed to ∞. We are now – after having cancelled the appropriate rows and columns – left with a (3×3)-matrix which can be reduced by 6 in row Ba. This yields a new lower bound of 253, so that we can ignore all tours of this branch in the decision tree and the algorithm terminates. By complete analysis of all possibilities, we have proved that our tour of length 250 is optimal. Figure 14.14 shows the whole decision tree.

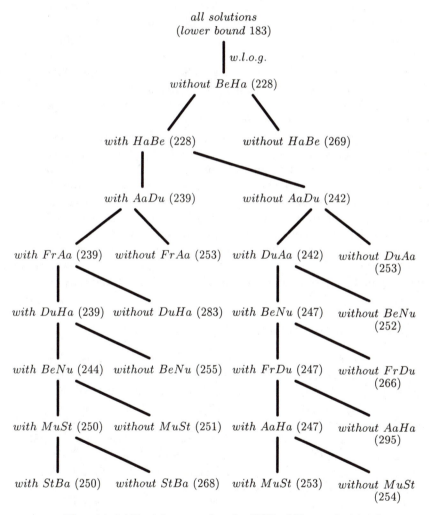

Fig. 14.14 Decision tree for the TSP of Example 14.1.2

The partial tour of the left branch can be completed in a unique way (which yields the known optimal tour of weight 250). Note that the branch with lower bound 253 indeed contains a tour of this weight; it can be obtained by exchanging the order of Aa and Du in the optimal tour. Analogously, the branch with lower bound 251 contains a tour of this length; this tour results from exchanging the order of Ba and St in the optimal tour.

We do not state the Algorithm of Little, Murty, Sweeney and Karel formally here, because the above example illustrates sufficiently how the algorithm works. An explicit formulation as well as a PASCAL program (and an example of size 6 for the ATSP) can be found in the book by Syslo, Deo and Kowalik (1983).

We close this section with some remarks concerning the algorithm presented here. The numbers we subtracted from rows and columns of the original weight matrix W define two vectors $\mathbf{u} = (8, 27, 29, 8, 20, 29, 17, 17, 19)$ and $\mathbf{v} = (0, 8, 0, 0, 1, 0, 0, 0, 0)$. The reduction process does not only change the weight of every tour by a constant (183 here), but, more generally, changes the weight of any diagonal of the matrix, that is, of any matching for the corresponding Assignment Problem. Thus, the bound of 183 ($= \sum(u_i + v_i)$) we found first is also a bound for the corresponding assignment relaxation (compare Section 14.2). This is not surprising: using the terminology of Section 13.2, $(\mathbf{u}, \mathbf{v})$ is a feasible node weighting for the corresponding Assignment Problem (in the minimization version which can be treated similar to Chapter 13: we always have $u_i + v_j \leq w_{ij}$). Thus, the Algorithm of Little, Murty, Sweeney and Karel (1963) works with a further relaxation of the assignment relaxation of the TSP (and therefore with rather weak lower bounds). Replacing certain entries by ∞ (that is, forbidding the corresponding edges) during the algorithm corresponds to forbidding non-cyclic permutations. If we omitted this feature, the algorithm would determine a complete matching of minimal weight instead of an optimal tour.

14.9 Concluding Remarks

We close our examination of the TSP with some remarks. As we mentioned in Section 14.2 D, the TSP could be solved by Linear Programming methods using the polytope Q defined by all tours. Recall that two vertices of a polytope are called *adjacent* if they are incident with a common edge. It can be shown that the unique minimal exact neighbourhood of some optimization problem is always given by adjacency in the corresponding polytope. For the TSP, the neighbourhood $N(f)$ of a tour f contains precisely those tours which are adjacent to f in Q (see Papadimitriou and Steiglitz (1982), §19.7). However, this does not help us in practice because the question whether two vertices of Q are adjacent is an NP-complete problem as well (see Papadimitriou (1978)). There is an amazing result for the polytope Q' corresponding to the ATSP: The diameter of Q' (in the graph theoretical sense, where we consider the vertices and edges of Q' as a graph called the *sceleton* of Q') is 2 (Padberg and Rao (1974)). This means that the distance between an arbitrary tour and a given optimal tour is 2 only. More about these questions can be found in Chapter 8 of Lawler, Lenstra, Rinnooy Kan and Shmoys (1985).

We mentioned already that even large instances of the TSP (consisting of several hundred cities) can nowadays be approximated very well, that is, it is routinely possible to find a solution which is not more than 1 % worse than the optimal solution. But how about determining optimal solutions? The first larger instance of a TSP for which an optimal solution was found was a problem of 49 cities (namely Washington, D.C. and the 48 capitals of the 48 states of the USA at that time), see Dantzig, Fulkerson and Johnson (1954). This problem was solved by first finding a good solution heuristically (this solution was in fact already optimal) and then using the LP relaxation (and adding appropriate inequalitities as described in Section 14.2). The paper of Dantzig, Fulkerson and Johnson (1954) is nowadays considered a milestone in the history of Combinatorial Optimization; it is more or less the forefather of all algorithms used at present for finding exact solutions of the TSP. The main part of these algorithms is the LP relaxation, which can be summarized as follows.

(1) Find an LP relaxation of the TSP and determine an optimal solution x for this relaxation.

(2) If x is not a tour, try to find one or more inequalities describing the polytope Q which are violated by x. Add these inequalitities to the LP and substitute x by a solution of the new LP. Repeat step (2) until no more inequalities are violated.

Using this method alone, Grötschel (1980) was able to solve a problem of 120 cities (German cities, where the distances were taken from the 'Deutscher Generalatlas') with only 13 iterations (without using a branch and bound technique). The results of Padberg and Hong (1980) and of Crowder and Padberg (1980) show that LP relaxation yields very good lower bounds, if not even an optimal solution, for the TSP. After having used LP relaxation, it is quite often possible to find an optimal solution with a branch and bound algorithm; solving problems of about 100 cities is nowadays more or less a matter of routine. Crowder and Padberg (1980) solved a problem of 318 cities using this approach; this was considered the 'world record' for several years. Meanwhile, this record was surpassed several times: Padberg and Rinaldi (1987) solved a problem of 532 cities (in the USA); Grötschel and Holland (1991) found the optimal solution for several large instances of the TSP using similar methods; one of these problems was a 'world tour' consisting of 666 cities. Finally, Padberg and Rinaldi (1991) solved two problems of 1002 and 2392 cities. Even though these results are quite impressive, the methods of Padberg and Rinaldi need an exponential number of steps in the worst case, see Cook and Hartmann (1990). The most recent 'TSP world record' has been published so far only as a research report:

Applegate, Bixby, Chvátal and Cook (1995) solved, among others, two problems consisting of 3038 and 4461 cities.

Using the problem with 532 cities mentioned above, we want to explain how important efficient heuristics are when using the LP relaxation method described above for finding the optimal solution. As the graph K_{532} contains precisely $141,246$ edges, the LP treated by Padberg and Rinaldi (1987) has just this number of (structural) variables (and some additional slackness variables). Now Padberg and Rinaldi applied the heuristic of Lin and Kernighan (1973) mentioned above to 50 initial tours chosen arbitrarily; the resulting locally optimal tours contained altogether 1278 edges only. The corresponding 1278 variables were used for the first LP relaxation (all other variables were defined as 0). Altogether, all the LP's occuring when solving this (rather large) problem used only 1520 (structural) variables and 815 lines!

For a more detailed description of the LP relaxation method which was merely sketched here, we refer in particular to Chapter 9 of Lawler, Lenstra, Rinnooy Kan and Shmoys (1985) and to Padberg and Rinaldi (1991). This technique is a special case of a general method which proved to be efficient for several other hard optimization problems as well. It belongs to the field of 'Polyhedral Combinatorics', a part of Combinatorial Optimization. We refer the reader to the interesting surveys of Pulleyblank (1983) and Grötschel (1984). Some other NP-hard problems have been approached successfully: Balas and Yu (1986) found maximal cliques in graphs with up to 400 vertices and 30000 edges; similar results exist for the corresponding weighted problem, see Balas and Xue (1991). We also recommend the book by Grötschel, Lovász and Schrijver (1993). A nice monograph on computational aspects of the TSP and its applications is due to Reinelt (1994).

14.10 Appendix: Some NP-Complete Problems

At the end of the present chapter, we collect some NP-complete problems which either appear in the text above or are closely related to the subjects treated in this book. A much more extensive list can be found in Garey and Johnson (1979).

CHINESE POSTMAN (comp. Section 13.5)

Let $G = (V, A, E)$ be a mixed graph, where A is the set directed edges and E the set of undirected edges of G. Moreover, let w be a non-negative length function on $A \cup E$ and c a positive number. Does there exist a cycle of length $\leq c$ in G which contains each edge at least once using the edges of A according to their given orientation? This problem was shown to be NP-complete by Papadimitriou (1976), even for G planar of maximal degree 3 and all edge lengths 1. However, it is polynomial for graphs or directed graphs (that is, $A = \emptyset$ or $E = \emptyset$, respectively), see Theorem 13.5.4 and Exercise 13.5.6.

CHROMATIC INDEX (comp. Section 8.3)

Let G be a graph. Is it possible to colour the edges of G with k colours, that is, does $\chi'(G) \leq k$ hold? Holyer (1981) proved that this problem is NP-complete for any $k \geq 3$; this holds even for the special case $k = 3$ and 3-regular graphs.

CHROMATIC NUMBER (compare Section 8.2)

Let G be a graph. Is it possible to colour the vertices of G with k colours, that is, does $\chi(G) \leq k$ hold? Karp (1972) showed that this problem is NP-complete for any $k \geq 3$. Even the problem restricted to $k = 3$ for planar graphs of maximal degree 4 is still NP-complete, see Garey, Johnson and Stockmeyer (1976). If P $\neq$ NP, there is not even a polynomial approximative algorithm which always needs less than $2\chi(G)$ colours, see Garey and Johnson (1976). For perfect graphs, the problem of determining the chromatic number is polynomial, see Grötschel, Lovász and Schrijver (1993).

CLIQUE (compare Exercise 2.8.3)

Let $G = (V, E)$ be a graph and $c \leq |V|$ a positive integer. Does G contain a clique consisting of c vertices? This problem is NP-complete in general according to Karp (1972). In particular, determining the clique number $\omega(G)$ is an NP-hard problem. Also, the related question whether G contains a clique with at least $r|V|$ vertices (for some given r with $0 < r < 1$) is NP-complete for any fixed r. The existence of a polynomial ε-approximative algorithm for determining a maximal clique implies already that P = NP, see Arora and Safra (1992). However, the problem can be solved in polynomial time for perfect (in particular for bipartite) graphs, see Grötschel, Lovász and Schrijver (1993).

DIAMETER (comp. Section 3.8)

Let $G = (V, E)$ be a connected graph and $c \leq |V|$ a positive integer. Determining the diameter of G (that is, the question whether $d(u, v) \leq c$ for all pairs u, v of vertices) is easy, see Section 3.8. However, the following two related problems are NP-complete.

(1) Does there exist a strongly connected orientation H of G with diameter $\leq c$? This result (which holds even for $c = 2$) is due to Chvátal and Thomasson (1978). Note that the Theorem of Robbins implies that it is easy to check whether any strongly connected orientation exists.

(2) Let C be a given set of at most $|E|$ non-negative integers. Does there exist a mapping $w : E \to C$ such that G has 'weighted diameter' $\leq c$, that is, such that any two vertices u, v have distance $d(u, v) \leq c$?

This problem is NP-complete even for $C = \{0,1\}$, as was shown by Perl and Zaks (see Garey and Johnson (1979)).

DISCRETE METRIC REALIZATION (compare Section 3.2)

Let $D = (d_{xy})$ be an $(n \times n)$-matrix with integral entries (representing distances). Is there a network (G, w) of total length $\leq k$ realizing D? Winkler (1988) proved that this problem – as well as the analogous real problem – is NP-complete.

DISJOINT PATHS (comp. Section 7.1)

Let $G = (V, E)$ be a graph, s and t two vertices of G and k and c two positive integers. Does G contain k pairwise vertex disjoint paths from s to t such that none of these paths contains more than c edges? Itai, Perl and Shiloach (1982) showed that this problem is NP-complete; this is even true for fixed $k \geq 5$ (whereas the problem is polynomial for fixed $k \leq 4$). Similar results hold for edge disjoint paths from s to t as well as for the analogous problems where each path should contain precisely k edges. Note that the maximal number of (edge or vertex) disjoint paths from s to t can be determined efficiently using the Theorem of Menger and its variations.

GRAPH PARTITIONING (comp. Section 8.1)

Let $G = (V, E)$ be a graph and c a positive integer. The question whether G can be partitioned into at most c subgraphs of a given type is NP-complete for many classes of subgraphs. For example, this holds for triangles and, more generally, for isomorphic subgraphs (for a given isomorphism type), for Hamiltonian subgraphs, for forests, cliques, and for matchings. We refer the reader to §A1.1 in Garey and Johnson (1979) and the references given there. In particular, determining the 'clique partition number' θ is an NP-hard problem in general; for perfect graphs, this problem can be solved in polynomial time, see Grötschel, Lovász and Schrijver (1993).

HAMILTONIAN CYCLE (comp. Sections 1.4 and 2.8)

Let $G = (V, E)$ be a graph. Does G contain a Hamiltonian cycle? This problem was proved to be NP-complete by Karp (1972). It is still NP-complete if we know a Hamiltonian path of G already (Papadimitriou and Steiglitz (1977), see Theorem 14.7.3). Even the special cases for bipartite graphs and for planar, 3-connected, 3-regular graphs are still NP-complete (see Krishnamoorthy (1975) and Garey, Johnson and Tarjan (1976), resp.). The analogous problem for directed Hamiltonian cycles in directed graphs is NP-complete as well (Karp (1972)), see Exercise 2.7.6.

HAMILTONIAN PATH (comp. Exercise 2.7.7)

Does the graph $G = (V, E)$ contain a Hamiltonian path? This problem and the analogous directed problem are NP-complete, even if the start and end vertices of the Hamiltonian path are fixed, see Garey and Johnson (1979).

INDEPENDENT SET (comp. Exercise 2.8.3)

Let $G = (V, E)$ be a graph and $c \leq |V|$ a positive integer. Does G contain an independent set with c elements? Note that the independent sets of G are precisely the cliques of $\overline{G}$. This problem is therefore NP-complete by Karp (1972), but polynomial for perfect (in particular for bipartite) graphs. The problem restricted to 3-regular planar graphs is still NP-complete, see Garey, Johnson and Stockmeyer (1976).

INDUCED SUBGRAPH

Let $G = (V, E)$ be a graph and c a positive integer. The problem whether G contains a (connected) induced subgraph of given type on c vertices is NP-complete for many classes of subgraphs. For example, this holds for cliques and independent sets (see 'Clique' and 'Independent Set'), but also for planar subgraphs, bipartite subgraphs, forests, etc. We refer to §A1.2 in Garey and Johnson (1979) and the references given there.

INTEGER PROGRAMMING (comp. Section 13.3)

Let A be an $(m \times n)$-matrix, $\mathbf{c} = (c_1, \ldots, c_n)$ and $\mathbf{b} = (b_1, \ldots, b_m)$ vectors with integral entries and d an integer. Does there exist an integral vector $\mathbf{x} = (x_1, \ldots, x_n) \geq \mathbf{0}$ such that $A\mathbf{x}^T \leq \mathbf{b}^T$ and $\mathbf{c}\mathbf{x}^T \geq d$? This problem is NP-complete according to Karp (1972), whereas the corresponding linear program (where $\mathbf{x}$ may have rational entries) can be solved in polynomial time.

LONGEST CYCLE

Let $N = (V, E, w)$ be a network with a non-negative length function w and c a positive number. Does N contain a cycle of length $\geq c$? This problem is NP-complete even if all edges have length 1, see Garey and Johnson (1979). The same is true for the analogous directed problem.

LONGEST PATH (comp. Section 3.1)

Let s and t be two vertices in a network $N = (V, E, w)$, where w is a non-negative length function, and c a positive number. Does there exist a path from s to t of length $\geq c$? This problem is NP-complete even if all edges have length 1 (similar to 'Longest Cycle').

MATCHING (comp. Section 7.2, Chapter 12 and Section 13.7)

As we saw above, a maximal matching (that is, a matching of maximal cardinality) in an arbitrary graph $G = (V, E)$ can be determined with complexity $O(|V|^3)$. However, a matching which cannot be extended does not have to have maximal cardinality in general. Determining a non-extendable matching of minimal cardinality, that is, the question whether G contains a non-extendable matching of cardinality $\leq c$ (for some given positive integer c) is NP-complete according to Yannakakis and Gavril (1978). This is true even for planar graphs and for bipartite graphs (even for maximal degree 3). The question whether G contains, for a given decomposition of E into subsets E_i $(i = 1, \ldots, k)$, a matching K with c edges such that $|K \cap E_i| \leq b_i$ holds for $i = 1, \ldots, k$ is NP-complete by Itai, Rodeh and Tanimota (1978) (even if all b_i are 1). See also 'Permanent Evaluation'.

MATROID INTERSECTION (comp. Section 5.4)

For three given matroids $(E, \mathbf{S}_i)$ $(i = 1, 2, 3)$ on the same set E and a positive integer $c \leq |E|$, does there exist a subset U of E of cardinality c which is an independent set for all three matroids? This problem is NP-complete. Note that, for example, determining a directed Hamiltonian path in a directed graph G is a special case of this problem, see Exercise 5.4.10. However, the analogous problem for the intersection of two matroids is solvable in polynomial time, even for the weighted case. This result is of fundamental importance, see Lawler (1975), Lawler (1976), Edmonds (1979), Cunningham (1986) and White (1987), for example.

MAX CUT (comp. Chapter 6)

Let $G = (V, E)$ be a graph with a non-negative capacity function c and b a positive number. Does there exist a cut (S, T) of G with capacity $c(S, T) \geq b$? This problem is NP-complete by Karp (1972). Yannakakis (1978) showed that this is true even if $c(e) = 1$ for each edge e and G has maximal degree 3. Therefore, determining a cut of maximal capacity is an NP-hard problem, whereas the analogous problem for cuts of minimal capacity is easy (using Network Flow Theory). Max Cut is polynomial for planar graphs, see Hadlock (1975).

MIN CUT (comp. Chapter 6)

Let $G = (V, E)$ be a graph with a non-negative capacity function c, s and t two vertices of G and $b \leq |V|$ and k two positive numbers. Does there exist a cut (S, T) of G with $s \in S$, $t \in T$, $|S| \leq b$, $|T| \leq b$ and capacity $c(S, T) \leq k$? This problem is NP-complete according to Garey, Johnson and Stockmeyer (1976), even if $c(e) = 1$ for all edges e. Note that 'Min Cut' without the bounds for $|S|$ and $|T|$ (that is, with $b = |V|$) is one of the fundamental easy problems.

MINIMUM k-CONNECTED SUBGRAPH (comp. Chapter 11)

Let $G = (V, E)$ be a graph and $k \leq |V|$ and $b \leq |E|$ two positive integers. Does there exist a subset E^* of E with $|E^*| \leq b$ such that $G^* = (V, E^*)$ is k-connected? Chung and Graham proved (see Garey and Johnson (1979)) that this problem – as well as the analogous problem for k-fold line connectivity – is NP-complete for any fixed $k \geq 2$. In other words: Determining a minimal k-connected subgraph of G is NP-hard. Note that the case $k = 1$ can be solved with complexity $O(|E|)$ using BFS, for example ($k = 1$ means that we want to find just a spanning tree of G).

MINIMUM SPANNING TREE (comp. Section 4.7)

Let $N = (V, E, w)$ be a network with a non-negative weight function w on a connected graph G. As we saw in Section 4.3, determining a minimal spanning tree T is one of the fundamental easy problems of Algorithmic Graph Theory. But, as for the problem of determining spanning trees in general, we obtain NP-complete problems by adding appropriate conditions, for example by restricting the diameter of T. We refer to Section 4.7 and to §A.2.1 in Garey and Johnson (1979) for more about these problems.

NETWORK FLOW (comp. Chapters 6 and 9)

The flow problems we treated in this book are solvable in polynomial time. However, by adding appropriate conditions, we obtain many NP-complete problems. We refer the reader to §A.2.4 in Garey and Johnson (1979) and the references given there.

NETWORK RELIABILITY (comp. Example 3.1.1)

Let $G = (V, E)$ be a graph, V^* a subset of V, p a mapping from E to the rational numbers between 0 and 1 (p is called 'failure probability') and $q \leq 1$ a positive rational number. Is the probability that any two vertices in V^* are connected by at least one *reliable* path (that is, a path which does not contain an edge which 'fails') at least q? This problem is NP-hard by Rosenthal (1977); see also Valiant (1979b) for related questions. Provan (1986) showed that it is NP-hard even to determine the probability for the existence of a reliable path from s to t in a planar acyclic directed graph G or in a planar graph G with maximal degree $\Delta(G) = 3$.

PERMANENT EVALUATION (comp. Section 7.4)

Let A be an $(n \times n)$-matrix with entries 0 and 1 and $k \leq n!$ a positive integer. Does per $A = k$ (or $\leq k$ or $\geq k$, respectively) hold? These problems are NP-hard by Valiant (1979a). As determining the number of perfect matchings in a bipartite graph is equivalent to determining the permanent of an appropriate matrix, this problem is NP-hard as well.

SATISFIABILITY (comp. Section 2.7)

Let $C_1 \ldots C_n$ be a logic formula in n Boolean variables in conjunctive normal form. Does there exist an assignment of the logic values true and false to the n variables such that the formula has value true? This problem is NP-complete even if each of the C_i contains precisely three of the Boolean variables (3-SAT); this was proved by Cook (1971).

SHORTEST CYCLE (comp. Sections 3.3 and 9.7)

Let $N = (V, E, w)$ be a network, where w is an arbitrary length function, and c an integer. Does G contain a cycle of length $\leq c$? This problem is NP-complete (see Garey and Johnson (1979)), but can be solved in polynomial time for non-negative length functions, see Itai and Rodeh (1978) and Monien (1983), for example. Similar results hold for the analogous directed problem. Determining a cycle of minimum cycle mean (for arbitrary w) is easy, see Section 9.7.

SHORTEST PATH (comp. Chapter 3)

Let s and t be two vertices in a network $N = (V, E, w)$, where w is an arbitrary length function, and c an integer. Does there exist a path from s to t of length $\leq c$? This problem is NP-complete, see Garey and Johnson (1979). However, as we saw in Chapter 3, if all lengths are non-negative, there are very good polynomial algorithms. Analogous statements hold for the corresponding problem for a network on a directed graph.

SPANNING TREE (comp. Chapter 4)

We know that a spanning tree in a connected graph G can be determined with linear complexity (with BFS or DFS, for example; see Sections 3.3 or 11.2, respectively). But the problem becomes NP-complete if we add certain conditions. For example, the questions whether G contains, for some given positive integer c, a spanning tree T with at least c leaves or with maximal degree $\Delta(T) \leq c$ are NP-complete, see §4.7 in Garey and Johnson (1979). Another condition which makes the problem NP-complete is the question whether the sum of distances $d(u, v)$ in T taken over all pairs (u, v) of vertices can be bounded by c, see Johnson, Lenstra and Rinnooy Kan (1978).

STEINER NETWORK (comp. Section 4.6)

Let $N = (V, E, w)$ be a network, where $V = R \overset{.}{\cup} S$. We want to determine a minimal spanning tree T for some induced subgraph whose vertex set has the form $R \cup S'$, where $S' \subset S$. This problem is NP-hard according to Karp (1972).

STEINER TREE (compare Section 4.6)

For a given set of n points in the Euclidean plane, we want to find a minimal Steiner tree, that is, a tree of minimal length with respect to Euclidean distances containing the given n points. This problem was shown to be NP-hard by Garey, Graham and Johnson (1977).

TRAVELLING SALESMAN PROBLEM (TSP) (comp. Chapter 14)

Let v_i $(i = 1, \ldots, n)$ be a set of n 'cities' and $d(v_i, v_j) > 0$ for all pairs i, j with $i \neq j$ the integral distance between v_i and v_j. For a given positive integer b, we want to find a tour (that is, a permutation of the cities) of total length $\leq b$. This problem served as the standard example for an NP-complete problem. It is still NP-complete in the metric case, in the asymmetric case, and for distance functions taking only 1 and 2 as values. Even the corresponding approximation problem is NP-hard in the general case, but easy in the metric case for $\varepsilon = 1/2$. However, the existence of an approximation scheme for the metric TSP would imply already that P = NP, see Arora, Lund, Motwani, Sudan and Szegedy (1992). The questions whether a tour is suboptimal or whether an optimal tour contains some given edge are NP-hard as well. We refer to Chapter 14 and to the book by Lawler, Lenstra, Rinnooy Kan and Shmoys (1985).

VERTEX COVER (comp. Section 2.8)

Let $G = (V, E)$ be a graph and $c \leq |V|$ a positive integer. Does G have a vertex cover of cardinality $\leq c$? Note that 'vertex cover' is equivalent to 'independent set', because the complement of a vertex cover is an independent set. This problem is NP-complete (see Theorem 2.8.2), but can be solved in polynomial time for perfect graphs (in particular for bipartite graphs).

A. Solutions

This appendix contains solutions or directions for solving almost all the exercises of this book. For difficult exercises, we give a more detailed solution, whereas for easy ones, we sometimes restrict ourselves to hints. If an exercise is a purely arithmetical problem, we state the result only. For some exercises, where the result is known already (from earlier considerations) or where the reader was required to do some experiments, we do not give any solution.

A.1 Solutions for Chapter 1

1.1.2 As $2n - 1$ is odd, $2i$ runs through all classes of remainders mod $2n - 1$ for $i = 1, \ldots 2n - 1$. Therefore, the E_i are pairwise disjoint. It is now immediate that each E_i is a factor of K_{2n}. Then, using counting arguments, $E_1, \ldots, E_{2n-1}$ must be a factorization.

1.1.3 Note $T_3 = K_3$. The graph T_4 is K_6 with one 1-factor removed. The complement of T_5 is drawn in Figure 1.12 (compare Exercise 1.5.10). A vertex $\{x, y\}$ of T_n is adjacent precisely to the $2(n - 2)$ vertices of the form $\{x, z\}$ and $\{y, z\}$ (where $z \neq x, y$). The vertices $\{x, y\}$ and $\{x, z\}$ for $y \neq z$ are adjacent precisely to the $n - 3$ vertices $\{x, w\}$ for $w \neq x, y, z$ and to $\{y, z\}$. Finally, $\{x, y\}$ and $\{z, w\}$ (for x, y, z, w pairwise distinct) are adjacent to $\{x, z\}$, $\{x, w\}$, $\{y, z\}$ and $\{y, w\}$.

1.1.4 For a given vertex x, there are precisely $a' = n - a - 1$ vertices which are not adjacent to x in G. If x and y are vertices adjacent in G, there are precisely $a - c - 1$ vertices which are adjacent to x but not to y, and precisely $(n - a - 1) - (a - c - 1)$ vertices which are adjacent neither to x nor to y. Thus, $\overline{G}$ has parameters $a' = n - a - 1$ and $d' = n - 2a + c$. It can be seen by similar arguments that $c' = n - 2a + d - 2$. To prove the validity of the given equation, choose some vertex x. Then there are $n - a - 1$ vertices z which are not adjacent to x. For each such vertex z, there are precisely d vertices y which are adjacent to x as well as to z. On the other hand, there are a vertices y adjacent to x, and for each such vertex y, there are $a - c - 1$ vertices z adjacent to y, but not adjacent to x.

1.2.1 Let $K = (v_0, \ldots, v_n)$ be a closed walk of odd length. If K is a cycle, there is nothing to show. Suppose there exists some index $i \neq 0, n$ such that $v_0 = v_i = v_n$. Then one of the closed walks $(v_0, \ldots, v_i)$ or $(v_i, \ldots, v_n)$ has odd length, so that the assertion follows with induction. In the general case, there are indices $i, j \neq 0, n$ with $i \neq j$ and $v_i = v_j$; in this case, the assertion follows with similar arguments as above. We obtain a closed walk of even length not containing any cycle if we append to some path W (from u to v, say) the same path W in opposite direction (that is, from v to u). In fact, any closed walk not containing a cycle is obtained by joining some examples of this kind.

1.2.2 For any two vertices x and y, the connected components of x and y contain at least $(n + 1)/2$ vertices and can therefore not be disjoint.

1.2.3 It is trivial that the condition is necessary. To show that it is sufficient as well, choose some vertex s in the connected component V_1. If $V_2 = V \backslash V_1$ were non-empty, there would exist (by hypothesis) an edge vw with $v \in V_1$ and $w \in V_2$. But then w would be contained in the same connected component as s.

1.2.4 If neither G nor $\overline{G}$ are connected, choose some vertex s and denote the connected components of G and $\overline{G}$ containing s by S and T, respectively. As each vertex $v \neq s$ is either adjacent to s in S or in T, we must have $V = S \cup T$. It can be seen by similar arguments that there cannot exist a pair (v, w) of vertices with $v \in S \backslash T$ and $w \in T \backslash S$, contradiction.

1.2.5 We know that $\sum_v \deg v = 2n - 2$ (see Lemma 1.1.1). Thus, there have to be at least two vertices v with $\deg v = 1$.

1.2.9 If $G \backslash e$ is connected, the assertion follows with induction on $|E|$. Otherwise, G consists of two connected components V_1 and V_2. Using induction on n, the assertion holds for the induced graphs $G|V_1$ and $G|V_2$ (which are connected). We get

$$|E| = |(E|V_1)| + |(E|V_2)| + 1 \geq (|V_1| - 1) + (|V_2| - 1) + 1 = n - 1.$$

1.2.15 The trees are shown in Figure A.1.

1.2.16 It can be seen that the symbol u occurs precisely $(\deg u - 1)$ times in $\pi_V(G)$; this is similar to the proof of Lemma 1.2.12. In particular, stars are precisely those trees G for which all entries of $\pi_V(G)$ are the same. Paths are the trees whose Prüfer code has pairwise distinct entries.

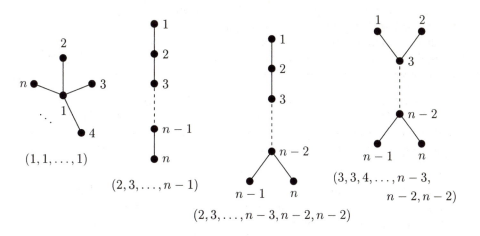

Fig. A.1 Exercise 1.2.15

1.2.17 As a tree on n vertices has precisely $n - 1$ edges, the condition is at least necessary. The solution of Exercise 1.2.16 yields that the degree of a vertex u in a tree T is equal to the number of entries u in the Prüfer code $\pi_V(T)$ plus 1. If $d_1, \ldots, d_n$ is a sequence of positive integers satisfying $d_1 + \ldots + d_n = 2(n - 1)$, trivially

$$(d_1 - 1) + (d_2 - 1) + \ldots + (d_n - 1) = n - 2.$$

Thus, each of the numbers $i \in \{1, \ldots n\}$ for which $d_i - 1 \neq 0$ holds can be used $d_i - 1$ times as entry in a vector of $n - 2$ components and the corresponding tree can be constructed using Theorem 1.2.13. For the degree sequence $(1, 1, 1, 1, 2, 3, 3)$, we get the Prüfer code $(5, 6, 6, 7, 7)$ and the tree shown in Figure A.2.

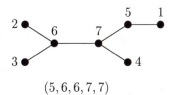

$(5, 6, 6, 7, 7)$

Fig. A.2 Tree with given degree sequence

1.3.3 Denote the vertices of odd degree by x_i and y_i (for $i = 1, \ldots, k$). Adding the edges $x_i y_i$ to G yields an Eulerian multigraph. We obtain the desired trails by omitting the edges $x_i y_i$ from a corresponding Euler tour.

1.3.4 Let uv be an edge of G, then uv is a vertex of $L(G)$ of degree deg u + deg v − 2. In particular, $L(K_{m,n})$ is $(m+n-2)$-regular. If x,y,z,w are pairwise distinct vertices of $K_{m,n}$, edges of the form xy and zw are always adjacent to precisely two edges in $L(K_{m,n})$. Edges of the form xy and xz are adjacent to $m-2$ or $n-2$ edges, depending on which part of $K_{m,n}$ contains x. Therefore, $L(K_{m,n})$ is an SRG precisely for $m = n$.

1.3.5 By Exercise 1.3.4, any edge uv of G has degree deg u + deg v − 2 in $L(G)$. By Theorem 1.3.1, $L(G)$ is Eulerian if and only if this number is always even, that is, if either all vertices of G have even degree or all vertices have odd degree. In particular, $L(K_{2n})$ is always Eulerian, even though K_{2n} is not.

1.4.4 As K_6 is Hamiltonian, G has to be Hamiltonian as well by Theorem 1.4.1. Therefore, G contains a cycle of length 6. We have to add at least two edges to this cycle to obtain a graph where deg u + deg $v \geq 6$ holds for any two non-adjacent vertices x and y. On the other hand, it is easy to check that the closure of this graph G is indeed K_6, so that 8 edges are necessary.

1.4.5 Suppose there exist vertices u and v with deg u + deg $v < n$, and u and v are not adjacent. Then $m < \frac{1}{2}(n-2)(n-3) + n = \frac{1}{2}(n-1)(n-2) + 2$.

1.4.6 Let $(e_1, \ldots, e_m)$ be an Euler tour of G; then the sequence $(e_1, \ldots, e_m, e_1)$ is a Hamiltonian cycle in $L(G)$. The converse is false; for example, K_4 is not Eulerian even though $L(K_4) = T_4$ is Hamiltonian.

1.4.8 We colour the squares of a chess board by turns black and white, as usual. Note that a knight always moves from a black square to a white one, and from a white square to a black one. Thus, in the corresponding graph, all edges connect a black and a white vertex. (This means that G is bipartite, compare Section 3.3.) Now it is obvious that G can only contain a Hamiltonian cycle if the numbers of white and black vertices are equal. Clearly, this is impossible if n and m are both odd, so that we have shown case (a). In case (b), this condition is satisfied; however, the cases $m = 1$ and $m = 2$ are trivially impossible. To show that a knight's cycle is still impossible for $m = 4$, we consider a further colouring of the chess board: The squares of the first and fourth row are green, whereas the squares in rows two and three are red. Then a knight can move from a green square only to a red square, whereas, from a red square, green squares as well as red squares are accessible. Now suppose there exists a knight's cycle. Then the knight has to reach and to move away from each of the green squares precisely once. As the green squares are only accessible from the red ones, the $2n$ moves from a red square always have to be moves to a green square, that is, red and green squares have to occur in turns in the knight's cycle. But white and black squares also occur in turns, and as the two colourings of the board are obviously distinct, this is impossible.

1.5.6 Any subdivision of a graph increases the number of vertices by the same value as the number of edges.

1.5.9 The Petersen graph G has girth $g = 5$. As G contains more than $40/3$ edges, G canot be planar by Theorem 1.5.3. Figure A.3 shows G (compare Figure 1.12) and a subgraph homeomorphic to $K_{3,3}$; here, the vertices of $K_{3,3}$ are indicated by bold circles and squares, whereas the vertices obtained by subdivision are drawn as small circles. Thus, Result 1.5.7 can be applied. Contracting each 'outer' vertex of G with the 'inner' vertex adjacent to it (see Figure A.3), we see that G can be contracted to K_5. Thus, Result 1.5.8 can be applied as well.

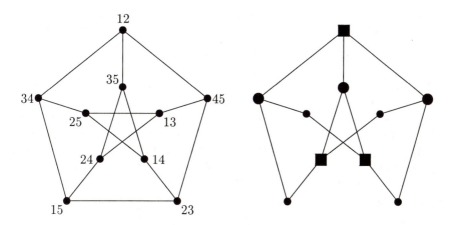

Fig. A.3 The Petersen graph

1.5.10 We write the 2-subsets $\{x, y\}$ of $\{1, \ldots, 5\}$ simply as xy. Then the vertices of T_5 are the xy, and xy and zw are adjacent in $\overline{T_5}$ if and only if x, y, z, w are four distinct elements. Now it is easy to check the isomorphism using the labelling of the vertices given in Figure A.3.

1.5.11 Any permutation α in S_5 induces an automorphism of T_5 (and thus an automorphism of the Petersen graph by Exercise 1.5.10) by mapping each 2-subset xy to $x^\alpha y^\alpha$. Actually, S_5 already yields *all* automorphisms of the Petersen graph; however, proving this requires a little more effort. (Hint: One can show that there are at most 120 automorphisms of the Petersen graph.)

1.5.12 For $n = 1, \ldots, 4$, K_n is already planar. For $n \geq 5$, K_n cannot be planar, because a planar graph with n vertices can have at most $3n - 6$ edges by Corollary 1.5.4. Thus, we have to remove at least $\frac{1}{2}n(n-1) - (3n-6) = \frac{1}{2}(n-2)(n-5) + 1$ edges. Using induction, it can be shown that there exists a planar graph with $3n - 6$ edges for each n; in fact, this graph can even be assumed to have a triangle as its 'outer border'. The induction basis ($n = 3, 4, 5$) and the recursive construction of placing a planar graph with n vertices and $3n - 6$ edges inside a triangle are sketched in Figure A.4.

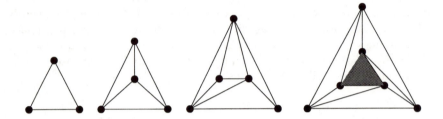

Fig. A.4 Maximal planar graphs

1.5.13 As $n - n_d$ vertices have degree at least $d + 1$, Corollary 1.5.4 implies $(n - n_d)(d + 1) \leq \sum \deg v = 2m \leq 6n - 12$ and hence the assertion. In particular, $n_5 \geq 2$ and $n_6 \geq n/7$; thus, more than 14 % of the vertices of a planar graph have degree at most 6. The given formula can be strengthened as follows: Any planar graph can be embedded in a planar graph (by adding appropriate edges) whose vertices have degree at least 3. For these planar graphs, the left hand side of the inequality can be increased by $3n_d$, and we obtain $n_d \geq \frac{n(d-5)+12}{d-2}$; in particular, $n_5 \geq 4$ and $n_6 \geq n/4$.

1.6.1 Let G be pseudo-symmetric. Choose some arbitrary edge $e_1 = v_0 v_1$, then some edge $e_2 = v_1 v_2$ and so on, always choosing edges which have not occured before. Now G is pseudo-symmetric, so that, for any vertex v_i which was reached using some edge e_i, there exists an edge e_{i+1} for leaving v_i. The only exception is $v_i = v_0$. Thus, the construction above yields a directed cycle C. Removing C from G yields a pseudo-symmetric graph H. Now the assertion follows by induction.

1.6.4 Obviously, any edge contained in a cycle cannot be a bridge. Conversely, let $e = uv$ be an edge which is not a bridge. Then the connected component containing u and v is still connected after removing e, that is, there exists a path W from u to v not containing e. Appending e to W yields the desired cycle.

1.6.5 G is Eulerian by Theorem 1.3.1. Let $(v_0, \ldots, v_m = v_0)$ be the sequence of vertices in an Euler tour $(e_1, \ldots, e_m)$ of G. Giving each edge e_i the orientation from v_{i-1} to v_i, we obtain an orientation of G, and $(e_1, \ldots, e_m)$ is a directed Euler tour for this orientation. Thus, this orientation is pseudo-symmetric and strongly connected.

A.2 Solutions for Chapter 2

2.1.3 Let G have the $n!$ permutations of $\{1, \ldots, n\}$ as vertices; two permutations are adjacent if and only if they differ only by a transposition. The case $n = 3$ is shown in Figure A.5; we use xyz to denote the permutation (x, y, z) of $\{1, 2, 3\}$. The sequence $(123, 132, 312, 321, 231, 213)$ is an ordering of the permutations of the desired kind.

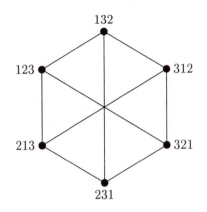

Fig. A.5 A graph for S_3

2.1.4 (a) First assume that $G\backslash v_0$ is acyclic, and let C be a maximal path starting at v_0. Then C is a cycle. If C were not an Euler tour, we could find a cycle C' in $G\backslash C$ as in Example 2.1.2. By hypothesis, C' would have to contain v_0, so that C would not be maximal. Thus, G is arbitrarily traceable from v_0. Conversely, suppose that G is arbitrarily traceable from v_0. If there exists a cycle C in $G\backslash v_0$, we can choose an Euler tour K of the connected component of v_0 in $G\backslash C$, so that K is a maximal path starting in v_0, a contradiction.

(b) Let w be a vertex of maximal degree $2k$ in G, and C an Euler tour for G. Then C can be divided into k cycles $C_1, \ldots, C_k$, each of which contains w only once. As $G\backslash v_0$ is acyclic by (a), v_0 has to occur in each of these cycles, and hence has degree $2k$ as well.

(c) Suppose G is arbitrarily traceable from u, v and w. (a) implies that each of these three vertices has to occur in any cycle of G. However, if G contains at least two cycles, it is easy to construct a cycle which contains only two of these vertices. Thus, G can contain at most one cycle, and hence G is a cycle itself.

(d) Choose two vertices u and v and connect u and v by $2k$ edges. Any subdivision of this multigraph is arbitrarily traceable from u and from v.

2.2.5 Use induction on h; the case $h = 1$ is trivial. Let $B = A^h$, then the (i, k)-entry of A^{h+1} is the sum of all terms $b_{ij}a_{jk}$ over $j = 1, \ldots, n$. By induction hypothesis, b_{ij} is the number of walks of length h from vertex i to vertex

j. Moreover, $a_{jk} = 1$ if and only if (j, k) is an edge (and $a_{jk} = 0$ otherwise). As any walk of length $h + 1$ from vertex i to vertex k consists of some walk of length h (from i to some vertex j) and some last edge (j, k), this implies the assertion.

2.2.6 By Exercise 2.2.5, the (i, j)-entry of the matrix A^2 is, for $i \neq j$, the number of paths of length 2 from i to j, and, for $i = j$, the degree of i. Denoting the matrix with all entries equal to 1 by J, this can be written as $A^2 = aI + cA + d(J - I - A)$.

2.3.2 A word $w = a_i \ldots a_{i+n-1}$ is the immediate predecessor of a word $v = a_{i+1} \ldots a_{i+n}$ in a de Bruijn sequence if and only if the edge v has the end vertex of w as start vertex. Therefore, the de Bruijn sequences correspond to Euler tours in $G_{s,n}$. It remains to show that $G_{s,n}$ satisfies the conditions of Theorem 1.6.1. First, $G_{s,n}$ is strongly connected, because vertices $b_1 \ldots b_{n-1}$ and $c_1 \ldots c_{n-1}$ are always connected by the directed path

$$(b_1 \ldots b_{n-1}c_1, b_2 \ldots b_{n-1}c_1c_2, \ldots, b_{n-1}c_1 \ldots c_{n-1}).$$

Moreover, as

$$d_{in}(x) = d_{out}(x) = s$$

holds for any vertex x, $G_{s,n}$ is pseudo-symmetric.

2.3.3 The directed graph $G_{3,3}$ is shown in Figure A.6. Using $s = 00$, the procedure TRACE(s, new; K) yields the cycle

$$K = (000, 001, 010, 100, 002, 020, 200).$$

Then all edges with start vertex 00 have been used, and $L = (00, 01, 10, 02, 20)$. In step (5) of EULER, vertex $u = 20$ is then removed from L. Now TRACE(u, new; C) yields the cycle

$$C = (201, 011, 110, 101, 012, 120, 202, 021, 210, 102, 022, 220).$$

This cycle is inserted in front of edge 200 into K by step (8) of EULER, so that then $K = (000, 001, \ldots, 020, 201, 011, \ldots, 220, 200)$ and $L = (00, 01, 10, 02, 11, 12, 21, 22)$. Next, $u = 22$ is removed from L in step (5), and the cycle $C = (221, 211, 111, 112, 121, 212, 122, 222)$ is constructed and inserted into K in front of edge 220 (this is done in step (8)). Now EULER finds out that all edges have been used by treating each vertex of L. The de Bruijn sequence corresponding to this Euler tour is 0001002011012021022111121222.

2.6.8 Let G be the empty directed graph with n vertices, that is, $E = \emptyset$. Then any algorithm using the adjacency matrix has to check at least one of the entries a_{ij} and a_{ji} (for each pair (i, j) with $i \neq j$); otherwise, edges (i, j) and (j, i) could be added to G and the algorithm would not realize that the graph is no longer acyclic. Thus, the algorithm has to check at least $n(n - 1)/2 = \Omega(n^2)$ entries.

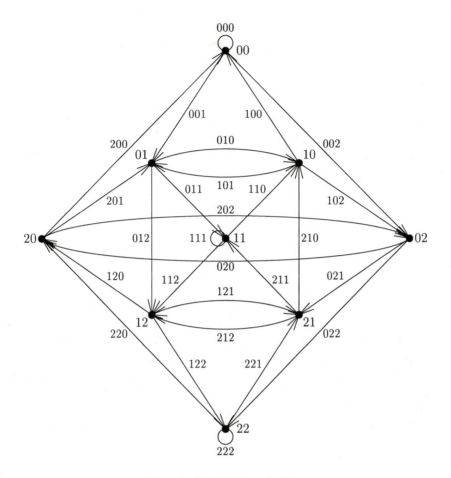

Fig. A.6 The digraph $G_{3,3}$

2.6.9 The algorithm first calculates ind(1) = 2, ind(2) = 0, ind(3) = 3, ind(4) = 1, ind(5) = 2, ind(6) = 4, ind(7) = 3, and $L = (2)$. Then vertex 2 is removed from L and the function ind is updated: ind(1) = 1, ind(3) = 2, ind(4) = 0, ind(7) = 2. Now 4 is appended to L. During the next iteration, 4 is removed from L, and we have ind(1) = 0, ind(3) = 1, ind(5) = 1, ind(7) = 1. Vertex 1 is appended to L and removed again during the next iteration. Continuing in this way yields the topological sorting $(2, 4, 1, 3, 5, 7, 6)$, see Figure A.7 (all edges are oriented from left to right).

2.7.6 DHC contains HC as a special case. (Consider the complete orientation of a given graph.)

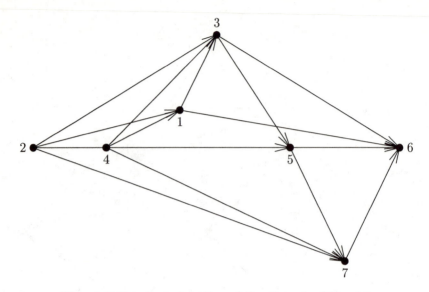

Fig. A.7 Topological sorting of the digraph of Fig. 2.2

2.7.7 We transform HC to HP. Let $G = (V, E)$ be a connected graph. We add three new vertices u, u' and w to G, and the edges uu' and wv_0 (where v_0 is a fixed vertex of G chosen arbitrarily) as well as, for each vertex v adjacent to v_0, an edge uv (see Figure A.8). Then the resulting graph G' has a Hamiltonian path if and only if G has a Hamiltonian cycle. (Note that the two 'external' edges of a Hamiltonian path of G' have to be the edges uu' and $v_0 w$.)

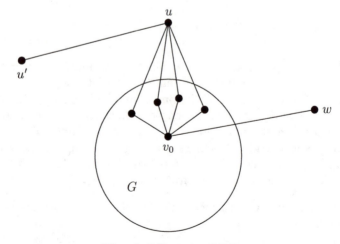

Fig. A.8 Exercise 2.7.7

2.8.3 Independent sets are precisely the complements of vertex covers. Thus, as VC is NP-complete, it follows immediately that IS is NP-complete as well. The cliques in a graph G are precisely the independent sets of the complementary graph $\overline{G}$. Therefore, 'Clique' is NP-complete.

A.3 Solutions for Chapter 3

3.1.2 Let $V = \{(j, k) : j = 1, \ldots, n; k = 0, \ldots, b\}$ be the vertex set of G. We choose all pairs $((j - 1, k), (j, k))$ as edges of length 0 (for $j = 2, \ldots, n$, $k = 0, \ldots, b$) and all pairs $((j - 1, k - a_j), (j, k))$ as edges with length c_j (for $j = 2, \ldots, n$, $k = 0, \ldots, b$ and $k \geq a_j$). Moreover, G contains a start vertex s and edges $(s, (1, 0))$ with length 0 and $(s, (1, a_1))$ with length c_1. Now the paths from s to (j, k) correspond to those subsets of $\{1, \ldots, j\}$ whose total weight is k (and whose value is the length of the path). Finally, we add an end vertex t and edges $((n, k), t)$ of length 0 (for $k = 0, \ldots, b$). Then paths from s to t correspond to subsets whose weight is at most b, and the length of a longest path from s to t is the value of an optimal solution for the knapsack problem.

3.2.3 The distances in the metric space have to be integral; moreover, $d(x, y) \geq 2$ always has to imply that a point z with $d(x, y) = d(x, z) + d(z, y)$ exists. It is clear that this condition is necessary. To show that it is sufficient as well, choose all pairs $\{x, y\}$ with $d(x, y) = 1$ as edges.

3.3.4 The connected components can be determined as follows (here, p denotes the number of connected components and $c(v)$ is the component of G containing $v \in V$).

Procedure COMP$(G; p, c)$

(1) $i \leftarrow 1$;
(2) **while** $V \neq \emptyset$ **do**
(3)   choose a vertex $s \in V$
(4)   BFS$(G, s; d)$
(5) $L \leftarrow \{v \in V : d(v) \text{ is defined}\}$; $V \leftarrow V \backslash L$;
(6)   **for** $v \in L$ **do** $c(v) \leftarrow i$ **od**;
(7) $i \leftarrow i + 1$
(8) **od.**

3.3.8 Let G be a graph containing cycles. Obviously, G contains a cycle which is accessible from some vertex s if and only if a BFS with start vertex s reaches a vertex w (for example when searching from a vertex v) such that $d(w)$ is defined already. Considering the point where such a vertex w occurs for the first time, we obtain a bound l for the length of a cycle accessible from s, namely $l \leq 2d(v) + 2$ if $d(w) = d(v) + 1$ and $l \leq 2d(v) + 1$ if $d(w) = d(v)$. (Note that this is indeed just a bound; the precise length can be determined by backtracking the paths from v and w to s in the BFS-tree T_s up to the first vertex they have in common. Obviously, this vertex does not have to be s). If $d(w) = d(v)$, the bound cannot be improved by continuing the BFS. However, if $d(w) = d(v) + 1$, the BFS should be continued until all vertices which are in the same layer as v have been examined, because l might still be decreased by one; after this, the BFS may be terminated. Having executed this procedure for all vertices s, l obviously contains the girth g of G. If we store the vertex s for which the BFS did yield the best value for l so far, it is easy to determine a cycle C of shortest length by a further BFS: we store the predecessor v of a vertex w at the point when w is labelled with $d(w)$ (in step (7) of BFS), that is, we execute the instruction $p(w) \leftarrow v$ at this point (v is the vertex from which w was reached). Using the predecessor function p, the BFS can be terminated as soon as an edge vw which closes a cycle C occurs. Then C is constructed as the union of the paths (in the BFS-tree T_s) from v and w to the root s and the edge vw. We leave it to the reader to write down such a procedure explicitly. As BFS has complexity $O(|E|)$, such a procedure has complexity $O(|V||E|)$. (If we want to check first whether G contains cycles at all, we may use the procedure COMP of Exercise 3.3.4 to determine the connected components, and then check the numbers of edges of the components using Theorem 1.2.8.)

3.4.4 Let u_i denote the length of a longest path from 1 to i. Then the following analogue of the Bellman equations has to be satisfied:

$$(B^*) \qquad u_1 = 0 \quad \text{and} \quad u_i = \max\{u_k + w_{ki} : i \neq k\} \qquad (i = 2, \ldots, n);$$

here, $w_{ki} = -\infty$ if (k, i) is not an edge of G. Theorems 3.4.1 to 3.4.3 carry over to this case (substitute w by $-w$ and apply the theorems to $(G, -w)$). If we do not want to require G to be acyclic, we still have to assume that G contains cycles of negative length only. The directed graph corresponding to the knapsack problem of Exercise 3.1.2 is acyclic, so that it is possible to determine a longest path from s to t – that is, a solution of the knapsack problem – with complexity $O(|E|)$. However, this is not a 'good' (that is, polynomial) algorithm for this problem, because the number of edges of G has order of magnitude $O(nb)$, so that it depends not only on n but also on b. Restricting the values of b yields a polynomial algorithm, but the general problem – without restrictions on b – is NP-hard (so that it is quite likely that it cannot be solved in polynomial time, see Karp (1972) and Garey and Johnson (1979)).

3.4.5 First let T be an SP-tree and uv an edge of G. Then, by definition, the path from s to v in T is a shortest path from s to v in G. On the other hand, appending edge uv to the path from s to u in T also yields a path from s to v in G. Therefore,

$$d_T(s, v) = d(s, v) \leq d_T(s, u) + w(uv),$$

that is, the given inequality holds. Conversely, suppose that

$$(*) \qquad d_T(s,v) \le d_T(s,u) + w(uv)$$

holds for all edges uv of G. If W is a shortest path from s to v in G (for $v \ne s$) and $e = uv$ is the last edge of W, then $W' = W \backslash e$ has to be a shortest path from s to u in G. (This follows – as in the proof of Theorem 3.4.6 – from the assumption that (G, w) does not contain any directed cycles of negative length.) Using induction on the number of edges of W, we may assume that $d(s, u) = w(W') = d_T(s, u)$. Then $(*)$ implies immediately

$$d(s,v) = d(s,u) + w(uv) = d_T(s,u) + w(uv) \ge d_T(s,v),$$

that is, $d_T(s,v) = d(s,v)$. Thus T is indeed an SP-tree.

3.4.7 Let (G, w) be a network containing a directed cycle K of negative length. Suppose there exists an SP-tree T (with root s) for (G, w). We choose a path W in T which has the minimal number of edges among all paths in T from s to a vertex of K. Denoting the end vertex of W by v, we have $d_T(s,v) = w(W) = d(s,v)$. Note that W cannot contain any edge of K because of the minimality property above. Thus, appending the cycle K to W yields a trail from s to v in G (note that this is not a path) of shorter length than W, a contradiction.

3.5.1 We obtain the network shown in Figure A.9 and the values $t_s = 0$, $t_1 = 0$, $t_2 = 0$, $t_3 = 8$, $t_4 = 25$, $t_5 = 25$, $t_8 = 25$, $t_6 = 34$, $t_7 = 46$, $t_9 = 52$, $t_{10} = 54$, $t_{11} = 55$, $t_z = 57$ and $T_z = 57$, $m_z = 0$; $T_{11} = 55$, $m_{11} = 0$; $T_{10} = 54$, $m_{10} = 0$; $T_9 = 52$, $m_9 = 0$; $T_7 = 46$, $m_7 = 0$; $T_6 = 37$, $m_6 = 3$; $T_8 = 39$, $m_8 = 14$; $T_5 = 25$, $m_5 = 0$; $T_4 = 28$, $m_4 = 3$; $T_3 = 32$, $m_3 = 24$; $T_2 = 24$, $m_2 = 24$; $T_1 = 0$, $m_1 = 0$; $T_s = 0$, $m_s = 0$. The critical path is $(s, 1, 5, 7, 9, 10, 11, z)$.

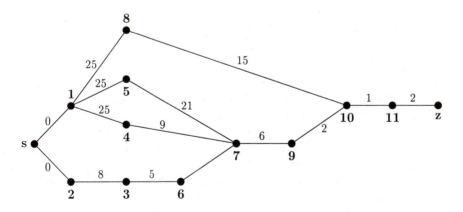

Fig. A.9 Project: Substitute production facility

3.5.2 Consider the network on G where all edges have length 1. If G is acyclic, the length of a longest path from s to v can be determined as in Section 3.5 (or as explained in the solution for Exercise 3.4.4) by recursively solving the equations (B^*) or (CPM), respectively (where G is assumed to be topologically sorted). Thus, a topological sorting of G has to be found first; this could be done by TOPSORT, for example. This procedure also checks whether G is acyclic. The whole method has complexity $O(|E|)$.

3.5.3 For the time being, we denote the rank function on G by r'. Then we have to show that, at the end of RANK, $r(v) = r'(v)$ holds for all v. This can be done using induction on the order in which r is defined. Note that $p(w)$ is the predecessor of w on a longest path from s to w; this function can also be used to find such a path: in reverse order, we get the path $(w, p(w), p(p(w)), \ldots, s)$. The values $d(v) = d_{in}(v)$ needed in step (3) can be determined from the A_w as in TOPSORT. Ordering the vertices of G by increasing rank yields a topological sorting of G; the order of vertices of the same rank is arbitrary. As each edge is examined exactly twice during RANK (once when d is determined in (3), and once in step (7)), this algorithm has complexity $O(|E|)$ as well.

3.6.3 We introduce a variable $p(v)$ which contains the predecessor of v on a shortest path (at the respective point of time) from s to v. $p(v)$ is initialized to be 0. We change step (6) as follows:

(6')   **for** $v \in T \cap A_u$ **do**
$\qquad\qquad$ **if** $d(u) + w_{uv} < d(v)$ **then** $d(v) \leftarrow d(u) + w_{uv}$; $p(v) \leftarrow u$ **fi**
$\qquad$ **od**

3.6.5 We obtain $d(1) = 0$, $d(5) = 1$, $d(3) = 2$, $d(4) = 6$, $d(2) = 9$, $d(8) = 13$, $d(6) = d(7) = 14$.

3.6.8 We may assume the given network to be connected; then planarity implies that $|E| = \Theta(|V|)$, see Example 2.5.1. Thus, the modified Algorithm of Dijkstra has complexity $O(|V| \log |V|)$.

3.6.9 We denote the values defined in (1) and (2) by $d_0(v)$ and the values defined during the k-th iteration of the **repeat**-loop by $d_k(v)$. Now we can show by induction that $d_k(v)$ is the length of a shortest path from s to v which has at most k edges. As (G, w) does not contain any cycles of negative length, a shortest path from s to v can contain at most $|V| - 1$ edges. Thus, the condition in (7) is satisfied at least for $k = |V|$. As one iteration of the **repeat**-loop requires $O(|E|)$ steps (using adjacency lists A'_v for the end vertices of the edges), we get a complexity of $O(|V||E|)$.

3.7.1 Determine the least common multiple T of all time cycles and substitute a line L with time cycle $T_L \neq T$ (say $T = m_L T_L$, $m_L \neq 1$) by m_L lines with time cycle T and times of departure s_L, $s_L + T_L$, $s_L + 2T_L$, etc.

3.8.3 Analogous to Algorithm 3.6.1, see Exercise 3.6.3.

3.8.5 The matrix we obtain finally is

$$D_7 = \begin{pmatrix} 0 & 4 & 5 & 7 & 12 & 10 & 12 \\ \infty & 0 & 6 & 3 & 8 & 6 & 8 \\ \infty & \infty & 0 & 4 & 9 & 7 & 9 \\ \infty & \infty & 3 & 0 & 5 & 3 & 3 \\ \infty & \infty & 7 & 4 & 0 & 3 & 2 \\ \infty & \infty & 9 & 6 & 2 & 0 & 2 \\ \infty & \infty & \infty & \infty & \infty & \infty & 0 \end{pmatrix}.$$

3.8.6 Substitute d in the procedure FLOYD by the adjacency matrix of G, that is, $d(i,j) = 1$ if ij is an edge and $d(i,j) = 0$ otherwise. Step (9) is changed to

$$(9') \quad d(i,j) \leftarrow \max\{d(i,j),\ \min(d(i,k),d(k,j))\};$$

alternatively, 'max' could be interpreted as the Boolean operation 'or', and 'min' as 'and'.

3.8.7 Let G be an acyclic directed graph; consider the network on G having all lengths equal to 1. If we calculate the maximum $\max\,(d(i,j),d(i,k)+d(k,j))$ in step (9) of the procedure FLOYD instead of the minimum, the lengths of longest paths between any two vertices are determined with complexity $O(|V|^3)$, because G is acyclic (this can be shown in a manner analogous to the proof of Theorem 3.8.2). However, we have to use the adjacency matrix of G instead of d, that is, we set $d(i,j) = 0$ if ij is not an edge of G. Then, at the end of the algorithm, we have $d(i,j) = 0$ if and only if there is no path from i to j. Otherwise, $d(i,j)$ is indeed the maximal number of edges on a path from i to j. We now choose all the edges ij with $d(i,j) = 1$ for G_{red}.

3.9.3 Define the values of the variables $d_k(v)$ as in the solution for Exercise 3.6.9. Then we can show that G contains a directed cycle of negative length which is accessible from s if and only if $d_{n-1} \neq d_n$. The reader should check this statement in all detail. Thus, the Algorithm of Bellman-Ford can be used to find cycles of negative length (because s is a root of G) by substituting the **repeat-until**-loop as given in Exercise 3.6.9 by a **for-do**-loop. Introducing a predecessor function $p(v)$, it is then possible to find either a directed cycle of negative length or an SP-tree with root s. We state the resulting procedure explicitly below; here, the A'_v are again (as in the solution for Exercise 3.6.9) the adjacency lists of G for the end vertices of the edges.

Procedure SPTREE $(G, w, s; d, p,$ neg, $T)$

(1) $d(s) \leftarrow 0$;
(2) $T \leftarrow \emptyset$;
(3) **for** $v \in V \backslash \{s\}$ **do** $d(v) \leftarrow \infty$ **od**;
(4) **for** $i = 1$ **to** n **do**
(5)   **for** $v \in V$ **do** $d'(v) \leftarrow d(v)$ **od**;
(6)   **for** $v \in V$ **do**
(7)   **for** $u \in A'_v$ **do**
(8)   **if** $d'(v) > d'(u) + w_{uv}$
(9)   **then** $d(v) \leftarrow d'(u) + w_{uv}, p(v) \leftarrow u$
(10)   **fi**
(11)   **od**
(12)   **od**
(13) **od**;
(14) **if** $d(v) = d'(v)$ for all $v \in V$
(15) **then** neg $\leftarrow$ false;
(16)   **for** $v \in V \backslash \{s\}$ **do** $T \leftarrow T \cup \{p(v)v\}$ **od**
(17) **else** neg $\leftarrow$ true
(18) **fi**.

3.9.4 Substitute the initial values $d(i, i) = 0$ in step (3) of procedure FLOYD by $d(i, i) = \infty$. Then, at the end of the algorithm, $d(i, i)$ states the shortest length of a directed cycle containing i.

3.10.2 The fact that $a = a \oplus o$ shows that $\geq$ is reflexive, and $a = b \oplus b'$ and $b = c \oplus c'$ imply $a = c \oplus (b' + c')$, so that $\geq$ is transitive as well. Suppose that $\oplus$ is idempotent. Then $a = b \oplus c$ and $b = a \oplus d$ imply

$$a = b \oplus c = b \oplus (b \oplus c) = b \oplus a = a \oplus b = a \oplus (a \oplus d) = a \oplus d = b;$$

it follows that $\geq$ is antisymmetric.

3.10.3 Let E be the matrix with diagonal entries 0 and all other entries ∞. Then we obtain the equation $D = D * W \oplus E$.

3.10.5 We have $(A')^k = \sum_{i=0}^{k} \binom{k}{i} A^i = \sum_{i=0}^{k} A^i = A^{(k)}$. Thus, $A^{(n)}$ can be calculated for $n = 2^a$ by a matrix multiplications:

$$A^{(1)} = A' = A \oplus E, A^{(2)} = (A')^2, A^{(4)} = (A^{(2)})^2, \text{etc.}$$

Assuming that the operations $\oplus$ and $*$ can be executed (in R) in one single step, we get a complexity of $O(n^3 \log n)$ for this method of calculating $A^{(n)}$. For the special case $(\overline{\mathbb{R}}, \oplus, *)$, we get – as explained in Lemma 3.10.4 – a technique alternative to the Algorithm of Floyd-Warshall, because $D = W^{(n-1)}$. However, the complexity of this technique is worse than what we found in

Theorem 3.8.2.

3.10.6 It is a matter of checking calculations to show that the matrices form a path algebra. For any solution Y of Equation (3.5), we have

$$Y = W * (W * Y \oplus B) \oplus B = W^2 * Y \oplus W^{(1)} * B;$$

so that, by induction,

$$Y = W^{k+1} * Y \oplus W^{(k)} * B \qquad \text{for all } k.$$

In particular, for $k = p$,

$$Y = W^{p+1} * Y \oplus W^* * B, \qquad \text{that is, } Y \geq W^* * B.$$

If the addition $\oplus$ on R is idempotent, then addition of matrices is idempotent as well, and Exercise 3.10.2 shows that, in this case, the corresponding pre-ordering on the set of matrices is even a partial ordering. Thus, the minimal solution $W^* * B$ of $(*)$ is unique.

3.10.10 Choose $R = \{a : 0 \leq a \leq 1\}$, $\oplus = \max$ and $* = \cdot$.

3.10.11 Note that A is stable if and only if $A^r = 0$ holds for some r from $\mathbb{N}$, because $A^{(r-1)} = A^{(r)} = A^{(r-1)} + A^r$ holds if and only if $A^r = 0$. Lemma 3.10.4 implies that this condition holds if G is acyclic, because then any walk contains at most $r - 1$ edges (where we choose r to be the number of vertices of G). In this case, A is a solution of the equation $A^* = A^*A + E$. As K is a field, this means $A^*(E - A) = E$, that is, $A^* = (E - A)^{-1}$. More generally, it is possible to show that A is stable if all cycles in G have weight 0 (with respect to w). The converse is false in general: it is easy to find an example with weights 1 and -1 such that A is stable, but G contains cycles of weight $\neq 0$. However, for $K = \mathbb{R}$ and positive weights, the converse statement is true.

A.4 Solutions for Chapter 4

4.1.2

(1) $\Rightarrow$ (2): Let e be any edge of the only cycle C contained in G. Then $G\backslash e$ is connected and acyclic, that is, $G\backslash e$ is a tree.

(2) $\Rightarrow$ (3): As any tree on n vertices has $n - 1$ edges and is connected, the statement in (3) follows.

(3) $\Rightarrow$ (4): As G is not a tree (G has one more edge than a tree could have), there are edges in G which are not bridges (see Lemma 4.1.1). Removing some edge e which is not a bridge yields a tree, so that e has to be contained in each cycle of G. Thus the set of all edges which are not bridges forms a cycle.

(4) $\Rightarrow$ (1): An edge e is not a bridge if and only if it is contained in some cycle (see Exercise 1.6.4). Thus G contains a unique cycle consisting of those edges which are not bridges.

4.1.3 The statement concerning the number of centers is clear for the trees K_1 and K_2. For any other tree T, remove all leaves of T, then the resulting tree T' has the same centers as T and the statement follows by induction. Denote the diameter of a tree T by d and the excentricity of a center by e. Then we have $d = 2e$ or $d = 2e - 1$, where $d = 2e$ holds if and only if T has only one center. This statement can be proved by induction as well.

4.1.4 Let W be a trail of maximal length in G. As G is acyclic, W has to be a path, and as W is maximal, the end vertices of W have degree 1. Thus, $G\backslash W$ is a forest containing $2k - 2$ vertices of odd degree. Now the statement follows by induction.

4.1.5 There are precisely 6 isomorphism types of trees on 6 vertices; representatives of these types are given in Figure 1.6. We denote these representatives by $T_1, \ldots, T_6$. Now let T be any tree on $\{1, \ldots, 6\}$. Then the image of T under any permutation $\sigma \in S_6$ is a tree isomorphic to T. By a well-known equation for permutation groups, the number of trees isomorphic to T is equal to the order of S_6 (that is, 6! = 720) divided by the order of the automorphism group of T. We obtain:

T_1 : cyclic group of order 2 (exchange the two leaves of the tree), 360 isomorphic trees;

T_2 : cyclic group of order 2 (exchange the two leaves at the 'bottom' of the tree), 360 isomorphic trees;

T_3 : symmetric group S_3 (acting on the 3 leaves at the 'bottom'), 120 isomorphic trees;

T_4 : cyclic group of order 2 (exchange the two branches in the lower half of the tree), 360 isomorphic trees;

T_5 : direct product of 3 cyclic groups of order 2 (exchange the two centers and exchange the two leaves at the 'top' or at the 'bottom' of the tree), 90 isomorphic trees;

T_6 : symmetric group S_5 (acting on the 5 leaves), 6 isomorphic trees.

The total number of trees is $360 + 360 + 120 + 360 + 90 + 6 = 1296 = 6^4$; this agrees with out result of Corollary 1.2.11.

4.1.6 Let x be a vertex of T, and let y and z be two further vertices which are contained in a different connected component of $\overline{T}$ than x. Then x is connected to y and z in T, and as T is a tree, yz cannot be an edge of T. Therefore, y and z are adjacent in $\overline{T}$, and the connected components of $\overline{T}$ are complete graphs. In a similar way, we see that $\overline{T}$ has at most two connected components, and if it has two components, one of them has to be an isolated vertex. Thus, T is a star in this case: There exists a vertex which is adjacent to all other vertices. The remaining assertion follows from Exercise 1.2.4 and Theorem 1.2.6.

4.2.10 By Theorem 4.2.9, the number of spanning trees of the complete bipartite graph $K_{m,n}$ is equal to the absolute value of the determinant of the matrix

$$A' = \begin{pmatrix} nI_m & -J_{m,n-1} \\ -J_{n-1,m} & mI_{n-1} \end{pmatrix},$$

where the indices give the numbers of rows and columns of the respective submatrices (and I denotes the unit matrix and J the matrix having all entries 1, as usual). Now it is just an exercise from Linear Algebra to show that $\det A' = n^{m-1}m^{n-1}$: by performing appropriate row and column transformations, it is easy to transform A' into a triangular matrix with diagonal entries $1, n \ldots, n, m, \ldots, m$.

4.2.11 The proofs of the results carry over, as now $1 + 1 = 0$, and thus $-1 = +1$.

4.2.12 First assume that G' is bipartite and the partition of its vertex set is $V = S \mathbin{\dot\cup} T$. Let M' be a square submatrix of M of order k, say. The case $k = 1$ is trivial, so let $k \neq 1$. First consider the case where each column of M' contains two entries 1. The k vertices corresponding to the rows of M' can be divided into two sets $S' \subset S$ and $T' \subset T$. Each column of M' corresponds to an edge of G which must have both end vertices in $S' \cup T'$ (using the above hypothesis). Thus, as G is bipartite, each column of M has one entry 1 in a row corresponding to S', and the other entry 1 in a row corresponding to T'. Therefore, the sum of the rows corresponding to S' is equal to the sum of the rows corresponding to T', so that the rows of M' are linearly dependent and $\det M' = 0$. Now suppose that M' contains a column with at most one entry 1, then the statement follows by using this column for determining $\det M'$ (by induction).

Conversely, suppose that M is totally unimodular and G is not bipartite. Then, by Theorem 3.3.5, G contains a cycle K of odd length, say

$$K = v_0 \xrightarrow{\ e_1\ } v_1 \ \ldots\ v_{2n-1} \xrightarrow{\ e_{2n}\ } v_{2n} \xrightarrow{\ e_{2n+1}\ } v_0.$$

Now simple calculations yield that the determinant of the submatrix M corresponding to the $2n + 1$ vertices and $2n + 1$ edges of K is 2, a contradiction.

4.2.13 By Corollary 1.2.11, the graph K_n has precisely n^{n-2} spanning trees. As each of these trees has $n - 1$ edges and each edge e has to be contained in the same number x of spanning trees, the number of spanning trees of $K_n \backslash e$ is $n^{n-2} - x = n^{n-2} - 2n^{n-3} = (n - 2)n^{n-3}$.

4.2.14 G has $p = n - m$ connected components.

4.3.4 Suppose G contains two minimal spanning trees T and T'. We number the edges of T and T' as

$$e_1, \ldots, e_{k-1}, e_k, \ldots, e_{n-1} \quad \text{and} \quad e_1, \ldots, e_{k-1}, e'_k, \ldots, e'_{n-1},$$

respectively, where

$$w(e_1) < \ldots < w(e_{n-1}) \quad \text{and} \quad w(e_1) < \ldots < w(e_k) < w(e'_k) < \ldots < w(e'_{n-1}).$$

Adding the edge e_k to T' yields a cycle $C_{T'}(e_k)$. As the weights of the edges are pairwise distinct, all edges $e \neq e_k$ of $C_{T'}(e_k)$ have to be contained among the first $k - 1$ edges $e_1, \ldots e_{k-1}$ of T'. But as these edges are contained in T as well, this means that T contains the cycle $C_{T'}(e_k)$, a contradiction.

4.4.13 Assign weight 1 to all the edges. Then, in the Algorithm of Boruvka, we can choose, for each connected component $U \in M$, any arbitrary edge e_u leading out of U. Thus, if there exist two connected components $U, U' \in M$ which can be connected by two different edges of G, choosing these two edges as e_u and $e_{u'}$ yields a cycle.

4.4.14 A minimal spanning tree has weight $2 + 13 + 21 + 35 + 51 = 122$.

4.4.15 The proof of Theorem 4.3.1 shows that the subgraph of the minimal spanning trees (for a given weight function w) is connected. If we assign weight $w(e) = 1$ to all edges e, we see that this implies that the whole tree graph is connected.

4.5.4 The edges $e_{15}, e_{14}, e_{13}, e_{12}, e_{11}, e_{10}$ and e_8 form a maximal spanning tree (of weight $28 + 27 + 26 + 24 + 10 + 9 + 8 = 132$). The edges are given in the order in which the Algorithm of Kruskal would find them.

4.5.5 The following characterization of maximal spanning trees follows from Theorem 4.3.1 by substituting w by $-w$: A spanning tree T is maximal if and only if, for each edge $e \notin T$, the condition

$$(*) \qquad w(e) \geq w(f) \quad \text{for all edges } f \text{ in } C_T(e)$$

holds. So let $e = uv$ be an edge of G not contained in T. Then, by hypothesis, the unique path W from u to v in T has capacity $w(W) \geq w(e)$. Obviously, $C_T(e) = W \cup \{e\}$, and this implies $(*)$. Now this characterization implies the assertion.

4.5.7 The directed graph shown in Figure A.10 yields an example.

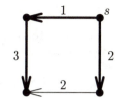

Fig. A.10 A digraph

4.7.7 Let T be an arbitrary spanning tree for G and x a center of T. Denoting the excentricity of x in T by $e_T(x)$, T has diameter $d_T = 2e_T(x)$ or $2e_T(x) - 1$ by Exercise 4.1.3. It is trivial that x can have excentricity at most $e_T(x)$ in G. Therefore, it is an obvious approach to look for spanning trees whose centers are centers of G as well. So let z be a center of G and T_z a spanning tree for G determined by a BFS starting at z. Note that T_z is an SP-tree for G with root z. Now, as z is a vertex of minimal excentricity for G, z indeed has to be a center of T_z (because of our considerations above). Therefore, T_z has diameter $d = 2e$ or $2e - 1$, where e is the excentricity of z in G. Moreover, any other spanning tree has diameter at least $2e - 1$. The tree T_z thus solves our problem; note that a center z (and then a tree T_z) can be determined with complexity $O(|V|^3)$ by Theorem 3.8.8. We mention that it is easy to find examples where a BFS starting at z could either find a tree of diameter $2e$ or a tree of diameter $2e - 1$ depending on the order in which adjacent vertices are examined.

A.5 Solutions for Chapter 5

5.1.5 The network in Figure A.11 has a maximal matching of weight 14, but the Greedy Algorithm constructs a matching of weight 12.

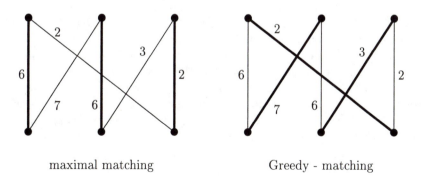

maximal matching   Greedy - matching

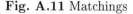

Fig. A.11 Matchings

5.2.3 Identify E with the set of columns of A.

5.2.4 Statements (1) and (2) are clear. To show that (3) holds, let J be a maximal independent subset of $A \cap B$ and K a maximal independent subset of $A \cup B$ containing J. Write $K = J \dot\cup X \dot\cup Y$ with $X \subset A$ and $Y \subset B$. Then $J \cup X$ and $J \cup Y$ are independent subsets of A and B, respectively, so that

$$\rho(A \cup B) + \rho(A \cap B) = 2|J| + |X| + |Y| = |J \cup X| + |J \cup Y| \le \rho(A) + \rho(B).$$

5.2.8 We have $\sigma(X) = \{e \in E : \rho(X \cup \{e\}) = \rho(X)\}$ by Theorem 5.2.7. Thus, (1) is clear. To prove (2), let J be a maximal independent subset of Y and K a maximal independent subset of X containing J. If $e \in \sigma(Y)$, then $e \in \sigma(X)$ (otherwise $K \cup \{e\}$ would be independent and $J \cup \{e\}$ would be independent as well, contradicting $\rho(J \cup \{e\}) = \rho(J)$), and (2) follows. By Theorem 5.2.7, $\sigma(X)$ is the unique maximal set containing X such that $\rho(\sigma(X)) = \rho(X)$; now (3) is clear. To show (4), let J be a maximal independent subset of X (and hence of $\sigma(X)$). As $y \notin \sigma(X)$ and $y \in \sigma(X \cup \{x\})$, $J \cup \{x\}$ and $J \cup \{y\}$ have to be independent sets. Moreover, $\rho(X \cup \{x\}) = \rho(X \cup \{y\}) = \rho(X \cup \{x,y\})$. But this implies $x \in \sigma(X \cup \{y\})$.

5.2.9 Let B be a basis of the matroid $M = (E, \mathbf{S})$. As $\rho(B) = \rho(E)$, Theorem 5.2.7 yields $\rho(B) = E$, so that B is a generating set for M. Now suppose B is not minimal, then there exists a proper subset C of B such that $B \subset E = \sigma(C)$. But then $\rho(E) = |C| < |B|$, which contradicts the fact that B is independent. Conversely, let D be a minimal generating set and A a maximal independent subset of D. Then $\rho(D) = |A|$ implies $D \subset \sigma(A)$ and (using Exercise 5.2.8) $E = \sigma(D) \subset \sigma(\sigma(A)) = \sigma(A)$. Thus, A is a generating set of M as well and the minimality of D implies $A = D$. Thus, D is independent. Now $\sigma(D) = E$, so that $|D| = \rho(E)$ and D is a basis of M.

5.2.13 Suppose there exist two cycles C, D and elements $x \in C \cap D$ and $y \in C \backslash D$ violating (2′); we may assume that $|C \cup D|$ is minimal for this counterexample. Theorem 5.2.12 implies that there exists a cycle $F_1 \subset (C \cup D) \backslash \{x\}$, but $y \notin F_1$. Note that the set $F_1 \cap (D \backslash C)$ cannot be empty (otherwise F_1 would be a proper subset of C). We choose $z \in F_1 \cap (D \backslash C)$ and consider the cycles D, F_1 and the elements $z \in D \cap F_1$ and $x \in D \backslash F_1$. As $y \notin D \cup F_1$, $D \cup F_1$ is a proper subset of $C \cup D$. Now we chose our counterexample to be minimal, so that there exists a cycle F_2 such that $x \in F_2 \subset (D \cup F_1) \backslash \{z\}$. Consider $C, F_2, x \in C \cap F_2$ and $y \in C \backslash F_2$. Again the minimality of our counterexample implies that there exists a cycle F_3 such that $y \in F_3 \subset (C \cup F_2) \backslash \{x\}$. But as $C \cup F_2$ is contained in $C \cup D$, this is a contradiction.

5.2.14

(a) Let A and B be two closed sets in M. Then we have $\sigma(A \cap B) \subset \sigma(A) \cap \sigma(B) = A \cap B \subset \sigma(A \cap B)$, so that $A \cap B$ is closed as well.

(b) Let A be a closed set containing X, then $\sigma(X) \subset \sigma(A) = A$. Thus, $\sigma(X)$ is contained in the intersection of all closed sets containing X. Now (a) implies that $\sigma(X)$ is equal to this intersection.

(c) If the condition $\rho(X \cup \{x\}) = \rho(X)$ holds for some $x \in E \backslash X$, then $x \in \sigma(X)$, so that X cannot be closed. The converse is shown by the same argument.

5.2.15 Let $\{x_1, \ldots, x_r\}$ be a basis of $(E, \mathbf{S})$. The 2^r subsets of this basis have 2^r distinct spans; these spans are obviously pairwise distinct closed sets.

5.3.5 By Theorem 5.3.1, we have $\rho(E \backslash A^*) = \rho^*(A^*) - |A^*| + \rho(E) = \rho(E)$ (because A^* is independent in M^*). As A is an independent subset of $E \backslash A^*$, A can be extended to a maximal independent subset (in M) of $E \backslash A^*$; we denote this subset by B. Then we have seen that $\rho(B) = \rho(E)$, that is, B is a basis of M. Therefore, $B^* = E \backslash B$ is a basis of M^* containing A^*.

5.3.6 First let B be a basis of M. Suppose that there exists a cocircuit C^* with $B \cap C^* = \emptyset$. Then $E \backslash B$ contains the cocircuit C^* and is dependent in M^*, which contradicts Corollary 5.3.2. Now suppose that a subset X of B intersects each cocircuit. Then $E \backslash X$ cannot contain any circuit of M^*, so that $E \backslash X$ must be independent in M^*. As $E \backslash X$ contains the basis $E \backslash B$ of M^*, we must have $X = B$. Thus, the bases are the minimal sets with the given property. The converse is shown analogously.

5.3.7 Suppose we have $C \cap C^* = \{e\}$. Then the two sets $A = C \backslash \{e\}$ and $A^* = C^* \backslash \{e\}$ are disjoint and independent in M and in M^*, respectively. By Exercise 5.3.5, A and A^* can be extended to bases B and B^* of M and M^*, respectively, and these bases are disjoint. It follows that $E = B \cup B^*$. But as C and C^* are dependent, e can be contained neither in B nor in B^*, a contradiction.

5.3.8 Let B be a basis of M containing $C \backslash \{x\}$. As $B^* = E \backslash B$ is a basis of M^*, $B^* \cup \{y\}$ has to contain a unique cocircuit C^* of M by Theorem 5.2.10. Obviously, y must be contained in C^*. Now $x \notin C^*$ would imply $|C \cap C^*| = 1$ contradicting the statement of Exercise 5.3.7. Thus, we must have $x, y \in C \cap C^*$, so that $C \cap C^* = \{x, y\}$.

5.4.6 By definition of the rank quotient, it suffices to find a subset A of E and two maximal independent subsets D and D' of A such that $2|D'| = n|D|$. We may assume $V = \{1, \ldots n\}$. Then

$$D := \{(i, i+1) : i = 1, \ldots, n-1\} \quad \text{and} \quad D' = \{(i, j) : i, j = 1, \ldots n \text{ and } i > j\}$$

and $A := D \cup D'$ have the desired property.

5.4.10 M is the intersection of the graphic matroid $M(G)$, the head-partition matroid and the tail-partition matroid of G.

5.5.7 Suppose w does not have to satisfy the triangle inequality. Then we may, for example, increase the weight of the edge of maximal weight in Example 5.5.6 by any value and thus make the solution the Greedy Algorithm yields as poor as we want.

5.6.3 Suppose that the axiom (CC) is violated by some feasible set A, elements $x, y \in \text{ext}(A)$ and a set $X \subset E \backslash (A \cup \text{ext}(A))$. Thus, there exists a basis B such that $A \cup X \cup \{x\} \subset B$, whereas $A \cup X \cup \{y\}$ is not contained in any basis. Consider the following weight function for E:

$$
w(z) := \begin{cases} 3 & \text{if } z \in A \\ 2 & \text{if } z \in X \\ 1 & \text{if } z = y \\ 0 & \text{otherwise.} \end{cases}
$$

Then the basis B has weight $w(B) = 3|A| + 2|X|$. The Greedy Algorithm begins by constructing (in some appropriate order) the feasible set A and then adds y (the elements of X have larger weight than y, but they are not contained in $\text{ext}(A)$). After that, the algorithm can add at most $|X| - 1$ of the elements of X, because we assumed that $A \cup X \cup \{y\}$ is not contained in any feasible set. Thus, the solution the Greedy Algorithm yields has weight at most

$$
3|A| + 1 + 2(|X| - 1) < w(B),
$$

a contradiction.

A.6 Solutions for Chapter 6

6.1.9 Substitute each vertex v by a pair (v, v') of vertices and each edge vw by $v'w$. Furthermore, add all edges of the form vv' and define $c(v'w) := c(vw)$ and $c(vv') := d(v)$. It is now easy to see that a flow f' on the new network corresponds to a flow f on N satisfying (F3). Now let (S, T) be a cut in the new network and E' the set of edges e with $e^- \in S$ and $e^+ \in T$. Each edge of type $v'w$ corresponds to an edge vw in N and each edge of type vv' corresponds to a vertex v of N. Thus, the set E' of edges of the cut (S, T) corresponds to a 'cut' in N in the following sense: a (generalized) cut is a set of edges and vertices ($\neq s, t$) of G such that, if we remove these edges and vertices, t is not accessible from s any more. The capacity of such a cut is the sum of all $c(e)$ and $d(v)$ for edges e and vertices v contained in the cut. Then the generalization of Theorem 6.1.6 is: The minimal capacity of a generalized cut is equal to the maximal value of a flow satisfying (F3). This theorem is easy to derive from Theorem 6.1.6 applied to the network defined above.

6.1.10 If we need k sources $s_1, \ldots, s_k$ (for which (F2) does not have to be satisfied and from which as much flow as possible should originate), for example, we add a new source s and all edges ss_i $(i = 1, \ldots k)$ with sufficient capacity.

6.1.11 Let W be the maximal value of a flow on N and (S, T) a minimal cut. Then, by hypothesis and by Theorem 6.1.6, we have $c(S, T) = W \neq 0$. If we remove an edge e with $e^- \in S$ and $e^+ \in T$ and $c(e) \neq 0$ from G, the capacity $c(S, T)$ and hence the value of a maximal flow is decreased by $c(e)$. Thus, it is an obvious approach to choose e as an edge of maximal capacity in a minimal cut. However, these edges do not have to be most vital: In the network shown in Figure 6.12, edge sa is obviously most vital, even though it is not contained in a minimal cut.

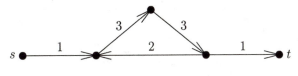

Fig. A.12 A flow

6.1.12 The capacities in the flow network of Figure A.12 define a flow which is obviously maximal, but which is not the sum of elementary flows.

6.1.13 First, in step (3) of Algorithm 6.1.7, we set $d(v) = 0$ for $v \neq s$. During the following labelling process, the labels are not permanent; similarly to the Algorithm of Dijkstra, the label of vertex v chosen in step (5) is made permanent at this point. As we want to construct augmenting paths of maximal capacity from s to all the other vertices, we choose in step (5), among all labelled vertices v with $u(v) = \text{false}$ (that is, v is not yet permanent), the vertex v for which $d(v)$ is maximal (initially, this is s). We do not want to change the flow as soon as t is reached, but want to wait until t is made permanent (that is, until t is chosen in step (5)). Therefore, we insert an **if** clause after step (5): if $v = t$, we may change the flow as in steps (16) to (28) of Algorithm 6.1.7 (where, of course, we have to set $d(v) = 0$ for $v \neq s$ in step (27)). Otherwise, that is, if $v \neq t$, the labelling process is continued from v. As in steps (6) to (9), we first consider all edges of the form $e = vw$. If $u(w) = \text{false}$ (that is, w is not yet labelled permanently) and $d(w) < \min\{d(v), c(e) - f(e)\}$, then $d(w)$ is replaced by this minimum and w is labelled with $(v, +, d(w))$ (so that the former label is replaced). Steps (10) to (13) for edges of the form $e = wv$ are changed analogously. Next, v is made permanent in step (14). We leave the further details and the task of writing down a formal version of the technique described above to the reader.

6.2.4 We use the algorithm described in the solution of Exercise 6.1.13. During the first iteration, the vertices chosen in step (5) are s with $d(s) = \infty$, a with $d(a) = 38$, d with $d(d) = 13$, c with $d(c) = 10$, f with $d(f) = 10$ and

t with $d(t) = 10$ (in this order). This yields an augmenting path of capacity
10; we obtain the flow f_1 of value 10 shown in Figure A.13 (the labels of the
first iteration are given as well).

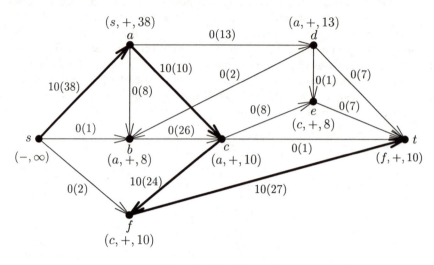

Fig. A.13 $w(f_1) = 10$

During the next iteration, the vertices s with $d(s) = \infty$, a with $d(a) = 28$,
d with $d(d) = 13$, b with $d(b) = 8$, c with $d(c) = 8$, f with $d(f) = 8$ and t
with $d(t) = 8$ are chosen in step (5). The corresponding augmenting path of
capacity 8 yields the flow f_2 shown in Figure A.14.

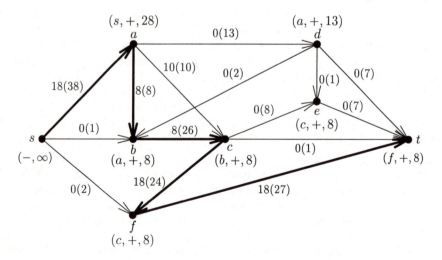

Fig. A.14 $w(f_2) = 18$

During the following iteration, the vertices chosen in step (5) are s with $d(s) = \infty$, a with $d(a) = 20$, d with $d(d) = 13$ and t with $d(t) = 7$. We obtain an augmenting path of capacity 7 and the flow f_3 shown in Figure A.15.

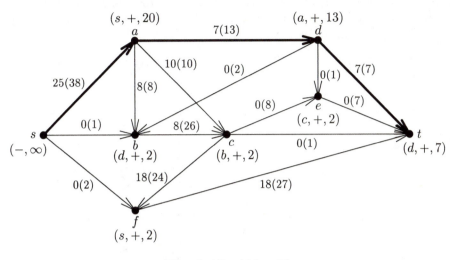

Fig. A.15 $w(f_3) = 25$

Four more iterations are needed; the augmenting paths constructed are $s — f — t$ of capacity 2, $s — a — d — b — c — f — t$ of capacity 2, $s — b — c — t$ of capacity 1 and $s — a — d — e — t$ of capacity 1. The resulting flow f with $w(f) = 31$ is shown in Figure A.16.

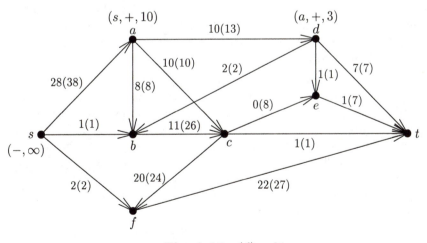

Fig. A.16 $w(f) = 31$

Thus, this algorithm needed 7 changes of the flow, whereas the Algorithm of Edmonds and Karp used in Example 6.2.3 made 9 flow changes. However, in the algorithm used here, the labelling process is somewhat more involved. Note that the maximal flows of Figures 6.12 and A.16 are not equal; there are other maximal flows as well, because there are several ways of distributing the flow coming out of vertex c.

6.2.5 The maximal value of a flow is 5; Figure A.17 shows a flow f with $w(f) = 5$ and a cut of this capacity.

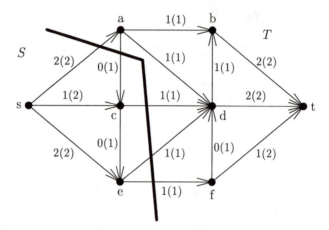

Fig. A.17 Solution for Exercise 6.2.5

6.2.6 Let f be the flow of value $W = w(f)$ which was found for the incorrect capacity $d(e)$, (S, T) a minimal cut, and denote the correct capacity by $c(e)$. These values can be used when calculating a flow for the correct capacity as follows. We distinguish two cases:

Case 1. $c(e) < d(e)$: If e is contained in (S, T) (that is, $e^- \in S$ and $e^+ \in T$), it is trivial that (S, T) is still a minimal cut. In the corrected network, (S, T) has capacity $c(S, T) - (d(e) - c(e))$, so that the maximal value of a flow is $W' = W - (d(e) - c(e))$. To find a flow of value W', consider all the augmenting paths (constructed before) containing e and decrease the value of the corresponding flow by $d(e) - c(e)$. If e is not contained in (S, T) and $f(e) \le c(e)$, there is obviously nothing to change. If $f(e) > c(e)$, we decrease the flow by $f(e) - c(e)$ (as before) and execute the algorithm again, using the decreased flow as the initial flow.

Case 2. $c(e) > d(e)$: If e is not contained in (S, T), then (S, T) is still a minimal cut and there is nothing to change. Otherwise, we execute the algorithm again, using f as the initial flow.

6.2.7 Edge $e = ac$ is contained in the minimal cut (S, T) shown in Figure 6.12. If $c(e) = 8$, (S, T) is still a minimal cut; the value of the flow has to be decreased to 29. A maximal flow of this value can be constructed, for example, from the flow of Figure 6.12 by decreasing the value of the flow by 2 for all edges of the augmenting path shown in Figure 6.7. For $c(e) = 12$, the same augmenting path can be used for increasing the value of the flow to 33.

6.2.8 First, the capacity of ac is increased to 12, so that the value of the flow can be increased to 33 as in Exercise 6.2.7 (by increasing $f(e)$ by 2 for each of the edges $e = sa, ac, cf, ft$). As edge ad is not contained in (S, T), increasing the capacity of this edge does not change anything. Next, we delete edge de. As this edge is contained in (S, T), the value of the flow has to be decreased by 1, say for the path $s \mathbin{\!-\!} a \mathbin{\!-\!} d \mathbin{\!-\!} e \mathbin{\!-\!} t$. Finally, ct is removed. The value of the flow is not changed, because the flow of value 1 which used ct can now use the path $c \mathbin{\!-\!} f \mathbin{\!-\!} t$. We obtain the flow of value 32 shown in Figure A.18; (S, T) is still a minimal cut.

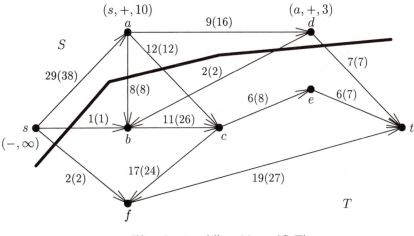

Fig. A.18 $w(f) = 32 = c(S, T)$

6.3.5 By definition, $c'(S, T)$ is the sum of all $c'(x)$ for $x^- \in S$ and $x^+ \in T$. Now if $x = e'$ corresponds to a forward edge e, we have $c'(x) = c(e) - f(e)$. Otherwise, if $x = e''$ corresponds to a backward edge e, then $c'(x) = f(e)$. Thus,

$$c'(S, T) = \sum_{e^- \in S, e^+ \in T} c(e) - \sum_{e^- \in S, e^+ \in T} f(e) + \sum_{e^- \in T, e^+ \in S} f(e),$$

that is, using Lemma 6.1.2, $c'(S, T) = c(S, T) - w(f)$. We see that the capacity of a minimal cut in N' is smaller by $w(f)$ than the capacity of a minimal cut in N. The assertion now follows by applying Theorem 6.1.6 to both networks.

6.3.8 Execute a BFS on the directed graph with opposite orientation starting at t and remove all vertices which are not reached during the algorithm.

6.3.9 The network N'' and a blocking flow are shown in Figure A.19.

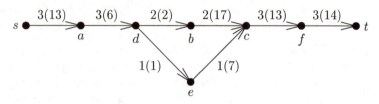

Fig. A.19 A blocking flow

6.3.10 Consider Example 6.3.7: The blocking flow g on N'' of value 10 is maximal here; the flow f has value 10. However, the maximal value of a flow on N is $31 \neq 10 + 10$ (see Example 6.2.3).

6.3.13 The layered auxiliary network with respect to g on $N'(f)$ is shown in Figure A.20; the layered auxiliary network with respect to g on $N''(f)$ is shown in Figure A.21. The flow determined on N by f and g is the flow $h = f_6$ of Figure 6.9. Therefore, $N''(h)$ is equal to the network of Figure A.20.

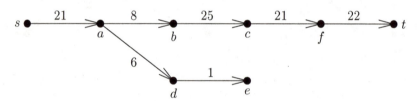

Fig. A.20 layered auxiliary network for $N'(f)$

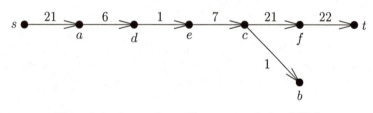

Fig. A.21 layered auxiliary network for $N''(f)$

6.3.18 Substitute step (16) of procedure AUXNET (Algorithm 6.3.14) by

(16′)   **if** $t \in V''$ **then** max $\leftarrow$ false; $d \leftarrow i$ **else** max $\leftarrow$ true;
$S \leftarrow V''; T \leftarrow V \backslash S$ **fi.**

6.4.5 A blocking flow constructed by Algorithm 6.4.1 is shown in Figure A.22. If there were several possibilities for choosing the edge $e = uv$ in step (5), the alphabetical order of the vertices u was used. The algorithm constructed the paths corresponding to the sequences (s, a, d, f, t), (s, b, d, f, t), (s, c, d, f, t), (s, c, d, g, t), (s, a, e, h, t), (s, a, e, k, t) in this order; the capacities of these paths are 3, 2, 4, 3, 1, 10. The total value of the flow is 23.

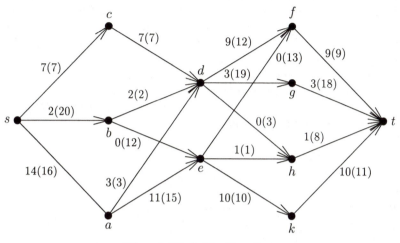

Fig. A.22 A blocking flow

6.4.10 Four iterations are needed in Algorithm 6.4.6: the vertices of minimal potential are h with $p(h) = 4$, c with $p(c) = 7$, d with $p(d) = 2$ and e with $p(e) = 10$. The resulting blocking flow of value 23 is shown in Figure A.23.

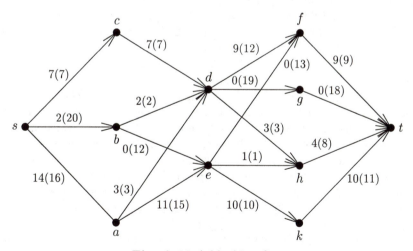

Fig. A.23 A blocking flow

6.5.5 Let G be the bipartite graph on $S \cup T$ (where $S = \{1, \ldots, m\}$ and $T = \{1', \ldots, n'\}$) such that $\{i, j'\}$ is an edge if girl i and boy j' know each other. Then the desired arrangement for a dance obviously corresponds to a matching of maximal cardinality in G (which can be determined using Exercise 6.5.6).

6.5.6 Define a directed graph H as follows: Add two new vertices s and t to $S \cup T$. The edges of H are all the sx for $x \in S$, all the xy for which $\{x, y\}$ is an edge of G and all the yt for $y \in T$. All edges are assigned capacity 1. Then the edges $\{x_i, y_i\}$ of any matching ($i = 1, \ldots, k$) induce a flow of value k by defining $f(e) = 1$ for all edges $e = sx_i$, $e = x_i y_i$ and $e = y_i t$ (for $i = 1, \ldots, k$). Conversely, any 0-1-flow of value k yields a matching consisting of k edges. By Theorem 6.5.4, a maximal 0-1-flow can be determined with complexity $O(|V|^{1/2}|E|)$ for our network, that is, the complexity is at most $O(|V|^{5/2})$. This yields the following algorithm[1]:

Procedure MATCH $(G; K)$

(1) let s and t be two new vertices; $V' \leftarrow S \cup T \cup \{s, t\}$;
(2) **for** $e \in E$ **do if** $e = \{x, y\}$ **then** $e' = xy$ **fi od**;
(3) $E' \leftarrow \{sx : x \in S\} \cup \{e' : e \in E\} \cup \{yt : y \in T\}$;
(4) **for** $e \in E'$ **do** $c(e) \leftarrow 1$ **od**;
(5) $H \leftarrow (V', E')$, $N \leftarrow (H, c, s, t)$, $K \leftarrow \emptyset$;
(6) MAXFLOW $(N; f)$
(7) **for** $e \in E$ **do if** $f(e') = 1$ **then** $K \leftarrow K \cup \{e\}$ **fi od**.

6.5.7 Let $A \subset S$ and $X \subset A$ an independent subset of maximal cardinality of A, say $|X| = k$. Consider the network N constructed from G in the solution of Exercise 6.5.6. Remove all vertices of $S \backslash A$ and the edges incident with them from N and denote the resulting network by N_A. Moreover, let M be a matching of G with $X = \{e^- : e \in M\}$. As we saw in Exercise 6.5.6, M induces a flow of value k on N_A. Now let Y be any maximal independent subset of A, say $Y = \{e^- : e \in M'\}$ for some matching M'. Then, by hypothesis, $|Y| \leq k$. Suppose we have $|Y| < k$. Then the flow on N_A corresponding to M' cannot be maximal, so that it can be changed to a maximal flow f (for example using the Algorithm of Edmonds and Karp) by constructing $k - |Y|$ augmenting paths in N_A. It is easy to see that, for each change of the flow, there is a matching corresponding to an independent subset of A which contains Y. Thus, Y cannot have been maximal, a contradiction. Hence, any two maximal independent subsets of A have the same cardinality k, so that $(S, \mathbf{S})$ satisfies condition (3) of Theorem 5.2.1 and therefore is a matroid.

---

[1] Note that backward edges may occur during the algorithm, but they do not interfere with the solution, because $c(sv) = c(wt) = 1$ holds for all v and w, so that at most one edge of the form vw incident with v or w, respectively, can carry a non-zero flow.

Such matroids (called 'transversal matroids') are studied in Section 7.3. We have given an 'algorithmic' proof for the fact that $(S, \mathbf{S})$ is a matroid, because we showed in a constructive way that condition (3) of Theorem 5.2.1 is satisfied. In a similar way, the validity of condition (3) can be proved (using the language of Transversal Theory) using the Algorithm of Hall (1956), see Section 7.3.

6.6.17 The algorithm FIFOFLOW yields (after nine phases) the maximal flow of Figure 6.12. It needs four more RELABEL- and five more PUSH-operations than HLFLOW (that is, about one third more operations altogether).

A.7 Solutions for Chapter 7

7.1.3 We use the Algorithm of Edmonds and Karp. Suppose there exists an augmenting path containing a backward edge, then let W be the first such path and $e = uv$ the last backward edge in W. Thus, when W is constructed, we must have $f(e) \neq 0$. Let Z be the last augmenting path constructed before W such that $f(e)$ was changed (that is, $f(e)$ was increased). Then W and Z have the form

$$W \;=\; s \;\xrightarrow{\;W'\;}\; v \;\text{------}\; u \;\xrightarrow{\;W''\;}\; t \quad \text{and}$$

$$Z \;=\; s \;\xrightarrow{\;Z'\;}\; u \;\text{------}\; v \;\xrightarrow{\;Z''\;}\; t,$$

respectively. Denote the capacities of W and Z by γ and δ, respectively. Suppose first that $\gamma \leq \delta$. Then we may substitute Z and W by the following paths:

$$s \;\xrightarrow{\;Z'\;}\; u \;\text{------}\; v \;\xrightarrow{\;Z''\;}\; t \quad (\text{with capacity } \delta - \gamma)$$

$$s \;\xrightarrow{\;Z'\;}\; u \;\xrightarrow{\;W''\;}\; t \quad (\text{with capacity } \gamma) \quad \text{and}$$

$$s \;\xrightarrow{\;W'\;}\; v \;\xrightarrow{\;Z''\;}\; t \quad (\text{with capacity } \gamma).$$

Now W'', Z' and Z'' contain forward edges only and the sum of the capacities of the three paths above is $\gamma + \delta$, so that we have removed the backward edge e from W. For $\gamma > \delta$, we use similar arguments: substitute W and Z by three paths such that the sum of their capacities is $\gamma + \delta$. However, the backward edge e is not removed in that case (because we need the path W with capacity $\gamma - \delta$), but the capacity of W is decreased, so that the algorithm has to terminate. Therefore, as the Algorithm of Edmonds and Karp is finite, we get a finite technique for constructing a maximal flow by using augmenting paths consisting of forward edges only. In Example 6.2.3, the only backward edge occurs in the last augmenting path which has capacity 1 (see Figure 6.11):

$$W \;=\; s \;\text{———}\; a \;\text{———}\; d \;\text{———}\; e \;\text{———}\; c \;\text{———}\; f \;\text{———}\; t$$

The backward edge is ce. Here, Z is the following augmenting path:

$$Z \;=\; s \;\text{———}\; a \;\text{———}\; c \;\text{———}\; e \;\text{———}\; t;$$

it has capacity 7 (see Figure 6.6). As described above, we may replace W and Z by the three augmenting paths $s \text{——} a \text{——} c \text{——} e \text{——} t$ (of capacity 6), $s \text{——} a \text{——} c \text{——} f \text{——} t$ (of capacity 1) and $s \text{——} a \text{——} d \text{——} e \text{——} t$ (of capacity 1).

7.1.6 If any two vertices of G are connected by at least k vertex disjoint paths, then G obviously has to be k-connected. So suppose conversely that G is k-connected. By the Theorem of Menger, any two non-adjacent vertices of G are connected by k vertex disjoint paths. So let s and t be adjacent and denote the graph which results from removing the edge st from G by H. Then obviously H is at least $(k-1)$-connected. Again by the Theorem of Menger, s and t are connected in H by $k-1$ vertex disjoint paths. Now st is the k-th path from s to t.

7.1.7 If G is k-connected, then Exercise 7.1.6 implies that any two vertices are connected by k vertex disjoint paths. In particular, any vertex must have degree at least k. However, by Exercise 1.5.13, any planar graph contains vertices of degree at most 5. The graph with six vertices shown in Figure A.4 (see the solution for Exercise 1.5.12) is 4-connected. If G is a 5-connected graph, any vertex of G must have degree ≥ 5. As in the solution for Exercise 1.5.13, we get the following bound on the number n_5 of vertices of degree at most (and therefore equal to) 5:

$$6(n - n_5) + 5n_5 \leq 12n - 6,$$

that is, $n_5 \geq 12$, and hence $n \geq 12$. The icosahedron (see Figure A.24) is an example on 12 vertices.

7.1.8 Add two vertices s and t to G and add all edges sx for $x \in S$ and all edges yt for $y \in T$. Now the assertion follows from Theorem 7.1.4.

7.2.2 Any matching K' which cannot be extended must have at least $k/2$ edges: otherwise, at least one of the k edges of K could be added to K'. It is easy to construct examples which show that this bound is best possible.

7.2.7 The Petersen graph (see Figure 1.12) is 3-regular, but does not have a 1-factorization.

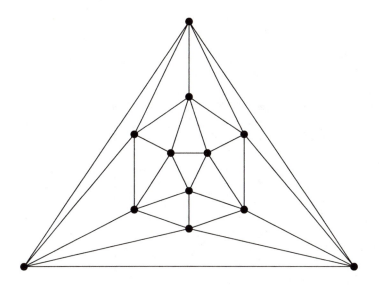

Fig. A.24 The icosahedron

7.2.9 We choose the disjoint union of the sets $R = \{r_1, \ldots, r_{2n}\}$, $S = \{s_1, \ldots, s_{2n}\}$ and $T = \{t_1, \ldots, t_{2n}\}$ as the vertex set of K_{6n}. Moreover, let K_{ST} denote the complete bipartite graph on $S \cup T$ and F_{ST} the 1-factor $\{s_i t_i : i = 1, \ldots, 2n\}$ of K_{ST}. By Corollary 7.2.6, $G_{ST} := K_{ST} \backslash F_{ST}$ can be decomposed into $2n - 1$ factors and by Exercise 1.1.2, the complete graph K_R on R can be decomposed into $2n - 1$ factors. By choosing an arbitrary bijection between these two sets of $2n - 1$ factors, we get $2n - 1$ factors of K_{6n} (merging the two corresponding factors of G_{ST} and of K_R); these factors together contain precisely all the edges of type $s_i t_j$ and $r_i r_j$ (for $i \neq j$). The same method yields (for the two cyclic permutations of the sets R, S and T) $4n - 2$ further factors of K_{6n}. The remaining edges (not occuring in one of these $6n - 3$ factors) of type $r_i s_i$, $r_i t_i$ and $s_i t_i$ (for $i = 1, \ldots, 2n$) obviously form a Δ-factor.

7.2.10 We denote the nine vertices by ij (for $i, j = 0, 1, 2$). Then the edges where i (or j) is constant form three triangles; these six triangles together form a Δ-factor. The remaining two Δ-factors are uniquely determined (see Figure A.25, where triangles are shown as arcs). This unique decomposition of K_9 into Δ-factors is – using geometrical terminology – just the affine plane of order 3 (see Beth, Jungnickel and Lenz (1998), for example).

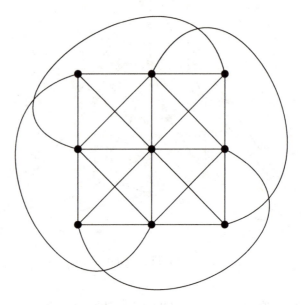

Fig. A.25 Decomposition of K_9 into triangle factors

7.2.11 Choose $2n - 1$ factors of a 1-factorization of K_{6n-2} (see Exercise 1.1.2) and denote the graph formed by these factors by G. Then $\overline{G}$ is a $(4n - 2)$-regular graph and can be decomposed into 2-factors by Theorem 7.2.8. Now choose a bijection between these two sets of $2n - 1$ factors and use the union of corresponding factors.

7.3.2 The assertion is clear for $n = 1$. So let $n \neq 1$. Choose $x_1 \in A_1$ and define $\mathbf{B} := (B_2, \ldots, B_n)$, where $B_i := A_i \backslash \{x_1\}$. If $\mathbf{A}$ does not contain any critical subfamily, then the union of any k sets in $\mathbf{A}$ contains at least $k + 1$ elements, so that $\mathbf{B}$ obviously satisfies (H'). Thus, $\mathbf{B}$ contains a transversal T, then $T \cup \{x_1\}$ is the transversal of $\mathbf{A}$ we are looking for. Now suppose that $\mathbf{A}$ contains a critical subfamily, say $\mathbf{A}' = (A_1, \ldots, A_m)$. By the induction hypothesis, $\mathbf{A}'$ contains a transversal T'. Define $\mathbf{C} := (C_{m+1}, \ldots, C_n)$, where $C_i := A_i \backslash T'$. Now we can check that $\mathbf{C}$ satisfies condition (H') as well, and therefore $\mathbf{C}$ has a transversal T''. Then $T' \cup T''$ is a transversal of $\mathbf{A}$.

7.3.3 It is obvious that the maximal cardinality of a matching of G cannot exceed the minimal cardinality of a vertex cover of G. Now suppose that $X = S' \cup T'$ (where $S' \subset S$ and $T' \subset T$) is a minimal vertex cover. We apply Theorem 7.3.1 in the terminology used in Theorem 7.2.4. Consider the bipartite graph G' induced on the set $(S\backslash S') \cup T'$. We want to show that G' satisfies condition (H). Suppose it does not. Then there exists a subset J of T' with $|\Gamma(J)| < |J|$ and the set $S' \cup \Gamma(J) \cup (T'\backslash J)$ is a vertex cover for G which has smaller cardinality than $|X|$. This contradicts our assumption above and proves that G' satisfies (H). Now, by Theorem 7.2.4, G' has a matching of cardinality $|T'|$. Analogously, the bipartite graph G'' induced on the set $S \cup (T\backslash T')$ contains a matching of cardinality $|S'|$. Then the union of these two matchings of G' and G'' forms a matching of cardinality $|X|$ of G.

7.3.6 The maximal cardinality of a matching in a bipartite graph (on vertex set $S \cup T$) is $|T|$ - max $\{|J| - |\Gamma(J)| : J \subset T\}$.

7.3.10 Consider the family **A** which consists of d_i copies of A_i for $i = 1, \ldots, k$. Then **S** is precisely the set of partial transversals of **A**, so that the assertion follows using Theorem 7.3.8.

7.3.13 Let G be the bipartite graph with vertex set $S \cup T$ corresponding to **A**. Then, as in Exercise 6.5.7, there is also a matroid induced on T. Using the terminology of set families, the independent sets of this matroid are precisely those subsets of the index set T for which the corresponding subfamily of **A** has a transversal.

7.3.17 Let **B** be the family consisting of p_i copies of A_i for $i = 1, \ldots, n$. Then the existence of sets X_i with the desired properties is equivalent to the existence of a transversal of **B**. Now condition (H') for **B** is precisely the condition given in the exercise, so that the assertion follows from the Marriage Theorem.

7.4.12 The assertions of Corollaries 7.4.6 and 7.2.6 are equivalent.

7.4.13 Let D be a diagonal with entries $d_1, \ldots, d_n$ such that $d_1 \ldots d_n \geq n^{-n}$ holds. The inequality between the arithmetic and the geometric mean implies

$$(d_1 \ldots d_n)^{1/n} \leq \frac{d_1 + \ldots + d_n}{n}, \quad \text{that is,} \quad d_1 + \ldots + d_n \geq 1.$$

(For a proof of the inequality mentioned above and of a more general inequality due to Muirhead (1903) using methods of Transversal Theory, we refer the reader to Mirsky (1971b), Theorem 4.3.3.)

7.4.14 Let **T** be the set family as described in the 'hint'. Then **T** satisfies condition (H'), because the ktr entries 1 in any given k rows of A have to be contained in at least kt columns of A (note that A has column sums $\leq r$). Therefore, **T** has a transversal, that is, there exist pairwise disjoint t-subsets S_i of T_i for $i = 1, \ldots, m$. Then the matrix P with entries $p_{ij} := 1$ for $i \in S_j$ (and $p_{ij} = 0$ otherwise) has row sums t and column sums ≤ 1. Moreover, the matrix $\mathbf{A}' := A - P$ has row sums $t(r - 1)$. If we want to use induction on r, we still have to make sure that the set X of all those indices for which column j of A has sum r is contained in $S_1 \cup \ldots \cup S_m$ (so that $\mathbf{A}'$ has column sums $\leq r - 1$). By Corollary 7.3.9, it is sufficient to show that X is a partial transversal of $\mathbf{T}$. However, any k columns having sum r together contain precisely kr entries 1 and these entries have to be contained in at least k/t rows of A. As each T_i occurs precisely t times in $\mathbf{T}$, any k elements of X correspond to at least k sets in $\mathbf{T}$. Now Theorem 7.2.4 implies that X is a partial transversal.

7.4.15 Use the equivalence of 0-1-matrices and bipartite graphs discussed at the beginning of Section 7.4. We have to show that a bipartite graph of maximal degree r can be decomposed into r matchings. Let $S \cup T$ be the vertex set of G and denote the set of vertices of degree r in S (and in T) by S' (and T', respectively). Using Theorem 7.2.4, we can now show that there exist matchings K' and K'' of G which meet S' and T', respectively. Thus, by Corollary 7.3.12, there exists a matching K meeting $S' \cup T'$. Now $G\backslash K$ has maximal degree $r - 1$ and the assertion follows by induction.

7.4.16 We may assume $n \geq 3$. We show first that the subspace W of $\mathbb{R}^{(n,n)}$ spanned by the permutation matrices consists precisely of those matrices for which all line sums are equal. It is trivial that any linear combination of permutation matrices is contained in W and has constant line sum. Conversely, let A be a matrix with constant line sum. If A does not contain any negative entries, A is contained in W by Theorem 7.4.7. Otherwise, let $b := \max \{-a_{ij} : i, j = 1, \ldots, n\}$. Then the matrix $B := A + bJ$ (where J is the matrix with all entries 1) has non-negative entries and constant line sum. Therefore, J and B (and A as well) are linear combinations of permutation matrices. Now let W' be the subspace spanned by the $2n - 2$ matrices S_i and Z_i (for $i = 1, \ldots, n-1$) which have entry 1 in cell (n, i) or (i, n), respectively, and all other entries 0. Obviously, W and W' have only the zero matrix in common. If we can show that W and W' together generate the whole space $\mathbb{R}^{(n,n)}$, it follows that dim $W = n^2 - 2n + 2$. So let A be any matrix of $\mathbb{R}^{(n,n)}$. By adding appropriate multiples of S_i or of Z_i to A, we can obtain a matrix C with the property that the first $n - 1$ rows and columns have a fixed sum s. Then the last row and column of C must have the same sum, say x. Adding aS_i and aZ_i to C, the sum s can be changed to $s' = s + a$; simultaneously, x is changed to $x' = x + (n - 1)a$. Now, as $n \neq 2$, we can determine a in such a way that $x' = s'$ and the resulting matrix C' has constant line sum. Thus, C' is contained in W, so that A is contained in $W + W'$.

7.5.4 Suppose G is a minimal counterexample for the assertion we want to prove and let $\mathbf{D}$ be a dissection of G consisting of as few paths as possible. Then $\mathbf{D}$ contains at least $\alpha + 1$ paths. Suppose we have $|\mathbf{D}| \geq \alpha + 2$. We omit a path W from $\mathbf{D}$. Then $G\backslash W$ has (because G is minimal) a dissection into at most α paths, say $\mathbf{D}'$. But then $\mathbf{D}' \cup \{W\}$ is a dissection of G into $\alpha + 1$ paths contradicting our assumption above. Thus, we must have $|\mathbf{D}| = \alpha + 1$, say $\mathbf{D} = \{W_1, \ldots, W_{\alpha+1}\}$. Denote the start vertex of path W_i by p_i. By definition of α, two of the p_i have to be connected by an edge; suppose $p_1 p_2$ is an edge. If W_1 consists of p_1 only, we may omit W_1 and substitute W_2 by $(p_1 p_2)W_2$, so that G would be decomposable into α paths. Therefore, W_1 cannot be trivial. Let W_1' be the path we obtain by omitting the first edge $p_1 p_1'$ from W_1. As G is a minimal counterexample, the graph $H = G \backslash p_1$ satisfies the assertion. Now $\{W_1', W_2, \ldots, W_{\alpha+1}\}$ is a dissection of H, so that we can find a dissection $\{Z_1, \ldots, Z_k\}$ of H into $k \le \alpha$ paths such that the start vertices of these paths are contained in $\{p_1', p_2, \ldots, p_{\alpha+1}\}$. If p_1' is the start vertex of one of the paths Z_i, Z_i can be substituted by $(p_1 p_1')Z_i$, which yields a dissection of G into at most α paths. If $k < \alpha$, we may add the trivial path $\{p_1'\}$ to the Z_i. If none of these two conditions holds, we must have $k = \alpha$ and the start vertices of the Z_i are precisely the vertices $p_2, \ldots, p_{\alpha+1}$. Thus p_2 is the start vertex of some Z_h. Substituting Z_h by $(p_1 p_2)Z_h$ again yields a dissection of G into at most α paths. Therefore, G cannot be a counterexample and the assertion of the theorem is true in general.

7.5.5 As a tournament is an orientation of a complete graph, the maximal independent sets have only one element in this case. Thus, the assertion follows immediately from Exercise 7.5.4. However, there is a direct proof (not using Exercise 7.5.4) which is much easier. Choose a directed (simple) path of maximal length in G, say

$$W \quad = \quad v_1 \text{——} v_2 \text{——} \ldots \text{——} v_k.$$

If W is not a Hamiltonian path (that is, $k < n$), then there exists a vertex v not on W. As W is maximal, G cannot contain the edge vv_1 or the edge $v_k v$. Thus, G must contain edges $v_1 v$ and vv_k. Hence, there must be some index i $(1 < i < k)$ such that G contains the edges $v_i v$ and vv_{i+1}. But then, we could substitute edge $v_i v_{i+1}$ in W by these two edges and W is not maximal, a contradiction.

7.5.9 Let k be the maximal cardinality of a chain in M. Moreover, let A denote the antichain of the maximal elements of M. Then the maximal cardinality of a chain in $M \backslash A$ is $k - 1$ and the assertion follows by induction.

7.5.10 Let $\mathbf{A} = (A_1, \ldots, A_n)$ be a family of subsets of $\{x_1, \ldots, x_m\}$ satisfying (H'). We define a partial ordering on $M := \{x_1, \ldots, x_m, A_1, \ldots, A_n\}$ by

$$u < v \quad :\Longleftrightarrow \quad u = x_i, \quad v = A_j \quad \text{and} \quad x_i \in A_j \quad \text{(for appropriate } i, j).$$

Now let s be the maximal cardinality of an antichain and suppose (w.l.o.g.) that $\{x_1, \ldots, x_h, A_1, \ldots, A_k\}$ is an antichain (where $h + k = s$). Then we have $k \le |A_1 \cup \ldots \cup A_k| \le m - h$, that is, $s = h + k \le m$. The Theorem of Dilworth implies that $(M, \le)$ can be decomposed into s chains, say $\{x_1, A_1\}, \ldots, \{x_i, A_i\}$, $\{A_{i+1}\}, \ldots, \{A_n\}$, $\{x_{i+1}\}, \ldots, \{x_m\}$. But then

$s = m + n - i$, so that $n = s - m + i \le i$, that is, $n = i$ and $\{x_1, \ldots, x_n\}$ is a transversal of **A**.

7.7.2 Use Theorem 7.7.3.

7.7.5 We have seen that Theorem 7.7.1 follows from Theorem 6.1.6 by constructing the flow network N as described at the beginning of Section 7.7. If c, a and n are integral, the capacity function on N is integral as well. Thus, if there exists a feasible flow at all, Theorem 6.1.5 implies that there exists an integral solution as well.

A.8 Solutions for Chapter 8

8.1.5 Let $(M_0, M_1, \ldots, M_k = M_0)$ be the sequence of vertices defining a cycle of length $k \ge 4$ in an interval graph; moreover, let $M_i = (x_i, y_i)$ for $i = 0, \ldots, k-1$. (The case of closed intervals can be treated analogously.) We may assume w.l.o.g. $x_0 < x_1$. If $M_2 M_0$ is an edge, this edge is a chord of the cycle (because $k \ge 4$). Otherwise, if $M_2 M_0$ is not an edge, $M_2 \cap M_0 = \emptyset$ and $M_2 \cap M_1 \ne \emptyset$ imply that $x_1 < y_0 \le x_2 < y_1$. Thus, if the cycle does not have a chord, the lower bounds of the intervals M_i have to form a monotonously increasing sequence. But then $M_{k-1} M_0$ cannot be an edge. Thus, G must be triangulated.

8.1.9 As any induced subgraph of a bipartite graph is bipartite again, it is sufficient to show that $\alpha(G) = \theta(G)$ holds for any bipartite graph G. However, for a bipartite graph, the number $\theta(G)$ of cliques is simply $|V| - \alpha'(G)$, where $\alpha'(G)$ denotes the maximal cardinality of a matching. The independence number $\alpha(G)$ is $|V| - \beta(G)$, where $\beta(G)$ is the minimal cardinality of a vertex cover (see Lemma 7.5.1). Then Theorem 7.2.3 implies that $\alpha(G) = \theta(G)$. (Verifying $\chi(G) = \omega(G)$ is even easier: both numbers are 2 for bipartite graphs, compare Example 8.1.1).

8.3.1 It is obvious that $\chi'(G)$ is the minimal number of matchings into which G can be decomposed. Thus, we have to show that a bipartite graph of maximal degree r can always be decomposed into r matchings. But this is true by Exercise 7.4.15 (compare the solution for that exercise).

8.4.6 It is clear that $G = G(H, S)$ is regular of degree k, where k is the cardinality of S. Now consider any two elements x and y of H; we have to determine the number of elements z of H which are adjacent to both x and y. As H acts regularly on G, we may assume $y = 1$. By definition, z is adjacent to both 1 and x if and only if $z^{-1}, xz^{-1} \in S$. If we put $d := z^{-1}$ and $c := xz^{-1}$, we may use (8.1) to re-write the preceding condition as

$$x = cd^{-1}, \quad z = d^{-1} \quad \text{with} \quad c, d \in S.$$

Hence the number of elements z of H which are adjacent to both 1 and x equals the number of 'quotient representations' of x from S. Noting that x is adjacent to 1 if and only if x belongs to S, it is clear that condition (2) in the statement of the exercise holds if and only if G is strongly regular with parameters λ and μ.

A.9 Solutions for Chapter 9

9.1.6 For any directed edge e of G, set $b(e) = c(e) = 1$; any undirected edge $e = \{u, v\}$ is substituted by two directed edges $e' = uv$ and $e'' = vu$ with $b(e') = b(e'') = 0$ and $c(e') = c(e'') = 1$. Denote the directed multigraph thus obtained by H. It is trivial that any Euler tour of G yields a circulation on H. Conversely, let f be a feasible circulation on H. If, for some undirected edge e of G, we have either $f(e') = 1$, $f(e'') = 0$ or $f(e'') = 1$, $f(e') = 0$, substitute e by e' or by e'', respectively. We get a mixed multigraph G' which has the additional property that, for any vertex v, the number of directed edges with start vertex v is equal to the number of directed edges with end vertex v. But in that case, an Euler tour can be constructed using the methods of Chapter 1 (see 1.3.1 and 1.6.1).

9.1.7 We use the following vertices: a source s, a vertex 0 (which represents the person selling the napkins), vertices $1, \ldots, N$ (corresponding to the dirty napkins which are sent away to be cleaned; we assume that all napkins are washed for $i \leq N - n$) and vertices $1', \ldots, N'$ (which represent the supply of clean napkins needed for the N days) as well as a sink t. The edges are: $e = s0$ with $b(e) = 0$, $c(e) = \infty$, $\gamma(e) = 0$; all si with $b(si) = c(si) = r_i$, $\gamma(si) = 0$; all $0i'$ with $b(0i') = 0$, $c(0i') = \infty$, $\gamma(0i') = \alpha$; all $e = i(i + m)'$ with $b(e) = 0$, $c(e) = r_i$, $\gamma(e) = \beta$; all $e = i(i + n)'$ with $b(e) = 0$, $c(e) = r_i$, $\gamma(e) = \delta$; all $i't$ with $b(i't) = c(i't) = r_i$, $\gamma(i't) = 0$. For $i + m > N$ (and $i + n > N$, respectively), the edge $i(i + m)'$ has to be interpreted as it, so that the cost of this edge has to be changed to 0. Finally, add all edges $e = i'(i + 1)'$ with $b(e) = 0$, $c(e) = \infty$, $\gamma(e) = 0$ (these edges represent the possibility of saving unused napkins for the next day).

9.2.3 As before, we set $c'(e) := c(e) - b(e)$. Moreover,

$$c'(sv) := \sum_{\substack{e^+ = v \\ b(e) > 0}} b(e) - \sum_{\substack{e^- = v \\ b(e) < 0}} b(e); \quad c'(vt) := \sum_{\substack{e^- = v \\ b(e) > 0}} b(e) - \sum_{\substack{e^+ = v \\ b(e) < 0}} b(e).$$

Then Theorem 9.2.1 remains valid without changes: a feasible circulation on G exists if and only if the maximal value of a flow on N is given by $W = \sum b(e)$.

9.2.6 First determine – if possible – a feasible flow as in Example 9.2.2. Next, a maximal flow can be found as in Chapter 6. To make sure that this flow is still feasible, we have to substitute the condition $f(e) \neq 0$ in step (10) of Algorithm 6.3.14 (when determining the auxiliary network) by $f(e) > b(e)$ and replace the assignment in step (11) by $c''(e) \leftarrow f(e) - b(e)$. We denote the changed procedure by LEGAUXNET. We may now proceed as in Algorithm 6.3.17. (Note that the Algorithm of Ford and Fulkerson with similar changes would likewise serve the same purpose.) We obtain the following algorithm of complexity $O(|V|^3)$ (setting $N = (G, b, c, s, t)$ and using the MKM-Algorithm for determining a blocking flow).

Procedure MAXLEGFLOW $(N; \text{legal}, f)$

(1) Add the edge $r = ts$ to G; $b(r) \leftarrow 0$; $c(r) \leftarrow \infty$;
(2) LEGCIRC$(G, b, c; f, \text{legal})$;
(3) **if** legal $=$ true **then**
(4)   remove edge $r = ts$ from G;
(5)   **repeat**
(6)   LEGAUXNET$(N, f; N'', \text{max}, d)$;
(7)   **if** max $=$ false **then** BLOCKMKM$(N''; g)$;
                   AUGMENT$(f, g; f)$ **fi**
(8)   **until** max $=$ true
(9) **fi**.

9.2.9 Apply the criterion of Theorem 9.2.7 to the directed multigraph H defined in the solution for Exercise 9.1.6 using the capacity functions b and c given there; this yields the following theorem: Let G be a connected mixed multigraph. Then G has an Euler tour if and only if the following two conditions hold:

(i) Any vertex of G is incident with an even number of edges.
(ii) For any subset X of V, the difference between the number of directed edges e with $e^- \in X$ and $e^+ \in V \backslash X$ and the number of directed edges e with $e^+ \in X$ and $e^- \in V \backslash X$ is at most as large as the number of undirected edges connecting X and $V \backslash X$.

9.2.10 It can be seen, similarly to the proof of Theorem 9.2.8, that the minimal value of a feasible flow is given by

$$\max \left\{ \sum_{e^- \in S, e^+ \in T} b(e) - \sum_{e^+ \in S, e^- \in T} c(e) : (S, T) \text{ is a cut on } N \right\},$$

where the return arc r has $c(r) = v$, $b(r) = -\infty$. To determine a minimal flow, a feasible flow found before can be changed by methods similar to those used in Chapter 6. To find a path along which the value of the flow can be decreased, we admit forward edges e in the auxiliary network if and only if $b(e) < f(e)$ (and backward edges are admitted if and only if $f(e) < c(e)$). Then the bounds on the complexity are the same as in Chapter 6. We leave the details to the reader.

9.2.11 First suppose that G has a feasible circulation. Let $e = uv$ be some edge of G. Moreover, let S be the set of all vertices s from which u is accessible. If $v \notin S$, $(S, V \backslash S)$ is a cut such that all edges of the corresponding cocycle are oriented from S to $V \backslash S$. Such a cut would violate the condition of Theorem 9.2.7, because $b(e) > 0$. Therefore, there must be a directed path W from v to u, and thus e is contained in the directed cycle $u \xrightarrow{\quad e \quad} v \xrightarrow{\quad W \quad} u$. Conversely, suppose that any edge of G is contained in a directed cycle. Then any cocycle has to contain edges in both possible directions, so that the condition of Theorem 9.2.7 is satisfied (because $c(e) = \infty$ for all e). Removing the return arc $r = ts$, we get, for any flow network with $c(e) = \infty$ and $b(e) > 0$ for all e, the following condition for the existence of a feasible flow: Any edge is contained in a directed cycle or in a directed path from s to t.

9.3.4 Part (a) follows immediately from (Z1):

$$
\begin{aligned}
f(S, T) &= \sum_{e^- \in S, e^+ \in T} f(e) = \sum_{v \in S} \sum_{e^- = v, e^+ \in T} f(e) \\
&= \sum_{v \in S} \Big(\sum_{e^- = v} f(e) - \sum_{e^- = v, e^+ \in S} f(e) \Big) \\
&= \sum_{v \in S} \Big(\sum_{e^+ = v} f(e) - \sum_{e^- = v, e^+ \in S} f(e) \Big) \\
&= \sum_{v \in S} \Big(\sum_{e^+ = v, e^- \in T} f(e) + \sum_{e^+ = v, e^- \in S} f(e) - \sum_{e^- = v, e^+ \in S} f(e) \Big) \\
&= f(T, S).
\end{aligned}
$$

To prove part (b), let $f \neq 0$ be a circulation and $e = uv$ an edge in the support of f. Suppose e is a bridge. Then $G \backslash e$ has at least two connected components S and T, say $u \in S$ and $v \in T$. Then e is the only edge in the cocycle $E(S, T)$, so that

$$
f(S, T) = f(e) \neq 0 \quad \text{and} \quad f(T, S) = 0,
$$

which contradicts part (a).

9.3.7 We may assume that each of the elementary circulations f_e in the proof of Theorem 9.3.6 satisfies the condition $f_e(e) = 1$. (Otherwise multiply f_e by -1.) Now set

$$
g := f - \sum_{e \in G \backslash T} f(e) f_e \qquad \text{(where f is an arbitrary circulation);}
$$

then the support of g is contained in T. Now Corollary 9.3.3 yields $g = 0$.

9.3.8

(a) Denoting the vector in $\mathbb{R}^m$ corresponding to $\delta q : E \to \mathbb{R}$ by $\delta\mathbf{q}$, we have

$$\delta\mathbf{q} = \sum_{i=1}^{n} q(v_i)\mathbf{a_i},$$

where $\mathbf{a_i}$ denotes the i-th row of A corresponding to vertex i. Then P corresponds to the row space of A and Theorem 4.2.4 implies $\dim P = \operatorname{rank} A = n - p$.

(b) Let (S,T) be a cut of G. We set $q(v) = 1$ for $v \in S$ and $q(v) = 0$ for $v \in T$. Then we have $\delta q(e) = +1$ or $= -1$ for all edges e contained in the cocycle corresponding to (S,T). For all other edges, $\delta q(e) = 0$.

(c) Let T be a tree and T' the corresponding cotree (that is, $T' = E\backslash T$). By Lemma 4.3.2, there exists, for each edge e of T, a unique cut such that the corresponding cocycle C_e contains, except for e, edges of T' only. By part (b), there is a potential difference δq_e for C_e whose support are precisely the edges of C_e. Thus, the δq_e (with $e \in T$) are $n - 1$ linearly independent potential differences and are, by part (a), a basis of P. (As G is connected, we have $p = 1$.)

9.5.4 For any feasible circulation, the value

$$M := \sum_{\substack{e \\ \gamma(e) > 0}} \gamma(e)c(e) + \sum_{\substack{e \\ \gamma(e) < 0}} \gamma(e)b(e)$$

is an upper bound for the cost. Defining m as in the proof of Lemma 9.5.2, $M - m$ is an upper bound for the number of iterations needed.

9.6.4 First consider the problem of how to determine, for any real number $v \leq M$ (where M is the maximal value of a flow on N), the optimal cost $\gamma(v)$. Denote the largest integer $\leq v$ by w and let f be an optimal flow of value w constructed by Algorithm 9.6.2. Moreover, let W be an augmenting path of least possible cost from s to t in the auxiliary network N' for f (with respect to the cost function γ'). As W has integral capacity, f can be augmented along W by $\delta := v - w < 1$ (with cost $\delta\gamma'(W)$). It can be shown as in the proof of Lemma 9.6.1 that the resulting flow of value v is optimal. Therefore, the cost function is linear between any two integers w and $w + 1$. As the cost of an augmenting path is always non-negative, the cost function is always monotonously increasing. Finally, for any two feasible flows f and f' of values v and v', respectively, and for λ with $0 \leq \lambda \leq 1$, the linear combination $\lambda f + (1 - \lambda)f'$ is always a feasible flow of value $\lambda v + (1 - \lambda)v'$, so that we get

$$\gamma(\lambda v + (1 - \lambda)v') \leq \lambda\gamma(v) + (1 - \lambda)\gamma(v').$$

Thus, the cost function is a monotonously increasing, piecewise linear, convex function.

9.6.5 In Example 9.1.4 we proved that the Assignment Problem can be reduced to the determination of an optimal flow of value n on a flow network with $2n + 2$ vertices. All capacities are integral in that network (in fact, they are always 1) and the cost function is non-negative. Thus, by Theorem 9.6.3, the Algorithm of Busacker and Gowen can be used for determining an optimal flow with complexity $O(|V|^2 n) = O(n^3)$, so that the Assignment Problem has complexity at most $O(n^3)$. The Assignment Problem will be studied more thoroughly in Chapter 13.

9.7.2 A possible solution is the following procedure.

Procedure RESIDUAL $(G, c, f; H)$

(1) $E' \leftarrow \emptyset$;
(2) **for** $e \in E$ **do**
(3)   **if** $c(e) > f(e)$ **then** $E' \leftarrow E' \cup \{e\}$ **fi**
(4) **od**;
(5) $H \leftarrow (V, E')$.

9.7.8 Let f be an ε-optimal pseudoflow on (G, c) with respect to the cost function γ. We construct the auxiliary graph H_f described in the proof of Theorem 9.7.6 with cost function $\gamma^{(\varepsilon)}$ and then proceed by determining an SP-tree for $(H_f, \gamma^{(\varepsilon)})$ using the procedure SPTREE given in Exercise 3.9.3. Now the desired potential is just the distance function we calculated. The procedure below does the job; s is a vertex not contained in G.

Procedure POTENTIAL $(G, c, \gamma, f, \varepsilon; p)$

(1) RESIDUAL $(G, c, f; H)$;
(2) $V^* \leftarrow V \cup \{s\}$; $E^* \leftarrow E'$;
(3) **for** $e \in E$ **do** $\gamma^*(e) \leftarrow \gamma^*(e) + \varepsilon$ **od**;
(4) **for** $v \in V$ **do** $E^* \leftarrow E^* \cup \{sv\}$; $\gamma^*(sv) \leftarrow 0$ **od**;
(5) $H^* \leftarrow (V^*, E^*)$;
(6) SPTREE $(H^*, \gamma^*, s; p, q, \text{neg}, T)$.

Note that p is (as needed according to Corollary 9.7.7) the distance function d_T in the arborescence T. The other output variables (that is, the predecessor function q for the SP-tree T and the Boolean variable neg) are not needed here. We could, of course, use the question whether neg $=$ false to check whether the given pseudoflow was indeed ε-optimal (by Theorem 9.7.6).

9.7.12 In the following procedure, s is a vertex not contained in H and $n-1$ denotes the number of vertices of H.

Procedure MEANCYCLE $(H, w; \mu, K)$

(1) TOPSORT $(H; \text{topnr, acyclic})$;
(2) **if** acyclic = true
(3) **then** $\mu \leftarrow \infty$
(4) **else** $V^* \leftarrow V \cup \{s\}$; $E^* \leftarrow E$; $F(0, s) \leftarrow 0$;
(5)   **for** $v \in V$ **do**
(6) $E^* \leftarrow E^* \cup \{sv\}$;
(7) $w(sv) \leftarrow 0$; $F(0, v) \leftarrow \infty$
(8)   **od**;
(9)   **for** $k = 1$ **to** n **do**
(10)   **for** $v \in V^*$ **do**
(11) $F(k, v) \leftarrow \min \{F(k-1, u) + w(uv) : uv \in E\}$
(12) $q(k, v) \leftarrow u$, where $u \in V$ is an element such that
                     $F(k-1, u) + w(uv) = \min \{F(k-1, x) + w(xv) : xv \in E\}$;
(13)   **od**;
(14)   **od**;
(15)   **for** $v \in V^*$ **do**
(16) $M(v) \leftarrow \max \{\frac{F(n,v) - F(k,v)}{n-k} : k = 0, \ldots, n-1\}$
(17)   **od**;
(18)   choose v with $M(v) = \min \{M(x) : x \in V\}$;
(19) $\mu \leftarrow M(v)$;
(20)   determine a walk W of length $F(n, v)$ from s to v consisting
             of n edges;
(21)   determine a cycle K contained in W
(22) **fi**.

To prove that this procedure is correct, we use the proofs of Theorem 9.7.10 and Corollary 9.7.11. The procedure TOPSORT checks – according to Theorem 2.6.6 – whether H^* is acyclic (then H is acyclic as well) and, if it is, μ is set to ∞. Otherwise, H contains directed cycles. In that case, the **for**-loop in steps (9) to (14) determines the minimal length $F(k, v)$ of a directed walk from s to v consisting of precisely k edges (for all k and v). This is done recursively. Then, in steps (15) to (19), the minimum cycle mean μ of a directed cycle in H is calculated according to Theorem 9.7.10. Now consider – as in the proof of Theorem 9.7.10 – the changed weight function w' defined by $w'(e) := w(e) - \mu$ (for all $e \in E$). The second part of the proof of Theorem 9.7.10 shows that the corresponding values $F'(k, v)$ and the vertex v chosen in step (18) satisfy the condition

$$\max \{\frac{F'(n, v) - F'(k, v)}{n - k} : k = 0, \ldots, n-1\} = 0.$$

Thus, the network (H, w') has minimum cycle mean 0. Now the first part of the proof of Theorem 9.7.10 shows that

$$F'(n, v) = F(n, v) - n\mu$$

is the shortest length of a directed walk from s to v (and therefore is equal to the distance from s to v) in (H^*, w'). In step (20), a directed walk W from s to v having this length and consisting of n edges is determined; this is done recursively using the function $q(k, v)$ defined in step (12). (The last edge of W is uv, where $u := q(n, v)$; the edge before the last is $u'u$, where $u' := q(n, u)$ and so on.) As W consists of precisely n edges, W has to contain a directed cycle K which is determined in step (21) (this can be done, for example, by a labelling process while W is traced from s to v). Then $W \backslash K$ is a directed walk from s to v as well and this walk must have length at least $F'(u, v)$ in (H^*, w'). Therefore, $w'(K)$ must be 0; otherwise, $w'(K)$ would be positive because of $\mu' = 0$, so that $w'(W \backslash K) < w'(W)$. It follows that $w(K) = \mu$.

9.7.14 Using Exercise 9.7.12 and Theorem 9.7.13 we obtain the following algorithm:

Procedure TIGHT $(G, c, \gamma, f; \varepsilon)$

(1) RESIDUAL $(G, c, f; H)$;
(2) MEANCYCLE $(H, \gamma; \mu, K)$;
(3) **if** $\mu \geq 0$ **then** $\varepsilon \leftarrow 0$ **else** $\varepsilon \leftarrow -\mu$ **fi**.

9.9.9 Define the function Φ as given in the hint. At the beginning of Algorithm 9.9.1, we have $\Phi \leq |V|$, because the admissible graph G_A does not contain any edges at this point, so that $\Phi(v) = 1$ holds trivially for any vertex v. A saturating PUSH-operation, say PUSH(u, v), can increase Φ by at most $\Phi(v) \leq |V|$ (if v becomes active by this operation), so that all the saturating PUSH-operations together can increase Φ by at most $O(|V|^2|E|)$ (because of Lemma 9.9.7). A RELABEL(v)-operation might add new edges of the form vu to G_A, so that Φ might be increased by at most $|V|$. Note that RELABEL(v) does not change the values $\Phi(w)$ for $w \neq v$, because, as we saw in the proof of Lemma 9.9.8, G_A does not contain any edges with end vertex v after this operation. Thus, Lemma 9.9.6 implies that all the RELABEL-operations together can increase Φ by at most $O(|V|^3)$; this value is dominated by $O(|V|^2|E|)$. It remains to consider the non-saturating PUSH-operations. A non-saturating PUSH(u, v)-operation makes u inactive, whereas v might become active. Thus, such a PUSH decreases Φ by $\Phi(u)$ and increases Φ (possibly) by $\Phi(v)$. However, we have $\Phi(u) \geq \Phi(v) + 1$, since any vertex in G_A which is accessible from v is accessible from u as well, but u is not accessible from v (because G_A is acyclic by Lemma 9.9.8). Note that a PUSH-operation does not add any edges to G_A according to the proof of 9.9.8. Thus, each non-saturating PUSH decreases Φ by at least 1. It follows that the total number of non-saturating PUSH-operations is bounded by the total increase of Φ during the algorithm, which is $O(|V|^2|E|)$.

9.10.6 The circulation f constructed during the initialization of Algorithm 9.10.1 is trivially C-optimal, that is, $\varepsilon(f_0) \leq C$. By Lemma 9.10.3, $|E|$ consecutive iterations decrease $\varepsilon(f)$ by at least a factor of $1 - 1/|V|$. Theorem 9.7.5 states that the algorithm terminates – and yields an optimal circulation f – as soon as $\varepsilon(f) < 1/|V|$. Therefore, it suffices to decrease $\varepsilon(f)$ by a total factor of value $< 1/(C|V|)$. Now Theorem 9.7.4 yields that $|E||V|$ iterations decrease $\varepsilon(f)$ by at least a factor of $1/2$, so that the algorithm has to terminate with an optimal circulation after at most $O(|V||E| \, (\log C|V|))$ iterations.

A.10 Solutions for Chapter 10

10.1.4 As the proof of Theorem 10.1.1 shows, any maximal spanning tree for (G, w) is also an equivalent flow tree for $N = (G, c)$. Now suppose conversely that T is an equivalent flow tree for N. It is obvious that the flow value $w_T(x, y)$ between x and y in the network (G, w) is equal to the capacity $w(W_{xy})$ of the unique path W_{xy} from x to y in T. By hypothesis, we have $w_T(x, y) = w(x, y)$ for all $x, y \in V$. It follows (as in the proof of Theorem 10.1.1) that W_{xy} is always a path of maximal capacity from x to y in the network (G, w). Now Exercise 4.5.5 yields that T is a maximal spanning tree for (G, w).

10.1.5 We use induction on the number n of vertices. The case $n = 2$ is trivial. So let $n \geq 3$. Choose a pair (x, y) of vertices such that $w(x, y)$ is maximal and remove one of these vertices, x say. We may assume by induction that the smaller flow network on $G\backslash x$ can be realized on a path W, say

$$W: \quad x_1 \text{——} x_2 \text{——} \cdots \text{——} x_{n-1},$$

where $y = x_i$. We insert x after y in W and denote the resulting path by W'. As $w(x, y)$ is the maximal value of a flow on N, the flow values realized before on $G\backslash x$ are not changed thereby. We also get the correct flow value $w(x, y)$ between x and y. Now consider a vertex z with $z \neq x, y$. The maximality of $w(x, y)$ implies $w(x, z) = w(y, z)$, because the inequality (10.1) of Theorem 10.1.1 shows that

$$w(x, z) \geq \min\{w(x, y), w(y, z)\} = w(y, z)$$

and, analogously, $w(y, z) \geq w(x, z)$. Thus, W realizes all flow values $w(y, z)$ correctly, and so does W'. Applying this technique recursively, we obtain from the network of Figure 10.1 the flow networks on smaller trees shown in Figure A.26 (in the order shown there). These smaller flow networks can be realized (beginning with the trivial path on two vertices) on the paths shown below the corresponding tree.

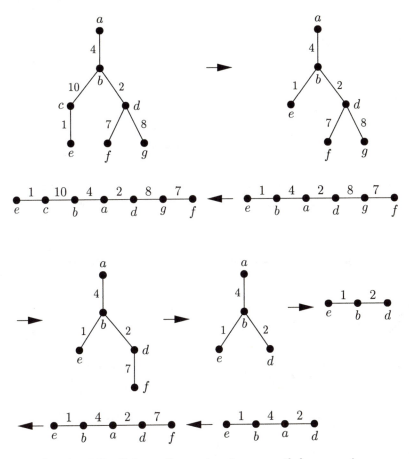

Fig. A.26 Realizing a flow network on a path by recursion

10.3.5 For the graph of Example 10.3.1, we get $u(a) = 13$, $u(b) = 13$, $u(c) = 12$, $u(d) = 12$, $u(h) = 13$, $u(g) = 15$, $u(f) = 15$, $u(e) = 11$. Then the increased flow requirements which can be realized with the minimal capacity of 52 given by r (see Figure 10.11) are given by $s(x, y) = \min \{u(x), u(y)\}$ according to the proof of Theorem 10.3.4. Using this weight function on K yields almost the same dominating tree T as in Example 10.3.1; only the weights are different (see Figure A.27). Now decompose T into uniform trees $U_1, \ldots, U_4$ (shown in Figure A.28) and construct the corresponding cycles, say (the order of the vertices is arbitrary) $C_1 = (a, b, c, d, e, f, g, h, a)$ with weight $11/2$, $C_2 = (a, b, c, d, f, g, h, a)$ with weight $1/2$, $C_3 = (a, b, f, g, h, a)$ with weight $1/2$ and the edge $C_4 = (g, f)$ with weight 2.

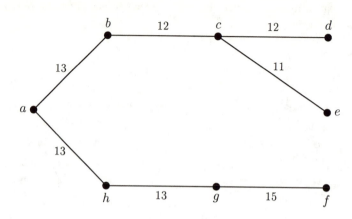

Fig. A.27 Dominating tree T

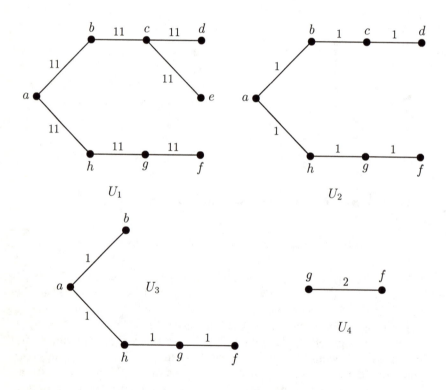

Fig. A.28 Partitioning T into uniform trees

We obtain the dominating network N shown in Figure A.29. N indeed allows higher flow values, for example $w(a,c) = 12$, whereas the network of Figure 10.11 has flow value $w(a,c) = 8$ only.

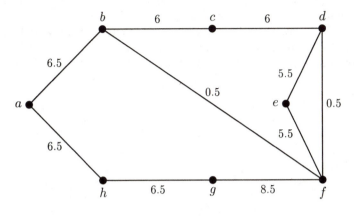

Fig. A.29 A dominating network

10.4.9 The network for the given values of the request function is shown in Figure A.30.

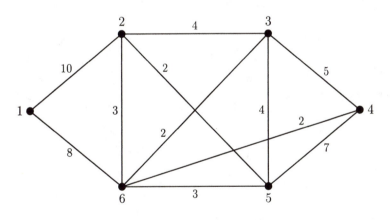

Fig. A.30 Symmetric network N for Exercise 10.4.9

By Theorem 10.4.6, we have to determine a cut tree T for (G, r); this is done using Algorithm 10.4.2. After initializing T as a star with center 1, we obtain $s = 2$, $t = 1$, $w = 18$ and $s = \{2, 3, 4, 5, 6\}$, so that $f(s) = 2$. The vertices $3, 4, 5$ and 6 are then cut off from 1 and connected to 2 instead. Next, we have $s = 3$, $t = 2$, $w = 13$ and $S = \{3, 4, 5\}$. We set $f(3) = 13$, cut off the vertices 4 and 5 from 2 and connect them to vertex 3. For $s = 4$, we have

$t = 3$, $w = 14$ and $S = \{4\}$. The tree T is not changed in this step; we set $f(4) = 14$. Now $s = 5$, $t = 3$, $w = 15$ and $S = \{4, 5, 6\}$. The vertices 3, 4 and 5 are removed from T, $s = 5$ is then connected to $p(t) = p(3) = 3$ and 3 and 4 are connected to 5. Also, $f(5)$ is now given the value $f(t) = f(3) = 13$ and $f(3)$ is changed to $w = 15$. In the last phase, we have $s = 6$, $t = 2$, $w = 17$ and $S = \{3, 4, 5, 6\}$; we set $f(6) = 17$. Vertex 5 is cut off from 2 and connected to vertex 6. The resulting tree has weight 77; it solves Problem 10.4.4 for the given request function r. Figure A.31 illustrates how the algorithm works.

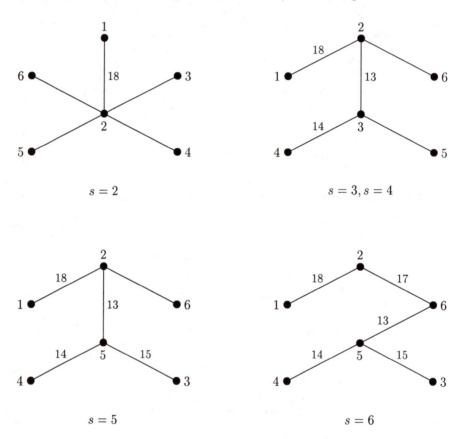

Fig. A.31 Determining a cut tree for N

10.5.2 The relevant part of the auxiliary network corresponding to the flow g of Figure 10.16 is drawn in Figure A.32; an augmenting path with cost 3 and capacity 15 is shown bold. Increasing the capacity of both the (bold) edges sb and ct by θ (for $\theta = 1, \ldots, 15$), we obtain a flow of value $v = 41 + \theta$. The total cost for the corresponding increase of the capacity is $20 + 3\theta$. In particular, we obtain the flow h of value 56 and cost 65 shown in Figure A.33.

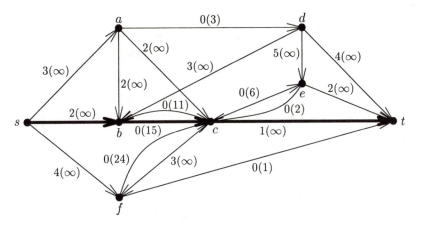

Fig. A.32 Auxiliary network for g

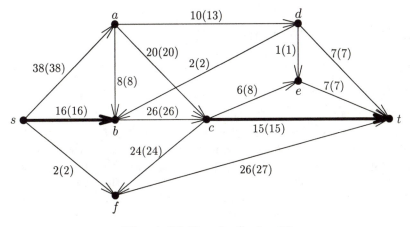

Fig. A.33 Flow h of value 56

The next step yields the auxiliary network shown in Figure A.34; again, an augmenting path is drawn bold. This time, it has cost 4 and its capacity is unlimited. Thus, we can now realize any flow value $v = 56 + \tau$ with total cost $65 + 4\tau$ by increasing the capacity of each of the edges sb, bc and ct by τ. Note that there are other paths of cost 4 in the auxiliary network of Figure A.34, but the capacity of these paths is not unlimited. We have now determined the cost function $z(v)$ completely by executing the iteration step of the Algorithm of Busacker and Gowen three times.

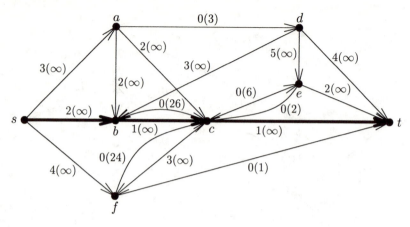

Fig. A.34 Auxiliary network for h

A.11 Solutions for Chapter 11

11.1.2

(a) $\kappa(K_{m,n}) = \min\{m, n\}$
(b) Each vertex has degree at least k.

11.1.3 Add a new vertex t and all edges xt for $x \in T$ to G. It is easy to show that the resulting graph H is k-connected as well (that is, there is no vertex separator for H consisting of $k-1$ vertices). Now Theorem 11.1.1 yields that there are k vertex disjoint paths from s to t; these paths have to contain all the k edges xt with $x \in T$. Deleting these edges, we obtain the desired paths in G.

11.1.6 The graph $K_{m,m+1}$ has connectivity $\kappa = m$ and independence number $\alpha = m + 1$. It cannot be Hamiltonian, because a Hamiltonian circuit would have length $2m + 1$ (but bipartite graphs cannot contain cycles of odd length, see Theorem 3.3.5).

11.1.7 Using the procedure BLOCK01FLOW of Lemma 6.5.2, we can determine the maximal value of a flow and a maximal flow as follows (analogous to Algorithm 6.3.17). Let G be a directed graph with two exceptional vertices s and t.

Procedure MAX01FLOW $(G, s, t; f, \text{val})$

(1) **for** $e \in E$ **do** $c(e) \leftarrow 1$; $f(e) \leftarrow 0$ **od**;
(2) $\text{val} \leftarrow 0$; $N \leftarrow (G, c, s, t)$;
(3) **repeat**
(4)   AUXNET $(N, f; N'', \text{max}, d)$;
(5)   **if** max = false **then** BLOCK01FLOW$(N''; g)$;
                AUGMENT $(f, g; f)$ **fi**
(6) **until** max = true;
(7) **for** $e \in A_S$ **do**
(8)   **if** $f(e) = 1$ **then** $\text{val} \leftarrow \text{val} + 1$ **fi**
(9) **od.**

The proofs of Theorems 7.1.1 and 7.1.4 imply that the maximal number of vertex disjoint paths from s to t in G is equal to the maximal value of a flow on the 0-1-network N on the directed graph H defined during the following procedure.

Procedure PATHNR $(G, s, t; k)$

(1) $V' \leftarrow \{s, t\}$; $E' \leftarrow \emptyset$;
(2) **for** $v \in V \backslash \{s, t\}$ **do** $V' \leftarrow V' \cup \{v', v''\}$; $E' \leftarrow E' \cup \{v'v''\}$ **od**;
(3) **for** $e \in E$ **do**
(4)   **if** $e = sv$ with $v \neq t$ **then** $E' \leftarrow E' \cup \{sv'\}$ **fi**;
(5)   **if** $e = tv$ with $v \neq s$ **then** $E' \leftarrow E' \cup \{v''t\}$ **fi**;
(6)   **if** $e = uv$ with $u, v \neq s, t$ **then** $E' \leftarrow E' \cup \{u''v', v''u'\}$ **fi**
(7) **od**;
(8) $H \leftarrow (V', E')$; MAX01FLOW $(H, s, t; \text{val}, f)$;
(9) **if** $st \in E$ **then** $k \leftarrow \text{val} + 1$ **else** $k \leftarrow \text{val}$ **fi**.

Theorems 7.1.1 and 7.1.4 show that this procedure is correct; note that s and t are not adjacent in H. If s and t are adjacent in G, we have to add one further path from s to t, namely the edge st itself. By Corollary 7.1.5, PATHNR has complexity $O(|V|^{1/2}|E|)$. Finally, if G is an undirected graph, we can – as in the proof of Theorem 7.1.1 – replace G by its complete orientation.

11.2.6 We define a graph G as follows. For each ramification of the maze, G has a vertex, where the entrance, the exit and dead ends are viewed as ramifications as well. The edges of G are those parts of paths of the maze which connect two ramifications; then the end vertices of such an edge are the corresponding ramifications. Figures A.35 and A.36 show the graph G corresponding to the maze of Figure 11.3. The labels of the vertices in Figure A.36 show how a DFS on G would work (beginning at the entrance of the maze which is represented by the vertex labelled 1); the algorithm terminates when the exit is reached (that is, the vertex labelled 64). The corresponding path through the maze is drawn in Figure A.37; for the sake of simplicity, we have omitted traversing the dead ends which occured during the DFS.

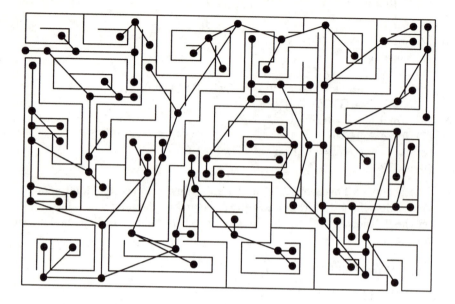

Fig. A.35 A maze with corresponding graph G

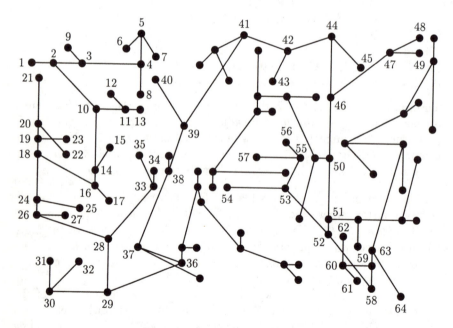

Fig. A.36 A partial DFS on G

Fig. A.37 A path through the maze

Of course, when we designed the above solution, we saw the maze from above and used this knowledge. However, it is not hard (if it is possible to label ramifications and paths in the maze when passing them) to find a rule which allows to apply a DFS to the maze without knowing it as a whole. We leave it to the reader to find such a rule.[2]

---

[2] In this context, the following citation from 'The name of the rose' by Umberto Eco is of interest (see Eco (1983), p. 176):

'At every new junction, never seen before, the path we have taken will be marked with three signs. If, because of previous signs on some of the paths of the junction, you see that the junction has already been visited, you will make only one mark on the path you have taken. If all the apertures of the junction are still without signs, you will choose any one, making two signs on it. Proceeding through an aperture that bears only one sign, you will make two more, so that now the aperture bears three. All the parts of the labyrinth must have been visited if, arriving at a junction, you never take a passage with three signs, unless none of the other passages is now without signs.'

This somewhat chaotic rule contains the basic idea of a depth first search, even though the hero of the tale, William of Baskerville, who says himself that he just cites 'an ancient text I once read', obviously confused the labelling rules a bit.

11.3.2 Consider two vertices u and v for which $d(u, v)$ is maximal. If v were a cut point, then $G \backslash v$ would consist of two components. In that case, it would be possible to choose a vertex w which is not contained in the same component as u. Then any path from u to w would have to contain v, so that the distance from w to u would have to be at least $d(u, v) + 1$, contradiction. Therefore, v and (analogously) u cannot be cut points. On the other hand, any path of length n contains precisely $n - 2$ cut points.

11.3.3

(a) If $bc(G)$ contained a cycle $(B_1, c_1, B_2, c_2, \ldots, B_k, c_k, B_1)$, it would be possible, after having removed c_k, to reach vertices in B_1 from vertices in B_k, a contradiction. This proves that $bc(G)$ is always acyclic. If G is connected, $bc(G)$ is obviously connected as well. Thus, in that case, $bc(G)$ is a tree.

(b) We may assume w.l.o.g. that G is connected, so that $p = 1$. Then $bc(G)$ is a tree and contains precisely $b(G) + c(G) - 1$ edges. Now each edge connects a cut point with a block, so that the number of edges is equal to the sum of all the $b(c)$ (over all cut points c). It follows that

$$b(G) + c(G) - 1 = \sum_c b(c) = \sum_c 1 + \sum_v (b(v) - 1) = c(G) + \sum_v (b(v) - 1),$$

because each vertex which is not a cut point is contained in precisely one block.

(c) can be proved analogous to b).

(d) We use induction on the number $c(G)$ of cut points. The case $c(G) = 1$ is trivial. For $c(G) > 1$, $bc(G)$ contains a leaf and any leaf B has to be a block. The only edge incident with B has a cut point c as its other end vertex. Removing B from the graph G corresponds to removing c and B from $bc(G)$. Now the assertion follows with induction (for appropriate choices of B and c).

11.3.4 Let $b(G) = k$. We denote the cardinalities of the blocks by $n_1, \ldots, n_k$ and the number of vertices of G by n. Then Exercise 11.3.3b) states that $n_1 + \ldots + n_k = k + n - 1$. By Exercise 11.3.3d), a graph with a maximal number of edges (for r cut points) has to have at least $r + 1$ blocks; obviously, each block has to be a complete graph on at least two vertices. Thus, the maximal number of edges is given by

$$\max \left\{ \sum_{i=1}^k \binom{n_i}{2} : n_1 + \ldots + n_k = n + k - 1; n_1, \ldots, n_k \geq 2; k \geq r + 1 \right\}$$

$$= \max \left\{ k - 1 + \binom{n + k - 1 - (2k - 2)}{2} : k \geq r + 1 \right\} = \binom{n - r}{2} + r.$$

This number is realized by a graph consisting of K_{n-r} with a path of length r appended.

11.3.10 We obtain the graph shown in Figure A.38. The first number written on a vertex v states the DFS-number $nr(v)$; the second number is $L(v)$. Algorithm 11.3.8 yields the cut points i, e, s and h in this order. The blocks are $\{k, j, i\}$; $\{i, e\}$; $\{e, f, b, a, s\}$; $\{l, h\}$; $\{h, d, g, c, s\}$. The edges of the DFS tree are drawn bold; cut points are indicated by a circle.

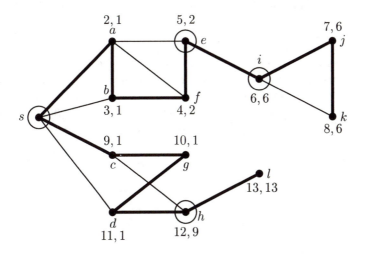

Fig. A.38 DFS-tree, blocks and cut points

11.4.3 As vertex u was reached later than v during the DFS, the examination of u has to take place during the examination of v.

11.4.4 If a back edge $e = vu$ occurs during the DFS, we obtain a directed cycle in G, because u is an ancestor of v. Conversely, suppose G contains a directed cycle. Let v be the first vertex of G examined during the DFS which is contained in a directed cycle and let $e = uv$ be an edge on such a cycle C. By the way we chose v, u is examined later during the DFS than v, so that e is neither a forward edge nor a tree edge. But as u is accessible from v (using C), u has to be a descendant of v. Thus, e is cannot be a cross edge, so that e must be a back edge.

11.5.2 Choose G to be a directed cycle or the complete orientation of a path, respectively.

11.5.3 Let C and C' be two distinct strong components of G. As G is connected, there exists an edge e connecting a vertex in C and a vertex in C'. Then e cannot be contained in a directed cycle, because that would imply $C = C'$ contradicting our hypothesis.

11.5.8 The vertices h, f and g each form a strong component with only one element; the remaining vertices together form a further strong component.

11.5.9 We define a directed graph to be strongly k-connected if it is the complete orientation of K_{k+1} or if any set S of vertices for which $G \backslash S$ is a directed graph which is not strongly connected has to contain at least k vertices. Then the analogous statement of Theorem 11.1.1 holds as well as the statement analogous to Theorem 11.1.9 (in both cases, $\kappa(v_i, w)$ as well as $\kappa(w, v_i)$ have to be calculated).

11.5.10 Suppose the strong components $C_1, \ldots, C_m$ are contained in a cycle of G'. Then there are edges $v_i v_i'$ with $v_i \in C_i$ and $v_i' \in C_{i+1}$ (where $m + 1$ is interpreted as 1). Now C_i contains a directed path from v_{i-1}' to v_i, so that we obtain a directed cycle and $C_1, \ldots, C_m$ have to be contained in a strong component, a contradiction. Therefore, G' has to be acyclic. Figure A.39 shows G' for the directed graph G of Figure 3.3.

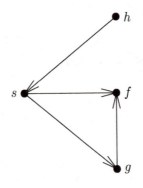

Fig. A.39 Condensed digraph for the digraph of Fig. 3.3

11.6.2 For $k = m = d$, we can choose $G = K_{d+1}$. For $k \neq d$, we need two copies of the complete graph K_{d+1} on two disjoint vertex sets S and T plus $2k$ vertices $x_1, \ldots, x_k, x_1', \ldots, x_k'$ and all the edges $x_i x_i'$. Moreover, each of the x_i (and the x_i', respectively) is connected to $d - 1$ vertices in S (or T, respectively) and we add $m - k$ further edges connecting the vertices in $S \cup \{x_2, \ldots, x_k\}$ to some of the x_i'. We illustrate the construction in Figure A.40.

11.6.3 Let E' be a minimal edge separator of G. Then $G \backslash E'$ has two connected components S and T and E' is the cocycle determined by the cut (S, T). We may assume w.l.o.g. that $x = |S| \leq n/2$. Then E' has to contain at least $x\delta - x(x - 1) = x(\delta - x + 1)$ edges. It is easy to check that, for $x = 1, \ldots, n/2$, we always have $x(\delta - x + 1) \geq \delta$ if $\delta \geq n/2$. Considering the graph consisting of two disjoint copies of K_d (connected by at most $d - 1$ edges) shows that nothing can be said for the case $\delta < n/2$.

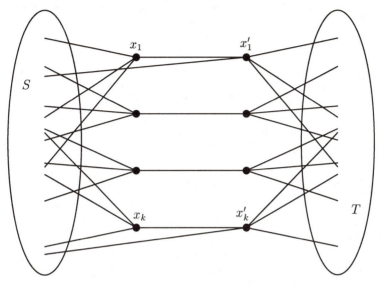

Fig. A.40 Graph constructed in Exercise 11.6.2

A.12 Solutions for Chapter 12

12.1.2 Suppose H is the graph which results from adding the edges of the complete graph on T to G. Obviously, G has a perfect matching if and only if H does. Thus, it suffices to show that the conditions (H) for G and (T) for H are equivalent. First suppose that (H) holds for G. Let $X \subset V$; we have to show that $p(X) \leq |X|$. This is clear for $X = \emptyset$, because H is connected and contains precisely $2n$ vertices. Now consider the case $X \subset T$ (and $X \neq \emptyset$); we set $J := T \backslash X$. Then the components of $H \backslash X$ are the set $Y = J \cup \Gamma(J)$ and the elements of $S \backslash \Gamma(J)$. If $|Y|$ is even, it follows that $p(X) = n - |\Gamma(J)|$ and $|X| = n - |J|$. But (H) implies that $|\Gamma(J)| \geq |J|$, so that $p(X) \leq |X|$ holds as desired. If $|Y|$ is odd, we have $|\Gamma(J)| \geq |J| + 1$ and the assertion follows accordingly. Now suppose that X is not a subset of T. If $T \subset X$, the assertion is trivial. Otherwise, let $X' = T \cap X$. Then

$$p(X) \leq p(X') + 1 \leq |X'| + 1 \leq |X|.$$

Thus, we have verified that (T) holds for (H). Conversely, (H) for G follows from (T) for (H) using a similar (but easier) argument.

12.1.3 Let S be a subset of V and denote the odd components of $G \backslash S$ by

$G_1, \ldots, G_k$. Moreover, let m_i be the number of edges connecting a vertex of G_i to a vertex of S (for $i = 1, \ldots, k$). As G does not contain any bridges, we always have $m_i \neq 1$. Now G is 3-regular, so that

$$\sum_{v \in G_i} \deg v = 3|G_i| \qquad \text{for } i = 1, \ldots, k.$$

This implies that

$$m_i = \sum_{v \in G_i} \deg v - 2|E_i|$$

(where E_i denotes the edge set of the graph induced on G_i) always is an odd number, so that $m_i \geq 3$. We get

$$p(S) = k \leq \frac{1}{3}(m_1 + \ldots + m_k) \leq \frac{1}{3}\left(\sum_{v \in S} \deg v\right) = |S|,$$

that is, condition (T) holds for G. Now the assertion follows from Theorem 12.1.1. Figure A.41 shows a 3-regular graph containing bridges which does not have a perfect matching, as $p(v) = 3$. Finally, the Petersen graph of Exercise 1.5.9 is a 3-regular graph without bridges which does not have a factorization (Petersen (1898)).

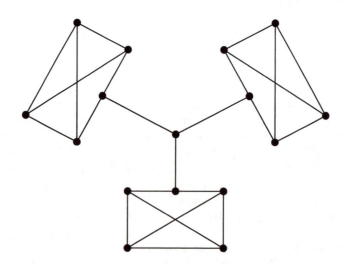

Fig. A.41 A 3-regular graph without a perfect matching

12.2.5 We show first that G is 2-connected. Suppose otherwise, then there exists a cut point v so that $G \backslash v$ has two components X and Y. Choose an edge of the form vx with $x \in X$ and extend it to a perfect matching K. Then $|Y|$ has to be even and X has to be odd. However, an analogous argument shows that $|Y|$ is odd and $|X|$ is even, a contradiction. Now we distinguish two cases.

Case 1: G is bipartite, say $V = S \cup T$. Suppose there are non-adjacent vertices $s \in S$ and $t \in T$; let W be a path from s to t. It is clear that W has odd length, so that the first, the third, ... and the last edge of W form a matching K which can be extended to a perfect matching K'. Then $K' \oplus W$ is a matching whose only exposed vertices are s and t. Now, as s and t are not adjacent, this matching cannot be extended, a contradiction. Therefore, we must have $G = K_{n,n}$.

Case 2: G is not bipartite. We show first that each vertex is contained in a cycle of odd length. Let v be any vertex of G and C any cycle of odd length (note that such a cycle exists by Theorem 3.3.5). We may assume that v is not contained in C. As G is 2-connected, we know by Exercise 11.1.3 that there are two paths W and W' with start vertex v and end vertex some vertex of C which have only the vertex v in common. Thus, W and W' together with one of the two paths in C connecting the two end vertices of W and W' form a cycle of odd length. We show next that any two vertices u and v of G are connected by a path of odd length. We may assume w.l.o.g. that u and v are not adjacent. Choose some cycle C of odd length containing v. If u is contained in C, the statement is clear. Otherwise, if u is not contained in C, we choose a path W with start vertex u and end vertex $w \neq v$ on C which does not contain any further vertices of C. Then W together with one of the two paths in C connecting w and v forms a path of odd length from u to v. Now suppose G contains two vertices u and v which are not adjacent. Then there exists a path W of odd length from u to v and we obtain a contradiction as in case 1. Thus, we must have $G = K_{2n}$.

12.2.6 Suppose C is a Hamiltonian circuit in a graph G on $2n$ vertices. Choosing every other edge of C, we obtain a perfect matching of G. Thus, any Hamiltonian graph having an even number of vertices has a perfect matching. Thus, the two conditions are sufficient for the existence of a perfect matching of G by Corollary 1.4.3 and Exercise 1.4.5, respectively.

12.4.2 Beginning the procedure at vertex r yields the alternating tree T shown in Figure A.42. When examining the edge 26, the blossom $B = \{2, 5, 6\}$ with base 2 is discovered and contracted. We obtain the graph $G' = G/B$ and the corresponding contracted tree $T' = T/B$ shown in Figure A.43. Next, when examining the pseudo node b, the blossom $B' = \{r, 1, 3, 4, b\}$ with base r is found (because of edge 64) and contracted. This yields the graph $G'' = G'/B'$ which consists of the edge $b's$ only. This edge forms a trivial augmenting path W''. Expanding this path from s, we obtain the augmenting path

$$W' : \quad s \text{ ——— } 1 \text{ ——— } b \text{ ——— } 4 \text{ ——— } 3 \text{ ——— } r$$

in G' and finally the augmenting path

$$W: \quad s \quad\text{---}\quad 1 \quad\text{---}\quad 2 \quad\text{---}\quad 5 \quad\text{---}\quad 6 \quad\text{---}\quad 4 \quad\text{---}\quad 3 \quad\text{---}\quad r$$

in G.

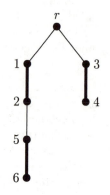

Fig. A.42 Alternating tree T for G

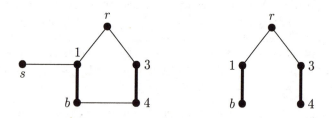

Fig. A.43 Contracted graph G/B with corresponding tree T/B

12.4.5 The graph G of Figure 12.23 is drawn again in Figure A.44 (on the left hand side). Obviously, $1 \text{---} 2 \text{---} 3 \text{---} 5$ is an augmenting path in G with respect to K. Contracting the blossom $B = \{2, 3, 4\}$, we obtain the graph $G' = G/B$ shown in Figure A.44 (on the right hand side); this graph has the matching $K' = \{b6\}$. Obviously, G' does not contain any augmenting path with respect to K'.

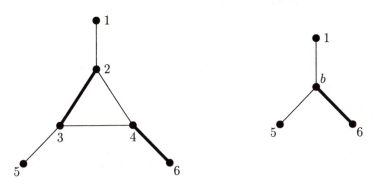

Fig. A.44 Graph G and contracted graph G/B

12.4.8 Let H be the graph with vertex set $V = \{1,\ldots,n\}$ which has an edge ij if and only if ij' (and then ji' as well) is an edge of G (for $i \neq j$). Then any matching in H consisting of k edges corresponds to a symmetric matching with $2k$ edges in G. Thus, a maximal symmetric matching of G can be determined by Algorithm 12.4.6 with complexity $O(n^3)$.[3]

12.5.3 Let G be the bipartite graph on $V = S \,\dot\cup\, T$ corresponding to $\mathbf{A} = (A_1,\ldots,A_n)$ (as defined in Section 7.3). Obviously, the partial transversals of $\mathbf{A}$ are precisely those subsets of S which are met by a matching of G. Therefore, the partial transversals of $\mathbf{A}$ form a matroid by Corollary 12.5.2.

12.5.4 As the maximal matchings of G induce the bases of the matching matroid $(V, \mathbf{S})$, the assertion follows from Theorem 5.2.5. However, the assertion can also be proved (with less theoretical effort) using Theorem 12.2.2: Extending a matching using an augmenting path (as in the proof of Theorem 12.2.2) leaves any saturated vertex saturated, so that the assertion follows by induction.

---

[3] The work of Kocay and Stone and Fremuth-Paeger and Jungnickel mentioned at the beginning of this chapter uses the reverse approach: A symmetric bipartite graph G (or a corresponding network, respectively) is used for constructing a maximal matching in the corresponding graph H.

A.13 Solutions for Chapter 13

13.1.2 Proceeding as outlined in Section 13.1, we obtain:

Procedure OPTMATCH $(n, w; K, M)$

(1) $W \leftarrow \max \{w_{ij} : i, j = 1, \ldots, n\}$;
(2) $V \leftarrow \{1, \ldots, n\} \cup \{1', \ldots, n'\} \cup \{s, t\}$;
(3) $E \leftarrow \{ij' : i, j = 1, \ldots, n\} \cup \{si : i = 1, \ldots, n\} \cup \{j't : j = 1, \ldots, n\}$;
(4) $G \leftarrow (V, E)$;
(5) **for** $i = 1$ **to** n **do**
(6) $\gamma(si) \leftarrow 0$; $\gamma(i't) \leftarrow 0$; **for** $j = 1$ **to** n **do** $\gamma(ij') \leftarrow W - w_{ij}$ **od**
(7) **od**;
(8) **for** $e \in E$ **do** $c(e) \leftarrow 1$ **od**;
(9) OPTFLOW $(G, c, s, t, \gamma, n; f, \text{sol})$;
(10) $K \leftarrow \{ij' : f(ij') = 1\}$; $M \leftarrow \sum\limits_{e \in K} w(e)$.

To achieve a complexity of $O(n^3)$, we have to use the Algorithm of Dijkstra for determining the shortest paths in step (7) of OPTFLOW (as explained before Theorem 9.6.3).

13.2.6 During the first four phases, we obtain (without any changes) the edges $\{1, 4'\}$, $\{2, 9'\}$, $\{3, 6'\}$ and $\{4, 1'\}$ in this order. Even the feasible node weighting $(\mathbf{u}, \mathbf{v})$ remains unchanged. During the fifth phase (where $i = 5$), the only vertex j' with $\delta_j = 0$ is $9'$, which is saturated already. Nothing is changed by $i = 2$, because mate$(9') = 2$ is the smallest vertex in Q. But next, for $i = 6$, we find the edge $\{6, 3'\}$. Analogously, during the phases 6 and 7, edges $\{7, 8'\}$ and $\{8, 7'\}$ are constructed. Up to now, $(\mathbf{u}, \mathbf{v})$ was not changed. During phase 8, we have $i = 5$, $i = 2$ (because of $\delta_9 = 0$, mate$(9') = 2$), $i = 9$ and $i = 7$ (because of $\delta_8 = 0$, mate$(8') = 7$). Now $J = \{2, 5, 7, 9\}$, $K = \{8', 9'\}$ and $\delta = 1$, so that the u_i and v_j have to be changed. We obtain the exposed vertex $5'$ with $\delta_5 = 0$, and the edge $\{9, 5'\}$ is added to the matching constructed so far. The ninth (and last) phase is the most complicated one. Again, we first have $i = 5$, $i = 2$ and $i = 7$. Then $(\mathbf{u}, \mathbf{v})$ has to be changed according to $J = \{2, 5, 7\}$, $K = \{8', 9'\}$ and $\delta = 2$. Now $\delta_4 = 0$ and mate $(4') = 1$, so that $i = 1$. Again, $(\mathbf{u}, \mathbf{v})$ has to be changed, this time for $J = \{1, 2, 5, 7\}$, $K = \{4', 8', 9'\}$ and $\delta = 3$. Three more changes of $(\mathbf{u}, \mathbf{v})$ follow: for $J = \{1, 2, 4, 5, 7\}$, $K = \{1', 4', 8', 9'\}$, $\delta = 1$; $J = \{1, 2, 4, 5, 7, 9\}$, $K = \{1', 4', 5', 8', 9'\}$, $\delta = 2$ and $J = \{1, 2, 4, 5, 7, 8, 9\}$, $K = \{1', 4', 5', 7', 8', 9'\}$, $\delta = 5$. Now $2'$ is exposed and we can complete the matching by adding the edge $\{5, 2'\}$. We show the values for $(\mathbf{u}, \mathbf{v})$ below; the entries corresponding to edges used in the construction are written in bold face. Note that indeed $w(K) = \sum(u_i + v_i) \ (= 603)$ holds.

$$
\begin{pmatrix}
0 & 31 & 24 & \mathbf{80} & 62 & 39 & 24 & 41 & 42 \\
31 & 0 & 0 & 34 & 54 & 5 & 51 & 45 & \mathbf{61} \\
24 & 0 & 0 & 31 & 32 & \mathbf{59} & 28 & 44 & 25 \\
\mathbf{80} & 34 & 31 & 0 & 65 & 45 & 25 & 44 & 47 \\
62 & \mathbf{54} & 32 & 65 & 0 & 38 & 48 & 66 & 68 \\
39 & 5 & \mathbf{59} & 45 & 38 & 0 & 8 & 25 & 18 \\
24 & 51 & 28 & 25 & 48 & 8 & 0 & \mathbf{71} & 66 \\
41 & 45 & 44 & 44 & 66 & 25 & \mathbf{71} & 0 & 69 \\
42 & \mathbf{61} & 25 & 47 & \mathbf{68} & 18 & 66 & 69 & 0
\end{pmatrix}
\quad
\begin{matrix}
69 \\ 47 \\ 59 \\ 72 \\ 54 \\ 59 \\ 57 \\ 66 \\ 61
\end{matrix}
$$

| 8 | 0 | 0 | 11 | 7 | 0 | 5 | 14 | 14 | $\mathbf{v}/\mathbf{u}$ |

Note that the matching consisting of the edges $\{1, 4'\}$, $\{2, 5'\}$, $\{3, 6'\}$, $\{4, 1'\}$, $\{5, 9'\}$, $\{6, 3'\}$, $\{7, 8'\}$ and $\{9, 2'\}$ is optimal as well.

13.2.7 The Algebraic Assignment Problem for the ordered semi-group $(\mathbb{R}_0^+, \min)$ yields the Bottleneck Assignment Problem.

13.2.8 During the first two phases, the edges $\{1, 3'\}$ and $\{2, 4'\}$ are found. In phase 3 for $i = 3$ we have $\delta_4 = 1$; as mate$(4') = 2$, we then find for $i = 2$ the exposed vertex $5'$ with $\delta_5 = 1$. Now the present matching is changed using $p(5) = 2$, mate$(2) = 4'$ and $p(4) = 3$; we obtain $\{1, 3'\}$, $\{2, 5'\}$ and $\{3, 4'\}$. In phase 4, the matching is changed again to $\{1, 3'\}$, $\{2, 5'\}$, $\{3, 4'\}$ and $\{5, 2'\}$. During the last phase, $(\mathbf{u}, \mathbf{v})$ has to be changed twice: First with $J = \{2, 3, 4\}$, $K = \{4', 5'\}$ and $\delta = 5/4$ and the second time with $J = \{2, 3, 4, 5\}$, $K = \{2', 4', 5'\}$ and $\delta = 36/35$. Now the matching is changed again to $\{1, 3'\}$, $\{2, 5'\}$, $\{3, 1'\}$, $\{4, 4'\}$ and $\{5, 2'\}$. The corresponding entries are printed bold in the matrix below. For checking our calculations, we determine $w(K) = \prod(u_i, v_i) = 15120$.

$$
\begin{pmatrix}
3 & 8 & \mathbf{9} & 1 & 6 \\
1 & 4 & 1 & 5 & \mathbf{5} \\
7 & 2 & 7 & 9 & 2 \\
3 & 1 & 6 & \mathbf{8} & 8 \\
2 & \mathbf{6} & 3 & 6 & 2
\end{pmatrix}
\quad
\begin{matrix}
9 \\ 35/9 \\ 7 \\ 56/9 \\ 35/6
\end{matrix}
$$

| 1 | $\frac{36}{35}$ | 1 | $\frac{9}{7}$ | $\frac{9}{7}$ | $\mathbf{v}/\mathbf{u}$ |

This product-optimal matching is equal to the optimal matching of Example 13.2.5. Exercise 13.2.10 shows that this is not always the case.

13.2.9 Denote the given weight matrix by $W := (w_{ij})$ and set $W' := (\log w_{ij})$. Then the product-optimal matchings with respect to W are precisely the optimal matchings with respect to W'. However, this is not interesting for practical applications. When executing calculations with W' using a computer, errors occur because of rounding (logarithms are irrational in general), and this means we cannot check our solution by comparing $w'(K)$ with $\sum(u_i' + v_i')$. However, if we do the calculations *symbolically*, that is, if we merely do operations such as replacing $\log p + \log q$ by $\log pq$, we may as well use the version of the Hungarian Algorithm modified for $(\mathbb{R}^+, \cdot)$. However, the above transformation yields an immediate proof for the correctness of this approach.

13.2.10 For the matrix

$$\begin{pmatrix} 3 & 1 & 1 \\ 1 & 4 & 5 \\ 6 & 1 & 4 \end{pmatrix},$$

the matching given by the bold entries has weight $12 = 1 + 5 + 6$ and is obviously optimal. However, it is not product-optimal. Conversely, the matching containing the entries 3, 4 and 4 is product-optimal but not optimal.

13.3.2

(a) Let A be the incidence matrix of a directed graph G. Lemma 9.3.1 states that the vector $\mathbf{f} = (f_e)_{e \in E}$ is a circulation if and only if $A\mathbf{f}^T = 0$. Therefore, we get the ILP

Minimize $\gamma \mathbf{x}^T$ subject to the restrictions $A\mathbf{x}^T = \mathbf{0}^T$, $\mathbf{b} \le \mathbf{x} \le \mathbf{c}$.

(b) As a spanning tree of a graph G on n vertices contains $n - 1$ edges and is acyclic, we can use the following ZOLP (which is not interesting because it contains too many inequalities):

Maximize $\mathbf{w}\mathbf{x}^T$ subject to the restrictions $\mathbf{1}\mathbf{x}^T = n - 1$ and
$$\sum_{e \in C} x_e \le |C| - 1 \text{ for any cycle } C \text{ of } G,$$

where $\mathbf{x} = (x_e)_{e \in E}$.

13.4.6 Let G be a regular bipartite multigraph with vertex set $V = S \cup T$, where $|S| = |T| = n$. We define the matrix $A = (a_{ij})_{i,j=1,\dots,n}$ corresponding to G to have the number of edges of G with end vertices i and j' as entry a_{ij} (we assume w.l.o.g. $S = \{1, \dots, n\}$ and $T = \{1', \dots, n'\}$). Then A is a matrix having non-negative integral entries and its row and column sums are constant. Now Theorem 7.4.5 (and its proof) allows us to write A as a sum of permutation matrices. As each permutation matrix corresponds to a 1-factor of G, this decomposition of A yields a factorization of G.

13.4.7 Obviously, we have $\mathbf{L}(G) \subset \mathbf{H}(G) \cap \mathbb{Z}^E$. Conversely, let $\mathbf{x}$ be a vector in $\mathbf{H}(G) \cap \mathbb{Z}^E$. Choose some positive integer k which is larger than the absolute value of $\mathbf{x}$. Then $\mathbf{x}' = \mathbf{x} + \sum k\mathbf{m}$ is an element of $\mathbf{H}(G) \cap \mathbb{Z}^E$ as well, where $\mathbf{m}$ runs over the incidence vectors of the perfect matchings of G. Moreover, $\mathbf{x}' \ge \mathbf{0}$ holds. We define a regular bipartite multigraph G' by substituting each edge e of G by x'_e parallel edges. G' is indeed regular, because $\mathbf{x}'$ is contained in $\mathbf{H}(G)$. By Exercise 13.4.6, G' can be decomposed into 1-factors. As each 1-factor of G' induces a 1-factor of G, x' has to be a linear combination of incidence vectors of perfect matchings of G with non-negative integral coefficients. But this means that $\mathbf{x} = \mathbf{x}' - \sum k\mathbf{m}$ is contained in $\mathbf{L}(G)$ as well.

13.5.6 Obviously, any closed walk of G containing each edge at least once induces a circulation $\mathbf{f}$ on G: Define f_e as the number of times e occurs in the given walk. Then we have $\mathbf{f} \geq \mathbf{1}$. Conversely, any circulation $\mathbf{f}$ with $\mathbf{f} \geq \mathbf{1}$ induces a closed walk on G containing each edge at least once: Replace each edge e by f_e parallel edges. The resulting pseudosymmetric directed graph contains an Euler tour by Theorem 1.6.1 and this Euler tour induces the desired walk. Note that G is obviously connected. Thus, a shortest directed closed walk corresponds to an optimal circulation with respect to the capacity constraints $b(e) = 1$ and $c(e) = \infty$ and the cost function $\gamma(e) = w(e)$ (for each edge e). Therefore, this problem can be solved using the Algorithm OPTCIRC from Section 9.8, for example.

13.6.5 A shortest $\{s,t\}$-path is $W : s \ \text{---} \ c \ \text{---} \ t$ of length -1. The corresponding f-factors are

$$F = \{\{a,a\}, \{b,b\}, sc, ct\} \quad \text{and} \quad F' = \{\{a,a\}, \{b,b\}, sc, ct, c_g b_g, a_e b_e\};$$

the corresponding perfect matching is $K = \{a'a'', b'b'', sc', c''t, a_e b_e, c_g b_g\}$.

13.6.6 If (G, w) contains cycles of negative length, the method yields a shortest *simple* $\{s,t\}$-path (which is not necessarily the shortest trail from s to t).

13.6.9 Use the following change of the transformation of Theorem 13.6.7: Any edge of the form tv is now substituted by an edge tv'' (instead of tv') and the edge st (if it exists) is removed. For the graph G of Example 13.6.8, the even $\{s,t\}$-path

$$W \ : \ s \ \text{---} \ u \ \text{---} \ v \ \text{---} \ a \ \text{---} \ t$$

corresponds to the perfect matching

$$K \ = \ \{su', u''v'', v'a', a''t, b'b'', c'c''\}$$

in the auxiliary graph G'', see Figures A.45 and A.46.

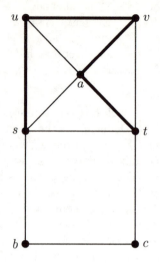

Fig. A.45 A path of even length in G

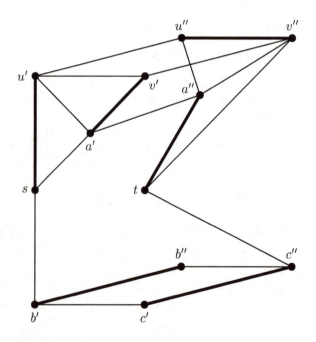

Fig. A.46 The corresponding perfect matching in G''

13.7.2 Define the weight function w on H by

$$
w_e := \begin{cases}
0 & \text{for } e \notin E \\
c - 1 & \text{for } e \in E_1 \\
c & \text{for } e \in E \backslash E_1.
\end{cases}
$$

Suppose K is an optimal matching of H with respect to this weight function. Then K consists exclusively of edges of G if and only if $w(K) \geq n(c-1)$, where $|V| = 2n$. In this case, the number of edges of K contained in E_1 is $cn - w(K)$. Thus, the problem RPM1 has a solution if and only if $cn - w(K) \leq b_1$. As $w(K)$ can be determined with complexity $O(n^3)$ by Result 13.4.5, the assertion follows.

13.7.4 Define $E_1 := R$, $E_2 := E \backslash R$, $b_1 := b$ and $b_2 := n - b$ (where $|V| = 2n$). Now the perfect matchings of G satisfying condition (13.12) of Problem 13.7.1 for these values are precisely the desired solutions of EPM, because any perfect matching contains precisely n edges.

A.14 Solutions for Chapter 14

14.2.2 Suppose ij is the edge of minimal weight w_{ij} in a perfect matching of minimal weight. Then, in the symmetric case, we have $w_{ij} = w_{ji}$. If the remaining weights are much larger, the edge ji occurs as well. This means that, in the symmetric case, it is much more likely that a pair of antiparallel edges occurs than in the asymmetric case.

14.2.5 Let T be the minimal spanning tree for the given TSP (see Figure 14.2). Then we obtain the minimal 1-tree for $1 = Aa$ by adding the edge $AaFr$, so that the weight is $186 + 26 = 212$. Similarly, we obtain for $1 = Ba$ a weight of $186 + 34 = 220$ and for $1 = Mu$ a weight of $186 + 22 = 208$. For $1 = Du$, a minimal spanning tree on the remaining 8 vertices consists of the edges $BeHa$, $HaAa$, $AaFr$, $FrSt$, $StBa$, $StNu$ and $NuMu$; the weight of the 1-tree here is $187 + 8 + 23 = 218$. For the remaining cases, we give the weight of a minimal 1-tree only: $184 + 20 + 22 = 226$ for $1 = Fr$; $158 + 29 + 43 = 230$ for $1 = Ha$; $172 + 17 + 19 = 208$ for $1 = Nu$ and $176 + 19 + 20 = 215$ for $1 = St$.

14.2.6 By Corollary 1.2.11, there are $(n-1)^{n-3}$ spanning trees on the remaining $n - 1$ vertices distinct from 1. To each of these trees, we could add $(n-1)(n-2)/2$ pairs of edges incident with 1, so that the total number of 1-trees of K_n is $\frac{1}{2}(n-2)(n-1)^{n-2}$.

14.2.7 The given inequality holds because, in a tour, each vertex i is incident with two edges whose weight is at least $s(i) + s'(i)$. This yields a lower bound of 214 for the TSP of Example 14.1.2 (note that w is integral).

14.5.4 We begin with $s = Fr$ as in Example 14.5.3. In the first step, we obtain the partial tour (Fr, St, Fr) of length 40 and in the next (Fr, St, Nu, Fr) of length 61. Now Mu is inserted, so that we get (Fr, St, Mu, Nu, Fr) of length 81. The next step yields (Fr, Du, St, Mu, Nu, Fr) of length 125. Inserting Aa between Du and St yields a partial tour of length 138. We proceed with $(Fr, Du, Aa, Ba, St, Mu, Nu, Fr)$ of length 176 and then by inserting Ha between Fr and Du which yields a partial tour of length 246. Finally, we obtain the tour $(Fr, Be, Ha, Du, Aa, Ba, St, Mu, Nu, Fr)$ of length 281.

14.6.4 In the first step, the edges $AaMu$ and $FrBe$ are replaced by $MuBe$ and $AaFr$. This reduces the weight of the tour of Figure 14.7 by $64 + 56 - (60 + 26) = 34$; the resulting tour of weight $307 - 34 = 273$ is $(Aa, Du, Ha, Be, Mu, Nu, Ba, St, Fr, Aa)$. Next, the edges $NuBa$ and $FrSt$ are substituted by $BaFr$ and $StNu$. This reduces the weight of the resulting tour $(Aa, Du, Ha, Be, Mu, Nu, St, Ba, Fr, Aa)$ by $(43 + 20) - (34 + 19) = 10$ to 263. Finally, the edges $StNu$ and $BeMu$ are exchanged with $StMu$ and $NuBe$. This yields the (optimal) tour of length 250 of Figure 14.9; the weight of the tour was reduced in this step by $(19 + 60) - (22 + 44) = 13$.

14.7.7 As $\mathbf{A}'$ is an ε-approximative algorithm for TSP, we can use $\mathbf{A}'$ to solve the problem HC as in the proof of Theorem 14.4.1. Note that each iteration of the algorithm $\mathbf{A}'$ (that is, each application of $\mathbf{A}$ to a neighbourhood $N(f)$) decreases the weight of the present tour (except for the last application of $\mathbf{A}$, which merely finds out that the tour constructed in the last step is locally optimal). As the weight function defined in the proof of Theorem 14.4.1 takes only two values, there can be only $n + 1$ distinct lengths of tours. Therefore, $\mathbf{A}'$ cannot need more than $O(n)$ iterations of $\mathbf{A}$. Now, as $\mathbf{A}$ is polynomial, $\mathbf{A}'$ would be a polynomial algorithm for HC, so that P=NP by Result 12.2.2.

14.7.8 Suppose the given problem could be solved polynomially. We show that this implies that we can find an optimal tour in polynomial time as well. We may assume w.l.o.g. that all weights are ≥ 2. Now we check whether some chosen edge e_1 is contained in an optimal tour. If the answer is yes, we reduce $w(e_1)$ to 1; this has the effect that (for the changed problem) e_1 has to be contained in any optimal tour. More precisely, the optimal tours for the new problem are precisely those optimal tours for the old problem which contain the edge e_1. Continuing this procedure, we can construct an optimal tour (for the original problem) with $O(n^2)$ calls of the decision problem we assumed to be polynomial.

B. List of Symbols

B.1 General Symbols

This first part of the list contains some general symbols which are more or less standard. The special symbols of Graph and Matroid Theory will be treated in the next section.

Sets

$A \cup B$	union of the sets A and B
$A \,\dot\cup\, B$	disjoint union of the sets A and B
$A \cap B$	intersection of the sets A and B
$A \times B$	Cartesian product of the sets A and B
$A \backslash B$	A without B
$A \oplus B$	symmetric difference of A and B, that is, $(A \backslash B) \cup (B \backslash A)$
2^A	power set of A
$\overline{A}$	complement of A (with respect to a given base set)
A^t	set of ordered t-tuples with elements from A
$\binom{A}{t}$	set of t-subsets of A
$|A|$	cardinality of A
$A \subset B$	A is a subset of B
$\emptyset$	empty set

Mappings

$f : A \to B$	f is a mapping from A to B
$f(x)$	image of x under the mapping f

$f(X)$	$\{f(x) : x \in X\}$ for $f : A \to B$ and $X \subset A$
supp f	support of f

Numbers

$\sum_{i=1}^{n} a_i$	$a_1 + \ldots + a_n$
$\prod_{i=1}^{n} a_i$	$a_1 a_2 \ldots a_n$
$\lceil x \rceil$	smallest integer $\geq x$ (for $x \in \mathbb{R}$)
$\lfloor x \rfloor$	largest integer $\leq x$ (for $x \in \mathbb{R}$)
$n!$	$n(n-1)(n-2)\ldots 1$ (for $n \in \mathbb{N}$)
$\binom{n}{t}$	number of t-subsets of an n-set
e	base of the natural logarithm

Matrices

A^T	transposed of the matrix A
J	matrix with all entries 1
I	unit matrix
$\mathrm{diag}(a_1, \ldots, a_n)$	diagonal matrix with entries $a_{11} = a_1, \ldots, a_{nn} = a_n$
(a_{ij})	matrix with entries a_{ij}
$\det A,\ |A|$	determinant of the matrix A
per A	permanent of the matrix A

Sets of Numbers and Algebraic Structures

$\mathbb{N}$	set of natural numbers (not including 0)
$\mathbb{N}_0$	set of natural numbers including 0
$\mathbb{Z}$	ring of integers
$\mathbb{Z}_n$	ring of integers modulo n
$\mathbb{Q}$	field of rational numbers
$\mathbb{Q}^+$	set of positive rational numbers
$\mathbb{Q}_0^+$	set of non-negative rational numbers
$\mathbb{R}$	field of real numbers

$\mathbb{R}^+$	set of positive real numbers
$\mathbb{R}_0^+$	set of non-negative real numbers
K^*	multiplicative group of the field K
K^n	n-dimensional vector space over the field K
$K^{(n,n)}$	ring of $(n \times n)$-matrices over the field K
S_n	symmetric group acting on n elements

Miscellaneous

$x := y,\ y =: x$	x is defined to be y
$x \leftarrow y$	x is assigned the value of y

B.2 Special Symbols

This second part of the list contains symbols from Graph Theory and the symbols introduced in this book.

Graphs and Networks

$\overline{G}$	complementary graph for the graph G
G_{red}	reduced digraph for the digraph G
$G|U$	subgraph of G induced on the vertex set U
$G\backslash T,\ G\backslash v$	subgraph of G induced on the set $V\backslash T$ or $V\backslash\{v\}$, resp.
$G\backslash e$	G without edge e
G/B	contraction of the graph G with respect to the blossom B
G/e	contraction of the graph G with respect to the edge e
$|G|$	multigraph underlying the directed multigraph G
(G)	underlying graph for the multigraph G
$\overrightarrow{G}$	complete orientation of the graph G
$[G]$	closure of the graph G

$bc(G)$	block-cutpoint graph of G
$G(H, S)$	Cayley graph corresponding to the group H and the set S
$G_{s,n}$	de Bruijn graph
$H_{\mathbf{u},\mathbf{v}}$	equality subgraph for G with respect to $(\mathbf{u}, \mathbf{v})$
K_n	complete graph on n vertices
$K_{m,n}$	complete bipartite graph on $m + n$ vertices
$L(G)$	line graph of G
$N', N'(f)$	auxiliary network for N (with respect to the flow f)
$N'', N''(f)$	layered auxiliary network for N (with respect to the flow f)
$T(G)$	tree graph of the connected graph G
T_n	triangular graph

Parts of Graphs

$C_T(e)$	cycle determined by the spanning tree T and edge $e \notin T$
$a \overset{e}{\rule{2em}{0.4pt}} b$	edge $e = ab$
e^-	start vertex of edge e
e^+	end vertex of edge e
$E(S), E(X, Y)$	edge set corresponding to the cut $S = (X, Y)$
$E\|V'$	edge set induced on the vertex set V'
F_ε	set of ε-fixed edges (with respect to a given circulation)
$S_T(e)$	cut determined by the spanning tree T and the edge $e \in T$
$\Gamma(J)$	neighbourhood of the vertex set J
$\Gamma(v)$	neighbourhood of the vertex v

Parameters for Graphs

$\deg v$	degree of vertex v
$d_{in}(v)$	indegree of vertex v
$d_{out}(v)$	outdegree of vertex v
g	girth of G
n_d	number of vertices of degree d
$\alpha(G)$	independence number of G

$\alpha'(G)$	maximal cardinality of a matching of G
$\beta(G)$	minimal cardinality of a vertex cover of G
$\delta(G)$	minimal degree of a vertex of G
$\Delta(G)$	maximal degree of a vertex of G.
Δ	minimal number of paths in a dissection of G, Dilworth number
$\theta(G)$	clique partition number of G
$\kappa(G)$	connectivity of G
$\lambda(G)$	edge connectivity of G
$\nu(G)$	cyclomatic number of G
$\chi(G)$	chromatic number of G
$\chi'(G)$	chromatic index (also called edge chromatic number) of G
$\omega(G)$	maximal cardinality of a clique in G

Mappings on Graphs and Networks

$a(x)$	supply at vertex x
$b(x)$	demand at vertex x
$b(e)$	lower capacity constraint for edge e
$c(e)$	capacity of edge e
$c(W)$	capacity of the path W
$c(S,T)$	capacity of the cut (S,T)
$d(a,b)$	distance between the vertices a and b
$d_H(a,b)$	distance between vertices a and b in the graph H
$f(S,T)$	flow value for the cut (S,T) with respect to the function f
$m(K)$	mean weight of the cycle K
$p(v)$	flow potential at vertex v
$p(S)$	number of odd components of $G \backslash S$
$r(v)$	rank of vertex v in an acyclic digraph
$w(e)$	weight (or length) of edge e
$w(f)$	value of the flow f
$w(P)$	weight of the optimal solution for problem P

$w(X)$	weight (or length) of a set X of edges
$w(\pi)$	weight of the tour π
$w_A(P)$	weight of the solution for problem P determined by algorithm A
$w(s,t)$	flow function of a symmetric network
$\gamma(e)$	cost of edge e
$\gamma^{(\varepsilon)}(f)$	cost of edge e increased by ε
$\gamma_p(e)$	reduced cost of edge e (with respect to the potential p)
$\gamma(f)$	cost of the circulation or the flow f
$\gamma(K)$	cost of the perfect matching K
$\gamma(v)$	cost of an optimal flow with value v
δq	potential difference
$\varepsilon(f)$	optimality parameter for the circulation f
$\epsilon(v)$	excentricity of vertex v
$\kappa(s,t)$	maximal number of vertex disjoint paths from s to t
$\lambda(s,t)$	maximal number of edge disjoint paths from s to t
$\mu(G,w)$	minimum cycle mean in the network (G,w)
$\pi_V(T)$	Prüfer code of the tree T on the vertex set V

Matroids and Independence Systems

$\mathrm{lr}(A)$	lower rank of the set A
$M(G)$	graphic matroid corresponding to G
M^*	dual matroid of the matroid M
$\overline{M}$	hereditary closure of the set system M
$\mathrm{rq}\,(M)$	rank quotient of the independence system M
$\mathrm{ur}\,(A)$	upper rank of the set A
$\mathbf{S}|N$	restriction of the set system $\mathbf{S}$ to the set N
$\rho(A)$	rank of the set A
$\sigma(A)$	span of the set A

Matrices

A	adjacency matrix of a graph
A'	degree matrix of a graph
M	incidence matrix of a graph or a digraph
$\rho(A)$	term rank of the matrix A

Miscellaneous

A_v	adjacency list for vertex v
A'_v	reverse adjacency list for vertex v
$d(\mathbf{a})$	deficiency of the set family $\mathbf{A}$
$t(\mathbf{A})$	transversal index of the set family $\mathbf{A}$
$O(f(n))$	upper bound on the complexity
$\Omega(f(n))$	lower bound on the complexity
$\Theta(f(n))$	rate of growth

References

Aarts, E. and Lenstra, J. K. (1997): *Local Search in Combinatorial Optimization*. Wiley, New York.

Abu-Sbeih, M. Z. (1990): On the number of spanning trees of K_n and $K_{m,n}$. *Discr. Math.* **84**, 205-207.

Aho, A. V., Hopcroft, J. E. and Ullman, J. D. (1974): *The Design and Analysis of Computer Algorithms*. Addison Wesley, Reading, Mass.

Aho, A. V., Hopcroft, J. E. and Ullman, J. D. (1983): *Data Structures and Algorithms*. Addison Wesley, Reading, Mass.

Ahuja, R. K., Goldberg, A. V., Orlin, J. B. and Tarjan, R. E. (1992): Finding minimum-cost flows by double scaling. *Math. Progr.* **53**, 243-266.

Ahuja, R. K., Kodialam, M., Mishra, A. K. and Orlin, J. B. (1992): Computational testing of maximum flow algorithms. Sloan working paper, Sloan School of Management, MIT.

Ahuja, R. K., Magnanti, T. L. and Orlin, J. B. (1989): Network flows. In: *Handbooks in Operations Research and Management Science, Vol 1: Optimization* (Eds. G. L. Nemhauser, A. H. G. Rinnooy Kan and M. J. Todd). North Holland, Amsterdam, pp. 211-369.

Ahuja, R. K., Magnanti, T. L. and Orlin, J. B. (1991): Some recent advances in network flows. *SIAM Review* **33**, 175-219.

Ahuja, R. K., Magnanti, T. L. and Orlin, J. B. (1993): *Network Flows: Theory, Algorithms and Applications*. Prentice Hall, Englewood Cliffs, N.J.

Ahuja, R. K., Mehlhorn, K., Orlin, J. B. and Tarjan, R. E. (1990): Faster algorithms for the shortest path problem. *J. ACM* **37**, 213-223.

Ahuja, R. K. and Orlin, J. B. (1989): A fast and simple algorithm for the maximum flow problem. *Oper. Res.* **37**, 748-759.

Ahuja, R. K. and Orlin, J. B. (1992): The scaling network simplex algorithm. *Oper. Res.* **40**, Suppl. 1, pp. S 5 - S 13.

Ahuja, R. K. and Orlin, J. B. (1995): A capacity scaling algorithm for the constrained maximum flow problem. *Networks* **25**, 89-98.

Ahuja, R. K., Orlin, J. B., Stein, C. and Tarjan, R. E. (1994): Improved algorithm for bipartite network flow. *SIAM J. Computing* **23**, 906-933.

Ahuja, R. K., Orlin, J. B. and Tarjan, R. E. (1989): Improved time bounds for the maximum flow problem. *SIAM J. Comp.* **18**, 939-954.

Aigner, M. (1984): *Graphentheorie. Eine Entwicklung aus dem 4-Farben-Problem*. Teubner, Stuttgart.

Aigner, M. (1997): *Combinatorial Theory*. Springer, New York.

Alon, N. (1990): Generating pseudo-random permutations and maximum flow algorithms. *Inform. Proc. Letters* **35**, 201-204.

Althöfer, I. (1988): On optimal realizations of finite metric spaces by graphs. *Discr. and Comput. Geom.* **3**, 103-122.

Anderson, I. (1990): *Combinatorial Designs: Construction Methods.* Ellis Horwood Ltd., Chichester.

Anderson, I. (1971): Perfect matchings of a graph. *J. Comb. Th.* **10**, 183-186.

Anderson, L. D. (1977): On edge-colorings of graphs. *Math. Scand.* **40**, 161-175.

Anderson, S. S. and Harary, F. (1967): Trees and unicyclic graphs. *Math. Teacher* **60**, 345-348.

Anstee, R. P. (1985): An algorithmic proof of Tutte's f-factor theorem. *J. Algor.* **6**, 112-131.

Appel, K. and Haken, W. (1977a): Every planar map is 4-colorable - 1: Discharging. *Illinois J. Math.* **21**, 429-490.

Appel, K. and Haken, W. (1977b): Every planar map is 4-colorable - 2: Reducibility. *Illinois J. Math.* **21**, 491-567.

Applegate, D., Bixby, R., Chvátal, V. and Cook, W. (1995): Finding cuts in the TSP (A preliminary report). DIMACS Technical Report 95-05, March 1995.

Applegate, D. and Cook, W. (1993): Solving large-scale matching problems. In: *Network Flows and Matching* (Eds. D. S. Johnson and C. C. McGeoch). Amer. Math. Soc., Providence, pp. 557-576.

Arkin, E. M. and Papadimitriou, C. H. (1986): On the complexity of circulations. *J. Algor.* **7**, 134-145.

Arora, S., Lund, C., Motwani, R., Sudan, M. and Szegedy, M. (1992): Proof verification and hardness of approximation problems. *Proc. 33th IEEE Symp. on Foundations of Computer Science*, pp. 14-23.

Arora, S. and Safra, S. (1992): Probabilistic checking of proofs: A new characterization of NP. *Proc. 33rd IEEE Symp. on Foundations of Computer Science*, pp. 2-13.

Ausiello, G., Italiano, G. F., Marchetti Spaccamela, A. and Nanni, U. (1991): Incremental algorithms for minimal length paths. *J. Algor.* **12**, 615-638.

Avis, D. (1978): Two greedy heuristics for the weighted matching problem. *Congr. Numer.* **21**, 65-76.

Avis, D. (1983): A survey of heuristics for the weighted matching problem. *Networks* **13**, 475-493.

Babai, L., Fortnow, L., Levin, L. A., and Szegedy, M. (1991): Checking computations in polylogarithmic time. *Proc. 23rd ACM Symp. on Theory of Computing*, pp. 21-31.

Babai, L., Fortnow, L. and Lund, C. (1991): Nondeterministic exponential time has two-prover interactive protocols. *Comput. Complexity* **1**, 3-40.

Bäbler, F. (1953): Über eine spezielle Klasse Eulerscher Graphen. *Comment. Math. Helv.* **21**, 81-100.

Bachem, A. and Kern, W. (1992): *Linear Programming Duality. An Introduction to Oriented Matroids.* Springer, Berlin.

Bachmann, F. (1989): *Ebene Spiegelungsgeometrie.* B.I. Wissenschaftsverlag, Mannheim-Wien-Zürich.

Baker, R. D. and Wilson, R. M. (1977): Nearly Kirkman triple systems. *Util. Math.* **11**, 289-296.

Balas, E. and Fischetti, M. (1993): A lifting procedure for the asymmetric traveling salesman polytope and a large new class of facets. *Math. Progr.* **58**, 325-352.

Balas, E. and Xue, J. (1991): Minimum weighted coloring of triangulated graphs, with application to maximum weight vertex packing and clique finding in arbitrary graphs. *SIAM J. Comp.* **20**, 209-221.

Balas, E. and Yu, C. S. (1986): Finding a maximum clique in an arbitrary graph. *SIAM J. Comp.* **15**, 1054-1068.

Balinsky, M. L. and Gonzales, J. (1991): Maximum matchings in bipartite graphs via strong spanning trees. *Networks* **21**, 165-179.

Balinski, M. and Ratier, G.: On stable marriages and graphs, and strategy and polytopes. *SIAM Review* **39**, 575-604.

Ball, M. O. (1985): Polynomial algorithms for matching problems with side constraints. Research report CORR 85-21, University of Waterloo.

Ball, M. O. and Derigs, U. (1983): An analysis of alternate strategies for implementing matching algorithms. *Networks* **13**, 517-549.

Ball, W. W. R. and Coxeter, H. S. M. (1947): *Mathematical Recreations and Essays.* Macmillan, New York.

Bandelt, H.-J. (1990): Recognition of tree matrices. *SIAM J. Discr. Math.* **3**, 1-6.

Bar-Ilan, J., Kortsarz, G. and Peleg, D. (1993): How to allocate network centers. *J. Algor.* **15**, 385-415.

Barahona, F. (1990): On some applications of the chinese postman problem. In: *Paths, flows and VLSI-Layout* (Eds. B. Korte, L. Lovász, H. J. Prömel and A. Schrijver). Springer, Berlin, pp. 1-16.

Barahona, F. and Pulleyblank, W. R. (1987): Exact arborescences, matchings and cycles. *Discr. Appl. Math.* **16**, 91-99.

Barahona, F. and Tardos, E. (1989): Note on Weintraub's minimum-cost circulation algorithm. *SIAM J. Comp.* **18**, 579-583.

Baranyai, Z. (1975): On the factorization of the complete uniform hypergraph. *Proc. Erdös-Koll. Keszthely 1973*, North Holland, Amsterdam, pp. 91-108.

Barnes, T. M. and Savage, C. D. (1995): A recurrence for counting graphical partitions. *Electronic J. Comb.* **2**, # R 11.

Bauer, F. L. and Wössner, H. (1982): *Algorithmic Language and Program Development.* Springer, Berlin.

Bazaraa, M. S., Jarvis, J. J. and Sherali, H. D. (1990): *Linear Programming and Network Flows (2nd edition).* Wiley, New York.

Bazaraa, M. S., Sherali, H. D. and Shetty, C. M. (1993): *Nonlinear Programming: Theory and Algorithms (2nd edition).* Wiley, New York.

Bellman, R. E. (1958): On a routing problem. *Quart. Appl. Math.* **16**, 87-90.

Bentley, J. L. (1990): Experiments on traveling salesman heuristics. *Proc. First SIAM Symp. on Discr. Algorithms*, pp. 91-99.

Berman, P. and Ramaiyer, V. (1994): Improved approximations for the Steiner tree problem. *J. Algor.* **17**, 381-408.

Berge, C. (1957): Two theorems in graph theory. *Proc. Nat. Acad. Sc. USA* **43**, 842-844.

Berge, C. (1958): Sur le couplage maximum d'un graphe. *C.R. Acad. Sci. Paris* **247**, 258-259.

Berge, C. (1973): *Graphs and Hypergraphs.* North Holland, Amsterdam.

Berge, C. and Chvátal, V. (1984): *Topics in Perfect Graphs.* North Holland, Amsterdam.

Berge, C. and Fournier, J. C. (1991): A short proof for a generalization of Vizing's theorem. *J. Graph Th.* **15**, 333-336.

Berge, C. and Ghouila-Houri, A. (1962): *Programmes, Jeux et Réseaux de Transport.* Dunod, Paris.

Berman, P. and Ramaiyer, V. (1994): Improved approximations for the Steiner tree problem. *J. Algor.* **17**, 381-408.

Bermond, J. C. (1978): Hamiltonian graphs. In: *Selected topics in graph theory* (Eds. L. W. Beineke and R. J. Wilson). Academic Press, New York, pp. 127-167.

Bermond, J. C., Ed. (1992): *Interconnection Networks.* North Holland, Amsterdam.

Bertsekas, D. P. (1993): A simple and fast label correcting algorithm for shortest paths. *Networks* **23**, 703-709.

Beth, T. (1974): Algebraische Auflösungsalgorithmen für einige unendliche Familien von 3-Designs. *Le Matematiche* **29**, 105-135.

Beth, T., Jungnickel, D. and Lenz, H. (1998): *Design Theory (2nd ed.)*. Cambridge University Press, Cambridge.

Bien, F. (1989): Constructions of telephone networks by group representations. *Notices AMS* **36**, 5-22.

Bienstock, D., Brickell, E. F. and Monma, C. N. (1990): On the structure of minimum-weight k-connected spanning networks. *SIAM J. Discr. Math.* **3**, 320-329.

Biggs, N. L. (1993): *Algebraic Graph Theory (2nd edition)*. Cambridge University Press, Cambridge.

Biggs, N. L., Lloyd, E. K. and Wilson, R. J. (1976): *Graph Theory 1736-1936*. Oxford University Press, Oxford.

Birkhoff, G. (1946): Tres observaciones sobre el algebra lineal. *Univ. Nac. Tucumán Rev. Ser. A* **5**, 147-151.

Bjørner, A., Las Vergnas, M., Sturmfels, B., White, N. and Ziegler, G. M. (1992): *Oriented Matroids*. Cambridge University Press, Cambridge.

Bjørner, A. and Ziegler, G. M. (1992): Introduction to greedoids. In: *Matroid applications* (Ed. N. White). Cambridge University Press, Cambridge, pp. 284-357.

Bland, R. G. and Shallcross, D. F. (1989): Large traveling salesman problems arising from experiments in x-ray crystallography: A preliminary report on computation. *Oper. Res. Letters* **8**, 125-128.

Boesch, F. and Tindell, R. (1980): Robbins theorem for mixed multigraphs. *Amer. Math. Monthly* **87**, 716-719.

Bollobas, B. (1978): *Extremal Graph Theory*. Academic Press, New York.

Bondy, J. A. and Chvátal, V. (1976): A method in graph theory. *Discr. Math.* **15**, 111-135.

Bondy, J. A. and Murty, U. S. R. (1976): *Graph Theory with Applications*. North Holland, Amsterdam.

Book, R. V. (1994): Relativizations of the P =? NP and other problems: developments in structural complexity theory. *SIAM Review* **36**, 157-175.

Booth, S. and Lueker, S. (1976): Testing for the consecutive ones property, interval graphs, and graph planarity using PQ-tree algorithms. *J. Comput. System Sc.* **13**, 335-379.

Borchardt, C. W. (1860): Über eine der Interpolation entsprechende Darstellung der Eliminationsresultante. *J. Reine Angew. Math.* **57**, 111-121.

Borgwardt, K. H. (1987): *The Simplex Method. A Probabilistic Analysis*. Springer, Berlin.

Boruvka, O. (1926a): O jistém problému minimálním. *Acta Societ. Scient. Natur. Moravicae* **3**, 37-58.

Boruvka, O. (1926b): Príspevek k resení otázky ekonomické stavby elektrovodních sítí. *Elektrotechnicky obzor* **15**, 153-154.

Bosák, J. (1990): *Decompositions of Graphs*. Kluwer Academic Publishers, Dordrecht.

Boyd, E. A. and Faigle, U. (1990): An algorithmic characterization of antimatroids. *Discr. Appl. Math.* **28**, 197-205.

Brooks, R. L. (1941): On colouring the nodes of a network. *Proc. Cambridge Phil. Soc.* **37**, 194-197.

Brucker, P., Burkard, R. E. and Hurink, J. (1990): Cyclic schedules for r irregularly occuring events. *J. Comp. Appl. Math.* **30**, 173-189.

Bryant, V. and Brooksbank, P. (1992): Greedy algorithm compatibility and heavy-set structures. *Europ. J. Comb.* **13**, 81-86.

Bunemann, P. (1974): A note on the metric properties of trees. *J. Comb. Th. (B)* **17**, 48-50.

Burkard, R. E. (1986): Optimal schedules for periodically recurring events. *Discr. Appl. Math.* **15**, 167-180.

Burkard, R. E., Hahn, W. and Zimmermann, U. (1977): An algebraic approach to assignment problems. *Math. Progr.* **12**, 318-327.

Busacker, R. G. and Gowen, P. J. (1961): A procedure for determining a family of minimum cost flow networks. ORO Techn. Report 15, John Hopkins University.

Camerini, P. M., Fratta, L. and Maffioli, F. (1979): A note on finding optimum branchings. *Networks* **9**, 309-312.

Camerini, P. M., Maffioli, F., Martello, S. and Toth, P. (1986): Most and least uniform spanning trees. *Discr. Appl. Math.* **15**, 181-197.

Cameron, P. J. (1976): *Parallelisms of Complete Designs*, Cambridge University Press, Cambridge.

Cameron, P. J. and Van Lint, J. H. (1991): *Designs, Graphs, Codes and their Links*. Cambridge University Press, Cambridge.

Campbell, D. M. and Radford, D. (1991): Tree isomorphism algorithms: Speed versus clarity. *Math. Magazine* **64**, 252-261.

Carpaneto, G., Fischetti, M. and Toth, P. (1989): New lower bounds for the symmetric travelling salesman problem. *Math. Progr.* **45**, 233-254.

Carré, P. A. (1971): An algebra for network routing problems. *J. Inst. Math. Appl.* **7**, 273-294.

Carré, P. A. (1979): *Graphs and Networks*. Oxford University Press, Oxford.

Catlin, P. A. (1979): Hajós' graph coloring conjecture: variations and counterexamples. *J. Comb. Th. (B)* **26**, 268-274.

Cayley, A. (1889): A theorem on trees. *Quart. J. Math.* **23**, 376-378.

Chandrasekaran, R., Aneja, Y. P. and Nair, K. P. K. (1981): Minimal cost reliability ratio spanning tree. *Ann. Discr. Math.* **11**, 53-60.

Chandrasekaran, R. and Tamir, A. (1984): Polynomial testing of the query 'Is $a^b \geq c^d$' with application to finding a minimal cost reliability ratio spanning tree. *Discr. Appl. Math.* **9**, 117-123.

Chartrand, G. (1966): A graph-theoretic approach to communication problems. *SIAM J. Appl. Math.* **14**, 778-781.

Chartrand, G. and Harary, F. (1968): Graphs with described connectivities. In: *Theory of graphs* (Eds. P. Erdös and G. Katona). Academic Press, New York, pp. 61-63.

Chartrand, G. and White, A. T. (1970): Randomly transversable graphs. *Elem. Math.* **25**, 101-107.

Cheng, C. K. and Hu, T. C. (1992): Maximum concurrent flows and minimum cuts. *Algorithmica* **8**, 233-249.

Cheriton, D. and Tarjan, R. E. (1976): Finding minimum spanning trees. *SIAM J. Comp.* **5**, 724-742.

Cheriyan, J. and Hagerup, T. (1989): A randomized maximum flow algorithm. *Proc. 30th IEEE Conf. on Foundations of Computer Science*, pp. 118-123.

Cheriyan, J. and Hagerup, T. (1995): A randomized maximum flow algorithm. *SIAM J. Computing* **24**, 203-226.

Cheriyan, J., Hagerup, T. and Mehlhorn, K. (1996): A $o(n^3)$-time maximum flow algorithm. *SIAM J. Computing* **25**, 1144-1170.

Cheriyan, J. and Maheshwari, S. N. (1989): Analysis of preflow push algorithms for maximum network flow. *SIAM J. Comp.* **18**, 1057-1086.

Cherkassky, B. V. and Goldberg, A. V. (1995): On implementing Push-Relabel method for the maximum flow problem. In: *Integer programming and combinatorial optimization* (Eds. E. Balas and J. Clausen). Springer, Berlin, pp. 157-171.

Cheung, T. Y. (1980): Computational comparison of eight methods for the maximum network flow problem. *ACM Trans. Math. Software* **6**, 1-16.

Christofides, N. (1975): *Graph Theory: An Algorithmic Approach*. Academic Press, New York.

Christofides, N. (1976): Worst-case analysis of a new heuristic for the travelling salesman problem. Report 388, Grad. School of Ind. Admin., Carnegie-Mellon University.

Chu, Y. J. and Liu, T. H. (1965): On the shortest arborescence of a directed graph. *Sci. Sinica* **14**, 1396-1400.

Chung, F. R. K. (1986): Diameters of communication networks. *Proc. Symp. Pure Appl. Math.* **34**, 1-18.

Chung, F. R. K., Garey, M. R. and Tarjan, R. E. (1985): Strongly connected orientations of mixed multigraphs. *Networks* **15**, 477-484.

Chvátal, V. (1983): *Linear Programming*. Freeman, New York.

Chvátal, V. (1985): Hamiltonian cycles. In: *The travelling salesman problem* (Eds. E. L. Lawler, J. K. Lenstra, A. H. G. Rinnooy Kan and D. B. Shmoys). Wiley, New York, pp. 403-429.

Chvátal, V. and Erdös, P. (1972): A note on Hamiltonian circuits. *Discr. Math.* **2**, 111-113.

Chvátal, V. and Thomasson, C. (1978): Distances in orientations of graphs. *J. Comb. Th. (B)* **24**, 61-75.

Colbourn, C. J. (1987): *The Combinatorics of Network Reliability*. Oxford University Press, Oxford.

Colbourn, C. J., Day, R. P. J. and Nel, L. D. (1989): Unranking and ranking spanning trees of a graph. *J. Algor.* **10**, 271-286.

Cole, R. and Hopcroft, J. (1982): On edge coloring bipartite graphs. *SIAM J. Comp.* **11**, 540-546.

Conrad, A., Hindrichs, T., Morsy, H. and Wegener, I. (1992): Wie es einem Springer gelingt, Schachbretter von beliebiger Größe zwischen beliebig vorgegebenen Anfangs- und Endfeldern vollständig abzureiten. *Spektrum der Wiss.*, Februar 1992, pp. 10-14.

Conrad, A., Hindrichs, T., Morsy, H. and Wegener, I. (1994): Solution of the knight's Hamiltonian path problem on chessboards. *Discr. Appl. Math.* **50**, 125-134.

Cook, S. A. (1971): The complexity of theorem proving procedures. *Proc. 3rd ACM Symp. on the Theory of Computing*, pp. 151-158.

Cook, W. and Hartmann, M. (1990): On the complexity of branch and cut methods for the traveling salesman problem. In: *Polyhedral combinatorics* (Eds. W. Cook and P. D. Seymour). American Mathematical Society, Providence, pp. 75-81.

Corman, T. H., Leiserson, C. E. and Rivest, R. L. (1990): *Introduction To Algorithms*. MIT Press, Cambridge, Massachusetts.

Cornuejols, G. and Nemhauser, G. L. (1978): Tight bounds for Christofides' traveling salesman heuristic. *Math. Progr.* **14**, 116-121.

Coxeter, H. M. S. (1973): *Regular Polytopes (3rd ed.)* Dover, New York.

Croes, G. A. (1958): A method for solving traveling-salesman problems. *Oper. Res.* **6**, 791-812.

Crowder, H. and Padberg, M. W. (1980): Solving large-scale symmetric travelling salesman problems to optimality. *Management Sc.* **26**, 495-509.

Cunningham, W. H. (1986): Improved bounds for matroid partition and intersection algorithms. *SIAM J. Comp.* **15**, 948-957.

Cunningham, W. H. and Marsh, A. B. (1978): A primal algorithm for optimal matching. *Math. Progr. Stud.* **8**, 50-72.

Cvetkovic, D. M., Doob, M., Gutman, I. and Torgasev, A. (1987): *Recent Results in the Theory of Graph Spectra*. North Holland, New York.

Cvetkovic, D. M., Doob, M. and Sachs, H. (1980): *Spectra of Graphs*. Academic Press, New York.

Dantzig, G. B., Ford, L. R. and Fulkerson, D. R. (1956): A primal-dual algorithm for linear programs. In: *Linear inequalities and related systems* (Eds. H. W. Kuhn and A. W. Tucker). Princeton University Press, Princeton, pp. 171-181.

Dantzig, G. B., Fulkerson, D. R. and Johnson, S. M. (1954): Solution of a large-scale traveling-salesman problem. *Oper. Res.* **2**, 393-410.

de Bruijn, N. G. (1946): A combinatorial problem. *Indag. Math.* **8**, 461-467.

de Bruijn, N. G. and van Aardenne-Ehrenfest, T. (1951): Circuits and trees in oriented linear graphs. *Simon Stevin* **28**, 203-217.

de Werra, D. (1980): Geography, games and graphs. *Discr. Appl. Math.* **2**, 327-337.

de Werra, D. (1981): Scheduling in sports. *Ann. Discr. Math.* **11**, 381-395.

de Werra, D. (1982): Minimizing irregularities in sports schedules using graph theory. *Discr. Appl. Math.* **4**, 217-226.

de Werra, D. (1988): Some models of graphs for scheduling sports competitions. *Discr. Appl. Math.* **21**, 47-65.

de Werra, D., Jacot-Descombes, L. and Masson, P. (1990): A constrained sports scheduling problem. *Discr. Appl. Math.* **26**, 41-49.

Deo, N., Prabhu, G. M. and Krishnamoorthy, M. S. (1982): Algorithms for generating fundamental cycles in a graph. *ACM Trans. Math. Software* **8**, 26-42.

Derigs, U. (1988): *Programming in Networks and Graphs.* Springer, Berlin.

Derigs, U. and Heske, A. (1980): A computational study on some methods for solving the cardinality matching problem. *Angew. Inform.* **22**, 249-254.

Derigs, U. and Meier, W. (1989): Implementing Goldberg's max-flow algorithm - A computational investigation. *ZOR* **33**, 383-403.

Derigs, U. and Metz, A. (1991): Solving (large scale) matching problems combinatorially. *Math. Progr.* **50**, 113-121.

Dijkstra, E. W. (1959): A note on two problems in connexion with graphs. *Numer. Math.* **1**, 269-271.

Dilworth, R. P. (1950): A decomposition theorem for partially ordered sets. *Annals Math.* **51**, 161-166.

Dinic, E. A. (1970): Algorithm for solution of a problem of maximum flow in networks with power estimation. *Soviet Math. Dokl.* **11**, 1277-1280.

Dirac, G. A. (1952): Some theorems on abstract graphs. *Proc. LMS (3)* **2**, 69-81.

Dixon, B., Rauch, M. and Tarjan, R. E. (1992): Verification and sensitivity analysis of minimum spanning trees in linear time. *SIAM J. Computing* **21**, 1184-1192.

Domschke, W. (1989): Schedule synchronization for public transit networks. *OR Spektrum* **11**, 17-24.

Dress, A. (1984): Trees, tight extensions of metric spaces, and the cohomological dimension of certain groups: A note on combinatorial properties of metric spaces. *Adv. Math.* **53**, 321-402.

Du, D.-Z. and Hwang, F. (1990a): An approach for proving lower bounds: Solution of Gilbert-Pollak's conjecture on Steiner ratio. *Proc. 31st Annual Symp. on Foundations of Computer Science*, Los Alamitos, Cal., IEEE Computer Society, pp. 76-85.

Du, D.-Z. and Hwang, F. (1990b): The Steiner ratio conjecture of Gilbert and Pollak is true. *Proc. National Acad. of Sciences USA* **87**, 9464-9466.

Du, D.-Z. and Zhang, Y. (1992): On better heuristics for Steiner minimum trees. *Math. Progr.* **57**, 193-202.

Dueck, G. (1993): New optimization heuristics: The great deluge algorithm and record-to-record travel. *J. Comput. Physics* **104**, 86-92.

Dueck, G. and Scheuer, T. (1990): Threshold accepting: a general purpose optimization algorithm appearing superior to simulating annealing. *J. Comput. Physics* **90**, 161-175.

Eco. U. (1983): *The Name of the Rose.* Harcourt Brace Jovanovich, Inc. and Martin Secker & Warburg Limited.

Edmonds, J. (1965a): Maximum matching and a polytope with 0, 1-vertices. *J. Res. Nat. Bur. Stand. B* **69**, 125-130.

Edmonds, J. (1965b): Paths, trees and flowers. *Canad. J. Math.* **17**, 449-467.

Edmonds, J. (1967a): An introduction to matching. Lecture Notes, Univ. of Michigan.

Edmonds, J. (1967b): Optimum branchings. *J. Res. Nat. Bur. Stand. B* **71**, 233-240.

Edmonds, J. (1970): Submodular functions, matroids and certain polyhedra. In: *Combinatorial structures and their applications* (Ed. K. Guy). Gordon & Breach, New York, pp. 69-87.

Edmonds, J. (1971): Matroids and the greedy algorithm. *Math. Progr.* **1**, 127-136.

Edmonds, J. (1973): Edge disjoint branchings. In: *Combinatorial algorithms* (Ed. R. Rustin). Algorithmics Press, 91-96.

Edmonds, J. (1979): Matroid intersection. *Ann. Discr. Math.* **4**, 39-49.

Edmonds, J. and Fulkerson, D. R. (1965): Transversals and matroid partition. *J. Res. Nat. Bur. Stand. B* **69**, 147-153.

Edmonds, J. and Giles, R. (1977): A min-max relation for submodular functions on graphs. *Ann. Discr. Math.* **1**, 185-204.

Edmonds, J. and Giles, R. (1984): Total dual integrality of linear systems. In: *Progress in combinatorial optimization* (Ed. W. R. Pulleyblank). Academic Press Canada, 117-129.

Edmonds, J. and Johnson, E. L. (1973): Matching, Euler tours and the Chinese postman. *Math. Progr.* **5**, 88-124.

Edmonds, J. and Karp, R. M. (1972): Theoretical improvements in algorithmic efficiency for network flow problems. *J. ACM* **19**, 248-264.

Edmonds, J., Lovász, L. and Pulleyblank, W. R. (1982): Brick decompositions and the matching rank of graphs. *Combinatorica* **2**, 247-274.

Egerváry, E. (1931): Matrixok kombinatorius tulajdonságairól. *Mat. Fiz. Lapok* **38**, 16-28.

Egoritsjev, G. E. (1981): Solution of van der Waerden's permanent conjecture. *Adv. Math.* **42**, 299-305.

Elias, P., Feinstein, A. and Shannon, C. E. (1956): Note on maximum flow through a network. *IRE Trans. Inform. Th.* **IT-12**, 117-119.

Engel, K. (1997): *Sperner Theory.* Cambridge University Press, Cambridge.

Eppstein, D. (1994): Offline algorithms for dynamic minimum spanning tree problems. *J. Algor.* **17**, 237-250.

Erdös, P. and Szekeres, G. (1935): A combinatorial problem in geometry. *Compos. Math.* **2**, 463-470.

Ervolina, T. R. and McCormick, S. T. (1993): Two strongly polynomial cut cancelling algorithms for minimum cost network flow. *Discr. Appl. Math.* **46**, 133-165.

Etzion, T. (1986): An algorithm for construction m-ary de Bruijn sequences. *J. Algor.* **7**, 331-340.

Euler, L. (1736): Solutio problematis ad geometriam situs pertinentis. *Comment. Acad. Sci. Imper. Petropol.* **8**, 128-140.

Even, S. (1973): *Combinatorial Algorithms.* Macmillan, New York.

Even, S. (1977): Algorithm for determining whether the connectivity of a graph is at least *k*. *SIAM J. Comp.* **6**, 393-396.

Even, S. (1979): *Graph Algorithms.* Computer Science Press, Rockville, Md.

Even, S., Garey, M. R. and Tarjan, R. E. (1977): A note on connectivity and circuits in directed graphs. Unpublished manuscript.

Even, S., Itai, A. and Shamir, A. (1976): On the complexity of timetable and multicommodity flow problems. *SIAM J. Comp.* **5**, 691-703.

Even, S. and Tarjan, R. E. (1975): Network flow and testing graph connectivity. *SIAM J. Comp.* **4**, 507-512.

Faigle, U. (1979): The greedy algorithm for partially ordered sets. *Discr. Math.* **28**, 153-159.

Faigle, U. (1985): On ordered languages and the optimization of linear functions by greedy algorithms. *J. ACM* **32**, 861-870.

Falikman, D. I. (1981): Ein Beweis der van der Waerdenschen Vermutung über die Permanente einer doppelt-stochastischen Matrix (Russian). *Mat. Zametki* **29**, 931-938.

Farahat, H. K. and Mirsky, L. (1960): Permutation endomorphisms and a refinement of a theorem of Birkhoff. *Proc. Cambridge Phil. Soc.* **56**, 322-328.

Fiechter, C.-N. (1994): A parallel tabu search algorithm for large traveling salesman problems. *Discr. Appl. Math.* **51**, 243-267.

Fiedler, M. and Sedlacek, J. (1958): O W-basich orientovanych grafu. *Casopis Pest. Mat.* **83**, 214-225.

Fishburn, P. C. (1985): *Interval Orders and Interval Graphs: A Study of Partially Ordered Sets*. Wiley, New York.

Fisher, M. L. (1981): The Langrangian method for solving integer programming problems. *Management Sc.* **27**, 1-18.

Fleischner, H. (1983): Eulerian graphs. In: *Selected topics in graph theory 2* (Eds. Ed. L. W. Beineke and R. J. Wilson). Academic Press, New York, pp. 17-53.

Fleischner, H. (1990): *Eulerian Graphs and Related Topics, Part 1, Vol. 1*. North Holland, Amsterdam.

Fleischner, H. (1991): *Eulerian Graphs and Related Topics, Part 1, Vol. 2*. North Holland, Amsterdam.

Floyd, R. W. (1962): Algorithm 97, Shortest path. *Comm. ACM* **5**, 345.

Ford, L. R. (1956): *Network Flow Theory*. Rand Corp., Santa Monica, Cal.

Ford, L. R. and Fulkerson, D. R. (1956): Maximal flow through a network. *Canad. J. Math.* **8**, 399-404.

Ford, L. R. and Fulkerson, D. R. (1957): A simple algorithm for finding maximal network flows and an application to the Hitchcock problem. *Canad. J. Math.* **9**, 210-218.

Ford, L. R. and Fulkerson, D. R. (1958a): Constructing maximal dynamic flows from static flows. *Oper. Res.* **6**, 419-433.

Ford, L. R. and Fulkerson, D. R. (1958b): Network flow and systems of representatives. *Canad J. Math.* **10**, 78-84.

Ford, L. R. and Fulkerson, D. R. (1958c): A suggested computation for maximum multi-commodity network flows. *Management Sc.* **5**, 97-101.

Ford, L. R. and Fulkerson, D. R. (1962): *Flows in Networks*. Princeton University Press, Princeton, N. J.

Frank, A. and Tardos, E. (1988): Generalized polymatroids and submodular flows. *Math. Progr.* **42**, 489-563.

Frederickson, G. N. (1985): Data structures for on-line updating of minimum spanning trees, with applications. *SIAM J. Comp.* **14**, 781-798.

Frederickson, G. N. (1987): Fast algorithms for shortest paths in planar graphs. *SIAM J. Comp.* **16**, 1004-1022.

Fredman, M. L. and Tarjan, R. E. (1987): Fibonacci heaps and their uses on improved network optimization algorithms. *J. ACM* **34**, 596-615.

Fredman, M. L. and Willard, D. E. (1994): Trans-dichotomous algorithms for minimum spanning trees and shortest paths. *J. Comp. Syst. Sc.* **48**, 533-551.

Fremuth-Paeger, C. and Jungnickel, D. (1998a): Balanced network flows I. A uni-
fying framework for design and analysis of matching algorithms. To appear in
Networks.

Fremuth-Paeger, C. and Jungnickel, D. (1998b): Balanced network flows II. Simple
augmentation algorithms. To appear in *Networks.*

Fremuth-Paeger, C. and Jungnickel, D. (1998c): Balanced network flows III.
Strongly polynomial augmentation algorithms. To appear in *Networks.*

Fremuth-Paeger, C. and Jungnickel, D. (1998d): Balanced network flows IV. Duality
and structure theory. Submitted to *Networks.*

Fremuth-Paeger, C. and Jungnickel, D. (1998e): Balanced network flows V. Cycle
canceling algorithms. Submitted to *Networks.*

Frobenius, G. (1912): Über Matrizen aus nicht negativen Elementen. *Sitzungsber.
Preuss. Akad. Wiss.* **1912**, 456-477.

Fujishige, S. (1986): An O(m^3 log n) capacity-rounding algorithm for the minimum-
cost circulation problem: A dual framework of Tardos' algorithm. *Math. Progr.*
35, 298-308.

Fujishige, S. (1991): *Submodular Functions and Optimization.* North Holland, Amsterdam.

Fulkerson, D. R. (1956): Note on Dilworth's decomposition theorem for partially
ordered sets. *Proc. AMS* **7**, 701-702.

Fulkerson, D. R. (1959): Increasing the capacity of a network: The parametric
budget problem. *Management Sc.* **5**, 472-483.

Fulkerson, D. R. (1961): An out-of-kilter method for minimal cost flow problems.
J. SIAM **9**, 18-27.

Gabow, H. N. (1976): An efficient implementation of Edmonds' algorithm for maximum matchings on graphs. *J. ACM* **23**, 221-234.

Gabow, H. N. (1990): Data structures for weighted matching and nearest common
ancestors with linking. *Proc. First Annual ACM-SIAM Symposium on Discrete
Algorithms*, Philadelphia, SIAM, pp. 434-443.

Gabow, H. N., Galil, Z., Spencer, T. and Tarjan, R. E. (1986): Efficient algorithms
for finding minimum spanning trees in undirected and directed graphs. *Combinatorica* **6**, 109-122.

Gabow, H. N. and Kariv, O. (1982): Algorithms for edge coloring bipartite graphs
and multigraphs. *SIAM J. Comp.* **11**, 117-129.

Gabow, H. N. and Tarjan, R. E. (1988): Algorithms for two bottleneck optimization
problems. *J. Algor.* **9**, 411-417.

Gabow, H. N. and Tarjan, R. E. (1989): Faster scaling algorithms for network
problems. *SIAM J. Comp.* **18**, 1013-1036.

Gabow, H. N. and Tarjan, R. E. (1991): Faster scaling algorithms for general graph-
matching problems. *J. ACM* **38**, 815-853.

Gale, D. (1957): A theorem on flows in networks. *Pacific J. Math.* **7**, 1073-1082.

Gale, D. (1968): Optimal assignments in an ordered set: An application of matroid
theory. *J. Comb. Th.* **4**, 176-180.

Gale, D. and Shepley, L. S. (1962): College admissions and the stability of marriage.
Amer. Math. Monthly **69**, 9-15.

Galil, Z. (1980): Finding the vertex connectivity of graphs. *SIAM J. Comp.* **9**,
197-199.

Galil, Z. (1981): On the theoretical efficiency of various network flow algorithms.
Theor. Comp. Sc. **14**, 103-111.

Galil, Z., Micali, S. and Gabow, H. (1986): An O(EV log V) algorithm for finding
a maximal weighted matching in general graphs. *SIAM J. Comp.* **15**, 120-130.

Galil, Z. and Schieber, B. (1988): On funding most uniform spanning trees. *Discr.
Appl. Math.* **20**, 173-175.

Galil, Z. and Tardos, E. (1988): An $O(n^2(m+n \log n)\log n)$ min-cost flow algorithm. *J. ACM* **35**, 374-386.

Gallai, T. (1964): Elementare Relationen bezüglich der Glieder und trennenden Punkte eines Graphen. *Magyar Tud. Akad. Mat. Kutato Int. Kozl.* **9**, 235-236.

Gallai, T. (1967): Transitiv orientierbare Graphen. *Acta Math. Acad. Sc. Hungar.* **18**, 25-66.

Gallai, T. and Milgram, A. N. (1960): Verallgemeinerung eines graphentheoretischen Satzes von Redéi. *Acta Sc. Math.* **21**, 181-186.

Gallo, G., Grigoriades, M. D. and Tarjan, R. E. (1989): A fast parametric maximum flow algorithm and applications. *SIAM J. Comp.* **18**, 30-55.

Gallo, G. and Pallottino, S. (1988): Shortest path algorithms. *Annals of Operations Research* **13**, 3-79.

Garey, M. R., Graham, R. L. and Johnson, D. S. (1977): The complexity of computing Steiner minimal trees. *SIAM J. Appl. Math.* **32**, 835-859.

Garey, M. R. and Johnson, D. S. (1976): The complexity of near-optimal graph coloring. *J. ACM* **23**, 43-49.

Garey, M. R. and Johnson, D. S. (1979): *Computers and Intractability: A Guide to the Theory of NP-Completeness.* Freeman, New York.

Garey, M. R., Johnson, D. S. and Stockmeyer, L. J. (1976): Some simplified NP-complete graph problems. *Theoret. Comp. Sc.* **1**, 237-267.

Garey, M. R., Johnson, D. S. and Tarjan, R. E. (1976): The planar Hamiltonian circuit problem is NP-complete. *SIAM J. Comp.* **5**, 704-714.

Ghinelli, D. and Jungnickel, D. (1990): The Steinberg module of a graph. *Archiv Math.* **55**, 503-506.

Ghouila-Houri, A. (1962): Caractérisation des graphes non orientés dont on peut orienter les arêtes de manière à obtenir le graphe d'une relation d'ordre. *C.R. Acad. Sc. Paris* **254**, 1370-1371.

Gilbert, E. N. and Pollak, H. O. (1968): Steiner minimal trees. *SIAM J. Appl. Math.* **16**, 1-29.

Gilmore, P. C. and Hoffman, A. J. (1964): A characterization of comparability graphs and of interval graphs. *Canad. J. Math.* **16**, 539-548.

Glover, F., Klingman, D. and Phillips, N. V. (1992): *Network Models in Optimization and their Applications in Practice.* Wiley, New York.

Godsil, C. D. (1993): *Algebraic Combinatorics.* Chapman and Hall, New York.

Goecke, O. (1988): A greedy algorithm for hereditary set systems and a generalization of the Rado-Edmonds characterization of matroids. *Discr. Appl. Math.* **20**, 39-49.

Goldberg, A. V., Grigoriadis, M. D. and Tarjan, R. E. (1991): Use of dynamic trees in a network simplex algorithm for the maximum flow problem. *Math. Progr.* **50**, 277-290.

Goldberg, A. V., Plotkin S. A. and Tardos, E. (1991): Combinatorial algorithms for the generalized circulation problem. *Math. Oper. Res.* **16**, 351-381.

Goldberg, A. V., Tardos, E. and Tarjan, R. E. (1990): Network flow algorithms. In: *Paths, flows and VLSI-layout* (Eds. B. Korte, L. Lovász, H. J. Prömel and A. Schrijver). Springer, Berlin, pp. 101-164.

Goldberg, A. V. and Tarjan, R. E. (1988): A new approach to the maximum flow problem. *J. ACM* **35**, 921-940.

Goldberg, A. V. and Tarjan, R. E. (1989): Finding minimum-cost circulations by canceling negative cycles. *J. ACM* **36**, 873-886.

Goldberg, A. V. and Tarjan, R. E. (1990): Solving minimum cost-flow problems by successive approximation. *Math. of Oper. Res.* **15**, 430-466.

Goldfarb, D. and Grigoriadis, M. D. (1988): A computational comparison of the Dinic and network simplex methods for maximum flow. *Ann. Oper. Res.* **13**, 83-123.

Goldfarb, D. and Hao, J. (1990): A primal simplex algorithm that solves the maximum flow problem in at most nm pivots and $O(n^2m)$ time. *Math. Progr.* **47**, 353-365.

Goldfarb, D. and Hao, J. (1991): On strongly polynomial variants of the network simplex algorithm for the maximum flow problem. *Oper. Res. Letters* **10**, 383-387.

Golomb, S. W. (1967): *Shift Register Sequences.* Holden-Day, San Francisco.

Golumbic, M. C. (1980): *Algorithmic Graph Theory and Perfect Graphs.* Academic Press, New York.

Gomory, R. E. and Hu, T. C. (1961): Multi-terminal network flows. *J. SIAM* **9**, 551-570.

Gomory, R. E. and Hu, T. C. (1962): An application of generalized linear programming to network flows. *J. SIAM* **10**, 260-283.

Gomory, R. E. and Hu, T. C. (1964): Synthesis of a communication network. *J. SIAM* **12**, 348-369.

Gondran, M. and Minoux, N. (1984): *Graphs and Algorithms.* Wiley, New York.

Gonzaga, C. C. (1992): Path-following methods for linear programming. *SIAM Review* **34**, 167-224.

Goulden, I. P. and Jackson, D. M. (1983): *Combinatorial Enumeration.* Wiley, New York.

Graham, R. L. and Hell. P. (1985): On the history of the minimum spanning tree problem. *Ann. History of Comp.* **7**, 43-57.

Greene, R. C. and Kleitman, D. J. (1978): Proof techniques in the theory of finite sets. In: *Studies in combinatorics* (Ed. G. C. Rota). 22-79. MAA.

Griggs, J. R. (1988): Saturated chains of subsets and a random walk. *J. Comb. Th. (A)* **47**, 262-283.

Griggs, T. and Rosa, A. (1996): A tour of European soccer schedules, or testing the popularity of GK_{2n}. *Bull. ICA* **18**, 65-68.

Grigoriadis, M. D. and Kalantari, B. (1988): A new class of heuristic algorithms for weighted perfect matching. *J. ACM* **35**, 769-776.

Grötschel, M. (1980): On the symmetric travelling salesman problem: Solution of a 120-city problem. *Math. Progr. Studies* **12**, 61-77.

Grötschel, M. (1984): Developments in combinatorial optimization. In *Perspectives in mathematics: Anniversary of Oberwolfach 1984* (Eds. W. Jäger, J. Moser and R. Remmert). Birkhäuser, Basel, pp. 249-294.

Grötschel, M. (1985): *Operations Research I.* Vorlesungsskript, Universität Augsburg.

Grötschel, M. and Holland, G. (1985): Solving matching problems with linear programming. *Math. Progr.* **33**, 243-259.

Grötschel, M. and Holland, O. (1991): Solution of large-scale symmetric travelling salesman problems. *Math. Progr.* **51**, 141-202.

Grötschel, M. Jünger, M. and Reinelt, G. (1991): Optimal control of plotting and drilling machines: a case study. *ZOR* **35**, 61-84.

Grötschel, M., Lovász, L. and Schrijver, A. (1984): Polynomial algorithms for perfect graphs. *Ann. Discr. Math.* **21**, 325-356.

Grötschel, M., Lovász, L. and Schrijver, A. (1993): *Geometric Algorithms and Combinatorial Optimization (2nd edition).* Springer, Berlin.

Guckert, M. (1996): *Anschlußoptimierung in öffentlichen Verkehrsnetzen - Graphentheoretische Grundlagen, objektorientierte Modellierung und Implementierung.* Ph. D. Thesis, Universität Marburg.

Guldan, F. (1980): Maximization of distances of regular polygones on a circle. *Appl. Math.* **25**, 182-195.

Gusfield, D. (1987): Three fast algorithms for four problems in stable marriage. *SIAM J. Comp.* **16**, 111-128.

Gusfield, D. (1988): The structure of the stable roommate problem: Efficient representation and enumeration of all stable assignments. *SIAM J. Comp.* **17**, 742-769.

Gusfield, D. (1990): Very simple methods for all pairs network flow analysis. *SIAM J. Comp.* **19**, 143-155.

Gusfield, D. and Irving, R. W. (1989): *The Stable Marriage Problem. Structure and Algorithms.* The MIT Press, Cambridge, Mass.

Gusfield, D., Martel, C. and Fernandez-Baca, D. (1987): Fast algorithms for bipartite network flow. *SIAM J. Comp.* **16**, 237-251.

Gusfield, D. and Naor, D. (1991): Efficient algorithms for generalized cut-trees. *Networks* **21**, 505-520.

Hadley, G. (1961): *Linear Algebra.* Addison-Wesley, Reading, Mass.

Hadlock, F. O. (1975): Finding a maximum cut of a planar graph in polynomial time. *SIAM J. Comp.* **4**, 221-225.

Hadwiger, H. (1943): Über eine Klassifikation der Streckenkomplexe. *Viertelj. Schr. Naturforsch. Ges. Zürich* **88**, 133-142.

Hajós, G. (1961): Über eine Konstruktion nicht n-färbbarer Graphen. *Wiss. Z. Martin-Luther-Univ. Halle-Wittenberg, Math.-Nat. Reihe* **10**, 116-117.

Hakimi, S. L. and Yau, S. S. (1964): Distance matrix of a graph and its realizability. *Quart. Appl. Math.* **22**, 305-317.

Hall, M. J. (1956): An algorithm for distinct representatives. *Amer. Math. Monthly* **63**, 716-717.

Hall, M. J. (1986): *Combinatorial Theory (2nd edition).* Wiley, New York.

Hall, P. (1935): On representatives of subsets. *J. LMS* **10**, 26-30.

Halmos, P. R. and Vaughan, H. E. (1950): The marriage problem. *Amer. J. Math.* **72**, 214-215.

Hamacher, H. W. and Ruhe, G. (1994): On spanning tree problems with multiple objectives. *Ann. Oper. Res.* **52**, 209-230.

Harary, F. (1962): The maximum connectivity of a graph. *Proc. Nat. Acad. Sci. USA* **48**, 1142-1146.

Harary, F. (1969): *Graph Theory.* Addison Wesley, Reading, Mass.

Harary, F. and Tutte, W. T. (1965): A dual form of Kuratowski's theorem. *Canad. Math. Bull.* **8**, 17-20 and 173.

Hassin, R. and Johnson, D. B. (1985): An $O(n \log^2 n)$ algorithm for maximum flow in undirected planar networks. *SIAM J. Comp.* **14**, 612-624.

Hausmann, D. and Korte, B. (1981): Algorithmic versus axiomatic definitions of matroids. *Math. Progr. Studies* **14**, 98-111.

Held, M. and Karp, R. (1970): The travelling salesman problem and minimum spanning trees. *Oper. Res.* **18**, 1138-1162.

Held, M. and Karp, R. (1971): The travelling salesman problem and minimum spanning trees II. *Math. Progr.* **1**, 6-25.

Held, M., Wolfe, P. and Crowder, H. P. (1974): Validation of subgradient optimization. *Math. Progr.* **6**, 62-88.

Helman, P., Mont, B. M. E. and Shapiro, H. D. (1993): An exact characterization of greedy structures. *SIAM J. Discr. Math.* **6**, 274-283.

Hierholzer, C. (1873): Über die Möglichkeit, einen Linienzug ohne Wiederholung und ohne Unterbrechung zu umfahren. *Math. Ann.* **6**, 30-32.

Hilton, A. J. W. and Jackson, B. (1987): A note concerning the chromatic index of multigraphs. *J. Graph Th.* **11**, 267-272.

Hitchcock, F. L. (1941): The distribution of a product from several sources to numerous localities. *J. Math. Phys.* **20**, 224-230.

Ho, J.-M., Lee, D. T., Chang, C.-H. and Wong, C. K. (1991): Minimum diameter spanning trees and related problems. *SIAM J. Computing* **20**, 987-997.

Hochbaum, D. S., Nishizeki, T. and Shmoys, D. B. (1986): A better than 'best possible' algorithm to edge color multigraphs. *J. Algor.* **7**, 79-104.

Hoffman, A. J. (1960): Some recent applications of the theory of linear inequalities to extremal combinatorial analysis. In: *Combinatorial analysis* (Eds. R. E. Bellman and M. Hall). AMS, Providence, pp. 113-127.

Hoffman, A. J. (1974): A generalization of max flow-min cut. *Math. Progr.* **6**, 352-359.

Hoffman, A. J. (1979): The role of unimodularity in applying linear inequalities to combinatorial theorems. *Ann. Discr. Math.* **4**, 73-84.

Hoffman, A. J. and Kruskal, J. B. (1956): Integral boundary points of convex polyhedra. In: *Linear inequalities and related systems* (Eds. H. W. Kuhn and A. W. Tucker). Princeton University Press, Princeton, N. J., pp. 233-246.

Hoffman, A. J. and Kuhn, H. W. (1956): On systems of distinct representatives. *Ann. Math. Studies* **38**, 199-206.

Hoffman, A. J. and Markowitz, H. M. (1963): A note on shortest path, assignment and transportation problems. *Naval Research Logistics Quarterly* **10**, 375-379.

Holyer, I. J. (1981): The NP-completeness of edge-coloring. *SIAM J. Comp.* **10**, 718-720.

Hopcroft, J. and Karp, R. M. (1973): An $n^{\frac{5}{2}}$ algorithm for maximum matching in bipartite graphs. *SIAM J. Comp.* **2**, 225-231.

Hopcroft, J. and Tarjan, R. E. (1973): Dividing a graph into triconnected components. *SIAM J. Comp.* **2**, 135-158.

Hopcroft, J. and Ullman, J. D. (1979): *Introduction to Automata Theory, Languages and Computation.* Addison Wesley, Reading, Mass.

Horton, J. D. (1987): A polynomial time algorithm to find the shortest cycle basis of a graph. *SIAM J. Comp.* **16**, 358-366.

Hu, T. C. (1961): The maximum capacity route problem. *Oper. Res.* **9**, 898-900.

Hu, T. C. (1974): Optimum communication spanning trees. *SIAM J. Computing* **3**, 188-195.

Huang, C., Mendelsohn, E. and Rosa, A. (1982): On partially resolvable t-partitions. *Ann. Discr. Math.* **12**, 160-183.

Hung, M. S. and Divoky, J. J. (1988): A computational study of efficient shortest path algorithms. *Computers and Operations Research* **15**, 567-576.

Huppert, B. (1967): *Endliche Gruppen I.* Springer, Berlin-Heidelberg.

Hwang, F. K., Richards, D. S. and Winter, P. (1992): *The Steiner Tree Problem.* North Holland, Amsterdam.

Imai, H. (1983): On the practical efficiency of various maximum flow algorithms. *J. Oper. Res. Soc. of Japan* **26**, 61-82.

Imrich, W., Simões-Pereira, J. M. S. and Zamfirescu, C. M. (1984): On optimal embeddings of metrics in graphs. *J. Comb. Th. (B)* **36**, 1-15.

Irving, R. W. (1985): An efficient algorithm for the 'stable roommates' problem. *J. Algor.* **6**, 577-595.

Irving, R. W. and Leather, P. (1986): The complexity of counting stable marriages. *SIAM J. Comp.* **15**, 655-667.

Irving, R. W., Leather, P. and Gusfield, D. (1987): An efficient algorithm for the 'optimal' stable marriage. *J. ACM* **34**, 532-543.

Itai, A., Perl, Y. and Shiloach, Y. (1982): The complexity of finding maximum disjoint paths with length constraints. *Networks* **12**, 277-286.

Itai, A. and Rodeh, M. (1978): Finding a minimum circuit in a graph. *SIAM J. Comp.* **7**, 413-423.

Itai, A., Rodeh, M. and Tanimota, S. L. (1978): Some matching problems in bipartite graphs. *J. ACM* **25**, 517-525.

Itai, A. and Shiloach, Y. (1979): Maximum flow in planar networks. *SIAM J. Comp.* **8**, 135-150.

Jarník, V. (1930): O jistém problému minimálním. *Acta Societ. Scient. Natur. Moravicae* **6**, 57-63.

Jarrah, A. I. Z., Yu, G., Krishnamurthy, N. and Rakshit, A. (1993): A decision support framework for airline flight cancellations and delays. *Transportation Sc.* **27**, 266-280.

Jenkyns, T. A. (1976): The efficacy of the 'greedy' algorithm. *Proc. 7th Southeastern Conf. Combinatorics, Graph Theory and Computing*, pp. 341-350.

Jensen, T. R. and Toft, B. (1995): *Graph Coloring Problems*. Wiley, New York.

Jensen, K. and Wirth, N. (1985): *PASCAL User Manual and Report (3rd edition)*. Springer, New York.

Johnson, D. B. (1975): Priority queues with update and minimum spanning trees. *Inf. Proc. Letters* **4**, 53-57.

Johnson, D. S. (1986): The NP-completeness column: An ongoing guide. *J. Algor.* **7**, 289-305.

Johnson, D. S., Lenstra, J. K. and Rinnooy Kan, A. H. G. (1978): The complexity of the network design problem. *Networks* **8**, 279-285.

Johnson, D. S. and McGeoch, C. C., Eds. (1993): *Network Flows and Matching*. American Mathematical Society, Providence.

Johnson, D. S. and Venkatesan, S. M. (1982): Using divide and conquer to find flows in directed planar networks in $O(n^{\frac{3}{2}} \log n)$ time. *Proc. 20th Allerton Conf. on Communication, Control and Computing.*, Urbana, Univ. of Illinois, pp. 898-905.

Jungnickel, D. (1979a): A construction of group divisible designs. *J. Stat. Planning Inf.* **3**, 273-278.

Jungnickel, D. (1979b): Die Methode der Hilfsmatrizen. In: *Contributions to geometry* (Eds. J. Tölke and J. M. Wills). Birkhäuser, Basel, pp. 388-394.

Jungnickel, D. (1986): Transversaltheorie: Ein Überblick. *Bayreuther Math. Schriften* **21**, 122-155.

Jungnickel, D. (1993): *Finite Fields*. B.I. Wissenschaftsverlag, Mannheim.

Jungnickel, D. and Leclerc, M. (1988): A class of lattices. *Ars Comb.* **26**, 243-248.

Jungnickel, D. and Leclerc, M. (1989): The 2-matching lattice of a graph. *J. Comb. Th. (B)* **46**, 246-248.

Jungnickel, D. and Lenz, H. (1987): Minimal linear spaces. *J. Comb. Th. (A)* **44**, 229-240.

Kahn, A. B. (1962): Topological sorting of large networks. *Comm. ACM* **5**, 558-562.

Kalaba, R. (1960): On some communication network problems. In: *Combinatorial analysis* (Eds. R. E. Bellman and M. Hall). AMS, Providence, pp. 261-280.

Karger, D. R. (1997): Using random sampling to find maximum flows in uncapacitated undirected graphs. Preprint, MIT Laboratory for Computer Science.

Karmarkar, N. (1984): A new polynomial-time algorithm for linear programming. *Combinatorica* **4**, 373-396.

Karp, R. M. (1972): Reducibility among combinatorial problems. In: *Complexity of computer computations* (Eds. R. E. Miller and J. W. Thatcher). Plenum Press, New York, pp. 85-103.

Karp, R. M. (1978): A characterization of the minimum cycle mean in a digraph. *Discr. Math.* **23**, 309-311.

Karzanov, A. V. (1974): Determining the maximal flow in a network with the method of preflows. *Soviet Math. Dokl.* **15**, 434-437.

Kasteleyn, P. W. (1967): Graph theory and crystal physics. In: *Graph theory and theoretical physics* (Ed. F. Harary). Academic Press, New York, pp. 43-110.

Kay, D. C. and Chartrand, G. (1965): A characterization of certain ptolemaic graphs. *Canad. J. Math.* **17**, 342-346.

Khachiyan, L. G. (1979): A polynomial algorithm in linear programming. *Soviet Math. Dokl.* **20**, 191-194.

King, V., Rao, S. and Tarjan, R. (1994): A faster deterministic maximum flow algorithm. *J. Algorithms* **17**, 447-474.

Kirchhoff, G. (1847): Über die Auflösungen der Gleichungen, auf die man bei der Untersuchung der Verteilung galvanischer Ströme geführt wird. *Ann. Phys. Chem.* **72**, 497-508.

Kirkman, T. P. (1847): On a problem in combinatorics. *Cambridge and Dublin Math. J.* **2**, 191-204.

Kirkman, T. P. (1850): Query VI. *Lady's and gentleman's diary* **147**, 48.

Klein, M. (1967): A primal method for minimal cost flows, with applications to the assignment and transportation problems. *Management Sc.* **14**, 205-220.

Kleitman, D. J. and West, D. B. (1991): Spanning trees with many leaves. *SIAM J. Discr. Math.* **4**, 99-106.

Klingman, D. and Philipps, N. V. (1986): Network algorithms and applications. *Discr. Appl. Math.* **13**, 107-292.

Knuth, D. E. (1967): Oriented subtrees of an arc digraph. *J. Comb. Th.* **3**, 309-314.

Knuth, D. E. (1981): A permanent inequality. *Amer. Math. Monthly* **88**, 731-740.

Kocay, W. and Stone, D. (1993): Balanced network flows. *Bull. ICA* **7**, 17-32.

Kocay, W. and Stone, D. (1995): An algorithm for balanced flows. *J. Comb. Math. Comb. Comp.* **19**, 3-31.

König, D. (1916): Über Graphen und ihre Anwendungen auf Determinantentheorie und Mengenlehre. *Math. Ann.* **77**, 453-465.

König, D. (1931): Graphen und Matrizen (Hungarian with a summary in German). *Mat. Fiz. Lapok* **38**, 116-119.

Korte, B. and Hausmann, D. (1978): An analysis of the greedy heuristic for independence systems. *Ann. Discr. Math.* **2**, 65-74.

Korte, B. and Lovász, L. (1981): Mathematical structures underlying greedy algorithms. In: *Fundamentals of computation theory* (Ed. F. Gécseg). Springer, Berlin, pp. 205-209.

Korte, B. and Lovász, L. (1984): Greedoids and linear objective functions. *SIAM J. Algebr. Discr. Math.* **5**, 229-238.

Korte, B., Lovász, L., Prömel, H. J. and Schrijver, A. (1990): *Paths, Flows and VLSI-Layout*. Springer, Berlin.

Korte, B., Lovász, L. and Schrader, R. (1991): *Greedoids*. Springer, Berlin.

Korte, B., Prömel, H. J. and Steger. A. (1990): Steiner trees in VLSI-Layout. In: *Paths, flows and VLSI-layout* (Eds. B. Korte, L. Lovász, H. J. Prömel and A. Schrijver). Springer, Berlin, pp. 185-214.

Korte, N. and Möhring, R. H. (1989): An incremental linear-time algorithm for recognizing interval graphs. *SIAM J. Comp.* **18**, 68-81.

Krishnamoorthy, M. S. (1975): An NP-hard problem in bipartite graphs. *SIGACT News* **7:1**, 26.

Kruskal, J. B. (1956): On the shortest spanning subtree of a graph and the travelling salesman problem. *Proc. AMS* **7**, 48-50.

Kuhn, H. W. (1955): The hungarian method for the assignment problem. *Naval Res. Logistic Quart.* **2**, 83-97.

Kuhn, H. W. (1956): Variants of the hungarian method for the assignment problem. *Naval Res. Logistic Quart.* **3**, 253-258.

Kuich, W. and Salomaa, A. (1986): *Semirings, Automata, Languages.* Springer, Berlin.

Kuratowski, K. (1930): Sur le problème des courbes gauches en topologie. *Fund. Math.* **15**, 271-283.

Kwan, M.-K. (1962): Graphic programming using odd and even points. *Chines. Math.* **1**, 273-277.

Lamken, E. (1987): A note on partitioned balanced tournament designs. *Ars Comb.* **24**, 5-16.

Lamken, E. and Vanstone, S. A. (1987): The existence of partitioned balanced tournament designs. *Ann. Discr. Math.* **34**, 339-352.

Lamken, E. and Vanstone, S. A. (1989): Balanced tournament designs and related topics. *Discr. Math.* **77**, 159-176.

Las Vergnas, M. (1972): *Problèmes de couplages et problèmes hamiltoniens en théorie des graphes.* Dissertation, Universitè de Paris VI.

Lawler, E. L. (1975): Matroid intersection algorithms. *Math. Progr.* **9**, 31-56.

Lawler, E. L. (1976): *Combinatorial Optimization: Networks and Matriods.* Holt, Rinehart and Winston, New York.

Lawler, E. L., Lenstra, J. K., Rinnooy Kan, A. H. G. and Shmoys, D. B., Eds. (1985): *The Travelling Salesman Problem: A Guided Tour of Combinatorial Optimization.* Wiley, New York.

Lawler, E. L., Lenstra, J. K., Rinnooy Kan, A. H. G. and Shmoys, D. B. (1993): Sequencing and scheduling: Algorithms and complexity. In: *Logistics of production and inventory* (Eds. S. C. Graves, A. H. G. Rinnooy Kan and P. H. Zipkin). Elsevier, Amsterdam, pp. 445-522.

Leclerc, M. (1986): *Polynomial time algorithms for exact matching problems.* M. Math. thesis, University of Waterloo, Dept. of Combinatorics and Optimization.

Leclerc, M. (1987): *Algorithmen für kombinatorische Optimierungsprobleme mit Partitionsbeschränkungen.* Dissertation, Universität Köln.

Leclerc, M. and Rendl. F. (1989): Constrained spanning trees and the travelling salesman problem. *Europ. J. Oper. Res.* **39**, 96-102.

Lehman, A. (1964): A solution of the Shannon switching game. *SIAM J. Appl. Math.* **12**, 687-725.

Lengauer, T. (1990): *Combinatorial Algorithms for Integrated Circuit Layout.* Wiley, New York.

Lenstra, J. K. and Rinnooy Kan, A. H. G. (1975): Some simple applications of the travelling salesman problem. *Oper. Res. Quart.* **26**, 717-733.

Lesk, M., Plummer, M. D. and Pulleyblank, W. R. (1984): Equi-matchable graphs. In: *Graph theory and combinatorics* (Ed. B. Bollobas). Academic Press, New York, pp. 239-254.

Lesniak, L. and Oellermann, O. R. (1986): An Eulerian exposition. *J. Graph Th.* **10**, 277-297.

Lewandowski, J. L., Liu, C. L. and Liu, J. W. S. (1986): An algorithmic proof of a generalization of the Birkhoff-Von Neumann theorem. *J. Algor.* **7**, 323-330.

Lewis, H. R. and Papadimitriou, C. H. (1981): *Elements of the Theory of Computation.* Prentice Hall, Englewood Cliffs, N. J.

Lin, S. (1965): Computer solutions of the travelling salesman problem. *Bell Systems Techn. J.* **44**, 2245-2269.

Lin, S. and Kernighan, B. W. (1973): An effective heuristic algorithm for the travelling salesman problem. *Oper. Res.* **31**, 498-516.

Linial, N., Lovász, L. and Widgerson, A. (1988): Rubber bands, convex embeddings and graph connectivity. *Combinatorica* **8**, 91-102.

Little, J. D. C., Murty, K. G., Sweeney, D. W. and Karel, C. (1963): An algorithm for the travelling salesman problem. *Oper. Res.* **11**, 972-989.

Lomonosov, M. V. (1985): Combinatorial approaches to multiflow problems. *Discr. Appl. Math.* **11**, 1-93.

Lovász, L. (1970a): Problem 11. In: *Combinatorial structures and their applications* (Eds. R. Guy, H. Hanani, N. Sauer and J. Schönheim). Gordon and Breach, New York, pp. 497.

Lovász, L. (1970b): Subgraphs with prescribed valencies. *J. Comb. Th.* **8**, 391-416.

Lovász, L. (1972): Normal hypergraphs and the perfect graph conjecture. *Discr. Math.* **2**, 253-267.

Lovász, L. (1976): On two minimax theorems in graph theory. *J. Comb. Th. (B)* **21**, 96-103.

Lovász, L. (1979): Graph theory and integer programming. *Ann. Discr. Math.* **4**, 141-158.

Lovász, L. (1985): Some algorithmic problems on lattices. In: *Theory of algorithms* (Eds. L. Lovász and E. Smerédi). North Holland, Amsterdam, pp. 323-337.

Lovász, L. (1987): The matching structure and the matching lattice. *J. Comb. Th. (B)* **43**, 187-222.

Lovász, L. and Plummer, M. D. (1986): *Matching Theory*. North Holland, Amsterdam.

Lucas, E. (1882): *Récréations Mathématiques*. Paris.

Lüneburg, H. (1982): Programmbeispiele aus Algebra, Zahlentheorie und Kombinatorik. Preprint, Universität Kaiserslautern.

Lüneburg, H. (1989): *Tools and Fundamental Constructions of Combinatorial Mathematics*. Bibliographisches Institut, Mannheim.

Ma, S. L. (1994): A survey of partial difference sets. *Designs, Codes and Cryptography* **4**, 221-261.

Maculan, N. (1987): The Steiner problem in graphs. *Ann. Discr. Math.* **31**, 185-212.

MacWilliams, F. J. and Sloane, N. J. A. (1977): *The Theory of Error-Correcting Codes*. North Holland, Amsterdam.

Mader, W. (1979): Connectivity and edge-connectivity in finite graphs. In: *Surveys in combinatorics* (Ed. B. Bollobás). Cambridge University Press, Cambridge, pp. 66-95.

Magnanti, T. L. and Wong, R. T. (1984): Network design and transportation planning: models and algorithms. *Transportation Sci.* **18**, 1-55.

Malhotra, V. M., Kumar, M. P. and Mahaswari, S. N. (1978): An $O(|V|^3)$ algorithm for finding maximum flows in networks. *Inform. Proc. Letters.* **7**, 277-278.

Mansour, Y., and Schieber, B. (1989): Finding the edge connectivity of directed graphs. *J. Algor.* **10**, 76-85.

Marcus, M. and Minc, H. (1965): Diagonal products in doubly stochastic matrices. *Quart. J. Math. (2)* **16**, 32-34.

Marcus, M. and Ree, R. (1959): Diagonals of doubly stochastic matrices. *Quart. J. Math. (2)* **10**, 296-302.

Martin, A. (1992): *Packen von Steinerbäumen: Polyedrische Studien und Anwendung*. Dissertation, Technische Universität Berlin.

Matsui, T. (1995): The minimum spanning tree problem on a planar graph. *Discr. Appl. Math.* **58**, 91-94.

Matula, D. W. (1987): Determining edge connectivity in $O(mn)$. *Proc. 28th Symp. on Foundations of Computer Science*, 249-251.

Mehlhorn, K. (1984): *Data Structures and Algorithms*. Springer, Berlin.

Mehlhorn, K. and Schmidt, B. H. (1986): On BF-orderable graphs. *Discr. Appl. Math.* **15**, 315-327.

Mendelsohn, E. and Rosa, A. (1985): One-factorizations of the complete graph - a survey. *J. Graph Th.* **9**, 43-65.

Mendelsohn, N. S. and Dulmage, A. L. (1958): Some generalizations of the problem of distinct representatives. *Canad. J. Math.* **10**, 230-241.

Meng, D. H. C. (1974): *Matchings and Coverings for Graphs.* Ph. D. thesis, Michigan State University, East Lansing, Mich.

Menger, K. (1927): Zur allgemeinen Kurventheorie. *Fund. Math.* **10**, 96-115.

Micali, S. and Vazirani, V. V. (1980): An $O(\sqrt{|V|}|E|)$ algorithm for finding maximum matchings in general graphs. *Proc. 21st IEEE Symp. on Foundations of Computer Science*, pp.17-27.

Michalewicz, Z. (1992): *Genetic Algorithms + Data Structures = Evolution Programs.* Springer, Berlin.

Miller, G. A. (1910): On a method due to Galois. *Quart. J. Pure Appl. Math.* **41**, 382-384.

Minc, H. (1978): *Permanents.* Addison-Wesley, Reading, Mass.

Minc, H. (1988): *Nonnegative Matrices.* Wiley, New York.

Minty, G. J. (1960): Monotone networks. *Proc. Royal Soc. London (A)* **257**, 194-212.

Minty, G. J. (1966): On the axiomatic foundations of the theories of directed linear graphs, electrical networks and network programming. *J. Math. Mech.* **15**, 485-520.

Mirkin, B. G. and Rodin, N. S. (1984): *Genes and Graphs.* Springer, New York.

Mirsky, L. (1969a): Hall's criterion as a 'self-refining' result. *Monatsh. Math.* **73**, 139-146.

Mirsky, L. (1969b): Transversal theory and the study of abstract independence. *J. Math. Anal. Appl.* **25**, 209-217.

Mirsky, L. (1971a): A dual of Dilworth's decomposition theorem. *Amer. Math. Monthly* **78**, 876-877.

Mirsky, L. (1971b): *Transversal Theory.* Academic Press, New York.

Mirsky, L. and Perfect. H. (1967): Applications of the notion of independence to problems of combinatorial analysis. *J. Comb. Th.* **2**, 327-357.

Mohar, B. and Poljak, S. (1993): Eigenvalues in Combinatorial Optimization. In: *Combinatorial and graph-theoretic problems in linear algebra* (Eds. R. Brualdi, S. Friedland and V. Klee). Springer, New York, pp. 107-151.

Monien, B. (1983): The complexity of determining a shortest cycle of even length. *Computing* **31**, 355-369.

Moore, E. F. (1959): The shortest path through a maze. *Proc. Int. Symp. on Theory of Switching Part II*, Cambridge, Mass., Harvard University Press, pp. 285-292.

Mühlenbein, H., Gorges-Schleuter, M. and Krämer, O. (1988): Evolution algorithms in combinatorial optimization. *Parallel Computing* **7**, 65-85.

Muirhead, A. F. (1903): Some methods applicable to identities and inequalities of symmetric algebraic functions of n letters. *Proc. Edinburg Math. Soc.* **21**, 144-157.

Müller-Merbach, H. (1966): Die Anwendung des Gozinto-Graphs zur Berechnung des Roh- und Zwischenproduktbedarfs in chemischen Betrieben. *Ablauf- und Planungsforschung* **7**, 189-198.

Müller-Merbach, H. (1969): Die Inversion von Gozinto-Matrizen mit einem graphenorientierten Verfahren. *Elektron. Datenverarb.* **11**, 310-314.

Müller-Merbach, H. (1973): *Operations Research, 3rd edition.* Franz Vahlen, München.

Naddef, D. (1990): Handles and teeth in the symmetric travelling salesman polytope. In: *Polyhedral combinatorics* (Eds. W. Cook and P. D. Seymour). American Mathematical Society, Providence, pp. 61-74.

Nemhauser, G. L. and Wolsey, L. A. (1988): *Integer and Combinatorial Optimization.* Wiley, New York.

Nijenhuis, A. and Wilf, H. S. (1978): *Combinatorial Algorithms (2nd edition)*. Academic Press, New York.

Nishizeki, T. and Chiba, N. (1988): *Planar Graphs: Theory and Algorithms*. North Holland, Amsterdam.

Nobert, Y. and J.- C. Picard (1996): An optimal algorithm for the mixed Chinese Postman Problem. *Networks* **27**, 95-108.

Oellermann, O. R. (1996): Connectivity and edge-connectivity in graphs: a survey. *Congr. Numer.* **116**, 231-252.

Or, I. (1976): *Traveling salesman-type combinatorial problems and their relation to the logistics of regional blood banking*. Ph. D., Northwestern University, Evanston, Ill.

Ore, O. (1951): A problem regarding the tracing of graphs. *Elem. Math.* **6**, 49-53.

Ore, O. (1955): Graphs and matching theorems. *Duke Math. J.* **22**, 625-639.

Ore, O. (1960): Note on hamiltonian circuits. *Amer. Math. Monthly* **67**, 55.

Ore, O. (1961): Arc coverings of graphs. *Ann. Mat. Pura Appl.* **55**, 315-322.

Orlin, J. B. (1993): A faster strongly polynomial minimum cost flow algorithm. *Oper. Res.* **41**, 338-350.

Orlin, J. B. and Ahuja, R. K. (1992): New scaling algorithms for the assignment and minimum cycle mean problems. *Math. Progr.* **54**, 41-56.

Orlin, J. B., Plotkin, S. A. and Tardos, E. (1993): Polynomial dual network simplex algorithms. *Math. Progr.* **60**, 255-276.

Oxley, J. G. (1992): *Matroid Theory*. Oxford University Press, Oxford.

Padberg, M. and Sung, T.-Y. (1991): An analytical comparison of different formulations of the travelling salesman problem. *Math. Progr.* **52**, 315-357.

Padberg, M. W. and Hong, S. (1980): On the symmetric travelling salesman problem: A computational study. *Math. Progr. Studies* **12**, 78-107.

Padberg, M. W. and Rao, M. R. (1974): The travelling salesman problem and a class of polyhedra of diameter two. *Math. Progr.* **7**, 32-45.

Padberg, M. W. and Rinaldi, G. (1987): Optimization of a 532-city symmetric travelling salesman problem. *Oper. Res. Letters* **6**, 1-7.

Padberg, M. W. and Rinaldi, G. (1991): A branch-and-cut algorithm for the resolution of large-scale travelling salesman problems. *SIAM Rev.* **33**, 60-100.

Papadimitriou, C. H. (1976): On the complexity of edge traversing. *J. ACM* **23**, 544-554.

Papadimitriou, C. H. (1978): The adjacency relation on the traveling salesman polytope is NP-complete. *Math. Progr.* **14**, 312-324.

Papadimitriou, C. H. (1992): The complexity of the Lin-Kernighan heuristic for the traveling salesman problem. *SIAM J. Comp.* **21**, 450-465.

Papadimitriou, C. H. and Steiglitz, K. (1977): On the complexity of local search for the travelling salesman problem. *SIAM J. Comp.* **6**, 76-83.

Papadimitriou, C. H. and Steiglitz,K. (1978): Some examples of difficult travelling salesman problems. *Oper. Res.* **26**, 434-443.

Papadimitriou, C. H. and Steiglitz, K. (1982): *Combinatorial Optimization: Algorithms and Complexity*. Prentice Hall, Englewood Cliffs, N. J.

Papadimitriou, C. H. and Yannakakis, M. (1982): The complexity of restricted spanning tree problems. *J. ACM* **29**, 285-309.

Papadimitriou, C. H. and Yannakakis, M. (1993): The traveling salesman problem with distances 1 and 2. *Math. of Oper. Res.* **18**, 1-11.

Pape, U. and Conradt, D. (1980): Maximales Matching in Graphen. In: *Ausgewählte Operations Research Software in FORTRAN* (Ed. H. Späth). Oldenbourg, München, pp. 103-114.

Peltesohn, R. (1936): *Das Turnierproblem für Spiele zu je dreien*. Dissertation, Universität Berlin.

Petersen, J. (1891): Die Theorie der regulären Graphen. *Acta Math.* **15**, 193-220.

Petersen, J. (1898): Sur le théorème de Tait. *L'Intermed. de Mathémat.* **5**, 225-227.

Peterson, P. A. and Loui, M. C. (1988): The general maximum matching algorithm of Micali and Vazirani. *Algorithmica* **3**, 511-533.

Plummer, M. D. (1994): Extending matchings in graphs: a survey. *Discr. Math.* **127**, 277-292.

Plummer, M. D. (1996): Extending matchings in graphs: an update. *Congr. Numer.* **116**, 3-32.

Prim, R. C. (1957): Shortest connection networks and some generalizations. *Bell Systems Techn. J.* **36**, 1389-1401.

Prisner, E. (1996): Line graphs and generalizations – a survey. *Congr. Numer.* **116**, 193-229.

Provan, J. S. (1986): The complexity of reliability computations in planar and acyclic graphs. *SIAM J. Comp.* **15**, 694-702.

Prüfer, H. (1918): Neuer Beweis eines Satzes über Permutationen. *Arch. Math. und Physik (3)* **27**, 142-144.

Pulleyblank, W. R. (1983): Polyhedral combinatorics. In: *Mathematical Programming: The state of the art* (Eds. A. Bachem, M. Grötschel and B. Korte). Springer, Berlin, pp. 312-345.

Pym, J. S. and Perfect, H. (1970): Submodular functions and independence structures. *J. Math. Anal. Appl.* **30**, 1-31.

Qi, L. (1988): Directed submodularity, ditroids and directed submodular flows. *Math. Progr.* **42**, 579-599.

Rado, R. (1942): A theorem on independence relations. *Quart. J. Math.* **13**, 83-89.

Rado, R. (1957): Note on independence functions. *Proc. LMS* **7**, 300-320.

Radzik, T. and Goldberg, A. V. (1991): Tight bounds on the number of minimum mean cycle cancellations and related results. *Proc. 2nd ACM – SIAM Symp. on Discrete Algorithms*, pp. 110-119.

Ralston, A. (1981): A new memoryless algorithm for de Bruijn sequences. *J. Algor.* **2**, 50-62.

Ramachandra Rao, A. (1968): An extremal problem in graph theory. *Israel J. Math.* **6**, 261-266.

Ray-Chaudhuri, D. K. and Wilson, R. M. (1971): Solution of Kirkman's school girl problem. *Proc. Symp. Pure Appl. Math.*, Providence, R.I., AMS, pp. 187-203.

Recski, A. (1989): *Matroid Theory and its Applications.* Springer, Berlin.

Redéi, L. (1934): Ein kombinatorischer Satz. *Acta Litt. Szeged* **7**, 39-43.

Rees, R. (1987): Uniformly resolvable pairwise balanced designs with block sizes two and three. *J. Comb. Th. (A)* **45**, 207-225.

Reinelt, G. (1994): *The traveling salesman.* Springer, Berlin.

Reingold, E. M. and Tarjan, R. E. (1981): On a greedy heuristic for complete matching. *SIAM J. Computing* **10**, 676-681.

Rényi, A. (1959): Some remarks on the theory of trees. *Publ. Math. Inst. Hungar. Acad. Sc.* **4**, 73-85.

Rieder, J. (1991): The lattices of matroid bases and exact matroid bases. *Archiv. Math.* **56**, 616-623.

Robbins, H. (1939): A theorem on graphs with an application to a problem of traffic control. *Amer. Math. Monthly* **46**, 281-283.

Roberts, F. S. and Xu, Y. (1988): On the optimal strongly connected orientations of city street graphs I: Large grids. *SIAM J. Discr. Math.* **1**, 199-222.

Robertson, N., Sanders, D. P., Seymour, P. and Thomas, R. (1997): The four-colour theorem. *J. Comb. Th. (B)* **70**, 2-44.

Robertson, N., Seymour, P. and Thomas, R. (1993): Hadwiger's conjecture for K_6-free graphs. *Combinatorica* **13**, 279-361.

Rosenkrantz, D. J., Stearns, E. A. and Lewis, P. M. (1977): An analysis of several heuristics for the traveling salesman problem. *SIAM J. Comp.* **6**, 563-581.

Rosenthal, A. (1977): Computing the reliability of complex networks. *SIAM J. Appl. Math.* **32**, 384-393.

Rueppel, R. (1986): *Analysis and Design of Stream Ciphers*. Springer, New York.

Ryser, H. J. (1957): Combinatorial properties of matrices of zeros and ones. *Canad. J. Math.* **9**, 371-377.

Sahni, S. and Gonzales, T. (1976): P-complete approximation problems. *J. ACM* **23**, 555-565.

Schnorr, C. P. (1978): An algorithm for transitive closure with linear expected time. *SIAM J. Comp.* **7**, 127-133.

Schnorr, C. P. (1979): Bottlenecks and edge connectivity in unsymmetrical networks. *SIAM J. Comp.* **8**, 265-274.

Schreuder, J. A. M. (1980): Constructing timetables for sport competitions. *Math. Progr. Studies* **13**, 58-67.

Schreuder, J. A. M. (1992): Combinatorial aspects of construction of competition Dutch professional football leagues. *Discr. Appl. Math.* **35**, 301-312.

Schrijver, A. (1983a): Min-max results in combinatorial optimization. In: *Mathematical Programming: The state of the art* (Eds. A. Bachem, M. Grötschel and B. Korte). Springer, Berlin, pp. 439-500.

Schrijver, A. (1983b): Short proofs on the matching polyhedron. *J. Comb. Th. (B)* **34**, 104-108.

Schrijver, A. (1984): Total dual integrality from directed graphs, crossing families, and sub- and supermodular functions. In: *Progress in combinatorial optimization*. (Ed. W. R. Pulleyblank). Academic Press Canada, 315-361.

Schrijver, A. (1986): *Theory of Integer and Linear Programming*. Wiley, New York.

Schwenk, A. J. (1991): Which rectangular chessboards have a knight's tour? *Math. Magazine* **64**, 325-332.

Schwenk, A. J. and Wilson, R. (1978): On the eigenvalues of a graph. In: *Selected Topics in Graph Theory* (Eds. L. Beineke and R. Wilson). Academic Press, London, pp. 307-336.

Seymour, P. (1979): Sums of circuits. In: *Graph Theory and related topics*. (Eds. J. A. Bondy and U. S. R. Murty). Academic Press, New York, pp. 341-355.

Shannon, C. E. (1949): A theorem on colouring lines of a network. *J. Math. Phys.* **28**, 148-151.

Shapiro, J. F. (1979): A survey of Langrangian techniques for discrete optimization. *Ann. Discr. Math.* **5**, 113-138.

Shimbel, A. (1955): Structure in communication nets. *Proc. Symp. Information Networks*, New York, Polytechnic Institute of Brooklyn, pp. 199-203.

Shmoys, D. B. and Williamson, D. P. (1990): Analyzing the Held-Karp-TSP bound: A monotonicity property with application. *Inform. Proc. Letters* **35**, 281-285.

Shor, N. Z. (1985): *Minimization Methods for non-differentiable Functions*. Springer, Berlin.

Sierksma, G. and Hoogeveen, H. (1991): Seven criteria for integer sequences being graphic. *J. Graph Th.* **15**, 223-231.

Siklóssy, L. and Tulp, E. (1989): Trains, an active time-table searcher. *ECAI '89*, 170-175.

Simões-Pereira, J. M. S. (1988): An optimality criterion for graph embeddings of metrics. *SIAM J. Discr. Math.* **1**, 223-229.

Sleator, D. D. (1980): *An $O(mn \log n)$ algorithm for maximum network flow*. Ph. D. thesis, Stanford University.

Sleator, D. D. and Tarjan, R. E. (1983): A data structure for dynamic trees. *J. Comput. System Sci.* **26**, 362-391.

Sperner, E. (1928): Ein Satz über Untermengen einer endlichen Menge. *Math. Z.* **27**, 544-548.

Spinrad, J. (1985): On comparability and permutation graphs. *SIAM J. Comp.* **14**, 658-670.

Stern, G. and Lenz, H. (1980): Steiner triple systems with given subspaces: Another proof of the Doyen-Wilson theorem. *Bolletiono U.M.I. (5)* **17**, 109-114.

Stoer, J. and Bulirsch, R. (1993): *Introduction to Numerical Analysis (2nd edition).* Springer, New York.

Stong, R. A. (1985): On 1-factorizability of Cayley graphs. *J. Comb. Th. (B)* **39**, 298-307.

Sumner, D. P. (1979): Randomly matchable graphs. *J. Graph Th.* **3**, 183-186.

Suzuki, M. (1982): *Group Theory I.* Springer, Berlin-Heidelberg-New York.

Syslo, M. M., Deo, N. and Kowalik, J. S. (1983): *Discrete Optimization Algorithms.* Prentice Hall, Englewood Cliffs, N.J.

Taha, H. A. (1992): *Operations Research (5th edition).* Macmillan Publishing Co., New York.

Takács, L. (1990a): On Cayley's formula for counting forests. *J.Comb.Th. (A)* **53**, 321-323.

Takács, L. (1990b): On the number of distinct forests. *SIAM J. Discr. Math.* **3**, 574-581.

Takaoka, T. (1992): A new upper bound on the complexity of the all pairs shortest path problem. *Inf. Process. Lett.* **43**, 195-199.

Tardos, E. (1985): A strongly polynomial minimum cost circulation algorithm. *Combinatorica* **5**, 247-255.

Tardos, E. (1986): A strongly polynomial algorithm to solve combinatorial linear programs. *Oper. Res.* **34**, 250-256.

Tarjan, R. E. (1972): Depth first search and linear graph algorithms. *SIAM J. Comp.* **1**, 146-160.

Tarjan, R. E. (1977): Finding optimum branchings. *Networks* **7**, 25-35.

Tarjan, R. E. (1983): *Data Structures and Network Algorithms.* SIAM, Philadelphia.

Tarjan, R. E. (1984): A simple version of Karzanov's blocking flow algorithm. *Oper. Res. Letters* **2**, 265-268.

Tarry, G. (1895): Le problème des labyrinthes. *Nouv. Ann. de Math.* **14**, 187.

Tassiulas, L. (1997): Worst case length of nearest neighbor tours for the euclidean traveling salesman problem. *SIAM J. Discr. Math.* **10**, 171-179.

Terlaky, T. (1996): *Interior Point Methods of Mathematical Programming.* Kluwer, Dordrecht.

Thomassen, C. (1981): Kuratowski's theorem. *J. Graph Th.* **5**, 225-241.

Toft, B. (1996): A survey of Hadwiger's conjecture. *Congr. Numer.* **115**, 249-283.

Trietsch, D. and Hwang, F. (1990): An improved algorithm for Steiner trees. *SIAM J. Appl. Math.* **50**, 244-264.

Turing, A. M. (1936): On computable numbers, with an application to the Entscheidungsproblem. *Proc. LMS (2)* **42**, 230-265.

Turner, J. S. (1988): Almost all k-colorable graphs are easy to color. *J. Algor.* **9**, 63-82.

Tutte, W. T. (1947): The factorization of linear graphs. *J. LMS* **22**, 107-111.

Tutte, W. T. (1948): The dissection of equilateral triangles into equilateral triangles. *Proc. Cambridge Phil. Soc.* **44**, 203-217.

Tutte, W. T. (1952): The factors of graphs. *Canad. J. Math.* **4**, 314-328.

Tutte, W. T. (1954) A short proof of the factor theorem for finite graphs. *Canad. J. Math.* **6**, 347-352.

Tutte, W. T. (1984): *Graph Theory.* Cambridge University Press, Cambridge.

Vaidya, P. M. (1989): Geometry helps in matching. *SIAM J. Comput.* **19**, 1201-1225.

Valiant, L. G. (1979a): The complexity of computing the permanent. *Theor. Comp. Sc.* **8**, 189-201.

Valiant, L. G. (1979b): The complexity of enumeration and reliability problems. *SIAM J. Comp.* **8**, 410-421.

van der Waerden, B. L. (1926): Aufgabe 45. *Jahresber. DMV*, 117.

van der Waerden, B. L. (1927): Ein Satz über Klasseneinteilungen von endlichen Mengen. *Abh. Math. Sem. Hamburg* **5**, 185-188.

van der Waerden, B. L. (1937): *Moderne Algebra (2nd edition)*. Springer, Berlin.

van Lint, J. H. (1974): *Combinatorial Theory Seminar Eindhoven University of Technology*. Springer, Berlin.

van Lint, J. H. and Wilson, R. M. (1992): *A Course in Combinatorics*. Cambridge University Press, Cambridge.

Vazirani, V. V. (1994): A theory of alternating paths and blossoms for proving correctness of the $O(V^{\frac{1}{2}}E)$ general graph matching algorithm. *Combinatorica* **14**, 71-109.

Vizing, V. G. (1964): Über eine Abschätzung der chromatischen Klasse eines p-Graphen (Russian). *Diskret. Analiz.* **3**, 25-30.

Volgenant, T. and Jonker, R. (1982): A branch and bound algorithm for the symmetric travelling salesman problem based on the 1-tree relaxation. *Europ. J. Oper. Res.* **9**, 83-89.

Voß, S. (1992): Steiner's problem in graphs: heuristic methods. *Discr. Appl. Math.* **40**, 45-72.

Wagner, K. (1936): Bemerkungen zum Vierfarbenproblem. *Jahresber. DMV* **46**, 26-32.

Wagner, K. (1937): Über eine Eigenschaft der ebenen Komplexe. *Math. Ann.* **114**, 170-190.

Wagner, K. (1960): Bemerkungen zu Hadwigers Vermutung. *Math. Ann.* **141**, 433-451.

Wallis, W. D. (1992): One-factorizations of the complete graph. In: *Contemporary design theory: A collection of surveys* (Eds. J. H. Dinitz and D. R. Stinson). Wiley, New York, pp. 593-639.

Wallis, W. D. (1997): *One-Factorizations*. Kluwer Academic Publishers, Dordrecht.

Warshall, S. (1962): A theorem on Boolean matrices. *J. ACM* **9**, 11-12.

Weintraub, A. (1974): A primal algorithm to solve network flow problems with convex costs. *Management Sc.* **21**, 87-97.

Welsh, D. J. A. (1968): Kruskal's theorem for matroids. *Proc. Cambridge Phil. Soc.* **64**, 3-4.

Welsh, D. J. A. (1976): *Matroid Theory*. Academic Press, New York.

White, N., Ed. (1986): *Theory of Matroids*. Cambridge University Press, Cambridge.

White, N., Ed. (1987): *Combinatorial Geometries*. Cambridge University Press, Cambridge.

White, N., Ed. (1992): *Matroid Applications*. Cambridge University Press, Cambridge.

Whitney, H. (1932a): Congruent graphs and the connectivity of graphs. *Amer. J. Math.* **54**, 150-168.

Whitney, H. (1932b): Non-separable and planar graphs. *Trans. AMS* **54**, 339-362.

Whitney, H. (1933): Planar graphs. *Fund. Math.* **21**, 73-84.

Whitney, H. (1935): On the abstract properties of linear dependence. *Amer. J. Math.* **57**, 509-533.

Wilson, L. B. (1972): An analysis of the stable marriage assignment problem. *BIT* **12**, 569-575.

Wilson, R. J. (1986): An Eulerian trail through Königsberg. *J. Graph Th.* **10**, 265-275.

Wilson, R. J. (1989): A brief history of Hamiltonian graphs. *Ann. Discr. Math.* **41**, 487-496.

Winkler, P. (1988): The complexity of metric realization. *SIAM J. Discr. Math.* **1**, 552-559.

Wirth, N. (1976): *Algorithms + Data Structures = Programs*. Prentice Hall, Englewood Cliffs, N.J.

Yannakakis, M. (1978): Node- and edge-deletion NP-complete problems. *Proc. 10th ACM Symp. on Theory of Computing*, New York, ACM, pp. 253-264.

Yannakakis, M. and Gavril, F. (1978): Edge dominating sets in graphs. Unpublished manuscript.

Yao, A. C. (1975): An $O(|E| \log \log |V|)$ algorithm for finding minimum spanning trees. *Inform. Proc. Letters* **4**, 21-23.

Yap, H. P. (1986): *Some Topics in Graph Theory*. Cambridge University Press, Cambridge.

Young, N. E., Tarjan, R. E. and Orlin, J. B. (1991): Faster parametric shortest path and minimum-balance algorithms. *Networks* **21**, 205-221.

Yuster, R. and Zwick, U. (1997): Finding even cycles even faster. *SIAM J. Discr. Math.* **10**, 209-222.

Zadeh, N. (1972): Theoretical efficiency of the Edmonds-Karp algorithm for computing maximal flows. *J. ACM* **19**, 248-264.

Zadeh, N. (1973a): A bad network problem for the simplex method and other minimum cost flow algorithms. *Math. Progr.* **5**, 255-266.

Zadeh, N. (1973b): More pathological examples for network flow problems. *Math. Progr.* **5**, 217-224.

Zimmermann, U. (1981): *Linear and Combinatorial Optimization in Ordered Algebraic Structures*. North Holland, Amsterdam.

Zuckerman, D. (1996): On unapproximable versions of NP-complete problems. *SIAM J. Computing* **25**, 1293-1304.

Index

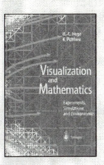

Algorithms and Computation in Mathematics

Volume 4
A.M. Cohen, H. Cuypers, H. Sterk (Eds.)
Some Tapas of Computer Algebra

1998. Approx. 350 pp.
Hardcover DM 79,-
ISBN 3-540-63480-0

A variety of topics in computer algebra at an accessible (upper undergraduate/graduate) level with a view towards recent developments. For those wanting to acquaint themselves somewhat further with the material, the book also contains seven 'projects', which could serve as practical sessions related to one or more chapters. The contributions focus on topics like Gröbner bases, real algebraic geometry, Lie algebras, factorisation of polynomials, integer programming, permutation groups, differential equations, coding theory, automatic theorem proving, and polyhedral geometry. A must-read for everybody interested in computer algebra.

Volume 3
N. Koblitz
Algebraic Aspects of Cryptography

1998. IX, 206 pp. 7 figs.
Hardcover DM 98,-
ISBN 3-540-63446-0

A comprehensive and systematic account on the Carathéodory and Kobayashi distances, hyperbolic complex spaces and holomorphic mappings with geometric methods. A very complete list of references should be useful for prospective researchers in this area.

Please order from
Springer-Verlag Berlin
Fax: + 49 / 30 / 8 27 87- 301
e-mail: orders@springer.de
or through your bookseller

Springer

Springer-Verlag, P. O. Box 14 02 01, D-14302 Berlin, Germany.

Gha.

Springer
and the
environment

At Springer we firmly believe that an international science publisher has a special obligation to the environment, and our corporate policies consistently reflect this conviction.

We also expect our business partners – paper mills, printers, packaging manufacturers, etc. – to commit themselves to using materials and production processes that do not harm the environment. The paper in this book is made from low- or no-chlorine pulp and is acid free, in conformance with international standards for paper permanency.

 Springer

Printing: Mercedesdruck, Berlin
Binding: Buchbinderei Lüderitz & Bauer, Berlin